PERSPECTIVES ON WRITING
Series Editor, Susan H. McLeod

PERSPECTIVES ON WRITING
Series Editor, Susan H. McLeod

The Perspectives on Writing series addresses writing studies in a broad sense. Consistent with the wide ranging approaches characteristic of teaching and scholarship in writing across the curriculum, the series presents works that take divergent perspectives on working as a writer, teaching writing, administering writing programs, and studying writing in its various forms.

The WAC Clearinghouse and Parlor Press are collaborating so that these books will be widely available through free digital distribution and low-cost print editions. The publishers and the Series editor are teachers and researchers of writing, committed to the principle that knowledge should freely circulate. We see the opportunities that new technologies have for further democratizing knowledge. And we see that to share the power of writing is to share the means for all to articulate their needs, interest, and learning into the great experiment of literacy.

Other Books in the Series

Charles Bazerman and David R. Russell (Eds.), *Writing Selves/Writing Societies* (2003)

Gerald P. Delahunty and James Garvey, *The English Language: From Sound to Sense* (2009)

Charles Bazerman, Adair Bonini, and Débora Figueiredo (Eds.), *Genre in a Changing World* (2009)

David Franke, Alex Reid, and Anthony Di Renzo (Eds.), *Design Discourse: Composing and Revising Programs in Professional and Technical Writing* (2010)

Martine Courant Rife, Shaun Slattery, and Dànielle Nicole DeVoss (Eds.), *Copy(write) : Intellectual Property in the Writing Classroom* (2011)

Doreen Starke-Meyerring, Anthony Paré, Natasha Artemeva, Miriam Horne, and Larissa Yousoubova, *Writing in Knowledge Societies* (2011)

Andy Kirkpatrick and Zhichang Xu, *Chinese Rhetoric and Writing: An Introduction for Language Teachers* (2012)

WRITING PROGRAMS WORLDWIDE: PROFILES OF ACADEMIC WRITING IN MANY PLACES

Edited by

Chris Thaiss
Gerd Bräuer
Paula Carlino
Lisa Ganobcsik-Williams
Aparna Sinha

The WAC Clearinghouse
wac.colostate.edu
Fort Collins, Colorado

Parlor Press
www.parlorpress.com
Anderson, South Carolina

The WAC Clearinghouse, Fort Collins, Colorado 80523-1052
Parlor Press, 3015 Brackenberry Drive, Anderson, South Carolina 29621

© 2012 by Chris Thaiss, Gerd Bräuer, Paula Carlino, Lisa Ganobcsik-Williams, and Aparna Sinha. This work is licensed under a Creative Commons Attribution-Noncommercial-No Derivative Works 3.0 United States License.

Printed in the United States of America

Library of Congress Cataloging-in-Publication Data

Writing programs worldwide : profiles of academic writing in many places / edited by Chris Thaiss ... [et. al].
   p. cm.
  Includes bibliographical references and index.
   ISBN 978-1-60235-343-5 (pbk. : acid-free paper) -- ISBN 978-1-60235-344-2 (hardcover : acid-free paper) -- ISBN 978-1-60235-345-9 (adobe ebook) -- ISBN 978-1-60235-346-6 (epub)
  1. Academic writing--Cross-cultural studies. I. Thaiss, Christopher J., 1948-
  P301.5.A27W75 2012
  808.02--dc23
                         2012028435

Copyeditor: Don Donahue
Designer: Mike Palmquist
Series Editor: Susan H. McLeod

This book is printed on acid-free paper.

The WAC Clearinghouse supports teachers of writing across the disciplines. Hosted by Colorado State University, it brings together scholarly journals and book series as well as resources for teachers who use writing in their courses. This book is available in digital format for free download at http://wac.colostate.edu.

Parlor Press, LLC is an independent publisher of scholarly and trade titles in print and multimedia formats. This book is available in paperback, cloth, and digital formats from Parlor Press at http://www.parlorpress.com. For submission information or to find out about Parlor Press publications, write to Parlor Press, 3015 Brackenberry Drive, Anderson, South Carolina 29621, or e-mail editor@parlorpress.com.

CONTENTS

1. Origins, Aims, and Uses of *Writing Programs Worldwide*: Profiles of Academic Writing in Many Places 5
   By Chris Thaiss

2. Teaching Academic Literacy Across the University Curriculum as Institutional Policy: The Case of the Universidad Nacional de General Sarmiento (Argentina) 23
   By Estela Inés Moyano and Lucia Natale

3. Writing to Learn Biology in the Framework of a Didactic-Curricular Change in the First Year Program at an Argentine University 35
   By Ana De Micheli and Patricia Iglesia

4. Developing Students' Writing at Queensland University of Technology . 43
   By Karyn Gonano and Peter Nelson

5. Teaching Academic Writing at the University of Wollongong 55
   By Emily Purser

6. The SchreibCenter at the Alpen-Adria-Universität, Klagenfurt, Austria . 69
   By Ursula Doleschal

7. The Academic Writing Research Group at the University of Vienna . . . 79
   By Helmut Gruber

8. From Remediation to the Development of Writing Competences in Disciplinary Contexts: Thirty Years of Practice and Questions 93
   By Marie-Christine Pollet

9. Academic Literacies in the South: Writing Practices in a Brazilian University 105
   By Désirée Motta-Roth

10. Writing Programs Worldwide: One Canadian Perspective 117
    By Roger Graves and Heather Graves

11. Department of Rhetoric, Writing, and Communications at the University of Winnipeg 129
    By Brian Turner and Judith Kearns

Contents

12. Xi'an International Studies University (XISU,西安外国语大学).... *139*
    By Wu Dan 吴丹

13. Training Experiences in Reading and Writing in a Colombian University: The Perspective of a Professor *147*
    By Elizabeth Narváez Cardona

14. The Progression and Transformations of the Program of Academic Reading and Writing (PLEA) in Colombia's Universidad Sergio Arboleda.... *157*
    Blanca Yaneth González Pinzón

15. From Working with Students to Working *through* Faculty: A Genre-centered Focus to Writing Development *169*
    By Lotte Rienecker and Peter Stray Jørgensen

16. The Department of Rhetoric and Composition at the American University in Cairo: Achievements and Challenges........................ *181*
    By Emily Golson and Lammert Holdijk

17. Providing a Hub for Writing Development: A Profile of the Centre for Academic Writing (CAW), Coventry University, England *189*
    By Mary Deane and Lisa Ganobcsik-Williams

18. Thinking Writing at Queen Mary, University of London *203*
    By Teresa McConlogue, Sally Mitchell, and Kelly Peake

19. The Teaching of Writing Skills in French Universities: The Case of the Université Stendhal, Grenoble III *213*
    By Francoise Boch and Catherine Frier

20. Literacy Development Projects Initiating Institutional Change...... *225*
    By Gerd Bräuer and Katrin Girgensohn

21. Writing at RWTH Aachen (Germany): Lessons from "Technik im Klartext" *239*
    By Vera Niederau and Eva-Maria Jakobs

22. Student Writing in the University of Madras: Traditions, Courses, Ambitions *251*
    By Susaimanickam Armstrong

23. The Regional Writing Centre at the University of Limerick *261*
    By Íde O'Sullivan and Lawrence Cleary

24. New Writing in an Old Land *271*
    By *Trudy Zuckermann, Bella Rubin, and Hadara Perpignan*

25. The Development of an Academic Writing Centre in the Netherlands *293*
    By *Ingrid Stassen and Carel Jansen*

26. Teaching Writing at AUT University: A Model of a Seminar Series for Postgraduate Students Writing Their First Thesis or Dissertation *301*
    By *John Bitchener*

27. Developing a "Kiwi" Writing Centre at Massey University, New Zealand *313*
    By *Lisa Emerson*

28. The Writing Centre at St. Mary's University College, Belfast, Northern Ireland *325*
    By *Jonathan Worley*

29. The Ups and Downs of the Interdisciplinary Writing Center of the InterAmerican University of Puerto Rico, Metropolitan Campus. . . . *333*
    By *Matilde García-Arroyo and Hilda E. Quintana*

30. Academic Writing at the University of Dundee: A Perspective from Scotland. *341*
    By *Kathleen McMillan*

31. Changing Academic Landscapes: Principles and Practices of Teaching Writing At the University of Cape Town *353*
    By *Arlene Archer*

32. Academic Communication Strategies at Postgraduate Level *365*
    By *Isabel Solé, Ana Teberosky, and Montserrat Castelló*

33. Multi-Disciplinary, Multi-Lingual Engineering Education Writing Development: A Writing Programme Perspective. *377*
    By *Magnus Gustafsson and Tobias Boström*

34. Shaping the Multimedia Mindset: Collaborative Writing in Journalism Education *389*
    By *Daniel Perrin*

35. The Place of Writing in Translation: From Linguistic Craftsmanship to Multilingual Text Production. *401*
    By *Otto Kruse*

36. A Writing Center Journey at Sabanci University, Istanbul. *417*
    By Dilek Tokay

37. Writing Programs Worldwide: Profile of the American University of
    Sharjah (AUS) *429*
    By Lynne Ronesi

38. The City University of New York: The Implementation and Impact of
    WAC/WID in a Multi-Campus US Urban University. *439*
    By Linda Hirsch and Dennis Paoli

39. Writing at UC Davis: Writing in Disciplines and Professions from the
    Undergraduate First Year through Graduate School. *455*
    By Chris Thaiss and Gary Goodman

40. Section Essay: Academic Literacy Development *467*
    By Gerd Bräuer

41. Section Essay: Who Takes Care of Writing in Latin American and Spanish
    Universities?. *485*
    By Paula Carlino

42. Section Essay: Reflecting on What Can Be Gained from Comparing
    Models of Academic Writing Provision *499*
    By Lisa Ganobcsik-Williams

About the Authors and Editors. *513*
Index *523*

Note: Chapters 2 - 39 are presented alphabetically by country.

WRITING PROGRAMS WORLDWIDE: PROFILES OF ACADEMIC WRITING IN MANY PLACES

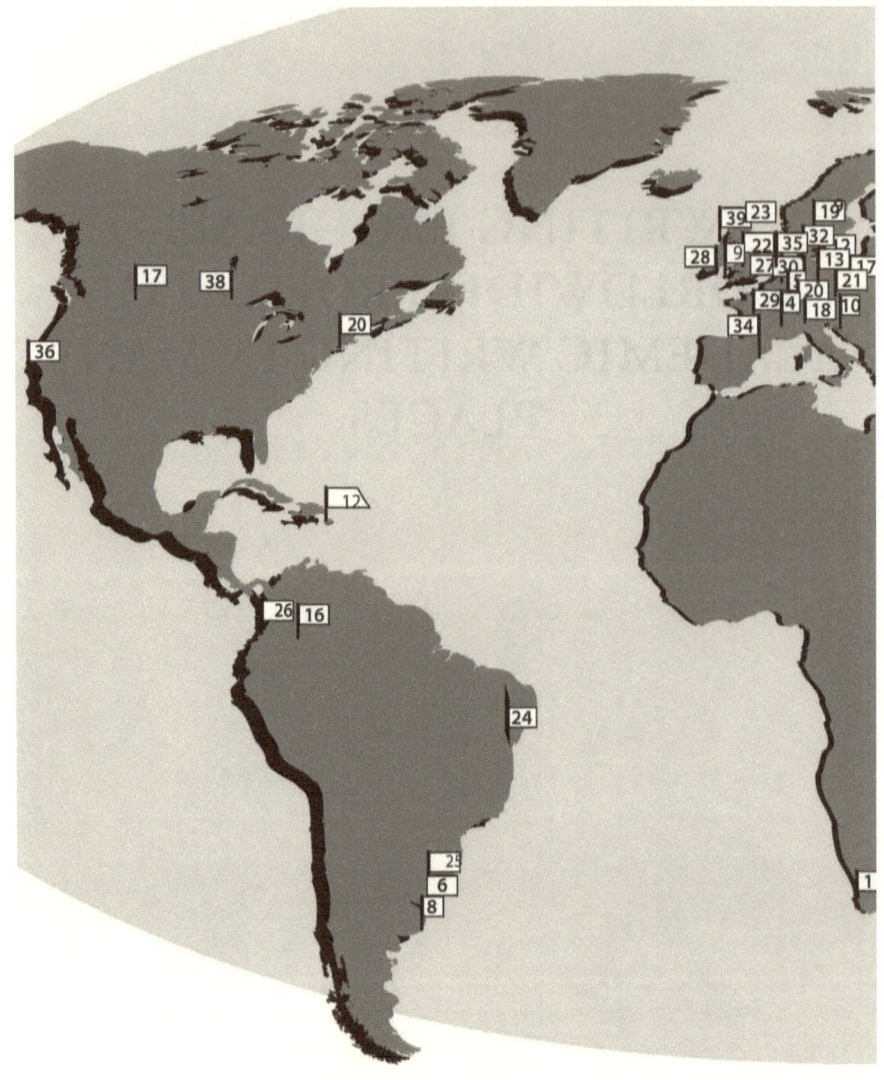

01	Archer - South Africa	11	Emerson - New Zealand
02	Armstrong - India	12	García-Arroyo & Quintana - Puerto Rico
03	Bitchener - New Zealand	13	Girgensohn - Germany
04	Boch & Frier - France	14	Golson & Holdijk - Egypt
05	Bräuer - Germany	15	Gonano & Nelson - Australia
06	Carlino - Argentina	16	González Pinzón - Colombia
07	Dan - China	17	Graves & Graves - Canada
08	De Micheli & Iglesiav- Argentina	18	Gruber - Austria
09	Deane & Gonabcsik-Williams - England	19	Gustafsson & Boström - Sweden
10	Doleschal - Austria	20	Hirsch & Paoli - United States of America

This map was created by Ray Summers, Centre for Academic Writing, Coventry University (England).

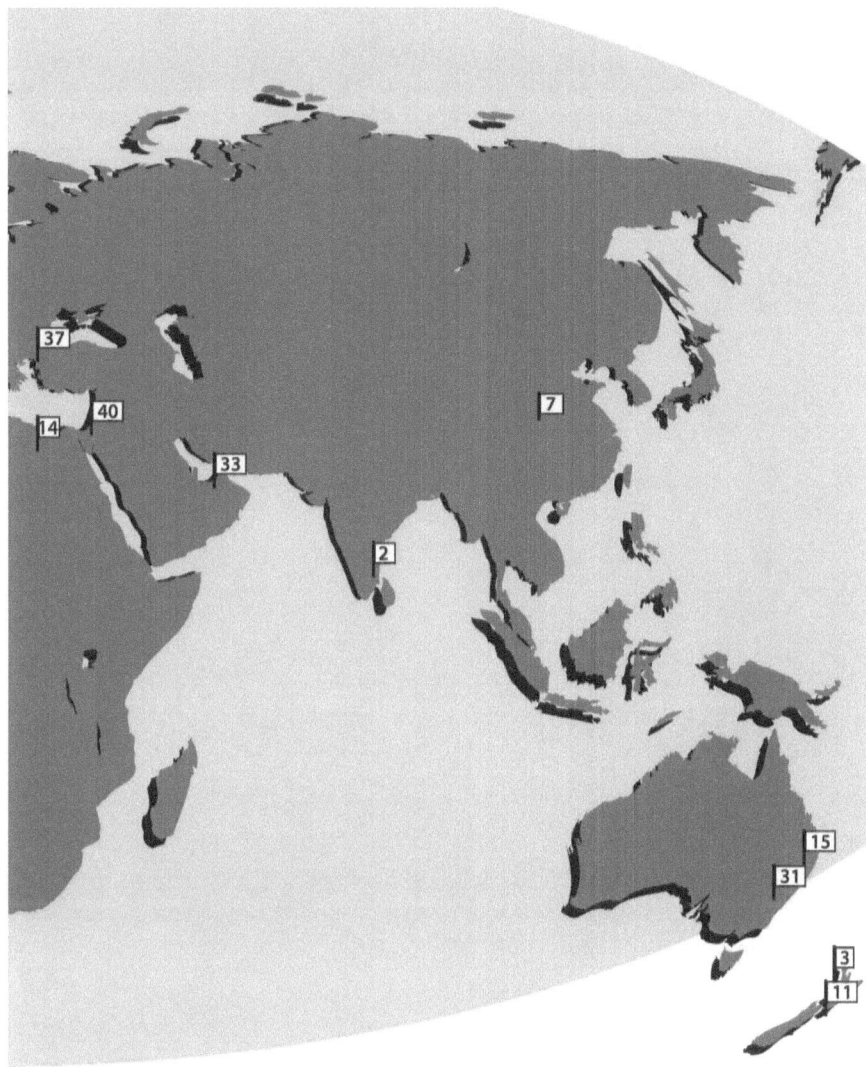

21 Kruse - Switzerland	31 Purser - Australia
22 McConlogue, Mitchell & Peake - England	32 Rienecker & Jørgensen - Denmark
23 McMillan - Scotland	33 Ronesi - United Arab Emirates
24 Motta Roth - Brazil	34 Solé, Teberosky, & Castelló - Spain
25 Moyano & Natale - Argentina	35 Stassen & Jansen - Netherlands
26 Narváez Cardona - Colombia	36 Thaiss & Goodman - United States of America
27 Niederau & Jakobs - Germany	37 Tokay - Turkey
28 O'Sullivan & Cleary - Ireland	38 Turner & Kearns - Canada
29 Perrin - Switzerland	39 Worley - Northern Ireland
30 Pollet - Belgium	40 Zuckermann, Rubin, & Perpignan - Israel

CHAPTER 1.

ORIGINS, AIMS, AND USES OF *WRITING PROGRAMS WORLDWIDE*: PROFILES OF ACADEMIC WRITING IN MANY PLACES

By Chris Thaiss
University of California, Davis (US)

To introduce Writing Programs Worldwide, *this essay describes and analyzes major reasons for this project to be undertaken and its primary goals. It also presents findings and analysis of the ongoing (since 2006) International WAC/WID Mapping Project, specifically of its "international survey" of writing programs and initiatives, which has received responses from more than 330 institutions on six continents. The essay describes how the survey results led to the choice of the universities invited to contribute profile chapters to this collection, as well as to the topics and emphases in the profiles themselves. The essay suggests reasons why teachers, program developers, administrators, and scholars might benefit from exploring the "many places" described and reflected on in the array of contributions to this ongoing project.*

We intend this book, in its print and online versions, to inform decision-making by teachers, program managers, and college/university administrators in regard to how writing is conceived of, managed, funded, and taught in higher education. We intend it, also, to contribute to the growing research literature in the shaping of writing programs.

In our title, "Writing Programs Worldwide," and in our subtitle, "Profiles of Academic Writing in Many Places," we have tried to join three aims of scholarship. The first of these, embodied in the term "worldwide," is to further the effort to build a transnational community of writing scholars, teachers, and program administrators who can share for their mutual benefit the discoveries of individuals and small teams. This aim has been exemplified by the growth of such collectives as the European Association for the Teaching of Academic Writing (EATAW), the International Writing Centers Association (IWCA), and the newly-formed (2011) International Society for the Advancement of Writing Research (http://www.isawr.org), formed by the transnational scientific committee of the conferences on Writing Research Across Borders.[1]

The second aim is to identify generalizable trends, patterns, and models that may be said to characterize initiatives in the teaching of academic writing at tertiary and postgraduate levels at this point in the transnational history of this growing movement. A main purpose of this introduction and of the three essays (at the end of the volume) by individual editors is to synthesize examples from many of the profiles toward such responsible generalizations. Later in this essay, for example, I will report trends from the International Survey of the International WAC/WID Mapping Project, this survey being instrumental in the development of this publishing project.

The third aim, embodied in the term "many places," is to honor the variety and rich complexity of persons, languages, traditions, geographies, conditions, and purposes that both inspire and constrain the writing pedagogies and research of these individuals and teams. To recognize the uniqueness of each effort described in this project, as the writers and editors have striven to do, works against the tendency to homogenize, hence reduce, all such efforts to a few "typical" principles and practices, motives and mechanisms. While there is, of course, value in the well-reasoned generalization, the presence of (in the case of this project) more than forty profiles of individual locales offers an alternative to *reductio ad absurdum*. The French winemakers' principle of *terroir* might be invoked to capture the feel of this respect for the local. Even if the palate—or the ability to read for nuance—limits one's ability to appreciate that uniqueness, accepting *terroir* means that, to read one of these profiles, one gains insight into the geographic, cultural, and personal histories and ambitions that have gone into creating each of these complex experiences. That this project makes use on our Web site of photos by our authors of their locales is meant to heighten this respect and feel for difference.

In "programs" (or its variant "programmes")[2] we've embodied our focus on how an institution—or at least some of its members—conceives of the needs of its students in regard to learning a discipline, "writing," that in basic ways crosses all disciplines and aids learning in all of them. Some of our essays describe individual classrooms and subjects; a few are able to describe individual students. But our overriding aim as individual (or team) writers has been to understand and to attempt to convey to a transnational readership how and why the universities in which we labor attend to (or have neglected) "academic writing" as a complex set of skills to be learned by students—and to be used as a vital tool in their learning of their major disciplines.

To look at the teaching of writing at the programmatic level is to engage in a rich subfield of writing research. This inquiry differs from, though it draws from, such other subfields of writing research as individual student learning and cognitive/social/emotional development, or description and assessment of specific teacher interventions. In regard to continental Europe, it is not much of a leap to say that the interest in how higher education systematically organizes its literacy education, including writing, goes back at least to Quintilian's *Institutio Oratoria* of 95 CE, and to Plato's much earlier critical comparison (e.g., in the Protagoras) of Socrates' school with the methods of the Sophists. In China, the ancient tradition of the written exams for the civil service, beginning before the sixth century CE, provoked intense interest in formal preparation for these exams and institutional structures to support it (Man-Cheong, 2004). Would that we could discover how the Mesopotamian bureaucracies of the fourth (and earlier) millennia BCE organized instruction in the learning of the earliest extant transcription system, the variously-shaped clay "counters" that Schmandt-Besserat (1996) has described as the first writing. We do know that by the third millennium BCE Sumerian culture had built a formal education system for scribes, young men (and some women) from wealthy families (Veldhuis, 1997; Robson, 2001).

In more recent centuries, in the United Kingdom, the highly-valued "tutorial system" of individualized/small-group teaching in place at Oxford and Cambridge historically has ensured that at these elite institutions students are provided with continuous feedback on their academic writing and that their writing develops in tandem with their disciplinary knowledge and learning (Palfreyman, 2008). In the United States, deep interest in the characteristics of organizational structures for the teaching of writing go back to well before the founding of the National Council of Teachers of English in 1919 (see, e.g., Brereton, 1996; Miller, 2011; Russell, 2002). As the reference lists of the individual profile essays show, research and theory from diverse traditions have been brought to bear in designing and sustaining these initiatives.

However, recent and truly international concern about structures for teaching writing has emerged from two primary sources: the internationalizing of the teaching of English for academic and professional purposes and the explosion of internet-accessible resources and models for the teaching of writing. In Europe, the Bologna Process, begun in 1999, has been another spur to transnational sharing of structural ideas, as universities have made their curricula accessible to students from across Europe.[3] These three related phenomena, of which the power of the internet is arguably the most important, have made possible and perhaps necessary the rise of the international organizations named earlier, as well as a burgeoning number of international conferences on many aspects of literacy. Further, national literacy-focused organizations have, because of the web and email, become *de facto* transnational, while the regional and even local have become noticed and relevant much outside their original terroir.

Particularly pertinent to this publishing project is the example of the former National (US) Network of Writing-across-the-Curriculum (WAC) Programs, which began in 1979 with a handful of US colleges and universities, gained Canadian members in the 1980s, and was centered on annual meetings at the (US) National Council of Teachers of English conventions and the conventions of the Conference on College Composition and Communication (Thaiss, 2006). It became the International Network after 2005, when it partnered with the Web-based WAC Clearinghouse (http://wac.colostate.edu) to extend its visibility across the digisphere. The research initiative spun off from the Network and named the International WAC/WID Mapping Project (http://mappingproject.ucdavis.edu), which began in 2006, has been to this point an almost-purely digispheric entity: the surveys, survey responses, requests for essays, essays themselves, Skype calls, photographs, and countless other messages traverse cyberspace and are "housed" in digital databases. The Mapping Project has come to terra firma only for physical presentations at conferences in Europe and North America. The transnationality of the group of editors and contributing writers and the translinguality of the survey and survey responses could only have happened through web reality.

WHY INTEREST IN THE SHAPES OF WRITING PROGRAMS ACROSS BORDERS?

A basic question to ask about this cross-borders interest in writing programs is why? –as in why should anyone be interested in how the teaching of writing is organized and formalized in settings outside one's own nation or region? (Editor Lisa Ganobcsik- Williams also takes up this question in her section essay in this volume, while the section essays by editors Gerd Bräuer and Paula Carlino describe specific transnational collaborations.) The whys may be obvious to those already convinced of the value of learning from traditions and practices in other cultures, or to those who see themselves helping to shape educational policy at a national level. But they may not be obvious to teachers focused on student learners in a given place, or to literacy scholars immersed in the methods of design in specific inquiries, or even to university and college department heads and administrators trying to understand and manage particular faculties and contend with ominous directives from supervisors.

The basic why is the increasing transnationality of most education, wherever it occurs. For example, many profiles in this project deal at least in part with the imposing presence of learning English, even if that language is not the medium of instruction in the university and the methods described in the profiles are not devoted to teaching writing in English. Moreover, the drives to become literate and, therefore, to teach literacy, usually in advanced forms, is sparked in almost every case by student and staff desires for academic recognition in the international research community or by desire for career success in the global economy. Third, the students and teachers in the universities profiled here, while sometimes representing a fairly homogeneous ethnicity, more often exemplify a range of linguistic and cultural backgrounds. Fourth, even in those locales where language and ethnicity are fairly uniform, students and teachers bring every day to their learning the internet and other mass culture influences that shape the writing educations they desire and are offered. Global social networking is but the latest dramatic manifestation of a long trend to bridge distances, borders, oceans, and mountains. Yet, its immediacy and its multi-sensory power, aided by translation software, to bring billions of individuals into literate contact with one another means that we cannot ignore how literacy is taught and learned around the world.

Other reasons also make a collection such as this intriguing and, we believe, useful:

- The desire of universities throughout the world to internationalize their student populations, whether through the Bologna Process or other forces, should spark interest in the cultural attitudes toward written literacy that students bring with them to new places and to very different learning environments.
- Transnational collaborations between universities that encourage movement of students and teachers, as well as creation of joint curricula and credit standards, need to be informed by understanding differing traditions and practices in literacy education.
- Lead teachers, administrators, and curriculum planners can learn from the experiences of their counterparts in different areas of the world who have faced struggles similar to their own—and the Internet makes surprisingly easy transnational and transoceanic conversation and collaboration. Language differences are somewhat of a barrier, but two factors: (1) the spread of versions of English and (2) the increasing accuracy of free or low-cost translation software, are making it much easier for willing and persistent conversants to overcome language differences.
- The profiles in this project describe a great variety of subject (course), modular, tutorial, collaborative, formal and informal organizational structures that can be adapted to different universities and learning environments. These may have derived from local conditions and traditions,

but reading about a successful curricular experiment in, say, the Netherlands, Canada, Argentina, China, South Africa, or Australia (among the 28 countries represented here) can spark the imagination of teachers and administrators in any country toward changes to better support student writing and learning development in their own universities.

THE MUTUAL INFLUENCES OF THE LOCAL AND THE GLOBAL

As you read the profiles, you will note how each of the authors tries to achieve this balance between, on the one hand, generalization and, on the other, concentration on the specific and local. While we have asked the writers to try to convey to our international audience, what is distinctive about institutional history, locale, and mission, and distinctive about the people of their particular university, the question itself asks for generalizations about these matters. Though we have not asked for a higher level of generalization, the authors frequently place their universities within their sense of the national or broader cultural and historical context: these writers conceive of their universities as not local or regional institutions only, but as having national and even international relevance--and striving for more.

Moreover, as scholars of literacy, they frequently explain their motives, theories, and practices within national, regional, or transnational research. Indeed, as you read these profiles, you will see that in most instances the writers are either explicitly aware of the transnational writing research community or are implicitly adapting goals and techniques that exist elsewhere. In order to give priority to their descriptions of place, history, and program structures, we have asked writers to be sparing in their citations. Nevertheless, even in profiles that offer very short lists of references, the influence of trends and models from other places is clear, though perhaps implicit within the body of the profile.

THE QUESTIONS AND TOPICS GUIDING THE PROFILES

In giving guidance to the authors who accepted our invitation to submit profiles, we asked that their essays address at least several of the following questions and topics. Items 4 through 7 derive directly from the International Survey of the International WAC/WID Mapping Project (http://mappingproject.ucdavis.edu). All of the questions and topics reflect the three aims described earlier. Given that we were restricting the profiles in length, we allowed authors to choose which of our questions and topics they would not be able to address. Moreover, we encouraged authors to focus more narrowly, if they wished, on specific initiatives within a larger program, or to explain their efforts more broadly but less deeply within the short-essay limits. Hence, some of the profiles clearly address many of the guiding questions, while others follow our guidance in spirit but list headings that fit their more specific focus. Nevertheless, in working with our authors on refinement of their drafts, we ensured that every essay addressed implicitly, if not explicitly, most of our guiding concerns. The questions and topics are as follows:

- The size, brief history, and mission of the institution
- Most salient geographic, economic, and cultural features of its location
- What "literacy" and especially "writing" mean to students and teachers in this institution: why they write, in what languages and dialects, in relation to what goals?
- Where and what students write in the institution—disciplines, genres, assignments*
- Who "cares" in the institution about student growth in and through writing? How is this concern—or lack of concern—shown in funding, requirements, attitudes, actions?*
- When and how have groups of teachers met to discuss and perhaps plan ways to help students grow as writers? What has resulted?*
- On what models, theories, authors, and principles have courses or methods been based?*
- What have been your and the institution's successes in teaching writing?
- What have been your unfulfilled ambitions in regard to student literacy/writing?
- Can you describe individual students or events that embody or illustrate these successes and frustrations?

---

* *Questions derived from the International Survey of the International WAC/WID Mapping Project*

EMERGENCE OF THE PROFILES FROM THE INTERNATIONAL SURVEY RESEARCH

The profile essays in *Writing Programs Worldwide* allow not only rich context, but encourage personal voices to emerge and the sense of the locale, the terroir, to come through. The profile essays may be thought of as delving more deeply into the evidence from the more than 350 responses (from 54 countries, 2007-10) to the International Survey *(*http://mappingproject.ucdavis.edu/preliminarysurvey*)*, much as interviews of a sample of respondents typically follow the collection of survey data. The question structure of this survey gives promise of a regularity and comparability of responses and language that encourages generalization, even as it also hints at the diversity and uniqueness beneath. While the survey responses did encourage generalizations (as shown in the following paragraphs), the profile essays, as described above and in the section "Choosing the Profiles" to follow, elaborate on the responses to the survey questions and encourage further questions from the reader. Where the survey responses to the five open-ended questions varied greatly in the depth and detail of the answers, and suggest a complexity that the question format did not allow, the profile allows the writer not only to address the questions more fully, but also to create an integrated essay with a vision of past, present, and future.

Background and Methods of the Survey

The idea of the survey began in 2005, as an offshoot of the National (US) WAC Network's becoming "international" in name as well as in fact, this change itself a result of the increasing attendance by scholars and teachers from diverse nations at the annual WAC Network meetings at the Conference on College Composition and Communication. I had begun planning survey work on characteristics of US and Canadian writing programs earlier that same year (Thaiss & Porter, 2010), and extending this work internationally seemed not only interesting but possible, given Internet accessibility. I asked the help of two colleagues, Terry Myers Zawacki (of George Mason University) and Christiane Donahue (now of Dartmouth College) in designing an appropriate international survey, and, following two very helpful focus groups conducted by Donahue in Europe in 2006, the questions and topics on the survey emerged.

With help from graduate student researchers Erin Steinke and Melissa Mack and from web designers Paul Nozicka and Elliott Pollard at the University of California, Davis, the survey established a presence on the web and began to attract respondents in 2007. It had been my intention from the beginning to have the survey available in multiple languages, and between 2007 and 2009, I was fortunate to have the assistance of the following colleagues in making the survey available in Spanish, German, French, Russian, and Chinese: Paula Carlino (Universidad de Buenos Aires, Argentina), Constanza Padilla (CONICET, Universidad Nacional de Tucumán, Argentina), Manuela Cartolari (CONICET, Universidad de Buenos Aires. Argentina), Ana Brown (Universidad de Buenos Aires, Argentina), Annette Verhein (Hochschule für Technik, Rapperswil, Switzerland), Céline Beaudet (Université de Sherbrooke, Canada), Sylvie Plane (Université Paris-Sorbonne, France), Nina Shevchuk-Murray (University of Nebraska, US), and Huahui Zhao (Umeå University, Sweden). Thus far, 82% of responses have been in English, with 15% in Spanish and 3% divided among the other four languages.

Recruiting respondents (2007-09) was handled in several ways:
- A paper survey completed by participants in a Mapping Project workshop in 2007 at the EATAW Conference in Bochum, Germany, plus several interviews conducted by Zawacki, Donahue, and me gave us the first twenty-five respondents.
- The initial email contact list was built by graduate researcher Steinke (2007) from the EATAW and European Writing Centers Association (EWCA) listserves and the speakers list from the 2008 Writing Research Across Borders conference (Santa Barbara, California, US)
- Study of university websites by Steinke and graduate researcher Melissa Mack (2008-09) added further contacts.
- By far the most successful method of recruiting respondents has been through friends and colleagues of respondents in professional and regional networks.

TRENDS IN THE SURVEY RESPONSES, BY QUESTION[4]

Total: 330 institutions (365 respondents), 54 countries
Most frequent responses, by country: 177 of the 330 institutions, 14 of the 54 countries represented

```
United Kingdom . . . . . . . . . . . . . . . . . . . . . . . . . . . . . . . . . . . . 45
Argentina. . . . . . . . . . . . . . . . . . . . . . . . . . . . . . . . . . . . . . . . . 19
Germany . . . . . . . . . . . . . . . . . . . . . . . . . . . . . . . . . . . . . . . . . 16
Colombia. . . . . . . . . . . . . . . . . . . . . . . . . . . . . . . . . . . . . . . . . 13
Australia. . . . . . . . . . . . . . . . . . . . . . . . . . . . . . . . . . . . . . . . . . 13
Spain . . . . . . . . . . . . . . . . . . . . . . . . . . . . . . . . . . . . . . . . . . . . 11
Switzerland . . . . . . . . . . . . . . . . . . . . . . . . . . . . . . . . . . . . . . . 11
Netherlands . . . . . . . . . . . . . . . . . . . . . . . . . . . . . . . . . . . . . . . 10
Israel . . . . . . . . . . . . . . . . . . . . . . . . . . . . . . . . . . . . . . . . . . . . . 8
Turkey . . . . . . . . . . . . . . . . . . . . . . . . . . . . . . . . . . . . . . . . . . . . 7
France . . . . . . . . . . . . . . . . . . . . . . . . . . . . . . . . . . . . . . . . . . . . 6
South Africa. . . . . . . . . . . . . . . . . . . . . . . . . . . . . . . . . . . . . . . . 6
Venezuela. . . . . . . . . . . . . . . . . . . . . . . . . . . . . . . . . . . . . . . . . . 6
Mexico. . . . . . . . . . . . . . . . . . . . . . . . . . . . . . . . . . . . . . . . . . . . 6
```

ANALYSIS OF RESPONSES TO EACH QUESTION:

Analyzing the responses by question allows the generalizations that follow.

1. Where are students writing in your institution, either in a first language of instruction or in English? In what genres and circumstances?

Seventy percent (70%) of the responses, from across countries, indicate that much writing is being required of undergraduate (tertiary) and graduate (postgraduate) students in all or most disciplines. This proportion may actually be higher, because in the remaining 30% of responses half (15%) either (1) focus their remarks on only one or two disciplines with which the respondents are associated (approx. 10%), or (2) do not address this question (5%). Only 10% of the total explicitly say that little or no writing is required of undergraduate (tertiary) students across their fields, or that writing is required only in language courses.

The length of the response largely determines the range and specificity of assignments named. A longer response, such as the following, might name several genres, differentiated by area of the curriculum:

> Technical and business writing predominate. Science and engineering students . . . are writing reports, experimental plans, and the rare essay. Business students are also writing reports. Academic essays are used in the social sciences and the humanities. In 2009, an academic writing course (a.k.a. FYC) will be required of all bachelor of arts students for the first time. Creative writing is taught as an elective to English majors and as a requirement of students in the bachelor of communications (a joint humanities and business degree). Oral communication is taught in many of the same courses as writing. There are, of course, variations on this quick gloss, but this is the most obvious profile of student writing.

Typical brief responses are the following:

> (Response 1) All departments, all engineering disciplines, in groups and individually, BSc-MSc-PhD level (i.e., writing in English)

> (Response 2) All years of study—1st to 5th. Genres: Essays, research papers, theses, (articles and web-)

Most respondents, even in shorter responses, describe writing in academic genres, usually appropriate to the discipline; for example, "essays" and "reports" of various kinds are mentioned, as well as "seminar papers," another popular term. "Exams" and "theses" are two other terms used in many responses. Writing for publication in disciplinary journals is frequently mentioned in responses that focus on postgraduate programs.

2. Who cares in your institution about the improvement of student writing or student learning through writing? Is improvement in student writing an objective of certain courses/modules/subjects in a discipline or of the overall curriculum? How and why?

Ninety-nine percent (99%) of responses are from language professionals who teach and/or conduct research in linguistics and/or literacy in various languages, are in teacher education, or work in academic writing/language support, such as writing centers. More than 50% of respondents feel that their own concern—"care"—for student writing development is not shared by many others in their institutions—even though, as the responses to Question 1 show, most of these institutions do require writing in most disciplines—and even though many of these universities have some form of writing support service.

What is important to keep in mind about these relatively negative responses is that lack of "care" is most often interpreted as lack of active attention or funding for programs—not as lack of awareness or concern. The following responses are typical:

> (Response 1) A few people: student service center: often a non-obligated course, for the "weak" writers, not related to curricula, for a few students. Language center: some courses, in other languages not related to the curricula, for a few students. We have a very small writing center, run by one of my colleagues (with no funding!), a couple of tutor-sessions per week. Some subject teachers here and there. Some managers here and there. Great diversity, no one and everyone.

> (Response 2) There is much complaining in our university about how the level of . . . student writing at the university level has deteriorated. Yet little is being done about the problem in the departments nor are there sufficient resources given to address the issue. The Language Centre of the university is mainly seen as the responsible element and yet we get insufficient money to create new courses.

In sharp contrast: in almost 40% of cases reported, writing growth is noted as an institutional goal and can take many curricular forms: tutoring, workshops, elective courses/modules, writing embedded in many disciplinary courses, modules attached to disciplinary courses, required courses/modules. Indeed, respondents from several countries, such as the United Kingdom, Australia, the Netherlands, and Norway, frame their own institutions' commitment within a national goal of building student communication competence.

As might be expected, the profiles in this book were more frequently invited from among this almost 40% of respondents, though not always so. We have striven to include a significant fraction from institutions where the authors perceive their concern for student writing unshared by most colleagues and rare in the region.

3. Have any teachers in/across disciplines met to talk about these issues or made an effort to plan curricula in relation to student writing?

Note that this question is very different from Questions 2 and 3, and gets at a precise concern related to an institution's sense of shared responsibility for student writing. It asks about explicit cross-faculties planning, not about programs or initiatives for writing instruction in the institution. Positive answers to Question 4 reflect collaboration by different faculties and offices rather than, for example, administrative funding of a writing initiative carried out by one unit or establishment of a student service. Thus, whereas almost 40% of responses to Question 2 were positive to enthusiastic, only 25% of responses to Question 4 were mild to emphatic "yeses"—and the responses to this question tended to be the shortest among the five categories surveyed, because, presumably, the respondents have relatively little to report about cross-departmental collaboration in planning for student writing instruction.

What I call "mild positives" include such statements as
- "A few teachers in ___ are talking"
- "We have regular meetings with___"
- "We co-plan with staff in ___ ___ ___"

The emphatic "yeses" (roughly 10% of the total) describe staff/faculty workshops, collaborative curriculum planning, and/or collaborative research.

In contrast, negative responses (75%) tend to be short and sharp, from terse "No" to mildly hopeful "Not yet" to more hopeful "Meetings are planned between . . . ."

Overall, taken together with the responses to Questions 2 and 3, the responses to Question 4 indicate that in this sample of 330 institutions, active attention to student writing development is most often carried out by staff and faculty members working independently or in small clusters or units. Truly collaborative efforts within an institution stand out within the sample. Again, the profiles in *Writing Programs Worldwide* tend to highlight such examples. Nevertheless, several of the profiles show individual teachers or small groups working mostly alone. These profiles show how the authors and perhaps a few colleagues have created structures to support student writing even in difficult circumstances.

4. What is the source of their interest and what models of student writing/learning development (e.g., articles, books, other documents), if any, help guide these discussions?

This question produced by far the most varied responses by type, though, as in answers to the other questions, responses varied greatly in length, and, therefore, in detail. Fifteen percent (15%) of respondents did not answer this question.

A shorter response might merely credit, for example, "books, articles, websites" as influences on the thinking of staff about teaching methods, whereas a longer response would name specific scholars or textbook authors. Indeed, close to one hundred authors were named in the approximately 25% of responses that include names, with no single author being named more than seven times.

Much more significant than specific texts or authors, and much more indicative of influences on the respondents' thinking, were two types of responses that follow from the phrasing of the question:

1. reasons for interest in student writing by teachers and administrators, and
2. theoretical/pedagogical models that guide the work of those designing centers and other initiatives.

In those responses that addressed reasons for interest, easily the most common (approx. 30% of total responses) was perception by teachers across disciplines of deficits in student writing proficiency. This perception was sometimes coupled in responses with explicit mention (10%) of certain pressures (proficiency exams, disciplinary accreditation, expectations of employers) that raised teacher anxiety about writing performance in disciplines. Less often mentioned (5% of responses) were the need to prepare students for publication in their fields and faculty members' awareness of the value of writing as a tool of learning in their disciplines. Thus, the drive to improve student writing proficiency within their disciplinary courses dominated teacher interest in supporting structures for writing.

When respondents articulated the theories that guided their work with colleagues across disciplines and their students, two terms appeared most frequently: "process" (10%) and "genre" (10%), with both sometimes appearing in the same response; for example,

> For engineers on their way out to industries, the programmes have needed to provide the necessary skills, like report writing and oral presentations. Predictably, they often assume there is a template. Our unwillingness to provide such templates has pushed us in the direction of genre-informed pedagogy and, of course, writing process pedagogy.

"Academic literacies," "English for Academic Purposes," "WAC," "ESL," and "linguistics" were among other terms appearing in a few responses in relation to guiding theories and methods. However, fewer than 50% of all responses named either a well-known approach or an author. Equally common were mentions of highly practical materials produced by a center or by a group of teachers for use only in the local context: e.g., sample student essays and reports, "writing guides," citation models, "teaching methods."

Overall, what comes through most strongly in answers to Question 5 is the respondents' conviction that they are trying, using whatever theoretical and practical means they know and can learn, to address a massive need in an atmosphere of anxiety about student preparedness. The responses across all the questions reinforce the sense of great variation in how well institutions are addressing this need. The profiles in *Writing Programs Worldwide*, while reflecting this range, in almost every case provide models intended to help institutions in this effort.

CHOOSING THE PROFILES

In building from these 350+ respondents the list of contributors to *Writing Programs Worldwide*, each of whom was invited by at least one of the editors, we were guided by several principles. Recognizing that the number of potential profiles far exceeded the scope of a print book and a reasonable publication schedule, we chose as a target forty articles, with no more than two from a given country, as a reasonable and representative number. We also kept in mind that in coordinating with the WAC Clearinghouse we were making possible and, we hoped, systematic, a way to expand the list of profiles after publication of the print volume.

Second, in striving for a representative collection, we wanted essays from six continents. Though, as you can see from our map (pp. 2-3), Western Europe is easily the most heavily-represented region in the book (as it is in survey responses), writing initiatives on all continents are represented, and, we hope, will increase interest in "filling in the map" through further publication.

Third, we wanted our collection of profiles to include (1) some that might serve as models for an institution's steady and thoughtful building over years of strong and diversified services to students and staff; (2) others that focused on a more recent initiative and its plans for expansion; (3) still others that saw themselves as new and quite limited, striving by small steps to affect a university culture in which "academic writing" was not yet regarded as a subject for serious study—or for university spending. Even in the case of the most-established programs, we wanted writers to convey honestly a sense of struggle, of unfulfilled ambitions, lest any reader think that any multi-faceted program had been born that way! Thus, even the contributors from the most successful programs clearly convey a realistic sense of the stability of their funding, especially in bad budget times.

Fourth, almost all the profiles come from among the 350+ respondents to the International Survey of the International WAC/WID Mapping Project, though some of those whom we invited were also previously known to one or more of the editors through their publications or their presentations on their initiatives at conferences. Several were invited based on the uniqueness of their initiatives or in order to broaden the geographic representativeness of the collection.

Fifth, we strove for balance and diversity in the features of the initiatives portrayed. It is safe to say that each profile is unique in its history and in the details of the functions described. However, we also strove to represent a range of broader structural categories: among them,

- Writing centers *(with diverse remits and components)*
- Subjects/courses/modules in aspects of writing
- Workshops and modules for specific faculties
- Peer tutoring and writing fellows
- Informal tutoring and consulting
- Writing instruction embedded in disciplinary courses
- Training for disciplinary teachers in how to assign and respond to student writing
- Writing "minors" and "majors"
- Postgraduate courses/subjects in theory and pedagogy
- Regional networks and consortia of universities

Individual profiles illustrate major differences within these categories. For example, there are described in the collection numerous "centers" that directly reach students in support of their growth as writers in their major disciplines. So it has been important for us that these "writing centers" be individualized in the profiles to show how really different they are in their histories, functions, and motives—how they address their specific student and staff populations, concerns, and political realities, even as they share some common practices.

THE PLACE AND PROJECTION OF *WRITING PROGRAMS WORLDWIDE* IN THE ONGOING RESEARCH

The publication of *Writing Programs Worldwide* in both print (Parlor Press) and digital formats (as part of the WAC Clearinghouse at http://wac/colostate.edu) signifies our intent to continue to build profiles of initiatives in the teaching of writing after publication. For many years, the Clearinghouse, under the imaginative leadership of Mike Palmquist, has served the WAC/WID movement in the US as a destination site for descriptions of college and university WAC/WID programs. De facto, the Clearinghouse is an international site, as its ever-increasing body of materials is accessed by users from many countries. We see *Writing Programs Worldwide* significantly augmenting the transnational content of the Clearinghouse—and providing a template for profiles of more and more institutions. Moreover, the online version of *Writing Programs Worldwide* will give us the flexibility to publish profiles in diverse languages, just as the WAC/WID Mapping Project has encouraged responses in several languages. In these ways, both this research project and the Clearinghouse will help to expand the international community of writing scholars, teachers, and program designers.

A NOTE ON VARIANTS IN SPELLING AND USAGE

The editors have retained as often as possible variants in spelling, as well as elements of syntax and usage, that reflect the different versions of English ("Englishes") most often used by our authors (or their translators) in their academic writing in that language. In most cases, readers will find a particular variant (e.g., "centre" or "center") used consistently within an essay. In a few instances, uses of more than one variant in an essay reflect the author's "code meshing" (Canagarajah, 2006) from different cultural contexts in the essay.

NOTES

1. The first conference of EATAW was held in 2000 (http://www.eataw.eu). The IWCA (http://writingcenters.edu) was founded in 1982 as the National (US) Writing

Centers Association and became the IWCA in 1998, with the founding of the affiliated European Writing Centers Association (http://ewca.sabanciuniv.edu). The initial Writing Research Across Borders Conference was held in 2008; the transnational steering committee was elected following the 2nd conference, held 2011 (http://www.writing.ucsb.edu/wrconf11).

2. See the "Note on Variants in Spelling and Usage" on the final page of this essay.

3. See the official website of the Bologna Process 2010-2012 (http://www.ehea.info/) for information on the history, key documents, and procedures of this ongoing initiative. The Bologna Declaration was signed by ministers of 30 European countries in 1999. As of 2011, there are 47 signatories. According to the website, "At its inception, the Bologna Process was meant to strengthen the competitiveness and attractiveness of European higher education and to foster student mobility and employability through the introduction of a system based on undergraduate and postgraduate studies with easily readable programmes and degrees" (http://www.ehea.info/article-details.aspx?ArticleId=3).

4. Summaries of partial results from this survey were published in *Zeitschrift Schreiben* (Thaiss 2008) and *Traditions of Writing Research*, eds Bazerman et al. (Thaiss 2010).

REFERENCES

Brereton, J. (1996). *The origins of composition studies in the American college, 1875-1925: A documentary history.* Pittsburgh: University of Pittsburgh Press.

Canagarajah, A. S. (2006). The place of world Englishes in composition: Pluralization continued. *College Composition and Communication, 57*(4), 586-619.

European Association for the Teaching of Academic Writing. (n.d.). *EATAW—European association for the teaching of academic writing.* Retrieved from http://www.eataw.eu European Higher Education Area website 2010-2020| EHEA. (n.d.). *European higher education area website 2010-2020| EHEA.* Retrieved from http://www.ehea.info/

Man-Cheong, I. (2004). *The class of 1761: Examinations, the state, and elites in eighteenth century China.* Palo Alto, CA: Stanford University Press.

Miller, T. (2011). *The evolution of college English: Literacy studies from the Puritans to the postmoderns.* Pittsburgh: University of Pittsburgh Press.

Palfreyman, D., ed. (2008). *The Oxford tutorial: "Thanks, you taught me how to think."* Oxford, UK: Oxford Center for Higher Education Policy Studies.

Plato (2008). *Protagoras.* (N. Denyer, Ed.). Cambridge, UK: Cambridge University Press.

Quintilian (1980). *Institutio oratoria: Books I-III* (Loeb Classical Library). (H. E. Butler, Trans.) Cambridge, MA: Harvard University Press.

Robson, E. (2001). The tablet house: A scribal school in Old Babylonian Nippur. *Revue d'Assyriologie et D'Archeologie Orientale 95*(1), 39-66.

Russell, D. (2002). *Writing in the academic disciplines: A curricular history. (2nd ed.)* Carbondale, IL: Southern Illinois University Press.

Schmandt-Besserat, D. (1996). *How writing came about.* Austin: University of Texas.

Thaiss, C. (2006). "Still a good place to be": More than twenty years of the National Network of Writing-across-the-Curriculum Programs. In S. McLeod & M. Soven (Eds.), *Composing a community: A history of writing across the curriculum.* West Lafayette, IN: Parlor Press, 126-41.

Thaiss, C. (2008). The International WAC/WID Mapping Project: Objectives and methods. *Zeitschrift Schreiben.* 18/6/2008. Retrieved from http://www.zeitschrift-schreiben.eu

Thaiss, C. (2010). The International WAC/WID Mapping Project: Objectives, methods, and early results. In C. Bazerman, et al. (Eds.), *Traditions of writing research (pp. 251-65).* New York & Oxford: Routledge.

Thaiss, C., & T. Porter (2010). The state of WAC/WID in 2010: Methods and results of the US survey of the International WAC/WID Mapping Project. *College Composition and Communication, 61*(3), 534-70.

Veldhuis, N. (1997). Elementary education at Nippur: The lists of trees and wooden objects. Ph.D. dissertation, University of Groningen.

CHAPTER 2.
TEACHING ACADEMIC LITERACY ACROSS THE UNIVERSITY CURRICULUM AS INSTITUTIONAL POLICY: THE CASE OF THE UNIVERSIDAD NACIONAL DE GENERAL SARMIENTO (ARGENTINA)

By Estela Inés Moyano and Lucia Natale
Universidad Nacional de General Sarmiento (Argentina)

The aim of this chapter is to briefly outline a genre-based academic literacy program (PRODEAC) across the university curriculum. Its major goal is to promote students' academic performance through the development of advanced literacy in institutional environments. From the theoretical perspective selected (systemic-functional linguistics), a genre-based pedagogy influences knowledge construction in disciplines and empowers students to engage academic, scientific and professional social activities. Two of the critical resources of the program's design will be described: the modality of implementation, which is a device called "negotiation among peers," and the institutional support during the process of installation. Some results in different areas of impact will be also summarized, such as the progress of the students and the university professors involved, as well as the progressive growth of the program itself to its present stability, plus new challenges this program faces.

The aim of this paper is to present an institutional program, developed at Universidad Nacional de General Sarmiento (UNGS), for teaching academic and professional literacy across the university curriculum. The UNGS is located in a suburban town 30 kilometers from Buenos Aires, Argentina. Most of the students of the university (around 60%) belong to the working class, with very low economic resources to cover basic needs and that do not satisfy either cultural or recreational needs. Their parents have had access only to the first levels of education: 55% of them have done complete or incomplete primary studies and 30% have finished secondary school (UNGS, 2003).

At the moment of its foundation, in 1993, UNGS highlighted the need of developing pedagogic strategies to enhance students' abilities in reading and writing in order to promote their success in obtaining a degree. As a result, two academic literacy courses have been implemented at the beginning of the university studies: the first of them as a mandatory condition to enter the university, as part of the University Adaptation Course (CAU); the second as a freshman subject that is part of the mandatory curriculum for all degrees.[1] These courses, the main goal of which is to develop students' skills in academic literacy, are taught by teachers of Spanish who hold university degrees and who also do research. Achievements in those mandatory courses, although very important, seem not to be enough to sustain five years of university studies, according to statements of professors and students themselves. First of all, texts students deal with during the first course have a low level of scientific or technical language, since the students can't yet handle more difficult academic texts. The second course—which meets thirty-two hours throughout the semester—offers them some examples of research articles from different disciplines and pays attention to structures and some prototypical formulations to be recognized in reading. It also reinforces some types of writing they have learned in previous courses. Students need to internalize generic models of academic writing, but this happens only after several opportunities to read and write them, which is not possible during the term of these two valuable experiences. On the other hand, academic activities increase in complexity through the university curriculum, demanding new genres not only to accomplish needs of the degree, but as preparation for professional life. These new genres—e.g., literature review, research projects, research reports, case analyses, and different types of professional reports—demand specific teaching-learning processes. Finally, the literature students have to read is highly specialized: they have to deal with density, abstraction, and technicality, specific grammar and discourse configurations as well as schematic structures they haven't experienced before (Halliday & Martin, 1993). It seemed to be necessary, therefore, to create a different stage of the teaching-learning process to meet the needs of students' academic literacy development.

After three (3) years of institutional negotiation, in February 2005 the Superior Council of the University, the higher collegiate organ of the university government, approved an institutional program with recurrent financial resources to promote students' increasing their academic and professional literacy. It was named "Program to Develop Academic Literacy across the Curriculum" (PRODEAC). [2]

PRODEAC'S FOUNDATION: A BRIEF HISTORY OF AN INSTITUTIONAL PROGRAM

During 2002, professors of subject matter in the degrees of Engineering and Economy taught in the Institute of Industry [3](UNGS) decided to take into account aspects of the students' writing when marking their assessments, in order to contribute to the development of their academic skills. As these lecturers found difficulties in achieving their goals, at the end of the year the head of the Institute of Industry consulted Estela Moyano, researcher in academic discourse analysis and educational linguistics at the Institute of Human Development (UNGS). In February 2003, a project designed by Moyano for the Institute of Industry was submitted to the university government. The project consisted of a proposal of joint work between subject matter professors and a linguist in order to teach academic literacy inside the subject matter classes, doing with the students detailed and reflexive analyses of the genres they had to write, helping them to plan their texts and to edit them until they had a final version that was good enough to be graded. However, this first proposal failed: the university denied financial support for this Program.

During this period, groups of students from different Institutes asked for advice from Professor Moyano to solve problems they found during the course of earning their degrees: new challenges required the development of higher literacy skills. As more lecturers expressed the same concern, the heads of the other Institutes in the Degree Cycle started to be worried about this issue. Nevertheless, a second presentation of the same proposal made at the beginning of 2004 was also rejected.

Two events contributed to the success of the third and last submission in 2005: (1) the determination of the three Institutes in the Degree Cycle to support the proposal, but now as a program to be applied to all university degrees, and (2) the presentation of a letter from students of the four (4) Institutes, asking for more opportunities to develop literacy skills. It is clear that the process begun in 2002 brought about this effect: the Superior Council includes the chair of the university, the heads of the four institutes, and representatives of the different university clusters: professors and assistants, students and graduates, administrative staff. The proposal had been discussed by these actors in their role as councilors, and probably the discussions went beyond the council meetings, thus creating consensus.

In 2005, PRODEAC was installed in the Degree Cycle of all the degrees at the UNGS, under the condition that it had to be evaluated during its first application. Since then, it has been monitored by research-action projects.

THE PROGRAM

PRODEAC is based on Systemic-Functional Linguistics (SFL) (Halliday & Mattiessen, 2004), genre and discourse theory in this frame (Martin, 1992; Martin & Rose, 2007 [2003]; 2008) and the Sydney School's pedagogic proposals (Martin, 1999; Martin & Rose, 2005) that have been adapted to Spanish and specific educational contexts (Moyano, 2007). It takes into account research on language of disciplines (Halliday & Martin, 1993; Martin & Veel, 1997; Wignell, 2007) and the dialogue between SFL and new Bernstenian sociology (Christie & Martin, 2007). The Program also acknowledges the very rich traditions of teaching academic writing and their theoretical bases in Writing Across the Curriculum, English for Specific Purposes, and experiences in Brazil and Argentina (Bazerman, Bonini & Figueredo, 2009; Carlino, 2005, 2006; Hyland, 2002; Hyon, 1996; Karwoski, Gaydeczka & Brito, 2006; McLeod & Soven, 1992; Swales, 1990; UNLu, 2001).

The Program assumes a collaborative design that includes linguists or language teachers[4] and lecturers of the specific subject matters of each degree curriculum. It carries out with students detailed and reflexive analysis of genres they have to write and the cultural contexts and social practices involved; it takes into account schematic structures of the texts and the characteristic uses of language in specific fields of knowledge.

Three main goals are pursued by PRODEAC: (a) to enlarge academic literacy abilities of students for improving their learning at the university and preparing them across the curriculum for future professional social activities; (b) to give assistance to lecturers of specific disciplines in planning and assessing written tasks proposed to students; (c) to prepare subject professors for teaching academic and professional literacy in their disciplines to impact the learning process and future professional performance. This work doesn't mean increasing curricular hours: the proposal implies doing the job as part of the subject and in the classes designed to teach its contents.

The modality of implementation supposes a partnership between a linguist/language teacher and a lecturer of a specific subject matter. These two actors are partners in the construction of particular activities in the class that are agreed on in a statement, or "device," of negotiation between peers,[5] whereby the partners discuss the reading and writing tasks to be proposed to students, the nature of the genres and their structure as well as the participation of the linguist partner in some classes and the criteria for evaluating students' texts. Further study is made in the Program to describe the genres selected to teach and the vocabulary of disciplines in Spanish.

This pedagogical project allows the improvement of ways of communication through interaction between experts of different disciplines in order to initiate students in a discourse community (Swales, 1990) and to enrich the scope of genres written at the university. Moreover, this process makes possible a profile of graduates the UNGS is interested in producing: a professional used to working inside inter- or multi-disciplinary teams for intellectual or technical production. This Program contributes to knowledge construction in disciplines, ways of producing and comprehending discourse, and strategies for cooperative work by modeling and scaffolding.

The work of each linguist-and-subject-matter-lecturer team lasts three periods of six months, until the subject-matter lecturer is able to do the job on his/her own, consulting the PRODEAC team when needed. Then, a similar process starts in other subject matters, until the entire university educational offering is covered. Nevertheless, some activities with different actors become recurrent, to enlarge experience across time.

There is consensus regarding the need for institutional support to implement literacy programs across the curriculum (Carlino, 2005; UNLu, 2001). A program proposing collaborative work inside subjects requires a high degree of institutional compromise to accomplish its goals and promote changes in teaching of disciplines. In fact, several layers of institutional actors participate in the process of determining particular implementations of the program in each Institute, and in tailoring the distribution of applications according to the needs and possibilities of each degree.

SOME RESULTS OF APPLICATION

Since its first implementation, PRODEAC has grown in several respects: in its institutional relevance, in the subject lecturers' and students' generic and linguistic awareness, and in the progress of the linguist-partners in developing strategies of implementation as well as their knowledge of academic and professional genres and discourse.

INSTITUTIONAL RELEVANCE

During the second semester of 2005, the first implementation of the Program took place in only six subjects of different degrees, while in the latest years PRODEAC has intervened in 20 subjects each semester, covering 16 of the 17 degrees offered in UNGS. This expansion has resulted from the high degree of institutionalization obtained and has been possible due to the creation of new posts of permanent researchers in linguistics that participate in the Program as linguist-partners. In 2005, the Program had assigned only two permanent researchers and two hired ad hoc language teachers; there are currently 7 researchers and two hired language teachers.

Subject Matter Lecturers

At the beginning of the implementation of the Program, most of the subject matter lecturers had been in some way compelled by authorities of the Institutes to participate in the Program. In many cases, they were reluctant to increase or systematize writing tasks across the subjects. The activities they usually proposed to students consisted of applying formulae, answering lists of questions, or writing traditional exams, with the only purpose being evaluation of knowledge reproduction. Most of these lecturers had low expectations of the possibility that their students could write long and complex texts in the subject. On the other hand, some expressed belief that genre-based teaching would limit students' creativity or freedom in writing. These kinds of resistance to the Program came from naturalized assumptions about the writing process and about teaching reading and writing that differed from the principles proposed by PRODEAC.

During the second semester of application in a subject some changes were noticed in lecturers' attitudes: they decided to demand more and different written tasks from students; for example, to produce more complex genres. These changes have been attributed to two main factors: (1) their finding students notably improved in their writing abilities because of their participation with the Program in teaching activities, and (2) the development of generic and linguistic awareness due to the negotiation process with their partner (Moyano, 2009; Natale, 2007; Natale & Moyano, 2006). At that point, the subject lecturers started to value in a positive way the role of the knowledge of genres in accomplishing social practices, especially for academic and workplace activities (Moyano, Natale & Valente, 2007). Due to this evolution, there is progress in performing the negotiation, which in turn impacts the process of collaborative teaching of literacy.

In fact, after one or two participations in the Program, some subject professors have made significant progress in relevant awareness. Consequenly, they started to intervene productively earlier in the teaching-learning process proposed by PRODEAC and were able to take on the teaching alone after the first cycle of collaboration. Nevertheless, lecturers can always consult with the PRODEAC team when needed, and may ask for a new intervention after a while. Also to speed the learning process, other professors have written descriptions of genres or materials for written tasks, and these have been prepared by the linguist-partners as bibliography in their subject matter programs.

Students

Students who have participated in the Program have experienced similar evolution. Although some of them recognized their need for systematic assistance in writing academic texts, others at first expressed that the Program meant an "extra load" to their duties. Their concern about writing had to do with the "content" of the texts, in the traditional sense of the term, disregarding the influence of writing on their process of construing knowledge. Nevertheless, their texts presented problems in both form and content. After several participations in the Program, when they could appreciate the benefits they received from the kind of intervention involved and their own progress in writing, students began to give positive value to PRODEAC and showed increasing understanding of the meaning of writing in disciplines.

These reactions have been observed through the consultations the students made in class as well as the comments they made on the texts of other students and on their own texts after a learning process. Students' awareness increased from considering graphical aspects and formalities of presentation (e.g., number of pages) to taking into account matters of information flow or register. They started to pay attention to social context and the need of adjusting discourse to it, the structure of the text, the kinds of information to include, and its organization. Moreover, they start to make spontaneous demands on such complex genres as research projects or reports and show awareness of some characteristics of written mode and particularities of language of different disciplines. This level of consciousness has consequences in the evolution of their abilities in writing (Giudice, Natale & Stagnaro, 2008; Giudice, 2009a, 2009b; Giudice & Moyano, 2009; Stagnaro & Natale, 2009).

PRODEAC Language Teachers

One challenge of the Program is the special training of the teachers of Spanish involved, who are expected to be familiar with descriptions of academic and professional genres and with accurate strategies for teaching academic and professional literacy in different areas of knowledge. As linguists, they need to be capable of doing further and detailed descriptions of those genres and specialized language in Spanish. They also need interpersonal and professional skills to participate in the negotiation device and to respond to lecturers' and students' demands in a productive way.

This profile is not easy to find, so the Program provides space for discussion in seminars, where members of the team share their experiences in different interventions, descriptions of the genres the students were asked to write, progress made in negotiating with subject lecturers, and problems in written texts of the students involved and improvements made by them. These instances make room for collective knowledge construction about matters related to PRODEAC, its development, and systematic work.

CONCLUSIONS

PRODEAC has been designed with the main goals of promoting improved students' performance in the university and preparing them for professional lives. According to Systemic Functional Linguistics theories of language, culture, knowledge construction, and learning, these goals are related to development of meaning potential and academic literacy skills.

The Program's original features include involving institutional actors of different hierarchies and disciplines, who provide institutional support of different kinds. The high commitment shown by these diverse individuals has been possible due to the fact that one of the main concerns of UNGS is to develop pedagogical tools, including reading and writing programs, which contribute to education of students who have grown up in disadvantaged social contexts (Coraggio, 1994).

This institutional support allowed the Program to expand their application field from six subject matters in the first semester of intervention to 20 in each of the latest semesters. In order to promote this expansion, the institution provided funding to create posts in PRODEAC to incorporate researcher-professors in linguistics. This action resulted in the formation of a group that controls the activities and ways of intervention and produces knowledge about different relevant aspects: e.g., accuracy of the pedagogic proposal, genre descriptions, features of academic writing in Spanish, evolution of students' abilities in academic and professional literacy, and evolution of linguistic and generic awareness by different disciplines' lecturers. Some of these developments have been made in the frame of new research projects in UNGS and in association with universities from abroad.

The challenge now is to continue research to improve performance in all the mentioned aspects of the Program, to produce teaching materials and publish them on the PRODEAC website,[6] and to produce knowledge about the languages of disciplines in Spanish as well as in other academic and professional genres.[7]

NOTES

1. Complete degrees in Argentina last five years or 10 semesters. In the Universidad Nacional de General Sarmiento, each degree has two cycles: the General University Cycle (the first five semesters) and the Degree Cycle (5 semesters more), with exception made for Teaching Degrees for the Secondary School Level, for which the Degrees Cycle lasts three semesters. Before starting their studies, students have to pass a mandatory University Adaptation Course (CAU), consisting of three subjects: Mathematics, Science, and a 92-hour Reading & Writing course (cf. http://www.ungs.edu.ar/areas/in_oferta_academica/n/academic-offer-.html).

2. The name of the Program in Spanish is "Programa de Desarrollo de Habilidades de Lectura y Escritura Académicas a lo largo de la Carrera".

3. UNGS is not organized in faculties but in institutes. One of them, the Institute of Sciences, is part of the General University Cycle of all the degrees and the other three are the responsibility of the Degrees Cycle, according to groups of degrees: Institute of Industry, Institute of Metropolitan Area Studies, and Institute of Human Development (cf. http://www.ungs.edu.ar/areas/in_inicio/n/home.html).

4. In Argentina, teachers of Spanish working at the university level must have at least a university degree or equivalent qualifications. Most of them (all of them at UNGS) are devoted to research in linguistics, applied linguistics, or literature.

5. For detailed description of the Negotiation device, see Moyano (2009; 2010).

6. http://www.ungs.edu.ar/prodeac/

7. For a more detailed explanation of further challenges, see Moyano (2010); Vian Jr., Anglada, Moyano & Romero (2009).

REFERENCES

Bazerman, C. Bonini, A., & Figueredo, D. (Eds.). (2009). *Genre in a changing world*. Fort Collins, Colorado & West Lafayette, Indiana: The WAC Clearinghouse and Parlor Press. Retrieved from http://wac.colostate.edu/books/genre/

Carlino, P. (2005). *Escribir, leer y aprender en la universidad. Una introducción a la afabetización académica.* Buenos Aires: FCE.

Carlino, P. (Ed.). (2006). *Procesos y prácticas de escritura en la educación superior.* Signo & Seña N° 16. Buenos Aires: Facultad de Filosofía y Letras, Universidad de Buenos Aires. Retrieved from http://www.escrituraylectura.com.ar/posgrado/revistas/SyS16.pdf

Christie, F., & Martin, J.R. (2007). *Language, knowledge and pedagogy: Functional linguistic and sociological perspectives.* London:Continuum.

Coraggio, J. (1994). Reforma pedagógica: Eje de desarrollo de la enseñanza superior. In *Documentos de Trabajo 1. Estudios de apoyo a la organización de la Universidad Nacional de General Sarmiento.* San Miguel:UNGS.

Giudice, J. (2009a). Apropiación por parte de alumnos universitarios de géneros académicos y del tipo de lenguaje propio de las ciencias sociales y humanas: Análisis evolutivo. Ponencia presentada en V Congreso ALSFAL, Universidad Nacional de Mar del Plata.

Giudice, J. (2009b). Implementación del Programa "Desarrollo de habilidades de escritura a lo largo de la carrera" (PRODEAC) en dos materias de la Licenciatura en Economía Industrial: Análisis evolutivo de casos. Ponencia presentada en Jornada de Intercambio de Experiencias Universitarias en el Desarrollo de Competencias Comunicativas. Universidad Tecnológica Nacional (UTN), Facultad Regional General Pacheco.

Giudice, J., & Moyano, E. (2009). Grado de apropiación del discurso de las ciencias sociales y humanas por alumnos universitarios: Una evaluación diagnóstica. Ponencia presentada en V Congreso Internacional de la Cátedra Unesco para el mejoramiento de la calidad y equidad de la educación en América Latina, con base en la lectura y la escritura, Caracas, Instituto Pedagógico de Caracas.

Halliday, M., & Martin, J.R. (1993). *Writing science: Literacy and discursive power.* Pittsburgh: University of Pittsburgh Press.

Halliday, M., & Matthiessen, C. (2004). *An introduction to functional grammar* (3rd ed.). London:Arnold.

Hyland, K. (2002). *Teaching and researching writing.* London:Longman.

Hyon, S. (1996). Genre in three traditions: Implications for ESL. *TESOL Quarterly, 30*(4), 693–722.

Karwoski, A., Gaydeczka, B., & Brito, K. (Org.) (2006). *Gêneros textuais: Reflexões e ensino.* (2ª Ed.) Rio de Janeiro:Lucerna.

Martin, J.R. (1992). *English text: System and structure.* Amsterdam: Benjamins.

Martin, J.R. (1999). Mentoring semogenesis: "Genre-based" literacy pedagogy. In F. Christie (Ed.), *Pedagogy and the shaping of consciousness: Linguistic and social processes* (pp.123-155). London: Continuum.

Martin, J.R., & Veel, R. (Eds.). (1998). *Reading science. Critical and functional perspectives on discourses of science.* London:Routlege.

Martin J.R., & Rose, D. (2007). *Working with discourse: Meaning beyond the clause.* (2nd Ed.) London:Continuum.

Martin J.R., & Rose, D. (2008). *Genre relations: Mapping culture.* London:Equinox.

Martin, J.R., & White, P. (2005). *The language of evaluation: Appraisal in English.* London: Palgrave.

McLeod, S., & Soven, M. (Eds.). (1992). *Writing across the curriculum: A guide to developing programs.* Sags Publications, Newbury Park, CA. Retrieved from http://wac.colostate.edu/books/

Moyano, E. (2007). Enseñanza de habilidades discursivas en español en contexto pre-universitario: Una aproximación desde la LSF. *Revista Signos, 40*(65) 573-608.

Moyano, E. (2009). Negotiating genre: Lecturer's awareness in genre across the curriculum project at the university level. In C. Bazerman, A Bonini, & D. Figueredo (Eds.), *Genre in a changing world* (pp. 242-264). Fort Collins, Colorado/West Lafayette, Indiana: The WAC Clearinghouse and Parlor Press. Retrieved from http://wac.colostate.edu/books/genre/

Moyano, E. (2010). Escritura académica a lo largo de la carrera: un programa institucional. *Revista Signos* , 43(74) , 465-488.

Moyano, E.; Natale, L., & Valente, E. (2007). ¿Género o actividad? La construcción del concepto de género y su realización en textos en una materia universitaria. In *Actas Primeras Jornadas Latinoamericanas de Lectura y Escritura. Lecturas y escrituras críticas: Perspectivas múltiples.* Facultad de Filosofía y Letras de la Universidad Nacional de Tucumán.

Natale, L. (2007). ¿Conciencia genérica en profesores universitarios?. Ponencia presentada en Tercer Congreso de la Asociación de Lingüística Sistémico Funcional de América Latina. Benemérita Universidad Autónoma de Puebla. Puebla, México.

Natale, L., & Moyano, E. (2006). Evolución de las conceptualizaciones sobre el lenguaje escrito como herramienta para el aprendizaje en algunos profesores de materias universitarias. In A.M. Rodi y M. Casco (Eds.), *Lengua-Investigación. Actas Primer Congreso Nacional "Leer, Escribir y Hablar Hoy."* Tandil:Universidad Nacional del Centro de la Provincia de Buenos Aires.

Stagnaro, D., & Natale, L. (2009). La construcción de respuestas de parcial en estudiantes universitarios. Análisis de las principales dificultades. V Congreso ALSFAL, Universidad Nacional de Mar del Plata.

Swales, J.M. (1990). *Genre Analysis: English in academic and research settings.* Cambridge Applied Linguistics. Cambridge, London: Cambridge University Press.

Universidad Nacional de General Sarmiento. (2003). *Informe sobre el perfil del estudiante*. Secretaría Académica, UNGS. Buenos Aires: Universidad Nacional de General Sarmiento.

Universidad National de Lujan. (2001). *La lectura y escritura como prácticas académicas universitarias*. Departamento de Educación, Luján, Bs. As., Argentina. Retrieved from http://www.unlu.edu.ar/~redecom/borrador.htm

Vian Jr, O.; Anglada, L.; Moyano, E.; & Romero, T. (2009). La gramática sistémico-funcional y la enseñanza de lenguas en contextos latinoamericanos. *D.E.L.T.A. 25*.

Wignell, P. (2007). *On the discourse of social science*. Darwin, Australia: Charles Darwin University Press.

CHAPTER 3.
WRITING TO LEARN BIOLOGY IN THE FRAMEWORK OF A DIDACTIC-CURRICULAR CHANGE IN THE FIRST YEAR PROGRAM AT AN ARGENTINE UNIVERSITY

By Ana De Micheli and Patricia Iglesia
Universidad de Buenos Aires (Argentina)

Reading and writing are essential practices for learning disciplines. Based on this idea, at biology courses of the first year at University of Buenos Aires (UBA) we have been working for ten years with writing to learn cellular biology. In this article we present the difficulties that students face when writing about biology, we describe our work during the classes with writing tasks and also we mention the challenges we continue to face as professors committed to our students' learning. Giving writing a space in the classroom represents an effort not only for students, but also for the teachers, especially when our teaching is done in large classrooms. Nevertheless, the results that we are obtaining in terms of the number of students who pass the class, in the quality of texts they write and in the students' commitment to their own learning are evidence that it is a worthwhile endeavor.

In order to understand the concepts of any field of knowledge and education, it is necessary to appropriate languages and specific ways of explaining, relating, representing, debating and communicating them. In contrast to what most university professors hold true, we believe that the practices of reading and writing—which are essential to the learning of any discipline—cannot be learned until the student experiences situations of written production and bibliographical research within the area (Carlino, 2005).

Based on this idea, in our Biology course within the Basic Common Cycle (CBC) at the University of Buenos Aires (UBA), we have been working for more than a decade on activities that incorporate writing as resources for learning about cellular biology, the discipline we teach. In this article, we present the difficulties that students face when writing about biology, the advances that we have made in implementing the didactic strategies aimed at facilitating such tasks, and the challenges we continue to face as professors committed to our students' learning.

THE INSTITUTIONAL CONTEXT

In 1985, the CBC was instituted as part of the democratic processes begun in 1983 in Argentina after a seven-year military government. The CBC is the first-year curriculum for the 70+ degrees offered by the UBA, the largest free public university in Argentina and also one of the most prestigious. At the CBC, twenty-two subjects are given each quarter; each student must take six of these subjects, based on the degree program that he or she has chosen. The student body of the CBC is heterogeneous in terms of its sociocultural level. In fact, the more than 50,000 students who enter the CBC each year come from both private and public high schools whose educational levels vary greatly. The students are distributed among ten different branches of the CBC in the capital city and Greater Buenos Aires. At each branch, the courses are organized by one or two professors and coordinated by a professor who is entrusted with establishing the educational guidelines.

In the last few years, CBC professors have reported that their students find reading and writing tasks more and more challenging. In spite of this problem, which can partially be attributed to the educational crisis at the high school level in Argentina, little has been done at the university to address it. Maybe one exception is the reading and writing workshop for students who choose a degree in the social sciences.

One of the subjects that is given at the CBC is biology, a class that is mainly focused on cellular biology. This subject is obligatory for all who are studying towards degrees related to living creatures, agricultural production, and health. Approximately 8,000 students take Biology each quarter at the ten branches of the CBC; the groups generally include over seventy students each. From the beginning, the teaching of this discipline was based on a reductionist approach to living structures and a transmissive didactical tradition. These concepts take form in lectures that involve scarce participation on the part of students, a great quantity of information on the subject and student examinations that are generally multiple choice.

This traditional approach to teaching biology sparks little interest among students, leading them to drop the class and evaluate the subject with disapproval. Due to our discontent with the results and our belief that what was being taught and the way it was being taught contributed little to educating students as citizens and future professionals, in 1996 the Biology professors at the North Region Branch of the CBC decided to work towards an innovative reform of the curriculum. This reform has been based on political, epistemological, and didactical considerations.

BASES FOR THE DIDACTICAL CHANGE IN THE CURRICULUM

First, we understand that as teachers committed to public education, it is our responsibility to facilitate the accommodation of a heterogeneous student body in the university sphere. At the same time, we should promote the learning of content important to their future careers and help them develop the cognitive abilities they require to do so.

Second, innovation is based on a systemic conception of living beings which, unlike the reductionist approach, conceives of them with a two-fold epistemological approach: as a whole with a historical, spatial dimension that interacts with its environment, and as the result of a great number of metabolic and physiological processes (Meyer et al., 1979; Morin, 1990; Lewontin, Rose, & Kamin, 1996). Our curriculum is based on analyzing cellular processes in order to understand the properties of the living beings, the relations among living beings, and connections between such beings and their environment. In this regard, instead of emphasizing the acquisition of a great quantity of information and terminology applicable to cellular biology, we organize relationships in hierarchies (organisms, cells, molecules) and on the articulation of different curricular topics in order to explain specific biological events. We are thus able to establish a dialectical relationship between theory and practice (Lucarelli, 2009).

Finally, our teaching rests on a constructivist conception of learning, which we understand as an event that results from continual, repetitive interaction between the experience of the subject, the student's previous knowledge, his/her emotional and cognitive structure, and the object of learning. In the process of learning a discipline, the following all play fundamental roles: the significance of the content to learn, its functionality, and the development of cognitive and meta-cognitive abilities and strategies (Giordan & De Vecchi., 1997). In addition, and based on the idea that the construction of disciplinary knowledge is a social event that involves appropriating a conceptual and methodological system, the learning of an area of knowledge requires that students develop a verbal language for the communicative interaction with others (Jorba, Gómez, Prat, 2000).

COMMUNICATION PRACTICES IN THE BIOLOGY CLASSROOM

Given the importance that we assign to communication in learning a discipline, we have organized different channels for oral and written communication in our classrooms. With respect to orality, we alternate moments of work-related lecture with small groups whose productions are then discussed in the lecture hall. These strategies make the class more dynamic and give students a feeling of belonging, facilitating the flow of information. However, there are several obstacles that make it difficult for individual learning to occur in large classes. On the one hand, few students dare to express their ideas before their classmates. In addition, oral communication allows for little time to reflect on what is heard and said. This feature of oral communication is counterproductive for a population of students who are unaccustomed to thinking before giving their opinions and to answering questions whose response requires some type of elaboration.

For their part, reading and writing are two important methods for accessing knowledge at the university level. However, it is generally believed that students at this level do not require guidance in order to read class texts or to produce academic papers. In our subject, we have been focused for many years on helping students utilize the written word in an interpretative way, and not as a labeling system that involves an endless list of processes, structures, and molecules (Sutton, 2003). To achieve this interpretive learning within the subject of the school and our assessments, we confront students with different problems and challenge them to write about these problems. Some of these activities are aimed at relating a certain molecular process with other events that occur in the same cell, in other cells within the organism, or in other living beings. Others are meant to have students explain biological events and/or justify whether statements on certain disciplinary issues are true or false. We believe that in activities of this kind, writing can become a practice with epistemic potential, an unbeatable resource in learning the subject from a systemic viewpoint.

For the biology professors, analyzing the texts of students and reflecting on the contributions that we can make to facilitate writing was a process of denaturalization, one that involved critical reflection on our own practices as writers and editors of biology-related texts. On this path, we established fruitful contacts with other university professors who incorporate writing practices when teaching their subjects. At the same time, some of the professors began post-graduate studies on writing and reading. Thus, through a recursive process between reflexive teaching practice and theory, we worked to construct a corpus of knowledge and questions that guided our work as professors.

WRITING IN BIOLOGY: OBSTACLES, DIDACTIC STRATEGIES, SUCCESSES AND CHALLENGES

For a long time, our only access to the written productions of students was through written examinations. By evaluating these products, we were able to identify different kinds of difficulties related to (a) the construction of disciplinary concepts, (b) the use of these concepts to explain specific biological cases, (c) the lack of knowledge of ways to explain that were characteristic of the natural sciences, and (d) linguistic problems that do not allow the professor to understand what it is that the student wants to communicate.

With the goal of helping our students confront these difficulties, five years ago we began to promote writing assignments throughout the quarter. This task was accompanied by suggestions on the possible strategies to be utilized as resources to plan the assignments. Some strategies are geared toward coming up with guidelines for relating different subject-related concepts. These include putting together a network that functions as a textual plan and the drafting of a conceptual aura of a certain term, a concept used by Giordan and De Vecchi (1997) to refer to expanding a concept. Other strategies are aimed at clarifying the characteristics of explicative tests and putting them into practice to streamline their use.

Experience has shown that students become committed to writing when the teacher is able to explain the importance of the task, provide students with continual feedback, and thus convince them and stimulate them to write. We are currently working with two types of texts written by students: (a) productions that are the result of some of the activities of the course material, geared to connecting subject-related concepts and (b) questions that the professor asks students to prepare after completing each subject unit in order to gather information on pending doubts and/or questions. With respect to the first type of writing, the assignments are returned with comments by the professor. Over time, we have varied the kind of feedback we provide as professors: at the beginning, we simply made corrections, but we now avoid intervening in the texts and instead make footnotes with suggestions, encouraging students to rewrite when necessary. Most of the suggestions are related to conceptual errors, lack of relevance, cohesion and/or coherence of certain parts of the text, and the lack of punctuation. For their part, the questions posed by the students are a very useful resource for the professor because questions give him/her a view into the aspects that have not been sufficiently explained during classes. After being analyzed, the questions are answered in the following class.

The students who respond favorably to the writing instructions and who read the professor's feedback express that writing helped them learn biology. Through semi-structured surveys, some of them stated that writing was useful when learning concepts, because it made them familiar with the subject-related vocabulary; for their part, the teacher's observations assisted them in detecting their mistakes. In addition, "When preparing the texts, it is necessary to reread the concepts and better understand them, and relate them with other processes." To put it differently, writing this type of text "helps [me] to relate the terms and thus better understand the concepts." Other students mentioned that writing offered them a different way to study than that which they were accustomed to; generally, they were limited to studying "book texts without providing my own explanations"; in these cases, texts were "simply memorized if I couldn't understand the explanation." On the other hand, this systematic work "helps me to avoid postponing." In addition, students admitted that writing helped them "be clearer and more coherent in terms of determining what is most important, what is least relevant, and also to express myself better." Similarly, teacher comments helped them "give the reader a context…not just act as if they already knew things, but explain everything." Finally, students valued the chance to prepare questions on the aspects they had not understood about each area and get answers to these questions because "I may have some of the same doubts as the other students."

In spite of the success in establishing writing as a way to learn biology, there are at least two challenges that remain which merit additional actions in the future. In the first place, we still have not managed to get all of the teachers in the course to address writing with their students. It appears evident that it is difficult for professors to diverge from the teaching models they learned and that doing it requires much critical reflection on the teaching practice. In this process, the joint work of two professors in each classroom proved highly useful. However, having two teachers in a classroom is not always possible due to institutional limitations; making this possible would help professors who are not as committed to their students' writing learn the strategies used by colleagues who are more aware of the importance of writing to learn.

The second challenge is related to the comments we make on students' written assignments. The form and content of the comments vary from professor to professor, depending on their own experiences as writers and their implicit or explicit conception of the role of professors in facilitating student tasks. This disparity necessitates activities aimed at reflection, perhaps in conjunction with specialized professionals who can help us give a name to the methods used by different professors in order to discuss and prepare a more rational strategy on which professors all agree.

CONCLUSIONS

The construction of knowledge is a social process in which communication and dialogue play fundamental roles.

The experience of professors and students suggests that in response to guidelines established in the subject in the framework of a didactical-curricular change, the practice of writing can have important epistemic value. This value grows when writing is inscribed in a dynamic dialogue: students write and professors return the papers with comments and/or suggestions or with verbal answers.

By concerning themselves with the writing of their students, the challenge for professors is twofold: it involves making students familiar with the kinds of writing within our subject area and denaturalizing our practices as "expert" writers to identify the strategies that we use and thus be able to teach them.

Finally, giving writing a space in the classroom represents an effort not only for students, but also for the teachers, especially when our teaching is done in large classrooms. Nevertheless, the results that we are obtaining in terms of the number of students who pass the class, the quality of texts they write, and the students' commitment to their own learning are evidence that it is a worthwhile endeavor.

REFERENCES

Carlino, P. (2005). *Escribir, leer y aprender en la universidad. Una introducción a la alfabetización académica.* Buenos Aires: Fondo de Cultura Económica

Giordan, A. and De Vecchi, G. (1997). *Los orígenes del saber. De las concepciones personales a los conceptos científicos.* Sevilla: Díada.

Jorba, J., Gómez, I. & Prat, A. (2000). *Hablar y escribir para aprender. Uso de la lengua en situaciones de enseñanza-aprendizaje desde las áreas curriculares.* Barcelona: ICE UAB. Síntesis.

Lewontin, R., Rose, S. & Kamin, L.J. (1996). *No está en los genes. Crítica del racismo biológico.* Barcelona: Crítica.

Lucarelli, E. (2009). *La teoría y práctica en la universidad. La innovación en las aulas.* Buenos Aires: Miño y Dávila.

Meyer F, Papert S, Nowinski C, & Piaget J. (Eds.). (1979). *Epistemología de la biología.* Buenos Aires: Paidós

Morin, E. (2001). *Los siete saberes necesarios para la educación del futuro.* Buenos Aires: Nueva Visión.

Sutton, C. (2003). Los profesores de ciencia como profesores de lenguaje. *Enseñanza de las Ciencias, 21*(1), 21-25.

CHAPTER 4.
DEVELOPING STUDENTS' WRITING AT QUEENSLAND UNIVERSITY OF TECHNOLOGY

By Karyn Gonano and Peter Nelson
Queensland University of Technology (Australia)

Identifying who is responsible for academic writing at QUT is a challenge. The message gained from many years of experience is that any writing program needs to be implemented from an institutional perspective and be both top down and bottom up. It must be well planned, well funded, and well integrated within the teaching and learning framework of the university. Written from the perspective of the Language and Learning Unit, whose work in prior years has primarily benefitted international students through various services, this profile essay outlines the Unit's more recent approach to meeting the writing needs of all students. As a central provider of academic writing the Unit is using the Australian government's DEEWR/AUQA Good Practice Principles in a multifaceted approach with faculties to position writing, not only as a core skill required to satisfactorily complete assessment tasks, but over the longer term, as a key graduate attribute.

QUT—AN OVERVIEW

Queensland University of Technology (QUT) is an Australian university with an applied emphasis on courses and research. Based in Brisbane, QUT has an enrolment averaging 40,000 students in undergraduate and postgraduate courses, including 6,000 from overseas. QUT has close links with industry, which complement theoretical learning with a practical perspective. Industry professionals contribute to course development, while academic staff also consult in industry.

QUT has three campuses. The main campus is located in the Central Business District while the Kelvin Grove campus (10 minutes by shuttle bus) houses the Creative Industries Precinct, Australia's first site dedicated to creative experimentation and commercial development in the creative industries. The Institute of Health and Biomedical Innovation is also at Kelvin Grove. Caboolture is one of Australia's newest campuses and is situated half-way between Brisbane and the Sunshine Coast.

What literacy and writing mean at QUT

QUT is structured to enhance students' learning and academic skills. Its approach to teaching and learning is articulated in the Manual of Policies and Procedures (MOPP), and the QUT Blue Print articulates the university's vision and goals to strengthen its reputation as a leading Australian university for quality teaching and learning, as well as to strengthen its distinctive national and international reputation by combining academic strength with practical engagement.

Who is responsible for academic writing at QUT?

While the importance of effective written and oral communication skills is identified broadly in the MOPP, it is not articulated clearly as an integral part of what academics should do in their daily teaching. It is not an uncommon expectation among academics that students should arrive at university with requisite written and oral communication skills firmly in place. Students who fail to meet this expectation are often seen as a problem for the support people in the library, International Student Services (ISS), or Learning Services. In other words, academics often see the professional staff as providing a remedial service to "fix the problem." One academic, who wishes to remain anonymous, confirmed this duality of teaching roles in a personal conversation in November 2009, when he stated, "I am a lecturer of economics, not a teacher of writing" (Nelson, 2009). It is clear therefore that addressing the issues around student writing requires a multifaceted approach that includes addressing the attitudes, focus, and perceptions of academic staff.

The approach to academic writing at QUT has historically been ad hoc. Apart from the occasional short-term funded project, there has been no coordinated attempt by the university to teach academic writing, even though it remains the most common form of assessment at undergraduate and postgraduate levels. It is interesting to note that QUT has no school or department of English or English Literature, and apart from the Faculty of Creative Industries—which offers Creative Writing and Literary Studies, Journalism, Media and Communication—there is no tradition of writing classes for undergraduate students. Since 2002, there has been no Faculty of Arts. Historically, the Language and Learning Unit within International Student Services has only provided ongoing academic writing support for international students and those from a non English-speaking background (NESB; these students in Australia are now referred to as CALD, culturally and linguistically diverse), while the library has traditionally provided academic writing support predominantly for domestic students.

One effort, however, to address the issue of student literacy occurred in 1992, when Ros Petelin (2002), responding to a University-wide call for Teaching and Learning initiative proposals, implemented at QUT 'the first Writing-across-the-Curriculum (WAC) program in the Australian Higher Education sector' (Petelin, 2002, p. 98). The program was funded by an initial grant of $45,000 and identified a need for a writing program through a survey of all full-time academic staff. As part of the WAC program, writing workshops were conducted "for faculty eager to learn and share strategies to integrate writing into their disciplines" (Petelin, 2002, p. 101). Handouts were developed, assessment tasks were redesigned for participating academics, faculty champions were brought on board, and "WAC designed and developed discipline-specific writing handbooks" for a number of schools (Petelin, 2002, p. 102).

Although many valuable activities and resources were developed as a result of this initiative, the program did not last. While feedback was positive, its lack of sustainability was attributed to a lack of resources for staffing and administrative support, particularly to maintain the development of materials and workshops in the classroom (Petelin, 2002, pp. 103-04).

In retrospect, it seems that writing development projects at QUT, including WAC, have not continued because they were very ambitious, not supported by all faculty academics, and rose and fell with the individuals driving them. Additionally, in terms of the WAC project, the unwillingness to link WAC with "the most obvious ally, the service units," meant the project could not capitalise on existing resources of staff, funding, and administration, a component Petelin (2002, p. 105) identifies to being critical to the sustainability of an academic writing program. While ISS today is working hard to remove the remedial tag, it is one of the major ongoing providers of academic writing support.

In the search to identify who in 2011 is responsible for academic writing at QUT, it is apparent that any writing program must be implemented from an institutional perspective and be both top down and bottom up. It must be well planned, well funded, and well supported by a champion at a high level within the university.

ROLES OF THE QUT LIBRARY AND OF THE LANGUAGE AND LEARNING UNIT OF ISS

The QUT Library now provides more extensive support for more students in more flexible ways. This model of service and support for learning skills is the result of restructuring in tertiary institutions that has taken place since 2004. The emphasis on flexible delivery means that library staff have assumed responsibility for point-of-need support and ongoing development of academic and information literacy skills. The library also provides valuable generic resources such as Cite|write and Studywell (http://www.studywell.library.qut.edu.au/).

At the same time, the Language and Learning Unit in ISS has increased its role substantially as a teaching unit for academic skills, particularly academic writing. Since its establishment in 1990, the unit has provided academic writing support for international students in the form of one-to-one sessions, adjunct academic writing classes within faculties (for example MBA, Accounting, Engineering), and introductory sessions during University orientation at the start of each academic year. In response to the increasing number of international students from culturally and linguistically diverse backgrounds enrolling in higher degree research (HDR) programs, the unit has also developed a range of programs to develop students' writing and research skills through intensive workshops and individual consultations. This central service model is now being expanded to include collaborative arrangements with faculties to provide embedded support for all QUT students. Our goal therefore at ISS is to make academic writing a part of the fabric of the faculties' teaching and learning practice for both international and domestic students.

WRITING—DISCIPLINES, GENRES, ASSIGNMENTS

Undergraduate degrees at QUT are both three and four year, and students enrol in four units (subjects) each semester. Each unit generally requires three pieces of summative assessment, including a written assignment and/or presentation; tutorial participation and/or activity; and an end of semester written examination, though this exam may be limited to short-answer and multiple choice questions. Academics have tended to leave students to their own devices when it comes to writing assignments, assuming they already know how to write and in what genre, and that they know what the lecturer is expecting. However, the government's Bradley Review, Transforming Australia's Higher Education System, was implemented in 2009 to widen participation in universities, resulting in an increasingly diverse range of students—with an equally significant range of experiences—who have to complete academic writing tasks.

Yet even today, academics are still reluctant to model examples of essays, for a variety of reasons, including a fear of plagiarism. Few appear to have the skills set to deconstruct texts and teach students how to write in their discipline. International students, however, have had greater access to academic writing support and can participate in generic academic writing programs presented by ISS during orientation week and the fourth week of each semester. These international students can make one-hour appointments to work with the Language and Learning Advisors in ISS, both face-to-face and online. The online service requires students to email their writing, task sheet, and criteria sheet to their Language and Learning Advisor by 9.00 AM on the day of their appointment. This service is used increasingly by the international students who work part time and/or find it difficult to access the university in the centre of the city. Feedback is via Microsoft Word "track changes," and Advisors provide detailed suggestions to students on how to improve their writing. During busy periods in the semester, when many assessment tasks are due, it is always a challenge for the Advisors to balance the urgency of students wanting to have their writing "checked" before it is handed in with their role as language developers.

> As noted earlier, the support for all students, particularly domestic, has increased with the new central services provided by the library. The library's Information Literacy Coordinator, Judith Peacock, has statedOne of the greatest attributes of this university is the extensive collaboration across the university, where the Library and ISS, for example, support each other in providing more comprehensive services for students via programs such as AusAid and Peer Mentoring. This institutional awareness of what particular groups or teams are doing across the university is exceptional, though personality driven. [...] However, we no longer have people in silos not sharing (Peacock, 2010).

PLANNING APPROACHES TO HELP STUDENTS GROW AS WRITERS

A community of practice has played a significant role in how we, as Language and Learning Advisors in ISS, meet to discuss ways to help students grow as writers. Close collaboration among a core team of full-time advisors has led to the development of a variety of programs. One such program is the Introductory Academic Program (IAP) for newly enrolled AusAid scholarship students. Another is IRIS, the Introduction to Research for International Students, which was also developed in response to champion academics asking for support in their classrooms. This program later developed into the faculty specific Language Development Program (LDP). These programs are detailed below.

SUCCESSES IN TEACHING WRITING AT QUT

AusAid scholarships are highly-valued and aim to contribute to the long-term development needs of Australia's partner countries by providing scholarship holders with leadership skills and knowledge to drive change and influence the development outcomes of their own country (Australian Government 2009, p. 1). AusAid is a five week course and includes a one week "settling in" component and a four week intensive academic program. This program is designed by the ISS Language and Learning Unit and conducted each January and June prior to each new academic semester. The program enables students to develop and practice language and learning skills needed for success in their academic studies. The main academic focus is a project which links directly to each individual student's intended course of study and leads students through a series of tasks, which include: principles of effective academic writing; understanding criteria for assessment; starting to research and find references; developing listening and note-taking skills (with different guest lecturers from faculties in which the students are enrolled); reading and research strategies; article summary writing; understanding and exploring their projects—developing useful research questions; identifying the structure of, and deconstructing a typical essay; text analysis; literature review and using literature to support an argument, as well as using references effectively; report writing, academic language, and style; learning styles and strategies; oral presentation strategies; and advanced powerpoint strategies.

Students are required to present a summary of selected readings, a draft essay outline, and a final essay of 2,000 words, as well as an oral presentation of 10 minutes with a five minute question session. The teaching team members each present different sessions in the program, providing students a variety of teaching styles and accents.

Students respond positively to the program and their comments have included:

> Great facilitation and support from the teachers in academic writing sessions.
>
> These sessions actually made me improve my capacities and understanding.
>
> A lovely program, makes me feel confident to take on the QUT challenge.

> IAP is excellent in giving us a better understanding of what is expected in terms of academic writing.
>
> IAP really improved my writing skills including planning and structuring. I've gained confidence in my work. (Song, 2010).

Student responses for the sessions on "Speaking in academic settings" have included:

> For the first time, I learned how to write my own speech for presentations.
>
> Helped a lot, especially the support and positive criticism was amazing.
>
> Really good session. It gave me a chance to speak my ideas, and learn the methods from my peers and the lecturer that I can use to improve myself. (Song, 2010).

Another success story is the IRIS program, established in 2003 to address the needs of QUT's international HDR students. All eligible students received an invitation to participate in the IRIS Program of six contact hours each week over seven weeks. Specifically, the program:

- supported newly-arrived international research students to adjust to the QUT academic culture
- provided practical experience in core written and oral communication skills critical to undertaking research at QUT
- established a positive and productive student/supervisor relationship. (Nelson, 2003.)

The IRIS Program experienced steady growth each year with 259 international HDR students successfully completing the program. Timely, relevant, and meaningful support was the key element, and content was framed to support students as they pursued their individual research projects. Engagement with the IRIS Program early in their candidature meant that these students developed a greater awareness of the requirements of their research proposal as well as greater confidence in communication (particularly with supervisors), plus a vital support network with other research students. The IRIS Program addressed the added challenges faced by HDR international students in terms of language difficulties, social and family dislocation, financial hardship, and adjustment to an unfamiliar educational and research culture.

The IRIS Program was conducted twice a semester over two campuses and acknowledged the rigours and challenges of cultural adjustment by incorporating specific sessions on work-study-life balance. The issues of finding direction at the beginning of their research journey and understanding their new academic requirements were addressed by adopting a learner-centred approach in a supportive environment underpinned by the principles and practice of:

- authentic models of research work
- guided practice and feedback followed by individual practice
- active participation and engagement through independent learning

An IRIS participant in 2008 stated that "the IRIS program helped to clarify the HDR student process for me. It gave me support so that I don't feel too isolated" (Nelson, Gonano, Lawson, & Reese, 2008). By providing collaborative learning opportunities, participants understood that they were part of a broader community of scholars. The Senior Student Forum allowed new and senior students to share, critique, and reflect on their respective postgraduate journeys. Students also supported "the short and sharp, relaxed cross-disciplinary environment", and said that "one of the overall strengths of this course is the opportunity of presenting in front of a large group, and getting feedback for our writing" (IRIS participant in Nelson et.al., 2008).

Overall, the IRIS program made a significant contribution to teaching and learning at QUT and in 2007 won the QUT Vice-Chancellor's Award for Excellence—in recognition of exceptional sustained performance and outstanding achievement in learning and teaching, client focus, and innovative and creative practice. It was subsequently nominated for a prestigious Carrick Award for Australian University Teaching in 2008.

THE NEW LANGUAGE DEVELOPMENT PROGRAMS

However, the rapidly increasing number of international HDR students caused the Language and Learning Advisors to review the IRIS model. Developing writing skills is a long-term process and while the introductory programs, even those of an intensive nature such as IRIS and AusAid, provide a solid foundation, it was felt that a series of faculty-based programs rather than a broad-based interdisciplinary program would better target and meet the needs of this diverse student population.

The new Language Development Programs (LDP), launched by ISS in 2009, are conducted each semester in the Engineering, Science/IT, Education, and Health Faculties and target the language needs, both written and spoken, of the international HDR student population as they work towards the milestones in their candidature: namely Stage 2 (LDP 1), Confirmation and Confirmation Presentation (LDP 2), Thesis (LDP 4) and Final seminar (LDP 5). LDP uses faculty-specific materials and detailed discourse analysis of authentic academic texts and student writing samples, along with an expanded range of support that includes oral communication skills, one-to-one (one hour) sessions and writing circles (LDP 3). These writing circles provide international students with a supportive peer-centred environment to meet in small groups within their community of scholars, where they can receive and offer non-judgemental feedback on their writing-in-progress. Continuing the momentum of the language development philosophy as established in LDP 1 and LDP 2, the ISS Language and Learning Advisors determined that students working together to support each other and facilitated by an Advisor would enable more students to become more independent writers. These writing circles are facilitated by an experienced Language and Learning Advisor who is able to highlight specific thesis writing tools and strategies.

Already the programs have been successful, as students understand that their PhD is actually a three-year research and writing journey. By participating in LDP they are better equipped to develop and edit their own writing. Professor Thambiratnam, who supervises a number of international HDR students, noted in an email to the Faculty of Built Environment and Engineering Research Officer that:

> The English classes have been a tremendous help to these students. I and some of my colleagues have seen the marked improvement in the English of these students. One of my students recently submitted a paper to me and to the other 2 supervisors for review. All 3 of us agreed that the paper was very well written. This student was previously struggling with his English. I am writing to thank you and the Faculty for organising these classes. They were much needed and I hope that they will continue. (Thambiratnam, 2009).

Students see the programs as timely in terms of acquiring strategies to develop their own writing and speaking (Nelson, 2009). Specifically, LDP focuses on writing the abstract, introduction, literature review, methodology, discussion, and results chapters as well as on presenting their confirmation and final defence. The Language and Learning teaching team also value LDP, as more students are participating in a writing program that is timely and developmental for each student. Contributing to the LDP's success is that one ISS teaching staff member is assigned to one faculty. The relationships built among the students, their supervisors, and the faculty are invaluable in helping students develop early on in their candidature the independence they need to write about their research. Meanwhile, the staff member develops a detailed understanding of faculty material, students' supervisors, and faculty organisers (as it is the faculty who promote the program, enrol the students and book the rooms and resources) to underpin this model of support.

LOOKING TOWARD THE FUTURE

2011 is a watershed year for academic writing at QUT. ISS staff are looking at ways to develop further the idea that academic writing is firmly embedded in the fabric of the university's teaching and learning. In 2010, we changed the name of our unit to the Academic Writing, Language and Learning Centre, with our ultimate aim to work as a key provider of academic writing development programs and to sustain an excellent level of support to all student writers.

Currently, the Language and Learning team is collaborating with the faculties of Health and Business on major programs to embed language and learning development within targeted units. These programs will serve as models of "good practice" based on the Australian government's DEEWR/AUQA Good Practice Principles (DEEWR/AUQA), which can be adapted for other ISS-Faculty collaborations across QUT. Significantly, they position writing, not only as a core skill required to satisfactorily complete assessment tasks, but over the longer term as a key graduate attribute.

These two programs include School-based/Unit-embedded workshops and activities developed in collaboration with unit lecturing staff and delivered at timely intervals throughout the semester. Cross-faculty language development workshops target key areas of need particularly in regard to professional and graduate skills development. These workshops are supplemented and extended throughout the semester by individual consultations and small-group writing circles.

When ISS and Language and Learning Advisors embed academic writing programs in the actual classroom or work with academics to incorporate a second-language perspective into their teaching, both international and domestic students benefit. Our goal to become an Academic Writing Centre for all students has evolved from our well-established and innovative language development programs and strategies.

Significantly in terms of sustainability, this work has now received funding from the highest levels of the university and has been included as part of the university's SISL (Support for International Student Learning) Project, a major initiative chaired by the Deputy Vice-Chancellor (International and Development). This commitment reflects the renewed focus in 2011 on the quality of education, particularly for international students. This level of support is also evidence of the growing recognition at the highest levels that writing for all students is a fundamental process of learning which is inextricably linked to developing deep learning; it is a process that can be taught and learned as an embedded skill within a targeted unit where modelling and deconstructing texts will enhance student writing, hence understanding.

REFERENCES

Australian Government. (2009). *Australian development scholarships handbook, 2009.* Australian Government . Retrieved from http://www.ausaid.gov.au/publications/pdf/adsmanual.pdf

Bradley Review of Australian Higher Education—Overview. (n.d.). *Department of Education, Employment and Workplace Relations.* Australian Government. Retrieved from http://www.deewr.gov.au/highereducation/Review/Pages/default.asp

DEEWR/AUQA Good Practice Principles. (n.d.). *Department of education, employment and workplace relations.* Austrialian Government. Retrieved from http://www.deewr.gov.au/HigherEducation/Publications/ Pages/goodpracticeprinciples.aspx

Nelson, P. (2003). IRIS teaching material. Brisbane: Language and Learning unit, ISS at QUT.

Nelson, P., K. Gonano, L. Lawson, & M. Reese. (2008). Carrick awards for Australian university teaching. Brisbane: Language and Learning Unit, ISS at QUT

Petelin, R. (2002). Another whack at WAC: Reprising WAC in Australia. *Language and learning across the disciplines,* 5(3), 98-109. Retrieved from http://wac.colostate.edu/llad/v5n3/v5n3.pdf

Song, Z. (2010). AusAID Introductory academic writing program report. Brisbane: International student support services at QUT.

QUT | Studywell. (n.d.). *QUT | Studywell.* Queensland University of Technology. Retrieved from http://www.studywell.library.qut.edu.au

CHAPTER 5.

TEACHING ACADEMIC WRITING AT THE UNIVERSITY OF WOLLONGONG

By Emily Purser
University of Wollongong (Australia)

Initiatives for the development of literacy at the University of Wollongong are growing within an Australian national commitment to increase overall tertiary enrollment, provide access to students from less-advantaged groups, and enroll more international students. While this essay describes successful programs within the Academic Services Division at Wollongong built to support student literacy, especially academic writing, it primarily emphasizes the work of a problem-solving task force on English language proficiency aimed at building consensus for a collaborative, cross-disciplinary paradigm of literacy growth that moves away from the traditional idea of separable services. The essay profiles a new initiative in the Master of Science program that exemplifies uses of technology to make literacy growth integral to every aspect of student learning and success, including the design of mainstream courses. This initiative and others like it depend on the collaboration of language teachers and researchers with teachers in the target disciplines.

THE INSTITUTIONAL CONTEXT

The University of Wollongong is a mid-sized Australian university, organised into nine faculties and various graduate schools and research institutes, with a population of approximately 23,000 students and 1,000 teaching academics at its main campus, and growing numbers at its various satellite education centres and offshore operations. In its relatively short history, the institution has made a good name for itself, and is very comfortably positioned in annual national "ratings" competitions that attract federal funding rewards for teaching and research. The institution's official story can be read through its website, but for the teaching of academic writing, and how specific programs for any aspect of language development are conceived and funded here, various specific contextual factors need to be outlined.

One important factor influencing programmed development of students' literacy is the university's overall educational mission statement on graduate qualities, which to be meaningful, has to be related to curricular design and teaching. It expresses the institution's sense of standards, and indicates five types of ability that students are expected to achieve, including effective communication. Another important influence on programming for literacy development is the institution's planning around recruitment. Perceptions of how best to help students stay, engage, and succeed in their studies depend very much on the profile and specific needs of incoming students. Other perhaps less well recognised, but equally important, influences on how literacy development needs are understood and responded to are policies and established practices in teaching and assessment across the disciplines, and what teaching academics generally do or do not know about the linguistic nature of academic work.

This chapter discusses implications of all these factors in relation to the practicalities of developing students' capacity to do academic work. It reports on some good educational experiences resulting from collaborative curriculum design and co-teaching, and responds to frequently asked questions about whether, when, where, how and by whom various aspects of "language" might need to be taught in the context of higher education.

POSITIONING OF LANGUAGE EDUCATION

UOW expects its students to become informed, independent yet co-operative, highly articulate and ethical problem-solvers (see http://www.uow.edu.au/student/qualities/index.html). This conception of the overall learning outcomes of any degree program at the university is also explicitly linked to grant and award incentives, to help teachers develop their own capacity and career around innovative, and where appropriate, collaborative, curriculum design and pedagogy. Creating a very visible profile for oneself as a teacher whose practice realises national goals and provides the sorts of measurable outcomes upon which good institutional ratings and funding currently depend is rewarded. Not that teaching is as valued as research, but it can play an important role in career development here, and increasing numbers of teachers participate each year in the complex and time consuming business of institutionally managed self promotion (see UOW Focus on Teaching—Octal awards webpage). Such emphasis on the development of teachers' capacity is crucial to the development of students' capacity in all aspects of tertiary level literacy, including writing. The matter of how students learn to communicate effectively, through all the various forms relevant to the production of new knowledge, needs to be seen as core business for all faculties, it is argued in this chapter.

Language as "Separable" from Content vs. a Collaborative Model

But while written communication may be a crucial dimension of academic work, discussing it (let alone teaching it), is not easy when "language" is conceived as separable from the "content" being taught and learned in the disciplines. So the chapter looks also at the benefits of viewing teaching, learning, and assessment practices as language development work, and as the most appropriate site for the application of expertise in language education. While the collaborative practices described may question some established assumptions and traditions, they are proving very effective and seem to warrant publicity.

Educators across the disciplines are not generally in the habit of thinking about themselves as actual or potential teachers of English language. The very notion strikes many as a ludicrous imposition on, or confusion of, their role and purpose in higher education. It can also strike a note of strange for many language teachers, who might feel their roles or job security challenged. But serious questioning around which aspects of the medium of instruction (English language) need explicit, programmed attention at tertiary level should involve serious analysis of the types of comprehension and performance problems that actually occur in real educational scenarios, and for that it helps to have people with expertise in educational linguistics as participant observers. It is less than ideal when the expertise of language researchers and teachers is confined to the margins of academic curricula, rather than closely associated with (or as is sometimes appropriate, positioned firmly within) the processes of their development and delivery. Such argumentation is quite strong at UOW anyway, where discussion of everything to do with language education has intensified recently, in response to moves at the national level.

The relative ease or difficulty that students experience, as they learn to be good thinkers, speakers, and writers in academic contexts, depends on how the teaching here relates to their previous experience. Whether the difference between their university experience here and their past is slight and exciting or an intimidating chasm has to do with both the recruitment directions taken by senior executive and the institution's marketing arm (in response to a complex range of external forces) and the ability and willingness of curriculum developers and teachers to adapt practices accordingly.

Means and Meaning of Support for Changing Cohorts

The federal government in Australia, as in many countries, wants to quite dramatically increase the overall number of citizens educated at tertiary level within the next two decades, and to increase the proportion of tertiary students coming from "low" socio-economic backgrounds and other traditionally disadvantaged social groups (DEEWR, 2008). At the same time, universities are required to attract a very substantial proportion of their funding from other sources. Philanthropic donations might develop into something of an income stream for some of the older universities with wealthy alumni (Allen Consulting, 2007, p. 7), but for the most part, the main source of non-government revenue is tuition fees on international students (Deloitte Access Economics, 2011, p. 6). And their education needs to be high quality, lest the international marketing of higher education become unsustainable (Phillimore & Koshy, 2010, pp. 1-2; Gillard, 2009). In the university's current planning cycle, the intention is to increase the overall number of students, and the proportion from specified equity categories, as well as to maintain or increase the number of international students (UOW Strategic Plan, 2011, pp. 6, 10, 17). New markets for our education are constantly being sought, and any falling numbers in one area (such as postgraduate coursework programs) are to be met with higher recruitment into undergraduate and research degree programs.

Such student recruitment goals have implications for retention and performance, recognition of which is reflected in forms of support being provided for students' development of academic literacy. But "support" still tends to be understood in limited terms. It is assumed to have more to do with additional programs and resources than with mainstream curricula and pedagogy across the disciplines. A proverbial elephant in the room at many curriculum review meetings, most discussion of such connections occurs in private conversations and in academic publications shared amongst a small number of scholars who are already in the habit of formulating such questions. The challenge remains to get adequate and appropriate support for the literacy development of current and future students into the design of mainstream disciplinary learning experiences. The situation is ripe for wider debate that includes those for whom it actually matters most.

The national quality auditing agency (AUQA) visited UOW in 2011 with two agreed questions: how do we support student transition into tertiary level education, and how do we support our international students? (imPAQT newsletter, 2010). Audits like this generate extensive documentation of current institutional practices, and in our case, urgent need was felt to come up with a coherent and visible statement of overall institutional "strategy" for supporting development of academic literacy, and responding appropriately to the various English language development needs of incoming university students. Funds were allocated in 2010 for a strategic project investigating English Language Proficiency at UOW, which is framed to check how the institution does or does not yet well implement the Good Practice Principles for English Language Proficiency in Australian Universities, endorsed by the Commonwealth Department of Education, Employment and Workplace Relations (DEEWR, 2009). The investigation behind that document began with a focus on international students using English as an additional language, but became a more general set of guidelines seen as relevant to all students.

THE DEFINITION OF LANGUAGE

The slippage between "English language" and "academic literacy" throughout this discussion of support for diversifying student populations is deliberately aiming to draw attention to common ground and theoretical problems. It is often assumed in discussions across the institution that separate discourses and sources of funding around notions of social inclusion and internationalisation relate necessarily to different sub-groups of students and separate educational programs. These assumptions tend not to be challenged when "language" is understood to refer only to vocabulary and rules of syntax, spelling, and punctuation. Such narrow definition of language goes hand in hand with the view that the conceptual "content" of a discipline is non-linguistic and disembodied (put "into" language, but existing independently of any specific socio-linguistic processes through which people come to know and negotiate meaning), and with the conception of language education as error correction and training in "generic skills," which might be taught outside the mainstream curriculum by "service" staff. When, on the other hand, language is understood to operate on multiple inter-related levels simultaneously, and to be the substance and instantiation of complex social contexts, fields of knowledge, subjectivities, and the ongoing reconstruction and negotiation of meaning, the very notion that "content" might be something other than language breaks down. When language education is conceived as examining the normal teaching and learning of an academic discipline from the perspective of language development processes, the relationship between those who best understand a discipline and those who best understand how language works and develops becomes quite different—and dramatically more useful to students' learning.

DISCUSSIONS AND HOPED-FOR RESULTS OF THE STRATEGIC PROJECT FOR STUDENT LITERACY

However broadly or narrowly we define language and literacy in this context, we at least now have a shared picture of our students' need for, and our provision of, teaching programs for the development of students' academic "literacy": in preparation for, alongside, and as part of the various academic disciplines being taught and learned at UOW. The strategic project formed around questions of English Language Proficiency at UOW was perhaps the first time that the various practices constituting our formal programming for the development of students' academic literacy have been discussed and described together. Discussion has been informative as participants have compared how different providers of language education operate, considered how the roles of language educators are institutionalized (and for what purposes their programs are designed), and heard various views on academic literacy and existing development programs from both language educators and the faculties. But throwing a spotlight onto questions of students' preparedness for academic work at tertiary level, and how we help them develop capacity while doing it, as English, is also political. A long felt sense of competition between providers of language education is no longer quietly latent, as the message was given that senior executive will fund whichever "model" wins the argument. Suddenly language educators sense they have to defend their practices and fight for their professional lives and income streams.

The development of students' academic literacy is not, however, simply a matter of economics, and models and programs are not theoretically neutral—they represent particular ways of thinking about language. While there is some shared philosophical ground, there are also interesting conflicts of belief and interest, and very different types and levels of experience shaping views. Another complicating factor is that the report of these deliberations being drafted appears similar to ones emerging in other universities, rather than to be representing the words and agreements of the committee here. We live in hope that the process is just messy rather than undemocratic, and expect to reach, if not agreement on the meaning of literacy and the role of language in academic learning, at least a workable compromise on the wording of any institutional strategy that is to appear online for the world to see.

QUESTIONS ARISING

Meanwhile, to those who think most seriously about it, it is clear there can be no simple or one-size-fits-all solution to the complex range of issues and questions that emerge around academic literacy, and of what language needs to be taught if students are to most effectively learn their chosen disciplines. The situation on the ground at this institution is and will no doubt remain more like a continuum of positions, hanging between two deeply dug-in poles of belief, jostled by voices blowing from various institutionalized roles and different histories in the teaching of English language. Language is everyone's business, and the more we talk about it, from any position, the better.

But key questions have emerged for this writer as a result of these high level institutional discussions, and shape the selective reporting of language teaching practices in this chapter, such as: Can a "free market" like ours, where various approaches to language education and learning support simply co-exist, supply the type and amount of literacy development demanded? Is it best to allow students and faculties to buy, try, and vote with their feet, or to centrally command? Should not programming decisions be based on reliable evidence of what provides students best support for learning the disciplines they come here to study—in terms of measurable learning outcomes within the students' target discipline itself? Within which model of practice are language education providers most likely to gather and report relevant evidence? Within which model of course design and delivery would academic writing instruction be most likely based on research into the linguistic reality of the disciplines taught and learned at UOW—a course provided for a fee by an Arts or Education faculty, or a project-based program tied to funding released on condition that data be gathered and outcomes reported to the institution? Are courses provided for a fee likely to be motivated by the students' actual needs, or by the provider's need to market their wares prêt-à-por·ter? Where are the target disciplines in the relationship between those selling and buying courses in language education? Whose interests are being served when educational policy and governance practice does not require mainstream courses in the disciplines to be designed in ways that are evidently most effective for the given students?

Perhaps the most important question to emerge out of the ongoing discussion of English language proficiency at UOW is how we model the qualities we want students to develop—how our own teaching, research, and governance practices reveal us as being well-informed, independent yet co-operative, highly articulate and ethical problem-solvers, whose work helps students develop appropriate academic knowledge and practice. The ethical dimension of language education here is not insignificant. About 30% of the operational budget of the institution is funded by the fees of international students, so we owe them a very great deal, and need to get their educational experience right. We also like to think that education has something important to do with the future of this nation and its people.

Collaboration in this problem-solving task force on English language proficiency at UOW has at least resulted in some broad assessment of risks and a good statement of principles and responsibilities, which officially represents the development of students' linguistic capacity as a responsibility to be shared by the whole university—students, all teaching academics, and systems. And as the written report morphs into something articulate enough for its harshest critics to accept, active participants in the process have at least become informed of the situation and the complexity of responding to it appropriately. The next section of this essay focuses on what this line of thinking means for academic literacy development in the disciplines, explaining programming choices that are proving particularly good for student learning.

THE TEACHING OF ACADEMIC WRITING IN MAINSTREAM CURRICULA ACROSS THE DISCIPLINES

Before zooming in on specific programs and practices developed with and for a particular discipline, it might help to quickly see the range of choices available to students at UOW for learning "about" academic writing and developing capacity to write academically: There are programs offered by a commercial college on campus as preparation to studies at the university proper (see UOW College website). There are some credit-bearing courses in academic writing provided by the Arts faculty on campus, which can be taken as electives within some degree programs (see ELL program webpage). And there are various options provided by a centrally-funded unit within the Academic Services Division (ASD) without charge to students. The ASD exists to support teaching academics and their students across the disciplines; the programs and services offered by its Learning Development unit range from introductory level extra-curricular workshops on specific aspects of common academic genres, to individual consultations about any aspect of academic work (and it is usually their writing that students want to talk about), to team-teaching arrangements in the disciplines and very varied and extensive curriculum development projects.

The more complex projects tend to be supported by additional funds allocated by senior executive, or by federal government grants, for specific strategic purposes, such as development of programs, scholarly discussion and publication of reports around first-year experience and transition, social inclusion, appropriate support for indigenous students, career development/work integrated learning, internationalization of curricula, and English language proficiency (see UOW's Teaching and Learning strategic projects site and its Focus on Learning website). It is through these sorts of collaborative teaching activities and curriculum development projects, focused as they are on the realities of learning and teaching academic disciplines here and now, and drawing as they do on very experienced informants that best practices in teaching academic writing tend to emerge.

USEFUL COLLABORATIONS WITH COLLEAGUES IN THE DISCIPLINES

Students also have various online options related to academic literacy, from the fairly generic resources for students (see UniLearning), to a wide range of subject-integrated blogs (on-campus access only) hosting scores of links to online language development resources and providing ongoing feedback. While there are and may always be situations where some form of add-on literacy development program based on some notion of "skills" is appropriate, increasing are the situations in higher education where it is recognized that a better approach to academic literacy (and oracy) development is to treat students' mainstream courses as opportunities for intelligent collaboration between those with expertise in the discipline and those with serious knowledge and experience in the design of language education that supports disciplinary learning. Much time and effort of the central Learning Development unit at UOW is devoted to engineering useful collaboration with colleagues in the disciplines, because while very many teaching academics are highly attuned to and interested in removing obstacles to student learning, they often find it difficult to make the changes that make the difference for students' development of literacy and learning. It is complex, and it is not possible to focus equally on research and teaching all of the time. UOW requires academics to prioritise (within limits) on an annual basis amongst the four elements of their core business (research, teaching, governance and professional association and/or community engagement), and provides various forms of academic support for the curriculum and teaching practice development activities prioritized, including its Academic Services Division.

Though not everyone is currently "singing from the same song sheet" on this matter or any other, there is growing consensus here as in the UK (see Ryan, 2011 and the Higher Education Academy's Teaching International Students project) that when the teaching of academic writing becomes a whole-of-institution approach, learning outcomes for students are bound to be better than when "writing" is conceived, and its teaching programmed, around notions of separable "skills" divorced from the dialogue, reading, thinking, and practice (educational and professional) that constitute an academic discipline. When a major issue with serious consequence for everyone is at stake, an inter-disciplinary approach is not only possible and probably more intelligent, it is a must. Whether the social issue is climate change or the standards of literacy and oracy across the disciplines through which we formally come to understand anything in academia, the sum total of outcomes is greater when collaboration between all stakeholders is well engineered and funded than when we develop and apply our expertise in silos.

As in any type of teamwork, the critical factor is professional management and funding. What we increasingly find at UOW is that big improvements are made for students when our activity around teaching academic communications is collaborative and focused on the design of mainstream assessment tasks, resources, and pedagogy within and for the students' target discipline. When two or a few informed and experienced heads work together, the development work is easier, quicker, more interesting, and satisfying for all concerned, and more fruitful, in terms of student learning outcomes. So this seems a model of practice providing lasting and exponentially multiplying returns from the initial investment.

LANGUAGE-FOCUSED LEARNING DESIGN: AN EXAMPLE FROM SCIENCE

Post-graduate coursework and research programs currently attract the greatest proportion of the international students at UOW, and so are a major focus of attention for some of UOW's Learning Development academics. Detail is given in other publications (e.g., Purser, 2011; Kupetz, in press), but one case of a purpose-built subject for post-graduate international students will illustrate points made throughout this chapter. In 2010, coinciding and aligned with the English Language Proficiency project, a project was internally funded to help document the development of learning designs for subjects delivered to international students. Based on principles developed in the AUTC learning designs project (2003) that describe learning sequences in terms of tasks, resources, and supports, the tasks in this case are engineered specifically to expand students' linguistic repertoire. The questions being asked in designing learning for language development in the disciplines are:

1. What types of assignment and learning activities help students notice disciplinary language and develop the academic literacy and oracy expected at UOW?
2. What kinds of learning material most help students complete such tasks?
3. What types of interaction best help students engage in learning, use resources effectively, and complete tasks successfully?

The pedagogical plans and resources are adaptable to a range of similar education scenarios at UOW or beyond. A subject developed for the beginning of the Master of Science program illustrates how the teaching of the target discipline is being approached from a language development perspective—an approach now shaping the design of other subjects at UOW.

Rather than the usual logic of course delivery, the approach being taken here is to foreground the students' learning activity, and to indicate visually throughout a website how the various informational resources are to be used to complete tasks, and what support will be given by teachers and peers. What is normally understood as course "content" is here presented as informational resources, to be drawn on in the guided process of completing specific tasks. Academic literacy, oracy and self-management are clearly fore-grounded as the major learning outcomes of the subject, and not treated as either "generic" or achievable outside the context of the teaching and learning of the target discipline. The whole science subject is presented to students as sets of inter-related processes of information searching, critical reading, text re-construction, and critical reflection on academic language and learning across their curriculum.

Each module within the eLearning site guides students through a sequence of necessary steps, scaffolding their awareness and control over the language involved and leading to greater communicative capacity and independence in organizing and completing the sorts of tasks routinely required throughout students' degree program.

Within each of these stages, students experience extensive modeling and guidance through annotated sample texts, process demonstration videos, integrated group discussion, regular feedback on drafts, and ongoing reflection on emerging practice. Students speaking voices are recorded and posted for group feedback and comparison against a model. A very wide range of lexico-grammatical possibilities in paraphrasing and summarising are demonstrated, discussed, and tested through the process of translating a published journal article into a visually supported spoken presentation and a poster.

In focusing on spoken presentation, students also develop understanding of good collaborative practice, by selecting one of the journal articles sourced for their literature review and, positioning themselves as a mock research team, translating the dense written text into a succinct visually-supported talk, in which each group member has equal time to speak.

Throughout the subject, students are guided to carefully observe and reflect on learning and academic language across the curriculum. The eLearning site in subjects like these is fundamental rather than ancillary, as it visualizes the design and guides the learning experience, freeing classroom time for intensive interaction, dialogue, trial and error, feedback and peer support. This is vital in the context, as the building of strong social networks in the students' first two months at UOW has proven a key element in how this type of subject makes a difference to the subsequent learning experience of the students throughout their chosen course of study (Purser, in Kupetz, in press). The designs emerging are quite easily adaptable across different Learning Management Systems, social networking technologies, and contexts.

CONCLUSION

This profile essay has described a context wherein learning is usually assessed through some form of prose writing, but where students may not "hit the ground running" when they encounter the realities of academic writing in the disciplines. It is an environment where a great deal of explicit teaching of academic writing occurs, but rarely in so-labeled classes. UOW recognizes the demands of academic literacy across the disciplines, and several staff here have developed good reputation nationally and internationally for their practice and leadership in teaching and research on academic literacy. But with current anticipation of ever more students finding academic discourse and practice per se quite new and strange, and a very significant proportion of students finding the doing of academic work *as English* to be new and challenging, it makes less and less sense to increasing numbers of teachers across the disciplines to address the literacy development needs of students in separate classes teaching so-called generic academic and language "skills." We might eventually stop regarding students' writing as evidence of *their* deficiencies altogether, and come to really understand how the teaching of academic disciplines can limit or liberate the linguistic repertoire of students entering a course of study.

REFERENCES

Allen Consulting Group. (2007). *Philanthropy in Australia's higher education system*. Australian Government. Retrieved from http://www.dest.gov.au/NR/rdonlyres/A12FE041-3589-4610-852B-8177303B6BD3/21550/PhilanthopyintheHigherEducationSystemFinalReportWe.pdf

Australian Universities Quality Agency.(n.d.). *Department of Education, Employment and Workplace Relations*. Australian Government. Retrieved from http://www.deewr.gov.au/HigherEducation/Programs/Quality/QualityAssurance/Pages/TheAusUniQualityAgency.aspx

Australian Universities Teaching Committee .(2003). *Project on ICT-based learning designs.* Australian Universities Teaching Committee. Retrieved from http://www.learningdesigns.uow.edu.au/project/learn_design.htm

Department of Education, Employment and Workplace Relations. (2008). *Review of Australian higher education report (The Bradley Review).* Australian Government. Retrieved from http://www.deewr.gov.au/HigherEducation/Review/Pages/default.aspx

Department of Education, Employment and Workplace Relations. (2009). *Good practice principles for English language proficiency for international students in Australian universities.* Australian Government. Retrieved from Australian Government http://www.deewr.gov.au/HigherEducation/Publications/Pages/GoodPracticePrinciples.aspx

Deloitte Access Economics. (2011). *Broader implications from a downturn in international students.* Universities Australia. Retrieved from http://www.universitiesaustralia.edu.au/resources/618/1100

English Language and Linguistics (ELL).(n.d.). *University of Wollongong.* Retrieved from http://www.uow.edu.au/arts/language/ELL/index.html

Gillard, J. (2009). *International education—its contribution to Australia.* Australian Government. Retrieved from http://www.deewr.gov.au/Ministers/Gillard/Media/Speeches/Pages/Article_090527_093411.aspx

The Higher Education Academy (THEA). (n.d.). *Teaching international students project.* Higher Education Academy. Retrieved from http://www.heacademy.ac.uk/international-student-lifecycle

Kupetz, R. (in press). *Interaction in CLIL scenarios.* London: Equinox.

Learning Development. (n.d.). *Student services at UOW.* University of Wollongong. Retrieved from http://www.uow.edu.au/student/services/ld/index.html

Phillimore, J., & Koshy, P. (2010). *The Economic implications of fewer international higher education students in Australia.* Australian Technology Network of Universities. Retrieved from http://www.atn.edu.au/newsroom/Docs/2010/August_2010_Economic_implications_of_fewer_international_higher_education_students_in_Australia.pdf

Purser, E. (2011). Developing academic literacy in context: Trends in Australia. In M. Deane & P. O'Neill (Eds.), *Writing in the Disciplines.* Palgrave: London.

Ryan, J. (2011, May 18). Academic shock: Thoughts on teaching international students. *The Guardian*; Higher Education Network. Retrieved from http://www.guardian.co.uk/higher-education-network/blog/2011/may/18/teaching-international-students

Stirling, J., & Rossetto, C. (2011, June). Walking the talk: From policy to practice. Presentation at the Critical discussion about social inclusion forum. University of Wollongong.

UniLearning. (n.d.). *University learning*. University of Wollongong. Retrieved from http://unilearning.uow.edu.au/main.html

University of Wollongong. (n.d.). *University of Wollongong*. Retrieved from http://www.uow.edu.au/index.html

UOW College. (n.d.). UOW. *English language programs*. University of Wollongong. Retrieved from http://www.uowcollege.edu.au/english_programs/academic_english#english_for_tertiary_studies

UOW Focus (n.d.). *UOW Focus on learning*. University of Wollongong. Retrieved from http://focusonlearning.uow.edu.au/index.html

UOW Focus on Teaching. (n.d.). *UOW Focus on Teaching*. University of Wollongong. Retrieved from http://focusonteaching.uow.edu.au/index.html

UOW Graduate Qualities. (n.d.). *UOW Graduate qualities*. University of Wollongong. Retrieved from http://www.uow.edu.au/student/qualities/index.html

UOW Learning Development .(n.d.). *Student services at UOW*. University of Wollongong. Retrieved from http://www.uow.edu.au/student/services/ld/index.html

UOW Strategic Plan .(2011). *Strategic Plan 2011-2013, Planning and Quality Office, 2011*. University of Wollongong. Retrieved from http://www.uow.edu.au/planquality/strategicplan/index.html

UOW Strategic Planning & Quality Office. (2010). *ImPAQT; Planning and quality at UOW*. University of Wollongong. Retrieved from http://www.uow.edu.au/content/groups/public/@web/@spq/documents/doc/uow088130.pdf

UOW Teaching and Learning. (n.d.). UOW *Teaching and learning strategic projects*. University of Wollongong. Retrieved from http://www.uow.edu.au/asd/executivedirector/projects/index.html

Wheeler, D. (2011). Philanthropy and higher education in Australia. *The Chronicle of Higher Education*. Retrieved from https://chronicle.com/blogs/worldwise/philanthropy-and-higher-education-in-australia/28220

CHAPTER 6.
THE SCHREIBCENTER AT THE ALPEN-ADRIA-UNIVERSITÄT, KLAGENFURT, AUSTRIA

By Ursula Doleschal
Alpen-Adria Universität Klagenfurt (Austria)

The writing centre (henceforward: "SchreibCenter") at the Alpen-Adria-Universität Klagenfurt was founded in 2004 and has since developed successfully, although it has been allotted only minimal financial means by the university. The history of the SchreibCenter is an example of how it is possible, in spite of minimal funding, to create an infrastructure and get appropriately entrenched in and acknowledged by the university. As will be shown, important steps to this goal are to find supporters and partners within faculty, acquire funds for teaching/courses, acquire funding for small projects, and find external partners and sponsors.

SIZE AND MISSION

The SchreibCenter at the University of Klagenfurt was founded in order to enhance the quality of written texts in the university. Its most prominent target group is of course students, but the mission statement in the statutes of the university (http://www.uni-klu.ac.at/rechtabt/downloads/Satzung_Teil_A.pdf, January 6, 2010) explicitly formulates that it is the aim of the SchreibCenter to "develop a high-quality writing standard in the university, in the first place with the students, but also with all other members of the university."[1]

The range of offers is thus directed at the different groups of university members and includes courses, tutoring and counseling for students as well as workshops for teachers and administrative personnel, and counseling for researchers, plus other pertinent measures that might enhance the quality of writing within but also beyond the university. The SchreibCenter is a rather small institution. The staff consists of one regular employee—the operative director (Carmen Mertlitsch) —along with the scientific director (Ursula Doleschal), who is at the same time full professor of Slavic linguistics. Teaching and tutoring is provided by 13 lecturers and nine tutors on the basis of contracts. These personnel are paid by the university, which makes available a moderate budget for daily business and other technical equipment. The university has also put one office room and one lecture room at the disposal of the SchreibCenter. For other financial needs, the SchreibCenter relies on external funding/fundraising.

Nevertheless, the SchreibCenter offers full-fledged courses, workshops, and individual counseling as well as tutorials accompanying courses in different disciplines.

Last year, for example, the SchreibCenter offered 20 courses,[2] which were attended by 230 students, three workshops for university staff, and about 100 hours of individual counseling and tutoring.

LOCATION AND AFFILIATION

Klagenfurt is the capital of the Austrian province of Carinthia (bordering both Slovenia and Italy) and is located in a bilingual area of a German-speaking majority (517,000 people) and a Slovene-speaking autochthonous minority (14,000). The city has 90,000 inhabitants. Economically, Carinthia depends very much on tourism, but there is also some industry (microtechnology, wood-processing, food) and agriculture. Culturally speaking, Carinthia is a traditionalist country with a remarkable number of folk musicians and choirs. As to education and literacy, they do not seem to be highly valued among the population, let alone among local politicians. In spite of the fact that Klagenfurt is the native town of Robert Musil and Ingeborg Bachmann, two of the most distinguished German-speaking writers of the twentieth century, and although every year a literary contest for the Ingeborg Bachmann prize is carried out, the city of Klagenfurt has no common public library (beside the Slovene library of studies, which offers literature in Slovene). Many students at the University of Klagenfurt come from families without higher education.

The University of Klagenfurt is a state university and a relatively young university; it was founded in 1970 and in the beginning offered only humanities and pedagogical studies. In 1990, a faculty of economics and IT was added, and lately, IT was enhanced by microtechnologies such as mechatronics, and a technical faculty was founded. In this way, undergraduate (bachelor) students can enroll either for humanistic studies, such as philosophy, philology, history, and applied cultural studies, or for more socially oriented studies: media communication, pedagogy, psychology; and for geography, mathematics, economics, and business studies, as well as information technology studies and microtechnologies. Besides, all these studies can also be enrolled in as graduate (master) and PhD programs.

The working language of the university is generally German. One master program is taught completely in English (information technology), and English is also an important working language for some other fields of studies, such as psychology, and especially for PhD studies. Currently about 10,000 students are enrolled in the Alpen-Adria-Universität (about 87% of whom are Austrian). Although Slovene is also an official language in parts of Carinthia, this is not reflected in language use at the university.

"LITERACY" AND "WRITING": WHY STUDENTS WRITE, IN WHAT LANGUAGES AND DIALECTS, IN RELATION TO WHAT GOALS?

During their studies, students have to write a number of course assignments and theses, usually in German, sometimes also in English; in the philologies they may also write their theses in the language they are studying. The exact number of written assignments differs significantly in terms of the respective field of studies; e.g., the undergraduate study of business administration currently has the least number (one thesis in the beginning and one—the bachelor thesis—at the end of the program of studies), whereas philological studies, such as Slavic studies, include at least six theses, including two bachelor theses. Theses are a compulsory part of Austrian academic education and aim at making students acquainted with doing research. As Otto Kruse (2009) contends, this tradition goes back to the Humboldtian reform of the university and the ideal of the unity of teachers and students, who in the nineteenth century worked together in the form of seminars. The course type of seminar is still seminal in German-speaking academia, although very often it is not a place of research any more, and neither are seminar theses. As a genre, seminar theses are usually modeled on the example of research articles. In some fields students also have to write reports (e.g., after an internship); students of pedagogy moreover have to master the genre of reflection ("Reflexionsarbeit"). At the Alpen-Adria-Universität, bachelor theses are usually understood as a form of seminar thesis, whereas master theses are considerably larger and tend to be seen as an autonomous contribution to research.

In contradistinction to the Anglo-Saxon practice and also to what pupils usually learn at school, essay writing is not common in German-speaking universities and not in Klagenfurt either (Stadter, 2003); neither is creative writing, though very recently there have been attempts in the realm of Germanistics and Media studies in Klagenfurt; these courses, however, are not part of the compulsory syllabus.

In these ways, students usually write in order to get credit for a course or toward receiving the final degree. It seems that many professors share this view and understand written assignments as a form of examination and not as an instrument of learning or research. In the teutonic tradition, writing is something one learns once and forever at school (cf. Čmejrková & Daneš, 1996). Therefore, professors expect their students to be able to write academic texts in a correct and adequate language. Students, on the other hand, come from a schooling system where style is seen as an individual, creative, and even artistic form of written expression (in the tradition of Leo Spitzer, cf. Fix, Poethe, & Yos, 2003, pp. 26-32) and where objective exposition has not been taught sufficiently,[3] perhaps with the exception of the text type "account." In university, they are faced with totally new genres, the sense of which is unclear to them, and so they often feel lost. When they try to transfer what they have learned in school, especially what they conceive of as "good style," the results do not usually meet the standards of academic texts. Professors are not a great help either; they often lack the instruments for adequate feedback on questions of text and style and therefore in the end resignedly accept what students deliver (cf. the interviews in Gruber et al., 2006).

THE LOBBY

Under such general conditions, the dean of the faculty of economics and informatics, Paul Kellermann, launched the idea of founding a writing centre in spring 2003, and so assistant professor Helmut Guggenberger from the department of sociology mustered a work group of about 10 volunteers—professors from different fields of study who were concerned and interested in students' writing, plus one graduate student—who discussed necessary measures and worked out a conceptual design and a schedule which were presented to the founding convent[4] in autumn. At that time a profound structural reform of the universities was being carried out in Austria, which proved a felicitous opportunity for the founding of new units. After a short period of lobbying by all members of the work group, the founding convent accepted the writing centre and included it in the new statutes, which were enacted on January 1, 2004. As a scholar of linguistics, I volunteered to be the scientific director of the writing centre, and this idea was accepted by the rector in February 2004, who in a conference with the work group commissioned us to start operating by the beginning of the autumn term, i.e., in October 2004, allotting the SchreibCenter a budget of € 15,000 for the academic year 2004/2005. It was also decreed that the writing centre should function as a pilot project for two years, after which an evaluation would take place.

Taking into account financial and human resources, the first step, in order to get started that autumn, was to begin with a course program and to develop other services, especially individual counselling. This approach was also a natural consequence of the fact that there were some people who were able and willing to teach writing courses at once. Most of them, especially Maria Nicolini, who for years was the only person in the university who regularly offered seminars on academic writing, relied on experience in this field.[5]

They argued for the pedagogical value of discussing the problems and facets of writing in groups. This teaching concept was built mainly on the findings of applied linguistics, taking into account on the one hand the academic proficiency of students, on the other disciplinary groupings. This approach draws on the writings of Ken Hyland (2004) and on projects in writing proficiency (especially the one carried out in Vienna under the guidance of Helmut Gruber, cf. Gruber et al., 2006, but also Pohl, 2007). Furthermore the findings of contrastive rhetoric (Clyne, 1987; Čmejrková & Daneš, 1997; Duszak, 1994, etc.) led to the designing of special courses both in English and in German for students with another native language. Last but not least, the differences among academic, journalistic, literary, and administrative styles, as studied by functional stylistics in the East European tradition (Fleischer & Michel, 1979; Mistrík, 1985; Riesel, 1959; Tošović, 1988) led to a differentiation between courses for academic writing and creative and/or journalistic writing. In the end, the possibilities and competencies of the people available on the spot were also taken into account. Therefore, the concept resulted in a pluralistic approach to individual teaching methods, which the newly constituted work group fervently discussed in many sessions and workshops.

These core concepts have been developed since and have resulted in variations as part of a three-layered program for beginners, intermediate students, and (postgraduate) students who are writing a qualification assignment (master or PhD thesis). This program is further differentiated into fields of studies, aiming at disciplinary groupings including business studies, philologies and history, technical studies, etc. But there are also courses for all students, regardless of their field of study, for academic, creative, and professional writing. Recently, a special form of peer tutoring was added, the "open writing lab" (Offene Schreibwerkstatt, cf. Halfmann, Perschak, & Doleschal, 2009), a course or forum where students from all disciplines and grades can discuss their problems and receive input and support from peer tutors. This innovation was designed by Carmen Mertlitsch drawing on Roth (1999).

The idea to work with student peer tutors goes back to a workshop with Gerd Bräuer in 2004, but only in 2006 were we able to start with a pilot project, and in 2007 with a first version of a training program (see Mertlitsch & Doleschal in press). Theoretically the work of the SchreibCenter continues to be based on applied linguistics. Therefore, the peer tutors, who come from different fields, are trained for identifying categories of language, such as text structure or elements of grammar and style, and design their feedback in accordance. Peer tutors are deployed for the open writing lab, tutorials, workshops, and individual counselling for students. The tutor is paid individually (currently € 15 per hour). At present we are educating a group of peer tutors to give support in English in collaboration with the English department.

Collaboration and networking have turned out to be the SchreibCenter's main key to success. In the pilot phase of the SchreibCenter (until 2007), when there was no regular staff, Carmen Mertlitsch and Jürgen Struger, who had graduated in linguistics and German from the University of Klagenfurt and ran a bureau for counselling and correcting academic texts,[6] worked for the SchreibCenter on a contract basis. They initiated a survey of demand regarding writing skills of students, during which the three of us sought conversations with faculty who were responsible for course programs. We learned about the concerns of professors and were at the same time able to make the new institution of a writing centre known among faculty and to propagate the idea of supporting students' writing skills. Reactions were very different, but some people were immediately in favour of the initiative and keen on getting support in their own fields. As a consequence we organized a workshop for a research group of PhD students and assistants and a tandem course with a seminar in psychology, both in English. In 2006, we succeeded in implementing tutorials with peer tutors for seminars, first in informatics, later in psychology. Furthermore, consultations were given to professors on how to care for students' writing skills, drawing on the model of dissemination proposed by Gerd Bräuer (cf. Bräuer, 2007).

It certainly helped that I was a member of the university senate and thus had the opportunity for informal talks with full professors and the rector. Both Carmen Mertlitsch and Jürgen Struger, on the other hand, were active among peers, trying out all forms of collaboration, such as projects for other departments (e.g., a practical guide for teachers, Mertlitsch, 2010), workshops for staff, individual counseling for staff, workshops for external partners, etc. These projects were at the time a vital source of funding, because until 2007 the SchreibCenter had to finance its workforce with the help of fundraising. At the same time, all these collaborations became the basis for external relationships, e.g., with the academies of health care, a post-secondary school, where 10-14 workshops for students have been carried out each year up to now, and which are financed by the governmental office of the province. Equally important, such projects were a challenge that called for and stimulated professional development in all members of the SchreibCenter.

SUCCESS AND UNFULFILLED AMBITIONS

The most sustainable success of the Klagenfurt SchreibCenter is probably that it initiated a process of consciousness among faculty and students. Especially younger professors actively take up advice and design their own courses in a way that includes writing assignments and feedback to the students. Others invite us to give input on academic writing in their seminars. As to students, they show a constantly growing interest in the courses and consultations of the SchreibCenter, especially in the open writing lab.

The second main success, to my mind, is that the SchreibCenter as a permanent and autonomous institution of the university is now beyond question. This was not always the case, since the idea that writing as a key competence should be learned before coming to university is still very much alive among professors.

Thirdly, it is a great success for me personally that Jürgen Struger got a regular job as assistant in the AEEC Deutsch ("Österreichisches Kompetenzzentrum für Deutschdidaktik") in 2006 and Carmen Mertlitsch was regularly employed at the SchreibCenter in 2007. Similarly, I consider it a great success that we can train students as peer tutors and advisors, and in this way give them the opportunity to do a job that is in demand—and earn money with linguistics.

Of course, there are also unfulfilled ambitions as to writing skills of students. Usually, students who have attended any activity of the SchreibCenter feel empowered and confident in their newly acquired skills. This is not congruent with my own rating of their competence; e.g., two of my own students went to workshops and tutorials and were convinced that they had learned a lot. The master theses they handed in, however, did not reflect this self-assessment; they were still rather badly written. On the other hand, I have to admit that they were able to revise their papers on the basis of my comments and then signed in very good theses. Reactions by faculty show that all people who attend courses of the SchreibCenter benefit from their learning of the revision process.

NOTES

1. Cf. The original: "Die professionelle Auseinandersetzung mit der Schreibtätigkeit ist eine Aufgabe einer auf internationale Wettbewerbsfähigkeit bedachten Universität.

Ziel des SchreibCenters der Universität Klagenfurt ist die Entwicklung eines qualitativ hochwertigen universitären Schreibstandards insbesondere bei den Studierenden aber auch bei allen anderen Universitätsangehörigen. Dies wird durch ein entsprechendes Kursangebot, durch Beratung sowie durch interdisziplinäre Zusammenarbeit gewährleistet. " (http://www.uni-klu.ac.at/rechtabt/downloads/Satzung_Teil_A.pdf, January 6, 2010).

2. Courses were financed by other departments, but organized and supervised by the SchreibCenter.

3. Although the syllabus for German in grammar schools gives equal significance to both subjective and objective text types (cf. Lehrpläne der AHS-Oberstufe http://www.bmukk.gv.at/schulen/unterricht/lp/lp_ahs_oberstufe.xml and "Deutsch" http://www.bmukk.gv.at/medienpool/11853/lp_neu_ahs_01.pdf), it seems that both teachers and pupils are on the whole more inclined to the genre of interpretation of literary texts (Saxalber Tetter, 2008).

4. "Gründungskonvent" —a work group of university members who had to formulate the statutes of the university on the basis of a new university-law.

5. See, e.g., Nicolini, 2001, 2008.

6. See Mertlitsch & Struger, 2007.

REFERENCES

Bräuer, G. (2007). Schreibdidaktische Beratung für Lehrende bei der Ausbildung von wissenschaftlich denkenden und handelnden Studierenden. In U. Doleschal & H. Gruber (Eds.), *Wissenschaftliches Schreiben abseits des englischen Mainstreams* (pp. 193-215). Frankfurt am Main: Peter Lang.

Clyne, M. (1987). Cultural differences in the organization of academic texts: English and German. *Journal of Pragmatics, 5,* 211-247.

Čmejrková, S. (1996). Academic Writing in Czech and English. In E. Ventola & A. Mauranen (Eds.), *Academic writing, Intercultural and textual issues* (pp. 137-145). Amsterdam: Benjamins.

Čmejrková, S., & Daneš, F. (1997). Academic writing and cultural identity: The case of Czech academic writing (pp. 41-62). In A. Duszak (Ed.), *Intellectual styles and crosscultural communication.* Berlin: deGruyter.

Duszak, A. (1994). Academic discourse and intellectual styles. *Journal of Pragmatics, 21,* 291-313.

Fix, U., Poethe, H., &.Yos, G. (2003). *Textlinguistik und Stilistik für Ginsteiger: Ein Lehr- und Arbeitsbuch. Unter Mitarb. von Ruth Geier.* 3., durchges. Aufl. Frankfurt am Main: Wien [u.a.]: Lang.

Fleischer, W. Michel, G. (1979). *Stilistik der deutschen Gegenwartssprache. unter Mitarb. von Rosemarie Gläser. 3., durchges.* Aufl. Leipzig: Bibliograph. Institut, VEB.

Gruber, H., Muntigl, P., Reisigl, M., Rheindorf, M., Wetschanow, K., &. Czinglar, C. (2006). *Genre, Habitus und wissenschaftliches Schreiben.* Münster: LIT Verlag.

Halfmann, C., Perschak, K, Doleschal, U. (2009, July). The Open Writing Lab—a way to improve the writing skills of students across all disciplines? Lecture held at the 5th EATAW Conference, University of Coventry. . Retrieved from http://wwwm.coventry.ac.uk/eataw2009/Pages/EATAW2009.aspx.

Hyland, Ken. (2004). *Disciplinary discourses: Social interactions in academic writing.* Ann Arbor: University of Michigan Press.

Kruse, Otto. (2009, November). Schreiben und kritisches Denken. Lecture held at the symposium Wissenschaftliches Schreiben 2: Writing across the curriculum. Alpen-Adria-Universität Klagenfurt.

Mertlitsch, Carmen. (2010). *Starke Texte Schreiben. Anregungen für Menschen im Arbeitsfeld Schule. Unter mitarbeit von Heimo Senger, Katharina Perschak, und Thomas Hainscho Klagenfurt.* Alpen-Adria-Universität Klagenfurt, Institut für Unterrichts- und Schulentwicklung.

Mertlitsch, C., Struger, J. (2007). Außeruniversitäres schreib-coaching von diplomand innen und dissertantInnen. In U. Doleschal & H. Gruber. (Eds.), *Wissenschaftliches Schreiben abseits des Englischen mainstreams* (pp. 193-215). Frankfurt am Main: Peter Lang.

Mertlitsch, C., & Doleschal, U.(in press). Individuelle Beratung und Begleitung von Schreibprozessen. Zum peer-tutoring am SchreibCenter der Alpen-Adria-Universität Klagenfurt. In A. Saxalber Tetter & U. Esterl (Eds.), *Schreiben: Schreibkompetenz und Lernbiographie (Ide extra 16).*

Mistrík, J. (1985). *Štylistika.* Bratislava: Slovenské pedagogické Nakladatel'stvo.

Nicolini, M. (2001). *Sprache, Wissenschaft, Wirklichkeit: Zum Sprachgebrauch in inter- und Transdisziplinärer.* Wien: Bundesministerium für Bildung, Wiss. u. Kultur.

Nicolini, M. (Ed.). (2008). *Wissenschaft, Helldunkler ort: Sprache im Dienst des Verstehens.* Wien: Braumüller.

Pohl, T. (2007). *Studien zur ontogenese wissenschaftlichen Schreibens.* Tübingen: Niemeyer.

Riesel, E. (1959). *Stilistik der deutschen Sprache.* Moskau: Verlag für fremdsprachige Literatur.

Roth, C. (1999). Wissenschaftliches Schreiben lernen in und mit der Gruppe. In O. Kruse, E. M. Hadara, & G. Ruhmann (Eds.), *Schlüsselkompetenz Sch-*

reiben: Konzepte, Methoden, Projekte für Schreibberatung und Schreibdidaktik an der Hochschule (pp. 135-146). Neuwied [u.a.]: Luchterhand.

Saxalber Tetter, A. (2008, November). Kann man schülerInnen zu guten schreiberInnen erziehen? Lecture held at the symposium Schreibkompetenz und Lernbiographie. Alpen-Adria-Universität Klagenfurt.

Stadter, A. (2003). Der Essay als Ziel und Instrument geisteswissenschaftlicher Schreibdidakitk. Überlegungen zur Erweiterung des universitären Textsortenkanons. In K. Ehlich & A. Steets (Eds.), *Wissenschaftlich Schreiben - lehren und lernen* (pp. 65-94). Berlin: Mouton-deGruyter,.

Tošović, B. (1988). *Funkcionalni stilovi.* Sarajevo: Svjetlost.

CHAPTER 7.
THE ACADEMIC WRITING RESEARCH GROUP AT THE UNIVERSITY OF VIENNA

By Helmut Gruber
University of Vienna (Austria)

In this paper, I describe 10 years of research on students' academic writing conducted at the University of Vienna. Furthermore, I describe the (small) success my team had in implementing the results of this research as a university-wide writing support program for doctoral students. Since 1999, I have carried out three successive research projects on students' academic writing. In the first two projects, textual characteristics of seminar papers, students' and instructors' views of students' writing, and student-instructor interaction in selected courses were investigated following the academic literacies approach. In the third project, the results of this previous research provided the basis for developing an academic writing course for students in a blended learning environment. We also developed a detailed concept for establishing a writing center at Vienna University that could not be realized in the intended form, but that at least resulted in establishing a series of university-wide writing courses for doctoral students.

I started my academic career in 1986 as an assistant professor ("Assistent") at the Applied Linguistics section of the Department of Linguistics at Vienna University. The first course I taught there was an "Introduction to text linguistics." Although I have never viewed text linguistics and discourse analysis as "applied" subfields of linguistics, students seemed to expect me to have an applied angle towards my teaching (and research) subjects, simply because I was part of the "Applied Linguistics" team at the department. So it was no surprise that every now and then students who had difficulties in writing their seminar papers[1] approached me in order to help them. And time after time, I also heard complaints from students who told me that "you are the specialist on text linguistics here at the department but you never teach us anything which we could use to improve our own writing." At first, I was a bit baffled about these complaints because my course had never been intended to teach students anything else than the basic concepts and theories of text and discourse analysis, but also because for me writing in academia had never posed a problem. Whenever I had had to master a new genre during my time as a student at university, I simply looked for texts which seemed (to me) to be good examples of the respective genre and then tried to bring together the demands of my actual writing task with the features of these texts—somehow I produced a text. From the feedback (or in most cases from the lack of feedback) and from the grades I received, I learned that I must have succeeded somehow in acquiring the relevant genres. But my students' complaints made me think about the way students learn to write academic texts in more general ways; they made me curious to know more about students' academic writing in the Austrian university system.

Up to the late nineties, the Austrian university system had much in common with the description of the German university system that Foster (2002) provides in regard to students' writing. The course system consisted of two major groups of courses: "lecture" courses in which an academic teacher presented the course content to their student- audience and in which students received their grades either through an oral or through a written exam; and (roughly speaking) "non-lecture" courses in which a lecturer could demand students to engage in several kinds of activities during and after the course which all could be made relevant for receiving a grade. In many of these latter courses, students had to write some kind of text (literature reviews, field or lab reports, shorter or longer seminar papers, etc.), which were in principle due at the end of the semester in which the course took place. However, a general regulation in the Austrian university law stipulated that written papers which served as a course requirement could be handed in up to four semesters after the end of a course; i.e., in principle students had two years for finishing their papers. Of course, some departments found ways to bypass this regulation by creating strict entry conditions for courses in subsequent semesters, which demanded students to provide evidence of positive grades from courses in the previous semester, etc. But in principle (if they could afford it in whatever respect) Austrian students had much time for fulfilling their writing tasks—time which they could use to experiment with new academic genres, revise their texts, seek model texts, or seek advice from peers and lecturers—or decide not to write the demanded paper when they found an equivalent course in which they could fulfill course requirements in an easier way. Thus, for dedicated students the Austrian system offered the opportunity to acquire new genres in a self-guided way, but for the other students it did not offer any support (except style-sheets which are provided by many departments and/or lecturers and which detail formal requirements like line spacing, margin widths, bibliographical styles, etc.[2]).

My own advice to students who had asked me for help with their papers up to this time had been based on the implicit and explicit knowledge I had of certain academic genres rather than on any systematic investigation of students' writing skills and/ or shortcomings. So in the summer semester 1999, I carried out an exploratory project in cooperation with the department of personnel management at the University of Economics and Business Administration in Vienna, in order to deepen my own understanding of students' writing. The cooperation with this department was partly triggered by methodological considerations, but also by opportunistic ones. From a methodological point of view, I did not want to investigate students' writing at my own department in order to avoid my potentially biased view of students' texts influencing the results of my study. Therefore, investigating students' texts from a different discipline with a social science background (which made them comparable to at least a big fraction of Linguistics students' texts) seemed to provide an unbiased way of investigating students' writing. The opportunistic aspect of this cooperation consisted in the fact that at this time my colleague Ursula Doleschal, who also has a strong interest in students' academic writing, held a position at the Business University and established a connection to the department of personnel management. This first exploratory project, in which 18 students' seminar papers from one seminar (i.e., a course for advanced students who would start working on their MA-theses after finishing this course) were investigated, established some themes which are still present in my theoretical and practical work concerning students' writing:

- The research followed a multi-methods approach: apart from the students' papers, instructor-student interaction in the seminar was investigated through participant observation by two student-research assistants, and interviews were conducted with all students in the seminar and the instructor in order to obtain students' and instructor's subjective views on the respective seminar, and on students' writing at the university in general. This approach made it possible to triangulate the results of the linguistic text analysis with results from participant observation and interview data. This methodology reflects the basic assumptions of the academic literacies approach (Jones, Turner, & Street, 1999; Lea & Street, 1998), which views students' writing as a complex social practice at the intersection of institutional demands, disciplinary constraints, and individual pre-dispositions.
- Textual analysis (and—later on—didactic implementation of the results of text analyses) was inspired by Systemic Functional Linguistics (SFL; Halliday, 1994), and especially by the register and genre approach (Eggins & Martin, 1997). SFL is a metafunctional approach to language that

assumes that each utterance conveys meaning on the ideational (=content), the interpersonal, and the textual level. The register and genre approach assumes a strong bi-directional relation between contextual variables and textual (generic) features. Genres are viewed as staged, goal-oriented, purposeful activities in which speakers engage as members of a culture (Eggins & Martin, 1997) and which are teachable to novices.[3] As no comprehensiv SFL model of German yet exists, the categories of analysis were partly taken from other functional approaches to language (e.g., functional pragmatics and rhetorical structure theory; Ehlich, 1985; Mann & Thompson, 1987).

- From the very beginning of my interest in students' writing, I dealt with the topic under an applied perspective. Thus, I have been interested in finding out strengths and weakenesses of students' texts and ways of improving students' writing in the institutional context of Austrian universities. And from the beginning I tried to investigate both aspects under two perspectives: first, by establishing linguistic evaluation criteria from the literature on academic writing. This first perspective provides an inventory of linguistic features of "adequate" or "well written" academic texts that were established in previous investigations of students' academic writing. But as the academic literacies approach cautions us not to generalize results from one context to another, and as most investigations of students' academic writing have been carried out in an anglophone context, the results of these studies cannot simply be transposed to the Austrian context. Thus, to avoid premature generalisations, a second perspective is necessary: in the interviews with instructors (and, if possible, in their written notes), their assessment criteria for students' texts were collected and "translated" into linguistic terms as far as possible. Additionally, each paper's grade was set into a relation to its textual properties and thus, a set of instructors' implicit evaluation criteria was established.

Because of the lack of personal and financial resources, the 18 students' papers, the interview data, and the protocols of the participant observation that were obtained in this first project, were analyzed qualitatively. Results showed that the departments' writing demands for students' seminar papers were communicated rather explicitly, albeit in a very short form and without offering students any support for their writing process. Results also showed that in this special seminar, a number of institutional difficulties and hurdles for students' working and writing processes had occurred, which partly were due to singular problems of this single seminar but partly were also characteristic of the institution as a whole. Both kinds of problems, of course, had a negative impact on students' motivation. The interview data also showed a mismatch between the motivations the instructors attributed to students for deciding to attend the seminar and students' actual motivations: whereas instructors thought that most students would attend the seminars at their department because of the high quality of teaching and students' support, all but one student simply choose the course because it fit well into their timetable. Accordingly, students did not invest too much time and effort into writing their papers, which instructors in turn interpreted as low achievement of (in their view) highly motivated students (Gruber, Wetschanow, & Herzberger, 1999).

Results of the textual analyses showed that, in their texts, most students tried to comply with the instructor's (and department's) most emphasized writing demand, namely to produce an explicit "problem formulation." Many students, however, did this in a rather superficial and formal manner and therefore all but one student produced texts which realized a descriptive, non-empirical genre which in a later publication was called "taxonomic report" (Gruber, et al., 2006). In this genre, students describe and/or elaborate some basic concepts which together constitute the topic of their papers (e.g., "Implementation and personnel management"). On the macro-structural level, two varieties of this genre occurred: (1) papers that employ a limited number of semantic relations ("is a," "has a") between headings (=main section) and sub-headings (=sub-sections), which results in clear and easily comprehensible overall content structures. In these papers, the content of the sub-sections elaborates the content of the main sections. (2) Papers that mainly employ an additive relation between successive sections, be it main- or sub-sections. These papers meander from one topic to the next without developing a clear overall content structure. As was to be expected, papers of the first group earned better grades than papers of the second group.

The descriptive genre of the majority of the papers resonates also on the micro-textual level: the major text organizing principle on the paragraph- and clause-level was called the "list-style" (Gruber, Wetschanow & Herzberger, 1999: 38ff.). In this kind of text organization, the elements of a list may come from different textual levels, i.e., word, clause, or paragraph, which results in word-, clause- or paragraph-lists respectively. Wordlists were the most frequent variant of this style. They resemble outlines, and in fact they were frequently used to summarize and represent the primary and secondary sources the students read. In many cases the terms in the list were hyponyms of those terms that functioned as "list headings." Word lists resemble also the descriptive tables of contents found on the macro-level of texts. Thus, similar textual devices occurred on the macro- and on the micro-level of the texts. The difference between the two devices is, however, that the table of contents is elaborated in the text, whereas the word-list is the text. In most cases word lists have negative consequences for the thematic progression of the texts. Especially if several word lists occur in a series, no systematic flow of information (thematic progression) can be developed. The resulting texts resemble an elaborate excerpt or outline, but not a proper text. Clause- and paragraph-lists resemble word lists. They are, however, constituted by clauses and paragraphs respectively, and thus allow for more elaborate thematic structures. The use of paragraph lists especially can result in an ordered and clearly arranged thematic structure, if they are introduced by topic sentences and closed by resuming sentences or paragraphs. All in all, the prevalent use of the list style and the lack of argumentation on the macro-structural level in most papers seem to indicate that most students followed a "knowledge-telling-strategy" rather than a "knowledge-transforming-strategy" (Scardamalia & Bereiter, 1987). Students' use of the list style (and all other micro-textual features), however, did not seem to have much impact on the grades the papers received (except in those cases where texts consisted mainly of word lists, which made the impression that the respective seminar paper was a compilation of bullet-point lists).

The results of this exploratory project were used to formulate a couple of more focused research questions on students' academic writing in the context of Austrian universities, and a bigger project was conducted (funded by the Austrian science foundation; FWF project P14720-G03). In this study (Gruber et al., 2006), students' writing practices in three social science disciplines (social history, business studies, business psychology) were investigated. The rationale behind this choice was that these three disciplines share a social science background and a common research area, namely economy and business, but they have different theoretical angles towards their research topics. It was therefore expected that the students' texts would exhibit parallels as well as discipline-specific differences. Following the multi-disciplinary approach already employed in the exploratory project, the study combined textual analyses with interview analyses and participant observation of three courses. The theoretical framework transcended the register and genre approach and combined Bourdieu's concepts of habitus and field (Bourdieu, 1992) with the academic literacies approach (Jones, et al., 1999). Following these theoretical considerations, a text production model was developed that differentiates between "text types" (abstract units on a rather general level), which are mainly influenced by the general social and institutional purposes they serve, and "genres," which are conceived as (semiotically enriched) realisations of text types in concrete institutional and social contexts. Text types and genres are related to the field specific habitus of persons insofar as the knowledge of the appropriateness of certain text types and genres for certain kinds of tasks in a field are relevant symbolic capitals. One general goal of the project was to investigate if students have already developed a discipline-specific habitus and hence if they produce texts which realise discipline-specific genres. A further major goal was to investigate if and which linguistic features of a seminar paper correlate with the grade it receives.

Quantitative and qualitative text analyses of all linguistic characteristics (generic and rhetorical structures, meta-communication, intertextuality, argumentation, modality, lexis) that were analysed showed that students in the three seminars produced different genres, which, however, belonged to one abstract text type which was coined "academic qualification text." This text type is located at the intersection of two social fields, namely the field of academia and the field of the university, respectively (Bourdieu, 1992). The results of the interview analyses showed that students are aware of the double institutional purpose of the text type in differing, yet systematically varying ways. Whereas social history students mainly oriented towards the academic purpose of a seminar paper and thus display the habitus of "apprentice scholars," management students and most of the business psychology students orient towards the assessment character of the texts they produce and thus display a "student habitus." The relationship between linguistic features of the texts and the grades the papers received was similar to results from the exploratory study. Most linguistic features of the micro-textual level did not show any correlation with the grades the papers received. Many features of the meso- and macro- textual level, however, did show rather systematic correlations with grades.

AN ACADEMIC WRITING COURSE DEVELOPED OUT OF THIS RESEARCH

In a follow-up project (FWF project L 179-G03), an academic writing course for (advanced) students, which was based on the results of the previous project, was developed in a blended learning framework (Apel & Kraft, 2003). The course design comprised the development of: (a) a web-based entrance module which consists of a self assessment for students' writing skills, and an investigation of the extent of their demand of assistance; (b) a general (discipline-independent) module containing information on academic writing; (c) two discipline-specific modules offering information on and training in academic writing (developed for Linguistics and Social and Economic History students).

The entrance module consists of a series of questions and tasks students have to complete and is designed to detect the individual students' level of previous writing experience and knowledge. This module was implemented on the e-learning platform of Vienna University. The results of the entrance module were used to decide whether individual students were advised to work through one (or several) chapters of the general module before attending the writing course, or if they could attend the writing course without additional pre-course instruction. For the purpose of developing didactic applications of the linguistic results of the previous projects, the linguistic concepts and categories were "translated" into "everyday concepts" of scholarly work with which students were expected to be familiar. The linguistic categories were mapped onto didactic domains as shown in Table 1.

Table 1: Linguistic Categories and Didactic Domains

Areas of linguistic analysis	Didactic domains
Macro-structure (SFL, RST)	Structure of a seminar paper, connecting text-segments, argumentation
Meta-communication	Structure of a seminar paper, connecting text-segments, general issues of academic writing
Intertextuality	Perspective
Argumentation	Explication and Argumentation
Modality	Difference between the language of everyday life and scientific language, Perspective, argumentation
Lexis	Difference between the language of everyday life and scientific language

The general module covers seven broad areas relevant for a functional understanding of the specifics of academic language and academic genres in the humanities and social sciences: "What is science?", "Scholarly work," "Academic language," "Differences between everyday language and academic language," "Structuring a paper," "Perspective," "Describing, Explaining, and Argumentation." The module was designed as a hypertext and is available online at http://www.univie.ac.at/linguistics/schreibprojekt/Grundlagen .

The two discipline specific courses elaborate the language-related aspects of the general module and comprise the following broad areas: "Structuring a paper," "Perspective," "Explanation and argumentation," and "The thematic thread." Their development followed a blended learning approach, which integrates face-to-face and online learning phases, and draws on theories of computer-mediated communication, cognitive psychology and education. The

following aspects were considered when developing course contents, exercises, and teaching materials:
- Mode of communication: face-to-face vs. online
- Pedagogical practice: instructing (lecture) vs. detecting (group work)
- Types of knowledge: conceptual vs. procedural vs. meta (linguistic)
- Types of exercises: detecting, classifying, correlating, sequencing, abstracting, modifying, focused variation, and composing

These four dimensions constitute a matrix in which all intended course content can be located, and which allows the appropriate type of content presentation to be chosen. Thus, the course design as a whole is based on a theoretically reflected, interdisciplinary combination of relevant areas of scholarship. In order to keep dependence on the e-learning platform to a minimum, course materials were mainly developed as written manuals and as MS-PowerPoint presentations The learning platform was only used for communication with and between students and for exercises.

The first instalment of the writing course was taught by two research assistants during the summer semester of 2008 at Vienna University. The whole course was evaluated by course participants via online feedback, questionnaires, and oral feedback at the end of the semester. Results of this feedback were used to redesign the entrance module and to implement slight changes in both the general and the two discipline specific modules.

CONSEQUENCES OF THE ACADEMIC WRITING COURSE

This project had consequences that go beyond the realm of academic research:

The teaching materials which were developed for modules one and two were used to produce an academic writing guide for German-speaking students of the Humanities and Social Sciences (Gruber, Huemer, & Rheindorf, 2009), which is intended to go further than many "how-to-do" writing books on the market currently. It provides readers with a short account of Merton's conception of science as a social system and then tries to derive various characteristics of academic communication and academic style from this (admittedly idealized) conception.

Both research assistants developed a competence as academic writing trainers and received numerous requests for writing courses that were eventually offered at the following institutions: Department of Linguistics (Vienna University), Department of Social and Economic History (Vienna University), Department of Human Resource Development of Vienna University, Competence Centre for the automobile industry (Villach), faculty of interdisciplinary research and advanced training (Klagenfurt University), writing centre of Klagenfurt University, and Department of Information Technology (Klagenfurt University).

Furthermore, in summer of 2008, the research team developed a detailed concept for a writing centre at Vienna University that was sent to all relevant administrative authorities of the university. Because the team anticipated that the university administration would not be able to cover all projected costs, they also contacted one of Austria's major banks and explored the possibility of external sponsorship there. As a matter of fact, the bank's public relation department showed an interest in financially supporting a writing centre, provided the university administration would also contribute their share. When the university officials met, the general feedback was positive, but the realisation of a writing centre was made dependent on the amount of funding the bank would provide. In the meantime, late September 2008 brought the international financial crisis to Austrian banks, and the bank withdrew their (oral) commitment to support a writing centre. As a consequence, the university administration no longer saw the whole project of a writing centre as realistic due to the general budgetary situation of the university.z

IMPACT OF THE "BOLOGNA PROCESS" ON PLANS FOR THE WRITING CENTRE

However, since 2005, Vienna University has gradually implemented the new MA-BA-PhD study programs in the course of the so-called "Bologna process." This means that the traditional tri-partite academic degree structure ("Magisterium" — "Doktorat" — "Habilitation") with its rather relaxed time constraints for students (cf. above) has been replaced by a rather tightly pre-scheduled course system. But whereas in the Anglophone university system (from which this study architecture has been transferred) students often receive institutionalised writing support, this institutional framework is missing at Vienna University. Administration officials are aware of this problem, but—as mentioned above—the budget for a university-wide writing centre is not available. As a consequence, a first small version of institutionalised writing support was implemented in the new PhD program of Vienna University, which started in fall 2009. In this university-wide program, the two former research assistants teach several courses on various aspects of academic genres (writing a proposal, writing an abstract, etc.).

Apart from this small institutional success, the research team initiated an interdisciplinary working group at Vienna University, which comprises participants from the faculties of history, philology, education, and the centre for translation studies interested in different aspects of students' academic writing. The working group set up an internet forum (http://homepage.univie.ac.at/markus.rheindorf/php/) in which teaching materials can be shared and which is intended to improve communication among interested faculty members of Vienna University. Furthermore, the group will organise regular meetings in which single members report on their current work.

CONCLUSION

Looking back on almost 10 years of research on students' academic writing and on the activities that have been intended to establish some practical consequences of this work, I cannot avoid having mixed feelings: On the one hand, the research group created some academic output in a research field that virtually did not exist in Austria before, and that group is now well integrated within the international research landscape (e.g., as part of COST action IS0703, http://www.cost-lwe.eu, which deals with improving writing on various levels in the European context). Furthermore, three former research assistants (Birgit Huemer, Markus Rheindorf, and Karin Wetschanow) teach academic writing courses in several institutions because they have been part of the academic writing research group. On the other hand, the degree of institutionalization of students' writing support at Vienna University is still low. Apart from the above-mentioned courses in the new PhD program, which is still in its early phases and some courses in MA study programs (linguistics, social and economic history), no institutional basis for students' writing support has been established so far. This might partly be due to the fact that Vienna University is by far the largest university in Austria, and with its 74,000 enrolled students resembles a supertanker which needs a very long time until it changes course.

NOTES

1. For the history and status of the seminar paper in the German university system see Kruse (2006) and also Foster (2002). Their accounts of the German university system hold—mutatis mutandis—also true for the Austrian university system.

2. This system has changed dramatically during the last years as Austrian universities had to introduce the BA-MA-PhD system in the course of the implementation of the so called "Bologna-study-architecture," an EU program which intends to harmonize the tertiary education systems of the EU member states. I will shortly discuss the consequences of this new framework at the end of the article.

3. This latter view marks a sharp distinction between the SFL-view of genre pedagogy and the proponents of the "New Rhetoric" movement who are very pessimistic about the explicit teachability of genres.

REFERENCES

Apel, H., & Kraft, S. (2003). Online lehren in der Weiterbildung. In H. Apel & S. Kraft (Eds.), *Online lehren* (pp. 7-15). Bielefeld North Rhine-Westphalia: Bertelsmann Verlag.

Bourdieu, P. (1992). *Homo academicus*. Frankfurt/Main: Suhrkamp.

Eggins, S., & Martin, J. R. (1997). Genres and registers of discourse. In T. van Dijk (Ed.), *Discourse studies. Discourse as structure and process* (Vol. 1, pp. 230-257). London, et al.: Sage.

Ehlich, K. (1985). Funktional-pragmatische Kommunikationsanalyse—Ziele und Verfahren. *Linguistische Studien, Reihe A, Arbeitsberichte, 149*, 15-40.

Foster, D. (2002). Making the transition to university: Student writers in Germany. In D. R. Russell & D. Foster (Eds.), *Writing and learning in cross-national perspective: Transitions from secondary to higher education* (pp. 192-241). Urbana, IL: National Council of Teachers of English.

Gruber, H., Huemer, B., & Rheindorf, M. (2009). *Wissenschaftlich Schreiben. Ein Arbeitsbuch für die Geistes- und Sozialwissenschaften*. Vienna: Böhlau.

Gruber, H., Muntigl, P., Reisigl, M., Rheindorf, M., Wetschanow, K., & Christine, C. (2006). *Genre, Habitus und wissenschaftlichess Schreiben*. Münster, North Rhine-Westphalia: LIT Verlag.

Gruber, H., Wetschanow, K., & Herzberger, P. (1999). *Wissenschaftliches Schreiben im universitären Kontext. Projektbericht*. Vienna: Institut f. Sprachwissenschaft.

Halliday, M. A. K. (1994). *An introduction to functional grammar* (2 ed.). London: Edward Arnold.

Jones, C., Turner, J., & Street, B. (Eds.). (1999). *Students writing in the university. Cultural and epistemological issues*. Amsterdam: John Benjamins.

Lea, M., & Street, B. (1998). Student writing and staff feedback in higher education: An academic literacies approach. *Studies in Higher Education, 23*, 157-172.

Mann, W., & Thompson, S. (1987). *Rhetorical structure theory: A theory of text organization* (No. ISI/RS-87-190). Marina del Rey, California: Information Sciences Institute.

Scardamalia, M., & Bereiter, C. (1987). Knowledge telling and knowledge transforming in written composition. In S. Rosenberg (Ed.), *Advances in applied psycholinguistics. Vol. 2: Reading, writing and language learning* (pp. 142-175). Cambridge: Cambridge University Press.

CHAPTER 8.
FROM REMEDIATION TO THE DEVELOPMENT OF WRITING COMPETENCES IN DISCIPLINARY CONTEXTS: THIRTY YEARS OF PRACTICE AND QUESTIONS

By Marie-Christine Pollet
Université libre de Bruxelles/ The Free University of Brussels (Belgium)

This profile essay focuses on writing provision at the Université libre de Bruxelles (ULB), or the Free University of Brussels, a French-speaking university situated in the Belgian capital. In 1979, the ULB established the Centre de Méthodologie Universitaire (CMU) (Centre for University Learning), the first initiative of its kind in French-speaking Belgium. The CMU situates its teaching and research within the context of the linguistic needs of first-year, French-speaking students. Through teaching in academic reading and writing, the CMU helps students to surmount the obstacles in language that are the preserve of university-level discourse communities, and enables first-year students to take part in what for them is a new discursive environment. This profile details the history and remit of the CMU and discusses various pedagogical approaches through which the centre has moved over the past thirty years.

THE INSTITUTIONAL CONTEXT

The Université libre de Bruxelles (ULB), or the Free University of Brussels, a French-speaking university situated in the Belgian capital, covers all disciplines, is divided into 11 faculties, and encompasses all modes of study including undergraduate and postgraduate.[1] In the 2010-2011 academic year, it had nearly

24,000 students, among whom more than 7,000 were in their first year of undergraduate study. ULB enrolls students who are native to Brussels, of course, but also a significant number of provincial students, while 29% of its entire student population comes from abroad (Free University of Brussels, 2011). In the eyes of those who live in Brussels, ULB students are characterized by diversity in their geographic, cultural, and social origins.

One can add to this diverse mix the variety of educational backgrounds, since, as in all institutions of higher education in Belgium (except for the Faculties of Applied Sciences), admission to university is not conditioned by any test (neither exam nor written application), as long as the student has obtained his or her diploma of general or technical secondary education ("technique de transition") through the transition stream.[2] Taking into account this particularity, the first-year student population in French-speaking Belgium is very heterogeneous and it is difficult to count on all students possessing more or less identical pre-requisites, including linguistic competence. This is what, in fact, led to the granting of ministerial subsidies for universities to improve rates of student success (The Bologna Accord of March 31, 2004) and then to the "decree democratizing higher education, working to promote the success of students and creating the Observatory of Higher Education" (July 18, 2008).

Therefore, we are currently in a political context where the promotion of student success has been, for the past few years, regulated by decree, which makes it possible for institutions to allocate funding for teaching initiatives which, until then, had not necessarily been amongst their first priorities. The ULB, however, had not awaited this decree for the university to take interest in the fate of its first-year students, and established instead Le Centre de Méthodologie Universitaire (CMU) (the Center for University Learning) in 1979, the first initiative of its kind in French-speaking Belgium exclusively to develop and support (beginning in the 1990s) disciplinary teaching guidance in most Faculties.

Even if, for historical reasons, the CMU is attached to the Faculty of Philosophy and Letters, at least insofar as the management of its personnel is concerned (hiring, careers, administrative framing), it is a cross-faculty center placed under the aegis of the Education Authority of the university and thus offers its services to the whole of the university community. The CMU situates its teaching and research within the context of the linguistic support for first-year students—French-speaking students, it is important to specify. It is indeed a question of helping them to overcome the obstacles in language which the university—and the new discursive environment that this embodies—has in store for them.

Originally called the "Center for French Language Improvement" —a name which speaks volumes about the normative approach and the purist vision of the Center's beginnings—the CMU now states clearly its will to acculturate students into university-level discourses, through interventions centered on the development of linguistic competences in disciplinary contexts. It is thus anchored resolutely in the theoretical and pedagogic field of Littéracies Universitaires or "University Literacies," which articulates the teaching and learning apprenticeship of writing at university in connection with the construction of disciplinary knowledge.[3]

This is why the CMU locates its pedagogic reflections and interventions at the heart of this articulation, as we shall see in what follows. First of all, the teaching team is made up of linguists and specialists in the various disciplines; then, the analysis of needs, the research of authentic documents, as well as the definitions of the main strands of the courses delivered by the CMU, are carried out in collaboration with colleagues (professors and/or assistants) in the various departments.

A BIT OF HISTORY: PRACTICES, QUESTIONS AND THE "PEDAGOGIC REVOLUTIONS" OF THE CMU

The CMU was created in 1979, following the publication by the Faculty of Sciences of the ULB of a report in which the authors attributed the main cause of students' failure in the first year to the poor knowledge of the language. According to their observations, these gaps in knowledge render "the students unable to follow the complexity of a scientific thought as much in a written text as in an oral lecture or class, to the extent to which 'the negligence of French-speaking students with respect to their language is such that they find themselves disadvantaged in relation to foreign students who have learned French recently but more rigorously.'"[4]

These are the catastrophist comments which led to the creation of a center called at the time "The Center for French Language Improvement," in charge of improving the linguistic performance of future students, through the use of language drills in order for students to master the command of the linguistic system as part of foundational courses as well as during the course of first-year exercise workshops. Through the years, these early practices evolved enormously from a logic of remediation to a logic of student education. The next section shows this evolution, indeed the "pedagogic revolutions" of the CMU. For a more complete discussion, see Pollet, 2001, 2008.) These changes reflect the limits of some practices, the teaching dead-ends with which we, the staff at the Center, confronted, as well as the reflections which led us to follow other paths. These revolutions at the CMU are the result of our experience, but also of the evolution of the research into the teaching of French in higher education, and thus, more recently, in the context of academic literacies, of the research in sociology and socio-linguistics.

The Normative Approach

For a long time, the command of language was considered from a normative perspective, through the reproaches formulated against students as well as the remedial type of solutions offered to them. These reproaches are well-known—poverty of vocabulary, ignorance of the most elementary syntax, appalling orthography—and led to the implementation of exercises whose objective was to develop micro-level skills.

However, no matter how generous and well-meant these practices were, they deserve questioning, First of all, these practices were in keeping with the so-called "compensatory" programmes, the main flaw of which was clarified by sociologists such as Jean-Claude Forquin (1990a, 1990b) and Christian Bachman (1993), who show all the difficulty, even impossibility, of grafting standard language codes on pupils coming from disadvantaged or notoriously harsh backgrounds. In other words, according to theorists, programmes based on linguistic drills are not fully adapted to the student audience that they target in the first place: on the contrary, they run the risk of discouraging students rather than aiding them.

Next, Bernard Lahire (1993) showed that school work on language—the reasoned exercises, the regulated practice, the perpetual work of repetition and correction—causes "practical resistance" [6] among those pupils in whose writing we find the famous spelling errors as well as the wobbly syntactic constructions. Moreover, certain researchers show the over-valuing of the influence of students' non-command of standard language on the difficulties of training. Thus, Elisabeth Bautier (1998) invites teachers and researchers not to grant too much importance to students' lexical or syntactic difficulties, because they often mask the difficulties "which represent deeper issues that differentiate pupils even more since they concern the use of language presupposed by school practices."

Finally—and this is not the least of limits to identify—this approach suffers terribly from decontextualization. The strongly reductive aspect of the teaching that targets the command of the linguistic system causes this type of remediation to result in the demotivation of students, and consequently in teaching failure. Obviously, it is not a question of ignoring the problems–orthographical, lexical, syntactic—of students, which are quite real. Rather, it is a question of thinking of other avenues than those represented by the language drill and the imposition of a norm. One such solution consists of locating the norm in the challenges of communication, by developing the critical and metalinguistic consciousness of students in relation to this language standard and its variations (Béguelin, 1998). By raising students' awareness in this way, they will undoubtedly grow to be more motivated to appropriate the tools that we can offer them.

The Technicist Approach

The recognition of the limits of the normative perspective such as it has just been briefly described led to the development of a technicist approach for achieving mastery of language and for its teaching in higher education. On the basis of recurring observations that students are not able to "distinguish the essential from the accessory," nor "to synthesize information," nor "to take notes," nor "to write a clear answer," the technicist approach acts to develop "techniques" and "methods," considered—wrongly it must be said—as general and transverse.

It is in this way that the programmes centred primarily on the improvement of language moved gradually towards the "working methods," investing primarily in strategies that concern the summarizing activity (plans, summaries, syntheses, note-taking). Like the normative approach, however, these practices also suffer from decontextualization, at least when they do not take into account the characteristics of the discourse to which they relate nor the analysis of assignment questions, in other words, when, as it is often the case, they are focused on the school exercise of summarising and its purely technical aspects of information reduction. The principal flaw of this approach is "to substitute a logic of technical skills for a logic of knowing and intellectual work" (Bautier, 1998, p. 22).

While this type of teaching can instil in students considerable non-negligible mechanisms such as the selection of important concepts, thanks to the identification of conceptual fields, it also runs the risk, however, of pushing students to take refuge behind automatisms. This approach will not support pragmatic reflection, which would enable them to stay open to the world of the discourse that surrounds them in the environment of their studies.

The Pragmatic Approach

This last approach, which is currently dominant, consists of developing writing competences in disciplinary contexts, and according to these contexts. Thus, the conception of "French in higher education" has been expanded to make room for its discursive and cognitive aspects. Moreover, "the mastery of the language" is considered from the angle of linguistic practices (reading-writing) in use in the medium of studies and the disciplinary field, and in connection with the modes of this disciplinary knowledge construction.

It is in the context of this pragmatic approach, initially developed due to the failures of the previous approaches and through a kind of pedagogic intuition, that the concept of "Littéracies Universitaires" came to be coined at the right moment. This concept, which made its way into the French-speaking world from the Anglophone countries, offers a genuine framework for us to inscribe our reflections, our research, and our practices. Indeed, this field of knowledge makes us consider the specificities of academic disciplines, and "taking into account these disciplines (of teaching or research) obliges us to articulate the analysis of writings and of writing with the various institutional spaces of discourse production, of academic or educational spaces with those of scientific research."[5] This also leads us to consider that it is within this space, of the "complex relation between university writing and the knowledge and know-how acquired in the disciplines," that it is appropriate to locate our pedagogic interventions (Donahue, 2010, pp. 43-44).

It is thus a question of supporting our students through their transition into their university literacy(ies), for there is more than one single academic literacy in keeping with the disciplines and types of discourse to comprehend and produce as part of their various strands of study. More precisely, it is advisable "to consider the connections between writing and knowledge in a discipline, as well as the epistemological role of the latter" (Delcambre & Lahanier-Reuter, 2010, p. 15) because "the writing and the object of the writing cannot be separated, and the learning of disciplinary writing will need to be done in connection with the teaching of the discipline itself" (Donahue, 2010, p. 57).

CONCRETELY: PRAGMATIC TEACHING APPROACHES OF THE CMU[2]

The CMU organizes various types of classes, according to the wishes, constraints or cultures of faculties and/or courses of study. This provision takes the shape of exercise sessions, practical work (which can be optional or heavily guided, or even subject to a "bonus" in terms of credits), or else courses taken as part of the students' degree programmes. Nevertheless, no matter the form the CMU teaching may take, certain fundamental principles guide the development and organization of its provision.

The Contextualisation of Interventions: the Analysis of Needs, Interdisciplinary Collaboration, and Team-teaching

The contextualisation of the CMU's teaching interventions involves a close cooperation with staff in academic departments, a deep analysis of students' needs, based on interactions with colleagues, but also on the observation of students' papers and work on authentic documents.

Moreover, most courses and/or practical work are delivered jointly by two teachers: one a linguist, the other a specialist in the discipline. This collaboration, which sometimes unsettles students at first, proves very profitable. Indeed, the complementarity of competences of each specialist renders the seminars rich, dynamic, complete, and legitimate, both on the linguistic and on the disciplinary level. The participation of disciplinary colleagues is paramount because only they make it possible "to clarify from within the epistemological dimensions of the writing, the interactions between the writing and the research methods, the challenges and the forms of the scientific communication" (Delcambre & Lahanier-Reuter, 2010, p. 15).

Recognition of the Need for Continued Training in Reading-writing, Including in Higher Education

It is the main tenet of the concept of literacies that is pinned down here, and that in itself allows for a change in the conception of teaching writing at university from the idea of remedial tuition to that of formation or education, at different strategic moments during the student's course of study, a kind of teaching that is normal with respect to the novelty of the environment. This also offers us the opportunity to envisage the articulation of reading/writing as integral to a single pedagogy of writing.

A Balanced Articulation between Theory and Practice

While the interventions of the CMU are meant to be especially practical and to lead students to exercise, above all, competences of reading comprehension and writing production, my colleagues and I believe, nonetheless, that the contribution of certain theoretical concepts represents a further means of developing students' metalinguistic consciousness, and their ability to transfer what they have learned into their courses. Therefore, it seems important to us to lead students to reflect on the concepts of discourse genres, textual or sequential typologies, cohesion/coherence, and enunciative modalities, as well as on practices of reported speech and problem-raising.

An Example from the Department of History

Among the courses or exercises taught by the CMU, we shall give here an example of a course which already has a long tradition and has recently been reorganized within the context of the latest reform of programs in the Department of History (2010) for it to adhere even more to the specificities of the discipline. Indeed, the course entitled "Exercises on the construction of historical knowledge," registered under this name with the programme for five years but existing informally for more than twenty, usually taught by a historian and a linguist, has been seen as being entrusted with the mission of anchoring, more than ever, work on writing in the discipline and its specificities, including those which are related to the practices of research. This demand for reinforcement thus led to an increase in ECTS course credits (10 instead of five out of 60 in total), to an increase in the number of tenured tutors (four instead of two), and to an enhanced collaboration with the unit teaching documentary research.

With regard to the implementation of this current draft of the course, a new analysis of needs was carried out based on three intersecting sources: the discussion of teachers in the department about their discipline and the students' needs; samples of the students' perspectives on the writing in their discipline and on their difficulties when confronted with the reception or the production of these discourses; and the characteristics of the various types of legitimated discourse circulating within this discipline (articles, books, and pedagogic discourses produced by teacher-researchers).

Afterwards, we cross-fertilised the various elements thus observed with certain reflections by "theorists of the history" of writing, the methods, and practices of research, from which we attempted to establish some characteristics of disciplinary discourses that cannot be ignored. The data thus collected make it possible to determine, besides the notions relevant to the discipline itself, the linguistic concepts to summon and the linguistic competences to develop in the students, in order thus to build a course centred on disciplinary writing, in which epistemological and heuristic specificities guide the choice of content.

SOME QUESTIONS BY WAY OF CONCLUSION...

The most important question concerns the status of this kind of course. First of all, do such courses have to be optional (either opted for by the students who wish to take them, or imposed by the institution on some students, following a test, for example), or obligatory (which is to say imposed on all the students by the requirements of the program)? If the pragmatic character and the formative aspect that we privilege cause us to show an inclination toward the obligatory, experience shows that these courses are not necessarily legitimate in the eyes of certain students ("I can read and write, nevertheless") nor, sometimes, it should be said, in the eyes of certain colleagues. We further add to this the problems which are encountered in all higher education French courses, including "techniques of expression," "methodology," and so on; these "weakened territories," to use again an expression of Michel Dabène and Claude Fintz (1998). To prevent this problem, it is necessary for this course to be a true project of the institution, but also of the department of study, to which all of the colleagues adhere. Moreover, the disciplinary anchoring must be very visible, which, very prosaically, implies an important reflection concerning the title of the course, which must signify this anchoring.

The question regarding the status of the course also arises insofar as the proportioning of theory and practice is concerned, and also in the mode(s) of assessment being used. These points, which require great flexibility and great adaptability on behalf of the CMU, must be tackled within the department, in keeping with the demand, the needs, the constraints, and the practices.

A second question concerns the cost, in all senses of the word: in terms of time, since the preparations are individualized according to the needs of the departments, but also in terms of money, since several people become involved in these courses. Institutional policy, therefore, must thus be very willing from this point of view.

The last question to be addressed relates to the most appropriate moments and objectives in students' courses for the organization of such teaching. In Belgium, the tendency is for such courses to be focused on the first year of study, and that is justified, of course, by the need to familiarize students with a new discursive environment. However, research in the field of University Literacies and our experiences in the field lead us to defend the idea of continuous teaching, focusing on the various genres of written and spoken discourse with which students are confronted throughout their courses.

NOTES

1. The editors wish to thank Dr. Catalina Neculai, Centre for Academic Writing, Coventry University, England, for translating Marie-Christine Pollet's essay from French to English.

2. For students who do not have this diploma, a university admission examination is organized by the institution, but these cases are relatively rare.

3. For a full definition of the term "Littéracies Universitaires" ("University Literacies"), see I. Delcambre and T. Donahue, "Academic Writing Activity: Student Writing in Transition," in M.Castelló and T. Donahue, eds. (2012).*University Writing: Selves and Texts in Academic Societies*. London: Emerald Group.

4. Enseignement des candidatures—Facteurs de réussite, Rapport du groupe de travail Faculté des Sciences—Enseignement secondaire [Teaching of the candidatures—Factors of success, Report of the Faculty of Sciences working group—Secondary education], ULB, 1975, p. 7.

5. Conference call « Littéracies universitaires: Savoirs, écrits, disciplines » [Academic Literacies: knowledge, writings, disciplines], Université Charles-de-Gaulle – *Lille 3*, 2-4 September 2010.

6. M.-C. Pollet, C. Glorieux, *Rapport d'activités du CMU* (rapport interne) [Activity Report of the CMU (internal report)], March 2010.

REFERENCES

Blondin, C. (2010). *Structures of education and training systems in Europe: Belgium (French Community 2009/10)*. Retrieved from http://orbi.ulg.ac.be/bitstream/2268/92473/1/041_BF_EN.pdf

Bachmann, C. (1993). Ecole et environnement: Actualité de l'interactionnisme [School and environment: Present-day interactionism]. In J.-F. Halté (Ed.), *Inter-actions* (pp. 41-60). Metz: CASUM.

Bautier, E. (1998). Pratiques langagières et démocratisation [Linguistic practices and democratization]. In G. Legros, M.-C. Pollet, J.-M. Rosier, & E. Gotto (Eds.), *Quels savoirs pour quelles valeurs ? Actes du 7ème colloque de la DFLM. [Which knowledge for which values? Acts of the 7th conference of the DFLM]* (pp. 16-17). Association pour la recherche en didactique du français langue maternelle (Association for research into the teaching of French in the native tongue)], Bruxelles.

Béguelin, M.-J. (1998). Le rapport écrit-oral. Tendances dissimulatrices, tendances assimilatrices [The Written-oral connection: Dissimulating tendencies, assimilating tendencies]. *Cahiers de linguistique française [Notebooks of French linguistics]*, *20*, 229-253.

Dabène, M. (1998). Preface. In C. Fintz (Ed.), *La didactique du français dans l'enseignement supérieur: Bricolage ou rénovation? [The pedagogy of French in higher education: Do-it-yourself or restoration?]*. Paris: L'Harmattan.

Delcambre, I., & Donahue, T. (2012). Academic writing activity: Student writing in transition. In M. Castelló and T. Donahue (Eds.), *University writing: Selves and texts in academic societies*. London: Emerald Group.

Delcambre, I., & & Lahanier-Reuter, D. (2010). Les littéracies universitaires: Influences des disciplines et du niveau d'études dans les pratiques de l'écrit [Academic Literacies: The Influences of the disciplines and of the level of studies in the practice of writing"]. *Diptyque*, 18.

Donahue, C. (2010). L'écrit universitaire et la disciplinarité: Perspectives états-uniennes» ["University writing and disciplinarity: Perspectives from the United States"], *Diptyque*, 18.

Fintz, C. (Ed.). (1998). *La didactique du français dans l'enseignement supérieur: Bricolage ou rénovation? [The pedagogy of French in higher education: Do-it-yourself or restoration?]*. Paris: L'Harmattan.

Forquin, J.-C. (1990a). La sociologie des inégalités de l'éducation : Principaux résultats depuis 1965 ["The sociology of the inequalities of education: Main results since 1965"]. In A. Coulon & J. Hassendorfer (Eds.), *Sociologie de l'éducation. Dix ans de recherché [The Sociology of education. Ten years of research]*. Paris: L'Harmattan.

Forquin, J.-C. (1990b). La nouvelle sociologie de l'éducation en Grande-Bretagne, orientations, apports théoriques, évolution », ["The new sociology of education in Great Britain, orientations, theoretical contributions, evolution"]. In A. Coulon & J. Hassendorfer (Eds.), *Sociologie de l'éducation. Dix ans de recherché [The Sociology of education. Ten years of research]*. Paris: L'Harmattan.

Free University of Brussells. (2011). *The Free University of Brussels website*. Retrieved from http://www.ulb.ac.be/ulb/presentation/uk.html

Lahire, B. (1993). *Culture écrite et inégalités scolaires. Sociologie de l' « échec scolaire » à l'école primaire [Written Culture and school inequalities. The Sociology of "school failure" in elementary/primary school]*. Lyon: Presses Universitaires de Lyon.

Pollet, M.-C. (2010, September). «Quels choix théoriques pour quels objectifs d'écriture disciplinaire? L'exemple de l'Histoire» ["Which theoretical choices for which objectives of disciplinary writing? The example of history"], communication au colloque Littéracies universitaires: Savoirs, écrits, disciplines, Université de Lille. [Paper presented at the conference Academic Literacies: Knowledge, writings, disciplines, University of Lille.]

Pollet, M.-C. (2008). La maitrise des compétences langagières: Remédier ou construire? ['The Mastery of linguistic competencies: To remedy or to build?']. *Enjeux, 71*, 77-86.

Pollet, M.-C. (2001). *Pour une didactique des discours universitaires [For a pedagogy of academic discourses]*. Bruxelles: De Boeck.

CHAPTER 9.
ACADEMIC LITERACIES IN THE SOUTH: WRITING PRACTICES IN A BRAZILIAN UNIVERSITY

By Désirée Motta-Roth
Federal University of Santa Maria (Brazil)

Paulo Freire (2000, p. 46), the renowned Brazilian educator, once stated that "one learns to read by reading." To understand what writing does, we need to experience interaction mediated by writing. In this essay I focus on the importance of learners' participation in academic activities for the development of academic literacies: the material and symbolic acts that (re)produce verified knowledge, associated with higher education. I will give an overview of the writing practices at the Federal University of Santa Maria (Universidade Federal de Santa Maria or UFSM), where I have been investigating and teaching academic writing since 1994. The essay starts with a brief history and mission statement about the university. The second section brings a general description of writing at UFSM in relation to why and in relation to what goals this writing occurs. In the third section, I analyze English undergraduate and Applied Linguistics graduate students' answers to a questionnaire about their literacy practices. The essay closes with a description of the principles for a writing program and a note on ambitions and frustrations regarding writing pedagogy in my local context.

THE SIZE, BRIEF HISTORY, AND MISSION OF UFSM

Founded on December 14, 1960, UFSM[1] (http://www.ufsm.br/) is located in an area of 4,593 acres on the outskirts of Santa Maria,[2] a city of 270,000 inhabitants, in the geographical center of Rio Grande do Sul, the southern-most state of Brazil.[3]

Through its 152 years, Santa Maria has become an important regional reference for agricultural and services sectors, especially medical and educational institutions. The city has education as one of its driving forces: one federal university and seven colleges for higher education, a school system (preschool to high school) that includes 80 city schools, 38 state schools, four federal schools, and a large number of private schools.

In its 50 years, UFSM has become paramount to the city's economic, cultural and social organization. Its mission is to construct and impart knowledge in order to make people able to innovate and contribute to the sustainable development of society as a whole, with the vision to become recognized as an institution of excellence. In the campus (total area of 4,593 acres, with 3,439,697 square feet of edification), 16,663 students pursue a degree in 10 colleges and 76 undergraduate programs in all areas (from Medicine to Education, from English Teaching to Business) and more than 50 graduate programs, taught by 1,397 professors organized in 200 research groups. Although UFSM is of medium importance and size if compared to major Brazilian institutions like the University of São Paulo,[4] some programs such as the ones in the Chemistry or the Rural Sciences (Agriculture and Veterinary) departments are among the best in the country.

Originally a rural university for the study and development of the local agricultural economic system and the field of medical services, UFSM has developed competencies in the areas of humanities, science, and technology. Although scientific publication and technological patent processing are two aspects of Brazilian academic life that need to grow exponentially in comparison to other developing countries like Argentina, publication and authorship have received a lot of attention. UFSM, in particular, has a policy to foster publication not only in Portuguese (Brazil's official language) but also in foreign languages. It allocates budget for each unit according to publication indexes, among other factors.[5]

WRITING AT UFSM: WHY, ABOUT WHAT, IN WHAT LANGUAGES, IN RELATION TO WHAT GOALS?

In departments with post-graduation programs, undergraduate writing for publishing is strongly advised if not demanded. Even though Brazil has an established tradition of publication in Portuguese and of translation of international material into Portuguese, UFSM departments tend to encourage reading of material in English or other languages (e.g., French or Spanish), as a way to keep updated with international research. Furthermore, some post-graduation programs (e.g., Chemistry) receive PhD candidates from other continents, so English is often used as the lingua franca in classes, labs, and publications.

Evidently the choice of the language is dependent on the object of study and research. While publishing in English may be the norm in Electrical Engineering or Physics, in the School of Arts and Languages, where a teaching degree in Portuguese is offered, reading theoretical/professional material in Portuguese is the norm. Academic activities for professors working at the Post-Graduation Program in Literature and Language Studies include publishing mostly theoretical books aimed at a readership in Brazil and Portugal, with few research papers in academic journals or in a foreign language.

In the Department of Foreign Languages, with teaching degrees in English and Spanish, and special courses in French, German, and Italian, research papers appear mainly in journals in Portuguese and Spanish. Writing in Portuguese is more comfortable, and the goal is to establish a local readership for the work of nationals and Latin-American colleagues, so that the Brazilian literature can be used as reference for further development of the area.

Although publication in international Applied Linguistics journals is a career asset, publishing in Portuguese is sometimes an affirmative action, according to email interviews with Brazilian applied linguists (Motta-Roth, 2002) about factors that constrained their academic writing:

> 20[6] - Obviously having a text accepted for publication in a prestigious international journal lends high status to the researcher, but in a new area such as ours I still think we have to democratically impart the results of our research projects in Brazil to Brazilian academics and school teachers.

> 28 - I'm convinced that especially in applied areas it is more important to publish in Portuguese in order to give Brazilians access to research results done about Brazilian issues. If not, you'll end up having to translate your own texts so that your work becomes known in Brazil.

In a large developing country such as Brazil,[7] creating a sense of disciplinary community for fostering theoretical elaboration is a political move, as is publishing in the native language.

> 29 - Many times, it's a one-way street. Almost no foreign researcher makes an effort to know what is being done in Brazil (. . .), while we are supposed to know what's going on in foreign countries (like US or UK). Many times what you see abroad is a concept that has been developed here first,

but since it has not been published in English, people do not acknowledge its previous existence.

While researchers in many areas aim at publishing in English,[8] applied linguists often feel that circulating their work in Portuguese is an act of resistance to "academic imperialism": the hegemony of Anglophonic scientific publication that legitimates research paradigms sometimes without further questioning (Phillipson & Skutnabb-Kangas, 1999, p. 31).

This "resistance" view can be disputed on several grounds and seldom extrapolates to students' discourse on writing. In fact, the average undergraduate has a relatively commonsensical view of the function of writing in life. A more articulate perspective that conceives writing as "social participation" is shown either by students who take part in undergraduate research opportunity programs with scientific initiation grants or graduate students doing research for their theses/dissertations. The answers to the survey conducted at the Reading and Writing Research and Teaching Laboratory (REWRITE) with undergraduate students from the English Teacher Education program and graduate students from the Applied Linguistics Program at UFSM are the focus of the next section.

WHERE AND WHAT STUDENTS WRITE AT UFSM: DISCIPLINES, GENRES, ASSIGNMENTS

Students have variable perceptions of how writing mediates their engagement in university activities and how these activities are significant to them. Perceptions of the role of writing in one's academic life depend on the model of writing and on the kind of learners' engagement in the activity/genre system that constructs their university environment.

Two very distinct kinds of undergraduate students' perceptions of the university arise: 1) learning mediated by teachers in regular classes and lectures or 2) education mediated by symbolic and material research activities. The kind of insertion students have in the discipline depends on how much they seek research opportunities and mentoring, beyond the lecture halls and classrooms.

"One has to live the process in order to be able to understand and practice it" (Freire, 2000, p. 46), as indicated by the results of a survey carried out at REWRITE with 41 students divided among four years of the English Teaching Degree Program. Questions regarded how often, about what, for what purpose, and in which situations students wrote, their greatest difficulties, and the relevance of writing activities in Portuguese and English to their everyday university or professional lives.

In their analysis of these data, Assis-Brasil and Marcuzzo (2009) argue that these undergraduate students have a clear perspective on the everyday written genres, since they identify them by such names as "e-mails," "letters," "notes" or "e-scraps." When referring to the production of academic texts, however, general terms emerge such as "texts" or "assignments" (p.171). For the authors, this distinction would demonstrate that these students know the genre-set pertaining to everyday life but lack metaawareness about academic genres.

Alternatively, I believe that, even though they mention everyday genres, these students tend to think of writing as a mechanical skill whose general aim is to "to express oneself" or "to communicate with others." There is no concept of genre systems exactly because of the lack of a general sense of literacy practices: the knowledge of the social practices mediated by the use of the written word (Lea, 1999, p. 106), of how living is mediated by tools and signs (texts) (Vygotsky, 2001).

First-year students express an imprecise perception of how often, when and why they write:

1/2 - Every day at work, in class, at home[9]

1/3 - Normally when I think of something that's controversial or interesting.

1/11 - To communicate with people that live far away

One could ask: to acquire vocabulary in what genre? To communicate with people in what capacity/role, for what purpose?

Most answers about writing situations and objectives are general: "chats" (1/1), "e-mail" (2/8), "assignments" (3/4), "notes" (4/1). At the time of the survey these students had not taken a course in academic writing and many expressed their frustration when trying to write an assignment because they lacked expressive resources. Although a writing course would certainly have made a difference, engagement in actual social research practices could have built awareness of the complex process through which written texts construct disciplinary knowledge. It could also help them understand how the very act of engaging in written practices specific to the discipline constructs a particular world of meanings, a particular mode of ratiocination (Bazerman, 1988).

These students have a "study skills model of writing" focused on "surface features of language form in terms of grammar, punctuation, spelling, etc," so that writing is considered a "technical skill" (Lea, 1999, p. 106).

This unfortunately is the writing model generally adopted in Brazilian schools and at UFSM, with few exceptions, as I will explain in the last section of this paper. In fact, writing difficulties are credited to lack of vocabulary and poor command of grammar and text organization skills, showing a structural perception of writing as the application of knowledge about language structures (Assis-Brasil & Marcuzzo, 2009, p. 173).

To understand complex academic writing practices and the role of writing in their everyday and academic lives, these students would need a model of "academic literacies" (Lea, 1999, p. 107): the social uses of alphabetical competencies by those who have appropriated reading and writing and have incorporated the social practices that demand them (Soares, 1999).

No respondent mentioned the specific literacy practices or genre systems that construct their field: essays for course assignments, articles originated in course papers, book reviews published in undergraduate journals with an appraisal of the literature in the area, teaching activities for teaching practice, research proposals submitted for approval, reports to present research data, final graduation papers, conference abstracts, e-mails with requests (e.g., for the copy of an article, for submitting a paper in a conference), letters and résumés for grant or job application, etc.

In contrast to this sample, another group of students from REWRITE were interviewed: two fourth-year students who hold a research scholarship in the English Teacher Education program, six master's students, and six PhDs students in the Applied Linguistics Program (who are either about to or have recently graduated). Of the seventeen questionnaires, fourteen were returned.

These students engage as authors in the complexity of academic written social practices, as part of the knowledge construction system at UFSM. They mobilize a repertoire of academic genres that allow them to negotiate a position as newcomers to the discipline.

The undergraduate students seem to have a precise view of what counts as a writing situation:

> 4/4 - I use writing in the university context: a) course assignments, b) tests, c) teaching material, d) teaching practice and research reports for scientific initiation, e) papers for conferences, f) administrative demands, e.g., a memo to ask permission to waive prerequisite(s) for an advanced course . . . I also write in everyday practices, such as i) notes for family members back home, j) messages in MSN, facebook, or to friends, . . .m) shopping lists.

They understand what writing does and how it does it in different contexts in terms of roles/relationships/purposes for the academic genres mentioned: "e-mail— to classmates—to make appointments for study meetings."

Post-graduate students have to practice academic writing on a daily basis and hold a clear perspective on the repertoire of genres that construct their professional activities.

> M/4 - I have been writing final papers for the post-graduation courses which later become articles that I submit to journals . . . later on they are edited and become parts of the thesis.[10]

> Dr/2 - In my teaching practice I write class plans, teaching materials . . ., tests and exams . . . As a researcher, I write book reviews…, research proposals, reports, memos, abstracts and papers to present results of my research in conferences, research articles . . . .

Although only eight respondents had taken the academic writing course I teach, those who had and were committed to research seemed to have the most articulate sense of how writing mediates their participation in the professional field:

> M/2 - . . . .writing is a way to open a niche from where to speak out in the academic environment. . . .

> M3 - . . .I write to maximize my CV and demarcate my presence in the academic environment.

Participation in research literacies generates a sense of authorship, which is one of the main attainments in academic writing teaching, as discussed below.

CONCLUSION: AMBITIONS AND FRUSTRATIONS, AND AN APPROACH TO THE TEACHING OF WRITING

The academic writing course whose principles are described here has been offered once a year since 1994 at REWRITE. Its three objectives are: 1) to raise novice academic writers' awareness of academic literacy practices, 2) to develop their reading and writing competencies by implementing a writing cycle that focuses on their own (real) work, 3) to encourage learners to develop discourse analysis abilities so that they can continue improving their written competencies throughout their academic lives in a cycle of reading/writing/revising/editing/publishing.

The course has been developed from three principles. First, academic literacies obtain from reading and writing: one attains a literacy state/condition by appropriating technologies to interact with the social context as reader/writer in order to participate in the knowledge society (Soares, 1999). People learn how to use language because they learn to interact in their social context (Halliday, 1994).

Second, one learns to write by engaging in literacy practices, by becoming an author. The course aims at developing learners' authorship by encouraging them to explore disciplinary literacy practices and fostering writing within events and genres that structure the academic life in which they want to participate. Authorship—as the writer's prerogative and responsibility to choose the aim, content, style, and readership of the text (Ivanic, 1998, pp. 26, 219, 341) —stems from the experience of this awareness. The concept of literacy(ies) depends on that of authorship.

Third, one learns to interact through language by becoming a discourse analyst (McCarthy & Carter, 1994, p.134), by developing a sense of how discursive practices are situated as genres (Bazerman, 2005). Students analyze the connections between contextual features (activity, identity, relations as well as the role performed by text in the situation) and their respective linguistic realizations (expression of content, instantiation of relationships between interlocutors, and organization of text).

The writing cycle taught in the course completes in three steps:
1. Context Exploration—collect genre exemplars, observe and report research practices, genres, concepts and problems from their labs (Which roles does language play in knowledge production practices in your discipline?);
2. Text Exploration—learners analyze genre systems for referential meanings (that make intelligible the activity system of their context), for interpersonal meanings (that represent the roles and relationships of the participants of that activity system), and for language itself (text form and content) (How does language construct context and vice versa?); and
3. Text Production—learners write, revise, and edit their own as well as others' exemplars of relevant genres (How is language used for engagement and participation in academic literacy practices? Who publishes where? Who reads what? Do you intend to publish your text? How can you do that?)

In the Context Exploration phase, learners go back to their laboratories to interview colleagues and advisors to identify relevant research topics, concepts, methodological approaches, and academic genres to structure their work. Learners already working on their dissertations are supposed to see their advisors in order to establish the writing priority for the course: to concentrate on writing a paper or one of their dissertation chapters (Rural Sciences learners, for example, often experience a hard time in writing their Review of the Literature chapter and tend to choose this text). The semantic map will evolve into the writing of the objectives and then into a tentative abstract that will serve as a guide to the writing of the longer text. The Text Exploration phase offers the learners the opportunity to analyze genre exemplars for referential meanings (relevant content for their research), interpersonal meanings (experienced authors' tone and style), and language itself (which linguistic choices produce these meanings, cohesion, and coherence).

We look at research articles from important journals or relevant research projects learners have identified with the help of advisors during the Context Exploration phase. The whole class analyzes each exemplar together in order to make contrasts among areas more evident and thus raise learners' awareness of language, text, and discourse features across disciplines.

Finally, in the Text Production phase learners write their drafts and bring copies, so the class reads and comments on them. As texts grow longer, we divide into revising teams and set a calendar so that every class a number of people bring their texts to be revised. After that they will have a fortnight or so to edit their texts and bring a new section or an extended version of their papers (or other genre). A textbook written especially for this course (Motta-Roth, 2001)[11] offers support for writing academic genres (explanations about aim, form, style, structure and linguistic choices).

This "Academic writing cycle"[12] is successful as long as learners are encouraged to experience disciplinary interaction as readers and writers (Russell, 1997). My academic literacy presupposes understanding how a system of written genres constructs a disciplinary context in different situations, how texts work differently in each field depending on the nature of the activities each area of study conducts and of the relations the participants maintain to produce knowledge. Awareness about the bi-directionality between text and context allows students to see how the texts they write are an integral part of academia so that they can situate their text in the system of discursive genres (Bazerman, 2005) that structure academic interactions.

One of my frustrations in relation to writing pedagogy at UFSM is the general lack of an institutional writing program that fosters undergraduate students' engagement in material and writing research practices from their very first year. Only sometimes is a special course offered as an initiative of the central administration or in one of the specific colleges, but no writing policy has yet been devised to significantly improve our publication levels. Institutional support of an extensive and inclusive writing program would be crucial. Specifically in the Language Teaching Program, the ambition would be to integrate into the teacher education process research and writing practices in academic genres, so that future teachers begin systematic thinking and writing from their freshman year forward.

NOTES

1. I thank Fabio Nascimento for the suggestions for the manuscript.

2. More at http://pt.wikipedia.org/wiki/Santa_Maria_(Rio_Grande_do_Sul).

3. About 680 miles from São Paulo, the major industrial and economic powerhouse of the Brazilian economy and the largest city in South America.

4. A leading institution in Latin-America and one of the 100 best universities in the world (http://www4.usp.br).

5. In 2009, UFSM had 603 articles indexed in the ISI Database and Web of Science, besides books, chapters, proceedings, etc.

6. A number identifies each interviewee.

7. The fifth largest country in the world, after Russia, Canada, China and the US, with a total area of 3,287,612 square miles.

8. The *Brazilian Journal of Medical and Biological Research* and the *Brazilian Journal of Physics* are in English.

9. Two numbers identified each respondent: the year they are studying in/their assigned number. Thus 1/3 corresponds to First year/Respondent no.3.

10. M (master's) and doctoral (PhD) students.

11. This material originally published by my laboratory has been updated, revised and extended for publication under a new title and publishing house as Motta-Roth & Hendges (2010).

12. See Motta-Roth (2009) for a detailed description of this pedagogic approach.

REFERENCES

Assis-Brasil, A. M. de & Marcuzzo, P. (2009). Um estudo sobre representações sociais de alunos de Letras sobre a produção escrita em inglês. *Expressão, 1,* 165-175.

Bazerman, C. (1988). *Shaping written knowledge.* Madison: The University of Wisconsin Press.

Bazerman, C. (2005). *Gêneros textuais, tipificação e interação.* A. P. Dionísio & J. C. Hoffnagel (trans.). São Paulo: Cortez.

Freire, P. (2000). *A importância do ato de ler—em três artigos que se complementam.* 39. ed. São Paulo: Cortez.

Halliday, M. A. K. (1994). *An introduction to functional grammar.* London: Arnold.

Ivanic, R. (1998). *Writing and identity: The discoursal construction of identity in academic writing.* Amsterdam/Philadelphia: John Benjamins.

Lea, M. R. (1999). Academic literacies and learning in higher education. In C. Jones, J. Turner, & B. Street (Eds.), *Students writing in the university: Cultural and epistemological issues—Studies in written language and literacy 8* (pp. 103-124). Amsterdam, Philadelphia: John Benjamins.

McCarthy, M., & Carter, R. (1994). *Language as discourse: Perspectives for language teaching.* London: Longman.

Motta-Roth, D. (2001). *Redação acadêmica: Princípios básicos.* 1. ed. Santa Maria: Imprensa Universitária.

Motta-Roth, D. (2002). Comunidade acadêmica internacional? Multicultural? Onde? Como? *Linguagem & Ensino, 5*(2), 49-65. Retrieved from http://rle.ucpel.tche.br/php/edicoes/v5n2/d_desiree.pdf.

Motta-Roth, D. (2009). The role of context in academic text production and writing pedagogy. In C. Bazerman, A. Bonini, & D. Figueiredo. (Eds.). *Genre in a changing world* (pp. 317-336). Fort Collins, Colorado, and West Lafayette, Indiana: The WAC Clearinghouse and Parlor Press. Retrieved from http://wac.colostate.edu/books/genre/chapter16.pdf.

Motta-Roth, D., & Hendges, G. (2010). *Produção textual na universidade.* São Paulo: Parábola Editorial.

Phillipson, R., & Skutnabb-Kangas, T. (1999). Englishisation: One dimension of globalisation. In D. Graddol & U. Meinhof (Eds.), *English in a changing world – L'anglais dans un monde changeant. AILA Review, 13,* 19-36. Retrieved from http://www.aila.info/publications/ailapublications/aila-review/downloads/aila-review-13.html

Russell, D. (1997). Rethinking genre in school and society: An activity theory analysis. *Written Communication, 14,* 504-554.

Soares, M. (1999). *Letramento: um tema em três gêneros.* Belo Horizonte, Minas Gerais, Brazil: Autêntica.

Universidade de São Paulo. (n.d.). *Universidade de São Paulo.* Retrieved from http://www4.usp.br

Vygotsky, L. S. (2001). *Pensamiento y palabra. Obras escogidas: Pensamiento y lenguaje.* 2ed. Primera Parte, Tomo II. Madri: A. Machado Libros.

CHAPTER 10.
WRITING PROGRAMS WORLDWIDE: ONE CANADIAN PERSPECTIVE

By Roger Graves and Heather Graves
University of Alberta (Canada)

The history of writing instruction in Canadian universities differs markedly from the US experience. In Canada, first-year writing was never required and even today is optional. Further, it has evolved out of a literature/composition hybrid course that continues to be taught in many institutions, including the University of Alberta. The key moment at the University of Alberta occurred with the establishment of the Writing Task Force in 2005. The task force made three major recommendations: a new Writing Centre; a Writing-Across-the-Curriculum Program (WAC); and a Writing Studies Program. These new initiatives joined three existing writing centres at Campus Saint Jean (the French-language campus); the Augustana campus, located 100 kilometers from Edmonton; and the existing writing tutorial service located in Student Services. The directors of all these units come together regularly at the University Writing Committee meetings to coordinate plans, share ideas, and listen to the concerns of faculty from across the institution.

The University of Alberta (enrollment 37,000; 18 faculties; established 1908; $500 million in research per year) has a long-standing commitment to improving student writing, but because this commitment arose out of the history of teaching writing in Canadian contexts, that commitment took form in ways unlike the pattern in the United States of America. Johnson (1988) summarized the differences, chief among them being the lack of first-year writing in Canada:

> In contrast to the much documented rise of the "Freshman Composition" course in English departments in the United States, the twentieth-century Canadian academy has never

> embraced the curricular concept of the "Comp" class per se; and, with remarkable hegemony, has persisted into the present decade in offering introductory English courses founded on a synthesis of composition instruction and training in critical analysis—a synthesis which was the distinctive legacy of nineteenth-century Canadian adaptations of British-style belletristic rhetoric. (869)

According to Johnson, an eighteenth-century British rhetorical education focuses on developing mental discipline, and the application of rhetorical principles to literature ("belles letters") results in the development of mental acuity and moral discipline. This combination of writing instruction in the context of literary analysis came to define the first-year literature course in many English departments in the early twentieth century, including the department at the University of Alberta (Graves 1994; Hubert 1994; Johnson 1991). This fusion of the two elements continues to dominate this department today, as unlikely as that may seem to American readers.

This tradition has come under pressure in the last few decades. Other universities, such as the University of Western Ontario, have largely abandoned the literature/composition hybrid and developed a writing program outside of the context of an English department. At the University of Winnipeg, the writing program has now become a department, and it now offers both undergraduate and graduate degrees, mirroring a trend in the United States towards "independent" writing programs (Kearns & Turner, 1997, and essay in this volume). While only one or two universities in Canada require first-year writing courses (the University of Winnipeg is one notable example), many offer an optional course or series of courses in writing. Another factor affecting first-year writing is the trend toward students transferring into a university after having done one or two years at a two-year college. Two-year colleges in Canada very often offer and even require a writing course or series of writing courses. At the University of Alberta, many students attend Grant MacEwen College/University (a hybrid institution) or Red Deer College before transferring to upper-year programs at the University of Alberta. At Grant MacEwen students may take a two-course writing sequence, the second of which mirrors the literature/composition synthesis favored at the University of Alberta. The recent development of exclusively writing courses has created a problem with assigning transfer credit: until very recently when the new Writing Studies courses were developed, there was no equivalent course at the University of Alberta.

KEY MOMENT: WRITING TASK FORCE (2005-2008)

As part of strategic planning for the University of Alberta, the Provost and Faculty of Arts jointly sponsored a large, university-wide task force to assess writing instruction and writing competencies from across the university. The task force researched the status of writing both within the university and across the continent to identify models that it might draw upon when proposing changes. The committee researched the literature/composition first-year English courses, examined the needs of second language writers, studied how much writing was being assigned in courses across the university curriculum, and wrote many documents as part of this process. Many of these documents, including the interim and final reports, are posted on the web: http://www.writinginitiatives.ualberta.ca/Writing%20Task%20Force.aspx

The task force gained widespread recognition for writing on campus and to some extent across the province because of the ramifications any changes would have for transfer credit from other institutions. Indeed, through conference presentations and the research of the participants, other writing studies scholars across the country were aware of its work. The task force made three major recommendations: a new, full-service, university-wide Writing Centre; a significant Writing-Across-the-Curriculum Program (WAC); and an interdisciplinary Writing Studies Program with a teaching/research mandate.

WRITING COURSES AT THE UNIVERSITY OF ALBERTA

While not officially a "program" (instead we are a "field of study") at the University of Alberta, Writing Studies offers a number of courses in writing through the Office of Interdisciplinary Studies (OIS), an administrative unit formed to house a number of programs, fields of study, and certificates in the Faculty of Arts, including Religious Studies, Comparative Literature, Humanities Computing, Middle Eastern and African Studies, and Science Technology and Society. These programs and fields of study are units housed in OIS for the purposes of administration, but all faculty who teach in these units are members of a "home" department; for example, faculty in Writing Studies have English and Film Studies as their home departments. A recent review of OIS raised questions about the future of this office, whether it should remain an administrative unit or be converted into something more, that is, whether it should be reconstituted as an academic unit.

In 2010, the Writing Studies unit offered a total of thirteen sections of six courses that were taught by four tenure-track or tenured faculty and one instructor—a very small program for an institution of 37,000 students. These courses included nine sections of the elective first year writing course (made up of seven sections of WRS 101, Exploring Writing, and two sections of WRS 103, Introduction to Writing in the Sciences); one section of a combined undergraduate- and graduate-level course that is a practicum for training tutors in the Centre for Writers (WRS 301/603); and three graduate level courses, Academic Writing for Graduate Students (WRS 500); Composition Theory (WRS 601); and Writing and Disciplinarity (WRS 604). Composition Theory has been offered at the University of Alberta for a number of years as an English and Film Studies Course; only in the last year or so has it been converted to a Writing Studies course. The other three courses (Writing for Graduate Students, the practicum for the Centre for Writers, and Writing and Disciplinarity) are either brand new or developed and offered in the last four years.

This number of courses is typical of our offerings for the past three years. Although there is significant demand for writing courses at both the undergraduate and graduate levels (we could probably fill a third section of WRS 103, An Introduction to Writing in the Sciences, and perhaps offer WRS 500, Academic Writing for Graduate Students, every term), the funding for offering additional courses is absent in part due to cost-cutting measures associated with the downturn in the provincial economy. Another factor is the cost of running 20-student courses in writing compared with the current 35-student literature/composition synthesis course; offering enough writing courses to replace composition courses would result in cost increases of about 40%. While we would like to see something like 30 or 40 sections offered each term, the additional costs will likely prevent that for the foreseeable future.

WRS 101: Exploring Writing

This first-year writing studies course, developed and supervised by Betsy Sargent (Director of Writing Studies), focuses on engaging students in the writing process using workshop and seminars in a small class (less than 20 students) setting. Students write often in class as well as following a process-driven approach to produce several larger documents that come together in a portfolio of writing that is evaluated at the end of the term. Part of the rationale for grading through portfolios is to delay finalizing the drafts students are working on; this then extends the time students spend drafting and revising—the invention part of the writing process.

The most novel feature of this course, however, is the focus on "writing about writing." This approach to teaching writing takes the stance that writing is the subject of study in a writing course; students read academic articles by composition scholars as their course material. Students here are both novices who are learning to practice the art of writing as well as students of a content area that focuses on knowledge about writing.

WRS 103, An Introduction to Writing in the Sciences

Writing Studies offered two distinct versions of first-year writing in 2010 because two sections of this course are reserved exclusively for first-year students in the Faculty of Science who are enrolled in Science 100. Science 100 is an innovative, interdisciplinary re-thinking of first-year science that was in its third year in 2010. The Faculty of Science consists of seven subject areas: Biological Sciences, Earth and Atmospheric Sciences, Physics, Computing Sciences, Mathematics and Statistical Sciences, Chemistry, and Psychology. This configuration of areas is an artifact of institutional history. Several years ago faculty in Science reconceptualized their first year curriculum into Science 100, a year-long, 27-credit course, in which they take an interdisciplinary approach to science, introducing students to all subject areas over the course of the year and taking an experimental/experiential approach to the various topics. The website describes the course like this: "SCIENCE 100 uses an integrated and interdisciplinary approach and employs the expertise of top science professors to deliver material from all seven Faculty of Science disciplines. The focus in SCIENCE 100's small classes is on in-depth teaching, conceptual understanding and practical mastery of the fundamentals": http://www.science.ualberta.ca/ProspectiveStudents/SCIENCE100/HowItWorks.aspx . In addition to Science 100, these students also take WRS 103, a three-credit course, in the fall term, which teaches them some of the concepts of writing that will contribute to their success over the course of their undergraduate education.

In 2008, the first year that Science 100 was offered, students took a modified version of WRS 101, Exploring Writing, a course developed for the general population of undergraduates at the University of Alberta; it has students read academic journal articles in writing studies and reflect on the implications this theory has for their own writing practices. WRS 101, Exploring Writing, was not well suited to the needs of undergraduate science students because the course's overt focus was on invention—helping students figure out what to write about in a given assignment. In fact, the assumption that students need help deciding on a topic is unwarranted with much science-related writing because it is experiment- and data-driven. Writers in science come to a text knowing what to write about--their interpretation of their findings. Consequently, faculty in writing studies developed a version of the first-year writing course that was tailored to the needs and interests of students in Science 100.

In WRS 103 students take a process approach to writing, and the central focus of activities is on analyzing audience, purpose, and genre. Audiences are not exclusively academic, with students writing for non-specialist and lay readers as well. Regarding purpose, the course focuses on two major purposes for writing in science: to inform and to persuade. Finally, assignments in WRS 103 are not exclusively essay-based, since undergraduates in science in Canada almost never write an essay of the variety routinely assigned in first-year composition courses in the US (a research essay). Instead, students in WRS 103 write one essay (a position argument) that uses explicit argument (in place of writing a grant proposal, which is the genre in which scientists argue most explicitly), two reports (that both argue for an interpretation and inform readers), and a newsletter article (writing for a non-specialist or lay reader). By discussing the varying requirements for structure, content, and style in these three different genres, students gain a greater awareness of how these elements shape writing as the writer moves from one genre to another, which is more useful to them in their academic careers than mastering the persuasive essay. There is some collaboration among instructors in Science 100 and the WRS 103 instructor to ensure connections are drawn between the writing done in both the writing and the science classes.

THE PHD PROGRAM PROPOSAL IN WRITING STUDIES AND RHETORIC

Rather than develop an undergraduate writing program, the faculty in Writing Studies decided to develop a PhD program because there are few doctoral programs in Writing Studies in Canada. Many writing-related programs in Canadian universities are staffed by non-academic faculty offered through Student Services. This situation is partly due to Canadian post-secondary administrators who continue to view writing as a "skill" that students can acquire with one or two hour-long workshops on academic writing or a handful of sessions with a poorly-paid writing tutor who works on a cost-recovery basis. It is also partly due to the lack of qualified academic faculty who could provide leadership and intellectual depth to the teaching of writing at Canadian post-secondary institutions.

To attempt to address the issue of limited qualified personnel for writing-related positions in Canada, the faculty in Writing Studies at the University of Alberta decided to create a doctoral program that would develop tenure-line professionals with expertise in three areas: Writing Centre research and administration; Writing Program research, development, and administration; and research and program development in writing in the disciplines/writing across the curriculum. When writing centres are housed in Student Services, administrators in charge of Student Services tend to lose sight of the fact that teaching writing has a strong intellectual and research foundation. When tutors and instructors are not equipped or rewarded for conducting research and expanding the field's understanding of the intellectual development entailed in the activity of writing, they obviously do not do it, to the detriment of the students they are charged with helping. Writing instruction that is drawn from cutting-edge knowledge in the field will be much better equipped to make a difference in students' lives than uninformed obsession with correcting grammar and punctuation errors in students papers. The proposed program will attempt to redress this ongoing issue in writing instruction in Canada.

Faculty in Writing Studies also decided to capitalize on the support at the instructional level for writing at the University of Alberta by developing options for graduate students to conduct research into writing in the disciplines. Recent research suggests that generic writing courses, such as are offered at the first-year level in composition, are not effectively generalizable across the academic disciplines, at least in Canadian universities and colleges. Research that explores the requirements for writing in various academic disciplines can help the field to offer instructional resources that better meet the needs of their students who come from disciplines across the university.

Early in 2010 Writing Studies faculty learned that the budget crisis at the University of Alberta would slow the funding of any new programs at any level of the university. It therefore appears that there is no money for developing this doctoral program in late 2010. This situation may change as the provincial, national, and global economies improve, however. In the meantime, the proposal is going forward with the hope that it might be approved and in place if and when funding becomes available.

CENTRE FOR WRITERS

When the student union presented its request to the Provost in 2006, he asked them to identify the one request they wanted most. They identified the Centre for Writers as their top priority. Now in its third full year of operation, the Centre for Writers is an established presence on campus. This success came despite some adversity, a fact that many writing centre directors might see as unremarkable. Now in its fourth year of operation, it has had three directors. The first director set up the office, hired an administrative assistant, taught the first peer-tutor training course, and oversaw the first term of tutoring sessions in Winter 2008 with about 180 students and 300 one-to-one sessions. After her resignation in the summer of 2008, Roger Graves served as interim director for the first full year of operations. Over 1300 students participated in a total of over 2500 one-to-one sessions. A staff of over 20 undergraduate peer tutors and graduate student tutors worked in the Center, which was relocated to a new, larger space for the 2009-10 year. During this first year, another permanent director was hired for the Centre, Lucie Moussu. In her first year as director and the second full year of operations, the Centre conducted over 4500 one-to-one appointments for over 1700 students. The web site for the Centre continues to add resources for students, and the tutoring desks in the Centre all have computers and print resources (handbooks, style manuals, dictionaries). It has become the vibrant, well-run, and important resource envisioned by the Writing Task Force.

The Centre for Writers is one of four independent (funded and run separately) writing centres at the university. Bilingual Writing Centre/Centre d'écriture bilingue (Campus Saint-Jean) works with French-language students at the French campus of the University of Alberta. The Augustana Writing Centre works with students at the Augustana campus, which is located approximately 60 miles from the main campus. Writing Resources (Academic Support Centre, Student Services) offers a similar tutorial service to the Centre for Writers as well as workshops for both undergraduates and graduate students. Writing Resources existed prior to the establishment of the Centre for Writers, and differs in that it is a fee-recovery unit: it charges students $20 per half-hour appointment and various amounts for workshops.

WRITING ACROSS THE CURRICULUM

The Writing Across the Curriculum program at the University of Alberta has engaged in four efforts: teaching about writing to classes in various disciplines (about 25 in 2009); one-to-one consultations as well as workshops and presentations for instructors, both faculty and graduate (18 workshops or presentations in 2009); research investigating the kinds of writing students are asked to engage in at the University of Alberta (5 studies completed or under way).

In an effort to engage and demonstrate how to teach students about the writing tasks set for them in courses, Roger Graves has visited classes to teach the session on getting started on the writing assignment. These sessions generally last 50 minutes (or whatever time the professor can allot to this activity) and involve parsing the assignment description; brainstorming topics for the assignment; drafting sample thesis statements; constructing evidence-based arguments in support of those thesis statements; writing summaries of research to include in essays. During these sessions, which are frequently held in classes of over 100 students, instructors and students talk back and forth about the nuances of the assignment—a conversation that might not take place outside this exchange or, if it did, sometimes too late in the writing process. Our goal at the end of these sessions is that students have a good understanding of the assignment; they know what kinds of strategies produce better writing (adopting a process approach; getting feedback; revising); and they know where to get help (at one of the four writing centres).

Invitations to visit classes for those kinds of presentations often come from writing-across-the-curriculum workshops and one-to-one conversations with faculty members. These sorts of activities are typical of WAC programs for faculty development. In addition, we have tried to work less on the broad scale of campus-wide workshops and more on a focused effort with specific curricular groups. The Faculty of Science has been an enthusiastic supporter of initiatives undertaken in Writing at University of Alberta. In additional to the collaboration between Writing Studies and Science 100 instructors, the science faculty has also been receptive to introducing more writing into some of their undergraduate science courses. Each department, for example, has a senior capstone course that involves a research project with a large writing component such as a senior honors thesis (e.g., earth and atmospheric science) or a work report following an Industrial Internship Program placement (e.g., computing science, biological sciences) or research report (e.g., biological sciences, including microbiology). In 2009, five faculty members in science consulted with Writing Studies faculty about ongoing capstone courses (two in biology, one in earth and atmospheric sciences) or during the process of developing a capstone course (mathematics and statistical sciences). In addition, a series of six workshops on writing-related topics (creating good writing assignments in science; grading rubrics for writing assignments; teaching writing in science classes, etc.) for faculty and graduate students in science in winter 2009 were well attended, with between 20 and 40 individuals at each one.

The third major component of our WAC work has been research into the writing assigned to students in various programs. Because most students do not take an extensive liberal arts component—many enter directly from secondary school into their major program of study—and very few have a writing or composition course, the writing they do is very much discipline-based. We have conducted studies here based on a previous study at another university where we collected every writing assignment from every course (Graves, Hyland & Samuels, 2010). We have replicated this study methodology for the Faculty of Nursing; Faculty of Physical Education, Recreation, and Leisure Studies; Faculty of Pharmacy; Department of Political Science; and Community Service Program. These data provide profiles of the writing that students in a particular program must do (Anson & Dannels, 2009). For example, we know that students in the RN program write 79 assignments in the required courses over the four years of the program, and we know which genres appear at each year in the program. The Nursing faculty has found this research to be extremely useful as a curriculum reform tool, and it has galvanized interest in writing and turned that interest into specific outcomes: re-written assignments; more and better scoring guides; workshops for instructors; writing workshops for peer research groups among the faculty.

STRATEGIZING FOR IMPACT

Much has been accomplished in the short time since the final report of the Writing Task Force in 2008. The Centre for Writers is established, effective, and growing. The WAC program teaches thousands of students about writing in their courses each year. The Writing Studies program has established writing courses at the University of Alberta. These new programs join the other writing centres at the university—at Campus Saint Jean, Augustana, and in Student Services—when we all meet once a month at the University Writing Council meetings to discuss strategy and coordinate efforts. In addition, a new group from across the province has been formed for professional development and to exchange program development news: the Campus Alberta Writing Studies group meets twice a year. Ultimately, each of these groups draws its funding from the government of the province of Alberta. Our hope is to coordinate our efforts in ways that magnify the impact of our individual efforts, from sharing costs for professional development events to sharing resources that we develop for our own writing centres.

REFERENCES

Anson, C.A., & Dannels, D. (2009). Profiling programs: Formative uses of departmental consultations in the assessment of communication across the curriculum. *Across the Disciplines, 6*. Retrieved from http://wac.colostate.edu/atd/assessment/anson_dannels.cfm

Graves, R. (1994). *Writing instruction in Canadian universities.* Winnipeg: Inkshed Publications.

Graves, R., Hyland, T., & Samuels, B. (2010). Undergraduate writing assignments: An analysis of syllabi at one Canadian university. *Written Communication, 27*(3), 293-317.

Hubert, H. (1994). *Harmonious perfection: The development of English studies in nineteenth-century Anglo-Canadian colleges.* East Lansing: Michigan State University Press.

Johnson, N. (1988). Rhetoric and belles lettres in the Canadian academy: An historical analysis. *College English, 50,* 861-73.

Johnson, N. (1991). *Nineteenth-century rhetoric in North America.* Carbondale, IL: Southern Illinois University Press.

Kearns, J., & Turner, B. (1997). Negotiated independence: How a Canadian writing program became a centre. *Writing Program Administrator, 21,* 31-45.

CHAPTER 11.
DEPARTMENT OF RHETORIC, WRITING, AND COMMUNICATIONS AT THE UNIVERSITY OF WINNIPEG

By Brian Turner and Judith Kearns
University of Winnipeg (Canada)

The University of Winnipeg's Department of Rhetoric, Writing, and Communications has the distinction of being the first independent writing program in Canada. Conceived in 1986 as The Writing Program, it underwent a review in 1993, separated from the English Department to become the Centre for Academic Writing, and then began offering a communications program in partnership with a local college. CAW launched a B.A. in Rhetoric and Communications in 2003; three years later, with fourteen full-time faculty, a writing centre, and a peer tutoring program, it was granted departmental status and took its current name. Evolution in our curriculum and institutional status have demanded compromise. Our chief concerns have been to strike a balance between rhetoric and writing and meet two objectives: to provide first-year students with the rhetorical skills necessary to disciplinary success, and to develop in upper-level students facilitas—the ability to assess a variety of rhetorical situations and respond both ethically and effectively.

With a population of approximately 670,000, the city of Winnipeg—the name comes from the Cree word win-nipi, meaning "muddy water" —is Canada's seventh largest municipality and home to more than half the residents of the province of Manitoba. It is located at the geographic centre of North America and the confluence of the Red and Assiniboine Rivers, on a site where First Nations people met and traded for centuries. After the Hudson's Bay Company established a strategic post there in the nineteenth century, the region experienced steady immigration from Europe and neighbouring Ontario. Residents of the modern city are mostly of European descent and primarily

English-speaking; however, Winnipeg has considerable ethnic diversity, including the largest French-speaking community west of Quebec and the highest proportion (about ten percent) of First Nations people of any Canadian city (http://www.statscan.gc.ca). The latter also constitute the fastest-growing ethnic group in the city and province. Improving the access of Aboriginal students to postsecondary education has consequently become an increasing concern for the province, one which the recently-established University College of the North is designed to address.

Though modest, Manitoba's diversified economy has remained relatively stable for decades; given its water resources and potential to export hydro-electricity, the province seems to have a promising future. Particularly noteworthy is the cultural life of its capital city. In addition to its several theatres, art gallery, provincial museum, and symphony hall, Winnipeg is home to an internationally recognized ballet company, to the Festival du Voyageur (the largest French winter carnival west of Quebec), and to large folk, jazz, fringe, film, and writers' festivals. Two universities and several colleges offer a variety of post-secondary options. The largest of these institutions is the University of Manitoba, with an undergraduate and graduate student population of about 26,000.

The smaller University of Winnipeg is one of the oldest post-secondary schools in western Canada. It was established as Manitoba College in 1871, merged with Wesley College in 1938 to become United College, then received its charter as a University in 1967. With approximately 9,000 full- and part-time students, the University has traditionally been an undergraduate institution, rooted in the liberal arts. In recent years, it has undergone a number of significant changes, including the development of joint programs with local colleges, several new departments, graduate studies, and a "global college" that, in the words of our current president, former Canadian Foreign Affairs Minister Lloyd Axworthy, aims to *"enhance and promote global citizenship in its many dimensions"* (http://www.uwinnipegcampaign.ca/academic/globalcollege).

HISTORY OF WRITING INSTRUCTION AT THE UNIVERSITY OF WINNIPEG

The Department of Rhetoric, Writing, and Communications—the academic unit with primary responsibility for writing instruction at the University of Winnipeg—has gone through several permutations over the past twenty-some years. Formally instituted by the university's senate as the Writing Program in 1986, it began operations the following year as a subdivision of the English Department, with a faculty of seven full-time instructors. It was seen and sold by administrators as a means of raising retention rates and of helping the university to improve access for historically under-represented groups. To this end, the Program relied mainly on a writing centre (equipped with computers, coordinated by faculty, and staffed by tutors who were meeting the practicum requirements of Education courses); and on two sequenced, pedagogically eclectic writing courses (part process-oriented, part expressivist, and part current-traditional), at least one of which was a requirement for any student who had graduated high-school with less than an honours standing in English. These were modest beginnings, certainly, but in Canada, where writing instruction at most post-secondary institutions was at best limited and first-year composition courses did not exist (Graves, 1994), the Writing Program garnered national recognition. In 1992 Canada's best-selling national magazine described it as "a model for universities across the country" ("Class options," 1992).

An extensive review of the Writing Program led to the formation of the Centre of Academic Writing (CAW) in 1995. This second phase marked an important advance, not only for the curriculum at the University of Winnipeg but to some extent for the status of post-secondary writing instruction in Canada, since CAW became the country's first independent writing program. We had a faculty of ten, all teaching writing and rhetoric courses exclusively. Guided by two main premises—that our university's heterogeneous population called for a diversity of approaches, and that our main task was, nonetheless, academic and disciplinary acculturation—we radically altered and expanded our curriculum. Students could now meet the writing requirement through a range of introductory courses (Academic Writing for broad discipline areas, such as the Social Sciences; courses with a multidisciplinary focus; courses "linked" with introductory sections in disciplines such as History and Environmental Studies; and extended courses, primarily for second-language students). CAW also began to develop a handful of upper-level writing and rhetoric courses.

With independence came greater institutional status and opportunities for curricular growth and diversification. In the second half of the decade, we teamed with a local college to develop a Joint Program in Communications aimed at students preparing for careers in journalism, advertising, or public relations. The enthusiastic response to this initiative, which combined a liberal arts focus with practical training, suggested further potential for communications studies. Accordingly, after extensive consultation about the kind of program that would best fit our faculty, students, and institution, we began in 2003 to deliver a new degree specialization (a "major") in "rhetoric and communications." Along with several core courses (in rhetorical criticism, professional editing, communication theory, and research methods), this major offered a variety of theoretical, analytical, and practical courses in writing and rhetoric. Together, the major and the Joint Program soon drew enough interest to make our student enrolment among the university's largest. In 2006, we appealed for and were granted department status, entering our third phase as the Department of Rhetoric, Writing, and Communications (re: http://rhetoric.uwinnipeg.ca).

THE DEPARTMENT OF RHETORIC, WRITING, AND COMMUNICATIONS

Like any historical synopsis, the above account leaves out many complicating details. The picture it creates of institutional harmony and steady progress towards departmental independence may be too sunny. It is true that writing instruction and instructors have been given unusual, even extraordinary support at the University of Winnipeg, particularly when considered in the context of Canadian higher education; however, the evolution of the Department of Rhetoric, Writing, and Communications has not always been smooth, nor has its current configuration been anything like an historical inevitability (Turner & Kearns, 2002). The process of becoming a full academic partner has required negotiations among competing demands, among them disciplinary ideals (i.e., "best practices"), institutional constraints, and local exigencies. Our success notwithstanding, becoming what we are has involved some compromises.

In what follows, we describe the current state of writing instruction at the University of Winnipeg—and in the process, consider some of these compromises—by examining three key topics: the focus on instructional delivery from within the Department of Rhetoric, Writing, and Communications rather than across the disciplines; the relationship between rhetoric and writing in the Department; and our Writing Centre.

WRITING INSTRUCTION: FROM A DEPARTMENT OR ACROSS THE CURRICULUM

In a 2006 report on trends in Canadian universities, Tanya Smith identifies three features of strong postsecondary writing instruction: the delivery of at least one course, early in the undergraduate programs of most students, focused mainly on academic writing, and of one or more additional writing courses at an advanced level, with a disciplinary or professional emphasis—in other words, a writing across the curriculum (WAC) component; a degree specialization or program devoted to academic or professional writing; and a supportive institutional culture. We are fortunate to enjoy an element of all three at the

University of Winnipeg, but we have faced some push and pull between the first and second features, even with institutional support. Commitment to a specialized degree program has necessarily reduced our capacity to foster advanced disciplinary writing instruction and similar WAC initiatives.

WAC once seemed a viable, even appealing option for the university. Writing Program and CAW faculty in the late 1980s and the 1990s produced a newsletter to promote the exchange of information about classroom practices and discussion of disciplinary rhetorics; we designed research projects on disciplinary grading practices; and, under the guidance of an interdisciplinary committee, we mounted writing workshops, arranged visits by prominent writing specialists, and began to define criteria for writing intensive courses. Rhetoric became a topic of interest, and colleagues spoke enthusiastically about "writing to learn." Early success of this kind is, however, difficult to sustain; attempts to foster WAC must be constantly re-invigorated, as many scholars have noted. Moreover, coming as they do from outside traditional departmental structures, such efforts depend heavily on "the individual commitment of faculty members" (Russell, 2009, p. 164). The burden for junior faculty working in a small Canadian university like ours proved especially demanding (Kearns & Turner, 1997). We were climbing mountains without much assistance or adequate equipment —struggling simultaneously to effect institutional change and to begin professional lives that might include research, even as we worked in a discipline for which we were not trained and in a country that lacked WAC models, strong national venues for rhet/comp scholarship, and "a concrete center for scholars to meet and exchange ideas" (Clary-Lemon, 2009). Tenure was waiting at the peak.

Professional survival meant that CAW needed to re-invent itself, in ways that drew more effectively on our strengths. This (and the increasing popularity of our courses) prompted the decision to design three- and four-year bachelor of arts degrees in Rhetoric and Communications (not, for instance, "Composition" or "Writing Studies"). Since most of us had, like the preceding generation of American compositionists, come to the teaching of writing from the study of literature,[1] it seemed sensible to emphasize courses that bridged the gap between text analysis and production, using the former as a means of facilitating the latter (see below). Movement in this direction was to some extent simultaneously a movement away from WAC and the constant, concomitant demands of work-shopping and consultation. Given our theoretical conviction about the value of WAC, this was, for some of us, a considerable loss.

But WAC was never abandoned altogether. Our first-year writing courses remain grounded in WAC principles (the versions of Academic Writing described above); and we continue to offer advanced courses such as Communicating Science, Strategies for Technical and Professional Communication, Professional Style and Editing, and Rhetoric in the Humanities and Social Sciences, which collectively appeal to students from across the university. It seems, moreover, that many of our colleagues are still committed to writing. A recent in-house survey indicates that faculty in nearly all departments (including such unlikely sites as math and physics) use writing assignments. Many report the allocation of class time to writing instruction (e.g., suggesting strategies or showing examples of effective student writing); an awareness of writing as process (giving opportunities to write multiple drafts, offering feedback on drafts, facilitating revision through conference and peer response); and the use of writing-to-learn activities (such as informal, exploratory writing). Our Writing Centre is also multi-disciplinary, both in the students who come seeking assistance and in the tutors who provide it. In this institution, writing is not seen as a concern of only the Humanities or the province of an English Department.

We suspect that, even without a full-fledged WAC program, the presence of an independent writing department helps sustain a climate of interest in writing. But we are aware that efforts of the sort just described may be primarily a happy consequence of the University of Winnipeg's traditionally small class sizes. Unfortunately, as in many universities, this is beginning to change, as several respondents noted. Indeed, caps for our own first-year writing classes have risen to 28—well over the number (20) recommended by the (US) National Council of Teachers of English (NCTE).

The decline of WAC, and with it the kind of oversight that WAC committees can provide, may be responsible for one further problem. When the Associate Dean recently analyzed first-year syllabi in the Arts, a somewhat startling fact emerged: the amount of writing and the proportion of final grades determined by writing assignments vary widely from section to section, even within a single department. Such inequities —certain to be noticed by students at some point, and rightly so—may undermine the attitudes to writing we are trying to foster.

RHETORIC AND WRITING

As much as the literature refers companionably to "rhetoric and composition" (or even "rhet/comp"), the relationship between the two has, in the US, often been vexed. In the 1970s, one scholar called it "obscure at best" (Douglas, 2009, p. 85); another described it in the 90s as "unstable" (Goggin, 1995). Being situated in Canada—and, we would add, in geographically isolated Winnipeg—has had its advantages in this respect. The very lack of a strong disciplinary tradition in writing or speech communication has given us greater license, making it possible to avoid some of the difficulties faced by American writing programs, even as we drew heavily on American theory and practice.

The key terms in our department name suggest our comfort with the rhet/comp relationship: they are intended to advertise our emphasis on rhetoric even as they reaffirm our long-standing commitment to writing. Indeed, the Department of Rhetoric, Writing, and Communications sees the two as inextricably linked, and still considers itself a "writing program." All our first-year courses and almost one third of our upper-level courses focus on academic writing. Despite differences in specifics, they have a larger common purpose: increasing our students' rhetorical awareness of academic and/or disciplinary styles, genres, and epistemic criteria in order to improve their own writing processes and written products.

In this sense, consistent with the classical tradition of "hermeneutical rhetoric" (Leff, 1997), a concern for student writing is also deeply embedded in the remaining two-thirds of our department's upper-level courses. In these, interpretive analysis and theory are not ends in themselves but a means "to enhance the reader's inventional skills as writer and speaker" (Leff, 1997, p. 199). Moreover, consistent with the tradition of small, liberal arts universities, we see the goal of enhanced inventional skills in broad, civic terms rather than discipline-specific or professional terms (Turner & Kearns, 2002). One of our main goals is to develop what Quintilian called facilitas—the ability to assess any rhetorical situation and respond appropriately, which is to say both effectively and ethically. For this reason, the focus of our rhetoric courses is as likely to be non-academic as academic discourses. Students may, for instance, analyze new journalism, nature essays, or magazine writing with the goal of producing a piece of their own; they may develop a communications strategy for an institution; or they may work with community organizations to produce other practical, "real-world" texts for a variety of audiences. [2]

Peer Tutoring

The presence of student supports for writing is a feature we share with most Canadian universities. In fact, the ubiquity of writing centres in Canadian universities led many to think that our former name, "the Centre for Academic Writing," represented a unit offering primarily tutorial assistance rather than credit courses and degree programs. That our writing centre has operated under the aegis of a department rather than within Student Services or the library, as is common elsewhere, has made all the difference: it has allowed faculty dedicated to writing to guide its evolution—not administrators, who often have quite different ideas about what such programs can and should do.

This has not, of course, meant complete autonomy. But it has meant a considerable degree of independence, allowing us to fund the writing centre securely and at the same time implement efficiencies that take disciplinary ideals into account. Originally, for instance, centre administration and the teaching of tutors required the time of two instructors; when we created a permanent staff position for the Computer Writing Lab, we not only freed up faculty time but also gained technological expertise and more efficient management of tutoring appointments. The decision to rely on paid tutoring also resulted in greater efficiency and helped compensate for the diminishment of WAC. At one time, the opportunity to tutor was available only to students taking an array of practicum courses, an arrangement that reduced our pool of tutors to Education and English students, prioritized the learning of the tutor over the learning of the tutee, limited tutoring time available to a few weeks each term (usually, Fall and Winter terms only), and drew heavily on department teaching resources. Combining paid tutoring with much shorter preparation courses opened the door to a wider range of students (including those in requirement-heavy science programs), increased tutoring hours, and significantly reduced the demands on faculty time. As a result, we now attract peer tutors from across the disciplines, well-prepared to address the diversity of student need (two-thirds of those who come to the Centre have been referred by colleagues in other departments). One faculty member alone is responsible for teaching, hiring, and supervising tutors and for what we might call "public relations": asking our colleagues to let good writers know about tutoring opportunities, weak students about opportunities for help, and keeping them well-informed about the principles and benefits of peer tutoring.

THE CURRENT STATE OF THE DEPARTMENT AND FUTURE DIRECTIONS

The Department now has a full-time faculty of fourteen. Six are instructors, with no contractual obligation to publish. For them, the development of a major has been professionally invigorating, providing new opportunities for research as they prepare for advanced courses. For the eight of us in the professoriate, teaching new courses has been similarly invigorating, and so too has teaching students who share our passion for rhetoric and composition. But just as important is that we have been relieved of the constant work of inventing a place for ourselves in the institution, now that independence, departmental status, and the major are faits accomplis. The result has been accelerated research productivity: we are publishing on visual rhetoric, journalism, gay and lesbian studies, critical pedagogy, literacy and social action, texting, the history of writing instruction, and composition—among other things. One of our newest colleagues was recently appointed editor of Composition Studies.

As a junior department, we may yet face obstacles from which other departments are generally exempt. While it is true that our tenure applications now proceed without undue complication, every one of our professoriate remains at the rank of assistant or associate professor. Indeed, to this point no one has applied for full professorship—partly because research productivity has been attenuated by the burdens described earlier, and partly (the authors suspect) because the experiences of our earliest tenure candidates has made some of us gun-shy (see Turner & Kearns, 2002). It seems that departmental status has been accompanied by greater respect within the university, and that colleagues from other departments appraise our work as they would their own. But when the time comes for our first application for promotion to professor, we will await the results with some trepidation.

The most recent initiative in the Department is a proposal for a graduate studies program, with a focus on rhetoric, writing, and public life. Its status remains uncertain, as does the status of grad studies generally at the University of Winnipeg; resources are an issue, as always, but so too are concerns that such a shift may undermine the university's real strengths, which lie in undergraduate education. There has also been talk of an undergraduate program in journalism. The authors feel some ambivalence, mainly for fear that such initiatives also risk over-taxing our resources. Yet re-invention of this kind may also prove again to be a stimulus to faculty, and in the case of Grad Studies, constitute another important step in the progress of writing and rhetoric studies in Canada.

NOTES

1. The proportion of degrees in English literature has been subsequently reduced, but it remains the case that most of us were trained in text analysis of some kind and learned to teach writing largely "on the job." Of eight PhDs, three are in English literature; three are in English with a focus on rhetoric (two from Canada, with a focus on rhetoric and/or text analysis, and one from the US, in rhet/comp); one is in rhetoric and professional writing (also from an American university); and one is in Education with a focus on cultural studies and critical pedagogy. Our most recent appointment at the instructor level has an MA in Communication Studies.

2. The meaning of our third key term, communications, is rather harder to explain. Since it refers to the dimension of our department that has the least to do with writing,

we've chosen not to grapple with it here. For a discussion of the difference between Communication Studies in Canada and the US, see Brent (2006).

REFERENCES

Brent, D. (2006). Same roots, different soil: Rhetoric in a communications studies program. In R. Graves & H. Graves (Eds.), *Writing centres, writing seminars, writing culture: Writing instruction in Anglo-Canadian universities* (pp. 175-198). Winnipeg, Manitoba: Inkshed.

Clary-Lemon, J. (2009). Shifting tradition: Writing research in Canada. *American Review of Canadian Studies, 39*(2), 94-111.

Class options. (1992, November 9). *Maclean's, 105*, 78.

Douglas, W. (2009). Rhetoric for the meritocracy: The creation of composition at Harvard. In S. Miller (Ed.), *The Norton book of composition studies* (pp. 74-97). New York: W.W. Norton. (Original work published 1976).

Goggin, M.D. (1995). The disciplinary instability of composition. In J. Petraglia (Ed.). *Reconceiving writing, rethinking writing instruction* (pp. 27-48). New York: Routledge.

Graves, R. (1994). *Writing instruction in Canadian universities.* Winnipeg, Manitoba: Inkshed.

Kearns, J., & Turner, B. (1997). Negotiated independence: How a Canadian writing program became a centre. *Writing Program Administration, 21*(1), 31-43.

Leff, M. (1997). Hermeneutical rhetoric. In W. Jost & M. Hyde (Eds.), *Rhetoric and hermeneutics in our time* (pp. 196-214). New Haven, Connecticut: Yale University Press.

Russell, D. (2009). American origins of the writing-across-the-curriculum movement. In S. Miller (Ed.), *The Norton book of composition studies* (pp. 151-170). New York, NY: W.W. Norton. (Original work published 1992).

Smith, T. (2006). Recent trends in writing instruction and composition studies in Canadian universities. In R. Graves & H. Graves (Eds.), *Writing centres, writing seminars, writing culture: Writing instruction in Anglo-Canadian universities* (pp. 319-370). Winnipeg, Manitoba: Inkshed.

Turner, B., & Kearns, J. (2002). No longer discourse technicians: Redefining place and purpose in an independent Canadian writing program. In P. O'Neill, A. Crow, & L. Burton (Eds.), *Field of dreams: Independent writing programs and the future of composition studies* (pp. 90-103). Logan, UT: Utah State University Press.

CHAPTER 12.
XI'AN INTERNATIONAL STUDIES UNIVERSITY (XISU, 西安外国语大学)

By Wu Dan 吴丹

Humboldt College at Xi'an International Studies University (China)

This essay introduces writing practice and related research conducted at Xi'an International Studies University (XISU), Shaanxi, China. As a university with foreign languages being the major disciplines, writing has been in the center of faculty teaching and student learning. Although the emphasis is more on language acquisition than on "writing-to-learn" concepts, writing practice and research have been the traditions here. With all the resources and possibilities provided by international collaborations, a majority of them being with US-based universities, XISU set up the first writing center in China, which has been housed in the School of English Studies and operated quite differently from writing centers in the US. This introduction of the US originated writing center concept and practice is among the new waves that XISU has contributed to higher education in China, as this model has begun to be adopted by a number of other institutions nationwide.

THE INSTITUTION

Xi'an International Studies University (XISU), formerly Xi'an Foreign Language University, was founded in 1952 as one of the first four foreign-language institutions of the People's Republic of China. It is located in Xi'an City, Shaanxi Province, with three campuses totaling 263 acres. XISU remains the only higher education institution in northwestern China that has all major foreign languages. XISU was accredited to award master's degrees in 1986, and in February, 2010, the Academic Degrees Committee of the State Council approved the PhD program application of XISU and granted three years for preparation before recruiting PhD students. The university also publishes three academic journals on foreign language education and human geography.

The major disciplines in XISU used to be only foreign languages, but now the university has been transformed to offer 39 undergraduate majors and seven minors in humanities, arts, social sciences, law, business management, education, and science. There are altogether 891 faculty members. The current enrollment is about 26,000, with half being undergraduate students and the other half graduate students, international students, and students in various training programs.

STUDENT WRITING IN XISU

Writing takes place in all disciplines and majors. Writing occurs in Chinese and English, as described below, as well as in the various other languages students take. Thesis writing is the last requirement for their four-year undergraduate study. They also write in administrative-related activities, such as filling out forms for their academic study, writing reports or proposals for student societies and interest groups, and communicating in such personal forms as e-mails, mobile phone texting, instant messaging, and blogs.

Foreign language education is the unique characteristic of this institution that appeals to students and parents, and the language(s) these students write in depend on their disciplines: students in different language departments write in both Chinese and the target languages they choose to specialize in. All students also write in English, the required foreign language for all majors. In all of the language-related majors, there are writing courses with emphasis on language skills. In lower-level courses, short papers or compositions are embedded in reading courses as response to the class content or as part of quizzes or exams. In upper-level courses, a final paper (in the target language) is often required at the end of the semester for final evaluation or as a supplement to the quizzes/exams.

English majors need to choose another foreign language to study; therefore, they also write in another foreign language in this part of their training, but with limited vocabulary and length due to the limited time devoted to this "second foreign language." In some courses such as College Chinese (focused mainly on literature), College Ethics, and Political Science, which are required for all majors, the professors normally require a final paper or an essay exam at the end of the semester; as the instruction of these courses is in Chinese, students write the papers and take the exams in Chinese, too.

Students write in Chinese for administrative-related activities. Student organizations always need to write proposals, plans, and reports on their activities.

These writing practices are in Chinese. Student organization leaders have more opportunities to practice their Chinese writing, and consequently their Chinese writing skills and other communication skills, such as speaking and giving presentations, are generally more satisfactory than those of other students. In the foreign-language-related clubs and student societies or interest groups, students write and speak in the language they choose for their activities. However, participation in these extra-curricular activities is voluntary, so not all students get a chance to practice their writing in these settings.

Foreign language education gives XISU tradition and prestige. Language teachers always pay much attention to writing, although sometimes they pay much more attention to accuracy and skills training rather than to the functions of writing in knowledge building and social construction. Almost all professors in language majors care about the improvement of student writing, and some of the faculty members in other disciplines have started to integrate more writing assignments into their courses.

However, because the main purpose for using writing has always been to evaluate students' learning, writing is still considered an assessment tool rather than a learning tool. Because a majority of the administrators of XISU have been promoted from professors in these disciplines, they also care about student writing. The most representative example of their commitment is the establishment of the Writing Center for English Majors in 2006, which was made possible by Dr. Hu Sishe, a French professor and President of XISU.

INTERNATIONAL COLLABORATIONS AND THE WRITING CENTER

The Writing Center at XISU is the first writing center in China. At present, it is dedicated to English writing. The establishment was largely due to a longstanding exchange program between XISU and Bowling Green State University, Ohio, US (BGSU), that began in 1985. Both of the universities have been sending one or two professors each year to study or teach in the other institution. The majority of the professors sent to BGSU by XISU have been English professors, and they were sponsored to conduct their two-year master's study in BGSU. All of the BGSU participants have taught English courses in XISU, in areas such as writing, speaking, reading, literature, and American culture.

There are two recent highlights of this exchange. First, Dr. William Coggin conducted a semester-long scientific and technical communication workshop for English faculty members in fall 2004. This was the first workshop of its kind in mainland China and started a new chapter for the exchange program, as three of the faculty participants in this workshop ended up studying in the MA program in Scientific and Technical Communication in the English Department of BGSU, which helped in forming an incomparable and promising faculty basis for possible technical communication courses in XISU. At the same time, Dr. Coggin taught a graduate seminar on technical communication to a class of students in the master's program in English studies.

The second highlight was the establishment of the Writing Center at XISU. Dr. Hu visited BGSU as part of a trip to the US in 2006. He was invited to visit the BGSU Writing Center and was convinced that this concept would be very beneficial to student learning and would help EFL (English as a Foreign Language) students in XISU. Thus, in 2006, XISU became the first university in mainland China to open a Writing Center. A second center has since opened (June 2010) at Zhejiang University.

The XISU Writing Center was built on the American model used by BGSU, but with its own characteristics. The Writing Center operates under the administration of the School of English Studies, but without a budget or staff members. As there has not been a systematic graduate assistantship program in Chinese higher education institutions by which to hire graduate students to work for departments, this writing center is run by volunteer faculty members. The first group of tutors was trained in XISU by Dr. Barbara Toth, Assistant Director of the BGSU Writing Center, in summer 2006. The following groups of tutors did not receive formal training as writing center tutors, but most of them are English professors teaching writing courses to different levels. Their participation is indeed voluntary, as they only get a very small amount of compensation, which should rather be regarded as a token of their contribution. Each semester, the Writing Center recruits interested professors to tutor a number of sessions according to their schedules; only because of the support and sacrifice of the professors can the Writing Center continue to serve the needs of the students. The tutoring group has been changing over these several years, but the passion for and devotion to student writing has remained.

Because there are no staff members, every week the Writing Center Director posts available sessions on the door of the office. Students then sign up for appointments by filling their names on the posted session table. Each session lasts 30 minutes, during which the student and the professor talk about the piece of writing brought in for improvement. Some of the pieces have been written for assignments in the courses, but the professors have found an increasing portion of overseas graduate school applications and job application materials, such as CVs, personal statements, and writing samples. As this is an English writing center, the students who come are mainly from the School of English Studies. Each semester, there are always several students who come to the center quite frequently, as they have found the service very helpful after trying it at the beginning of the semester. Some of them even have preferred professors to work with, so they particularly pick the sessions that these professors facilitate.

However, research and publication about this writing center have been limited by the fact that the director and other professors who work as tutors are full-time teachers. They do not have time to think about designing studies or collecting data from their practice in the center. Furthermore, none of these professors has received training in composition studies; most of them are either literature or linguistics specialists. Therefore, it is difficult for them to connect their practice with the theories or practices in composition and writing center studies without proper guidance or sufficient research interests. Another reason is that writing center practice has not yet been discovered by most Chinese higher education institutions, thus making it difficult for the research to find outlets in the journals published in China.

Although it has been a great success to have this writing center run without a budget for five years since its establishment, this condition will greatly impede its development and related research. And it would be very difficult to include attention to student writing in other languages, if there is no appropriate and healthy operation that is powered by research.

WRITING RESEARCH AND EXCHANGES

Improvement in student writing has been an objective in various language courses in all the languages departments, but it has not been stated as an objective of the overall curriculum. Faculty members discuss writing in the disciplines, but not much "across disciplines" practice or discussion has happened. There is no general education program in most of the Chinese higher education institutions, so there is little incentive for professors from different disciplines to come together to talk about teaching. The boundaries between the disciplines are clearly drawn, and upon entering the university the students start their study in the disciplines they choose to specialize in.

One exception to this pattern in XISU is the business school, in which Business English professors discuss student writing and their teaching of writing with business or management professors, as their curriculum is a combination of both fields. Therefore, although the faculty members are from the different disciplines of English and business, they have exchanges on writing because they work for the same school and the same group of students. However, this close relationship of two or more disciplines cannot be easily found in other schools.

Language professors put emphasis on writing because writing is regarded as one of the language skills for their students, but they do not really conceptualize writing as a tool to enhance learning and critical thinking, although the learning of languages is indeed improved through writing. Instead, the emphasis on writing has been promoted as "practice makes perfect." Professors in other disciplines employ writing assignments as evaluation tools and consider them as "by-products" of their courses, not as "writing to learn," as writing researchers would think of it. However, this seemingly "naïve" emphasis on and attention to writing has been passed down through generations of language teachers and should serve as a very solid foundation for introducing WAC (Writing-Across-the-Curriculum) research and practice. This lack of association of writing with learning is not a rejection of the concept, but simply evidence that WAC has not been introduced into China yet.

An example from a recent study (Wu, 2010) on faculty perceptions of student communication skills illustrates this point very well. One of the participants was a professor of international laws in XISU. He studied and conducted research in the US and was influenced by the writing components his professors used in their courses. He found these writing components very helpful for him in understanding and learning the course content, so he decided to practice in his own courses after he returned to XISU. However, he was distressed because his students complained about these "extra" writing assignments in their course evaluations and some of them even plagiarized by using documents downloaded from the Internet. He was so disappointed that he said he would not recommend this pedagogy to other professors, but he also said that he still wanted to try it by making adjustments to the assignments. This example illustrates the faculty interest in adopting and adapting educational innovations like WAC into their courses for better teaching and learning. However, it also warns that faculty interest can become faculty resistance if no proper support is provided.

Another reason why XISU or similar institutions would be such a good entry point for WAC research is that faculty and students in the languages disciplines, especially English, are the gatekeepers of writing research and practice. Many of the graduates of XISU are now middle school teachers or professors themselves, as education is the major career path for the students. Therefore, the introduction of WAC into XISU would not only benefit the current students but also the students of the students. XISU students will not only learn better through "writing to learn," but also will become "changing agents" and make the learning experience better for their students.

The majority of the current writing research in China has been done by linguistics professors. Some of the major studies are on ESL writing with focus on linguistic corpus (Yang, 2000) and China English (Du & Jiang, 2001), and the theoretical influences primarily come from Michael Halliday (1973), Noam Chomsky (1986), and Graeme Kennedy (1998).

A major achievement for English writing instruction and research is the National Award for Excellent Courses in 2009. The writing program in the School of English Studies at XISU was given this prestigious recognition for their efforts since 1984. Dr. Yang Dafu is the primary investigator and professor for this project, and Professor Guo Fenrong, the current Director of the Writing Center, is also a member of this research and teaching group. Also cited was a project funded by the Ministry of Education on the quality of English MA thesis writing in China and strategies to improve it. This project was started in 2009 and is still in progress; it is hoped that the results will be made available to colleagues in other countries.

The School of English Studies has also started another exchange program, with Raymond Walters College of the University of Cincinnati, Ohio, and has been sending professors both to conduct research and to teach writing courses there. This exchange program helps to build a better basis for understanding US rhetoric and composition; this better understanding has begun to influence XISU classrooms through a project funded by Shaanxi Province that focuses on renovating the curriculum for English majors from separate reading and writing courses to an integrated course with both writing and reading components. This curriculum experiment has gone on for two years in the School of English Studies, and the primary investigator, Dr. Dafu Yang, has collaborated with several colleagues toward reporting the results in an international conference. This goal was realized in February 2011, at the Writing Research Across Borders Conference (Fairfax, Virginia, US), the first time that writing research in XISU has been shared with the international writing research community.

International exchanges have pervasive influence on writing practice and research in XISU. However, researchers at XISU are finding that our research should not be limited to sharing with colleagues in China; the international research community might also benefit from these studies. Hopefully, challenges such as lack of budget and lack of information on research resources will not impede these exchanges; the unique research being carried out here in XISU needs to be available to all who are interested in writing and its development.

REFERENCES

Chomsky, N. (1986). *Knowledge of language: Its nature, origin, and use.* New York: Praeger.

Du, R., & Jiang, Y. (2001). "China English" in the past 20 years. *Foreign Language Teaching and Research, 33*(1), 37-41.

Halliday, M. A. K. (1973). *Explorations in the functions of language.* London: Edward Arnold.

Kennedy, G. (1998). *An introduction to corpus linguistics.* London: Addison-Wesley-Longman.

Wu, D. (2010). Introducing WAC into China: Feasibility and adaptation (Unpublished doctoral dissertation). Clemson University, South Carolina.

Yang, D. (2000). *EFL error patterns in China.* Xi'an, Shaanxi, China: Shaanxi People's Publishing House.

CHAPTER 13.
TRAINING EXPERIENCES IN READING AND WRITING IN A COLOMBIAN UNIVERSITY: THE PERSPECTIVE OF A PROFESSOR

By Elizabeth Narváez Cardona
Universidad Autónoma de Occidente (Colombia)

This paper emerges from the author's trajectory as a professor and researcher in the Reading and Writing field at a Colombian University. The study features three institutional experiences: teaching reading and writing in a course of professional training; a training proposal for professors; and training for beginning researchers as writers. The reflection on the pedagogic actions and tensions that emerged shows that the initiatives and trajectories of such experiences are derived from professional efforts of teaching and researching. Although these experiences are not necessarily dependant on institutional policies, it is evident that the professional connection between researching and didactic formation strengthens the existence and visibility of initiatives in the context of a South American university.

BRIEF CONTEXT

A review of the research literature on reading and writing in Colombia shows clearly that students need to become academic and professional writers.[1] The curricular policy at universities is for students to attend one or two courses on reading and writing only at the beginning of their education, in order to address unresolved issues that remain from education prior to university. The review shows that the theoretical perspectives that support teaching in these courses comes from the language sciences, specifically textual linguistics and analysis of discourse, as traditional research has come from these areas of knowledge. These courses run from 16 to 18 weeks; the textual production of argumentative papers is encouraged, mainly essays. The activities are organized from a psycholinguistic perspective: this means that a text is planned, drafts are checked, and the last draft is edited (Rincon, Narváez & Perez, 2009).

In this context stands the Universidad Autónoma de Occidente, which was founded as the Corporacion Universitaria in 1969 with undergraduates in Economics and Industrial, Electrical, and Mechanical Engineering. In the 1980s it opened undergraduate courses in Social Communications and Electronic Engineering. With the Development Plan created in the 1990s, the institution expanded its functions and, from 2003, it holds the academic charter of a university.[2]

The author of this chapter is a professor and researcher from the Languages Department, which was consolidated in 2004 in the Social Communications Faculty. She has recently completed the project entitled "Pedagogy and Didactics of Reading and Writing in Higher Education" as a member of an Education research group. Her duality as teacher and researcher in the university context has allowed her to develop three training experiences: i) teaching reading and writing in the Social Communications undergraduate course; ii) a training proposal for professors; and, iii) training for beginner researchers as writers. This paper presents the characteristics of these experiences, the pedagogical steps carried out, and tensions that emerged. Reflective analysis of these experiences reveals the characteristics of educational programs that exist within the distinctive framework of a Colombian university.

TEACHING READING AND WRITING IN A SOCIAL COMMUNICATIONS UNDERGRADUATE COURSE

In the course "Language," a theoretical foundation compulsory for training in Social Communication, it was decided to teach the students to "trust" the theoretical documents and encourage the need to use them in order to directly understand the authors, instead of working with the professor's oral discourse. The experience was developed during 2008 and 2009. It was supported by the teachers' academic background in language science, and their research in reading and writing in college and didactic understanding as a field of action, researching, and theorizing in teaching and learning (Camps, 2001).

The subject is taken between the third and fourth semesters[3] and it can be taken after a course on reading and writing. If the course is passed, students are able to enroll in Semiotics 1 and Semiotics 2. The frequency of class is two hours a week. The course introduces students to a reflection on linguistics as part of the theoretical foundation of human communication and its complexities. It employs the following practices in reading and writing:

1. The reading chapters assigned to the students are accompanied by a guide with explanations which the professor added to the author's ideas. It is an explanatory and supporting resource for reading as an assignment outside of the classroom. For example, a thought in the first chapter of "Nature of the Linguistic Sign" by Ferdinand de Saussure says: "(...) some people regard language, when reduced to its elements as a naming-process only—a list of words (...)." This passage has an addition by the professor which says: "Attention, What is Saussure implying with 'Language is not a LIST OF WORDS'?"
2. The ideas which are read in documents have to be used in the written explanations in cases related with social communication; for example, questions like "how would the pragmatic theory explain the title that the journalist chose for this piece of news?" The analysis of the answers during the class requires a re-read of the documents and also discussion.
3. The written explanations of the cases are supported by literal quotes from the chapters already read. To help students do this, in class, fragments of the documents are re-read in which the intellectual positions of the authors are evident.
4. The explanations written by students are evaluated among those in the classroom. The assignments with successful and problematic features are photocopied and distributed (without including the students' names), listing conceptual strengths and weaknesses related to theory as well as the manner in which to write about it.
5. The lack of understanding and misinterpretation of the ideas during class or in the written explanations are respected. During the revision workshops, the teacher underlines the problematic statements but does not cross them out, and instead asks the students questions that help them clarify and re-write the idea. All the written assignments, including the tests, can be re-written. That is why grading is done early in the process, starting with evaluation indicators previously presented to the students.
6. Re-reading and re-writing give the students the capability to question the authors and propose, on their behalf, possible alternatives.

The process achieved in the students the capability to identify misinterpretations in their writing; through the re-reading of their texts and chapters with two purposes: one, to make clear the inconsistencies in their drafting and, the other, to defend their explanations with literal quotes, they became conscious of the conceptual process achieved.

This experience shows that in the practice of reading and writing for conceptual learning, chaos and confusion are conditions typical of a discontinuous process in the clarifying of thinking. For this reason, the effect can be exhaustion and a desire to abandon the task (Carlino, 2006; Castelló, 2007; Perry, 1996). This explains some of the opinions expressed[4] by the students that show, on the one hand, the recognition of writing as a necessary and constitutive step in the process of comprehension of what was read. One student stated that in this subject they wrote because "writing an idea is much more complicated than saying it;" on the other hand, given that degree of difficulty, some of the students recognized the conflictive emotional dimension of the process: "it is boring but at the same time interesting since one goes through moments of intense desperation, rage, and relaxation."

For some students, in addition to realizing that reading and writing helped them to understand the way they were learning, the effort made was related to their development as academic individuals, as expressed by one of the students: "yes, I have learned, since I have understood a theorist's writing and how to take it apart and explain some phenomena from those perspectives. That is good for, in the future, facing other more complex theoretical positions that help me to progress in a study area."

However, for others, the experience did not have any relation to their identity as professionals: "regarding the way of reading and writing, I think that it is good, but I do not believe that to write in this way for a social communicator is the most appropriate." Effectively, this last student was right, if professional writing (Morales & Cassany, 2008) is understood as the process and the written products inherent to the performance of the professions; in the case of social communicators, for example the journalist writing news, opinion articles, or chronicles, writing practice differs from the academic genres such as reviews and scientific articles.

TRAINING UNIVERSITY TEACHERS

The command of discipline by university teachers is a very important condition; however, it is not sufficient for the practice of teaching in higher education. The graduate and research background the teacher holds is a plus and might contribute, but it does not suffice in preparing teachers to design and respond to reading and writing assignments (Narváez & Cadena, 2009).

Consequently, a research and training project[5] was developed. It included a program of teachers' training about academic reading and writing in the university context. The research teachers also designed and led this experimental program; they conducted it as a study using educational action research methodology.

An open call for teachers interested in the training and study within the institution was made once the proposal was completed. The response was from a

group of teachers who belonged to the schools of Administrative and Economic Sciences, Engineering, and Social Communication. The teachers attended the activities during their private time for the duration of two months. The objectives of the proposal were:
1. To understand that academic reading is a process of constructing meaning from the documents assigned to support the learning, and the reading process shows specificities that are not addressed during the students' previous educational stage.
2. To question the idea that a large bibliography and numerous reading activities will by themselves increase the quality of the specialized learning and knowledge of a specific field.
3. To recognize that the assigned papers for academic reading in university learning are specialized texts due to the complexity of their structure and the conceptual content which characterizes them.

The educational program showed the necessity of recognizing the value of academic reading as a practice interwoven with questioning and the oral and written conversation. For this reason, some activities were designed to place the teachers as beginners in the field of academic reading, as they tried to understand readings outside their disciplinary or professional areas.

During the first month of work, we conducted a guided group reading activity with discussion about two documents. The first document[6] presented a perspective opposed to this educational experience, in which university students' difficulties with reading and writing were blamed on "doubtful" training from basic education. The group expressed opinions about these assertions, some positive, some negative.

Subsequently, a second document[7] was assigned. It showed the position defended in the experience and argued in support of explicit attention to reading and writing skills in the university. In order to analyze both arguments, we asked the teachers to complete a conceptual map during a workshop. Subsequently, the teachers were asked to write about how they used the reading in their subject and to compare their practices with the arguments identified. Finally, participants were assigned to compare the positions of the documents with those of the participants and to discuss why and how readings of non-field-specific texts had been used.

The teachers who participated in the study identified the reading conditions that were useful to the "foreigners" in a specific field:
1. while the amount of reading diminishes, the time devoted to discussion increases;
2. students need to become aware of opposing arguments presented in the literature;

3. there should be guides with explicit questions that help the re-reading and conversation, as well as the contrast with personal experiences;
4. there should be direct confrontation with beliefs of the "foreigners" in the field.

The analysis of the collected audio and video data, as well as the building up of field diaries, showed that the planning and development of the first stage of the study influenced the teachers' beliefs, but that they still did not know how to transform "what is done" with the reading in the classroom; in other words, the teachers seemed to agree on the fact that there was "something" that had to be changed in the development of their subjects. However, they did not know how to do it. Therefore, this two-month study with eight in-class hours should be extended and needs support by institutional policy to make time in the teachers' working schedules; policy should also ensure that other activities can be carried out that contribute to transformations in the classroom, not just conceptually.

THE EDUCATION OF YOUNG RESEARCHERS AS WRITERS

As part of the program "School of Student Researchers" at the Universidad Autónoma de Occidente, educational experiences organized in three modules are being developed. One of the modules is academic reading and writing, which lasts 22 in-class hours and is developed in 11 two-hour sessions, a session per week, all during an academic semester. The students participate in this program voluntarily; it bears no addition to the enrollment fee, they may belong to different undergraduate -night and daytime- academic programs, and they may be in different stages of their professional training. The module offers the participants activities which allow them to put forward some of the reading and writing processes related to the formulation of a research problem (Narváez, 2009). Practices of reading and writing are developed in the following activities:
1. Identifying the academic quality criteria to be used for creating bibliographies.
2. Comparing introductions of various scientific articles in order to help students develop writing models for the proposal of a research problem.
3. Critically and meticulously revising each paragraph of scientific article introductions published in indexed magazines in order to anticipate reading and writing processes that precede the writing of a research problem.
4. Performing workshops in close reading of academic documents. This analysis is carried out in three ways: identifying the author(s)'s arguments; recognizing their attitude, audience, and purposes; and criti-

cally commenting to highlight ideas that were interesting and difficult, whether or not these are shared with the author.

Our study of this training thus far shows that those students who have already begun enrollment in research groups in order to carry out actual projects get more out of these structured activities than do those who have not yet become involved in their own research.

WHAT DO THESE EXPERIENCES SHOW?

The first experience, teaching reading and writing in a Social Communications undergraduate course, was based on the ability of a professor to recognize students as academic individuals in their training. For that reason the collective practice of reading in depth was introduced, rewriting was encouraged, and the teacher was obliged to co-evaluate so as to grade the learning. In institutional contexts in which the amount of information conveyed is evaluated as primary indicator of teaching quality, maintaining this type of experience is a challenge, as it decreases the number of issues to be addressed in a course, but increases the amount of time spent focusing on understanding and teaching the difficult construction of meaning through writing. Documenting these efforts, however, is a way to defend their presence and impact.

To support these kinds of experience, study should focus on how these activities lead to understanding the contents in a course and to knowledge in reading and academic writing. Such studies would be useful also in the process of university teacher training to help foster such enhanced learning. Also emerging from our study of this first experience is the value of considering the curricular distinction between courses that deal with the training of writers as academic professionals or scientists and those that focus on the written practices and genres of interaction with enterprises or companies. In one case, research genres would be the focus (e.g., research projects, presentations, posters), whereas the second case would feature business genres (e.g., technical reports, projects for bids, executive letters).

Regarding the second experience, the training of teachers in different subject areas, our study found remarkable power in the consolidation of collegiate teams. The interaction between teachers of disciplinary and professional fields and the language teachers was essential to our discussion of the diverse teaching practices with reading and writing. Otherwise, we could not have analyzed what is viable, possible, and pertinent in these diverse university classrooms. However, to keep these efforts will depend on the strengthening of institutional policies that treat as a priority the training of university teachers in an interdisciplinary way.

From the last study, the education of young researchers as writers, it is evident that training in the skills of reading and writing as part of the research process in the university setting is necessary. However, the impact of such training will differ depending on the public who would be the target, and so different kinds of training are necessary. One case is researchers who already belong to scientific and technical communities;[8] another is junior researchers. The analysis of this last study with undergraduate students shows that impact is greater when participants are linked to actual research processes in which academic writing is imperative.

In short, these three experiences have arisen from the initiative of the author of this chapter and colleagues more than from any institutional policy that favored them. They were made possible by the conjunction between two features of their own professional training: on the one hand, an interest in research in academic writing and, on the other hand, the interest in the didactic field as a discipline that studies relations between teaching and learning in specific contexts. The intersection of these two interests enabled the development of these rare experiences, which often are not supported in the context of South American universities.

NOTES

1. The original paper was written by the author in Spanish. Professors Edgar Meza and Hector Rivillas have translated the article into English. They belong to the Languages Institute at Universidad Autónoma de Occidente.

2. Taken from the Universidad Autónoma de Occidente Web page: http://www.uao.edu.co/

3. In Colombia, the majority of the undergraduate academic programs are developed in 10 semesters.

4. To explore and analyze, in part, the impact of the progress of the work, an anonymous written survey was given to all the students who participated in the experience. They were requested to answer in writing three (3) questions, as follows: "According to your own reading and writing experience in this subject, answer: 1. What did you read and write in this subject? 2. Do you think you have learned "something new" about how to read and write in college? What is that useful for? 3. What is your opinion about the way reading and writing is done in this subject? Is that way of doing it useful for a social communicator? Justify your answer."

5. The research project, carried out in conjunction with Professors Sonia Cadena Castillo and Beatriz Elena Calle, was named "Interactions and conceptions constructed from digital communication, within an experience of formation of teachers about academic reading," and was financed by the Administration of Research and Technological Development in the Universidad Autónoma de Occidente.

6. Lizcano, D. (2006).

7. Carlino, P. (2003).

8. Frequently Colombian universities offer courses, for professors, about scientific publications.

REFERENCES

Camps, A. (2001). *El aula como espacio de investigación y reflexión. Investigaciones en didáctica de la lengua.* Barcelona: Editorial Graó.

Carlino, P. (2003). Leer textos científicos y académicos en la educación superior: Obstáculos y bienvenidas a una cultura nueva. VI International Conference on Promotion of Reading and the Book, Buenos Aires . Retrieved from http://www.buenosaires.gov.ar/areas/educacion/bibleduc/pdf/paula_carlino.pdf

Carlino, P. (2006). La experiencia de escribir una tesis. Contextos que las vuelven más difíciles. *Revista Anales. 14, 15 & 16.* 41-62.

Carlino, P. (2008). Desafíos para hacer una tesis de posgrado y dispositivos institucionales que favorecerían su completamiento. Segundo Encuentro Nacional y Primero Internacional sobre lectura y escritura en la educación superior. Universidad Javeriana. Colombia.

Castelló, M. (2007). Escribir y comunicarse en contextos científicos y académicos. Conocimientos y estrategias. Capítulo 2. *El proceso de composición de textos académicos.* Cinco reglas de oro para escribir textos científicos (y no morir en el intento). Barcelona: Grao.

Lizcano, D. (2006). ¿Baja lectura y escritura en la universidad? "Notas de lengua y redacción" [Web log post]. Retrieved from http://notasdelenguayredaccion.blogspot.com/2006/10/la-lectura-y-el-universitario.html

Morales, O., & Cassany, D. (2008). Leer y escribir en la universidad: Hacia la lectura y la escritura crítica de géneros científicos. *Revista Memoralia*, Universidad Nacional Experimental de los Llanos Ezequiel Zamora (Unellez), Cojedes, Venezuela. En prensa. Retrieved from http://www.falemosportugues.com/pdf/leer_universidad.pdf

Narváez, E. (2009). Dimensionar las características de la escritura académica y anticipar su demanda: Un caso en la formación de jóvenes investigadores. III

Encuentro Nacional y II Internacional de lectura y escritura. Red de lectura y escritura en educación superior (REDLEES). Cali, Colombia.

Narváez, E., & Cadena, S. (2009). La enseñanza de la lectura académica: un Objeto de formación docente. *Lectura y Vida, 30*(1), 56-67.

Perry, C. (1996). *Cómo escribir una tesis doctoral. Traducción al español: José Luis Pariente.* Universidad Autónoma de Tamaulipas Centro de Excelencia. Con autorización del autor. Retrieved from http://www.excelencia.uat.edu.mx/pariente/Tesis/perry.pdf

Rincón, G., Narváez, E. y Pérez, M. (2009). Construyendo un proyecto de investigación sobre lectura y escritura, mientras leemos y escribimos. III Encuentro Nacional y II Encuentro Internacional de lectura y escritura. REDLEES. Colombia.

Universidad Autónoma de Occidente. (2008). La investigación formativa. Dirección de Investigaciones y Desarrollo Tecnológico.

CHAPTER 14.
THE PROGRESSION AND TRANSFORMATIONS OF THE PROGRAM OF ACADEMIC READING AND WRITING (PLEA) IN COLOMBIA'S UNIVERSIDAD SERGIO ARBOLEDA

Blanca Yaneth González Pinzón
Universidad Sergio Arboleda (Colombia)

This profile essay describes the evolution and current structure of the Program of Academic Reading and Writing (PLEA) at the Sergio Arboleda University in Bogota: from its inception in the 1980s as the "Grammar Program" to its current status as a two-semester compulsory course focused on university-level academic reading and writing. It also presents the most important results of the investigation conducted to recognize learning by the students in this first-year course of study, and the evaluation of this Program conducted among teachers of these courses and teachers of other subjects. New aspects of PLEA since the assessment, to extend the reach of the Program to higher-level students and to faculty in disciplines, are also described. The profile concludes by noting the first Colombian national conference on reading and writing in higher education and the formation of REDLEES, the Reading and Writing in Higher Education Network for Colombia.

THE BEGINNINGS AND DEVELOPMENT OF THE PROGRAM

In the second semester of 2004, the directors of the Universidad Sergio Arboleda, with the support of a CERLALC consultant (CERLALC: Regional Center for the Promotion of Books in Latin America and the Caribbean), proposed to expand the university language program's initial objectives.[1] Since its creation in 1984, the Program had followed a purely normative approach. Through a resolution of the Rector, a department was created with the goal of working on the issues of university reading and writing. Tutors were contracted to meet these new objectives. They were specialists in Language (10) and Philosophy (1); most had experience working with high school students.

Given that, at the time, there was scarce literature in Colombia about university level reading and writing, the Program drew on pedagogical approaches from various authors who have extensively discussed the topic at the primary and secondary school level. As is the case with many other institutional proposals, the Program's work to address concerns about student performance began with providing a single course of study. This approach has been questioned by many authors in diverse contexts (Carlino, 2005; González, 2010; Russell, 1995; Winsor, 1999); however, in 2004 it was seen as the most appropriate strategy.

The Program kept its original name, Grammar Program, from 2004 to 2006, and was scheduled to offer a course to first-year students from all the university's academic majors. During the first years of the Program's implementation, its main difficulty was finding harmony between the old normative-focused position of the department and the new communications-based approach that timidly showed its inclination towards professional and disciplinary texts.

From 2007 to 2009, this course was called Grammar – Academic Reading and Writing; since 2010: Academic Reading and Writing (LEA). The Department now is called PLEA (Program of Academic Reading and Writing).

It has been compulsory for students and makes up the basic training level of all the university's majors. While students are free to take the course at any point during their professional training in the university, the majority of majors put the course in the list of classes to be taken during the student's first year.

The course is two semesters long, one level per semester, meeting four hours per week (two hours per two sessions). The course uses a workshop format, wherein teachers provide a lecture at the beginning of the session, and then students do individual work in four basic areas: reading, writing, spelling, and formal aspects of language. In some assessment sessions, students work in pairs or in groups to self-evaluate and give each other feedback. Each class has no more than thirty students that come from the different majors.

Given that in Colombia there is an accreditation system (that is, students receive a set number of credits or certifications of approval per course), the LEA course gives two credits for having theory and practice (each academic course can provide no more than three credits). To receive these credits, students must attend 56 to 64 hours per course level and demonstrate the same amount of autonomous work outside the classroom. This last requisite means that the student must do homework and/or virtual classroom work, or whatever strategy the teacher selects.

At the beginning of the course, the students take a diagnostic test, and low-level achievers' results are used to personalize their assistance. Personal assistance sessions are a Program support strategy that complements class work. Every teacher offers ten hours per week of personalized assistance in an appropriate space to individually help students who need support. In these sessions, the teacher and student work with and revise the student's actual productions. A student can access this personalized assistance by directly asking the teacher, whether in class, via email, or a phone call. The assistance space lasts at least 40 minutes, and each student can schedule as many sessions as he or she likes.

CURRICULUM AND OBJECTIVES

The course's reading work concentrates on the development of reading logs and records, which are questionnaire-style guides with fifteen items and/or questions designed to orient the student in his/her in-depth analysis of the text. The published document titled "How do I make a reading log?" (González, 2004) is used to support this process. Reading exercises are supported by a reading plan, whose required texts are selected by the Program; the list of texts is expanded by the teacher. These texts include essays, journalistic articles, iconic texts, and texts about the students' disciplinary studies. Different types of texts are used to help students learn about different ways to approach a text. The objectives for the two semesters of coursework are listed in the course's syllabus, and seek to enable students to be capable of (1) recognizing the structure of ideas in a text and its argumentative plan; (2) deducing and inferring using textual contents; (3) relating text content to other texts; (4) recognizing their polyphony and contextualizing the text based on cultural, ideological, historical, stylistic, linguistic, etc., elements; (5) assuming a critical perspective of text content; (6) reading with specific objectives, such as research, synthesizing, separating fact from opinion, delving into a topic, or identifying information to organize in a text; and (7) gaining ownership of new terms and concepts.

In the writing section at the first level of the LEA course, the class is focused on the construction of sentences and, from there, on the production of paragraphs. Then it is oriented to the production of summaries and argumentative texts that require a critical position. These texts are produced out of the reading plan that was previously mentioned. Pursuant to a strict institutional disposition, the class has workshops on morpho-syntactic and grammatical aspects, which do not exceed more than 20% of the course, as outlined in the course schedule and syllabus.

In the second level of the LEA course, the teacher accompanies the students in re-writing exercises to produce an article or essay. They are able to pick from three topic areas provided for the assignment (themes related to their major, social issues and problems youth face). The reading plan provides the students with bibliographic sources and support.

If the student selects the thematic axis focused on his/her major, the teacher suggests seeking out support from professors from within the student's department. However, students rarely do so. As a strategy to link student writing to the topics from students' disciplines, the PLEA teachers encourage students to develop a writing assignment from their major coursework as their LEA course paper. However, this option has not achieved sustained disciplinary work because of two reasons: first, students are assigned very limited writing assignments during their first years in school; secondly, if a project in the student's other class work is identified as useful for the LEA writing process, we observe that the student often does not carry out the stages of writing that the Program teacher demands, because the assignment often has short deadlines, at most two weeks.

Reading in the second level of LEA continues with a similar process, using reading logs and records, which should support the production of the written document during the course of the semester. The syllabus states its goals in writing as follows: (1) produce texts with a clear basic structure: introduction, development, and conclusion; (2) achieve a logical connection between the thesis statement and the supporting arguments; (3) ask problem questions to develop argumentative texts; (4) consult, organize, and use a minimum number of sources for writing, and use standard referencing and citation norms; (5) balance the contributions coming from sources and the student's purposeful intention as a writer; (6) own the process of writing a text (documentation, contextualization, review, correction and rewrite); (7) use punctuation in context; (8) adequately use connectors and other cohesive devices; and (9) review the semantic precision and correspondence between the terms and concepts used, given that the student is entering a new profession and/or discipline and academic culture.

As a strategy to encourage students' independent writing and the dissemination of their work in the course, two anthologies have been created: Colombia: 21st Century Utopia (Noguera, L. et al., 2005) and Colombia: 21st Century Utopia 2 (Ballén, C. et al., 2007) were formed to collect the articles and essays produced by students, as selected by PLEA for publication. The electronic magazine *Altus* was also created (http://www.usa.edu.co/altus/index.htm). *Altus*' editorial committee is comprised of students, who select the texts to be published. Each year, around 1,400 students take the course, and only 40 to 45 (3%) publish their texts.

To monitor students' progress, rubrics were used for students' co-evaluation and self-evaluation. These evaluations were centralized in a personalized oversight called the Student Reading and Writing Registry (RELEE in Spanish). The registry and rubrics allowed teachers to share the students' results, their progress or lack of progress made during and by the end of the semester.

In PLEA's first years, there was very limited outreach to the rest of the university and academic spaces because it was generally considered sufficient to provide support to students in reading and writing in their first year. This perception, as will be discussed further on, slowly changed with time. This change was largely supported by the creation of the research group.

ASSESSMENT, ACHIEVEMENTS AND URGENT ADJUSTMENTS

From 2005 and through 2010, research projects were initiated, motivated by the much-needed reflections that permeated the discussions on these topics in Colombia. These discussions came from literature outside the country, namely from Paula Carlino in Argentina (2005), and from Bazerman (1988) and Russell (1990) in the Anglo Saxon context. The research papers included College Reading and Writing Practices: Five Majors as Case Studies at the Universidad Sergio Arboleda (González & Vega, 2010), and Assessment and Description of the Grammar Program – Academic Reading and Writing (PGLEA) in Colombia's Universidad Sergio Arboleda (González & Vega, 2011).

The second research project analyzed the Program's curricular and guiding documents, and included structured and semi-structured interviews with PLEA department members and with faculty from five other departments. Semi-structured interviews were used with 90 students in their ninth and tenth semesters from those departments to learn about their perceptions of the course they took and their own processes. We also analyzed student performance during and after their participation in the Program by comparing test results. Researchers compared the students' performance in levels I and II of the course with the results they achieved on a test similar to the Colombian government's required test for all students graduating from the university. The research also gathered tests of different types and from different courses for the analysis.

Perceptions of the Faculty in Charge of Developing the PLEA

The faculty in charge of the course emphasized the following in their narratives: (1) the absence of a clear position within the university's institutional policies, given the directors' continuous intervention; (2) that other professors from different departments are not interested in reading and writing issues, despite the frequent discussion and exchange spaces promoted by PLEA; (3) that students are not interested beyond "getting a certain grade" because the courses are seen as "a burden or obligation;" (4) that students see few transformations during such a short course; and (5) the small or null transfer of LEA contents to other areas.

PLEA teachers generally value their work in the Program as being positive. They state that the faculty is well-suited to the task given their knowledge and continual improvements in their work on the topic. Many of the faculty members compare their experience with the Universidad Sergio Arboleda to previous jobs and they see glimpses of improvement, new lessons learned, "evolving processes," and "interesting experiences."

Perceptions of the Faculty from the Five Departments

In general terms and among other topics, faculty members from other departments believed that some students (from the ninth and tenth semesters) show notable progress in communications, while others—the majority —still demonstrate serious difficulties in reading and "composition." Despite a continuous demand for reading and writing exercises assigned by professors, and the high standards placed upon students, the results are not satisfactory. These faculty members questioned PLEA's effectiveness, and consider several reforms and complementarities necessary.

Furthermore, several faculty members stated that they were unaware of the Program or doubted its usefulness. Faculty members expect students to be able to read, defend an argument, and continually improve their ability to interpret texts. They state that developing these skills in students is the responsibility of PGLEA teachers, and not the teachers within the majors. These professors rarely participated in discussions on reading and writing, in extension courses or other calls made by PGLEA with the Academic Vice Rector's support, to provide information and pedagogical support.

Perceptions of Last Semester Students

Student perceptions are the most abundant data that were gathered about the Program. The initial categories used to classify the perceptions and analyze the data were the following: weaknesses, strengths, opportunities, and threats[2] to PLEA; PLEA's quality, utility, and applicability; changes in reading and writing after taking PLEA; and contributions and suggestions.

It should be clarified that what some students mention as positive, other students classified as negative, and vice versa. This has made us reflect on the criteria, strategies, methodologies and concepts used in the course. Despite the clear intention of unifying criteria at the time (2004-2006), each teacher guided his/her course using his/her own vision about students' needs and the functionality of reading and writing.

When looking at the positive ratings given by interviewed students a full four years after having taken the course, the students marked positively:

- The relevance and quality of the Program components and contents (grammar, spelling, reading and writing, selections from the reading plan). These areas were considered sufficient for a complete and structured Program.
- The coursework was not only useful for the Department's courses, but also for other academic spaces and even professional work. Many students interviewed are already part of the workforce.
- Many stated that they formed habits after taking the Program that include checking information, referencing, and being aware of plagiarism.
- A generic improvement in "comprehension."
- Improvement in "composition" (they do not distinguish between composition and writing), spelling, coherence, use of connectors, use of paragraph types, and text structures (using those terms).

In contrast, another group of students mentioned negative aspects or weaknesses of the course:

- They easily forgot what they had studied in the Program and they did not develop the habit or ability to enjoy reading and writing. Being in the process of finishing their capstone projects, some students express that they are not able to use any of the strategies from the Program and that they did not use skills learned in the Program in other classes.
- Program contents are too generic and not specific or applicable.
- Some topic areas were similar to what they studied in high school.
- The course's timeframe is very short.

TRANSFORMATIONS UNDERTAKEN

Building and consolidating a program to strengthen university students' reading and writing, with a clear integration into the institutional academic dynamic, was a risky bet in Colombia in 2004. At that time, the Universidad Sergio Arboleda's proposal was a pioneer in its type, intention, and level of administrative disposition. This Program is perhaps a representative sample of the obstacles that need to be avoided or overcome in the country and its institutions to be able to consolidate an academic culture that supports writing processes.

Some faculty members' and directors' strong resistance to change has forced the Program to maintain some of its traditional contents during its development. The course's name (Grammar—Academic Reading and Writing) from 2007 to 2009 shows the mixture of the two tendencies (normative and oriented towards academic literacy). In 2010, the name of the course has been simplified to Academic Reading and Writing.

In this scenario, it must be recognized that the presence of a reading and writing program, such as the one described, gives a different value to these processes. It reveals reading and writing and saves these processes from becoming unnoticed mechanisms. The fact that research, observation, assessment, and self-analysis are part of this work justifies that initiatives such as these exist; any other way would not be worthwhile. However, due to the results of this evaluation process, the Program has recently undergone some significant changes: The initial group of eleven teachers was modified. Currently there are thirteen full-time teachers and two part-time. The seven language specialists have been joined by two specialists in literature, two specialists in communications, one philosopher, a lawyer, a psychologist, and a systems engineer. The intention behind these changes is to promote a cross-disciplinary view of the program.

Spaces for dialogue have been created to discuss the risks of understanding reading and writing as just an instructional plane. Often these processes are mere activity without theory behind them, and they end up mirroring the practices used in previous educational spaces, which moves them away from real production situations and instead prioritizes artificial practice.

Working within one specific Department continues to be the best strategy for consolidating an academic culture in the Universidad. This process has helped keep the discussion alive. Using the Program's space as an operations center, members come together to think through the alternatives necessary to overcome the dominant approach that believes a single course such as LEA is sufficient (what we call a single-department approach), instead of working throughout the institution to address reading and writing skills learning. For this reason, we have carried out alternative actions since 2006, some within the institution and others with the participation of communities outside the university, as a strategic mechanism to make the topic visible and to position the discussion, but which are not solutions themselves. These actions include:

- Constant review of methodological strategies used in the classroom. This review has included spaces in which the Department professors share materials and experiences they have in class.
- Expanding personalized work spaces, so that not only first-year students have access to personal assistance sessions, but also more advanced students and professors. The goal is to continue evolving the space into a writing center.
- Two courses held for teachers: *Writing for Publishing* and *Project-based Class Work*, to bring them closer to reading and writing processes.
- Publication and sharing of research work on the topic, made by a group of the PLEA teachers, under the leadership of the PLEA director.
- Support of pedagogical campaigns against plagiarism, and strategies to reinforce reading and writing skills for State exams.
- Personalized assistance tutoring to students to review their capstone projects for graduation, when they request it.
- Creation of virtual classrooms with 33 supportive workshops that are designed to support the individual tutoring work with online assistance.
- Forums held with high schools as an institutional outreach project with the goal of moving forward the dialogue between secondary schools and universities.
- Development of extension courses to train high school teachers and other universities in orienting reading and writing processes.
- Creation of two elective courses that are academic spaces built to support the writing processes of students working on their capstone projects, as well as the research processes of research groups, using "research nurseries" (more than 50). These spaces reflect advanced students' need and desire for a work space.

FORMATION OF THE REDLEES NETWORK

As a strategy to initiate a broader discussion on the national level, in 2007, an invitation was sent to sixteen institutions, and with the support of the Colombia Association of Universities (ASCUN), the First National Conference on institutional policies to develop reading and writing in higher education was held in the Universidad Sergio Arboleda. The universities that participated in the meeting formed the Reading and Writing in Higher Education Network (REDLEES, from its name in Spanish), with the objective of promoting institutional policies for the development of reading and writing in higher education. PLEA's participation in the academic network has contributed to strengthening of our discussion and enrichment of the Program, thanks to an exchange of experiences and research.

Precisely, following from the results of this research, members of REDLEES were invited to participate in an inter-institutional investigation: Initial training in reading and writing in the university: from secondary education to academic achievement in higher education, which will continue through 2012.

For us, the most important strategy implemented so far has been the recent work of an inter-disciplinary group of twelve professors from different majors that come from eight of the twelve schools in the university. The group's goals include thinking together about the basis of institutional policy for reading and writing in the university, and working together to develop classroom strategies.

NOTES

1. Research carried out by Blanca González and Violetta Vega, faculty researchers at the Universidad Sergio Arboleda.

2. SWOT analysis (strengths, weaknesses, opportunities, threats) used in organizational planning. (See http://www.quickmba.com/strategy/swot/.)

REFERENCES

Ballén, C. et al. (2007). *Colombia: Utopía Siglo XXI 2.* Bogotá: Fondo de Publicaciones Universidad Sergio Arboleda.

Bazerman, C. (1988). *Shaping written knowledge. The genre and activity of the experimental article in science.* Madison, WI: University of Wisconsin Press.

Carlino, P. (2005). *Escribir, leer y aprender en la universidad. Una introducción a la alfabetización académica.* Buenos Aires: Fondo de Cultura Económica.

González, B. (2004). *¿Cómo elaborar una ficha de lectura?* Bogotá: Fondo de Publicaciones Universidad Sergio Arboleda.

González, B. (2010). Strategies, policies and research on reading and writing in Colombian universities. In C. Bazerman, S. McLeod, R. Krut, K. Lunsford, S. Null, P. Rogers, & A. Stansell (Eds.), *Traditions of Writing Research.*(pp. 122-132). London: Routledge.

González, B., &Vega, V. (2010). *Prácticas de lectura y escritura en la universidad. El caso de cinco asignaturas de la Universidad Sergio Arboleda.* Bogotá: Fondo de Publicaciones Universidad Sergio Arboleda.

González B., & Vega, V. (2011). *Evaluación y descripción del Programa de Gramática / Lectura y Escritura Académicas (PGLEA) en la Universidad Sergio*

Arboleda. Unpublished manuscript, University of Sergio Arboleda, Bogatá, Columbia.

Noguera, L. et al. (2005). *Colombia: Utopía Siglo XXI.* Bogotá: Fondo de Publicaciones Universidad Sergio Arboleda.

Russell, D. (1995). Activity theory and its implications for writing instruction. In J. Petraglia (Ed.), *Reconceiving writing, rethinking writing instruction* (pp. 51-78). Hillsdale, NJ: Erlbaum.

Russell, D. (1990). Writing across the curriculum in historical perspective: Toward a social interpretation. *College English, 52*(1). 52-80.

Winsor, D. (1999). *Genre and activity systems: The role of documentation in maintaining and changing engineering activity systems.* Retrieved from http://wcx.sagepub.com/cgi/content/abstract/16/2/200

CHAPTER 15.
FROM WORKING WITH STUDENTS TO WORKING *THROUGH* FACULTY: A GENRE-CENTERED FOCUS TO WRITING DEVELOPMENT

By Lotte Rienecker and Peter Stray Jørgensen
University of Copenhagen (Denmark)

In this article we point to the core of the Academic Writing Centre's teaching of academic writing: a genre definition of research papers, and the research paper as a main genre. We model our teaching academic writing practice on a "pentagon model" of basic elements in the research paper as a highly formatted genre across disciplines on a structural level. The work with text formats and heuristics ("box- and fill-in-forms" pedagogy) lays the foundation of our favourite teaching activities at all educational levels from BA to PhD students. Students need to recognise standard structures and conventions before they will be able to break or supersede academic writing conventions successfully. Lastly, we focus on the current next step in our local version of teaching academic writing across the curriculum: mandatory accreditation courses for all thesis supervisors at our institution and our work with assessment-aligned, formative supervisor feedback on PhD students' drafts.

This article is about the Academic Writing Centre in the Humanities Department of a big Scandinavian university. We would like to start by sharing our best advice for the writing programme director or consultant. Our best advice: align your activities with your institution's most important assessed writing: genres, formats, criteria of quality, inquiry, reading and writing processes. Work genre-based: Break down the genres you teach into their basic elements: text types, structures, argumentation, documentation, language features, etc. Demonstrate tried-and-true templates that students may depart from as they develop their rhetorical practices. Your job is to relieve students (and faculty) from designing "deep plates" all over again. Write and publish textbooks, articles, research papers, reports, pamphlets, leaflets, websites. Write at least one textbook on (an aspect of) academic writing! Be a writer yourself, not merely a teacher of academic writing. Take the time for it. The last piece of advice is based on our experience of the impact our publications on academic writing and supervision had on our work. Especially our authorship of two textbooks: Rienecker & Stray Jørgensen et al. (2005): *Den gode opgave* [*The Good Paper, a research paper manual for students*], and Rienecker, Harboe & Stray Jørgensen (2005): *Vejledning. . .* [*Supervision of MA Theses, a handbook for supervisors*], and the many books and on-line materials that were authored by the Academic Writing Centre staff 1992—2010, became the foundation of our teaching-academic-writing activities today, as we will explore further in this article. These two publications reflected and set the platform for our work with students, especially thesis writers, and heralded the work we now do with and through the thesis writers' supervisors.

THE FOCUS, THE PROBLEM, THE QUESTION: MASTER'S THESIS WRITING AND COMPLETION

The foremost question that caused our university management to open our writing programme in 1992 was "How do we bring our master's thesis writers to timely completion, without selling out on the quality of their inquiries and their writing?" This is still probably the hottest issue in student writing in the eyes of university management and staff, even as one major change was implemented by the Research Ministry: a six-month deadline on thesis completion from the day a thesis contract is signed.[1] The six-month deadline was and is a revolution to a system that never worked under any time constraints until 2007. The role of faculty who supervise thesis writing is very pivotal. In the final six months of the masters degree program, many students and faculty members see the real development of the young disciplinary writer truly unfolding. The transition to writing under deadline pressure is not easy, and it brings to the fore any discrepancies there may be between supervisor expectations and student writing and project management competencies. By 2007, when the deadline was imposed, the writing centre staff was busy with MA Thesis Writers Workshops and tutorials. How our centre focuses this advising of students is the main subject of this essay.

We will later turn our attention to advising of thesis supervisors: how an accredited, mandatory 30-hour course for all thesis supervisors builds on the content of what we offer students; namely, research processes and the genre-bound documentation of the inquiry students do for the MA thesis. We will conclude this article with an account of the Academic Writing Centre's latest genre-based project: designing a feedback tool—a rubric—for supervisory feedback on PhD students' dissertation drafts.

> **Facts about Academic Writing and the Academic Writing Centre, University of Copenhagen**
>
> - The University of Copenhagen has 35,000 students, including 15,000 students in the Humanities Department, and approx. 500 faculty.
> - University educations in Denmark build heavily on the writing of long term papers, generally one or two long papers per semester. The Humanities are a monoculture with very few Danish as Second Language-students. Most writing is in Danish, though a substantial number of MA and PhD theses are now written in English.
> - There are no general, credit-giving writing courses in Denmark, and all activities are on a voluntary basis as extracurricular support services. In all of Danish higher education, there are fewer than 10 small units to support student writing (staffing by one to three academics, often on a part-time basis, no student tutors) offering courses, workshops, online writing labs (OWLs), one-on-one-tutorials on academic writing, study skills, and oral presentations. Subject teachers are in charge of writing and writing development, and it is up to their initiative to discuss writing during classes, in tutorials or on the intranet facilities, and to give feedback on writing. Supervision of major writing tasks is provided by faculty (typically two hrs. on a BA thesis, and five to seven hours one-on-one supervision on an MA thesis).
> - Student, faculty, and management interest in writing competency centers on the writing of the BA (25 pages) and especially MA thesis (80 pages) —that is: product- as well as process-centered, academic, scientific research paper writing. First and second year papers and essays attract some interest. Creative and professional writing are very minor issues.
> - The authors of this article initiated and ran the first writing centre in Scandinavia from 1992, with staffing at its high point by four academics. Student-centered writing activities are now part of Student Services, whereas faculty-centered activities reside in the Academic Writing Centre.

THE RESEARCH PAPER GENRE AS A BASIS FOR TEACHING UNIVERSITY WRITING

The core concept of our teaching and supervising is the notion of the research paper as a genre, defined below:

> The research paper should document the research of a *relevant problem,* using concepts, theories, and methods from scientific disciplines to argue a case and to convince a colleague of the validity of the results and the conclusions of the research in an exposition that is acceptable in the targeted discourse community. (Rienecker & Stray Jørgensen, 2005)

Students will be assessed on the degree to which they demonstrate
- learning and mastery of scientific inquiry and writing
- knowledge transforming (Bereiter & Scardamalia, 1987)

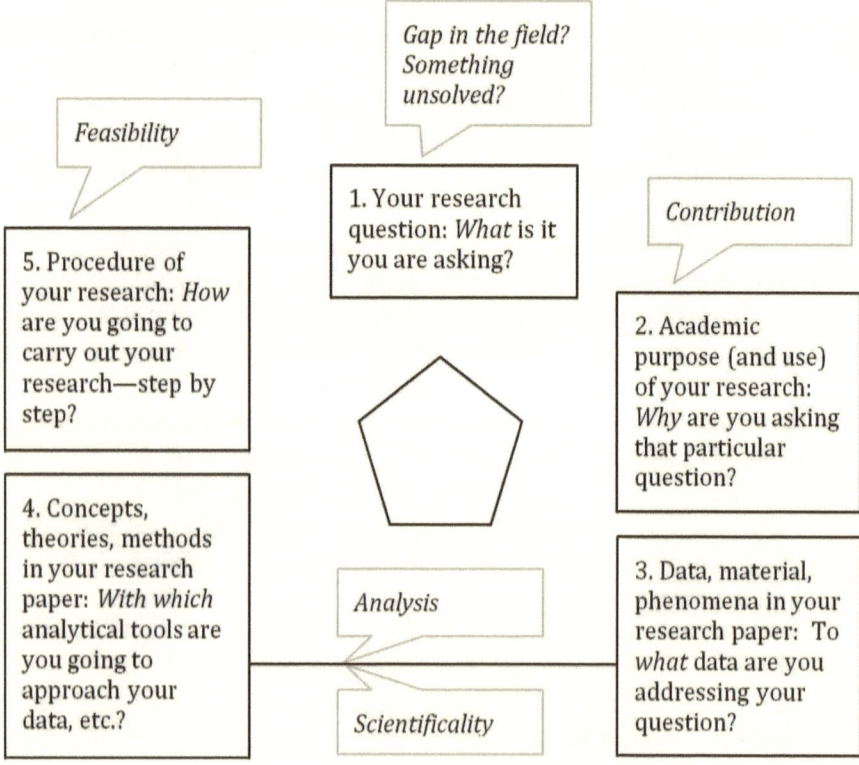

Figure 1. Pentagon model of the basic elements of the research paper.

- problem inquiry
- sound analysis
- explicit or at least clear methodology in data selection and analysis
- theory- or at least concept-based analysis and discussion
- documentation
- use and critical appraisal of sources
- coherent argumentation
- language suitable to the purpose

The master's thesis is meant to be a demonstration of the ability to research and write a small-scale model piece of conceptually and methodologically sound scientific work, even if that be not substantial enough to qualify as a "contribution to research." To simplify the core elements of the research paper genre, we use a pentagon (Rienecker & Stray Jørgensen, 2005) as a graphic model of the elements and choices every writer needs to consider before getting far into literature searches, reading, and drafting (Figure 1).

Figure 2 shows examples of kinds of information that might be in each corner. The first corner (the problem box) represents the problem to research, the gap in the field. The second corner (the purpose box) is the rhetorical corner where relevance to the field and the world at large, purpose, and targeted

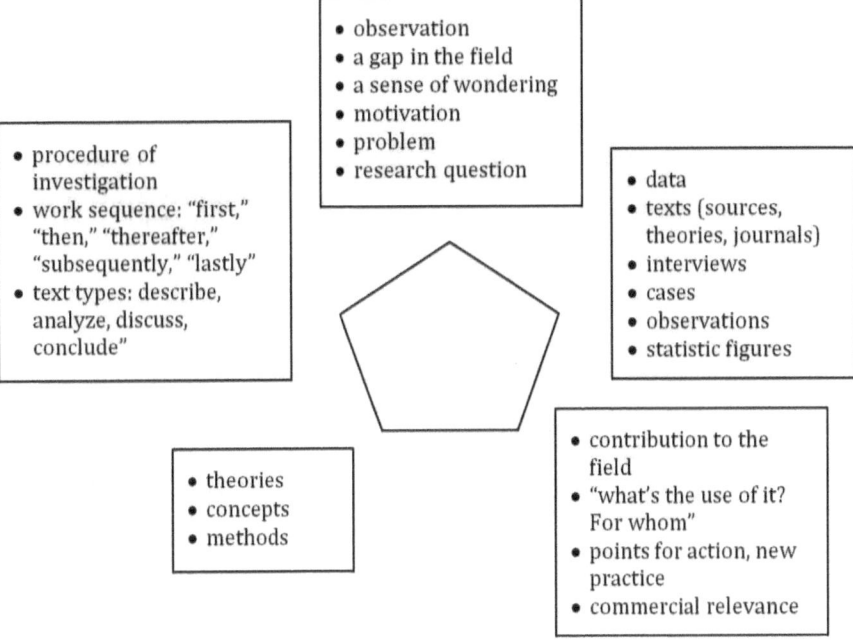

Figure 2. Pentagon model expanded.

audience should be stated. In the third corner (the databox) is an overview of the data, the objects to be examined. The fourth corner (the tool box) is the theories, concepts, and/or methods with which to collect, categorize, analyze, and interpret the data.

The science in the writing springs from the connection between the data corner and the discipline's tool corner. Tools from the writer's discipline (or adjacent, relevant disciplines) are used in the treatment of data (in the humanities: often primary sources, texts) and that connection secures that conceptualizations, points of analysis, results, your argument, and reasoning can be understood by others. The fifth corner (the methodology box) aims to set up a research design that is feasible, realistic, and logical. It often depicts the line of reasoning and argumentation —and the outline of the research.[2]

Writers and their teachers/supervisors may use the filling-in of the boxes at any stage of the design phase of writing a research paper or an extended piece of research, as a departure point for dialogue, or for more research. It is a planning and revising tool that has spurred a host of pedagogical activities, reflecting the need for early planning and supervision of student research. Experience has demonstrated amply for us that students who will experience serious problems with an MA thesis almost always have one or more "empty boxes" or vague formulations a long way into the designated six months' MA thesis time frame. Issues with genre and with higher order concerns (structure, argumentation, major elements such as methods, theories, data, etc.) are quite frequently the major writing issues of students, even at advanced levels; hence, that is where we have placed major effort. Even the language issues (lower order concerns) that we have seen presented at the writing centre often relate to the writer's being a novice to scientific writing, in the sense of having little available explicit knowledge about academic, scientific forms and formats for writing—even though they may very well have written many research papers prior to the MA thesis.

THE RESEARCH PAPER STRUCTURE

Another big concern over our years of tutoring thesis writers has been their difficulty structuring major written work (on both macro- and micro-levels). Therefore, principles and possibilities for structuring papers form a theme with supervisors who often find their students without ready models. Hence, we have designed a number of activities with students. Again we work with various fill-in-forms and preformatted standard structures that may later be tailored by the writers to their individual projects.

Box- and Fill-in-forms Pedagogy

A favourite workshop activity for all study levels, from first year to PhD, has been and still is for the writer in the planning stage to fill in a sheet or file with a format for research paper design, and we have made a number of forms (for all major elements of a research paper within a standard structure).

Fill-in-forms are on our website, can be mailed to students before tutorials, and are available to supervisors and can be filled in on the spot and discussed and shared in writing workshops. A piece of software, Scribo—A Guide to Research Questions and Literature Search (Rienecker & Pipa, 2009), on the intranet in many Danish universities and other higher education institutions represents the digital version of a comprehensive design tool for research papers' basic elements. The idea is not merely to regularize or mainstream students' writing, but to get their thinking and planning started within tried-and-true, working conventional frameworks that the writer can then always develop, challenge, expand, surpass, or discard if writers have other options that work better for their topics and material. A filled-in form is a short list that facilitates supervision and can lead to library searches, to more detailed structuring, drafting, and revision.

ACADEMIC WRITERS' DEVELOPMENT ACCORDING TO RESEARCH

A host of recent, major, empirical works on writer development underpins a genre approach to teaching university writing. Blåsjø (2000), Thaiss and Zawacki (2006), and Steinhoff (2007) support the idea that discernible writer development occurs from a pre-conventional stage (in which the novice writer is unaware of existing norms and conventions) to a conventional stage (in which the writer may rely too heavily on formats and "boxes" for required genres) to a post-conventional stage, where the student has become an academic writer: the desired end result of all education, in which the writer is able to use his or her judgement aptly to produce reader-oriented, suitable text for every occasion, using and transforming formats adequately. The development towards a rhetorical awareness of a multitude of textual possibilities is in fact aided by an awareness of genre conventions made explicit; our "boxes" and formats are helpful tools in passing from not knowing appropriate conventions for any given target audience to addressing each writing task with a rhetorical awareness of the specifics of the communicative content, purpose, and audience. Many students report benefiting from following preformatted schemata at least once: the template is just good to have in mind in contemplating subsequent tasks, but not needed as the final structure for the paper.

THESIS SUPERVISOR'S MANDATORY ACCREDITATION COURSES

Since 2009, the Academic Writing Centre has employed only faculty. We have fused with the Teaching and Learning Unit, and have the teaching of supervision, feedback to students, assessments, and teaching writing, as well as general teaching skills, as our work area. Part of our teaching portfolio is the MA Supervisors' Accreditation Course. Accreditation of supervisors is mandatory at our department and in the Department of Social Sciences at Aarhus University, Denmark, but is otherwise unique in Scandinavia. We have been commissioned by the dean's office to accredit all thesis supervisors at the department—i.e., the majority of faculty will go on a supervisor's course, totalling three hours plus preparation and essay writing on theses supervision. "Mandatory" means that successful completion of the course is a prerequisite in the department for supervising MA theses in the future. This means that we now teach, discuss, workshop, inform, and casework on themes related to academic inquiry, writing, project planning, etc. through the supervisors and comprehensively, getting in contact with each and every supervisor, as opposed to reaching a couple of hundred students each year out of the 15,000 in the department, and having only sporadic contact with staff. Through 2011, more than 80 out of some 500 supervisors will have been accredited. The supervisors' course focuses on the MA thesis genre and format requirement and criteria; on formative feedback on thesis designs and drafts; on supporting students through their research, reading, and writing work; on negotiating mutual expectations, and on problem writers and problem texts. The overall focus is on what individual supervisors and what departments can do to support timely and qualified submission. The course activities entail a number of case-based discussions with the theme "What can the supervisor do to assist the writing and the writer in this case?"

Many supervisors report that they adopt some of the activities with writers that served us so well, particularly using the heuristics of the pentagon model as the basis for the research paper/thesis. Supervisors request of thesis writers that they fill in and submit a pentagon for supervision early on, as a point of departure for the crucial discussion of research design and the alignment of research question with choice of data, concepts, and methods. Many supervisors also bring their own heuristics to the course, their lists of criteria for the good thesis, their supervisory practices, and their supervisory concerns, and these get shared in the course. We report the supervisor input back to heads of studies and the vice dean of education, in the hope that supervisor experiences and concerns will eventually affect curriculum design. We aim to ensure that every student is prepared through prior work and writing experiences for thesis writing, before the student signs a contract with a six-month deadline.

IN DIALOGUE WITH THESIS SUPERVISORS

How do the thesis supervisors in the Humanities Department—among the most apt and able writers and teachers of theses and dissertations and a host of other genres—react to the genre definitions and the rather restricted "box pedagogy," the formulaic and schematic suggestions concerning what the supervisor might ask for in text planning and production? We meet a range of supervisor angles and attitudes, from "but you don't quite seem to address the individual writer who happens to be an original, a young genius in the making, and who needs to be unbound by conventions and formats to freely explore his ideas in writing—and to have that very freedom in content and form acknowledged and supported by his supervisor" to "Thank you for this tool, I am going to use it" —and even further to "Yes, I've read your stuff and used it, and I have developed a tool myself, and I should like to have the supervisors' course participants' reactions to it." We welcome all input to the dialogue on writing from those who really own university writing: the writers and their supervisors/teachers. The mandatory accreditation of thesis supervisors has made possible the explicit foregrounding of the department's 500 supervisors as the true collaborators with students concerning thesis writing. We aid this process rather than substituting for absent supervisors. Accreditation courses for MA thesis supervisors are but one example of our work with academic writing with and through faculty.

THE PHD DISSERTATION AS A GENRE—AND A RUBRIC FOR FORMATIVE FEEDBACK TO PHD-STUDENTS

PhD supervision is a targeted area, not just for Danish, but for all European university education, and many institutions are implementing mandatory courses for PhD supervisors. It is our aim that the PhD dissertation as the most visible product of the PhD education should be thoroughly addressed in all supervisor preparation at our department. We want writers to explore textual options before submission rather than get negative summative feedback in the all-important assessments. We would welcome a systematic and pro-active supervisory style over a more reactive—and possibly more random—style, which is the local norm. New supervisors need to be prepared for helping their candidates plan, assess, and revise their research and their thesis, to be prepared for giving formative feedback on PhD drafts, for sitting on assessment committees, and for writing PhD assessments that are useful to the candidate, to the university, and to future employers. As a point of departure for PhD supervisor courses, we now work on a project of alignment (Biggs, 2007) of PhD assessments with the supervision of PhD students and the courses offered from the graduate school. The PhD assessments (five to ten page long summaries plus evaluation) and the PhD vivas are the most comprehensive assessments done in the university system, and when read/witnessed in bulk, give deep insight into the criteria used to assess, and also the lacunae in the desired learning outcomes when it comes to university writing. These documents reveal how well university candidates are able to write and communicate according to scientific standards, what they have learned and turned into practices of their own, and what they might not have absorbed. In our department's case, assessments from the years 2007-2008 show interesting patterns in strong and weaker features of scholarly writing. We analysed all of the departments' 2009 assessments, from which we record all evaluative remarks. The patterns emerging from the survey point to areas of (local? or more global?) PhD supervision and feedback practices that could be strengthened and reinforced to alert PhD writers to elements of dissertations that tend to be underdeveloped, and hence attract sometimes severe and clearly well-documented and justifiable criticism of dissertations.

Developing a Rubric for Feedback on PhD Drafts

The analysis of PhD assessments in a genre-frame results in a 25 page rubric feedback tool for PhD supervisors and candidates, inspired by and adjusted from Barbara Lovitt's work (2007) with feedback rubrics at the PhD level. The feedback tool alerts the feedback-giver and receiver to most-used assessment criteria, and even if all the rubrics in the feedback tool are not filled out or explicitly addressed in the supervision, they may serve as a reminder or checklist to be discussed, negotiated, embraced, or rejected as relevant, in each supervisory dyad.

The feedback tool is still under testing and revision, using several supervisor pairs as test-persons. This piece of work represents a juncture between our work until now on genre, on feedback and criteria for "the good paper," and on supervision of academic writing. It is embedded in our local Graduate School's larger scheme for enhancing the quality of dissertation writing, as well as the quality of supervision.

The integration of writing centre support with faculty activities toward student writing relies on political and management initiative and a steady drive from the dean's office to implement new routines, just as this integration relies on our work.

FUTURE TRENDS IN TEACHING ACADEMIC WRITING IN DENMARK

Supervisor education is certainly a central issue for higher education and for our policy makers. But also in other theatres of the educational system we observe movements: professional educations (e.g., teachers' and nurses' training) are becoming "academized," and also at the upper secondary level students write research papers, sometimes complete with scientific theory, research questions, data analysis, and discussion of methods. Inquiry and research become democratised and so does academic writing. Now everybody with a high school diploma has done mini-research, and with any luck they arrive at university with experience in writing in many genres--and also with a general knowledge of genres. In the next generation all our students might be adept not just at producing qualified work in one core genre but in juggling genres.

NOTES

1. The deadline can be expanded twice with an extra 3 months. This practice, however, is discouraged.

2. Similarly a pentagon model for the short essay (Signe Skov in Stray Jørgensen & Rienecker *Studiehaandbog* [*Study skills handbook*], 2009 serves as a heuristic and fill-in-form for essay writers.

REFERENCES

Bereiter, C., & Scardamalia, M. (1987). *The psychology of written composition*, Mahwah, NJ: Lawrence Erlbaum.

Biggs, J., & Tang, C. (2007). *Teaching for quality learning at university* (3rd ed.). Maidenhead, Berkshire, UK: The Society for Research into Higher Education & Open University Press.

Blåsjö, M. (2000): *Uppsatsens yta och djup. TeFa, 33.* Stockholm: Stockholms Universitet, Stockholm

Rienecker, L., & Pipa Buchtrup, T.(2009). Scribo—guide til problemformulering og litteratursøgning [Scribo—Guide to research question and literature search] Forlaget Samfundslitteratur, Frederiksberg, software. Retrieved from http://www.scribo.dk

Rienecker, L., & Stray Jørgensen, P. (2005). *Den gode opgave [The good paper].* Frederiksberg: Samfundslitteratur.

Rienecker, L., Harboe, T., & Stray Jørgensen, P. (2005). *Vejledningsbogen - en brugsbog for opgave- og specialevejledere på de videregående uddannelser. [Supervision of research papers and MA theses]* Frederiksberg: Samfundslitteratur.

Rienecker, L.& Stray Jørgensen, P. (2003). The (im)possibilities in teaching university writing in the Anglo-American tradition when dealing with continental student writers. In L. Björk, G. Bräuer,L. Rienecker, & P. Stray Jörgensen,(Eds.), *Teaching academic writing in European higher education.* Studies in Writing, 12 (pp. 101-112). Amsterdam: Kluwer Academic Publishers.

Rienecker, L., & Stray Jørgensen, P. (2003). The genre in focus, not the writer: Using model examples in large-class workshops. In L. Björk, G. Bräuer, L. Rienecker, & P. Stray Jörgensen (Eds.), *Teaching academic writing in European higher education.* Studies in Writing, Vol. 12 (pp. 59-74). Amsterdam: Kluwer Academic Publishers.

Steinhoff, T. (2007). *Wissenschaftliche textkompetenz sprachgebrauch und schreibentwicklung in wissenschaftlichen texten von studenten und experten [Academic textual competence. language use and the development of writing in academic texts by students and experts].* Berlin: De Gruyter.

Stray Jørgensen, P.& Rienecker, L. (2009). *Studiehåndbogen for studiestartere på videregående uddannelser. [Study skills handbook]* Frederiksberg: Samfundslitteratur.

Thaiss, C., & Zawacki, T. (2006). *Engaged writers and dynamic disciplines: Research on the academic writing life.* Portsmouth, NH: Heinemann.

CHAPTER 16.
THE DEPARTMENT OF RHETORIC AND COMPOSITION AT THE AMERICAN UNIVERSITY IN CAIRO: ACHIEVEMENTS AND CHALLENGES

By Emily Golson and Lammert Holdijk
American University in Cairo (Egypt)

This chapter traces the growth of the first department of Rhetoric and Composition in the Middle East from its initial stages as a six-credit freshmen seminar (1957) to its emergence as the first Department of Rhetoric and Composition in the Middle East (2007). The piece includes a summary of the demographics of the current department, a description of the pedagogy and philosophy that informs the curriculum, a summary of the creation of the Writing Minor (2009), a brief description of the Writing Center, and references to ancillary programs, such as the Undergraduate Research Conference and Community Based Learning Courses. The final part of the chapter articulates current challenges and future plans.

The American University in Cairo, founded in 1919, is a private university enrolling approximately 5,055 undergraduate and 1,148 graduate students per year (About AUC, 2011). The Department of Rhetoric and Composition is the largest Department in the School of Humanities and Social Sciences. As of this writing, it serves 4,000 students per year in lower-division courses and 200 in upper division courses, with 34 students enrolled in a new Writing Minor (Rhetoric and Writing Minor, 2011). A separate English language program, located in the English Language Institute, serves the needs of prospective students whose English language proficiency does not meet entry-level requirements (95-102 on the TOEFL iBT total score—Internet Based Test). Approximately 45% of the students enter the university through the English language program while the remaining 55% enter into one of three entry-level required writing courses. Students entering the university come from private international schools (American, French, German, British, Dutch) or enter directly from national schools.

The Department is responsible for three required writing courses and a growing Writing Minor. It employs 44-48 full time faculty who teach three courses per term. Ten percent of the current faculty hold PhDs in Rhetoric & Composition or related areas. The remaining faculty have degrees in creative writing, literature, history, theology, film studies, journalism, science, business, and TEFL (Teaching English as a Foreign Language). The required lower-division curriculum consists of three required writing courses, which use (US) WPA (Writing Program Administrators) Outcomes for First Year Composition as guidelines (http://www.wpacouncil.org/positions/outcomes.html) and include a heavy emphasis on rhetorical strategies—voice, analysis, audience and argument—to assist in critical thinking. The first course focuses on voice and analysis, the second on argument and audience, and the third on formal academic research. The Department's Writing Center offers tutorials to 3,500 undergraduate students annually and 110 graduate students; the Center sponsors 20 general and 10 discipline-specific workshops per semester for undergraduates and six general workshops and occasional customized courses for graduate students. The Department also sponsors an Undergraduate Research Conference, co-sponsors a linguistics conference every other year, and offers several Community Based Learning (CBL) courses.

HISTORY OF THE DEPARTMENT

As Egypt's national school curriculum rests on rote learning, many Egyptian students have difficulty with independent thinking. In general, students lack an awareness of the value of a liberal arts education, have little experience in reading and writing, have not been exposed to effective reasoning, and are unfamiliar with the concept of plagiarism. Although Egypt's International Schools provide an American/European education for those who can afford it, many of the faculty in these schools were not trained to specifically address the writing needs of students.

The history of AUC's effort to address these needs began in 1957, when AUC faculty voted for a six-credit freshman seminar consisting of a two-course sequence—101 (Freshman Composition) and 102 (Research Writing). At that time, the writing faculty was composed of three local hires with BAs in the humanities or social sciences. In the 1960s, the university added a second level of Freshman Composition (a new 102—three credits) and moved the Research Writing course to a sophomore offering (201—three credits), resulting in a total of nine credits for a three-course sequence—101, 102 and 201. In order to meet this commitment, the university asked English and Comparative Literature faculty to teach one to two writing courses per year. The most significant problem during this period was lack of consistency in grading. The need to confront this problem eventually persuaded the Literature department to consider establishing a Writing Program with specialized faculty teaching composition

The 1970s saw the beginning of a specialized Writing Program with a coordinator and enough office space for the addition of locally-hired faculty, most of whom held MAs in literature or TESOL. During this period, it was difficult to recruit native speakers from the US with specialized training in composition; consequently, local native speakers of English, with degrees in a variety of disciplines, provided additional instruction. This marked the beginning of a unit composed of a mixture of Egyptian, European, and American faculty with degrees in many different disciplines—this diversity continues to characterize the department to this day.

As the goal was to provide an intense writing experience, the three required English courses were condensed into two courses: ENGL 112, Rhetorical Modes (four credits) and ENGL 113, Research Writing (five credits). Grading for these courses was pass/fail. The above change was followed by the development of techniques and materials that drew from the growing body of TESOL and Composition literature in the US and UK. Recognizing that many of the students were not prepared to master the level of writing required in the new courses, the Director of the Writing Program, who was also the Chair of the committee that was in the process of creating a new Core Curriculum, created a remedial preparatory course, ENGL 111, later re-labeled ENGL 100, which eventually became an exit course on writing for the English Language Institute.

CHANGE AND EVOLUTION

In the eighties and nineties the Writing Program received limited support from faculty and students. Although writing faculty were stressing critical thinking, there was limited follow-up in subsequent academic courses. A survey revealed that many faculty were giving multiple-choice tests in lieu of assigning papers. Since writing was rarely assessed in humanities or non-humanities courses, students began to perceive writing as irrelevant to their academic work. In the mid nineties, as part of an effort to bring writing pedagogy in line with US composition pedagogy, the Writing Program attempted to introduce Writing Across the Curriculum (WAC). An expert consultant delivered a weeklong workshop, but the effort was eventually dropped because there was no incentive for faculty to change course requirements or delivery. By the year 2000, the Writing Program, with little support from colleagues in other disciplines, had become a series of loosely connected required courses on a variety of themes with, as earlier, no mechanism to assure fairness in grading. Some instructors graded for "content," while others addressed sentence-level issues, paragraph structure, vocabulary, and usage.

The next few years saw renewed attention to writing as a result of the grading question and several other needs:

- The Department of Engineering needed an advanced writing course to qualify for ABET accreditation
- Businesses reported that AUC graduates were not proficient in writing
- Writing pedagogy was not in line with US composition programs

In 2001, Faculty Senate Resolution 209 called for the restructuring of course offerings in writing to better reflect current US practices and to allow for easier integration with the credit-hour structure. This opened the way for a revision of the Program.

As the writing faculty began to move away from the influence of both TESOL and literature and toward a pedagogy that was informed by the discipline of Rhetoric/Composition, a new Writing Program began to take shape. Courses were streamlined to address differing competencies in language and thought. Classes were limited to 14 students. The curriculum was revised. ECLT 112 (four credits) and 113 (five credits) were replaced by ECLT 101, 102 and 103 (three credits each), and the name of the program was changed from the Freshman Writing Program to the Writing Program. A portfolio system was initiated. The grading system was changed from pass/fail to letter grades, with final papers graded by adjudication. New upper division courses in Business Communication, Technical Communication and Writing, and Writing in the Humanities and Social Sciences were created to answer the need for more specialized writing courses. In 2004, the Writing Program was granted an independent budget. In 2005, Writing Program administrators took control of hiring. In 2006, as a result of mandated, campus-wide self studies that called for stronger and more engaged writing, the Writing Program gained department status. To our knowledge, the Department is the first of its kind in the Middle East.

Department Struggles

In 2007, while the university prepared for extensive restructuring, the new Department, with full support from both Provost and Dean, began to revise its identity so that the discipline and the work of teaching Rhet/Comp would be perceived as equal to the work of other departments. When a new Provost took office in 2008, and the campus moved from its crowded downtown quarters to a sprawling state-of the-art desert complex located outside of the city, that effort intensified. The Department proposed a Writing Minor consisting of three emphasis areas—business, academic, and creative. Eleven new courses, offered on a rotating basis, were added to the standard upper division offerings. Faculty with creative writing backgrounds tapped into a hidden need for attention to creative expression, and within one year, the minor boasted 34 students, many of whom were creative writers.

During this period, those teaching business and technical writing began to strengthen the conceptual foundation of their courses by articulating rhetorical outcomes that had always existed below the surface of their teaching. In addition, Rhetoric and Composition's business writing faculty teamed up with allies in the Business School to work on a required under-division course for business majors. New faculty with degrees in Rhetoric proposed academic writing courses that either emphasized the rhetorical foundations of critical thought or focused on rhetorical engagement that cut across the disciplines. Meanwhile, the lower-division required courses enhanced WPA outcomes by adding a stronger emphasis on rhetoric to allow instructors to build on mastery of appropriate levels of critical engagement. As of this writing, RHET 101 now focuses on voice and analysis and RHET 102 on audience and argument. RHET 103 has now become RHET 201, a sophomore level research writing course. Portfolio requirements now allow faculty to concentrate on process, with low-stakes activities and exercises buttressing partial and final drafts. Norming sessions and outcomes now assure consistency and coherence of the offerings.

To assist in this transition, faculty take advantage of AUC's generous research, teaching enhancement, conference, and semester-long tenure and professional development grants to focus on their own writing and research projects. Creative writers attend writing residencies, and academic faculty travel to research facilities throughout Europe and the US In addition, faculty learn from each other through professional development sessions on the use of digital platforms, such as Blackboard, wikis, Moodle, and blogs, as well as new approaches to traditional writing classroom practices from fields such as epistolary writing, film studies, or public speaking.

CHALLENGES

Our faculty faces many challenges. While department status has given instructors more authority in the classroom and on university-wide, policy-making committees, it has also placed the Department at the forefront of attempts to introduce western pedagogy. There are few free public libraries in Egypt, and the public schools do not emphasize reading and writing. Because Egyptian culture privileges oral exchange over reading and writing, learning is primarily associated with memorization and repetition. As Egyptian society places a strong emphasis on conformity, class discussions often feature praise for those parts of a text that support student beliefs and silence during conversations or text readings that challenge those same beliefs. Even though exposure to the Internet has opened new possibilities for free-ranging discussion, progress is slow because of limited engagement with critical thinking, reading, or writing.

The shift from a Writing Program (often referred to as "English Classes" by Egyptian students) to a Department of Rhetoric and Composition was accompanied by a realization that most students (and most parents) had never heard of rhetoric and composition and were not familiar with its goals and outcomes. Therefore, one of the first duties of the new department was to inform students, parents, and faculty of the connection between rhetoric and critical thinking, and to introduce the community to the concept of writing as a form of engagement with thought. For the students, however, conversation often focused on grades. Although most AUC students come from the upper classes and have more personal freedom, better education, and greater exposure to Western ideas than their peers, they remain immersed in a culture that strongly supervises their activities. AUC students live at home and receive daily reminders of the need for high grades, which are sometimes linked to family honour rather than mastery of subject matter. For some students, the pressure can become so intense that they ignore learning. In the worst cases, students blatantly plagiarize. In the best cases, students rely too heavily on sources or turn to more accomplished friends for help with writing a paper. Even the best students negotiate to receive additional points on every completed assignment, no matter the quality.

The recent changes in curriculum and outcomes in the lower-division required courses have allowed faculty to take a different approach to issues of learning and academic integrity. Although the department has always been sensitive to plagiarism and used Turnitin software (an Internet tool that identifies plagiarized work) as a teaching tool, faculty now employ additional means to shift student attention from grades to learning. A new emphasis on voice and analysis in RHET 101 and argument and audience in RHET 102, when used in conjunction with several low-stakes assignments, now guides students through several stages of critical thinking. Constant attention to feedback through class discussion, peer evaluation, and conferencing now allows students to stay focused on learning instead of grades. And the gradual accumulation of pages and pages of writing that evidences increased cognitive awareness has helped to convince students that they are indeed capable of the complex written thought that accompanies engagement in the writing process.

The Department also attempts to educate parents by holding occasional parent conferences. In the event that a student and instructor cannot reach a resolution during a grade dispute, we request a meeting in which we invite parents, student, and instructor to meet with the Director or Associate Director to discuss approaches and goals of the course in conjunction with the student's earned grade. Although in all instances we have tactfully refused to change a grade, there has never been an instance in which a parent did not accept our judgement or leave an office dissatisfied.

Our second challenge is to make our diversity our strength. A third of our faculty are Egyptian, a third are from Europe (mainly the UK), and a third are American. They hold different types of degrees in many different majors. They come from the corporate as well as the education sector. Many have never taken a composition course nor have they been trained to teach composition. Although these faculty have much to contribute, they face the constant challenge of placing Rhetoric and Composition knowledge and pedagogy at the core of their teaching.

As a result, the department takes outcomes, normalizing, assessment, and professional development very seriously. Course co-ordinators meet with faculty to discuss outcomes at the beginning of each term. The assessment co-ordinator "normalizes" with faculty twice each term and oversees random portfolio evaluation once a year. A professional development coordinator oversees faculty development presentations given by those with expertise in a particular area of rhetoric or composition. And an informal "Seminar/Practicum" in Rhet/Comp theory and practice supports those with little experience in teaching Rhet/Comp. Also during the last few years, the Department has hired a Chair with extensive Rhet/Comp experience and three Rhet/Comp PhDs to assist in providing a sound disciplinary focus and intellectual resonance to the curriculum.

A final challenge is to deliver creative, coherent, quality writing instruction that will keep pace with the rapid changes in the university. We are the first Department of Rhetoric and Composition in the Middle East. We are housed in a university that has witnessed the creation of three new schools, several new graduate programs, and several new professional degree departments in the last three years. In all instances, there appears to be a shift away from the liberal arts toward professional degrees.

Our Provost and our Board of Trustees want to be assured that our approach is worth the effort invested by the university. Thus, we are under increased pressure to define "who we are" and "what we do." We are currently addressing this demand by encouraging collaboration with faculty in other AUC Schools as well as reminding officials of the strong need for training in and articulation of critical/creative thinking in all professions and disciplines. Thus far, the university has supported our efforts, but we are also constantly reminded that we are a "special" unit and must prove our worth.

CONCLUSION

The Department of Rhetoric and Composition was created to oversee training in the generation, articulation, development, exchange, and evaluation of ideas. Working in conjunction with other departments in the university, it attempts to provide a foundation for successful civic and social engagement to students who will one day take up leadership positions in the Middle East. As the department develops a deeper understanding of the needs of the students, it works to create a level of instruction that supports critical thinking and creative problem solving. Although still in its infancy, the Department has evolved to the point that it can deliver instruction that integrates disciplinary learning and understanding with personal, social, and civic engagement, a crucial part of AUC's mission. We now know who we are, and in order to meet current demands, we are constantly evaluating and revising what we do.

REFERENCES

American University in Cairo. (2011). *About AUC*. Retrieved *from* http://www.aucegypt.edu/about/Pages/default.aspx

American University in Cairo. (2011). *Rhetoric and Writing Minor.* Retrieved from http://catalog.aucegypt.edu/preview_program.php?catoid=15&poid=1780&returnto=475

CHAPTER 17.
PROVIDING A HUB FOR WRITING DEVELOPMENT: A PROFILE OF THE CENTRE FOR ACADEMIC WRITING (CAW), COVENTRY UNIVERSITY, ENGLAND

By Mary Deane and Lisa Ganobcsik-Williams
Oxford Brookes University and Coventry University (England)

Academic Writing is an emerging area for teaching and research in UK higher education. This profile essay outlines the work of the first centrally-funded UK writing centre, the Centre for Academic Writing (CAW) at Coventry University. The profile looks in detail at why and how CAW was established, and discusses the CAW model of a "hub" for three "spokes" of university writing development: student writing, staff development in the teaching of writing, and staff and postgraduate scholarly writing. The profile argues that to be effective and sustainable, writing provision and writing centres must evolve strategically to meet the needs of university students and staff.

The phoenix arising from the ashes is the symbol of the city of Coventry, England (Cheesewright, 2009).[1] Heavily bombed during World War II, Coventry was rebuilt and now celebrates its heritage as home of the British bicycle and automotive industry as well as a centre of peace and reconciliation (Richardson, 1972).[2] Coventry University, which also takes the phoenix as its emblem, developed in tandem with the city's regeneration. As one of the "new universities" to grow out of government changes to polytechnics in 1992, Coventry University places a strong focus both on teaching and applied research. Today, in 2011, the university encompasses three Faculties (Business, Environment and Society; Engineering and Computing; Health and Life Sciences) and the Schools of Art and Design and Lifelong Learning. The student body comprises approximately

18,800 undergraduates and 3,000 postgraduates, and 18% are international students (Turton, 2011). As noted on the university's website, "Coventry is an evolving and innovative university" that provides "a caring and supportive environment, enriched by a unique blend of academic expertise and practical experience" (Coventry University, 2011).

Within this educational and research environment a leading UK university writing centre is flourishing.[3] The Centre for Academic Writing (CAW), established at Coventry University in May 2004, provides writing support for undergraduate students, postgraduates, and academics. From its inception, CAW has promoted a strategy of "whole institution" writing development whose aim is to create a shared culture for valuing writing that enables students and staff to progress along a "continuum of writing development" (Ganobcsik-Williams, 2004, pp. 37-39, 2009). This approach is articulated in CAW's mission statement, in which CAW serves as the "hub" for three "spokes" of university writing development:

> The Centre for Academic Writing is an innovative teaching and research centre whose mission is to enable students at Coventry University to become independent writers, and to equip academic staff in all disciplines to achieve their full potential as authors and teachers of scholarly writing. (CAW, 2010)

This profile essay outlines the three spokes of CAW's work: student writing, staff development in the teaching of writing, and staff and postgraduate scholarly writing. In doing so, the profile aims to provide readers with a sense of what writing means to students and academics at Coventry University and of CAW's evolving role as a hub for Academic Writing development and research.

HISTORY OF THE CENTRE FOR ACADEMIC WRITING

The 2003 proposal to establish a writing centre at Coventry University resulted from over eight years of discussion about what could be done to help students strengthen their writing skills (Williams ,2004). The proposal was submitted by a committee chaired by the University Librarian and comprised of staff from the Student Disabilities Office, the English Language Unit, the Business School, the Library, and the Maths Support Centre. Dyslexia tutors identified the need for dedicated writing tuition because they had nowhere to send non-dyslexic students for writing advice, while staff at the English Language Unit, whose remit was to support non-native English speakers, increasingly found native English speakers seeking writing support (Williams, 2004; Wilkinson, 2004). Subject Librarians also reported that students were asking for help on structuring, argumentation, and referencing for written assignments (Rock, 2004). These "pockets of provision around the university" became a major factor leading to the proposal for a writing centre (Rock, 2004).[4] The centre's proposed remit was to improve students' writing skills, and its main features were to be "a dedicated space for students to visit," "dedicated staff to provide face to face support", "dedicated resources," and "a realistic budget" (Noon, 2003, pp. 1-3). The proposal also stipulated the necessity for "a supportive approach and a name that attracts without stigma":

> [A]ny name we give. . . must avoid terms such as "skills" or "study skills" and any sense of being a remedial centre . . . . If we want students to willingly use the centre either through referral or of their own volition it will need to project a supportive image that encourages students to see it as a normal part of their learning experience. (Noon, 2003, p. 3)[5]

A new permanent full-time post of Centre Co-ordinator, a set-up budget, and "a budget to deliver service . . . on a continuing basis" were also outlined (Noon, 4). The proposal was "strongly supported at Academic Executive and in the Vice-Chancellor's group" (Pennington, 2003), who decided the writing centre would run in its start-up phase as a project of the department responsible for staff development across the University: the Centre for Higher Education Development (CHED). This positioning within CHED, whose lecturers supported "the implementation of the [University's] Learning and Teaching Strategy" through collaborations with academic staff, staff development seminars, and a staff teaching certificate' (Learning, 10), gave the writing centre a staff development remit to "organise staff development activities to assist academic and academic-related staff in helping students to improve their academic writing" that went beyond the original proposal's direct student focus (Coventry University, 2003, p.1). In August 2003, Vice-Chancellor Michael Goldstein approved the proposal and allocated funding to found the new Centre for Academic Writing.[6] The proposal's success was made public in the job description for the Co-ordinator post in December 2003, which announced the Centre for Academic Writing as "a strategic priority within the university" (Coventry University, 2003, p. 1).

In 2004, Lisa Ganobcsik-Williams, co-author of this profile essay, was appointed Co-ordinator. She brought to the role her US university background in composition teaching, writing centre tutoring, and an MA and PhD in Rhetoric and Composition; experience of working in UK higher education as a postdoctoral research fellow in Academic Writing sponsored by the Royal Literary Fund and as Co-ordinator of Academic Writing for the University of Warwick Writing Programme; and links with the international writing research community. Within the first months of CAW's operation, she appointed two professional writing tutors and an administrator, Penny Gilchrist, who had previously managed the "Learning Zone" at a local Further Education college. Mary Deane, co-author of this profile, joined this small team as CAW's first Lecturer in Academic Writing early in 2005. In the seven years since CAW's founding, its staffing has grown exponentially and now comprises three full-time lecturers/senior lecturers, 10 part-time professional Academic Writing Tutors,[7] two full-time administrators, and two part-time receptionist/clerical staff. The Centre's remit has also expanded, not only to incorporate staff as well as student writing development, but to engage in writing research that is recognised internationally and that grows out of and informs CAW's work.

STUDENT WRITING

The first "spoke" of CAW's mission statement, "to enable students to become independent writers," aims to transform the student learning experience by teaching students to view writing as a process, including how to plan, structure, critique, revise and edit their own writing. CAW offers individualised/small-group writing tutorials focusing on students' own assignments. Fifty-minute tutorials enable students to meet with an Academic Writing Tutor to have in-depth discussions of writing assignments and to cover topics such as essay structure and argumentation. Twenty-minute bookable-on-the-day tutorials are available for students who need immediate advice to clarify a specific writing issue, problem, or question. Students at all levels of study and educational preparation attend CAW tutorials. At the conclusion of a tutorial, students give feedback via CAW's electronic recordkeeping system. Typical comments include:

> The tutor gave structured comments and feedback at a level I could understand. (Student 1, 2010)

> I feel confident to continue with my paper, taking on board the writing tutor's comments. (Student 2, 2010)

Research undertaken into the impact of individualised tutorials at CAW has found that these sessions help assist students to move from a writer-based perspective on their own work to a reader-based approach (Borg & Deane, 2009, p. 16). Students gain confidence and competence, and are encouraged to apply the writing strategies they learn to the rest of their studies.

Because student demand for writing tutorials is not scalable, and because CAW aims to provide an array of learning opportunities, CAW also offers credit-bearing writing modules, group workshops, paper-based and electronic writing resources, and "Protected Writing Time" sessions for students to work on their writing with an Academic Writing Tutor on-hand.[8] The Coventry University Harvard Reference Style Guide, a CAW project Mary Deane carried out in response to the need for a consistent, teachable system of referencing to be used in all undergraduate teaching and learning materials, is a resource that is particularly valued throughout the institution and is used by other UK universities.[9]

That CAW's work with students is well-regarded within the university is evidenced by the attitudes of students, academics and senior managers. Students have said: "I am very happy that such a one-on-one tutoring system exists" (Student 3, 2010) and "CAW is the most useful thing in the university because they really help students (Student 4, 2010). Colleagues have noted that "'Students who have attended CAW before resubmission of their coursework have improved dramatically" (Davies, 2009) and that CAW's teaching "has resulted in a higher proportion of doctoral students producing better quality written work" (de Nahlik, 2009). At a 2009 meeting of the university's Teaching and Learning Committee, Faculty Deans and other senior managers unanimously advocated the work of CAW (Watts 2010).

As part of a university-wide "Add+vantage" initiative to enhance student employability (Atkins, 1999), CAW also offers a range of undergraduate modules. Students attend a two-hour seminar each week for ten weeks, and learn about the theory and practice of writing for assessment, academic genres, and research, and are expected to apply these topics to studying in their own disciplines. As a result, most students gain confidence as scholars in their fields. For instance, a student gave this feedback:"I thank you for all the help you have given me, you have certainly made me a better academic writer because I have not just achieved a good grade in this coursework, but in other coursework as well" (Student 5, 2011).

Add+vantage modules are not the only kind of group writing development CAW offers. CAW lecturers also work in a staff development mode with academics in the disciplines to support their teaching of writing to undergraduate and postgraduate students (Deane & O'Neill, 2011).

STAFF DEVELOPMENT IN THE TEACHING OF WRITING

Staff development to "equip academic staff in all disciplines to achieve their full potential as teachers of scholarly writing," the second "spoke,' is central to CAW's mission. By working with academics on strategies for teaching writing, CAW lecturers reach large numbers of students in a cost-effective way (Purser et al., 2008). Subject experts who integrate explicit writing instruction into their courses are well placed to connect generic competencies with discipline-specific knowledge, so students have the most intellectually challenging and meaningful experience of academic writing development (Monroe, 2003). Furthermore, collaboration between writing specialists and disciplinary experts can lead to research and publication on academic genres and pedagogic approaches for supporting student writers, which can benefit the wider academic community (Samuels & Deane, 2008).

CAW lecturers provide nine hours per week of one-to-one staff writing consultancy by appointment. The format of these appointments varies according to the issues a colleague wishes to tackle, which can include designing written assessments, providing timely and constructive feedback, or supporting students with academic integrity and avoiding plagiarism. During an appointment, the Academic Writing lecturer asks the subject-based colleague about the strengths and weaknesses he or she has perceived in a particular cohort of students, and together they establish a goal for a targeted teaching intervention to address a priority issue. For instance, if they plan to improve the students' ability to produce well-structured written work that addresses the assignment brief, they may aim to introduce a formative assessment into a course to give students guided practice and feedback the students can implement in their summative assessment task. Writing specialists recommend readings and resources to support the intervention, helping to produce tailored teaching materials if required. Importantly, the discipline-based teaching interventions are led by subject specialists, because they are authoritative on the content students must also master. This is a good way to maximise the impact of writing development around the university, because subject experts develop additional expertise in writing pedagogies which they share with all the students they teach. This "Writing in the Disciplines" (WiD) approach embeds writing instruction into disciplinary teaching, and is beneficial for students because they learn how to construct and articulate arguments in the genres of their field (Bean, 2006).

One example of a WiD teaching intervention at Coventry is a collaboration between Law specialist Dr. Steve Foster and Academic Writing lecturer Dr. Mary Deane, who worked together to support Law students' transition to university and adoption of legal writing conventions, including referencing, analysis of cases, and formal expression (Strong, 2006, p. 8). Foster, in consultation with Deane, taught legal writing to 150 students on Coventry's LLB Law Degree in their first term at university through an intervention that lasted for five weeks of the 10-week long autumn term. The teaching was informed by the premise that academic study involves learning about genres as well as developing disciplinary knowledge (Monroe, 2003). Foster and Deane were also influenced by the Australian "Developing Academic Literacies in Context" (DALiC) approach to embedding the teaching of academic genres into subject courses (Skillen et al., 1999).

Compared to the previous year's cohort, the majority of students produced more structured assignments with more appropriate paragraphing, whilst many showed an improved ability to cite and evaluate legal sources. There was also evidence that the students were more capable of addressing and answering the set question than previous cohorts. Most of the students improved their basic legal essay writing as a result of this WiD intervention, and encouraged by this, Foster and Deane shared their methods with colleagues in the Law department, and Foster developed further resources to address issues they felt they had not fully resolved. This collaboration has also contributed to Foster and Deane's research profiles (e.g., Foster & Deane, 2011) and to CAW's eligibility to participate in Coventry University's submission to the UK's national Research Excellence Framework (REF) exercise.[10]

STAFF AND POSTGRADUATE SCHOLARLY WRITING

The third "spoke" of CAW's mission statement, "to equip academic staff in all disciplines to achieve their full potential as authors of scholarly writing," also contributes to the university's applied research and publication agenda and is valued by many academics and postgraduates. CAW facilitates staff and postgraduate writing development by offering writing consultations, Scholarly Writing Retreats and Protected Writing Time sessions that make it possible for participants to progress their writing projects and publications.

As noted in the previous section, CAW lecturers offer staff writing consultancy by appointment. In addition to obtaining advice about teaching writing, academics and postgraduates can attend these appointments for support with their own research and publication writing, including planning for submission, targeting publication outputs, responding to peer reviews, managing extended writing tasks, and preparing grant applications. The Academic Writing lecturer completes a record of these meetings, noting the main recommendations and action points. The lecturer reads the colleague's work-in-progress and works in a facilitative mode, asking questions to encourage the writer to strengthen key arguments and boost the audience appeal of a text in line with its purpose and genre.

In addition to individual staff consultations, CAW lecturers facilitate Protected Writing Time sessions for postgraduates and academics. Sessions usually last for two hours and the format is flexible but requires:

1. A writing specialist available to read work-in-progress
2. Participants with a plan for the session
3. A quiet space with no distractions

Participants are responsible for using this protected time efficiently, and facilitators have found that writers' productivity increases the more familiar they become with this time-bound and focused approach to writing (Murray, 2009). As this type of provision directly addresses CAW's mission to promote writers' independence, facilitators often adopt a non-interventionist approach (e.g., Clark, 2001), which can be surprisingly fruitful once participants have learnt how to develop realistic writing objectives.

Scholarly Writing Retreats, which CAW has been running since 2006, are an extended type of protected writing time that allows participants to establish a more sustained writing rhythm and the opportunity to fulfill a substantial writing objective (Murray, 2009). Retreats support writers in becoming more independent because they foster strategies for managing limited time to complete a specific writing task, and delegates often feel motivated when they realise just how productive they can be to use the strategies they learn on Retreats to inform their daily writing routines.

Participants attend a one-hour planning workshop a month before the event, where they identify the amount and type of writing they will produce during each half-day period. Participants are also informed that they will be expected to deliver a short presentation at the close of the Retreat about the writing they have produced and the extent to which they achieved their main goal. These presentations allow delegates to obtain feedback from peers and help them to stay focused by making Retreats outcome-orientated.

CONCLUSION

Within a national higher education climate in which the subject of "writing development" has only recently begun to be recognised, CAW has developed its mission and established writing provision to meet the needs of university students and staff.[11] Arising from this context, CAW has tried to be strategic in creating forms of provision that are targeted but flexible. The need for a fluid approach to writing development is paramount in the face of economic challenges that are now affecting the UK, with reduction in government funding for higher education heralding budget cuts across the sector. Whilst CAW will continue working toward the aims articulated in its mission statement, CAW staff are aware that in terms of sustainability, the means of achieving these aims may need to adapt and change. CAW's provision, therefore, will continue to evolve. One direction will be writing and technology, as CAW currently is preparing to introduce its online component, the Coventry Online Writing Lab (COWL), to offer synchronous and asynchronous online writing support.[12]

Another direction will be to launch an "MA in Academic Writing Theory and Practice," which will engage with the international community of Academic Writing scholars and practitioners and which CAW staff are taking through the university's course approval process at present.[13] A third direction may be to begin a student peer tutoring scheme, to fulfil the university's commitment to providing work opportunities for students and to enhancing students' employability by providing work experiences to help them to gain graduate jobs.

This profile essay has outlined the history and mission of CAW as well as the range of Academic Writing provision offered by this UK-based writing centre. In detailing the three spokes of CAW's existing activity—student writing, staff development in the teaching of writing, and staff and postgraduate scholarly writing—as well as its evolving possibilities, the profile has demonstrated how the active engagement by CAW staff in both teaching and research is integral to all areas of the writing centre's work. In each of these ways, the Centre for Academic Writing functions as a hub for writing development and research at Coventry University.

NOTES

1. The phoenix is a mythical bird that burns and is reborn from its own ashes. See, for example, R. van den Broek, The Myth of the Phoenix - According to Classical and Early Christian Traditions, Leiden: Brill, 1972.

2. On Coventry's motor industry heritage, see the Coventry Transport Museum http://www.transport-museum.com/. On Coventry's peace and reconciliation ethos, see the Peace and Reconciliation Gallery at Coventry's Herbert Art Gallery and Museum: http://www.theherbert.org/index.php/home/permanent-galleries/peace-and-reconciliation-gallery. Coventry University is home to the Centre for Peace and Reconciliation Studies (http://wwwm.coventry.ac.uk/researchnet/cprs/Pages/Home.aspx).

3. The "writing centre" is still a very new type of provision in UK higher education. As early as 1979 there was an attempt to set up a US-university-style writing cen-

tre modelled on those in US universities at Newcastle Polytechnic (now Northumbria University) (Hebron, 1984, p. 92), and another, in 2002, at the University of Glasgow, Crichton Campus. CAW was the first centrally-funded UK university writing centre and has served as a model upon which other universities have drawn (e.g., London Met, Gloucestershire, Liverpool Hope, Limerick).

4. Staff from Coventry University's Maths Support Centre, established in the early 1990s, contributed their experience of setting up and managing a centre to the university's conversation about a writing centre (Reed, 2004).

5. The name "Effective Academic Writing Centre" was recommended by the committee. Other names considered were "Literacy Centre," "Learner Development Centre," "Learning Skills Drop-in Centre," and "Academic Writing Skills Support Centre" (Noon, 2003).

6. A further factor enabling the creation of the centre was the existence of a vacant space in an old building and the plan to re-locate to a purpose-built suite of rooms upon completion of the university's new student centre building. This purpose-built space proving too small, in 2007 CAW was relocated instead to a self-contained annexe in a central ground-floor position adjacent to the Coventry University Library.

7. For a map of CAW's activities in support of student writing (2004-2010), see: http://curve.coventry.ac.uk/cu/items/c9110b81-0b1a-dfa6-23e9-6b96402d6ba0/1/AMENDED%20CAW%20Model%20v3%2015.3.10%20FINAL.pdf.

8. The Coventry University Harvard Reference Style Guide is officially used by the University of the Highlands and Islands and by Nottingham Trent University. It is now in its third version and is edited by CAW lecturer Dr. Catalina Neculai.

9. Originating as the RAE (Research Assessment Exercise) in the 1980s, the REF (Research Excellence Framework) is a system for assessing the quality of journal articles and other research outputs of UK higher education institutions (see http://www.hefce.ac.uk/research/ref/).

10. On the growth of Academic Writing as a field for teaching and research in the UK, see, for example Lillis, 2001; Bergstrom, 2004; and Ganobcsik-Willliams, 2006 and 2010.

11. One early effect of budget reductions in 2009, for example, was the restructuring of the staff development centre at Coventry University, which resulted in CAW becoming affiliated with the Library—a move which emphasised CAW's student and staff research support remit.

12. The COWL research project (2008-2010) was generously funded by JISC, a UK government-funded organisation whose purpose is to "inspire . . . UK colleges and universities in the innovative use of digital technologies," http://www.jisc.ac.uk/aboutus.aspx.

13. Indeed, this initiative was approved in Autumn 2011 and will be launched in Autumn 2012. It consists of three components: Coventry's new MA in Academic Writing Theory and Practice, Postgraduate Diploma in Academic Writing Theory and Practice, and Postgraduate Certificate in Academic Writing Development.

REFERENCES

Atkins, M. J. (1999). Oven-ready and self-basting: Taking stock of employability skills. *Teaching in Higher Education, 4*(2), 267-82.

Bean, J. C. (2006). *Engaging ideas: The professor's guide to integrating writing, critical thinking, and active learning in the classroom.* San Francisco: Jossey-Bass Publishers.

Bergstrom, C. (2004). The status of writing in the university. *English Subject Centre Newsletter 6,* 10-13.

Borg, E. & Deane, M. (2009). Interim report on individualised writing tutorials at Coventry University's Centre for Academic Writing (CAW). Unpublished report. Coventry: Coventry University.

Borg E. & Deane, M. (2011). Measuring the outcomes of individualised writing instruction: A multilayered approach to capturing changes in students' texts. *Teaching in Higher Education, 16,* 319-331.

CAW (2011). *Centre for Academic Writing Mission Statement.* Retrieved from http://www.coventry.ac.uk/cu/caw

Cheesewright, P. (2009). *The phoenix rises: A portrait of Coventry University and its city.* London: Third Millennium.

Clark, I. (2001). Perspectives on the directive/non-directive continuum in the writing center. *Writing Center Journal, 22*(1), 33-58.

Coventry University (2011). *Coventry University Website.* Retrieved from http://wwwm.coventry.ac.uk/university/Pages/TheUniversity.aspx

Coventry University (2003). Job Description: Co-ordinator: Centre for Academic Writing. Unpublished document. Coventry: Coventry University.

Coventry University (2002). Learning and teaching strategy. Unpublished document. Coventry: Coventry University.

Davies, B. (2009). Student feedback: Nursing students. [email] to Deane, M. [4 June 2009].

Deane, M., & O'Neill, P. (Eds.). (2011). *Writing in the disciplines.* Houndmills: Palgrave Macmillan.

De Nahlik, C. (2009). Centre for Academic Writing and doctoral students. [email] to Ganobcsik-Williams, L. [24 March 2009].

Foster, S. (2009). *How to write better law essays: Tools and techniques for success in exams and assignments.* Harlow: Longman.

Foster, S., & Deane, M. (2011). Enhancing students' legal writing. In M. Deane & P. O'Neill (Eds.), *Writing in the Disciplines* (pp. 88-102). Houndmills: Palgrave Macmillan.

Ganobcsik-Williams, L. (2004). *A Report on the teaching of academic writing in UK higher education.* London: Royal Literary Fund.

Ganobcsik-Williams, L. (Ed.). (2006). *Teaching academic writing in UK higher education: Theories, practices and models.* Houndmills: Palgrave Macmillan.

Ganobcsik-Williams, L. (2009, June). Supporting students along a continuum of writing development. Bridging the gap: Transitions in student writing. Symposium hosted by Flying Start, Write Now and LearnHigher. Retrieved from http://www.hope.ac.uk/latest-news-and-progress-reports/writing-symposium.html

Ganobcsik-Williams, L. (2010). Academic writing in higher education: A brief overview. *Research Intelligence, 113,*10-11. Retrieved from http://www.bera.ac.uk/files/2009/07/BERA_RI113_to-view.pdf.

Ganobcsik-Williams, L. (2011). The writing centre as a locus for WID, WAC and whole-institution writing provision. In M. Deane & P. O'Neill (Eds.), *Writing in the disciplines* (pp.252-64). Houndmills: Palgrave Macmillan.

Lillis, T. (2001). *Student writing: Access, regulation, desire.* London: Routledge.

Monroe, J. (2003). *Local knowledges ,local practices: Writing in the disciplines at Cornell.* Pittsburgh: University of Pittsburgh Press.

Murray, R. (2009). *Writing for academic journals. Maidenhead.* Berkshire, UK: Open University Press.

Noon, P. (2003). Creating a literacy centre. Unpublished proposal. Coventry: Coventry University.

Pennington, D. (2003). Academic writing skills support unit [email] forwarded to Ganobcsik-Williams, L. [14 July 2003].

Purser, E., Skillen, J., Deane, M., Donahue, J., & Peake, K. (2008). Developing academic literacy in context. *Zeitschrift Schreiben* Retrieved from http://www.zeitschrift-schreiben.eu/

Reed, J. (2004). Interview by L. Ganobcsik-Williams. Coventry University, 6 May 2004.

Richardson, K. (1972). *Twentieth-century Coventry.* London and Basingstoke: Macmillan Press Ltd.

Rock, C. (2004). Writing Centre Interview [interview by L. Ganobcsik-Williams] Coventry University, 19 May 2004.

Samuels, P. & Deane, M. (2011). Writing for mathematics education at doctoral level. In M. Deane & P. O'Neill (Eds.), *Writing in the disciplines* (pp. 140-54). Houndmills: Palgrave Macmillan.

Samuels, P. & Deane, M. (2008). Academic writing training for Mathematics Education PhD students. *Maths, Stats, and OR Connections, 8*(3), 41-44. Retrieved from http://mathstore.gla.ac.uk/headocs/8341_samuels_p_academicwriting.pdf

Skillen, J., Trivett N., Merten M., & Percy, A. (1999). Integrating the instruction of generic and discipline specific skills into the curriculum: A case study. In *Cornerstones: Proceedings of the 1999 HERDSA Conference, Canberra:* HERDSA.

Strong, S. I. (2006) *How to write law essays and exams.* Oxford: Open University Press.

Students 1-4 (2010). Tutorial Feedback. Centre for Academic Writing Feedback and Statistics. Unpublished report. Coventry University.

Student 5 (2011). Feedback on module [email] to Deane, M. [26 April 2011].

Turton, K. (2011). Coventry university monthly student number update [email] to Medlock, S. [12 May 2011].

Van den Broek, R. (1972). *The Myth of the phoenix - According to classical and early Christian traditions.* Leiden: Brill.

Watts, J. (2009). Minutes of the university teaching and learning committee. Unpublished document. Coventry: Coventry University.

Williams, S. (2004). Writing centre interview [interview by L. Ganobcsik-Williams] Coventry University, 5 May 2004.

Wilkinson, R. (2004) Writing centre interview [interview by L. Ganobcsik-Williams] Coventry University, 7 May 2004.

Wingate, U. (2011). A comparison of "additional" and "embedded" approaches to teaching writing in the disciplines. In M. Deane& P. O'Neill (Eds.), *Writing in the disciplines* (pp. 65-86). Houndmills: Palgrave Macmillan.

CHAPTER 18.
THINKING WRITING AT QUEEN MARY, UNIVERSITY OF LONDON

By Teresa McConlogue, Sally Mitchell, and Kelly Peake
Queen Mary, University of London (England)

In this contribution we outline and discuss the work of Thinking Writing at Queen Mary, University of London. Thinking Writing seeks, through a focus on writing, to facilitate professional development and enhanced teaching, assessment and curriculum design. We describe how the initiative has developed over a 10-year period, the range of activities it now encompasses, and the theoretical orientations and resources from which it draws. To explain the negotiated way in which the Thinking Writing team typically works, we give an account of our involvement with processes of change in a single department of the university. We note that our approach does not assume particular models of writing nor measure success in terms of the "written product"; and we consider the potential future impact on our work of new strategic initiatives that articulate "writing" as an explicit goal.

Queen Mary, University of London is a highly regarded research-intensive university in east London with 3,000 staff and 16,000 students in three faculties: Humanities and Social Science, Science and Engineering, and Medicine and Dentistry. Based centrally in the Language and Learning Unit (LLU), Thinking Writing (TW) is an established team whose activity centres on the development of writing as a pedagogical tool and outcome within the mainstream of disciplinary teaching and learning across the institution. The team is staff- rather than student-facing, its aim being to assist academic departments with their educational work (designing modules and programmes, setting and assessing assignments, enhancing student learning) specifically through the lens of writing. TW was begun in 2001 as a three-year project with a part-time coordinator. Drawing inspiration from Writing in the Disciplines at Cornell University, the project was made possible by Teaching Quality Enhancement funds allocated to UK higher education institutions and, in our case, bid for internally.[1] Since then it has grown significantly and now comprises the coordinator and a team of three permanent advisors.

The location of TW in the LLU has been a factor in its successful growth thus far; income-generating foundation programmes for international students are central to the LLU's remit and these have enabled Alan Evison (head of the LLU) and Nigel Relph, Director of Corporate Affairs (the organisational area in which the LLU sits) to demonstrate their commitment to TW's goals through financial cross-subsidy. Over the period of TW's existence, however, interest in issues of student writing has also moved higher up the institution's wider teaching and learning agenda. So in January 2009, for example, the Vice Principal for Teaching and Learning created a "Student Writing Working Group" charged with taking an overview of the current situation at Queen Mary, identifying priorities and making recommendations for future work. At the same time, the institution has also formulated a "Statement of Graduate Attributes," which includes a commitment to "developing graduates who use writing for learning and reflection" (QMUL, 2010).

These recent developments suggest a continuing and perhaps increasingly significant role for Thinking Writing at QM, and it is timely that we should have occasion, through the writing of this profile essay, to reflect on the kind of work we predominantly do, and why.

As the TW team has grown, we have been able to extend our range of activities, and these now include funding and supporting departmental working groups and professional development schemes, developing models of co-teaching, and conducting small scale research. This year we have begun to run "Urban Writing Retreats" for staff and postgraduate students, as a way of supporting their practice and productivity whilst encouraging reflection on the writing process and passing on ideas that may be incorporated into teaching. Hoping to enrich our insights into pre-university learning, we have also used small scale funding to work on writing with students and teachers in local schools. As we have done from the beginning, we continue to put on cross-disciplinary exchange of practice fora, but we have moved away from offering short workshops, designed and led by us, taking the view that although they provide some visibility for our ideas, they tend not to be very effective in establishing collaborative relationships over time.[2]

Most fundamentally our work is characterised by an ethnographic orientation; we do not expect to find sufficient meaning in textual objects themselves, but rather take the complex "natural habitat" in which writing occurs as the object of our understanding and activity (Geertz, 1983). Theoretically, this approach draws on insights from UK Academic Literacies work (see Lillis & Scott, 2008, for overview), though we have less focus on individual students than many studies in that field. In practice our holistic/contextual orientation means that, in some cases, our work centres on using writing to explore and express ideas in the subject, while in others it is more concerned with developing ways of improving students' texts, often by focusing on process. We've found that overreliance on the "learning to write/writing to learn" division can be unproductive because it doesn't offer a critique of the "products" students are learning to write and also detracts from the intense learning (shaping) that often needs to go on in writing successfully for a disciplinary reader. For this reason approaches and studies (e.g., Hewings, 2005; Ravelli, 2005) that offer linguistic explanations for perceived qualitative differences amongst student texts offer a useful resource for some of our work. More generally, we view learners as actively constructing their understanding of disciplinary concepts and articulating these through writing; it is through writing (at least in a UK context) that students can begin to participate in the discourse community of their academic discipline (Northedge, 2003).

HOW WE WORK – AN EXAMPLE

BACKGROUND

This section will bring to life the kind of developmental activity that is key to Thinking Writing's work with academic disciplinary staff and departments by presenting a skeleton account of work over the 2009-10 academic year with colleagues in the School of Biological and Chemical Sciences (SBCS). This work picks up on earlier involvement of TW with SBCS and is still evolving as we write. It is fairly characteristic in that it eschews any particular model of writing or writing development, and involves the negotiation of contested beliefs and practices, relating not only to writing but also to the way knowledge is conceived and curricula are designed.

When Sally Mitchell came to QM in 2001, an early meeting with the Head of Biology led to invitations to observe and talk with staff teaching on the Integrated Studies in Biological Sciences module (ISBS). Taught at second and third year level to all students in small tutorial groups, with the majority of academic teachers involved, the module aims to help students make connections across the sub-disciplines of biology. When Sally became involved, however, there was perceived dissatisfaction amongst staff and students, with the former disappointed by the quality of the essays students were producing. A plan was hatched to create a more structured and uniform approach to running tutorials with sequenced reading, writing and discussion activities; this was piloted by a group of volunteer staff. When the overall response was positive, all Biology staff were asked to adopt the approach. It was also decided to redesign a compulsory first year "skills" course, Essential Skills for Biologists (ESB), to introduce more reading and writing tasks. As for ISBS, these tasks, focussed on reasonably general, controversial topics, would be part of work in tutorial groups led by almost every member of the teaching staff. The assumption, incorrect as it turned out, was that all tutors would be comfortable addressing the chosen topics. The speedy development and apparent staff buy-in for the approaches and materials developed for these modules was on the face of it a success for TW. Nonetheless, Sally had reservations; for TW, "writing in the disciplines" implies that writing be fully part and parcel of an integrated curriculum, in which, as Barnett and Coate (2005, p. 56) put it, "disciplinary content" and "disciplinary skills . . . take in each other's washing." Separating the development of skills from the acquisition of disciplinary content and making writing (essays) the subject of the teaching rather than part of a process of wider learning, she felt that the ESB module in particular was at best "semi-integrated" (Warren, 2002) and in TW's terms, therefore, problematic. Once the revised modules were established, however, opportunities for critical re-engagement with TW dwindled and it was some time before Thinking Writing was able to re-engage in detailed discussion about work in Biology.

GETTING BACK INTO CONVERSATION

In summer 2009, however, the School initiated a review of ESB and ISBS and invited TW to participate. Early meetings threw up some key differences in the way TW and disciplinary staff were thinking about the modules.

The perception amongst SBCS staff was that the modules needed to cover more "transferable skills," including critical thinking. On the TW side we were more sceptical, questioning the educational justification for running modules focussing on skills (see North, 2005). In particular we were concerned that these modules were perceived as meeting the School's desire that students "learn to write," whilst simultaneously narrowing the definition of writing to the skills required to "write essays." With writing thus "fixed" in these modules, no attention was being paid to its development and potential uses in other modules; for example, in the production of text types such as lab reports, and for purposes such as developing and checking understanding of disciplinary processes or concepts.

Another concern of SBCS staff was that ESB in the first year should be streamlined and linked more clearly and formally to ISBS in the second and third year—thus emphasising a "vertical" skills development stream through the Schools' degree programmes. Ultimately ESB and ISBS should prepare students for their final year research project, particularly for undertaking an extended literature study. TW had reservations about overemphasising this vertical structure, sensing that the more important integration should be "horizontal;" that is, making links between ESB or ISBS and other modules that students are taking at the same time, particularly as the original purpose of ISBS had been to foster such horizontal orientation. Placing the onus on ESB and ISBS to prepare students for the research in the final year might, we felt, unhelpfully separate out "research skills" from the overall disciplinary development of students—leaving all other courses to be perceived as about "content" alone. The "content" of ESB itself was a further concern—how to find a common topic relevant to all students and staff from the wide range—ecology to microbiology—of specialist subfields in biological sciences.

Some Pivotal Events

The TW team felt we needed a longer involvement with SBCS tutors, in order to better understand their thinking and develop a relationship. So we sought the SBCS staff group's approval for a two-year plan, to work on reviewing the current modules and implementing and evaluating changes. Between October and December 2009 TW staff observed tutorials, had informal chats and formal audio-recorded interviews with staff and students, and collected samples of students' writing. Throughout this period, the TW team shared impressions and exchanged ideas on the best way forward. These discussions and an early analysis of the interview data formed the basis for a short report, proposing changes, which was sent to the SBCS staff group in December.

In this account we focus only on what happened in relation to ESB, leaving out ISBS, where more minor changes were suggested. Key Biology staff referred to are Brendan Curran and Caroline Brennan.

Caroline had made the suggestion that students' learning in ESB would be more active if a Problem Based Learning (PBL) approach were introduced. PBL is widely used in higher education in the UK. In PBL students are presented with "problem scenarios" (Savin-Baden, 2003, p. 2) which they usually work on in groups, deciding what information is needed and how they should go about addressing the problem. Typically these scenarios have no correct answer. Pursuing the PBL idea further, Caroline pointed out that in order to introduce PBL it would be necessary to identify some problems that all staff and students could relate to—a return to the vexed issue of the common topic. As we explored this issue, Caroline mentioned that all Biology students need a good grasp of experimental design; this is essential for their third-year projects and is an area that all staff have expertise in. We proposed therefore that tutors should think about a problem within their field and relevant to work in other first-year modules, present it to students and ask them to think about ways of solving it. The tutor would then guide students' thinking through questioning; e.g., "You want to investigate X, what would you do? What makes a good experiment?" and help students think about interpreting results—"What is this telling you?" To help students think through experimental design, tutors would devise exploratory writing tasks, similar to the current short writing tasks in ESB. Thus, we defined the "common topic" as a way of thinking, rather than a content area.

Following this discussion, TW organised an exchange of practice that gave Caroline the opportunity to present her thinking to colleagues from other disciplines and get their feedback. A further breakthrough occurred when Brendan secured funding to replace some ESB tutorial slots with an e-Forum, giving students opportunities for online group interaction. TW facilitated a meeting between Brendan and Caroline to discuss redesigning the new course, making aspects of experimental design the topic for online writing and discussion tasks. These tasks would begin to build towards the kind of thinking and writing students needed to do for third-year project work, while the new topic would provide an opportunity to move away from the emphasis on essay writing, and to introduce a new more discipline-specific text type, a mini-grant proposal.

At the time of writing this profile essay the proposed changes have been submitted to the SBCS staff group for approval and we will need a further meeting with the Head of School to agree on further TW work with Biology, including detailed planning of the revised module, and evaluation to provide tutors with evidence for future modifications.

Reflections

As our example indicates, the primary focus of TW's work is on supporting the professional development of colleagues involved in teaching and the enhancement of disciplinary teaching, curricula, and assessment. We may be distinct from many of our colleagues in the UK field of staff and educational development in that we use our various theoretically—and empirically—informed understandings of writing to think about issues in teaching and learning. Yet we have in common with this group an interest in understanding how change occurs in educational institutions (Wareing & Elvidge, 2007) and how we can develop thriving collaborative relationships with academic teachers, working towards creating enhanced opportunities for learning at university.

We hope the example illustrates what we have found about effective collaboration: that it requires time to establish relationships with tutors, to establish trust and to understand their concerns and the context in which they work.

Observations, informal and formal interviews with tutors and students, and developing a greater awareness of tutors' teaching contexts through collection of relevant documents (e.g., module descriptions, samples of students' written work) all help us to get a feel for the situation and to recognise the knowledge and expertise of our colleagues in their discipline and as teachers. We expect to challenge and question our colleagues, bringing in alternative understandings and ideas; and we expect to be challenged (about, for example, the practical constraints on teaching in contemporary higher education) and to glimpse (if not fully grasp) new insights into disciplinary thinking. Such partnership work is rarely straightforward, steady or completed, but is open to chance, and characterised by the kinds of stops and starts, twists and turns we experienced with Caroline in identifying a common topic (something we are still not sure will be acceptable to all tutors). The work is also heavily negotiated: in the example, some steps we advised, like a larger programme review, were dismissed as options, but at the same time elements previously unmoveable, like reliance on the essay as a default text for ESB, became more flexible.

Although we regard the 2009-2010 academic year as a positive collaboration with Biology we are aware that its practical outcomes remain uncertain. We have been working with only five SBCS tutors (two most closely), and plans still need to be formulated and presented to the wider staff for agreement. Moreover, as with the earlier design of ESB and ISBS, we will not know how the module structure and materials are actually being interpreted by the approx 25 tutors involved in running small group tutorials. The way in which handed-down teaching ideas and materials are "domesticated" by individual teachers is well acknowledged (Mangubhai et al., 2007) and we try to be aware of this in contributing to their design. It's also a fact that in the frequently changing structure of departments, staff often rotate teaching responsibilities, and the teaching materials and practices that are the result of collaboration with one group of teachers can be differently applied or conceived by new teachers on a course. At times this may happen in ways that are at odds with the original goals of the material or with TW philosophy, but may seem more appropriate for the new teacher or new context.

These insights bring us to the recognition that the virtue of collaboration does not so much lie in the artefacts (modules, materials) it generates, as in the ongoing transactions between individual teachers, students and those like us in the development role (see Peake & Horne, in press; also Cousin, 2008). Locating value here steers us away from a sense of "job done, problem solved" in accounting for our work.

As writing moves up the institutional agenda at QMUL we are a little cautious that its greater visibility in strategies and documents like the Statement of

Graduate Attributes may bring with it reductive demands to "solve the problem" of student writing, endorsing a view of writing as separate from learning more generally (see Mitchell, 2010). At the same time, however, our experience encourages us to be confident of our collaborative, negotiated approach to working with departments, our rejection of single or simple models of writing, and our emphasis instead on the potential for writing to play a highly integrative role in the complex jigsaw of university learning. In the next year or so we will see how the top-down agenda of the institution and the bottom-up practice in which we daily engage begin to marry up, and what adjustments we may need to make.

NOTES

1. A comprehensive account of the early history of Thinking Writing appears in Lisa Ganobcsik Williams' 2006 volume on teaching academic writing in the UK (Mitchell & Evison, 2006).

2. Others have reached similar conclusions. Peters (2009) reports on a qualitative study of staff development providers who report that "formal workshops" have been unsuccessful; Pilkington (2006, p. 304) suggests the cause may be "'workshop overload;"; and Layne et al. *(2002) that workshops are often one-off and "isolated" from the tutor's context, allowing "little interaction with peers."*

REFERENCES

Barnett, R., & Coate, K. (2005). *Engaging the curriculum in higher education.* Berkshire: SHRE and Open University Press.

Cousin, G. (2008). Threshold concepts: Old wine in new bottles. In R. Land, J. Meyer, & J. Smith (Eds.), *Threshold concepts in the disciplines.* Oxford: Routledge Falmer.

Geertz, C. (1983). *Local knowledge: Further essays in interpretive anthropology.* New York: Basic Books.

Hewings, A (2005). Developing discipline-specific writing: An analysis of undergraduate geography essays. In L.J. Ravelli & R. A. Ellis (Eds.), *Analysing academic writing: Contextualised frameworks* (pp. 131-152). London: Continuum.

Layne, J., Froyd, J., Morgan, J., & Kenimer, A. (2002, month?) Faculty learning communities. 32nd Annual Frontiers in Education Conference, 2002. F1A-13 to F1A-18. Retrieved from http://citeseerx.ist.psu.edu/viewdoc/download?doi=10.1.1.20.4847&rep=rep1&type=pdf

Lillis, T. & Scott, M. (2008). Defining academic literacies research: Issues of epistemology, ideology and strategy. *Journal of Applied Linguistics, 4*(1), 5-32.

Mangubhai, F., Marland P., Dashwood, A., & Son, J. (2007). Framing communicative language teaching for better teacher understanding. *Issues in Educational Research, 17.* Retrieved from http://www.iier.org.au/iier17/mangubhai.html

Mitchell, S. & Evison, A. (2006). Exploiting the potential of writing for educational change at Queen Mary, University of London. In L. Ganobcsik-Williams (Ed.), *Teaching academic writing in UK higher education* (pp. 68-84). Basingstoke: Palgrave Macmillan.

Mitchell, S (2010). Now you don't see it; now you do: Writing made visible in the university. *Arts and Humanities in Higher Education, 9*(2), 133-148.

Northedge, A. (2003). Rethinking teaching in the context of diversity. *Teaching in Higher Education, 8*(1), 17-32.

North, S. (2005). Different values, different skills? A comparison of essay writing by students from arts and science backgrounds. *Studies in Higher Education, 30*(5), 517-533.

Peake, K. & Horne, D. (2011). Writing hazards. In M. Deane & P. O'Neill (Eds.), *Writing in the Disciplines.* London: Palgrave MacMillan.

Peters, J. (2009). What is the purpose of a University CPD Framework? In M. Laycock & L. Shrives (Eds.), *Embedding CPD in higher education* (pp. 45-50). SEDA Paper 123.

Pilkington, R. (2006). Supporting lecturers to improve essay assessment. In C. Rust (Ed.), *Improving student learning through assessment* (pp. 295-307). Oxford: Oxford Brookes University, Oxford Centre for Staff and Learning Development.

QMUL Graduate Attributes Project. (2011). Retrieved from http://www.qmul.ac.uk/gacep/

Ravelli, L. (2005). Signalling the organisation of written texts: Hyper-themes in management and history essays. In L. J. Ravelli & R. A. Ellis (Eds.), *Analysing academic writing: Contextualised frameworks* (pp. 104-130). London: Continuum.

Savin-Baden, M. (2003). *Facilitating problem-based learning: Illuminating perspectives.* Maidenhead, Berkshire, UK: SRHE and Open University Press.

Wareing, S., & Elvidge, E. (2007). Educational development and strategic planning. In B. Tomlinson (Ed.), *Leading educational change* (pp. 21-28). London: SEDA Special.

Warren, D. (2002). Curriculum design in the context of widening participation in higher education. *Arts and Humanities in Higher Education, 1*(1), 85-99.

CHAPTER 19.
THE TEACHING OF WRITING SKILLS IN FRENCH UNIVERSITIES: THE CASE OF THE UNIVERSITÉ STENDHAL, GRENOBLE III

By Francoise Boch and Catherine Frier
Université Stendhal, Grenoble (France)

The article is divided into three parts. The first recounts the evolution of the teaching of writing skills in French universities since the 1980s and shows how university traditions in this matter have been subject to a profound shift in recent years. The second part gives a brief presentation of the Université Stendhal in Grenoble, which was required as of 2010, like all other universities, to put in place classes focusing on writing skills. Finally, the third part seeks to analyze the effects of a pedagogical measure that has been tested over the past three years at the Université Stendhal in the context of a class in the methodology of academic writing for first-year linguistics students. The pedagogical methods put into practice intend to bring together knowledge (academic learning), expertise (command of written skills), and interpersonal skills (construction of a point of view), whilst at the same time working both on engaging with the subject and respecting standards, and on graphic reason and graphic creation.

THE CHANGING FACES OF THE FRENCH UNIVERSITY

In France, the question of teaching writing skills at university level is relatively recent.[1] Until the 1990s, the teaching of writing skills was considered to be the remit of primary school (6-11 years old) and collège (12-15 years old). Pupils were supposed to have mastered all elements of writing, in particular the formal aspects (spelling and grammar), by the time they entered lycée education (15-18 years old). Thus, implicitly, it was assumed that students arrived at university with the requisite skills in this domain.

From the 1980s onwards, the situation in France slowly began to change.[2] Politically, the national aim was henceforth to attain 80% success at the baccalauréat[3] (end of secondary education diploma providing entrance to university, on a non-selective basis) in order to raise the level of education of the country within a more and more competitive global scene. In parallel, the socio-economic situation, characterized by a rise in unemployment, was pushing young people into a race for qualifications. This led to a massive increase in numbers of students attending university (referred to as the "democratization" of "mass" higher education), which in turn entailed a substantial modification of an audience that had hitherto been fairly homogenous. Henceforth, universities (in the Humanities and Social Sciences in particular) welcomed students from all backgrounds, including the less advantaged.

Yet from the mid 1990s onwards a decline in numbers at public universities began and continued in a worrying manner until 2008, with holders of the baccalauréat seeming to prefer selective vocational programmes. In addition, another process has been accelerating since 2000 and causing a profound shift in the demographics of higher education as it contributes to the dwindling numbers at university. The Grandes Ecoles,[4] formerly reserved for training the nation's elite, are attracting more and more young people from the middle and higher classes, who are eschewing university in favour of the classes préparatoires which offer training for the entrance exams to these prestigious institutions. In a context strongly affected by the economic crisis, there is a general desire to choose the right strategy for success. The sacrosanct university degree no longer affords sufficient protection against the soaring unemployment that affects first and foremost those in the 18-25 age group. Furthermore, the progressive withdrawal of state backing of public services (since 2008, government policy has indicated the aim of the non-renewal of one civil servant post in two [Conseil des Ministres, 2007]) has perhaps contributed to the deterioration of the image of universities in public opinion. That said, the most recent figures available would seem to indicate a rise in numbers for the academic year 2009/2010 (MESR- DGESIP, 2010).

In parallel, the national curriculum for French in primary and secondary school education has been far heavier since 1995 than was previously the case, and this goes hand-in-hand with a significant drop in contact hours given over to this subject. In other words, teachers are being asked to do far more in far less time. In such conditions, teachers of French in the collèges cannot have the same expectations regarding the normative correction of written work.

Since 2000, we, as researchers in linguistics and writing, have seen a growing awareness of the fact that students reach university with incomplete written skills in French. Indeed, the new students are often very surprised by the importance that is suddenly given to the linguistic aspect of their studies and the pressing necessity to improve their level. At the same time, academics, who often have little training in teaching writing skills, tend to consider that it is not up to the university to take this side of things in hand, and that it should be dealt with beforehand. However, failure rates, relatively substantial in the first years at university (one student in two fails their first year, according to MESR, 2011) have begun to call these assumptions into question. It is undoubtedly the implementation of the "Réussite en Licence" or 'Success in Undergraduate Degrees' project[5] by the Ministry of Higher Education in 2008[6] that has placed the question of written skills in Higher Education in the public eye, whereas previously it had remained in the background.

Due to a sudden and unexpected influx of funds, this highly publicised government project led to a large number of pedagogical initiatives within universities, with a view to better supporting students entering higher education, in particular through a substantial tutorial system. At least twenty of these universities chose to place the onus on the question of written expression and in particular upon spelling, which in France has traditionally been the locus of debates concerning written ability. This small revolution, echoed in the press at the start of the 2010/2011 academic year,[7] led to different innovative pedagogical experiments according to the university, with a general view to allowing students to better master the written work that they would be required to produce.

At the Université Stendhal, which will be our focus here, the question of teaching writing skills is somewhat older and grounded in research carried out from 2000 onwards by a team of lecturers in linguistics and pedagogy[8] (linguistic knowledge and skills, usage and representations) in a pedagogical perspective centered upon the writing subject, enabling the learner's relationship to writing to be taken into account and helped to evolve. Before outlining one of the measures put in place by this team as part of the "plan réussite en licence," we shall briefly describe the institution in question.

THE CASE OF THE UNIVERSITÉ STENDHAL, GRENOBLE III

Located in the Rhône-Alpes region (South-East France), the Université Stendhal is a medium-sized institution (approximately 12,000 students) that offers programmes grounded in the humanities: foreign languages and culture, linguistics, literature, and communication studies. Although, in accordance with institutional expectations on a national level, this university seeks to diversify and consolidate the professional prospects of its graduates, the skills envisaged by the study programmes remain traditionally strongly linked with written skills. Students enrolled in such "humanities-orientated" universities as the Université Stendhal are often destined for teaching (primary or secondary education, and language teaching, including French as a Foreign Language), translation, speech therapy, journalism or business communication. In these different domains the concours (competitive entrance examinations for training programmes, or for obtaining the professional qualification in question) are generally highly selective, and written skills are an essential criterion albeit a criterion that corresponds to different categories depending on the concours. In particular, "written skills" refers to the formal elements of writing (overvalued in France in comparison with other countries: in France spelling mistakes are particularly badly viewed) and the generic dimension of texts. Students in France are trained from the lycée onwards in the production of canonical academic writing such as essays or summaries.[9]

At the Université Stendhal in Grenoble, there was a desire to take this question of training in writing skills seriously, by offering courses allowing the combination of work on language (spelling and grammar) and the implication of the writer, through a measure focusing on a genre rarely used at university: academic fiction.

AN INNOVATIVE MEASURE: KNOWLEDGE BUILDING THROUGH THE WRITING OF ACADEMIC FICTION

THEORETICAL FRAMEWORK

In this section we shall outline and analyse the effects of a pedagogical measure that has been tested over the past three years at the Université Stendhal in the context of a class in the methodology of academic writing. This measure originates in our team's research in reading/writing practices as modes of knowledge building in Higher Education. This field has already given rise to numerous publications,[10] particularly in linguistics and didactics. This research places the onus on the difficulties facing young students when they are first confronted with specialist texts in their disciplines, difficulties that are essentially of two types:

- Difficulty in approaching the "theoretical knowledge," in integrating and reconstructing notions and concepts in a precise manner, in problema-

tizing, in objectivising knowledge and in including the words of others in their own discourse (Kara, 2004).
- Difficulty in taking up a point of view (Rinck, 2004) and in linking theory and practical experience in the field (Frier, 2004).

This research also focuses upon the heuristic function of the written text and on the reflexive dimension of writing practice that encourages knowledge building and the "written codification of knowledge" specific to "graphic reason" (Goody, 1979).

In this context, "graphic reason" is seen as the best tool for implementing the systematic classification of reality that then allows abstraction, distance, and scientific objectivity. Consequently, non-reflexive writing such as narration, viewed with some suspicion, is sometimes seen as antonymic to academic discourse. This no doubt explains at least in part that such texts are rarely worked upon at university.

However, recently another side of didactics is more specifically focusing upon the role played by narrative in the building of knowledge, and in particular of academic knowledge: in other words, the didactic function of narrative in different disciplines (Reuter, 2007). Indeed, studies of various horizons call into question the restrictive vision of scientific knowledge and how it is built, by giving a place to narrative in academic teaching.

Following Bruner's (2005) seminal works, we can formulate the following hypotheses:
- "Rational" thinking, imagination, and experience work in perpetual interaction in the process of elaborating academic knowledge.
- In order for knowledge to be appropriated, it must be made to have resonance with personal experience and understanding: a necessary link must be made between the singular and the generic (two spaces that are usually hermetically detached in the context of formal learning).
- It is by activating "ordinary creativity" (Chabanne & Dunas, 1999) that the mechanism of appropriating academic knowledge, in all its complexity and diversity, is set off.

The Pedagogical Project Put in Place[11]

The project in question is aimed at students enrolled in the first year of Language Sciences in a class on methodology of academic writing that entails 48 hours of contact time, divided into 24 sessions of 2 hours. This class is organized around 6 themes (The Origins of Language; The Acquisition of Language; Birth and Transformations of Writing; Natural Language Processing; Language and Deafness). The pedagogical methods put into practice intend to bring together knowledge (building of knowledge in an academic field), expertise (command of written skills) and interpersonal skills (demystifying theoretical knowledge and fostering confidence, appropriation of knowledge by the subject and construction of a point of view). Above and beyond these aims, the intention is also to combat the huge writerly insecurity at the beginning of undergraduate studies at university, to bring out the "unrecognized knowledge" (Penloup, 2007) of our students, to encourage their creativity and to get them to engage in and through writing on the path to knowledge.

Within this new pedagogical project, the text to be produced includes fiction (invented story) and narrative (situations, fictional characters or staging of the protagonists of different debates) and is thus supposed to entertain the reader. However, it is also a narrative showcasing ideas, a point of view on a question, an academic problem, as well as the fictional aspect. It therefore also has to inform the reader: the academic information has to be presented in different forms, and within this piece of writing extracts of academic writing are to be found: fragments of texts (quotes), notions, reformulated ideas, arguments, theoretical trends, names of authors, dates, etc., are inserted as the story unfolds. These two requirements (entertaining and informing) have to find a balance in the text. We chose to prepare students for, and support them in, the writing of this fictional text using writing workshops.

Promising Results[12]

The analysis of the corpus of fictional pieces gathered in the context of this project (2008-2011) shows that academic fiction is largely conducive to a tangible and solid evolution of the written abilities of students, if they are offered the correct support throughout the process. Each in its own way, these fictional narratives interweave with more or less competence the elements considered to be objective parts of academic knowledge (definitions, authors' names, theories, dates, etc.), the fictional elements supposed to provide a context for the question asked by the text, and elements of argumentation (point of view put forward). The systematic presence of these three intentions signifies, in our view, a considerable evolution of the abilities of the students who authored these texts, insofar as this capacity to navigate between different stances in language is progressively constructed through the texts produced throughout the year. The appendix includes some commented extracts from a text entitled "At the Origin of Writing," which illustrate this ability.

After completing this work, the students no longer write in the same way. Engaged over the long term both on an individual and collective level in a ritualized project of training/support in writing, they progressively become aware of the formal, but also enunciative and textual stakes of their productions. Paradoxically, it is through a psycho-affective implication in their writing that they manage to distance themselves from it in intellectual terms. The final quality of the texts is often surprising, both regarding creativity and the appropriation of academic knowledge. This is why this gamble of working in parallel on both engaging with the subject and on respecting norms, on both graphic reason and graphic creation, seems to have paid off in part within the context of this experiment.

These initial results need, of course, to be both qualified and examined in more depth. Narratives cannot be seen as a miracle solution that could allow students' erroneous representations, academic approximations, or methodological problems to be erased. However, it could be said that the implicational function of the narrative (Reuter, 2007) that allows and encourages the writing subject's engagement with his text makes it an efficient tool for bringing to the fore representations that can then be formalized, considered on a conscious level, and discussed with a view to possible evolution.

Our results show that the narrative, by linking the universe of concepts to that of the subject's affect, sensory perception, and dreams, contributes to combining "graphic creation" and "graphic reason." It generates emotions, sensations, and ideas all at once. This is why it should find a legitimate place alongside the other genres of writing used in building and assessing knowledge at university: by putting thought into movement, the narrative creates the right kind of chemistry for producing results and promoting discovery.

SUMMARY

The project described above is an example of a pedagogical initiative that has recently proven its worth. This initiative has become part of the curriculum for Language Sciences degrees. Moreover, our team is now writing a textbook for French teachers who would like to implement effective literacy pedagogy in their classes. However, in France this kind of initiative remains relatively marginal and localized. In the absence of training centres in teaching writing skills—unlike many other Western countries—and of national programmes in the subject, the French university system is not yet ready to respond in an organized fashion to students' weaknesses in the field of written work. Although descriptive analyses of students' written production abound in the emerging field of academic literacy, these only rarely give rise to carefully thought out pedagogical actions, which, moreover, remain on a local level and are not shared. We would therefore argue strongly in favour of the training of future higher education practitioners—training that remains insufficiently developed in France—to take this dimension into account. It is undoubtedly through training that pedagogical practice in academic writing and literacy has a chance of progressing.

NOTES

1. This article is drawn from a research project entitled "Ecrits Universitaires: inventaire, pratiques, modèles" funded by the Agence Nationale pour la Recherche 2007-2011, theme "Apprentissages" ; Project leaders: I. Delcambre (Théodile-Cirel) and F. Boch (Lidilem).

2. Between 1981 and 1997, the proportion of 18-24 year-olds enrolled in public higher education rose from 9,6% to 20% (INRP, 2005 :9).

3. This aim was declared in 1985 by the Minister of Education of the time, J.P. Chevènement.

4. The "*Grandes écoles*" are a French specificity. These highly selective establishments accept a very small number of students. The grandes écoles train high-level engineers and managers, but also specialists in art, literature and humanities. The programmes within the grandes écoles and specialist institutions generally take place over five years, including two initial years of training for the entrance examinations to these institutions. The very principle of the grandes écoles is controversial. They are criticized in particular for being a tool for social reproduction. Indeed, although the majority of grandes écoles are public and free (with the exception of those in business studies), the funding allocated per student by the state is considerably greater than at university, and the students in question tend in general to be from higher social classes: a sort of "back-to-front redistribution" to use Lebègue & Walter's (2008) phrase.

5. A *Licence* is the equivalent of an undergraduate degree: the diploma achieved, in the French system, after three years of university education.

6. The Minister for Teaching and Research "Valérie Pécresse outlined her pluriannual project for success in undergraduate degrees with a view to cutting in half the failure rates in the first year at university. Provided with 730 million Euros funding in total for 2008-2012, a 43% raise in funds in five years, this project makes provision for personalized support to be provided to students: five extra hours of weekly pedagogical contact per student, as well as a Faculty advisor for each year group, tutorials, etc." (Government press release: http://www.enseignementsup-recherche.gouv.fr).

7. Many major French national newspapers and magazines (such as Le Point, Télérama and Le Monde, etc.) and television channels (regional and national) devoted a feature or a programme to the question of the teaching of French language (and in particular

spelling) at university.

8. Laboratoire LIDILEM: linguistique et didactique des langues étrangères et maternelles, cf. http://w3.u-grenoble3.fr/lidilem/labo/web/presentation.php.

9. On the question of the written genres worked upon at French universities, cf. Delcambre & Reuter (2010).

10. Cf. Boch, Laborde-Milaa & Reuter (2004) for a summary.

11. Inspired by Sauzeau & Triquet (2004).

12. These results have given rise to a more detailed publication, cf. Frier & Chartier (2009).

REFERENCES

Boch, F., Laborde-Milaa, I., Reuter, Y. (Eds.). (2004). *Pratiques, les ecrits universitaires*. Metz : CRESEF.
Bruner, J. (2005). Pourquoi nous racontons- nous des histoires ? Le récit au fondement de la culture et de l'identité individuelle, Paris: **Agora-Pocket**.
Chabanne, J. P., Dunas, A. (1999). La créativité « ordinaire »: Penser et apprendre, c'est créer les formes singulières de sa pensée et de son savoir, *Le français aujourd'hui, 127,* 17-24.
Conseil des Ministres. (2007). *Communiqué du 20 juin 2007.* Retrieved from http://www.gouvernement.fr/
Delcambre, I., & Reuter, Y. (2010). The French didactics approach to writing, from elementary school to university. In C. Bazerman, et al. (Eds.), *Traditions of writing research* (pp. 17-30). New York and London: Routledge, Taylor & Francis.
Frier, C., & Chartier, A. (2009). Petite fabrique de la connaissance: Aborder le savoir scientifique en se racontant des histoires, *Pratiques, 143-144,* 154-168.
Goody, J. (1979). *La Raison Graphique, la domestication de la pensée sauvage.* Paris: Éditions de Minuit.
INRP (2005). *L'enseignement supérieur sous le regard des chercheurs. Les dossiers de la veille.* Retrieved from http://rsu.afev.org/pdf/ens_sup_regard_chercheurs.pdf
Kara, M. (2004). Pratiques de la citation dans les mémoires de maîtrise. *Pratiques, 121-122,* 111-142.
Lebègue, T., & Walter, E. (2008). *Grandes écoles: La fin d'une exception française.* Paris: Calmann-Levy.
Ministère de l'Enseignement Supérieur et de la Recherche (MESR) (2011). *Plan pour la réussite en licence: 730 millions d'euros d'ici 2012.* Retrieved from

http://www.enseignementsup-recherche.gouv.fr/cid20651/plan-pour-la-reussite-en-licence-730-millions-d-euros-d-ici-2012.html

MESR-DGESIP/DGRI SIES (2010), *Les effectifs d'étudiants dans le supérieur en 2009: La plus forte progression depuis 1993*. Note d'Information Enseignement supérieur & Recherche 10.08. Retrieved from http://media.enseignementsup-recherche.gouv.fr/file/2010/83/3/NIMESR1008_158833.pdf

Penloup, M. C. (Ed.). (2007). *Les connaissances ignores: Approche pluridisciplinaire de ce que savent les élèves*. Paris: INRP.

Reuter, Y. (2007). Récits et disciplines scolaires. Présentation du numéro. *Pratiques, 133-134*, 3-12.

Rinck, F. (2004). Construire la problématique d'un rapport de stage: Les difficultés d'étudiants du second cycle. *Pratiques, 121-122*, 93-110.

Sauzeau, C., and Triquet, E. (2006). L'atelier d'écriture d'un récit de fiction scientifique: Un dispositif interdisciplinaire pour un nouveau genre? Actes du 9 e Colloque international de l'AIRDF, 26-28 août 2004 [CD-ROM]. Québec: AIRDF.

APPENDIX: TEXT BY JULIE, A FIRST YEAR STUDENT IN LANGUAGE SCIENCES

The heroine of the story is a student who has been imprisoned following a raid and who, from the depth of her cell, is trying to understand what happened: who betrayed her and why. However, her efforts are in vain as, deprived of everything, and in particular of writing, she is unable to organise her ideas: "without a medium, I couldn't manage to sort out my thoughts. My anger got in the way of my ideas, and so did the fatigue. I needed to set things out, sort through what I could remember and structure my memory." The heroine's quest is thus to be able to write because writing alone can help her to find her past, to think and to move forward. The situation-problem raised by this narrative is thus clearly identified from the outset and placed in a double perspective: the question of finding a way to write and of recovering the primitive source of writing.

The explicative aim of the text alternates between two levels of response to these issues:

1) the first is grounded in matter and in reverie: "*For several days, I had been mechanically using my spoon to etch small vertical lines into the soft wood of the old plank that served as a bed for me, so as to count the days and try and regain some points of reference in time. I had done this without thinking. The*

primary graphic scratching was the only way for me to occupy my hands and my mind . . . I imagined that I was in a prehistoric cave, scratching small mammoths and sketching out the first steps of writing . . . ."

From a psychoanalytical point of view, the resonance of this extract with the notion of a return to limbo, a return to the original womb that precedes rational thought, can be underlined.

2) The second level of response refers to objective knowledge: *"I suddenly remembered a text by Jack Goody, an English anthropologist who, following his imprisonment in Italy during the Second World War, had written a book about writing. I seemed to recall that he referred to the difficulty of thinking and bringing together ideas without the medium of writing. In "The Consequence of Literacy," he had explained the veritable intellectual mutilation that was the impossibility of reading or writing . . . I had the remedy for my torture as an erudite!"*

These two extracts illustrate the way this text regularly shifts between a metaphorical, dreamlike thinking, grounded in the material nature of the elements (here soil) and a more rational mode of thinking, working on the basis of stable reference points (dates, author's name, title of book, concepts) and of objective facts. Hence the idea of obtaining some soil, in secret, on the daily outing in the prison courtyard so as to make slabs of clay from it in order to write: *"I threw myself to the ground on my stomach and began to scratch away at the moist soil so as to stuff large handfuls of it into the pockets of my trousers and coat. . . . With the end of my bent spoon, I implanted my alphabet into substance. . . . I felt like a modern Sumerian in Mesopotamia, engraving my clay tablets in 3500 BC!"*

The ending of the narrative excels at this intertwining and contrives to create an almost inextricable mixture of objective arguments imbued with concrete experience and traces of the initial reverie: *"And so I began again my cuneiform mixtures with each of the heaps I had kept under my bed, and once the tablets were full and dry I hid them beneath my covers, safe from harm. Each grapheme rooted in the earth freed my mind a little further and made room for a larger reflection. I could list names, reformulate my notes, and remember details without further cluttering my memory . . . Everything became more visual at last and far clearer. I could easily understand how our "civilisation of the written word" had been an intellectual leap for mankind—I was experiencing this revolution firsthand! The long Darwinian trains of my thought could now be uncoupled and recoupled on command. It was as if I were putting my brain in a computer and printing everything that was inside, so as to then be able to erase from my memory what was now before my eyes, leaving twice as much space as before! I had understood the technology of words. . . but above all, the name of the traitor now sprung to mind with clarity."*

CHAPTER 20.
LITERACY DEVELOPMENT PROJECTS INITIATING INSTITUTIONAL CHANGE

By Gerd Bräuer and Katrin Girgensohn
University of Education, Freiburg, and European University Viadrina Frankfurt/Oder (Germany)

In this chapter, two literacy development projects will be introduced as a means of initiating institutional development with regard to the role of writing in higher education and beyond. In the first portrait Katrin Girgensohn presents Gerd Bräuer's model of literacy management. Through Gerd's eyes, she will shed light on the role of a specialist, called "literacy manager," whose profile is taking shape in educational and professional settings as someone to initiate and facilitate substantial change not only in the daily practice of writers and readers but in the literacy culture of entire institutions. In the second portrait Gerd Bräuer presents Katrin Girgensohn as a pioneer of literacy management and her model of autonomous academic writing groups in Germany's higher education. Through Katrin's eyes, he will shed light especially on the role of the faculty and the writing center in facilitating such groups of writers.

PORTRAIT 1: GERD BRÄUER (AS PRESENTED BY KATRIN GIRGENSOHN)

When Gerd, who grew up in the former East Germany and had also lived for several years in Prague (Czech Republic), joined the University of Oregon in 1992 as a post-doctoral fellow, he had no clue about what literacy management could mean. As a matter of fact, at that time he had barely started to grasp a notion of writing pedagogy. As he says himself, looking back, at his research on US writing pedagogy during the early 1990s, writing pedagogy for him at that time was merely teaching methods and techniques related to creative writing.

Having worked on a PhD thesis in the late 1980s on the German dramatist Bertolt Brecht, he adapted Brecht's strategy of handling writing in the different literary genres as a means of constructing knowledge for his teaching in the field of German studies. Already at the time of his PhD thesis (1989), Gerd understood writing, based on Bertolt Brecht's aesthetic concept (Brecht, 1957), as a mode of learning that applies to the act of text production as well as to the act of receiving texts though the audience. While Brecht imagined this collaborative learning between those who write and those who read/watch as part of the theatre as a truly educational institution, Gerd envisioned this learning for schools and universities. With this vision he went to the US, where he hoped to learn from the rich experience of Anglo-Saxon writing pedagogy that he had started to encounter through his academic research.

It took Gerd about ten years of work and two monographs, one on US writing pedagogy (1996), one on adapting Anglo-Saxon writing pedagogy for the existing writing culture in the German-speaking countries (1998), before his ideas received some attention in his home country. In 2000, he was asked by a small university of education (Freiburg/Germany) to set up the first writing center in European teacher education. From the beginning of his work in Freiburg, his main focus was on "training the trainers" so that the changes he suggested for the role of writing in teacher education would trickle down the educational pyramid and trigger similar changes in primary and secondary education. Early he saw the need for providing knowledge to student teachers and in-service teachers with regard to strengthening sustainability of outcomes of individual projects on writing and reading. When Gerd started a certificate program for writing coaches at the Freiburg Writing Center in 2003, he not only wanted to foster the development of active writers and readers in various educational settings, but also intensify the impact of the many creative ideas of individual instructors in higher education and in professional training.

Despite the more than 100 graduates of the certificate program so far, he today sees the limitations of training that focuses solely on coaching writers. Too often in the past years he witnessed his graduates struggling and reaching their limits of professional development quickly, simply because they didn't know enough about how to initiate institutional change toward redefining the role of writing as a mode of learning instead of a mere mode of knowledge reproduction and presentation. He started to understand that these writing coaches also needed specific expertise in how to initiate and set up writing programs and/or writing centers.

He, therefore, coined the term literacy management (Bräuer, 2011) and conceptualized a specific training for literacy managers. Based on Gerd's description in our interview, literacy management aims for the optimization of the individual handling of information and of the flow of texts between writers and readers within and beyond institutional settings and local cultures of literacy. The International Literacy Management Consortium, initiated by Gerd and others, sees literacy management as an "emerging professional field at the intersection of literacy research, pedagogy of reading and writing, instructional design, and institutional development" (see homepage of http://www.international-literacy-management.org).

From my own experience as a writing pedagogue in secondary and higher education, I can clearly see the demand for literacy management is developing rapidly due to a profound transition from the so-called information age to the so-called knowledge age that is being initiated and shaped by a growing variety of literacies and the specific demands of each of them. As with labeling of any other emerging professional field, terminology to describe the specific features of literacy management has not been established yet. Therefore, different names, such as knowledge worker, writing coach, or educational analyst are currently in use synonymously to speak of the same area of interest.

So, what do literacy managers in Gerds's vision actually do? He says the contour of a field of practice becomes more alive when listing individual tasks and highlighting those that carve out a specific profile of action. Gerd sees literacy managers juggle the potential, demands, and challenges of the different literacies such as "computer literacy," "digital literacy," "multimodal literacies" (Jewitt & Kress, 2003), "visual literacies" (ibid.), and critical literacy in order to solve problems with efficient handling of information by individuals within the larger framework of schools, universities, companies, and/or organizations. For that, as Gerd tells me in his interview, literacy managers

1. Analyze the current state of both handling information in general and specifically in text production, distribution, and reception, including visual, audio, spatial, behavioral aspects of forms of representation of meaning, within their home institution and beyond;
2. Assess the quality of the latter processes and try to determine a price tag for any loss of information and/or understanding of texts in order to quantify the urgency of change;
3. Identify the current needs of the main stakeholders with regard to in-house communication and the flow of information beyond;
4. Develop concepts and prototypes for optimizing the management of literacies within the organization;
5. Test and assess procedures, methods, materials, and training programs in order to further develop and successfully implement them;
6. Initiate necessary structural change within the institution and facilitate steering groups in this matter.

(For applications of these principles in various German-speaking institutions, see the Bräuer essay in this volume.)

Gerd wants us to read this list also as an overview of expertise needed to support livelong learners in understanding and actively living local and global differences. In this process, literacy managers make strategic use of the differences each individual involved contributes to an institution. This way of seeing opens up not only new opportunities to understand one's own way of writing, reading, and handling of information, but to optimize existing literacy resources of an entire institution. Gerd in our conversation also stressed the role of literacy managers as change agents in shaping local cultures of readers and writers who interact with global practices. The list provided by Gerd above can also be read as an overall procedure in managing literacies. This procedure is based on the key principles of instructional design: (a) Analysis of learner characteristics and the learning environment; (b) Design of learning objectives and instructional approach; (c) Development of instructional frameworks and training materials (prototype); (d/e) Implementation and evaluation of the prototype in action.

As a result of this overall procedure the following tasks could be performed as part of literacy management projects: establishment of writing/reading centers; development of literacy programs and workshops for primary/secondary schools, colleges, and universities, and professional training; establishment of (e-) portfolio systems; conducting in-house staff/faculty training; development of self-learning material for students and instructors; research, assessment, and optimization of existing literacy processes in the institution; constructing an overall literacy culture in the institution that is beneficial for peer feedback and tutoring; development and testing of diagnostic procedures, methods, and materials.

To perform those tasks successfully, literacy managers need specialized training that Gerd several years ago had hoped to establish at the University of Education in Freiburg. However, realizing a vision of this scope requires patience and persistence, and the willingness to work within an institution's constraints. Gerd's experience at the University of Education/Freiburg illustrates typical challenges a literacy manager faces and offers an example of slow but steady progress.

To Gerd, the writing center at Education/Freiburg still plays a limited role in the institution. While he envisions the writing center as a place of instructing, coaching, and facilitating writers and readers from different literacy domains, the university still sees the center fulfilling the service function of providing hands-on help to beginning students in their status as rather inexperienced academic writers—despite the wide range of projects, publications, and expertise that resulted from the effort of the writing center team.

In order to make sense of this limitation, it is important to provide some information on the University of Education Freiburg, which is located in the South-western corner of Germany. The region of Freiburg borders France to the west and Switzerland to the south. The city of about 250,000 inhabitants is the home to a large research university and several small professional universities, one of them being the University of Education. There, teacher education for primary and secondary schools and professional training is offered. Like the other small professional schools in town, the University of Education puts a lot of effort into profiling itself against the large university in Freiburg. Instead of focusing this effort on what is known and performed best here—professional training—this college tries to raise attention with large-scale pedagogical research projects carried out by a few established faculty. Any entity of the University of Education that would not be able to carry out, for whatever reason, such large-scale research projects is doomed to stick to a rather limited profile of a service institution.

Nevertheless, the center has achieved a vital place in the university's culture. The writing center itself is a rather small but attractive space right next to the cafeteria and frequented daily by the majority of students and faculty. When Gerd accepted the university's invitation to develop a writing center in 2001, he urged the institution to provide this central location, which he saw as urgently necessary in order to get a new and mainly unknown entity such as a writing center off the ground. Gerd remembers his first day on campus, when the provost for teaching showed him around in order to find a decent place for the writing center:

> After the provost took me to two far-away locations on the edge of campus, which he suggested to me as possible places for the writing center, he was about to take me for lunch to the cafeteria in the heart of the campus. I spotted a room of about 50 qm, with all glass walls, right next to the entrance to the cafeteria. To my curious question about what this room was for, he answered with hesitation in his voice that is was reserved for staff meetings of the president's office. When I told him this would be the ideal place for getting a writing center started successfully due to its central location and its transparency, I noticed his body stiffening and he didn't comment at all. The next day, he called to tell me that the university president agreed to assign the room to the writing center. I was in awe and, at that time, very hopeful to also successfully move writing more toward the center of academic life in the years to come (Bräuer, 2002).

Nevertheless, what seemed promising in the beginning wasn't easy in the process of defining the role of the writing center beyond a "fixit shop" (North 1987). It was not before the success of an EU-sponsored project called "Scriptorium," which Gerd directed from 2005 until 2008 (see also Bräuer, 2009; and Bräuer, this volume) that the writing center gained substantial attention among the university's faculty. This project brought together teams of literacy specialists from eight European countries who developed a modularized training program for student teachers and in-service teachers in reading and writing development and support. As a result, high school writing/reading centers appeared in Poland, Denmark, Finland, Italy, Ireland, the Netherlands, Switzerland, and Germany. Training materials in the first languages of these countries as well as in French and English can be accessed through an e-learning platform (http://www.scriptorium-project.org) where teachers gather not only for in-house workshops but also exchange ideas and experience across the educational pyramid and across national borders.

With this training program in place, Gerd had hoped to lay the foundation for further steps in institutional development at the University of Education, Freiburg. The university, unfortunately, was neither able on a financial basis nor willing in conceptual terms to move on toward a full-fledged WAC and WID concept. Writing training remained isolated in German studies and in the writing center, although the latter instituted additional certificate courses on journalistic education and on portfolio instruction in secondary education. These courses are sometimes team-taught by colleagues from the German studies department, foreign languages department, and the departments of education and psychology. Gerd still hopes that this interdisciplinary effort will, in the near future, result in a more substantial change with regard to a more central role of writing in all parts of teacher education in Freiburg.

Symptomatic of this very slow pace in institutional development is what has been happening since 2007 with regard to implementing portfolios as an emerging genre of academic teaching and learning and an alternative form of individual and institutional assessment. Despite the fact that the university sponsored the development of a concept and testing of a prototype, the institution is currently not ready to engage in all consequences necessary to successfully implement a college-wide ePortfolio system; i.e., mandating a steering group by the university president. While some changes have already been made to the exam rules and guidelines, the university was not willing yet to make a firm commitment to a well-working ePortfolio web application. While recent portfolio research (e.g., Baumgartner et al., 2009) does provide enough evidence and guidance on the best digital applications, this research is not being discussed freely and openly among the faculty. The part of the administrative structure that is responsible for e-learning follows closely the recommendations provided by a central committee for all teacher colleges in the state of Baden-Württemberg. Since the discourse of this committee is not communicated openly with local faculty members, many of them feel disempowered and, therefore, discouraged to contribute to finding a solution that would meet the real needs with regard to ePortfolio in Freiburg's teacher training.

A similar situation can be witnessed with regard to further developing the literacy management approach established already some years ago with the Scriptorium training program. The development of a necessary MA program on literacy management has been postponed indefinitely and in the meantime Gerd has moved his initiative to the Zurich University of Applied Sciences in Winterthur (ZHAW) (Switzerland), a place much more open to substantial institutional development, as can be seen in the chapters in this book by Otto Kruse and Daniel Perrin, both faculty members of the ZHAW. The near future will unveil whether Gerd Bräuer's hope for Education/Freiburg will come true: for this new distance-learning program in Winterthur to further shape writing as a central means of academic training in Freiburg.

PORTRAIT 2: KATRIN GIRGENSOHN (AS PRESENTED BY GERD BRÄUER)

Before Katrin started working at the European University Viadrina Frankfurt/Oder (Germany), she used to hold writing courses and writing groups outside the university for more than 10 years. These groups sometimes belonged to community centers or other institutions for adult and continuing education. Others started outside the institution and met in cafés or other places. At that time, Katrin worked with people from different age groups and levels of writing experience: old and young, female and male, authors and people who had never written before. In order to meet the different needs of these diverse groups, she experimented with several methods and settings, such as presenting and discussing texts at a regular open stage;[1] group and performance work for women only; projects for writing and publishing books with autobiographical stories.[2] Through these projects Katrin expanded her understanding of different approaches to learning-to-write and to facilitating writing-practice groups.

In 2002, Katrin was asked by the European University Viadrina to teach writing seminars. This invitation followed from the university's realizing a need to foster academic writing. Since the opening of the university 15 years ago a stable number of about 30% of the student population at EUV is not of German decent and therefore represents either foreign or second language writers. Soon, Katrin realized in her writing seminars that there was low motivation for writing in general and academic writing in specific, and no willingness to freely share drafts and provide peer feedback. One of the reasons for that, she recognizes, is the teacher-centered seminar format practiced widely in higher education in Germany—a model that she saw herself obligated to follow at the beginning of her teaching career at the university. Katrin, from the beginning, felt the desire to bring to EUV her experience of working with writing groups outside higher education. When she finally followed her desire, she was very much aware that there has been no tradition at universities in Germany—and this is true also for the other German-speaking countries—with autonomous groups.

Let's mention a few additional facts about the European University Viadrina in order to better understand the circumstances of writing at EUV: this old university (originally created in the sixteenth century) reopened in 1995 with a new face, after about 150 years of mainly politically-motivated self-denial. The university is situated in Frankfurt—the "other" Frankfurt in Germany, located on the river Oder, which forms a physical border between Germany and Poland. Frankfurt/Oder is 80 km (about 50 miles) east of Berlin. EUV is a small public university with three faculties and about 6,000 students total.[3] Katrin Girgensohn is still the only faculty member at EUV with a distinct teaching profile in writing. When Katrin started at EUV, there was no writing center, no composition classes, nor any other form of writing instruction. Katrin's students have been mostly BA and MA students of cultural studies who can choose her writing seminars to obtain credit points in "practical skills." Besides writing in Katrin's courses, these students do not have to write very much other than take-home-exams at the end of the semesters and a thesis at the end of either BA or MA studies.[4] Looking back at the beginning of her teaching career at EUV, Katrin says:

> I worked at my university as an adjunct faculty for two semesters and tried to teach academic writing the traditional way in front of a class that was restricted to 25 students (from about 100 students who initially wanted to join the course but weren't allowed to sign up) and with a time budget of only 90 minutes per week.[5] This, to me, wasn't satisfying at all. I tried using various forms of group work and peer learning and I gave as many tips and tricks about academic writing as possible. However, what I was missing was students really thinking about their own writing and practising

> writing voluntarily, out of intrinsic motivation, so to speak. So, I began thinking about other ways of facilitating these writers and how I could transfer the experience I gathered with writing group work outside university to my courses at EUV (Girgensohn, interview, 2011).

Eventually, Katrin designed a concept for autonomous academic writing practice groups and started to experiment with it. Her understanding of writing practice groups is one that focuses more on writing together at the time of the group meetings than on giving each other feedback on drafts brought to the meeting. What follows is a list of aims she formulated for a new model of writing classes at the university: first of all and very simply, she wants the students to write more often and learn to enjoy writing. In other words, Katrin stresses what she calls a hedonistic approach to writing, which focuses first on the moment of happiness in the creation of texts (Girgensohn, 2007). From the perspective of instructional design and institutional development, her main concern is balancing the tendency in traditional German education to tackle the writers' weaknesses instead of acknowledging and making use of their individual strengths.

In Katrin's concept of autonomous academic writing groups, she wants

- students to write regularly,
- to offer encouragement for writing,
- to help students search for different ways, strategies, and methods of writing,
- to make students aware of their own writing processes,
- to encourage students to share their writing in progress,
- to give students a real audience for their writing,
- to leave responsibility for the learning process with the students themselves,
- and last but not least: to give the teacher a chance to really get to meet and know each individual writer in an otherwise large group of class participants.

In her 2005 presentation at the conference of the European Association for the Teaching of Academic Writing (EATAW), she named this obstacle of having to deal with large lecture classes and a very small classroom time budget "How to make a virtue out of necessity." Her autonomous writing groups are now offered as a regular credit-bearing course—not only in EUV but also in five large research universities throughout Germany. The term "autonomous writing group" follows Anne Ruggles Gere, who defines the term as follows (1987, p. 100):

> Although groups take a variety of forms, they can be categorized into three main types—autonomous, semi-autonomous and non-autonomous—depending upon locus and degree of authority. The voluntary constitution of writing groups within literary societies, young men's associations, women's clubs, and in a myriad other self-sponsored gatherings identifies them as autonomous. Authority resides within individual members of autonomous groups because they choose to join other writers with whom they are friendly, share common interests, backgrounds, or needs.

In Gere's opinion, university writing groups can never be autonomous "because of the authority invested in the educational institution and its representative, the instructor" (1987, p. 101). Nevertheless, Katrin Girgensohn had gained the experience—from her work outside university—that the autonomy of a writing group is the key for its success and the shaping of the individual desire to write: All members have to possess equal authority and must be "stage crew" and spectator at the same time. Katrin reflects on her experience in the first semester of putting this approach into practice:

> I decided to let the groups meet without me, the "representative authority." The groups are teacherless groups, which means that they are prepared and moderated alternately by all participating students. Furthermore, this decision solved my practical needs: I knew that I couldn't supervise several groups as a leader. With no more than 90 minutes of teaching time per week I would not be able to lead even one. At the beginning I worried a lot about students' development as writers and their willingness to collaborate with each other and, even more fundamental, to actually do their work without being closely supervised by me.

When Katrin started assessing process and outcome of the groups' work, she found this: both motivation for giving feedback and the quality of the feedback provided changed for the better. How come? First of all, she detected a certain natural curiosity in the students' reactions to each other's writing. Also, students showed more awareness of the writing process simply due to the fact that one can see in each other's actions what process writing is all about. There was also a stronger personal incentive for experimenting with writing strategies, settings, modes, and genres. All in all, Katrin witnessed a change of attitude regarding the responsibility for one's own writing and that of others.

How could she make the students work in a way they never did before? What she expects them to do is a lot. They are asked to constitute small groups with students they never met before. They are expected to write together—though most of them usually haven't written on their own initiative before joining the group. Katrin's concept requires them to read their own texts aloud in their small group and talk about their drafts as well as about their personal writing processes. All this they are expected to do without direct teacher guidance. There is a very important reason why Katrin's concept is actually working well: the idea of autonomy is taken seriously by transforming the role of the instructor into one of facilitating writers by challenging them to build confidence and trust with each other. This transformation is supported through the following additional elements of her concept:

- Katrin takes the idea of an *autonomous* writing group seriously: this means that the groups have to be self-elected. Furthermore, the students are free to choose the themes and methods or strategies *they* like. They can produce texts the way they like and they do not have to show Katrin the product of their work until the end of the semester—there is no pressure to hand in or publish the results of their work There is no doubt for them that *they* are responsible for their work. They are free to meet wherever they want—inside and outside the university. Katrin points out: "I don't grade their texts but instead I provide feedback on how the students engage in the writing process based on the information provided to me through team protocols and personal conversation during my office hours. The textbook they put together during the semester in each small group counts as group work. Nevertheless, I don't monitor how much each individual member contributes to the book."
- Her role as teacher is transformed: she becomes a facilitator, a resource for the students and their learning processes. She *offers* them help with preparing the group meetings. After the group meetings, Katrin receives a protocol, which, based on focus questions, helps students to reflect their individual work and the group processes.
- During an intensive kick-off writing weekend Katrin gives a hands-on introduction to writing group work and combines it with efforts to build confidence and trust among the students. This is happening mainly through a task called "Stationen-Schreiben," where students get a chance to explore their individual writing strategies, including an analysis of personal strengths and weaknesses. This leads them to

acknowledge not only their own current developmental state as writers but also to accept each other in their individuality. This Katrin sees as the foundation of individual confidence and trust among all members of the group.

In 2002, Katrin joined a group of writing pedagogues in Germany initiated by the Bielefeld University Writing Lab, with the goal of investigating the pedagogical potential of peer tutoring. In Bielefeld, Paula Gillespie and Harvey Kail presented a three-day workshop on peer tutoring. Katrin's experience of this workshop was one that opened her eyes to the larger community of writing pedagogues and the writing research related to peer learning in general (e.g., Bruffee, 1984) and peer tutoring of writing in specific. This experience, first of all, had a large impact on the further development of Katrin's concept of the autonomous academic writing group. It actually provided her with enough confidence to finally put it into practice in 2003.

At the same time she started to develop a concept for a peer-run writing center at EUV, including a training program for student writing tutors. Katrin wanted to provide a home base not only for the autonomous writing groups but also for other writing seminars and workshops to come and, last but not least, for individual peer-tutoring of writing. In the process of preparing for the opening of the center in 2007, Katrin spent several months visiting US writing centers. She also profited greatly from German writing pedagogues who had started their own writing centers in Bielefeld, Bochum, and Freiburg. Katrin also participated in the certificate program for writing coaches at the writing center of the University of Education Freiburg. Several alumni of this program started an informal network where people freely share their experience not only with coaching writers but also with initiating change with regard to writing in institutions of higher education.

After the opening of the writing center at EUV in 2007, Katrin initiated several developmental projects with great impact on redefining the role of writing at EUV. The most important for her is a course Katrin developed on collaborative writing as a mode of cultural learning. "Intercultural writing teams" is an innovative seminar model that is integrated into the curriculum of the cross-disciplinary master's degree in European Studies and arranges cross-cultural encounters based on creative writing methods. Students work in interculturally mixed small groups that meet regularly once a week during the semester. In addition, every two weeks all small groups join a seminar on academic writing. This mix of academic and creative-oriented teamwork aims at a more holistic academic socialization for both the international as well as the German master's students. Therefore, students aren't just practicing academic literacy skills, but also intercultural competence and team skills.

The growing impact Katrin has had on institutional development at EUV with regard to writing over the years doesn't stop at the gates of the university, but bridges the traditional gap between higher and secondary education. Through the project "high school writing coaches" she initiates and facilitates the development of high school writing centers staffed with high school students, an approach that has been developed in Europe through the Scriptorium project, led by the Freiburg Writing Center (Bräuer, 2009). Sponsored by the Robert Bosch foundation, high school students of two different partner schools visit the writing center at EUV and get a three-day training in peer tutoring methods. Afterwards, the high school students work for one year as peer tutors at their schools. They are supervised by two students of the EUV writing center. After one year a new group of high school students will be trained to become peer tutors in writing. Teachers of the schools are trained as well. A long-term goal is to establish writing centers at these high schools.

With this said, it becomes very obvious that Katrin's initiative for shaping autonomous academic writing groups laid the foundation for a slowly-changing role of writing in the university and the formation of new curricular structures supporting writers and creating sustainable support of writing.

NOTES

1. See ULR http://www.theodoras-literatursalon.de

2. See ULR http://www.girgensohn.schreibreisen.de

3. See ULR http://www.europa-uni.de

4. The German "Hausarbeit" causes many problems because students have to manage these demanding research papers without support during vacations.

5. For adjunct teachers, who tend to take on more and more university classes in Germany, this is all—you are not paid for the time you need to prepare the lessons or to read and comment on the papers, you just work for the honour of being a university teacher. Young teachers often are not paid at all.

REFERENCES

Baumgartner, P. (2009). Developing a taxonomy for electronic portfolios. In P. Baumgartner, S. Zauchner, & R. Bauer (Eds.), *The potential of e-portfolio in higher education* (pp. 13-44). Innsbruck: StudienVerlag.

Bräuer, G. (1989). *Lernen im Dialog. Untersuchungen zu Bertolt Brechts "Flüchtlingsgesprächen"*. Frankfurt am Main: Centaurus.

Bräuer, G. (1996). *Warum schreiben? Schreiben in den USA*. Frankfurt am Main: Peter Lang.

Bräuer, G. (1998). *Schreibend Lernen: Grundlagen einer theoretischen und praktischen Schreibpädagogik*. Innsbruck: Studienverlag.

Bräuer, G. (2002). Drawing connections across education: The Freiburg Writing Center model. *Language and Learning Across the Disciplines, 5*(3), 25-34.

Bräuer, G. (Ed.). (2009). *Scriptorium—Ways of interacting with writers and readers. A professional development program*. Freiburg i. Breisgau: Fillibachverlag.

Bräuer, G., & Schindler, K., (Eds.). (2011). *Schreibarrangements für Schule, Studium, Beruf.* Freiburg i. Breisgau: Fillibachverlag.

Brecht, B. (1957). *Schriften zum Theater. Über eine nicht-aristotelische Dramatik*. Frankfurt am Main: Suhrkamp.

Bruffee, K. (1984). Collaborative learning and the conversation of mankind. *College English, 46,* 635-52.

Gere, A. (1987). *Writing groups. History, theory and implications*. Carbondale and Edwardsville, IL: Southern Illinois University Press.

Girgensohn, K. (2007). *Neue Wege zur Schlüsselqualifikation Schreiben. Autonome Schreibgruppen an der Hochschule*. Wiesbaden: VS Research.

Jewitt, C. & Kress, G. (2003). *Multimodal literacy*. New York: Peter Lang.

North, S. (1984). The idea of a writing center. *College English, 46*(5), 433-446.

CHAPTER 21.
WRITING AT RWTH AACHEN (GERMANY): LESSONS FROM "TECHNIK IM KLARTEXT"

By Vera Niederau and Eva-Maria Jakobs
RWTH Aachen (Germany)

This article introduces the measurements and aims of the "TiK" (Technik im Klartext) project at the RWTH Aachen; the project flourished from 2001 to 2005 and has been recently restructured. Focused on popular writing about science, TiK aims to build interest in science and engineering careers among pre-university students and to teach university students important skills in reaching wider audiences. Some chosen components of the (teaching) concept will be presented. The impact of the project will be reflected on, problems and conditions discussed, and prospects for the future given.

Conveying science to a broad audience occupies an important place in Germany. The public as well as research foundations increase their support for it and it is seen as an essential component of communication. The transfer of knowledge and research results to society (industry, politics, public) is especially important for technical universities such as the RWTH Aachen. It should be an integral part of strategic public relations and academic education. It is crucial that students develop the ability of knowledge transfer and know about differentiated instruments and measurements for the presentation of knowledge to various target groups. There is a lack of practical courses in which teachers and students learn how to teach central skills such as the transfer of knowledge and the transfer of scientific topics for different target groups.

One important target group are scholars—pre-university students. On the one hand, they represent an important source of the rising generation of engineers; they are also the future social decision-makers. Scholars should be led to science and technology in order to awaken their interest for technical professions. Scholars not only gain information through teachers and media: important sources for scholars to shape their opinions are the articles of other scholars at the same age, for example in school newspapers. The subject of this profile is a project at the RWTH Aachen, which aims at new forms of knowledge transfer between university and school. The motto is: "Scholars Write for Scholars about Technology." They are accompanied and guided by various groups (researchers, teachers, and students of the university as well as teachers in schools). The learning places are different as well. One part of the project takes part at the university, another part at the schools. University teachers and students as well as teachers in their schools are competent contacts for them. The concept is that the transfer of knowledge goes from university to the schools.

The TiK project was initiated, developed, and carried out by the Department of Textlinguistics and Technical Communication of the RWTH Aachen in cooperation with the press office of the university. The department coordinates an interdisciplinary study course—technical writing. It combines systematically two subjects: one engineering subject, such as mechanical engineering or electrical engineering, and communication studies. The intent is to train specialists for the transfer of technology. The basic idea of the project is to integrate popular science writing into university and school studies in two ways. Students learn how to write popular science texts and at the same time learn to transfer their knowledge to others.

A basic aim of the project is to awaken interest for technical research by students, scholars, and teachers. In the centre of the project is writing about technology and basic skills such as research, phrasing, and revising. The project contains several measurements (seminars, workshops, building of networks etc.), which provide students, scholars (14-19 year olds of all schools), and teachers with the ability to convey knowledge in a popular-science way and sensitize them and awaken their interest for natural and engineering science. Another aim of the project is to make public the innovations, academic plans, and research results of the RWTH Aachen nationwide.

DESCRIPTION OF THE "TECHNIK IM KLARTEXT" PROJECT

With the "TiK" project the RWTH had successfully pursued new methods to convey teaching contents. The Department for Textlinguistics and Technical Communication developed the idea and the concept. The project was realized in cooperation with the press office of the RWTH and school newspapers from various German schools. All in all, 800 schools took part in the project. The rector of the RWTH financed it. The project was supported by an advisory board, which contains students, upper school scholars, teachers, subject teachers, and local journalists. The advisory board guided—among other things—the school newspapers and contributed considerably to the conception of the scholar/teacher workshops. The concept was realized for the first time in 2002-2003. The first phase included writing workshops and layout-seminars for technical communication students; in the second phase, writing workshops and layout-seminars for scholars and teachers. In agreement with and with support by the "Lehrerbildungszentrum" of the RWTH, the teachers were trained.

The project is based on various components. The first component combines innovative teaching forms (project-based learning) with new information- and communication offerings addressed to students. Usually the course includes four credit hours per week. In academic courses the participants have the opportunity to learn about the basics of popular science writing, which they have to use in a realistic context. The topics arise out of the research environment of the university. Every department with interesting research projects may apply. The project leader collects the suggested topics and the students decide which project and department they want to write about. They start research about their topic and have the opportunity to contact the researchers to gain material for their articles, to interview them, to visit laboratories, and to observe experiments. Their task is to prepare the collected material for writing a popular science article. The produced articles will be collected in a database for school newspaper editorials.

The young journalists from the participating schools have access to a web-based platform and may use the texts as basic material for their own texts. The database concept derives from the idea of news agencies; the platform offers relevant and current information about research and teaching in nature and engineering science—from news about innovative developments to current research projects and perspectives on various occupational areas. The knowledge transfer is supported by a second format: a newsletter, which is made by students under the guidance of teachers from the department and of journalists from the RWTH press office. The RWTH Aachen was the first German university to provide nationwide school newspaper editorials every semester with information about research.

The second component aggregates the academic and scholastic training in interactive forms. It includes several day-lasting events, where scholars and teachers learn the basics of popular science writing and layout design for school newspapers. The third component integrates experience-driven offerings: scholars have the opportunity to visit test beds, factories, and laboratories as extraordinary teaching spaces.

In the following sections of the profile, some chosen measurements of the project will be introduced, as well as distinctive attributes of teaching and learning forms.

DISTINCTIVE ATTRIBUTES OF THE ACADEMIC TEACHING AND LEARNING CONCEPT

The course "Popularisieren: Schreiben in Medien und Öffentlichkeit" [Popularising: Writing for Media and Public] has four credit hours per week and additionally a three-day-seminar. The course had been offered for four years in both summer and winter terms. The maximum number of participants was 30 students. The course was led by a teacher from the Department for Textlinguistics and Technical Communication and by the head of the press office. One part of the learning process results from frontal teaching. It was complemented by numerous working sessions of the students' project groups. There is a huge work involvement by all participants, because the innovative design of the course requires intensive cooperation. The students are mainly motivated by the possibility to transfer the learned theory into practice and to gain vocationally-orientated qualifications during their studies.

PROJECT-BASED LEARNING

Project work in this context means a long-term and complex examination within the curricular course. It is a dynamic combination of theory and practice. In the sense of experienced learning (Gudjons, 1997; Apel & Knoll, 2001) an academic course should combine theory and practice as equal and mutual elements. The project-based dealing with the topic requires interdisciplinary consultations and cooperation. The course participants come from various disciplines of humanities, nature, and engineering science. The task of the course participants is to process engineering subjects and humanities research through genuine scientific methods and measurements. This includes the reception of theory and writing of diverse texts as well as creating a layout and the allocation of keywords in the database.

The content of the project, which focuses on "establishing a news agency by students for scholars," is based on the idea that students write for school newspapers. The focus of this reality-based situation is the use of knowledge resources (public relations, phrasing, editing, etc.), which—in conjunction with other activities (such as public relations, event preparation and implementation, supervision of writing workshops, etc.) —forms a specifically engineered action system. The basis for practical work in the real-life situation is the development of theoretical knowledge in science journalism and public relations. During the seminar the following areas are covered:

- Goals/ Strategies and features/ techniques of popular science writing (see Niederhauser, 1997, 1998, 1999)

- Analysis of popular science texts as compared to scientific texts
- Instruments and measures of public relations (Faulstich, 1992)
- Techniques/methods of information gathering and processing systems (Haller, 2001)
- Writing theory and writing strategies (see Jakobs, 1997, 1999a, 2009; Molitor, 1985; Perrin, 1997, 1998)

Theoretical knowledge is applied in practical work: Participants write short and long versions of research on the subject. They learn to deal intensively with their texts to make changes in perspective and to give each other specific feedback. Students reflect together on their progress and the results of their work. The role of teachers is to be informative, advisory, supportive, and encouraging.

Intensive Seminar with Accompanying Tutorials

The intensive seminar is based on team-teaching (lecturers, tutors, students). The project-themes about which the students want to write are specified and the project teams created. The students' project teams plan workflow. They determine simultaneously both the individual areas of responsibility of team members, as well as share learning processes such as different forms of collaborative writing (see Bleich ,1995; Jakobs, 1997; Lean, 1999; Sharples, 1999; Schindler, 2007). Contents of the intensive seminar are theory and teaching of writing strategies, as well as training and flexibility through techniques (Molitor, 1985; Jakobs, 1999; Perrin, Böttcher, & Kruse, 2003). A major challenge is the border between factual accuracy and entertainment value of the journalistic text. They learn to deal with discipline-specific discourse patterns as well as with conflicts.

The main aim of the intensive seminar is to revise the articles for the newsletter. The text revising takes place as simulated editorial meetings. The course participants discuss the draft texts by using predetermined objective criteria. The group discussion is held at eye level. Everyone will be taken seriously. In addition, there is a tutorial for writing for the Internet. The students deal with the specifics of web formats, and practice by using given materials.

Combination of Teaching and Public Relations

A special feature of the project is the substantive and personal link between teaching and public relations. The strong involvement of the press office and their staff gives the seminar authenticity and practical relevance. The students learn about working practices of journalism and get professional advice and feedback. The students can also take advantage of the strong contact network of public relations. Conversely, the press benefits from the perspective of students and the challenge of adapting discussion of journalistic writing to the target group scholars. Important impulses arise from the confrontation between theory and practice. In the journalist's contact with the students, experienced processes of research and journalistic text production, as well as the setting of target values and criteria, must be questioned. The task to develop writing workshops with students and teachers for scholars and their teachers, as well as discussing the themes, research, and text products, leads to intense discussions and a repeated change of perspectives. Current topics of the younger generation will find—stronger than before—the entrance to public relations. Critical feedback from seminar participants means that instruments and measures of public relations are considered and analyzed—for the public relations work of the university, this is a valuable form of evaluation.

Moreover, the press office can cover many results of student research and text production. The university is nationally visible through the newsletter. A secondary effect of the publications through media about the project is the resultant inquiries from interested schools and institutions.

PROJECT EVENTS: CONGRESS FOR SCHOLARS, WITH WORKSHOPS

In November 2001, the first TIK congress for scholars was held: scholars from all over North Rhine-Westphalia took part in four day-long writing workshops in which practical tips for work were offered to school newspapers. The results of the writing workshops were put together in a conference newspaper. In small groups, specific issues for school newspapers were discussed, for example, writing, illustrating, and web-design.

WRITING WORKSHOPS

The TiK writing workshops give young editors the possibility to practice journalistic writing about scientific topics. The scholars are introduced to science-teaching strategies and techniques of research. In a subsequent research phase in a research institute of the RWTH Aachen, scholars can visit projects to experience and learn science in a personal discussion with scientists. For most scholars this is the first opportunity to look at a university from the inside. The personal contact breaks down barriers and helps to break down clichés about science and the work of scientists.

After visiting the departments, the writing phase begins. In order to initiate the process of writing, the scholars test methods of creative writing (Böttcher, 1999a, 1999b; Böttcher & Czapla, 2002). The actual writing process occurs either alone or collaboratively. Each workshop ends with a text optimization phase. In small groups, participants receive constructive feedback. They use the notes for the final editing. The output of the seminar is not only new experiences and an increase in skills, but also a number of texts that are the subject of further processes and workshops.

Layout Workshops

In TiK layout workshops, the participants learn to make their text products visually interesting. The design is based primarily on printed school newspapers. The workshops also address the needs of online newspapers and opportunities they offer. Graphic designers introduce the participants to the basics of professional layout design. During the workshop, not only young editors are addressed, but also their teachers, who work together with the students to learn innovative methods of design of school newspapers. The theoretical principles are put into practice with the help of exercises. The guidelines are applied to the layout of their own school newspapers. This part is especially valued. The participants receive a briefing on the use of various computer programs such as "Adobe Photoshop" or "InDesign." In small groups, their own ideas can be creatively implemented on a computer. All workshops are evaluated and the results are recorded in a report. The evaluations are used iteratively for optimization of teaching and learning forms and other aspects of information and knowledge.

REFLECTION ON THE PROJECT

The long-term project approach results in a heterogeneous stock. The project's content and method are as extraordinarily successful as its inner and external impact. Negative outcomes include the high costs in time, people, and finances, as well as the fluctuation of the scientific staff and personnel.

Achievements and Positive Feedback

The response to the project has been very positive. This is shown by external and internal evaluations, such as evaluations of university teaching by students, resonance analysis in schools, and the evaluation of the project by

Stifterverband, the business community's innovation agency for the German science system.

The project shows that by working closely with young editors, a long-term commitment arises: interesting contributions generate curiosity, interest, and possibly a desire for further information—in some cases to study a science or engineering discipline. Interest and information are augmented by the personal approach and the continuous emotional contact. Young people who are interested in public relations or in science journalism are specifically encouraged. Some former scholarly editors have decided on the basis of the TIK-project to study at the RWTH Aachen. By training the target groups, there are also multiplier effects: the interest in technology will be transported via school newspapers and spread in the schools.

From winter term 2001/02 to winter term 2004/05, over 180 students successfully completed the project course: "Popularisieren: Schreiben in Medien und Öffentlichkeit." As noted in course evaluations, the students especially appreciated the motivational content of the course, the opportunity to practice interactive forms of learning within the team, and the close relation between the theoretical and scientific education and practical relevance.

The commitment of the students was higher than the average. The registration numbers for each course were more than 100 applicants. The commitment was above the planned six hours per week. The students volunteered extensively to support the organization of the student congress by teams who occupied the conference office and participated in the preparation of the conference sessions, workshops, etc. Some course participants have managed to write a script for a short film about TiK and to design a radio program, from manuscript to on-air production. A student group was engaged in sponsorship, another has written a play about TiK and presented it. Since winter term 2003/04, students took over two sponsorships of newspapers at regional schools. Another volunteer activity was that experienced students conducted advice sessions with new students.

The results of the research and interviews of students in the RWTH institutes were excellent. Overall, the text corpus includes 250 target group specific texts in short-and long version (newsletter and database). The response from the school newspapers is extremely positive. The project convinced the business community's innovation agency for the German science system: TiK was established in 2001 as one of 12 outstanding actions nationwide with extraordinary marketing efforts and awarded financial support.

The text products as well as the response show that the cooperation has been successful on both sides, as well as the learning process for students.

PROBLEMS AND CONSTRAINTS

The negative outcome begins with the framework for sustainability and continuity of the project work. It refers to the heavy workload and the flow of information from the schools into the project, as well as the institutional conditions in universities. The personnel fluctuation for the school newspapers is high; the constant change leads to social difficulties and the need for ongoing reconciliation and thus intensive contact. Most documents are sent with a considerable time lag. Specific measures have helped to reduce these confounding factors: the platform has been made significantly more service oriented. Twinning arrangements between students and school newspapers allow the maintenance of personal contacts.

Academic teaching requires a high level of personal effort of teachers, who are exchanged by temporary contracts. Personnel change always means a loss of knowledge and networks. On the part of the university, the high level of preparation, implementation, and follow-up effort for such holistic teaching and learning is often underestimated: successful project implementation requires substantial financial, time, and personnel resources. The university supported the project with an initial funding of approximately €10,000 over two years; achievements of the Institute and the press office were added. Despite the positive evaluation of all project partners the funding ended in 2005. Overall, the project ultimately foundered on personnel and financial resources. The latter is especially important in times where competition among higher education programs determines the daily work routine. If the payment is oriented on graduate numbers, funding, and scientific publications, there is no room for a volunteer commitment.

CONCLUSION AND OUTLOOK

Currently we are working at the Department for Textlinguistics and Technical Communication to take up the project idea again in a changed configuration. The main innovation is a broad national orientation and financial security of measurements. In the future, the project will rely on a network of stakeholders from business, universities, and schools. The learning places should become more diverse. The range of topics will be broader. The themes will come from industry and research. Other changes relate to the methods of media preparation and writing for various communication channels. The technological development shows that printed school newspapers represent only one of many different media variants. All in all, we are convinced that the idea is a very interesting approach to teach text production skills. Added values are created by the combination of innovative learning environments and themes, the connection between theory and practice and the diversity of persons involved. Therefore, we continue: the seminar "Populariseren: Schreiben in Medien und Öffentlichkeit" was offered again in summer 2010 by the Department for Textlinguistics and Technical Communication in cooperation with the press office of the RWTH Aachen, with the aim to develop the concept further.

REFERENCES

Apel, H. J., & Knoll, M. (2001). *Aus Projekten lernen. Grundlegung und Anregung.* Munich: Oldenbourg.

Baurmann, J. (2006). *Schreiben—Überarbeiten— Beurteilen. Ein Arbeitsbuch zur Schreibdidaktik.* Seelze (Velber), Lower Saxony, Germany: Kallmeyer.

Becker-Mrotzek, M., & Schindler, K. (Eds.). (2007). *Texte schreiben.* Duisburg: Gilles & Francke [Kölner Beiträge zur Sprachdidaktik; 5].

Bleich, D. (1995). Collaboration and the pedagogy of disclosure. *College English, 57*(1), 43-61.

Böttcher, I. (1999a). *Kreatives Schreiben. Grundlagen und Methoden. Beispiele für Fächer und Projekte—Schreibecke und Dokumentation.* Berlin: Cornelsen.

Böttcher, I. (1999b). *Kreatives Schreiben. Grundlagen und Methoden. Beispiele für Fächer und Projekte—Schreibecke und Dokumentation.* Berlin: Cornelsen.

Böttcher, I., & Czapla, C. (2002). Repertoires flexibilisieren. Kreative Methoden für professionelles Schreiben. In D. Perrin, I. Böttcher, O. Kruse & A. Wrobel (Eds.), *Schreiben. Von intuitiven zu professionellen Schreibstrategien* (pp. 182-201). Wiesbaden: Westdeutscher Verlag.

Faulstich, W. (1992). *Grundwissen Öffentlichkeitsarbeit: Kritische Einführung in Problemfelder der Public Relations.* Bardowick, Lower Saxony, Germany: Wissenschaftler-Verlag (IfAM-Arbeitsberichte ; 6).

Gudjons, H. (1997). *Handlungsorientiert lehren und lernen: Schüleraktivierung, Selbsttätigkeit, Projektarbeit. 5.* Bad Heilbrunn, Bavaria, Germany: Klinkhardt.

Haller, M. (2001). *Recherchieren—Ein Handbuch für Journalisten. 5., völlig überarb. Aufl., [Reihe Praktischer Journalismus, Bd. 7].* Konstanz: UVK Medien.

Jakobs, E.-M. (1997). Textproduktion als domänen- und kulturspezifisches Handeln. Diskutiert am Beispiel wissenschaftlichen Schreibens. In K. Adamzik, G. Antos, & E. M Jakobs. (Eds.), *Domänen- und kulturspezifisches Schreiben* (pp. 3, 9-30). Frankfurt am Main: Textproduktion und Medium.

Jakobs, E.-M. (1999a). Online-Zeitungen. Potentiale und Prozesse. In H. Von Strohner, L. Sichelschmidt, & M. Hielscher (Eds.), *Medium Sprache*. Frankfurt am Main: Lang (Forum Angewandte Linguistik; 34).

Jakobs, E.-M. (1999b). *Textvernetzung in den Wissenschaften. Zitat und Verweis als Ergebnis rezeptiver, reproduktiver und produktiver Prozesse*. Tübingen, Baden-Württemberg, Germany: Niemeyer [RGL; 210].

Jakobs, E.-M. (2009). Schlüsselqualifikation Rede und Schreiben in der universitären Ausbildung. In U. Fix, A. Gardt, & J. Knape, J. (Eds.), *Rhetorik und Stilistik. Ein internationales Handbuch historischer und systematischer Forschung. [Rhetoric and Stylistics. An international handbook of historical und systematic research.]* (pp. 58-68). Berlin, New York: Mouton-de Gruyter.

Lehnen, K. (1999). Kooperative Textproduktion. In O. Kruse, E.-M. Jakobs & G. Ruhmann (Eds.), *Schlüsselkompetenz Schreiben. Konzepte, Methoden, Projekte für Schreibberatung und Schreibdidaktik an der Hochschule* (pp. 147-170). Neuwied, Rhineland-Palatinate , Kriftel, Hesse, Germany: Luchterhand.

Lilienthal, B. (1999). Hypertextartige Strukturen in der Regionalpresse und neue Möglichkeiten in der Gestaltung von Online-Zeitungen. In H. Strohner, L. Sichelschmidt, & M. Hielscher, M. (Eds.), *Medium Sprache* (pp. 109-121). Frankfurt am Main: Lang.

Molitor, S. (1985). Personen- und aufgabenspezifische Schreibstrategien. *Unterrichtswissenschaft, 13,* 334-345.

Niederhauser, J. (1997). Das Schreiben populärwissenschaftlicher Texte als Transfer wissenschaftlicher Texte. In E.-M. Jakobs & D. Knorr (Eds.), *Schreiben in den Wissenschaften* (pp. 107-122). Frankfurt am Main: Lang.

Niederhauser, J. (1998). Darstellungsformen der Wissenschaften und populärwissenschaftliche Darstellungsformen. In L. Danneberg & J. Niederhauser (Eds.), *Darstellungsformen der Wissenschaften im Kontrast. Aspekte der Methodik, Theorie und Empirie* (pp. 157-188). Tübingen, Baden-Württemberg, Germany.

Niederhauser, J. (1999). *Wissenschaftssprache und populärwissenschaftliche Vermittlung*. Tübingen, Baden-Württemberg, Germany: Narr.

Perrin, D. (1997). Kompressionsfaktor 100. Strategien journalistischer Textproduktion optimieren. In G. Antos, K. Adamzik & E.-M. Jakobs. (Eds.), *Domänen- und kulturspezifisches Schreiben* (pp. 167-203). Frankfurt am Main: Lang [Textproduktion und Medium; 3], 167-203.

Perrin, D. (1998). *Journalistische Schreibstrategien optimieren*. Bern/Stuttgart/ Vienna: Verlag Paul Haupt.

Perrin, D., Böttcher, I., & Kruse, O. (2003). *Schreiben. Von intuitiven zu professionellen Schreibstrategien*. Wiesbaden, Hesse, Germany: Westdeutscher Verlag.

Portmann, P. (2005). Schreiben und Überarbeiten von Texten. In U. Abraham, C. Kupfer-Schreiner & K. Maiwald (Eds.), *Schreibförderung und Schreibererziehung. Eine Einführung für Schule und Hochschule* (pp. 174-186). Donauwörth, Bavaria, Germany: Auer.

Rau, C. (1994). *Revisionen beim Schreiben. Zur Bedeutung von Veränderungen in Textproduktionsprozessen*. Tübingen, Baden-Württemberg, Germany: Niemeyer.

Schindler, K. (2005). ... und immer an den Leser denken!? Anmerkungen zur Rolle des Adressaten beim Schreiben. *Fachjournalist, 16*(8), 11-14.

Sharples, M. (1999). *How we write: An account of writing as creative design* (Chapter 11: Writing together). New York and London: Routledge.

Wrobel, A. (1997). Zur Modellierung von Formulierungsprozessen. In E.-M. Jakobs & D. Knorr (Eds.), *Schreiben in den Wissenschaften* (pp. 15-24). Frankfurt am Main/ Berlin/ New York/ Paris/Vienna: Lang (Textproduktion und Medium, Bd. 1).

Wrobel, A. (2002). Schreiben und Formulieren. Prätext als Problemindikator und Lösung. In D. Perrin, I. Böttcher, O. Kruse, O. & A. Wrobel. (Eds.), *Schreiben. Von intuitiven zu professionellen Schreibstrategien* (pp. 83-96). Wiesbaden, Hesse, Germany: Westdeutscher Verlag.

Ziefle, M., & Jakobs, E.-M. (2009). Wege zu Technikfaszination. Sozialisationsverläufe und Interventionszeitpunkte. Unter Mitarbeit von: Katrin Arning, Patrick Elftmann, Anne Kursten, Felix Langness, Vera Niederau [acatech diskutiert]. Berlin/Heidelberg: Springer.

CHAPTER 22.
STUDENT WRITING IN THE UNIVERSITY OF MADRAS: TRADITIONS, COURSES, AMBITIONS

By Susaimanickam Armstrong
University of Madras (India)

Writing courses and related initiatives at the University of Madras make available to the students the skills of writing. According to their programs and interests, students are trained in many forms of writing, including professional, creative, and research. This profile describes some techniques and assignments used as part of these writing opportunities in various disciplines. It attempts to critically understand the role of the university in forwarding new trends in writing and communication that play a major role in establishing careers of students and that are shaping the development of the academic and creative world. The author describes in detail his own expanded uses of writing in a literature course. Further, the essay spells out the progress of "soft skills" programs in several languages, by which students gain new horizons in language acquisition. Finally, it projects a range of new writing/communications initiatives by which the university can expand its importance in the burgeoning economy of its region.

The 153-year old University of Madras (UOM) is the mother of almost all the old universities of Southern India. It is an affiliated, state university under the Government of Tamil Nadu. The university area of jurisdiction has been confined to three districts of Tamil Nadu in recent years. This is consequent to the establishment of various universities in the state and demarcation of the university territories.

Through its long history, the university has diversified its teaching and research. UOM has produced two presidents for the Government of India and has three Nobel laureates to her credit. The university imparts both undergraduate and post-graduate education through over 100 affiliated institutions that are spread over the districts of Chennai, Thiruvalluvar, and Kancheepuram. Apart from teaching, research activities in arts, humanities, science, management, and technology are the main portals of the university.

The 68 university departments of study and research are spread over four campuses organized into 18 schools, each of which offers post-graduate courses in part-time and full-time PhD programs and diploma and certificate programs (http://www.unom.ac.in/). Addressing education needs of an even larger population of the country, the university offers both undergraduate and post-graduate education through the Institute of Distance Education (IDE). Some of the courses offered by IDE have no parallel in this country.

HISTORY AND HERITAGE

The Public Petition dated 11 November 1839 initiated the establishment of the Madras University. In January 1840, with George Norton as its President, the University Board was constituted, but it was not until 1857 that the university was established by an act of the Legislative Council. The university was organized on the model of the University of London (Hunter, 1886; Mahalingam, 1974; University of Madras, 2001). By 1912, endowments were made to the university to establish departments of Indian History, Archaeology, Comparative Philology, and Indian Economics. In all there were 17 University departments, 30 University teachers, 69 research scholars, and 127 University publications in that year. Later, the research and teaching functions of the university were encouraged by the Sadler Commission, and the gains of the university were consolidated by the enactment of the Madras University Act of 1923. About this time, the territorial ambit of the Madras University encompassed from Berhampur of Orissa in the North, Trivandrum of Kerala in the Southwest, Bangalore and Mangalore of Karnataka in the West and Hyderabad of Andhra Pradesh in the South. However, Indian independence in 1947, the setting up of the University Grants Commission in 1956, and changes in the political, social, and cultural milieu brought several amendments to the University of Madras Act of 1923 to permit qualitative and quantitative changes in its jurisdiction and functions.

MOST SALIENT GEOGRAPHIC, ECONOMIC, AND CULTURAL FEATURES OF ITS LOCATION

UOM is located in Chennai, formerly known as Madras, the capital city of the Indian State of Tamil Nadu. Chennai is the fourth most populous metropolitan area and the fifth most populous city in India. Located on the Coromandel Coast of the Bay of Bengal, Chennai city had a population of 4.34 million in the 2001 census. The urban agglomeration of metropolitan Chennai has an estimated population of over 8.2 million people.

Chennai's economy has a broad base of auto, computer, technology, hardware manufacturing, and healthcare industries. The city is India's second largest exporter of software, information technology, and information-technology-enabled services. A major chunk of India's auto manufacturing industry is based in and around the city. Chennai Zone contributes 39 per cent of the State's GDP. Chennai accounts for 60 per cent of the country's automotive exports.

Chennai is an important centre for folk songs and Carnatic music and hosts a large cultural event, the annual Madras Music Season, which includes performances by hundreds of artists. The city has a vibrant theatre scene and is an important centre for the Bharatanatyam, a classical dance form. The Tamil film industry, one of the largest in India, is based in the city; the soundtracks of the films dominate its music scene.

The University of Madras is spread over six campuses, viz., Chepauk, Marina, Guindy, Taramani, Chetpet, and Maduravoyal. The main campus of the University of Madras is located in Chepauk. The stately and historic Senate House, the Library building with its imposing clock tower, the spacious Centenary Auditorium, and the massive Centenary Building are some of the important buildings of the university campus at Chepauk. Most of the science departments are located in the Guindy Campus of the university. The campus at Taramani houses the Dr. A. Lakshmanaswamy Mudaliar Post-Graduate Institute of Basic Medical Sciences. The Oriental and Indian languages departments, the Post-graduate Hostel for Men and the University Guesthouse are located in the Marina Campus. The University Union for Sports and its pavilion are on the Spur Tank Road in Chetpet. The Botanical Garden of the University is located in the Maduravoyal campus.

WHAT "LITERACY" AND ESPECIALLY "WRITING" MEAN TO STUDENTS AND TEACHERS IN UOM: WHY THEY WRITE, IN WHAT LANGUAGES AND DIALECTS, IN RELATION TO WHAT GOALS?[1]

By and large, the students and teachers of the University of Madras (UOM) assume that "literacy" and especially "writing" mean only writing sessional tests and end-of-semester examinations. Writing practice here is clubbed with examination of students' memory and understanding of their subjects. English is the medium of instruction at UOM, but is a second language for the students, who bring with them a broad range of first languages: Hindi (national language), Tamil (regional mother tongue), Malayalam, Telugu, Kannada, Sanskrit, North Eastern Tribal languages, Arabic, Persian, and Urdu. UOM also admits international students who speak English, French, Sinhalese, Chinese, Japanese, Tibetan, and other languages. Is writing practice different from examination of subject knowledge? It remains a question here. Proper attention for writing practice is not professionally administered in universities such as UOM in India. Students write their three sessional tests per semester and end-semester examinations in English, except for the students in their respective language departments. For the most part, the goal of students here is to score top-ranking marks and not to improve their writing skills. However, there are a few elective courses in writing, described below, that serve other student goals.

WHAT STUDENTS WRITE IN THE INSTITUTION: DISCIPLINES, GENRES, ASSIGNMENTS

Though the medium of instruction in UOM is English, students write in other Indian and regional languages depending upon the respective language departments in the campuses. Students answer objective type or multiple-choice questions in one word; they also write short notes in 50 words, paragraphs in 150 to 200 words, and essays in 500 words or more. This is the general examination pattern in UOM. In science disciplines, students write lab experiment reports of two or three pages, do statistical analysis, and submit a Record Book as a part of general examination writing. Data-based reports, field studies, interview transcriptions, and media reports are some of the assignments given in the departments of Archeology, Journalism, Economics, Econometrics, Statistics, and Management Studies. The departments of Literatures, Languages, Geography, History, Politics, Psychology, and other human sciences assign book reviews. Some of the Departments of Indian Languages in UOM encourage students who are interested in creative writing in their respective mother tongues, among them English, Tamil, and Malayalam.

Writing per se is the subject in several courses offered by Journalism and English. For example, Journalism offers a course in technical communication that includes manual writing, flier design, and brochure design and writing. A core course in Journalism introduces writing for radio, television, TV news, cinema, and the Internet. Peer review is an important element of this course. The objective of the course in Copy Editing is to introduce the students to the basic skills of editing as applicable in the field of publishing and journalism. The

Department of English offers an elective course in Writing Skills that features thesis writing, proposals, and research writing. Other courses offered by English will be described in later sections of this essay.

WHO "CARES" IN THE INSTITUTION ABOUT STUDENT GROWTH IN AND THROUGH WRITING? HOW IS THIS CONCERN—OR LACK OF CONCERN—SHOWN IN FUNDING, REQUIREMENTS, ATTITUDES, ACTIONS?

UOM does not have an official body in charge of students' growth in and through writing. The respective research supervisors during the preparation of research dissertations for post-graduate degrees, the Master of Philosophy in various disciplines, and doctoral degrees will normally address the writing and editing skills of the student scholars. For sessional or periodical tests, end-semester examinations, and submitted assignments, the respective course coordinators take care of the evaluation of writing.

The University Students Advisory Board (USAB), which is funded by the university and partly supported by the Government of Tamil Nadu, and the Dr. B. R. Ambedkar Centre for Economic Studies, fully funded by the Government of India, conduct writing courses for the socially disadvantaged students of the university and her affiliated colleges. This Centre periodically conducts coaching classes for students to take up various job-oriented competitive examinations. Subject experts do conduct writing practices in their respective fields. USAB is very much interested in helping students get suitable job placements; they very often conduct job fairs in collaboration with leading Info Tech companies. USAB also facilitates student-oriented programs, such as remedial coaching classes, and conducts training for students who aspire for competitive examinations. Ample writing exercises are given to test students' writing skills. Neither USAB nor the Ambedkar Centre has a writing program per se, but developing such courses in the near future is a possibility.

ONE ILLUSTRATION OF SUCCESS IN TEACHING WRITING IN A DISCIPLINE

I trained a set of 14 pre-doctoral (Master of Philosophy in English) students who opted an elective course entitled "Discourses of Domination, Resistance, and Emancipation: Race, Caste, and Gender" during the academic year 2007-2008. This course focused more on writing skills than others I have previously taught. The students had to prepare two assignments, and then present them as papers. After presentation, students were asked to share the presented papers for peer review. After this step, they were asked to interview experts on the topics of research that they had prepared, presented, and peer reviewed (e.g., Gajendran, 1998; Guru, 1998). These interviews were later transcribed and prepared in a format fit for publication. My task as the coordinator of this course was to compile all of this work as an anthology having the following features:

- Broad division of chapters containing individual papers
- Bibliographic essay on race, caste, and gender (to which three students contributed)
- Compilation of the interviews with experts, relevant to the themes of the student papers
- Compilation of official/archival/gubernatorial documents gathered by the students as additional information on their themes.

For example, a student who presented a paper on trans-gender interviewed a trans-gender leader in Chennai, who in turn directed the student to the government office where an order issued in favor of trans-gender was available. The student annexed this document to the proposed anthology for the benefit of future researchers. This student also contributed to the section of the bibliographic essay on genders.

For the M. Phil. students of the Department of English at the University of Madras this was a new educational experience. Normally, students of literature will not go out for field study here. In this course, students shared that they had enriching experiences during interviews with subject experts, activists, writers, critics, and political leaders. One of the students interviewed a Minister for Social Welfare. For her, it was a thrilling experience. Some of them told me that they learned the art of interviewing through transcribing the recorded interviews. Students who felt very shy in the class benefited from going out to attend seminars and present papers with the help of their peers. I wanted to give a social science perspective to literary and cultural studies research such as this. Normally, some of the best social science work will have a literary touch. I wanted to experiment with this type of research with my team of students, and this fusion worked out very well, as I could see this in the writings and the interesting titles given by the students to their papers.

Through this complex assignment, students developed the following:
- Interviewing skills
- Book review skills
- Research paper writing methods
- Proposal writing methods
- Looking at literature through a social science perspective

- Team research skills
- Self-editing skills

WHEN AND HOW HAVE GROUPS OF TEACHERS MET TO DISCUSS AND PERHAPS PLAN WAYS TO HELP STUDENTS GROW AS WRITERS? WHAT HAS RESULTED?

Though there is no professional group of teachers to teach writing skills to students of their respective departments, the Department of English has been offering courses on technical writing and copy editing for the past five years as electives for the students of all disciplines in UOM. The coordinator of these courses has received overwhelming response from various departments. Students are made aware of the importance of mastering the nuances of the written language. Examples are taken from real life work scenarios. For example, the students are shown examples from the print media where errors have been overlooked. Thus, they are trained to be sensitive to language use. The students go through a very result-oriented training program in different kinds of writing assignments. The results of this training have been positive. Select students in a class exhibit enthusiasm to become flawless writers.

NEW INITIATIVES IN TEACHING WRITING

The University of Madras has been offering the Soft Skills program for its students. It is mandatory for every student in the MA, MSc, MCom, and MBA programs of the university to acquire eight credits from this program to successfully complete their post-graduation degree. The objective of the program is to enable students to understand and produce the target language accurately and fluently. Emphasis is on the four skills/modules—listening, speaking, reading and writing—with writing given the most emphasis. The Soft Skills program is offered in English, Spanish, French, German, and Italian. The students learn grammar rules and new vocabulary. They write answers to reading and listening comprehension questions and also take a written test. The students are trained in spelling and punctuation at the level of word and sentence, with later emphasis on content and organization.

In the Communication and Soft Skills program in English, the modules define the various principles of communication and demonstrate its importance using the four skills. The objective of the written skills module is to enable the students to link spoken words and thoughts to writing, demonstrate the importance of writing without errors, and discuss the process and result of a written work. The students are given ample time during the course to practice writing with precision, accuracy, and clarity of thought. The learners are monitored closely by the faculty, who guide them to successfully process their ideas. They practice writing through such tasks as narrating stories; drafting letters, emails, and reports; writing their resumes and curriculum vitae; writing book reports, reviews, personal stories, job applications, news reports, etc.

The University of Madras has recently (July 2010) outsourced this program to a private educational company. As a University Coordinator for this program, I have control over what is taught. On behalf of the university, I prescribe the syllabus and monitor the company's tutoring; University faculties evaluate the examination given by the company faculty. Thus far, the program has been successful, and I have received many positive responses from the students.

PROPOSED/UNFULFILLED AMBITIONS IN REGARD TO STUDENT LITERACY/WRITING

1. Training in writing for **M.Phil.** and **PhD** students: The students enrolled in the Master of Philosophy (pre-doctoral degree) and PhD (doctoral) in various science, arts, and humanities courses at the University of Madras do not have a separate training program for writing skills, and their writing activity is limited to writing dissertations with the guidance of respective research supervisors. A program related to writing for these research students would be an ambitious venture for any member of faculty here, and efforts are being made to draft a program that combines purposeful and original writing with precise and orderly presentation.
2. Writing and translation: The Department of English is conceiving plans for a program for Writing and Translation in consultation with the authorities of the university and other volunteering members from affiliating colleges of the University of Madras.
3. Technical writing and content development: To prepare materials such as websites, user manuals, training manuals, reports, proposals, etc., there is a huge demand for technical writers in software companies, financial institutions, and many other organizations. UOM plans to conduct courses in the above program shortly for students across all disciplines, in collaboration with interested professional and educational institutions in India and abroad, particularly with a corporation in the US
4. Publishing: There is a lacuna in the publishing industry in India due to a shortage of copy editors, proof readers, etc. This area requires excellent

writing skills, error detection and correction skills, and reading comprehension. Opportunities are aplenty in Chennai itself. UOM in collaboration with leading publishing companies plans to launch a program on publishing in consultation with experts in the university and affiliating colleges.
5. Translation: this is an up-and-coming enterprise as part of the publishing industry. UOM has separate departments for Tamil literature, Tamil language, Telugu, Kannada, Hindi, and Sanskrit, as well as programs for French, Spanish, Italian and German. Efforts are being made to make translation an academic discipline. The faculty has given suggestions on how to accommodate translation into the relevant university curricula.
6. E-publishing: A combination of publishing and technical writing will be floated for the students of UOM in future to train them to enrich their occupational and professional skills. Writing practice related to E-publishing alone will be a focal point of this program.
7. Writing for the screen: Chennai, home of UOM, is known for production of films of international quality. There are opportunities for students to step into the movie industry if they master this form of writing at UOM. A proposal has been submitted to the Asian College of Journalism and the Tamil Nadu Film Institute in Chennai for a possible joint venture to float a course on Script Writing for the students of UOM and her affiliated colleges.

NOTE

1. The author wishes to thank the individuals at the University of Madras whom he interviewed regarding writing across disciplines at this university. These interviews are listed in the References.

REFERENCES

Arasu, V. Personal Interview. 13 July 2010.
Arumugam. M. Personal Interview. 20 September 2010.
Beulah,T. Personal Interview. 17 September 2010.
Gajendran, A. (1998). Transforming Dalit Politics. Seminar, 471, 24-27.
Guru, G. (1998). The Politics of Naming. Seminar, 471, 14-17.
Hunter, W. W. (1886). *The Imperial Gazetteer of India, Volume IX*, 2nd ed. London: Trubner & Co.
Karunanidhi, S. Personal Interview. 15 September 2010.

Leo, A. Personal Interview. 18 September 2010.
Mahalingam, T.V. (1974). *Early South Indian Paleography*. Madras: University of Madras Press.
Murugan. E. Personal Interview. 30 September 2010.
Narayanan, S. Personal Interview. 9 September 2010.
Ravindran, G. Personal Interview. 15 August 2010.
University of Madras. (2001).*University of Madras: The Calendar, The Madras University Act, 1923 Volume I and University Laws of the University (Statues and Ordinances)*. Madras: University of Madras Press.
University of Madras (2011). *Welcome to the University of Madras—150 Years of Excellence.* University of Madras. Retrieved from http://www.unom.ac.in
Venkataramanan.D. Personal Interview.19 September 2010

CHAPTER 23.
THE REGIONAL WRITING CENTRE AT THE UNIVERSITY OF LIMERICK

By Íde O'Sullivan and Lawrence Cleary
University of Limerick (Ireland)

In April 2007, Ireland's first Regional Writing Centre at the University of Limerick was launched. This chapter outlines the various international, European, national, regional, and institutional winds to which the growing Centre responded. Trailing UL's Regional Writing Centre through its path from inception to fruition, the profile reveals the influences that have shaped its ethos, guided its development and served to sustain it. Furthermore, the profile outlines the Centre's variegated approach for achieving what it hopes to be a more systematic approach to undergraduate, postgraduate, and professional writing development at UL and the region.

The University of Limerick (UL) is one of Ireland's youngest universities. Established as the National Institute for Higher Education (NIHE) in 1972, the institute attained its current university status in 1989. Describing itself as "an independent, internationally-focused university"(University of Limerick, 2009, p. 1), UL is often referred to as more of an "American-style" university. Proud of its record of innovation in education and excellence in research and scholarship, the university's mission is "to promote and advance learning and knowledge through teaching, research, and scholarship in an environment which encourages innovation and upholds the principles of free enquiry and expression" (University of Limerick, 2009, p. 1). In 2011, 1,300 staff strive to qualify UL as an exceptional, vibrant learning environment for 11,300 students.

Astride two sides of the River Shannon, the UL campus ranges over 130 hectares in Counties Limerick and Clare. Its recreational, cultural and sporting facilities are renowned, enhancing the university experience for students, staff and the wider, surrounding community. Further augmenting the university experience, the Regional Writing Centre at UL, formed in April of 2007, is a relatively new addition to campus life. Central in all aspects, the Writing

Centre is situated in the Main Building, roughly equidistant from all other campus localities.

As with most third-level institutes around the world, participation in a global economy and moves toward a mass education have changed the context into which learning is facilitated (Ivanič and Lea, 2006). Increased attention has been given to the link between education and career opportunities. In its mission statement (University of Limerick, 2009, p. 1), the university stresses its relationship to Ireland's national goal of preparing its citizens to participate in a global, highly competitive knowledge economy. In an effort to upskill its workforce, Ireland's third-level institutes strive to be more inclusive. As a result, student populations include an ever-increasing number from backgrounds that do not include the cultural and economic support systems that students from more traditional backgrounds might take for granted. In order to accommodate spatial and temporal varieties, such as distance learners, and encourage institutional collaborations, greater emphasis has been placed on teaching with technology. Additionally, with state aid diminishing, there is a greater reliance on international students for revenue, infusing the facilitation of learning and, in particular, meaning-making tasks with further language and cultural challenges. Funding challenges also inspire a greater interest in the link between scholarly research and entrepreneurial development. Finally, in an effort to increase enrolment and to improve retention rates, attention has shifted to the student experience. Educators are subject to a mounting pressure to evidence the quality of their performance. Against this backdrop, the Regional Writing Centre has taken shape and has thus far survived and, in some respects, even thrived.

FROM INCEPTION TO FRUITION

Prior to the establishment of the Regional Writing Centre, there had been a growing concern among faculty at UL about the writing competencies of their students. Initial responses to anecdotal concerns included ad hoc writing clinics and seminars. Much of that response came via UL's Language Support Unit. Strong support for a university-wide initiative on writing was evidenced by the intensity of the interest. An interdisciplinary working group was formed to investigate the means that this support might take. The disciplinary diversity of the interest was reflected in the make-up of that initial working group, which included representatives from each of the four Faculties; namely Arts, Humanities and Social Sciences; Education and Health Sciences; the Kemmy Business School; and Science and Engineering. The efforts of those interested in developing a writing initiative culminated in:

- a week-long consultation with visiting Professor Jim Henry of Virginia's (US) George-Mason University. Jim led a series of workshops on writing and, with interested parties, explored how that university-wide support could be translated into a systematic, comprehensive approach to writing, while addressing individual, disciplinary concerns;
- a student and academic staff audit of attitudes to writing, writing practices, and writing needs;
- several submissions for funding for a UL initiative; and,
- eventually, the establishment of a consortium of higher education institutions in the Shannon region and a Higher Education Authority Strategic Innovation Fund (SIF) award for the establishment of the Shannon Consortium Regional Writing Centre in April 2007.

This UL-led initiative, now located within the Centre for Teaching and Learning, resulted in two Writing Consultants being employed to run the Shannon Consortium Regional Writing Centre in UL and to collaborate with colleagues in Teaching and Learning support services across the Consortium to develop writing initiatives in each of these institutions: Limerick Institute of Technology, the Institute of Technology Tralee and Mary Immaculate College, Limerick. The two Writing Consultants (authors of this article) have always had an interest in developing their careers as writing developers. Lawrence has a strong background in writing, including rhetoric and composition, from Illinois State University, while Íde's doctoral research was in the area of applied linguistics, with an important influence from the European tradition in academic literacies. The combined approach that they bring to the Centre has resulted in a unique blend of the New Rhetoric (Berlin, 1982) and Academic Literacies (Lea and Street, 1998), influencing the direction the Centre has taken. This has led to the Writing Centre practicing a non-invasive, inductive approach to writing development, utilising peer tutors and experts who work with both students and staff to identify their writing practices in order to assess and improve strategic effectiveness, thus producing "better writers, not better writing" (North, 1984, p.438).

In this national context, into which early Writing Centre initiatives were introduced, writing was recognised as a central skill in preparing students for the knowledge economy. All other benefits were, and to a large extent still are, subsumed into writing's contribution to knowledge creation, dissemination and storage. Writing Centre support would be student-centred and augment a positive student experience. Writing Centre support would assist with recruitment efforts and increase student retention. International and non-traditional students would be attracted to the university by the support, and that same support would give hope to a population of students that might otherwise have given up. Research students would receive support in the complexities of research writing, and faculty would have somewhere to turn to help them in their endeavours to enhance student writing development. With more students signing on and more students staying on-board, more students publishing research and increased utilisation of writing expertise in classrooms, writing would make its contribution to the upskilling of the nation.

In addition to the broader cultural, economic and political contexts informing the approach that writing development would take, the working group took into account the results of the student and staff surveys of writing needs. The analysis of the surveys revealed that students recognised the importance of writing for both their academic careers and for their future professional development. Furthermore, the need and the desire for a systematic approach to the development of writing became obvious. The multiplicity of writing-related needs was evident in the surveys, and it was agreed that a writing centre that would incorporate a multidimensional approach would best meet those needs.

A Regional Writing Centre at the University of Limerick would be the first of its kind in Ireland. The Writing Centre would serve as a vital nexus of university writing activities at UL and across the Consortium. The factors motivating such a choice are explored in depth in Cleary, Graham, Jeanneau and O'Sullivan (2009, p. 4.12):

> The establishment of a Writing Centre is an important and, in the Irish HE context, ground-breaking step. It provides a centralised locus for the provision of a systematic discipline-specific writing support and development programme. The Writing Centre responds directly to the writing needs identified in the staff and student surveys carried out at UL and corroborating evidence from students and faculty surveys replicated in the other three institutions in the Shannon Consortium. While initial writing support was provided on an ad hoc basis, the move now is clearly towards a *Writing in the Disciplines* approach with elements of the *Writing Across the Curriculum* and *Writing to Learn* approaches being incorporated. The *academic literacies* approach, encapsulating both the study skills and acculturation models, has also been influential. Such an eclectic approach satisfies the multiplicity of writing needs of UL students identified in the online surveys.

Responding to the multiplicity of demands meant that the Writing Centre was charged with supporting the development of academic writing among undergraduates, postgraduates and researchers and with supporting staff in their teaching of academic writing. The objectives of the Centre, as set out in the first phase of the SIF project (2007-2009), were as follows:

- Improve writing skills of students in the collaborating institutions to assist them with current studies and future professional lives.
- Support course and curriculum design/development.
- Foster meta-cognitive thinking about writing.
- Bolster recruitment and retention efforts, by supporting students with particular needs, specifically mature students, first years, students in Access programmes.
- Conduct ongoing evaluation of interventions.
- Initiate a site for action research output related to writing.
- Share existing expertise and experience to date among collaborating institutions.

Charged with the responsibility to design, deliver and evaluate writing-support interventions and to assist with the development of an academic plan for the continued development of the Writing Centre, the two Writing Consultants set about developing Ireland's first Regional Writing Centre.

A first priority for the Writing Centre was to support student writers. With the goal of bolstering student recruitment and retention, strong emphasis has been placed on facilitating first-year students' acculturation into the academic community, while also reaching out to targeted groups of students with particular needs. This goal has been achieved through the following media:

- *Writing Interventions in Disciplinary Modules:* The two Writing Consultants have worked closely with subject specialists to design such interventions in a significant number of disciplines. Such interventions are delivered by the Writing Consultants or trained tutors or teaching assistants from within the discipline.
- *One-to-one Tutorial Assistance:* The number of one-on-one sessions in the Writing Centre has been steadily increasing since our inception. In accordance with this, the number of tutors and the disciplines they represent has also increased. Undergraduate peer-tutors are recruited from the module Peer-tutoring in Academic Writing, based on their performance in that module. Postgraduates are selected based on an interview and an evaluation of their writing and, subsequently, trained in our Writing Centre tutoring techniques.
- *Stand-alone Workshops:* These generic writing initiatives include essay-writing workshops, academic-writing workshops and writing support for mature students, facilitated by the two Writing Consultants and trained tutors.

- *Online Resources:* Online resources are developed by the two Writing Consultants, with assistance from the Technology Enhanced Learning Advisor from the Centre for Teaching and Learning.

In addition to the above activities, further initiatives have been created specifically for postgraduate students, who seek support not only for the development of their own writing, but also training in best practice for tutoring writing. These postgraduate initiatives include writing workshops, for example thesis writing and writing-for-publication; writers' groups for postgraduate and post-doctoral researchers; and peer-tutoring and tutor training in writing.

The third key focus of the Centre has been on faculty development on best practices for teaching with writing. The aim has been to assist faculty in developing student writing, while also developing their own academic writing. Events have been organised to facilitate staff development in teaching with writing; for instance, writing-in-disciplines and writing-to-learn workshops and a symposium on writing entitled Research on Writing Practices: Consequences for the Teaching of Writing and Learner Outcomes. The number of staff participating in writing-in-disciplines initiatives has increased; equally, Writing Centre staff have been involved in the training of tutors on several discipline-specific modules. In 2009, the Writing Centre also made a successful bid to host the 2011 EATAW (European Association for the Teaching of Academic Writing) conference, not only demonstrating the growing international status of the Centre, but also providing our staff with access to current research on best practices in teaching writing. Faculty development is an area that would certainly need to be developed further in order to incorporate writing into the curriculum in a meaningful way. The Centre would like to provide regular workshops to faculty on different areas of best practice for teaching and researching writing.

In relation to the professional development of writing amongst staff, the Centre for Teaching and Learning has been successfully supporting these writers for some time prior to the existence of the Writing Centre. This support has been primarily in the form of staff development workshops and writers' retreats, for which the theory and pedagogy have been developed by Professor Sarah Moore (2003), now Associate Vice-President at UL, through her collaborations with Professor Rowena Murray at the University of Strathclyde, Scotland, who has provided models for postgraduate and academic staff writing development (Murray & Moore, 2006).

Finally, in order to ensure the goal to initiate a site for action research and publication, Writing Centre staff conduct and publish action research to contribute to the body of scholarship on academic writing and the teaching of writing (Cleary & O'Sullivan 2008; Cleary, Graham, Jeanneau & O'Sullivan, 2009). Academic writing development in the Shannon region continues to be based on researched best practices in writing and writing pedagogy, as evidenced by recent Writing Centre staff publications and the Centre's growing national and international links with writing programme directors and scholars.

CHALLENGES FOR THE REGIONAL WRITING CENTRE

As the Centre grew, so did some of the challenges facing the Centre. Interestingly, our challenges did not relate to interest in the Centre or issues of visibility. In truth, the interest was so great, we were struggling to cope with the demand. At its inception, interest came only from a few departments in each of the faculties; now requests were coming from a vast range of departments across all four faculties. However, given the relative absence of a writing culture or writing programmes in the university, it was difficult to envisage from where the writing expertise to sustain the demand would emerge. We recognised that the development of this culture was going to be a slow process. To this end, in addition to the initiatives described above, it was decided that the development of writing modules would help to further the development of a culture in writing from which the required expertise would eventually emerge.

The development of a writing culture began with the development of a range of modules in writing, each assigned an individual code commencing with AW (Academic Writing), thus establishing an important identity for the Writing Centre modules. Academic Literacies 1 and 2 (AW4001 and AW4002) are offered to first-year students in the arts, humanities and social sciences. The aim of these modules is to facilitate the transition to university for students in this faculty. More importantly, these modules foster an awareness of writing among students at an early stage of their academic careers. The Writing Centre is responsible for training the tutors who are recruited from appropriate disciplines within the faculty, an activity which again fosters an important awareness of writing, while equally fostering a systematic approach.

Another module, Peer-tutoring in Academic Writing (AW4006), is offered as an elective module to students wishing to enhance their writing skills, while training to become peer-tutors in the Writing Centre. Again, this accredited module fosters an awareness of writing among students but, equally, it provides the Centre with a panel of well-trained peer-tutors to work in the Writing Centre. The development of two modules entitled Research Planning and Preparation and Scholarly Presentation and Dialogue in Research and Academic Writing, delivered as part of the Specialist Diploma in Teaching, Learning and Scholarship, is a third illustration of how expertise in writing is nurtured among our future teachers.

SUSTAINABILITY OF THE REGIONAL WRITING CENTRE

Another responsibility of the Writing Consultants, in addition to developing student writing, was to assist with the development of an academic plan for the continued development of the Writing Centre. The most important aspect of this plan was the sustainability of the Writing Centre in the post-SIF (Strategic Initiative Fund) period. Throughout the SIF-funded period, the aim of the Centre was to ensure the development of initiatives that would be valued so greatly that the institutions would not want to do without them. However, as the SIF project neared an end in June 2009, the possibility of further SIF funding to sustain the Shannon Consortium Regional Writing Centre diminished as the economic climate weakened. The focus for future funding turned toward the individual institutions for sustainability. UL contributed matching SIF funding to sustain the Regional Writing Centre at the university for a further year, until June 2010. The efforts of the Centre staff in that year were to ensure that the funding for the Writing Centre would come from core budget. Embedding Writing Centre activity in core curricula, it was advised, was the means to ensuring sustainability. In addition to continuing the initiatives outlined above, the Centre was involved in the design and development of further modules to ensure its presence in the core activities of the university; for instance, the development of modules entitled Thesis Writing, Advanced Technical Communication for Engineers, and Educational Guidance have been developed in conjunction with the MA programme in English Language Teaching, the MEng in Mechanical Aeronautical Engineering and the pre-university Access programme respectively. It was hoped that these modules, alongside ever-increasing intervention within disciplinary modules, would be enough to ensure our sustainability in the university.

Efforts to ensure the sustainability of the Writing Centre have resulted in the Centre growing quite rapidly and in many diverse directions. Such diversity ensured the visibility of the Centre in its infancy and built goodwill amongst faculty and staff. However, with limited resources, such diversity and rapid growth would be difficult to maintain. Following the external evaluation of the Writing Centre in July 2008,[1] carried out by Professor. Terry Myers Zawacki, former Writing Center Director and currently Director of the Writing Across the Curriculum (WAC) Program at George Mason University, it was recommended that the scope of activities and initiatives the Centre had developed in the SIF-funded period be narrowed in order to ensure the sustainability of the Centre and to grow the Centre in the two areas central to its core mission, namely to assist students with their writing, through one-on-one and group support, as a way to bolster both recruitment and retention efforts; and, secondly, to assist faculty across disciplines in their efforts to teach with writing.

In moving forward and developing new initiatives, we have been careful to ensure that they do indeed enhance these two areas of our core mission. As we continue to develop writing interventions in disciplinary modules, we will recruit postgraduate students from within the disciplines to help create and deliver such interventions, a task which will become easier as the culture of writing is developed. In her evaluation, Professor Zawacki recommended the development of a Writing Fellows programme to this end. Equally, we will strive to help staff to nurture these important writing skills in their own classrooms rather than always calling on the experts to intervene. This will entail supporting disciplinary staff through ongoing workshops on teaching with writing and by populating our website with useful support materials and resources.

CONCLUSION

The primary research carried out at the inception of the project highlighted evidence of a non-systematic approach to writing development and support; it suggested that writing was not getting the attention it needed, despite its centrality to success at third level and its impact on students' professional lives. The Regional Writing Centre at UL now provides a coordinated, systematic approach to the teaching, learning and research of academic writing and to academic writing support across the region, supporting undergraduate and postgraduate student writers and collaborating with faculty to expand writing-based curriculum innovations. The Writing Centre's activities work towards enhancing the quality and effectiveness of teaching and research across the region, while enhancing the student experience. In its short existence, the Writing Centre has become an essential part of the regional landscape and is now recognised as a unique centre of expertise and knowledge in Ireland.

All of the efforts to ensure sustainability highlighted herein culminated in the presentation of a three-year business/academic plan for the Writing Centre to the University Executive Committee. At the time of the writing of this profile, it was announced that the Executive Committee, after much time and deliberation, had agreed to mainstream the Regional Writing Centre at UL. Consortium partners may wish to invest in the writing expertise offered by the Regional Writing Centre at UL, following a shared-services model, thereby benefiting from, yet avoiding the full cost of, programmes developed through UL writing expertise. Writing Consultants from UL will work with staff in each of these institutions to develop writing initiatives therein. Such expertise may well be extended beyond the Consortium partners to the National University of Ireland, Galway, which has recently formed a new alliance with UL. Moving forward will bring new and exciting challenges for the Regional Writing Centre in its ever-expanding regional profile.

NOTE

1. Following the original consultation with Professor Jim Henry, now Director of Writing across the Curriculum at the University of Hawaii, and formerly of George Mason University, it was agreed that a follow-up consultation in the form of an external evaluation would inform the future direction of the Writing Centre at UL.

REFERENCES

Berlin, J. (1982). Contemporary composition: The major pedagogical theories. *College English, 44*(8), 765-77.

Cleary, L., Graham, C., Jeanneau, C., & O'Sullivan, Í. (2009). Responding to the writing development needs of Irish higher education students: A case study. *The All Ireland Journal of Teaching and Learning in Higher Education, 1*(1), 4.1-4.16.

Cleary, L., & O'Sullivan, Í. (2008). Innovations, activities and principles for supporting student writing. In Moore, S. (Ed.), *Supporting academic writing among students and academics* (pp. 15-20), SEDA Special (24).

Ivanič, R., & Lea, M. R. (2006). New contexts, new challenges: The teaching of writing in UK higher education. In L. Ganobcsik-Williams (Ed.), *Teaching academic writing in UK higher education: Theories, practices and models* (pp. 6-15). Basingstroke, Hampshire, UK: Palgrave / Macmillan.

Lea, M., & Street, B. (1998). Student writing in higher education: An academic literacies approach. *Studies in Higher Education, 23*(2), 157-172.

Moore, S. (2003). Writers' retreats for academics: Exploring and increasing the motivation to write. *Journal of Further and Higher Education, 27*(3), 333-42.

Murray, R., & Moore, S. (2006). *The handbook of academic writing: A fresh approach.* Maidenhead, Berkshire, UK: Open University Press.

North, S. M. (1984). The idea of a writing center. *College English, 46*(5), 433-446.

University of Limerick. (2009). *University of Limerick: A Profile 2009.* Retrieved from http://www2.ul.ie/pdf/290515567.pdf

CHAPTER 24.
NEW WRITING IN AN OLD LAND

By Trudy Zuckermann, Bella Rubin, and Hadara Perpignan
Achva Academic College of Education, Tel Aviv University, and Bar-Ilan University (Israel)

This essay covers the history of academic writing development in Israel (vertically) and the landscape and diversity of the present programs (horizontally). It explains why Israel was slow in developing programs in either Hebrew or English, although there were academic institutions in the country even before the establishment of the State. It describes the foresight of our first prime minister, David Ben-Gurion, in his realization that some students need extra support in order to succeed academically, the contribution of Eliezer Ben Yehudah in the development of the modern Hebrew language, and the insight of the sponsors of the Wolfson Family Charitable Trust in the need for scientists and social scientists to write for the global community. The picture is one of slow growth, recent innovations, attempts to develop programs in spite of budgetary cuts, and dreams for a better future. The establishment of IFAW, the Israel Forum for Academic Writing, and the attempts to connect with like-minded educators throughout the world through international conferences are bright spots on the horizon.

In preparation for the symposium at the 2007 EATAW conference, "Historical Roots of National Writing Cultures," we began doing research on the state of academic writing and its history in the modern State of Israel. We were amazed, even then, about how many different programs exist in English and in Hebrew, and how little we knew about what other people were doing, even within the same institution. It was this situation that encouraged us to organize what has become IFAW, the Israel Forum for Academic Writing, and to continue our research in this area. The following profile essay is one result of these efforts.[1]

THE BEGINNINGS: INSTITUTIONS OF HIGHER EDUCATION IN ISRAEL

Israel is an old-new country. The history of Israel is at least 3,000 years old; on the other hand, the modern State of Israel was born only 63 years ago. Even before the State of Israel was established in 1948, three institutions of higher education had been founded: the Israeli Institute for Technology (the Technion) in 1914; the Hebrew University of Jerusalem in 1925, and the Weizmann Institute of Science (then called the Daniel Sieff Research Institute) in 1934.

The first universities in modern Israel were based on European models, with the idea that the cultured, intellectual community should be able to learn and to spread knowledge to the masses throughout the nation and the world. There were very few books available in those days; so the system was based mainly on lectures and discussion, the professors being the privileged few who had already breathed the air of the European university tradition. In pre-state Israel and even after the establishment of the State, studying at a university was a privilege of the very few.

The Weizmann Institute of Science opened its doors in 1934. This was to be a different kind of academic institution, namely a research center for graduate students who would devote their lives to using science for the benefit of humanity. Scientists and professors were expected to publish the results of their research, and it was assumed that they knew how to do this. Many of them did.

Students who did enter Israeli universities were expected to know how to write academic papers without being trained and without getting feedback on their writing. It was assumed that if you were accepted to a university, then you knew how to write academic papers. Thus, Israeli universities never developed a tradition of Freshman Composition or Writing across the Curriculum, either in Hebrew or in English. It is only within the last few years that freshman composition courses have begun to appear in the universities, and that a greater concern about writing instruction in general has manifested itself among Israeli educators.

Today, there are numerous tertiary institutions in Israel. Four additional universities (Bar-Ilan University, 1955; Tel Aviv University, 1956-1963; University of Haifa, 1963; Ben-Gurion University, 1969) as well as the Open University began operating in Israel during the first decades of the State. In addition, private institutions such as IDC (the Herzliya Interdisciplinary Center) were established, and numerous colleges have been granted the right to issue bachelors' and masters' degrees by the Council of Higher Education. In the Palestinian Authority, twenty institutions of higher learning are listed on the Internet, all established since 1967. Bethlehem University, founded in 1973, the first university established in the West Bank, can trace its roots to 1893, when the De La Salle Christian Brothers opened schools in Bethlehem, Jerusalem, Jaffa, and Nazareth, as well as in Turkey, Lebanon, Jordan, and Egypt.[2] Al-Quds University was established in 1984 with the purpose of providing education to Palestinian students from Jerusalem and other parts of Palestine. Since then, Al-Quds University has expanded to encompass 10 faculties and sixteen institutes and centers, and serves a student body of more than 5000.[3]

With such a wide range of tertiary institutions, it is very difficult to ascertain where there is any type of writing program and in what languages. We have begun our own mapping project, but it is incomplete. What is clear is that today's students in all institutions need professional guidance in order to cope with their writing tasks.

The remainder of this paper will trace the developments of writing instruction in Israel, according to the information we have been able to gather thus far, and will describe the directions and goals of the present programs as well as our hopes for the future.

Table 1: Chronology of Events Relevant to Academic Writing Instruction from Pre-State Israel until Today

Year	Event
1881	Arrival in Palestine of Ben-Yehuda, the founder of Modern Hebrew
1884	Publication of Hebrew language newspaper, "Hatzvi"
1890	Founding of the Hebrew Language Council (now the Hebrew Language Academy)
1893	Opening of the De La Salle Christian Brothers schools in Bethlehem, Jerusalem, Jaffa, Nazareth
1898	Establishment of six all-encompassing Hebrew schools and 14 part time Hebrew schools
1900	Publication of the first method book for teaching Hebrew
1906	Founding of the first Hebrew high school in Jaffa
1910	Publication of first six volumes of Ben-Yehuda's Hebrew language dictionary
1914	Beginning of classes at the Technion
1919	Laying of the cornerstone of the Hebrew University
1921	Recognition by the British Mandate Authority of Hebrew, as well as Arabic and English, as official languages
1925	Opening of classes at the Hebrew University of Jerusalem
1934	Opening of the Daniel Sieff Research Institute (Now the Weizmann Institute of Science)
1948	Establishment of the State of Israel

1955	Establishment of Bar-Ilan University
1956	Sponsoring of three Tel Aviv University Institutes by the City of Tel-Aviv
1959	Posthumous publication of the complete 17 volumes of Ben-Yehuda's Hebrew language dictionary by his 2nd wife and son
1963	Opening of Tel-Aviv University as an independent institution
1963	Founding of University of Haifa
1968	Opening of the Center for Pre-Academic Studies, the preparatory program of the Hebrew University in Jerusalem; Requirement of "scientific" writing for all students
1969	Opening of Ben-Gurion University
1973	Founding of Bethlehem University, the first university established in the West Bank
1973	Founding of the Open University of Israel
The early 1980s	Introduction of first academic writing courses in EFL in Israel, but only for English majors
1984	Founding of Al-Quds University
1986	Beginning of the Wolfson Pilot Project
The 1990s	Introduction of Academic Writing in the Teachers' Colleges
1994	Opening of the IDC (Inter-Disciplinary Center of Herzliya)
1995	Opening of Sal'Or Writing Center—Kibbutzim College
2007	Founding of IFAW
2007	Beginning of IFAW Mapping Project
2007	Establishment of first "Freshman Hebrew" course required of all incoming humanities students at Hebrew University
2008	Hebrew University EAP Initiatives
2009-2010	Celebration of the Year of the Hebrew Language
2009-2010	Ministry of Education emphasis on Hebrew writing courses in K-12 system
2010	IFAW International Conference

A BIT OF A DIGRESSION: THE STRUGGLE FOR HEBREW

Eliezer Ben-Yehuda, the pioneer and prophet of the modern Hebrew language, was born in 1858 in Lithuania.[4] Like most Jewish children of the time in Eastern Europe, he began learning Hebrew for prayer and Bible study at an early age in the hope that he would become a great rabbi; instead he became a product of the "Haskalah," the Enlightenment movement in Europe. Ben-Yehuda and many other promising young Jews of Eastern Europe at the time left the Talmudic academy and entered a Russian gymnasium and/or a European university.

Hebrew had been used throughout the ages for religious purposes—prayer and Bible study—especially by male Jews in Eastern Europe, North Africa, and Yemen. In addition, even as far back as the medieval period, secular literature in Hebrew, especially poetry and philosophy, existed. By the nineteenth century, there were also a number of Hebrew periodicals in Europe, and a few people were beginning to write poetry, short stories, and essays in the ancient tongue. Interestingly enough, during all this time, Hebrew was only a written language and not a spoken tongue. It was Ben-Yehuda's dream to make it a spoken language as well. Today the process is reversed. Almost everyone in Israel speaks and understands Hebrew. What is necessary is to educate people to write in Hebrew as well.

When Ben-Yehuda arrived in Palestine in 1881, he had already published his first article on the importance of reviving the Hebrew language. He immediately began work on his three-pronged plan of action: Hebrew in the Home; Hebrew in the School, and Hebrew for Adults. It was not an easy plan to carry through. Members of the religious community objected to using the holy tongue for secular purposes, and the Turks, who ruled the country at that time, objected to the official use of any language other than Turkish. In spite of many hardships, Ben-Yehuda and his supporters persisted and eventually succeeded in their goal.

In the Ben-Yehuda home, it was forbidden for children to hear any language other than Hebrew. Others followed his example. As a child, sixty years after Ben-Yehuda had arrived in the country, Amos Oz writes that his parents knew many different languages, but they taught him only Hebrew (Oz, 2004). This was the general trend for many immigrant families.

Ben Yehuda believed that in order for the younger generation to begin speaking Hebrew freely, it would be necessary to have Hebrew become the language of instruction in all Jewish schools in the country. This was not an easy task, as there were vested interests in maintaining instruction in French, German, English, and Yiddish. Ben Yehuda began by insisting that all kindergarten teachers learn Hebrew so that very quickly the children would became native speakers of Hebrew. By 1898, there were six all-encompassing Hebrew schools in the country, and fourteen part time Hebrew schools, with a total enrollment of 2,500 pupils. In 1900, the first method book for teaching Hebrew was published, and in 1906, the first Hebrew high school was founded in Jaffa (St. John, 1952; Cooper-Weill, 1998).

With the establishment of the Technion in 1913-14, the first major language war took place. The founders of the Technion from Germany insisted that it was logical for instruction to take place in German, since the language of science at the time was German and students needed to communicate with the scientific community throughout the world. Many scientific and technical terms did not even exist in Hebrew at the time. However, the students and instructors went on strike and refused to return to classes unless Hebrew became the language of instruction. They won the battle: the language of instruction in all universities in the country was to be Hebrew. In 1921, the Mandate authority recognized Hebrew, as well as Arabic and English, as official languages (Bein, 1971; Spolsky and Shohamy, 1999).

Finally, Ben-Yehuda wanted the Hebrew language to permeate the entire society. He had begun publishing his own Hebrew newspaper, called "Hatzvi," in 1884. Here, as well as in many speeches, discussions, and meetings, he propagandized for the use of Hebrew in the home, in schools, in the workplace, in the marketplace; in fact, all over. However, in a sense, the founders of the Technion were correct. Not only scientific terms, but also many modern concepts and ideas did not exist in nineteenth century Hebrew. Ben-Yehuda began introducing new words in his newspaper. By a careful study of ancient and medieval texts, he was able to coin new terms from the old roots and to spread his ideas and linguistic coinages to Hebrew readers throughout the world. The words he entered in his seventeen-volume dictionary, which was completed only after his death by his wife and son, followed strict philological rules. Ben-Yehuda founded the Hebrew Language Council in 1890, the forerunner of the present Hebrew Language Academy, which continues to introduce new words and concepts into modern spoken and written Hebrew, to solve various linguistic problems in the Hebrew language, and to set acceptable standards for the use of the language.

Ben-Yehuda and his followers succeeded in reviving the ancient Hebrew language into a vital, modern language in everyday use. There is no doubt that this is an impressive achievement. Unlike most countries, where monolingual policy originates and is enforced by powerful, political forces (Kibner, 2008), the Hebrew-only initiative was a grassroots movement, which, for many years, needed to struggle against the powers-that-be. Today, however, when the Hebrew language is clearly the lingua-franca of most Israelis, the necessity of insisting on Hebrew-only policies is questionable. Was it necessary, for instance, during 2009, designated by the Ministry of Education as the year for the Hebrew language, for the Ministry to instruct schools to begin playing only Hebrew songs during school recesses and in all school events and activities? Why did the President of the Hebrew Language Academy express such strong opposition concerning a proposed graduate course at the Technion to be conducted in English in order to attract foreign students? (How could this happen at the Technion, he wanted to know, where the first major battle in academia for the Hebrew language took place?)

Achva Academic College of Education, Tel Aviv University, and Bar-Ilan University (Israel)

According to some, the imposition of Hebrew only is a mixed blessing (Shohamy, 2009). We shall touch on this problem as we continue to discuss the development of writing programs in higher education in Israel today.

WRITING "A NATURAL PHENOMENON: NO NEED FOR INSTRUCTION"

Amos Oz states in his autobiography, "All Jerusalem, in my childhood, in the last years of British rule, sat at home and wrote. Hardly anyone had a radio in those days, and there was no television or video or compact disc player or Internet or e-mail, not even the telephone. But everyone had a pencil and a notebook" (Oz, 2004, p.285). Later, even when he moved to the kibbutz, he found that farmers devoted to manual labor often wrote modest articles and sometimes even poetry (Oz, 2004, p.468).

Perhaps one reason for the lack of attention to specific writing skills in Israel until recently, whether in the elementary and secondary grades or in the universities, was that writing seemed to be a natural phenomenon, like sleeping or breathing. Even though most people did not attend university, many people wrote. In those days, people wrote in many languages. However, their children, the second generation, wrote only in Hebrew. No matter what their occupation at the time, members of the first generation were, like Ben Yehuda himself, products of the "Haskalah" or "Enlightenment" movement. Others, who had not been exposed to European secular education, were, nevertheless, products of a literate tradition: the Bible, the Mishnah, etc. The style was argumentative and sometimes poetic, not the traditional Western, academic writing we know today. Nevertheless, if these people entered the university, they were able to survive without a freshman composition course.

What has happened since then to the culture of writing in Israel? We know that many of our students who enter institutions of higher education have difficulty writing, and some enter with writer's block. Is it because of the failure of the school system (large classes, discipline problems, matriculation exams, poor planning, too many subjects, poor teaching)? Is it the conditions of life today: technology, Internet, TV, many more activities and distractions?

We do know that higher education in Israel no longer belongs to the privileged few. More students come from non-academic backgrounds. Members of the Ethiopian and Bedouin communities come from oral-aural cultures where writing played no part. Students with learning differences are accepted into colleges and universities. In addition, for some students, Hebrew is a third or fourth language, and English (which is a requirement for the Bachelors' degree) may be a fourth or fifth language.

It is true that professors throughout the ages have always complained that some of their students do not know how to write properly. But today's concern seems more acute, both about students writing in their native language, Hebrew, and certainly about their writing skills in English. Those of us who have worked with such students, whether at the beginning of their college career or at the post-graduate level, have long realized that those entering higher education are in need of professional guidance in order to cope with their writing tasks.

BEN-GURION AND THE PREPARATORY PROGRAMS (THE "MECHINOT")

The realization that some students needed additional support in order to succeed in higher education came from our first prime-minister, David Ben-Gurion. One of his dreams was to integrate the many non-Western immigrants into Israeli society as equal citizens. They, too, should have a chance in higher education, he believed. In order to do this, these students, who did not have the advantages of a European education or the educational background of their peers, needed extra preparation and support before they could enter the university. For this purpose, the first preparatory program was established at the Hebrew University in Jerusalem. It was probably the first place in Israel where academic writing in Hebrew was taught. The Saltiel Center for Pre-Academic Studies continues to flourish to this day, as do many other preparatory programs throughout the country.

Among the required courses during this preparatory year, all students in the program take a course called "Scientific Writing." Depending on their level, students study writing four, six, or eight hours a week. The present student population is somewhat different from the original group of students in 1968. It consists both of very strong students who are interested in improving their matriculation grades so they can enter prestigious departments such as medicine, law, or psychology, and very weak students, some of whom come from an oral culture where they were never expected to write at all.

Some students at the Center know how to write, but not academically; some lack worldly knowledge. For some, it is an embarrassment to take writing courses in Hebrew, which is their mother tongue. The influence of culture on writing is also very strong. For example, it is very difficult for Arab students to write summaries without injecting an interpretation of their own.

In all courses, the connection between reading academic texts and academic writing is stressed, as the need is felt for students to broaden and deepen their knowledge before they begin to write. Organization strategies and thinking skills are taught. Students then study text types and the hierarchy structure within texts, and practice writing summaries. Before they write definitions of their own, they analyze different types of definition within texts. They must learn to give ideas their exact designation. Finally, they work on the development of their own ideas through paragraph structure and organization of larger texts. Later in the course, the use of sources is covered. As a final project, students from the higher levels in all divisions and all social science students are required to write a paper of about 3,000 words.

ADDITIONAL HEBREW WRITING PROGRAMS

Many colleges in Israel offer academic degrees today, and in so doing have attempted to develop academic writing programs in both Hebrew and English. Students preparing to become teachers are expected to do both conventional, academic writing and reflective writing within the framework of the academy. They are often confused when suddenly encouraged to express their own ideas and feelings and use the first person singular. They see the academic context and expectations of essay writing established within the wider institution as inhibiting their ability and willingness to reflect in writing (Zuckermann, 2007). In addition to these two different aspects of academic writing, future teachers must prepare themselves to teach their own pupils how to write. Even native speakers of a language may find these requirements formidable. For teachers college students who may be writing in a language that is not their mother tongue, the task is many times more difficult.

A varied number of programs have been developed in the teachers colleges. Some programs are similar to the skills-based program described in the university preparatory program above. Others, like the David Yellin College in Jerusalem, have developed experimental programs where students in each department of the college are required to take an introductory course in their discipline during their first year of studies. This course includes a unit on academic writing in that discipline, a kind of combination of WAC (Writing across the Curriculum) and WID (Writing in the Disciplines).

In another institution, the Kibbutzim College, a writing center has been successfully established in place of the Hebrew academic writing courses. As far as we know, this is the only fully-developed writing center in Israel in spite of many attempts to establish such a center in the universities. The SAL'OR Writing Center is one section of the three-tier complex of the alternative learning centers at Kibbutzim College. These are all housed together in one building, which contains a concentration of library activities and a counseling center. It is hoped that students will learn to use the facilities of the center as an aid in their academic work. SAL'OR and the other two centers in the building are part of the trend of "alternative learning" or mentoring systems for academic activities.

The first academic writing program at Kibbutzim College was a one-semester course for all students, which did not seem to be meeting the goals of having students properly prepared to do the writing they were expected to do at the college. In 1995, all academic writing courses at the college were cancelled, and the staff was moved to the new SAL'OR center.

The center is open five full days a week. Sessions last one half hour each; study sessions are arranged ahead of time. Students come on a voluntary basis as frequently or infrequently as they like. Some come because they feel a technical need to complete an assignment; some are completely overwhelmed by their assignments and don't know where to begin; some are more knowledgeable and want specific guidance. Students do not receive academic credit for attending sessions; nor is there any grade assessment given at the center for the completion of assignments: the grade is given by the course instructor. However, both oral and written formative assessment is given to the students on the process of their writing, and there is detailed record-keeping of each student's progress. All the mentors are experienced lecturers at the college, with knowledge and some training in academic literacy as well as expertise in at least one other subject. They receive salaries from the original budget allotted to the semester courses in academic literacy that were cancelled.

About 10 percent of the students in the regular four-year program come to the center voluntarily. In addition, special sessions are arranged for students from different language and cultural backgrounds and those with learning disabilities and other difficulties. Students in the English department also receive tutoring in English academic writing.

The staff of the center works to ensure contact with other staff members of the college. Department heads and lecturers are consulted to coordinate specific needs and norms of writing in their disciplines. Sometimes mentors from the center are invited by lecturers to give workshops to groups of students or an entire class. Often, some of these students arrive at the center afterwards for individual help. The center has also given courses to other members of the college staff who are interested.

A special project was conducted with experienced teachers in the field who returned to the college to earn a BEd or upgrade their education in some other way. Many of them felt overwhelmed by the many writing assignments they received at the college. A combination of group mentoring and one-to-one tutoring was used. By the end of the course, most participants had become more confident about their writing and were very enthusiastic about the work at the center.

Colleges other than teachers colleges have also developed writing programs in recent years. In some cases, it has been difficult to obtain administrative support for these programs. In other cases, administrators have come to realize the importance of helping students professionally in their writing tasks and those they will face after leaving the academy.

THE WOLFSON PROJECT—ACADEMIC WRITING IN ENGLISH

In the early days of the State, students had to write seminar papers and theses, but mostly in Hebrew. Later students were being asked to publish in English for international journals during their graduate studies, especially in the sciences. The students, however, wrote only in Hebrew. As there were no courses in academic writing, PhD advisors were expected to teach their students how to write in English, how to publish, and how to enter the international scientific community.

We know of two courses in English composition, one at the Hebrew University, and the second at Tel-Aviv University (TAU). The Hebrew University course was taught gratis and served only faculty members, not students. The TAU course was funded directly from the Rector's office and served a handful of PhD students and some faculty members. Both of these courses were taught by teachers with no writing instruction background or experience and with little or no theoretical framework.

There were also composition courses in the English literature departments, but only for literature students whose native language, on the whole, was English. In the early 1980s, a "bridge course" was designed at TAU, the purpose of which was to help Israeli students improve their writing in English and eventually be accepted into the English Literature Department. This course ran for years and was actually one of the first English academic writing courses for foreign language students in Israel, but it served only literature and some linguistic students. Other Israelis who wished to publish in international journals generally hired English-speaking immigrants to translate and/or edit their work, a grueling but profitable task for the lucky British, Americans, or South Africans.

Soon after the establishment of the State, the teaching of English for Academic Purposes became an established field. However, the focus was primarily on reading comprehension. By this time, there were more books imported from abroad available, and although courses were taught in Hebrew, students had to cope with bibliographies and textbooks that were written in English. The universities reluctantly took on some of the responsibility for helping students do so, but the dominant attitude was that students who couldn't cope with their reading assignments in English did not belong in the university. As to writing, it was assumed that if students could read in English, they could also write in English. Indeed, if people were studying at universities, they certainly knew how to write in Hebrew, the national language, and therefore, they could do so in English.

These were the dominant attitudes for many years by those who made pedagogical decisions. Then in 1986, the Wolfson Family Charitable Trust, which had previously given financial support in the sciences to institutions of higher education in Israel, approached the University Teachers of English Language in Israel (UTELI) and offered to sponsor a pilot project to teach Israeli PhD students to improve their writing in English. It seemed to the sponsors that Israeli academics were losing ground in the international scientific community.

In its earliest stage, the Wolfson Project consisted of three selected writing instructors who were to design their own syllabi and create their own instructional materials, with guidance from the project coordinator. The courses were originally designed for PhD and post-doctoral students, since undergraduate courses in Israel are taught in Hebrew. The major aim was to prepare students to write research papers and minimally to make conference presentations. The original project was extended to all the universities in Israel, following which most academic institutions agreed to support the teaching of writing in English and eventually to take over the financial support. Thus, the first generation of organized English academic writing courses in Israel was born.

The program was based, above all, on the principle of authenticity. Students used real data, no matter the discipline, in the main writing tasks they did. They wrote authentic abstracts for conferences and/or articles; grant proposals; parts of their thesis; book chapters; experimental research reports; conference papers; review articles; even academic correspondence . . . and CVs. Most courses were geared either to the biological sciences, exact sciences, humanities, or social sciences, but some were mixed. Although the graduate students in the project had to produce real-world texts, the process approach was used and criteria were developed for assessment and evaluation without using grades. The project coordinator and participating teachers insisted on individual student conferences and maintaining contact with subject specialists/PhD advisors. However, many university administrators were not willing to accept conferences as an integral part of the course syllabus, an issue of contention that remains.

Today's practices, based on the original Wolfson Project, reflect the development of academic writing research in the twenty-first century and vary somewhat in the different institutions throughout Israel. In general, although class size is no longer limited to twelve students, emphasis is still placed on one-to-one student-teacher conferences/tutorials and e-mail. E-learning and virtual courses have been developed. Today, program evaluation is more systematized and performed both during the courses and after they end. In addition to instructor assessment, peer review is encouraged, and criteria for judging written work are developed by both students and instructors. There is more refined emphasis on audience: readership of journals, members of academic committees, conference organizing committees, journal editors, etc. Students may choose their own scientific articles in their specific fields of research to be used as model texts. Many more genres are dealt with (e.g., grant proposals, thesis chapters, conference presentations, e-mail, letters to journal editors, CV writing, use of PowerPoint). Since conference presentations also involve oral presentation skills, students may participate in mini-conferences where they practice with PowerPoint and videos. Emphasis is placed on authentic texts based on actual data which students are intending to publish and on content-based courses with actual tasks students are required to complete for their subject courses. There is better contact with subject specialists, student advisors, and university administrators.

DEVELOPMENTS FROM 1990 TO THE PRESENT

Today there is greater recognition of the need for writing courses in Hebrew, as well as in English, throughout Israel. Composition courses for Arabic speakers writing in Arabic seem to be at a minimum, however. The attitude of administrators, including those in Arab colleges, seems to be that students will need to write in Hebrew in order to get along in Israeli society, and in English in order to publish internationally; so why waste precious resources on teaching Arab composition? In the Arab Institute of Beit Berl Academic College of Education, whereas Arabic as a first language is scheduled for up to six hours a week for all three-year BEd students, the emphasis is on reading comprehension, not writing. It will probably take a few more years to convince the policy makers that writing in the mother tongue is a necessary prerequisite to writing in other languages.

As far as Hebrew writing goes, the necessity for more concentrated instruction seems to have filtered down into the K-12 school system. Previously, writing was not mandated to be taught by the Ministry of Education until the eleventh or twelfth grade. Creative writing was not included in the official curriculum at all. Of course there were some teachers who provided opportunities for written expression even in the elementary grades, but nothing was mandated officially.

Beginning in 2010, pupils in the seventh and eighth grades are given a subject called "Ivrit" (Hebrew) six hours a week, instead of the old language and written and oral expression courses which were taught two to three hours a week altogether. In our opinion, this is a positive development, showing an increased awareness of the need for developing writing skills as early as possible. There is still a long way to go, but this is a beginning, and we hope that our efforts on the tertiary level will eventually influence the elementary grades.

In regard to activity in Hebrew on the tertiary level, since 2007 freshmen in the humanities division of the Hebrew University in Jerusalem are required to take a course called "Introduction to Hebrew Composition." In the Master's Degree Program of the Hebrew University Nursing School of Hadassah Hospital, a Hebrew writing course has been operating since 2008. Other departments of the university, mainly in the social sciences, require some writing instruction. Many instructors help their students step-by-step in producing a project or a research paper, for instance.

The Rothberg School for International Students of the Hebrew University in Jerusalem offers a one-year preparatory program for non-native Israeli students. Since 2000, students in the two upper levels of their mandated Hebrew language courses are required to take a one-semester course in academic writing in conjunction with their mandatory history course. Because students are required to write a paper as a final project in history, they are motivated to learn the skills necessary for such an endeavor. The instructors in the academic writing courses are the history teachers who have been trained especially for this purpose.

Students in the lower levels of the Hebrew language courses also study history, but in their native languages. In 2006, academic writing was introduced as an accompaniment to the history course in these languages: Russian, Arabic, French, Spanish, or English, and taught by former immigrant instructors, PhD or post-doctoral students from the country of their origin. The final history paper is written in the language of the course. During the second semester, all students are required to write a paper in their field of specialty in Hebrew as well, and if they continue on in the Hebrew University in the humanities division, they will also take an academic writing course in Hebrew.

There are still some negative attitudes toward writing courses in Hebrew, as exemplified by one of the deans of Ben-Gurion University during our mapping project. When one of our members, a faculty member of the university, approached the dean in an attempt to find out what writing courses are given and in what languages, he answered, "Of course only in English. We do want to encourage our students to do research and to publish internationally. Why would they need to write in Hebrew?"

There are courses in English composition and academic writing in English departments in colleges and universities throughout Israel, but because of budgetary cuts, some programs are becoming smaller. Today there is also some writing done in many EAP courses that have traditionally covered reading comprehension exclusively.

RECENT INNOVATIONS

Among recent innovations in various programs are the Technical Writing Course for the MSc in Engineering developed by Bella Rubin, and the Technical Writing Course for the PhD in Engineering developed by Prof. Reuven Boxman, both at Tel Aviv University; courses for biology students at the Weizman Research Institute taught by a PhD in biology who has also become an expert in academic writing, and a writing course for chemistry students at Weizman taught by a lecturer with a PhD in linguistics. At Haifa University, in an attempt to bridge the gap between the fields of composition studies and of EAP or EFL, an applied linguist, Dr. Hadara Perpignan, was recruited to guide the teaching of writing about literature to Arabic- and Hebrew-speaking English majors. At Bar Ilan, in addition to the PhD program, all masters degree students who do not show exemption mastery are required to take academic writing courses in English.

At the Technion, beginning in 2010, the Graduate School Dean has extended the PhD academic writing program to the master's level as well. This course is still an elective as students have to fulfill graduate English reading comprehension proficiency requirements as a prerequisite to the advanced course. For PhD students, the one-semester Academic Writing Course is a requirement as before. There is also a high level, undergraduate writing course titled Communication in English for Scientists and Engineers. This is an elective that focuses on both writing and presentation skills. It grew out of the specific request by the high-tech industry to offer a course at the Technion that would provide graduates with the skills they will need when they enter the professional world.

Since 2000, two graduate-level writing courses were offered by the Dept. of EFL at Ben-Gurion University at its two campuses in Beer-Sheva and Sde-Boqer. Students at Sde-Boqer—both Israeli (Jews and Arabs) and international (from Europe, Asia, Africa, Latin America, and Jordan) —study all their courses in English. Both academic writing courses were opened as a result of specific requests by the Faculty of Science and the Jacob Blaustein Institute for Desert Research/Albert Katz International School for Desert Studies. Both courses were, in fact, open to all graduate students at BGU, regardless of faculty of study. In practice, most of the students came from the faculties of technology and social sciences in addition to the natural sciences, and rarely from humanities. There is also an undergraduate writing elective for business administration students, and the School of Business Administration is eager to train students in professional writing from early on. Unfortunately, because of budgetary cuts, the graduate course on the Beer Sheva campus did not open in 2010.

The administration of the Herzliya Interdisciplinary Center, a private institution which opened in 1994, has always paid serious attention to writing skills. Professor Reichman, the dean, expects law school graduates, for instance, to be able to write "decent and intelligible" formal legal letters and case notes (briefs), as well as mini-contracts, short wills, and a research paper, so that students can learn to utilize the language of law in English fully. Similarly, at the other Herzliya programs, the administration has supported programs in academic writing.

At the Ruppin Academic Center, Business English is a compulsory, semester (28-hour) course for undergraduate students of business administration in their third year of studies. It is also offered as an optional course for second- and third-year students of economics. The course was designed following consultation with the heads of the Departments of Business Administration and Economics. In accordance with their requirements, emphasis is placed on writing skills in general, and on written commercial correspondence in particular. The course is organized around two main threads, one relating to text types and the other relating to business content. With regard to major text types, students learn memos, formal letters, and e-mails, and practice these texts extensively. A wide range of genres that are most prevalent in the business world defines the content of the students' writing. These include cover letters, requests and enquiries, notifying and informing, making and addressing complaints, organizing business trips, etc. Course requirements include participation in classroom and homework activities, a portfolio including drafts, final products, and reflection, a mid-term exam and a final exam. All course content and activities are on the e-learning platform, Moodle. Student feedback has revealed that the vast majority of participants believe that the course sets them in good stead for their future business careers.

RESPONDING TO BUDGETARY CHALLENGES

Private efforts have also pioneered new directions in business writing and writing for the high-tech sector. There is increased awareness that beyond the academy, students will need these skills.

Because of the present budgetary situation confronting all institutions of higher education in Israel, many official writing programs have been curtailed. In view of this situation and the continuing needs of the students, the present head of the EAP department of Hebrew University has initiated some voluntary activities. Her first step was to train all the instructors in the department to become writing instructors. She has developed a mini-library in the staff room with relevant journal articles and books, etc. She has initiated a series of workshops on teaching writing given by people with varied experience in the field. She has started a journal club in which teachers of the department, even those with no prior experience in the teaching of writing, are asked to present material from current journals on teaching writing. In addition, in order to get a feel for the needs of the students, teachers of the department give tutorials on a voluntary basis to PhD students in the social sciences.

Besides the individual tutorials, workshops in writing are available for interested students, during which both faculty members and peers have helped the students revise their work. In addition, two courses in writing are currently being taught by the EAP teachers.

The department has presented a proposal to the administration of the university to establish a formal writing center with the following possibilities for students: (a) workshops, (b) individual tutorials, (c) courses in specific kinds of writing, and (d) supervised group work experience in which a guide would work with the group, and the students would work together.

Table 2. A Sampling of Academic Writing Instruction Opportunities in Israel

Academic Writing in English

PhD + Faculty	Early days	Hebrew University	English composition
		Tel Aviv University	Academic Writing
BA	1980s until today	TAU and other universities	EFL Writing course for English majors only
PhD	From 1986 to the present	All major universities	Academic writing courses and teacher training in the teaching of writing established by the Wolfson Family Charitable Trust
MA	The 1980s to the present	Bar-Ilan University	1-3 semesters Academic writing for all non-exempt MA candidates
BA	1994	IDC—Interdisciplinary Center of Herzliya	Strong emphasis on writing for legal purposes in English for law students

BSc	From 2000	Technion—Israel Institute of Technology	Elective course in writing and presentation skills: "Communication in English for scientists and engineers"
MA/PhD	The late 1990s until today	Weizman Institute	Scientific writing courses taught by a teacher with a PhD in biology, as well as by teachers with linguistic training
Graduate and undergraduate students	From 2000	Ben-Gurion University	Writing courses in EFL for students whose main program is Hebrew and courses for Israelis and international students, whose main program is taught in English; Elective course in writing for business administration students
BA	2002-2006	University of Haifa	Addition of an applied linguistics component to the teaching of writing to English literature majors
MSc	2004	Tel Aviv University	Technical Writing course for engineering students
PhD and all other interested students	From 2008	Hebrew University EAP Department	Alternatives to writing courses sought in order to fill the gap created by budgetary cuts: workshops, tutorials
PhD	From 2008	Tel Aviv University	Required Academic Writing course for students at the Porter School of Environmental Studies
MA	2009	Technion Israel Institute of Technology	One semester elective in academic writing
BA		Ruppin Academy	Required Business English course with strong emphasis on writing for Business administration students using the e-learning platform Moodle for writing; Elective for Economics students

Academic Writing in Hebrew

Level	Approximate Date	Institution(s)	Description of program
Pre-academic	From 1968 until today	Center for Pre-Academic Studies, Hebrew University of Jerusalem	"Scientific Writing"—first Hebrew academic writing program in Israel
B.Ed	Early 1990s until today	Academic Teachers' Colleges	One or two semester skills-based writing courses

B.Ed and up-grading teaching certificate	From 1995	Hakibbutzim Academic Teachers College	Cancellation of required writing courses: establishment of Sal'Or Writing Center Special group mentoring and one-to-one tutoring project and tailor-made courses for students and staff
B.Ed	From 1996	David Yellin Academic College of Education	Experimental writing programs, at first called "A Drop in the Sea," combining WAC and WID
Preparatory Program— Pre-Academic	From 2000	Rothberg International School—Hebrew University	Two-hour one semester course taught by the history instructors in conjunction with the history course to students in higher Hebrew language levels
BA-incoming students	From 2007	Hebrew University Faculty of Humanities	Introduction to Hebrew composition
Master's Degree Students	From 2008	Hebrew University Hadassah Nursing School	Writing course for nurses

Academic Writing in Other Languages

BA	From 2006	Rothberg International School—Hebrew University of Jerusalem	Academic writing taught in the language of the immigrant student: courses in Russian, English, Arabic, Spanish, French, etc.
BA and above		Hebrew University German Department; Department of Romance Languages	Academic writing taught in advanced German language courses; Academic writing taught as one element in Spanish, French, and Italian language courses

IFAW AND BEYOND, INCLUDING OUR FIRST INTERNATIONAL CONFERENCE

Inspired by the symposium at the 2007 EATAW conference, "Historical Roots of National Writing Cultures," we decided to establish an organization for people engaged in academic writing instruction. Its purpose was to share resources and insights and ultimately provide the best possible writing instruction for Israel's wide variety of students. We were encouraged by the fact that our first meeting at Tel Aviv University in November, 2007, was attended by about forty people from colleges and universities throughout Israel involved in both English and Hebrew academic writing. It was decided at that meeting to meet several times a year face-to-face and to communicate by email as well. Since then, our organization has grown—we now have over 150 members on our mailing list. We have succeeded in establishing a communication network and made connections among people in our field. We have had five face-to-face meetings during each of the first two years of the organization—in 2010, we held only four as we had many more activities in preparation for our international conference in July. At our meetings, we have had workshops, visiting lecturers, research presentations, practical applications, and discussions, addressing such issues as responding to and assessing student writing, the use of technology in the teaching of writing, and how to gain administrative support for our programs. Members from all over the country, from colleges and universities, and from Hebrew, English, and German departments have attended. We have found a home for our organization, MOFET, the Institute of Research, Curriculum and Program Development for Teacher Education, an already existing and respected institution.

The first international conference on academic writing in Israel, "Academic Writing and Beyond in Multicultural Societies," took place at the MOFET Institute in Tel-Aviv on July 28 and 29, 2010. Some 200 participants, from the US, Canada, the UK, Germany, Switzerland, Hungary, China, Russia, Italy, Turkey, and Cyprus, as well as from Israel attended the conference. One hundred twenty presentations were given in Hebrew and English and included panel discussions, workshops, and individual papers. Keynote speakers were John Harbord of the Central European University in Hungary, Chris Anson of North Carolina State University, Otto Kruse of the Zurich University of Applied Sciences, and Deborah Holdstein of Columbia College, Chicago. Topics covered included the development of writing centers, writing in the disciplines, writing across the curriculum, how to deal with plagiarism, bridging the gap between high school writing and writing in the university, the use of technology in teaching academic writing, giving feedback, and the connection between creativity and academic writing. For this first conference in Israel, we wanted to appeal to as wide an audience as possible. The conference succeeded in connecting us with like-minded educators throughout the world, and we hope that it widened the horizons of those of us engaged in the teaching and research of academic writing in Israel.

We hope that the conference will advance the goals of our organization. We have not yet succeeded in locating all the existing programs in academic writing in Israel. Nor have we arranged to publish a journal or set up a permanent internet site, both of which are included in our long term goals. We would also like to initiate a national writing project in Israel together with the Ministry of Education and the Council for Higher Education. To the best of our knowledge, there has never been such a project, either for Hebrew or English or Arabic writing. Even at the universities, there has very rarely been central funding directly from the Rector's office. The trend has been to have individual faculties or departments (e.g., Humanities, Engineering) support writing courses in L1 or L2.

What we would like to see in all our institutions is a combination of writing courses, writing centers, and writing taught by all instructors according to the needs of their disciplines. Writing centers, such as the one at Kibbutzim College, are ideal, in that they meet the needs of the students as they perceive them, but if they meet the needs of only 10 per cent of the student body, what about the other 90 per cent? Similarly, setting standards in academic writing in the various languages we teach is important, but we must guard against standardization. Each group of students is different, and each institution should develop its own program.

Although the people of Israel are known as "the people of the Book," and although many books and journal articles are published in Israel each year, we know that supporting student writers at all levels of study is still a pedagogical imperative. Beyond the academy, in today's world of research and globalization, writing skills are a necessity for all who wish to advance professionally. In the modern State of Israel, where academic writing is no longer the prerogative of the privileged few, we make it our purpose, by drawing on Israel's ancient roots, to empower all of its citizens to become fully accomplished people of the book.[5]

NOTES

1. Unfortunately, our dear friend and colleague, Hadara Perpignan, passed away on December 25, 2010, after a difficult illness. Hadara was senior lecturer in the department of English as a Foreign Language at Bar-Ilan University (Israel), where she taught writing for academic purposes to doctoral candidates. She developed writing programs at Bar-Ilan University and the University of Haifa, as well as at the Catholic University of Rio de Janeiro, Brazil. Her research centered on teacher-written feedback to student writing, affective and social outcomes of writing instruction, and genre analysis of literary criticism. Hadara was an active member of our team in researching and writing this article, and we would like to dedicate it to her memory.

2. Retrieved from http://www.bethlehem.edu/about/history/shtml

3. Retrieved from http://www.medea.be/? page=28 and http://en.wikipedia.org.wik

4. Sources for the life and influence of Ben-Yehuda include Bein, 1971; Cooper-Weill, 1998;; Fellman, 1998; Lang, 2008; St. John, 1952; Weisgal, 1944, and Weizmann, 1949.

5. We wish to thank our colleagues at a range of Israeli institutions, among them Susan Holzman, Sharon Hirsch, Sara Hauptman, Yochi Wolfensberger; Ruwaida Aburass, Monica Broido, Michal Schleifer, Ilana Shilo, Dana Taube, Ruth Burstein, Elana Spector Cohen, Ziona Snir, and Tamar Weyl, for their input on this chapter.

REFERENCES

Bein, Alex (Ed.). (1971.). *Ruppin, Arthur: Memories, diaries, letters.* Jerusalem: Weidenfeld & Nicolson.

Bethlehem University (2010). *Bethlehem University in the Holy Land—Brief History.* Retrieved from http://www.bethlehem.edu/about/history.shtml

Cooper-Weill, J. (1998). Early Hebrew schools in Eretx-Israel. *The Israel Review of Arts and Letters, 1997, 104.*

Fellman, J. (1998). Eliezer Ben-Yehuda—A language reborn. *The Israel Review of Arts and Letters, 1997, 104.*

Kibler, A. (2008). Speaking Like a "Good American": National identity and the legacy of German-language education. *Teachers College Record, 110*(6), 1241-1268. Retrieved from http://www.tcrecord.org/Home.asp

Lang, J. (2008). *Speak Hebrew: The life of Eliezar Ben Yehudah.* Jerusalem: Yad Ben Zvi.

Oz, Amos. (2004). *A tale of love and darkness.* London: Vintage.

Spolsky, B., & Shohamy, E. (1999). *The languages of Israel: Policy, ideology, and practice.* Clevedon, England: Multilingual Matters LTD.

St. John, R. (1952). *Tongue of the prophets.* North Hollywood, CA: Wilshire Book Co.

Weisgal, M. (Ed.). (1944). *Chaim Weizmann: Statesman, scientist, builder of the Jewish Commonwealth.* New York: Dial Press.

Weizmann, C. (1949). *Trial and error.* New York: Harper & Brothers.

Zuckermann, T. (2007). The history of writing instruction in Israeli. Presentation at EATAW conference, Bochum, Germany.

CHAPTER 25.
THE DEVELOPMENT OF AN ACADEMIC WRITING CENTRE IN THE NETHERLANDS

By Ingrid Stassen and Carel Jansen
Radboud University Nijmegen and Stellenbosch University)

Radboud University Nijmegen was the first university in the Netherlands to have a writing centre. Founded in February 2004, the Academic Writing Centre Nijmegen (ASN) was based on the outcomes of a feasibility study that demonstrated that at Radboud University Nijmegen writing problems were often not recognized as such, and that faculty could not always give students proper individual coaching, due to lack of time or expertise. The feasibility study also revealed that both students and faculty felt positive about the concept of the writing centre that was proposed, and in its basic philosophy that not the writing product but the writing process would deserve primary attention. The ASN has proven to serve a clear need: the number of consultation sessions has grown to an average of 45 sessions per week. Some three years after its start, more than 50 percent of the students knew about the writing centre's existence. Evaluation studies consistently show that after visiting the writing centre students are highly satisfied with the help that is provided. Supervisors of students who consulted the ASN generally felt that both their students and they themselves as staff members had profited from the services offered at the writing centre. In spite of these positive evaluations the university board decided in June 2011, in view of the need to cut university expenses, that central financing will have to end by 2013 and that from then on other means of financing have to be found.

In the past few decades academic writing has gained considerable attention at Radboud University Nijmegen in the Netherlands.[1] Courses in general communicative skills (including composition), writing intensive courses, and online facilities such as WorldWideWriting and WritingStudio have grown into important tools to help students to improve their academic writing.[2]

Since 2004, the university also houses a writing centre: the Academic Writing Centre Nijmegen (from here: ASN, the abbreviation for the name in Dutch: Academisch Schrijfcentrum Nijmegen). In this chapter the development and the (still short) history of the ASN will be sketched, and the results of the work done in the ASN since it started offering its services will be discussed.

In 2003, after having been introduced to the newly founded writing centre at Stellenbosch University (South Africa), the second author of this chapter asked the University Board to be allowed to investigate the possibilities for creating a similar writing centre at Radboud University Nijmegen, taking into account, among other things, the favourable experiences of American universities such as Colorado State University, Purdue University, and the University of Maryland with their writing centres.

After some discussion between the University Board and the Assembly of Faculty Deans, financial means were granted for a feasibility study as asked for, to be carried out by the first author of this chapter together with her then colleague, Vincent Boeschoten. As a result of this feasibility study, which included interviews with students and staff members at the Nijmegen campus and consultation of international colleagues in the field of the teaching of writing, a proposal for founding a writing centre was put forward, including a business plan for an experimental period of two years. The proposal was well received, and the University Board decided to give permission and financial means to start the first writing centre ever at a Dutch university.[3] For a first experimental period of two years, a total of 250,000 euros was granted to cover the costs of hiring personnel (part time manager, part time office manager, and tutors) and decorating the space that was made available (for free) in the university library. This made it possible to offer services to students and staff members without having to charge them, or their faculties.

There were some clear criteria, however, that had to be met if the ASN was to continue after the experimental period.

First of all, the ASN needed to maintain an academic status. Only university students could have access to its services, and these services could not be extended to students from other types of higher education, even if they would be willing to pay for it. Furthermore a full professor in communication (i.e., the second author of this chapter) would have to be prepared to carry the academic responsibility for the work in the ASN, and there would have to be frequent contact with experts in this field from universities abroad, for example Professor Dr. Leon de Stadler from Stellenbosch University (South Africa). The second criterion set by the University Board was that after one year, a total of at least 250 visits from students would have to be registered. That number would have to grow into at least 750 after two years. The final criterion to play a role in the decision to continue or discontinue the ASN pertained to the evaluation of the services offered by the ASN: both students and staff members who had been in touch with the ASN would have to think favourably of what the ASN had done for them.

KEY ROLE FOR TUTORS

Following the basic philosophy of the writing centres in the US (and also in Stellenbosch, South Africa) the coaching in the ASN was, and still is, done by tutors who are in majority graduated students and PhD-candidates at Radboud University Nijmegen.

A welcome source of inspiration for the approach taken at the ASN was the work in the writing lab at Purdue University, as discussed in Harris (1995). As Harris points out, the primary responsibility of a writing centre is to work one-to-one with writers, and not to duplicate or usurp writing classrooms. The uniqueness of a writing center is its setting with "a middle person, the tutor, who inhabits a world somewhere between student and teacher". It is in this specific setting that students are encouraged to think independently, to gain confidence in themselves as writers, and to put their theoretical knowledge into practice as they write. If only because of the power structure in academia as it is perceived by many students, the institutional authority automatically ascribed to the teacher often prohibits the collaborative atmosphere that is typical for tutor sessions in a writing centre (cf. Harris, 1995, pp. 27; 35-36; 40).

Not all faculty members are equally convinced of the importance of giving feedback that is directed at stimulating the student's development into a good writer, rather than at providing quick fixes of an imperfect draft. And even if they are willing to give development-directed feedback, where the writer is the one who recognises and solves the problem, supported by non-directive questions from the coach, they often do not have enough time available to do so. In a survey among teachers of the Faculty of Arts at Radboud University Nijmegen, it emerged that several interviewees also indicated that they felt uncertain about their expertise on this type of commentary (Stassen & Wilbers, 2006). Stassen and Wilbers also point at the advantages of development-directed feedback. In a qualitative study, seven students were observed in a total of 10 tutor sessions at the ASN. Although the results were based on a relatively small number of observations and therefore need to be interpreted with care, the study suggests that the tutor sessions did influence the strategic writing process of the students. Non-directive, development-directed tutor behavior led to a positive situational norm and independent student behavior. Students who distilled their own strategies from the development-oriented feedback of their tutors proved to use these strategies when working independently on their writing tasks (Stassen & Wilbers, 2006).

From the beginning, ASN tutors were thoroughly trained in providing development-directed feedback and in supporting various forms of academic writing by the manager of the ASN and by other experts in the field of writing education, for example Gerd Bräuer, University of Education Freiburg, and Leigh Ryan, University of Maryland. The manager of the ASN also offered support for faculty by asking questions on, for instance, how to improve their students' writing skills, how to assess their students' texts, and how to create programmes for writing across the curriculum. Furthermore, the ASN organised workshops, both for students and for teachers, about subjects such as writing effectively, collecting relevant information when writing an academic text, avoiding plagiarism, and developing writing assignments. Part of these workshops were, and still are, conducted by experts such as Cheryl Glenn, Pennsylvania State University.

To draw the attention of the target groups (i.e., students and staff from all faculties) to the ASN and to its basic philosophy, a number of marketing activities have been undertaken. There were "guest performances" of tutors in regular classes in all kinds of academic programmes, special lunches were organised to introduce staff members to the services of the ASN and to show them its location, a website including a short video clip was launched (http://www.ru.nl/asn), a newsletter was issued, advertisements were placed in the university magazine, favourably-priced memory sticks (including information on the ASN) were offered to students who paid the ASN a visit, and posters and flyers were distributed on campus, all stressing the basic ASN philosophy: better thinking produces better writing, and vice versa.

RESULTS

Since its start in 2004, the ASN was evaluated on several occasions. Each time the results were positive. Based on these outcomes the University Board decided in early 2006 to extend the first, experimental ASN period for two more years, until March 2008. By the end of 2007 it was decided to extend this period for another two years (providing for additional means to cover all expenses until March 2010), with the perspective that by 2010 a definitive decision would be made about the possible inclusion of the ASN in the university structure. Below the most important results from the evaluation studies are presented.

Students' Familiarity with the ASN

In a questionnaire study carried out in 2006 among a sample of 1,012 students at Radboud University Nijmegen, it was found that 54% were familiar with the existence of the ASN. Especially students from the Faculties of Arts

(80%), Management (76%), and Philosophy (75%) knew about the ASN; students from the Faculties of Science (41%) and Medicine (25%) were less aware of its existence. Those students who knew about the existence of the ASN were also asked if they knew that the ASN offered individual help with a diversity of writing tasks (90% said yes), if they knew that this service was for free (66% said yes), and if in the 24 months before the date of this study, they had ever felt the need for assistance in their writing processes (24% said yes).

Consultation Numbers

From the start in March 2004, the total number of consultation sessions in that year was 301. One year later the number had grown to 1,001. In 2010, the total number of consultation sessions had reached 1,861, and based on the numbers from the first five months in 2011 a total of 2,100 consultation sessions are predicted (see Figure 1). On average, a student visiting the ASN has three to four consultation sessions; by implication, by the end of 2011 some 600 students are expected to have visited the ASN in that year.

Most students visiting the ASN prove to come from four faculties: Social Sciences(40%), Arts (25%), Management (14%), and Law (10%). This result does not really come as a surprise, in view of the relatively high numbers of students enrolled in programmes in these faculties, and in view also of the importance that these faculties traditionally attach to adequate writing skills.

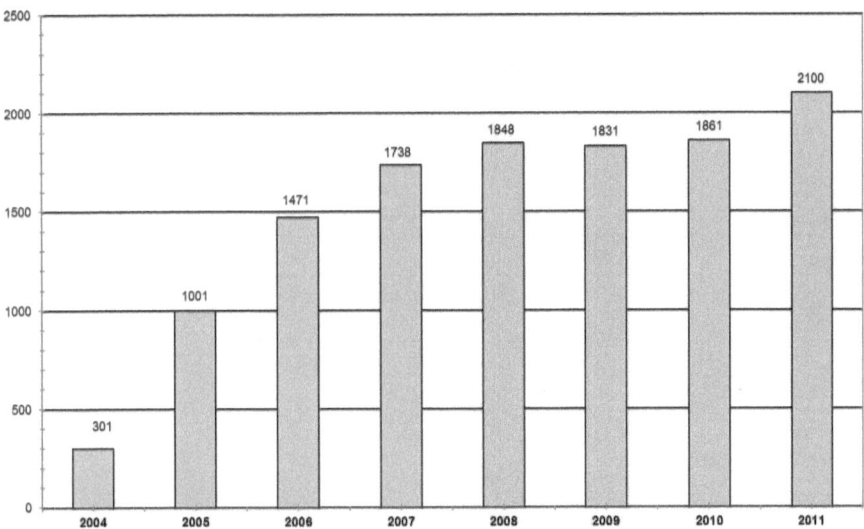

Figure 1. Number of consultation sessions per year.

Most sessions (72.0%) are in Dutch; English (20.2%) is second. Most visitors (55.5%) to the ASN are graduates; 44.5% are undergraduates.

STUDENTS' SATISFACTION

In the period 2008-2010, 150 students who received one or more consultation sessions were asked to fill out a questionnaire about the general quality of the services provided by the ASN, the extent to which they felt the consultations helped them, the effect they thought the consultations had on their writing skills, and the role that the input of the tutor played in all this. All questions had the format of statements followed by five answering options, ranging from very negative to very positive. Table 1 shows the results of this evaluation.

QUALITATIVE OUTPUT

Due to the large number of consultation sessions, the different text genres, and the variety of academic discourse themes that are discussed, the ASN has gained more specific insights into the special demands of academic discourse. This expertise is a breeding ground for the development of different strategies to

Table 1. Results from Evaluation Questionnaire ASN (2008-2010)

Question	Scores	Percentage
Structure of the tutoring sessions	good or very good	88.6 %
Tutor's feedback	clear or very clear	90.7 %
Alignment of tutoring sessions with own needs	good or very good	82.7 %
Perceived atmosphere during tutoring sessions	pleasant or very pleasant	96.7 %
Usefulness of tutor's input	useful or very useful	87.3 %
Motivation after the tutoring sessions	improved or much better	86.7 %
Improvement of text after the tutoring sessions	better or much better	83.3 %
Improvement of writing process after the tutoring sessions	easier/faster or much easier/faster	69.4%
Improvement in enjoying writing after the tutoring sessions	more fun or much more fun	46.7 %
Services like contact, information, etc.	good or very good	96.7 %
Physical room of the writing center	pleasant or very pleasant	71.4 %

optimize the writing processes of academic texts. In April 2011, for instance, a workshop was organized for staff members about efficiently supervising writing to make optimal use of, often limited, coaching time. Another theme of this well-attended workshop, directed by Jude Carroll (Oxford Brookes University), was the coaching of writing in a second language. Recently the present ASN manager, Dr. Joy de Jong, published a handbook on Academic Writing (J. de Jong, 2011) that was based, among other things, on insights gained in the ASN.

OPINIONS FROM SUPERVISORS

Not only students, but also staff members who supervised students being coached at the ASN, were asked for their opinions on the effects of tutor-coaching. In an MA thesis, communication student Christa de Jong conducted 14 interviews with supervisors. It appeared that a large majority of the supervisors felt that the work done in the ASN had an added value, that the text versions that their students handed in after their consultation sessions clearly had improved, and that the students in general had learned to be more critical toward their own writing products. Most supervisors also felt that the ASN relieved them from their tasks by helping the students to clearly structure and formulate their theses, so that in their own discussions with the students they could concentrate more on the academic merits of the research presented in the text (C. de Jong, 2005).

OVERVIEW: INFLUENCE ON DEVELOPMENT OF WRITING CENTRES IN THE NETHERLANDS

The first seven years of the ASN have shown that a writing centre can play an important role in improving students' writing skills. The formula of individual consultation sessions focusing on possible ways to improve the writing process has proven to be successful—not only in terms of the fast-growing numbers of students visiting the ASN but also in the quality of the services rendered, as perceived by these students and their supervisors. Combined with other forms of writing education, such as traditional composition courses, writing-intensive courses, and modern online facilities, the services offered by the ASN have a clear added value. In view of all this, it is not surprising that the work in the ASN has drawn the attention of other universities. In 2004 and 2008, after the example of the ASN, the second and the third academic writing centres in the Netherlands were founded at the University of Groningen and the University of Tilburg. In mid 2011, the University of

Twente and Maastricht University were in the process of developing academic writing centres.

In spite of all this, the Nijmegen University board decided in June 2011, in view of the need to cut university expenses, that central financing of the Centre will have to end by 2013, and that from then on other means of financing have to be found. May there indeed be other means to keep the ASN up and running!

NOTES

1. Radboud University Nijmegen is a university located in the eastern part of the Netherlands, near the German border. It is the fourth Dutch university in numbers of students (some 16.000), and offers educational programmes and research facilities in seven Faculties: Arts, Law, Science, Medicine, Philosophy, Theology and Religion Studies, Management, and Social Sciences.

2. See http://www.worldwidewriting.eu and http://www.writingstudio.eu.

3. The financial and organisational responsibility is carried by Radboud into Languages, the Language and Communication Centre of Radboud Nijmegen University, supervised by Liesbet Korebrits (director) and by José Bakx (vice-director) for matters concerning the ASN. The first manager of the ASN was Ron Welters; in 2005 he was followed by Vincent Boeschoten. Since 2007, Joy de Jong supervises and coordinates the activities in the ASN.

REFERENCES

Jong, C. de (2005). *De effecten van tutorbegeleiding aan het Academisch Schrijfcentrum Nijmegen op het strategisch schrijfproces van studenten.* (Unpublished master's thesis.) Nijmegen: Radboud University Nijmegen.

Jong, J. de. (2011). *Handboek academisch schrijven.* Bussum: Coutinho.

Harris, M. (1995). Talking in the middle: Why writers need writing tutors. *College English, 57*(1), 27-42.

Stassen, I.M.A.M., & Wilbers, U.M. (2005, June). The development of academic writing: Work in progress. Longitudinal research on the development of academic writing. In *Teaching writing on line and face to face. 3rd Conference of the European Association for the Teaching of Academic Writing*, Hellenic American Union, Athens.

CHAPTER 26.
TEACHING WRITING AT AUT UNIVERSITY: A MODEL OF A SEMINAR SERIES FOR POSTGRADUATE STUDENTS WRITING THEIR FIRST THESIS OR DISSERTATION

By John Bitchener
AUT University, Auckland (New Zealand)

This essay describes and comments on a series of seminars that were designed by the author to meet the discourse needs of postgraduate students writing their first thesis or dissertation in English at AUT University, Auckland, New Zealand. In New Zealand, a dissertation is seen as a smaller report on research that has been carried out by a student in a bachelor honours programme, whereas a thesis may be at either master's or doctoral level. (Hereafter, the term 'thesis' should be understood to also refer to "dissertation.")

AUT University was originally the largest polytechnic in New Zealand, but just over 10 years ago, in 2000, it was granted university status. Postgraduate students at the institution had been writing theses well before it became a university. The University comprises five faculties (Applied Humanities, Business, Design and Creative Technologies, Health and Environmental Sciences, Te Ara Poutama) and each of these houses a number of schools and departments. According to the Director of the Postgraduate Centre, the overall student population at the university is in excess of 27,000, and 2,250 of these are postgraduate students (Banda, 2011). Depending on the programme they are enrolled in, not all postgraduate students are required to write a thesis, but more than half do. Since 2005, over 400 students have graduated with a master's degree that included a thesis and over 140 have graduated with a doctoral degree.

The university has a multi-national and multi-cultural population: 42% pakehas (white New Zealanders), 10% Maori (indigenous New Zealanders), 11% Pasifika (Pacific Islanders), 27% Asians (East and South Asian countries) and 10% others (Banda, 2011). While many of the students who enrol in a thesis are New Zealand residents who have completed undergraduate programmes at the university or at another New Zealand university, a growing number from other countries and, therefore, from other educational backgrounds may also enrol in a thesis at the university. Consequently, a number of these students are non-native speakers/writers of English, but before they are accepted as thesis students they are required to have an IELTS (International English Language Testing System) score (or similar) with at least 6.5 in Reading, Speaking, and Listening and 7.0 in Writing.

This range of backgrounds means that the university must cater for the diverse needs of its equally diverse student population. Students who have completed short research projects and written up reports on this work before enrolling in postgraduate programmes often have a head start in knowing generally what is required in conducting and reporting on research. Even though these students bring a certain amount of knowledge, skill, and experience to their postgraduate study, their understanding of what is required at this level is sometimes quite different from what is expected at a New Zealand university. This difference can become an issue for those who have completed an honours or master's degree by thesis from a university in another country where different requirements and expectations exist. When a university such as ours accepts a student into a thesis-based programme, it needs to accept responsibility for ensuring that students have every chance of succeeding. Aware of the need to take responsibility for each of its students, AUT University established a Postgraduate Centre in the mid 1990s to coordinate all aspects of postgraduate study at the university, including that which is undertaken by faculties, schools, and departments.

WRITING SUPPORT FOR UNDERGRADUATES

Before describing what the Postgraduate Centre offers its students, it is worth noting that the university also provides writing support opportunities for its undergraduate students. Students in these earlier years of study are able to access various forms of writing support when required. For instance, the university's Keys Workshops are available to those seeking a credit-bearing certificate in generic writing skills. Te Tari Awhina, a writing support unit for one-on-one and small group conferences and workshops that is available to all students, is another section of the university that provides one-on-one and small group support to both undergraduate and postgraduate students. Each of these provisions were offered by the university when it was a polytechnic. At the faculty level, students are also able to access on-line writing support given by academics in the disciplines. Postgraduate students and staff who are upskilling their qualifications are able to obtain one-on-one feedback at writing retreats.

ROLES OF THE POSTGRADUATE CENTRE

One of the many roles of the Postgraduate Centre is to provide courses, seminars and workshops on skills (e.g., computer and statistics packages) that postgraduate students will need during their course of study. One of the needs that was identified in the early years of becoming a university was an understanding of what is involved in the writing of a thesis. Although individual schools, departments, and supervision staff understand that this is a role they must take responsibility for, the Postgraduate Centre felt there was a need to offer students an introductory seminar or workshop on the generic, non-discipline specific requirements of thesis writing, so that those writing their first thesis could begin the task with some understanding of what would be expected. The series of seminars that are now offered on writing the various part-genres or chapters of an empirically-based thesis (to be described below) originated in 2004 with a one-off workshop on the writing of a literature review. Seminars and workshops offered by the Centre are open to students across the faculties; attendance is voluntary.

Participation in these sessions cannot earn grades for degree programmes or coursework papers. Inevitably, this means that students who might benefit most from these sessions are the ones who choose not to attend, and those who have sufficient knowledge and experience come to all sessions. The overwhelming success of the first workshop (in the number of students who attended, the positive feedback given in the evaluation forms at the end of the workshop, and the feedback from staff across the university who had heard about the workshop from their students) meant that other workshops were scheduled. Many of the evaluation forms revealed a desire for seminars and workshops on other aspects of thesis-writing. This, of course, meant that the staff member facilitating the seminars was required to give more of his time and that the Centre had to fund his release time from the school in which he is employed as a fulltime staff member.

Since 2006, the series has included the writing of (1) an introduction chapter, (2) a literature review chapter(s), (3) a methodology chapter(s), (4) a presentation of results chapter, (5) a discussion of results chapter and (6) a conclusion chapter. Over the last three years, other seminars related to thesis research and writing have been offered, including (1) preparing a thesis proposal and (2) writing a journal article from a section of a thesis. These initiatives have come about as a result of students and staff requesting support in these high-stakes areas.

The typical needs of first-time thesis writers have been identified by both students and supervisors in the literature on students' needs and difficulties (Bitchener, 2010; Bitchener & Basturkmen, 2006; Casanave & Hubbard, 1992; Cooley & Lewcowicz, 1997; Dong, 1998; Paltridge & Starfield, 2007). While the needs of students at one university may be a little different from those at another university (this, for example, may be the result of certain disciplines being offered by some universities and not others), there tends to be a common need amongst students to understand (1) the type of content that should be included in the separate chapters or sections of a thesis, (2) ways to most effectively or rhetorically organise this material and (3) the register/language expected by the general academic community and by the discipline in which students are studying.

USING A GENRE APPROACH IN THE SEMINARS

Charged with the responsibility of deciding how the seminars/workshops could meet the typical needs of thesis writers, the member of staff who was asked to design and deliver the seminars decided that a genre approach would be the most effective. As Swales (2004) and Devitt (2004) explain, a genre is a text that has, amongst other characteristics, particular and distinctive communicative functions and recognisable patterns and norms of organisation and structure. Discourse analyses, reported in the literature of discipline-specific journal articles and thesis part-genres, reveal the inter-relationship amongst the function(s) of a text, its content, and structure. Kwan (2006), for example, explains that the crucial starting point for a "discourse move" analysis (that is, understanding the units of content required) is to consider the purposes or functions of the target genre (chapter or section) that regulate the choice of content, its schematic pattern (or organisational structure) and characteristic linguistic features. Discourse analyses also reveal that "discourse moves" are staged or organised through the use of various "sub-moves" (sometimes referred to as "strategies" or "steps"). Empirical evidence reveals that these moves and sub-moves, employed within the various theme or topic sections of a part-genre, should be seen as options rather than as prescriptive requirements and that there may be a considerable recycling of moves and sub-moves within and across theme/topic sections.

The next section of this essay illustrates how this approach underpinned the content provided in the seminar/workshop on writing a "discussion of results" chapter. It should be noted that some theses combine the presentation and discussion of results in one chapter, that others have more than one results or discussion chapter, and that others include the conclusion of the thesis with the discussion of results. The seminar presenter makes this variety clear to students and explains how the content presented in the session can be applied just as effectively to whichever format is chosen.

The discussion of results seminar/workshop, like those for the other part-genres, takes approximately three hours (depending on the amount of interactive discussion and the number of analyses of sample texts considered) and is divided into the following sections: the approach taken (the genre approach), the purpose(s) or function(s), the content and its structure, key linguistic characteristics, frequently asked questions, and further activities and reading.

1. *The approach*

The genre approach and reasons for its use are explained to the students.

2. *The purpose(s) and function(s) of the discussion of results chapter*

This section includes the following stages: (1) participants discuss in pairs what they understand to be the purpose(s) and function(s) of the discussion of results chapter; (2) a plenary reporting back on the key ideas; (3) a presentation of the chart shown in Figure 1. Attention is drawn to the importance of functions 4 and 5.

---

1. An overview of the aims of the research that refers to the research questions or hypotheses
2. A summary of the theoretical and research contexts of the study
3. A summary of the methodological approach for investigating the research questions or hypotheses
4. A discussion of the contribution you believe your results or findings have made to the research questions or hypotheses and therefore to existing theory, research and practice (i.e. their importance and significance)
5. This discussion will often include an interpretation of your results, a comparison with other research, an explanation of why the results occurred as they did, and an evaluation of their contribution to the field of knowledge

---

Figure 1. Functions of a thesis discussion of results chapter.

Moves	Sub-moves
1. Provide background information	a. restatement of aims, research questions, hypotheses
	b. restatement of key published research
	c. restatement of research/methodological approach
2. Present a statement of result (SOR)	a. restatement of a key result
	b. expanded statement about a key result
3. Evaluate/comment on results or findings	a. explanation of result—suggest reasons for result
	b. (un)expected result—comment on whether it was an expected or unexpected result
	c. reference to previous research—compare result with previously published research
	d. exemplification—provide examples of result
	e. deduction or claim—make a more general claim arising from the result, e.g., drawing a conclusion or stating a hypothesis
	f. support from previous research—quote previous research to support the claim being made
	g. recommendation—make suggestion for future research
	h. justification for further research—explain why further research is recommended

Figure 2. Move and sub-move options.

3. *The content & structure of the discussion of results chapter*

The presenter explains that the discourse analyses of discussion of results chapters in the literature have identified a series of typical moves (content units) and sub-moves used to create each main move (see Figure 2). It is emphasised that these are options and that a recycling of moves and sub-moves is characteristic of the part-genre.

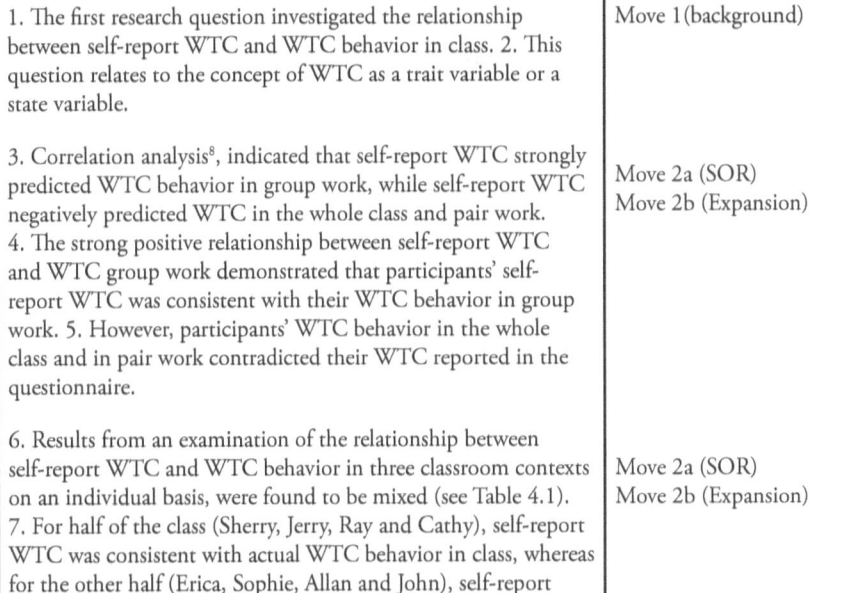

1. The first research question investigated the relationship between self-report WTC and WTC behavior in class. 2. This question relates to the concept of WTC as a trait variable or a state variable.	Move 1 (background)
3. Correlation analysis[8], indicated that self-report WTC strongly predicted WTC behavior in group work, while self-report WTC negatively predicted WTC in the whole class and pair work. 4. The strong positive relationship between self-report WTC and WTC group work demonstrated that participants' self-report WTC was consistent with their WTC behavior in group work. 5. However, participants' WTC behavior in the whole class and in pair work contradicted their WTC reported in the questionnaire.	Move 2a (SOR) Move 2b (Expansion)
6. Results from an examination of the relationship between self-report WTC and WTC behavior in three classroom contexts on an individual basis, were found to be mixed (see Table 4.1). 7. For half of the class (Sherry, Jerry, Ray and Cathy), self-report WTC was consistent with actual WTC behavior in class, whereas for the other half (Erica, Sophie, Allan and John), self-report WTC contradicted classroom WTC behavior.	Move 2a (SOR) Move 2b (Expansion)

Figure 3. Text of first research question discussion.

The text shown in Figure 3 is used to illustrate the extent to which the moves in Figure 2 were employed. It is explained that the sample material comes from an applied linguistics thesis on the willingness to communicate of second language learners in the language learning classroom. This particular thesis was chosen because it is an excellent example of an empirically-based thesis. It won a special award from the New Zealand applied linguistics community. It is also explained that the content is quite accessible for those unfamiliar with the topic or the discipline area. Participants are also reminded that the discourse analytical skills applied in the analysis of the move structure of the text can be transferred to texts in any other discipline area so that similarities and differences in what typically characterises the writing of such texts can be identified. Other sample texts that can be analysed are referred to in section 6 of this profile essay.

4. *Key Linguistic Characteristics of the Discussion of Results Chapter*

The following stages can be employed when discussing the linguistic characteristics to which students' attention should be drawn: (1) for illustrative purposes, the text in Figure 4 can be used to draw their attention to the use of hedging (reducing the degree of assertiveness) when making claims and offering explanations about certain findings; (2) the presenter defines hedging verbs (seems; appears) and modal verbs (may) and illustrates their use in the first paragraph of the text. It is also pointed out that adjectives such as "possible" might also be used for hedging purposes (e.g., It is possible that. . . .). Other samples can then be analysed by the participants and these can be from any discipline.

5   *Frequently Asked Questions*

The frequently asked questions shown in Figure 5 are then discussed. Often, they will be addressed during the course of the seminar/workshop but it is useful to return to them towards the end of the session.

6.   *Further Activities and Reading*

It is useful to have samples and/or recommendations of other textual material for participants to use in a classroom context or in their own time. Some

---

1. Whether L1 or L2 was used as the medium of communication also *appeared* to exert an influence on learners' WTC. 2. As MacIntyre et al. (1998, p. 546) have suggested, the differences between L1 and L2 WTC *may* be due to "the uncertainty inherent in L2 use," and the level of linguistic competency can be one differentiating factor existing in L1 and L2 WTC. 3. In this study, Jerry noted that a lack of linguistic competence in L2 inhibited communication, but when L1 was used, such a problem was not present. 4. Cathy also considered a lack of lexical resources in L2 as a factor affecting her perceived competence, which in turn influenced willingness to communicate at times. 5. This *seems* to support House's (2004) claim that lack of actual linguistic competence in L2 can prevent communication.

6. Differences in L1 and L2 WTC were also detected in task engagement in pair work. 7. Dörnyei and Kormos (2000) found that learners' relationships with their interlocutor had a considerable impact on the extent of their engagement in the task in L1, but this relationship failed to emerge in an L2 task. 8. They suggested that when L2 was used as the medium of communication, the challenge of trying to express one's thoughts using a limited linguistic code in addition to decoding the interlocutor's utterances, created an emotional state different from the communication mode in L1, which *may* "alter one's perceptions of the constraints of the interaction" (Dörnyei & Kormos, 2000, p. 293). 9. Differences in WTC in pair work in both L1 and L2 were, however, beyond the scope of this study and were not, as a consequence, examined. 10. It *appears* to be another area for further research.

Figure 4. Text illustrating hedging possibilities.

students may also be interested in the literature informing the content presented in the seminar/workshop. Examples of further activities and reading can be found in Bitchener (2010).

EVALUATION OF THE APPROACH

The approach described here is one approach. It has proven to be effective for those who have been introduced to it, as several different types of evidence reveal. First, the approach has been used with postgraduate students at a number of overseas universities (e.g., Brock University, Edith Cowan University, Nanyang Technological University, University of Melbourne, Murcia University, Michigan State University, Purdue University, University of California). Evaluative feedback (using a 7-point Likert scale to determine level of perceived usefulness from the programme employing the approach) from a total of 840 participants over a seven-year period at AUT University reveal an extremely high level of satisfaction: 92% rated it at level 7 (extremely useful), 6% at level 6 (very useful) and 2% at level 5 (useful). In the evaluations, qualitative assessments were also sought. As an example of the type of statement made, four from a recent seminar commented as follows:

> Course provided a solid foundation structure for both masters and doctoral style thesis construction and useful for all disciplines

> Handouts and format of the session was brilliant—feel very confident to approach my thesis now—thanks John!

---

1. Can I introduce any new literature in the discussion of results section?
2. How much of the literature review do I need to refer to when comparing one of my results with those of a study referred to in the literature review?
3. To what extent do the ideas presented in the discussion chapter have to be based on the literature presented in the literature review?

Figure 5. Frequently Asked Questions.

> After attending John's workshops, I took on board his comments, information provided and would like to advise that I got an "A"
>
> The veil has now lifted!

Empirical evidence (for example, Bitchener & Banda, 2007; Cheng, 2007; Turner & Bitchener, 2009) also attests to its effectiveness.

The approach described here is one that can be easily adapted if a less presenter-centred style is preferred and if time permits a more deductive approach. Group sessions can be in the form of seminars, workshops, and classroom-based lessons. Illustrative textual material can be drawn from any discipline. Greatest value for students tends to result if they are required to analyse textual material as soon as sample analyses have been discussed. Finally, it needs to be remembered that the genre approach presented in this essay draws upon the research findings of numerous journal articles reporting empirical investigations of what are typically the requirements and expectations for each of part-genres of theses in specific discipline areas.

CONCLUSION: ISSUES TO CONSIDER

While the implementation of this approach and the seminar series generally has been largely trouble-free, there are a couple of issues that might be usefully highlighted. First, some students have commented that they would have liked to have had the seminar time extended so that more attention could be given to analysis and discussion of sample texts, but not all students shared this view. A credit-bearing course based on this approach would be one way of meeting this request. Second, scheduling the seminars to suit a wide range of students can be problematic, especially if they are offered during a typical working week. Some students are distance-learners and not able to attend sessions, and others may be working part-time or fulltime and are only able to attend some sessions.

The solution to these issues has been to offer the seminars on the weekend. Six hours on Saturday and another six hours on Sunday proved popular with some students, but others felt this schedule was too much over two days. In recent years, we have spread the seminars over two consecutive weekends, with six hours on the first Sunday for the Introduction, Literature Review, and Methodology chapters and the second six hours the following Sunday for the Results, Discussion, and Conclusion chapters.

Finally, it is worth mentioning that the success of the seminar series is to a large extent the result of not only the content that is provided and the way in which it is delivered, as well as the willingness of the Centre and the presenter to respond to suggestions given in the evaluations completed at the end of each session, but also of the support given by supervisors across the University who strongly recommend that their students attend the seminars.

REFERENCES

Banda, M. (2011). AUT University Postgraduate Centre Director. Face-to-face interview with Bitchener. (15 February 2011, 9-11am).

Bitchener, J. (2010). *Writing an applied linguistics thesis or dissertation: A guide to presenting empirical research.* Hampshire, UK: Palgrave Macmillan.

Bitchener, J., & Banda, M. (2007). Postgraduate students' understanding of the functions of thesis sub-genres: The case of the literature review. *New Zealand Studies in Applied Linguistics, 13*(2), 61-68.

Bitchener, J., & Basturkmen, H. (2006). Perceptions of the difficulties of postgraduate L2 thesis students writing the discussion section. *Journal of English for Academic Purposes, 5,* 4-18.

Casanave, C., & Hubbard, P. (1992). The writing assignments and writing problems of doctoral students: Faculty perceptions, pedagogical issues, and needed research. *English for Specific Purposes, 11,* 33-49.

Cheng, A. (2007). Transfering generic features and recontextualizing genre awareness: Understanding writing performance in the ESP genre-based literacy framework. *English for Specific Purposes, 26,* 287-307.

Cooley, L., & Lewkowicz, J. (1997). Developing awareness of the rhetorical and linguistic conventions of writing a thesis in English: Addressing the needs of ESL/EFL postgraduate students. In A. Duszak (Ed.), *Culture and styles of academic discourse* (pp. 113-140). Berlin: Mouton de Gruyter.

Devitt, A. (2004). *Writing genres.* Carbondale, IL: Southern Illinois University Press.

Dong, Y. (1998). Non-native graduate students' thesis/dissertation writing in science: Self-reports by students and their advisors from two US institutions. *English for Specific Purposes, 17,* 369-390.

Swales, J. (2004). *Research genres: Exploration and applications.* Cambridge: Cambridge University Press.

Turner, E., & Bitchener, J. (2009). An approach to teaching the writing of literature reviews. *Zeitschrift Schreiben* Retrieved from http://www.zeitschrift-schreiben.eu.11.6.2008

CHAPTER 27.
DEVELOPING A "KIWI" WRITING CENTRE AT MASSEY UNIVERSITY, NEW ZEALAND

By Lisa Emerson
Massey University (New Zealand)

This essay outlines how the teaching of writing has been introduced into the curriculum of a New Zealand university over the last 20 years. Starting with a description of her accidental introduction to teaching writing, the author outlines early initiatives such as the development of a WAC programme in the sciences, and New Zealand's first OWLL. Despite this early promise, recent years have seen the emergence of uncoordinated initiatives in the teaching of writing that have led to various groups competing for ground. Nevertheless, a promising new development—New Zealand's first Writing Centre—aims not only to support students, but also to teach writing theory to a first generation of students. The author sees "becoming an ethnographer of your home campus" as an essential aspect of developing a writing programme, and describes the writing centre initiative as "something unique: not a transplanted idea but a kiwi writing centre . . . which will be informed by international theory and experience but emerge out of unchartered antipodean ground."

GETTING STARTED

A little over 20 years ago, in 1989, I unwittingly took my first steps towards developing a "Kiwi"[1] Writing Centre at Massey University, in Aotearoa New Zealand. A colleague had returned from sabbatical in the US fired up with a mission to start a writing centre to improve students' writing skills in the College of Business. She rang me to see if I would take on the job as sole tutor on a .5 position. I pointed out that, as a recent MA in Victorian literature, I knew nothing about teaching writing and even less about business writing—and had no idea what a Writing Centre was. "No worries," said my colleague airily, "we think you have the kind of personality needed for the job," as if that were the only qualification needed to teach writing.

As it happened, no one in New Zealand would have been more qualified than I was to take on New Zealand's first writing centre work. At that time, writing was not a part of the New Zealand tertiary curriculum: most universities had no writing courses of any kind, there were no PhDs in Rhetoric and Composition, no WAC programmes, no freshman composition, no writing centres. And so I stepped uncertainly into a new space as a pioneer—and soon became passionately committed not just to making my little Centre work for my students but also to making the teaching of writing an uncontested, integrated part of the university's curriculum.

I had no idea what a Writing Centre could or should be. This was before the Internet revolutionised our ability to access information, and, because it was not a research field in New Zealand, our University library carried scant resources on writing pedagogy, let alone writing centre theory. I discovered the Writing Center listserv in 1990-91[2]—it was a lifeline at times, and I was overwhelmed by the generosity of list members who took the time to send me resources. More often than not, though, reading the e-mail discussions felt more like eavesdropping on a conversation on an alien planet. The conversation may have been in English, but the largely American cultural context in which it took place was beyond my comprehension: the terminology was opaque, and the assumption that a whole institutional infrastructure around writing was in place was unimaginable at that time in a New Zealand context. So I had to invent my role as writing tutor. My students, and some faculty, certainly had an expected role for me which could only be described as a combination of proof reader and magician.[3] I was not entirely familiar with the concept of peer tutoring at this time—but the role I carved out for myself was, in effect, that of a peer tutor, puzzling over assignments with the students who found their way into my office, talking to faculty, listening, reading, asking questions.

Early on I came across Elaine Maimon's comment (in McLeod & Soven, 1992, p. xi): "Those who would change curriculum must become ethnographers of their home campuses," and this resonated strongly with what I wanted to achieve in a New Zealand writing programme: something that drew on international scholarship but emerged out of the context of a New Zealand university, something unique and carefully crafted to meet the needs of New Zealand students. To do this, I needed to pay attention to the political, educational, and cultural context in which I worked.

This profile essay outlines the development of a writing centre in a New Zealand university over a 20-year period, within the context of writing instruction emerging within the Aotearoa New Zealand university curriculum.

BECOMING AN ETHNOGRAPHER: UNDERSTANDING THE CONTEXT

New Zealand (Aotearoa is the Maori name) is located in the South Pacific with a population in 2011 of approximately 4.2 million people (Index Mundi, 2010). Although 70% of the population are of European origin (Statistics New Zealand, n.d.), New Zealand considers itself to be a bicultural nation, with both English and Maori (the language of the indigenous people) as official languages, although the language of tuition in most tertiary institutions is primarily English. We also have a growing Asian population, as well as attracting international students primarily from Asia and the Pacific. New Zealand university education was established in the 1870s and has a tradition similar to that of the British university system (Degrees Ahead, n.d.): most students enrol in a three-year degree (there are some exceptions in the applied sciences) and specialise from first year. An unusual feature of the New Zealand university system, and one that, until recently, it has prided itself on, is that it has an open entry policy for students over 20 years of age.[4]

My primary interest has been to develop a writing programme at Massey University. Massey is situated on three campuses: the original and most established campus in Palmerston North, in the lower North Island of New Zealand; Albany (near Auckland); and Wellington (the nation's capital). It offers a full spectrum of academic programmes from undergraduate to PhD and has an unusual student profile by New Zealand standards, due partly to its role as New Zealand's biggest distance education provider; in 2009, it had 34,000 students enrolled, of whom 60% were mature students (over 25), 50% were part-time, and 48% were distance students. It has more Maori students than any other New Zealand university and only 31% of its student population are recent school leavers.

FIRST STEPS: 1980-1999

While the idea for a writing centre came from a colleague who had encountered a North American writing centre, that the initiative took root can largely be attributed to the impact of a time of transition for New Zealand universities, which led to a perceived need for writing instruction within the curriculum. New Zealand was undergoing an economic and political upheaval between 1985 and 1995, which led to a change in the student population. Mature students, many affected by redundancy, were coming to the university to retrain. At the same time, changing social investment and attitudes meant that there was concern to support equitable access to universities, particularly increased representation from Maori and lower socio-economic groups. Open admissions for mature students meant that for the first time large numbers of students without academic preparation were entering the university system.

The response to this transition took two forms at Massey University. First, the small writing centre in the College of Business became the core of a university-wide Student Learning Centre (SLC) in 1996, funded by government "equity" funding. The SLC developed a range of programmes, from learning skills to remedial maths and science, and writing support for both on-campus and distance students. Writing support in these early years was offered by tutors who were usually either experienced high school English teachers or who held post-graduate qualifications in English or Education. The support offered comprised primarily one-on-one support for both on-campus and distance students, and lectures to undergraduate classes. In the early years, the status of the SLC was considered remedial, and its legitimacy as university business questioned. Of particular significance was the fact that staff employed in the SLC was designated as non-academic staff, with a reporting line through Student Services.

Second, the opportunities presented by the economic and social upheavals of the 1980s and 1990s, combined with the identity crises of many English departments in the 1980s and 1990s,[5] led to the development of writing courses as market opportunities. Massey University's School of English and Media Studies showed a particularly early entrepreneurial spirit, with an undergraduate academic writing degree course emerging in the early 1980s. Because we had no "homegrown" PhDs in rhetoric and composition in New Zealand at that time, suitably qualified faculty (with qualifications in applied linguistics and, later, in rhetoric and composition) were re-located from overseas to direct the academic writing course, with faculty from the literature programme retraining to contribute to the course. Fulbright scholars from the US[6] with an interest in WAC also had an influence on the development of the course in the mid-1980s. The development of this course was contentious, with some faculty of the view that this was an inappropriate function of an English Department; however, most English faculty engaged with the course and taught into it at some stage in its early development.

DEVELOPING DISTINCTIVENESS: 1990-2000

Between 1990 and 2000, Massey University's writing programme developed further to incorporate two distinctive features that clearly established writing instruction as developmental rather than remedial.

One of the most distinctive features of Massey University's writing initiatives has been the commitment of the College of Science (CoS) to integrating the teaching of writing into its programmes. In the mid-1990s, a survey of employers of science graduates showed a particular concern with the generic skills of science graduates and in particular graduates' writing skills, and the then Dean began to champion the inclusion of writing in the new degree (Anderson, 1991). Prior to this, the College of Science had taken a range of approaches to integrating writing into its curriculum, but with the advent of a new degree programme in the applied sciences in 1995, which included a first year writing course (Anderson, 1995), the college took the opportunity to introduce writing as a core component of its curriculum through a first year science writing course and a "Writing Across the Curriculum" (WAC) programme (see Emerson et al, 2002, 2006).

Both aspects of this programme are unusual in that they emerged out of a collaboration between myself (a writing teacher from the SLC) and faculty from the College of Sciences as part of a PhD programme using an action research methodology (Emerson et al, 2006). In the first years of the first-year writing course, it was taught entirely by faculty from the CoS, who re-trained with my support as a writing teacher. The WAC component of the programme was intended to further extend science students' writing skills throughout the disciplines, using both a "Writing in the Disciplines" (WiD) and a "Writing to Learn" (WtL) approach. In particular, two Departments within the college developed whole-of-major approaches (modelled on Holyoak, 1998) to integrate writing into their undergraduate programmes (Emerson et al., 2002; MacKay et al., 1999)

In 2000, the science writing course was made compulsory for all students enrolled in any undergraduate science programme, and the course became domiciled in the School of English and Media Studies, under my direction.

A second distinctive aspect of Massey University's developing writing programme was the early development and extension of its OWLL (Online Writing and Learning Link[7])—again, a first for New Zealand universities (Emerson et al, 2000; MacKay et al, 2000). This was developed out of the SLC in 1996, through a large grant from the Fund for Excellence and Innovation in Teaching, and has a distinctive feature in its focus on the needs of distance students. It has been through several iterations, with intensive investment and development in the last decade, and is now an extensive resource, providing static learning resources, interactive resources, and tutor-driven resources, including an asynchronous tutor-review service (called the pre-reading service), which enables distance students to engage with writing tutors and gain a similar level of support as that experienced by on-campus students (see http://owll.massey.ac.nz/).

By 2000, then, Massey had developed a range of writing programmes, located in two distinct areas: academic writing and science writing courses within the School of English and Media Studies, and support for writing in the SLC through face-to-face tutoring, a pre-reading service for distance students, and the OWLL. While the two parts of the programme reported separately, through quite distinct reporting lines, there was, at this time, some communication between the two groups, and a relatively straightforward distinction in function.

There was also the first sign that an institutional approach to writing might emerge, when, in 1998, Council approved the university's Learning and Teaching Plan, which included, as one of the attributes of a Massey graduate, that students be able to "communicate clearly and fluently with all individuals and groups with whom they will interact professionally" (cited in Massey University, 2005, p.1).

FRAGMENTATION: 2000-2010

Following these initial successes, however, in more recent years, a University-wide approach to writing instruction has not been achieved. Instead, the provision of writing instruction has diversified and boundaries have blurred—and while the university has made progress with supporting students' writing, the writing programme continues to face a number of challenges.

On the positive side, in response to the university's Learning and Teaching Plan (1998), the academic board in 2005 adopted a proposal for graduate literacy and numeracy requirements. Despite this, no centralised plan was put in place to operationalise the proposal—but literacy and writing development initiatives continued to develop in an ad hoc way. In 2008, the College of Humanities and Social Sciences made the academic writing course taught by the School of English and Media Studies compulsory for all students studying for a BA degree, which meant that by 2009 all students enrolled in the College of Sciences and the College of Humanities and Social Sciences were required to take a writing course as part of their first year programme. At the same time, the SLC diversified its writing programmes, including the development of writing support programmes for post graduates, and continued to extend its resources on academic writing for both distance and on-campus undergraduates. Also, in 2003, the SLC, in conjunction with the Halls office (the unit responsible for student residences on campus), developed a PASS (Peer Assisted Study Sessions) programme (Wilkinson, 2009a, 2009b), partly as a way of improving the academic profile of the Halls; while this programme was primarily designed to support first-year science and business students, it signalled a commitment to peer tutoring programmes, which would become significant in future years.

However, there have been trends that suggest a need for vigilance. The university has developed a preparatory academic writing course positioned as pre-tertiary level within the Centre for University Preparation and English Language studies (CUPELS), and there are indications that programmes are looking to transfer writing instruction from their academic programme to the pre-tertiary programme. This may be a matter for concern, since such a move would position writing instruction within a remedial rather than developmental context. This concern, that writing could be seen as a remedial rather than developmental function of student learning, also emerged when the SLC, despite its programmes becoming more developmental, was amalgamated with Disability Services. Changed government funding policy, which looks to fund universities on the basis of completions while retaining open admissions, has led to a proposal to develop a literacy testing or pre-entry literacy course requirement for all students. Whether this will eventuate, and what its impact on developmental academic writing programmes might be, is yet to be seen. The challenge is to distinguish between pre-entry expectations and the academic writing skills rightly taught within the disciplines.

Those of us engaged in teaching writing now face a number of difficulties. First is the fact that writing instruction is now so fragmented in so many parts of the university (within different Colleges, in the SLC, and in CUPELS), with almost no coordination or communication, that we are often competing for ground. The second is that, while writing instruction has been established as part of the curriculum, there is little understanding or articulation of the theory of writing instruction or the relationship between writing, learning, and thinking within the disciplines.

A PEER TUTORING CENTRE

Looking squarely into this situation, I have found my thoughts returning to my earliest experience of teaching writing, to the notion of a Writing Centre—and in particular a peer tutoring centre.

In 2008, I was invited to spend a semester as visiting lecturer at the Sweetland Writing Centre at the University of Michigan in the United States. Like my colleague 20 years ago, I came home with a passion to create a peer-tutoring writing centre at Massey as part of our WAC strategy and to build bridges within my home context.

Two practical factors have worked together to support the development of a peer-tutoring centre. First, the School of English and Media Studies was keen to develop its courses on academic writing beyond first year. Second, the SLC was reviewing its commitment to the PASS programme, and looking for new ways to extend the notion of peer-supported learning.

For the first time, the School of English and Media Studies and the SLC are actively working together. The peer review centre will be domiciled in and funded by the SLC with an academic affiliation with the School of English and Media Studies. I am writing two peer tutoring courses—Writing Centre: Theory and Practice and a Writing Centre Practicum. Because the centre is conceived as part of our WAC strategy, we anticipate inviting students from across the university who have demonstrated outstanding writing skills to apply to enrol in these courses. The courses will be offered for the first time in 2011 with the peer tutoring centre established at the start of the second semester in July 2010. We hope to have the peer tutoring writing centre in full operation by 2012, staffed by 10-20 fully trained part-time peer tutors.

I am ambitious for this project. I aim to make connections between the SLC and the School of English and Media Studies in a way that facilitates communication, coordination, and development. We cannot have a university-wide writing programme without coordination: this is one step towards this process. I also hope to engage a first generation of Kiwi students with an ability to see writing as an integral part of thinking and learning within the disciplines. My hope is that as these ideas become current within the New Zealand curriculum, they may come to influence long-term strategy for integrating writing into the curriculum.

Finally, what I hope to achieve is something unique: not a transplanted idea but a Kiwi writing centre. A straight transplant could never be a possibility. As just one example, most Writing Center texts are geared for a North American readership, making assumptions about student experience and institutional structures that are not applicable in Aotearoa. And while these texts may discuss the needs and experiences of specific indigenous peoples in their transition into academia, there can be no assumption that their experiences match those of Maori. There are no texts that address the needs and experiences of Maori in a writing centre context, or the needs of kiwi students more generally. We may have to make our own.

So the centre we are establishing, while it will be informed by international theory and experience, will emerge out of unchartered antipodean ground. I hope to do this through an unusual pedagogical approach: I plan to run the courses using an action research model, and in this way I hope to take my students with me, so that we can become, together, "ethnographers of our home campuses." Together, we will analyse our own context and develop a model for peer tutoring that is informed by international scholarship, but grounded in Aotearoa New Zealand.

The last 20 years have seen exciting opportunities for writing to emerge within the tertiary curriculum in Aotearoa New Zealand. We do not, at Massey University, yet have a university-wide, coordinated writing programme. But we have taken huge strides—and we are contributing to the wider conversation in New Zealand universities concerning the integration of writing into the curriculum. The challenge now is to retain the legitimacy of writing as part of the academic programme and to develop coordinated approaches that are rooted in writing pedagogy. The new peer tutoring centre is one step to achieving these goals.

NOTES

1. "Kiwi" is a term used by New Zealanders to describe themselves (i.e. as a noun) and to describe a New Zealand context (i.e., as an adjective). It is a reference not to the fruit, but to the flightless nocturnal bird that is indigenous to these Islands.

2. The Writing Center listserv is a mailing list run through what is now the International Writing Center Association (IWCA); see http://writingcenters.org/resources/starting-a-writing-cente/#Mail

3. "Fix the writing, fix the writer—preferably in one 30 minute consultation" would be another way of describing the expectations on me.

4. Recent initiatives to cap university placements mean that this policy is currently under review.

5. During this time, enrolments in English literature programmes in New Zealand decreased, leading to a revision, in many places, of the curriculum.

6. Richard Adler, Richard Young and, later, Ruie Pritchard

7. The notion of an online writing lab did not make sense in a New Zealand context because we had no history of writing labs. Hence, we did not make use of the common term "OWL" or "online writing lab."

REFERENCES

Anderson, R. D. (1991). Building a smarter agriculture: A New Zealand perspective. The Australian Institute of Agricultural Science 1991 National

Conference. Paper presented at the National Conference of the Australian Institute of Agricultural Science, Canberra.

Anderson, R. D. (1995). Science, technology and education: The challenge to education. *Agricultural Science, 8,* 37-40.

Degrees Ahead (n.d.) *Universities in New Zealand.* Retrieved from http://www.degreesahead.co.uk/degrees/content/category/5/107/188/

Emerson, L. E., MacKay, B. R., MacKay, M. B., Funnell, K. A. (2002). Writing in a New Zealand tertiary context: WAC and action research. *Language and Learning across the Disciplines, Special Edition: WAC in an international context, 5*(3), 110-133.

Emerson, L. E., MacKay, B. R., MacKay, M. B., Funnell, K. A. (2006). A team of equals: Teaching writing in the sciences. *Educational Action Research, 14*(1), 65-81.

Emerson, L., MacKay, B.R., Falconer, K.R., & Billany, T. J. H. (2000). *The Massey University OWLL: Providing learning support on-line. DEANZ.* Retrieved from: http://www.deanz.org.nz/home/index.php/journal/51-general/48-the-journal-of-distance-learning

Holyoak, A. R. (1998). A plan for writing throughout (not just across) the biology curriculum. *The American Biology Teacher, 60*(3), 186-190.

Index Mundi (2010) *New Zealand demographics profile.* Retrieved from http://www.indexmundi.com/new_zealand/demographics_profile.html

MacKay, B.R., Emerson, L., Funnell, K.A., MacKay, M.B., and Welsh, T.E. (1999). Challenging the pedagogy of tertiary level horticulture. *HortTechnology 9*(2), 272-276.

MacKay, B. R., Emerson, L., Falconer, K. R., & Billany, T. J. H. (2000). T*he Massey OWLL: Sustainable on-line systems. DEANZ.* Retrieved from http://www.deanz.org.nz/home/index.php/journal/51-general/48-the-journal-of-distance-learning

Massey University (2005). Proposal for graduate literacy and numeracy requirements, Unpublished paper, Academic Board, Massey University, New Zealand.

McLeod, S. H., & Soven, M. (Eds.). (1992). *Writing across the curriculum: A guide to developing programs. T*housand Oaks, California: Sage Publications.

Statistics New Zealand (n.d.). *Ethnic groups in New Zealand.* Retrieved from http://www.stats.govt.nz/Census/2006CensusHomePage/QuickStats/quickstats-about-a-subject/culture-and-identity/ethnic-groups-in-new-zealand.aspx

Wilkinson, L. (2009a, November) PASSing on the secrets —a first year study group programme. Association of Tertiary Learning Advisers Aotearoa New

Zealand (ATLAANZ), November 19, 2009, Massey University, Albany Campus, NZ.

Wilkinson, L. (2009b, November) Peer supported study sessions: An academic support programme running in the halls of residence. New Zealand Association of Tertiary Education Accommodation Professionals Conference. , Palmerston North, NZ.

CHAPTER 28.
THE WRITING CENTRE AT ST. MARY'S UNIVERSITY COLLEGE, BELFAST, NORTHERN IRELAND

By Jonathan Worley
Saint Mary's University College, Belfast (Northern Ireland)

This essay describes how my experience of teaching in writing programmes in the US influenced my development of Northern Ireland's first Writing Centre, established in the spring of 2002. I discuss particular influences and how they led to specific pedagogical practices. The experience of moving from an American to a UK academic culture, and the contrasts that the move revealed, were an especially important part of the formation of my personal pedagogy, with insights, I believe, for writing centres on both sides of the Atlantic. As this essay indicates, I remain strongly committed to the student-centred tutorial practices advocated by Donald Murray of the University of New Hampshire and the close, critical scrutiny of student texts, as advocated by Kurt Spellmeyer of Rutgers. Central to this narrative is the belief that critical writing is a significant element of social and political practice.

Opening up a writing centre at St. Mary's University College on the Falls Road in Belfast was in many ways the fulfillment of an unanticipated dream. It was an "unanticipated" fulfillment because, like many of my American colleagues, I had dreamt initially of becoming a lecturer in English. I had planned to share my love of literature with students who would then become enlightened and improved, thereby fulfilling Matthew Arnold's high argument about the place of literature in education.[1] My gradual disaffection with Arnold's lofty claims, combined with my subsequent exposure to pedagogies for teaching writing, ultimately converted me to a lecturer in academic writing, one who made a good fit with the liberal arts degree being offered at St. Mary's.

What does that dream look like in reality? In reality, St. Mary's University College is a close-knit community of approximately 1,000 students, lecturers, management and staff. The community is self-effacing but quietly confident about its place in Northern Irish society. Students were initially friendly and welcoming when I began teaching there, and they became more so the better I came to know them. Management was supportive of the importance of a writing programme to the liberal arts degree, and with their assistance, a colleague from the English department and I were able to obtain substantial additional funding to establish a writing centre.

Lest that reality appear utopian, it came with a significant set of challenges. First, the liberal arts degree at St. Mary's had a strong commitment to widening access, which meant that many of our students were likely to be first-generation university attenders, unfamiliar with the culture and academic practices of tertiary education. Secondly, the heavy commitment to standardised testing in the North—the 11-plus, GCSE and A-level exams—meant that students graduating from high school sorely needed to develop further competence in critical approaches to research, reading, and writing. Finally, if my American impressions of Irish students were correct, they were reluctant to express their critical opinions publicly. The challenges, then, were to develop writing courses that could effectively encourage these students to develop the critical sophistication required for university work and to get them into a writing centre where they could talk about their writing.

A brief history of my development as a writing lecturer will help to explain the practices that I have come to hold dear and which I believe are suited to St. Mary's. In the United States, many graduate students in English Literature begin their teaching by being assigned first-year courses in academic writing, often known as "Freshman English" or "Freshman Composition." As an American graduate student, I began apprenticeship as a composition instructor at the University of New Hampshire (UNH) in 1985. Their writing programme, which had achieved prominence primarily through the work of Donald Murray, emphasised a writing process pedagogy that made use of one-on-one teacher-tutor conferences (individual tutorials) and classroom workshops (full-class discussions of students' essays). The programme encouraged students to write personal narratives and was memorably enthusiastic about the act of writing.

While my own reserved personality probably attenuated some of this enthusiasm, the programme provided an important reminder that writing ideally should be enjoyable, and I began to develop a more restrained vocabulary: "engagement," "struggle," "accomplishment," "absorption," "insight," and "competence." These conceptions proved valuable in my one-on-one tutorials with students, and as I began to learn to draw them out about their own writing and looked for ways to encourage their interest, I gradually shifted from being a "lecturer" to being a "responder." As Murray put it, "The instructor responds to the student's response and to the student's suggestions for improvement."[2]

Beyond Murray's emphasis on the importance of listening and responding in the one-on-one tutorial, he also provided a good scaffold for the writing process, which encouraged students to think of writing as a series of activities. Students could learn that in any piece of written work, there are a multitude of possible interventions. I still cling possessively to my first edition of Murray's text on student writing, *Write to Learn*, and I continue (facetiously) to tell my students to memorise Murray's model for the writing process—collect, focus, order, draft, clarify—each stage associated with a number of possible developments of their texts.[3]

However, good writing involves more than enthusiasm and an awareness of writing as a process, as important as these elements are. Through my experience at UNH, I realised that students could become effective writers about their personal experience, such as winning a football match or going to a formal dance. If they were to venture further, into persuasive forms of writing, their arguments often, frustratingly, were predictable and lacked engagement: they would write familiar arguments about familiar issues in familiar ways. The issues did not even appear interesting to them because they were on safe ground. Very little of this writing did more than reflect their own positions within their dominant culture; that is, they tended to write unproblematically about their experience of the world around them. If they were to abstract values from their experience, these were generally culturally accepted ones. For example, a football match was about "good sportsmanship," a formal dance was the "best day of my life," abortion was simply "murder"—all familiar cultural subject positions.

My dissatisfaction with this kind of writing gained theoretical underpinnings when I studied academic writing under Kurt Spellmeyer at Rutgers University.[4] In his classes we read student texts through the lens of critical theory. While my own interpretations undoubtedly err on the side of pragmatism and reductionism, I found real power in the use of these theorists. Foucault's structuralism, for example, became a commentary on how students were lulled through the discourse that surrounded them into constructing safe and predictable arguments.[5] In contrast, Derrida's views on deconstruction helped me to see how students' tightly held arguments might be the consequence of rigid binary oppositions.[6] Finally, Raymond Williams' (1977) Marxist theory demonstrated that student texts could be productive of social change, but also might very well participate in an ideological false consciousness that preserved the status quo.

Critical theory enabled me to look at students' texts from a fresh perspective: what kind of meaning could emerge from the student text? This perspective turned me into a kind of Sherlock Holmes of student writing: in the presence of larger cultural constructs, what meanings were students attempting to make? This perspective kept student texts fresh and interesting and took me away from an overemphasis on essay structure. Instead of endlessly looking for thesis statements and well-structured arguments, I searched for emerging meaning.

Arriving on Irish shores, my initial experience of teaching at Queen's University Belfast (1994-2002) was that there was not much interest in writing pedagogy. Students were expected to have come to university as competent writers. My experience, however, was that even at prestigious universities such as Queen's, a significant number of students were under-developed as independent learners and writers. For example, when I assigned my class to read Hamlet, one promising student said, "You mean go off and read the whole thing?" In secondary school, such students had been taken step-by-step through literary texts in preparation for their pre-university exams and, additionally, some were told exactly what to say about them. A history student told me that in preparing a critical question upon whether World War I led to World War II, he was told that there was only one correct answer.

Fortunately, at Queen's, I was able to collaborate with another American colleague who had a keen interest in developing a writing programme. He garnered provisional funding for pilot programmes in the teaching of writing from the Queen's School of English. A series of writing seminars ran for two years before devolving to a smaller programme in individualised tutoring. My colleague and I would sit together in our shared office and meet individually with students interested in improving their writing. The high level of appreciation from them for this work, and our developing skill with the one-on-one tutorial, made us keen to expand the programme.

That opportunity arrived when we moved to St. Mary's University College, a teacher training college associated with Queen's that had just established a new degree in the liberal arts. This degree incorporated the teaching of writing as a central element of its programme, and I found myself with the unexpected luxury of teaching students in the classroom on a regular basis. I made use of Murray's writing process model, and, to foster engagement, supplied students with the kinds of critically challenging texts that I hoped would encourage them to problematize their experience. I further deployed strategies of small group work, combined with a myriad of writing activities, in an attempt to develop classroom discussions. These classrooms were not always as lively as comparable American ones, but student reviews showed that they thought I was an 'energetic' teacher and that the texts were interesting.

My American colleague provided a superb start for our mutual ambition to establish a peer tutoring programme in writing by securing an initial grant from the English Subject Centre.[7] We began to establish the programme by drawing upon essential lessons learned at Queen's. We had come to believe that the one-on-one tutorial was central, that tutorial discussions should centre upon what the student wanted to do, and that, because of this focus upon the writer, the concept of having students tutor other students was essentially sound. It was sound because our peer tutors were not going to put themselves forward as experts, but rather as fellow writers who could listen and offer suggestions. As another American colleague, Kathleen Shine Cain, continually asserts, "Writing is a social process." Students may retreat to a solitary location to write—the so-called "ivory tower"—but they are probably deceiving themselves if they believe they do not need the criticism and support of fellow writers. Bolstered by our experience, the training of peer tutors became grounded in student-centred tutoring and the writing process.

Additionally, based on my education at Rutgers, I encourage my tutors to see themselves in the detective role I imagine for myself: Sherlock Holmes searching for emerging meaning in student texts. When we practice reviewing pieces of student writing, I encourage tutors to emphasise content. If, for example, tutors comment that an essay needs a thesis statement, I encourage them to go one step further and ask what the particular thesis statement should be. Thus, in the tutoring session, queries such as, "Are you saying that Marxist political theory does not address the issue of central government?" are much better than, "Where is your thesis statement?"

After three years of initial support from the English Subject Centre, my colleagues and I were in the excellent position of having enough experience to speak with some authority when applying for a grant to be designated as a Centre for Excellence in Teaching and Learning in Northern Ireland. Our application was successful and in 2006 our funding increased fifty-fold. A significant benefit of this funding was that we were more fully able to develop a relationship with Dr. Kathleen Cain, who directs the Merrimack College Writing Centre in Massachusetts, US Kathy came to St. Mary's for a year as a visiting lecturer and was able to contribute her expertise to the further development of our writing centre. The contrasts between the practices of American and UK educational systems proved productive in our thinking about how to develop writing centre pedagogy, and Kathy and I have developed a number of joint conference presentations on the subject of this difference. The second significant benefit was that we were able to move into a larger teaching space with a connected suite of rooms: a peer tutor office, a teaching classroom, and an office for me as director. The willingness of St. Mary's to provide us with this space was one of the most significant aspects of our success: we became an obvious physical presence at the college and students began not only to come to tutorials, but to begin to "hang out" at the centre and study and collaborate on their writing. The rooms are not pre-possessing, but the space itself is excellent. I am able to confer with peer tutors in an informal atmosphere, and the space is an excellent design emphasising collaboration rather than formal teaching. As one of the peer tutors commented: "There is no hierarchy in the writing centre."

When I meet with peer tutors individually at the end of each academic year, I am greatly encouraged and pleasantly surprised by their insights. My colleagues and I learn from them. My dream had been transformed from teaching the appreciation of literature into the opportunity to see students empowered by their ability to engage in the process of writing: not empowered merely because they had mastered writing skills, but because through writing they could learn to be effective and engaged social participants in a larger world. The writing centre that we have set up at St. Mary's is good value because students, very properly and naturally, tutor other students. Staffed by twenty-five student peer tutors, we can handle up to 100 sessions per week, and last academic year we had close to 700 tutorials. Each session is a unique opportunity for a significant discussion about writing. In the writing centre students do what should be a normal part of the learning process: they learn from each other.

NOTES

1. See, especially, Matthew Arnold (1869/2009), *Culture and Anarchy*.

2. Donald Murray, *A Writer Teaches Writing* (1968, p. 148). Chapter 8, Conference Teaching: The Individual Response , represents the foundation for our tutoring strategies.

3. Donald Murray (1985, p. 57). Note that the text has gone through seven subsequent editions: the first edition uses the process described in this essay.

4. To get a good sense of this kind of pedagogic practice, see Kurt Spellmeyer (1993).

5. See, especially, Michel Foucault (1986).

6. To get a sense of the theory behind the deconstruction of texts, see Jacques Lacan (1982a, 1982b, 1984).

7. As part of the national Higher Education Academy, The English Subject Centre supported the teaching and learning of English Literature, English Language and Creative Writing across UK Higher Education. For more information on St. Mary's funded project "Exploring the Potential of Peer-Tutoring in Developing Student Writing" see http://www.stmarys-belfast.ac.uk/downloads/writing%20centre/cetl/documents/ESC%20Report%201.pdf.

REFERENCES

Arnold, M. (1869/2009). *Culture and anarchy*. Oxford: Oxford University Press.

Foucault, M. (1986). The discourse on language. In H. Adams (Ed.), *Critical theory since 1965* (pp. 148-62). Tallahassee, FL: University Presses of Florida.

Lacan, J. (1982a). Différence. In A. Bass (Ed.), *Margins of philosophy* (pp. 1-28). Chicago: University of Chicago Press.

Lacan, J. (1982b). Signature, event, context. In A. Bass (Ed.), *Margins of philosophy* (pp. 307-30). Chicago: University of Chicago Press.

Lacan, J. (1994) Structure, sign, and play in the discourse of the human sciences. In D. Keesey (Ed.), *Contexts for criticism* (pp. 347-58). London: Mayfield.

Murray, D. (1968). *A writer teaches writing*. New York: Houghton Mifflin.

Murray, D. (1985). *Write to learn*. New York: Harcourt.

Spellmeyer, K. (1993). *Common ground: Dialogue, understanding, and the teaching of composition*, New York: Prentice Hall.

Williams, R. (1977). *Marxism and literature*. Oxford: Oxford University Press.

CHAPTER 29.
THE UPS AND DOWNS OF THE INTERDISCIPLINARY WRITING CENTER OF THE INTERAMERICAN UNIVERSITY OF PUERTO RICO, METROPOLITAN CAMPUS

By Matilde García-Arroyo and Hilda E. Quintana
InterAmerican University of Puerto Rico, Metro Campus

This profile describes the eventful history over twenty-five years of the Interdisciplinary Writing Center of the InterAmerican University of Puerto Rico. The Center, the first in Puerto Rico and committed to developing students' writing in both Spanish and English, flourished for several years, closed, then re-opened in 2008 to a new mandate. The authors analyze persistent attitudinal challenges the Center continues to face, even as it has succeeded in its mission of reaching students across disciplines.

The Metropolitan Campus was founded in 1962 as part of the InterAmerican University of Puerto Rico (IAUPR, founded in 1912), a private, coeducational nonprofit teaching institution with a Christian heritage and an ecumenical tradition. IAUPR was accredited in 1944 by the Middle States Association of Colleges and Schools, thus becoming the first four-year liberal arts college to be accredited outside the continental limits of the United States. At present, our campus serves an average of 10,600 students, who are enrolled in one of four faculties: Sciences and Technology, Education and Behavioral Professions, Business and Economic Administration, and Humanistic Studies. It offers all levels of study from certificates to doctoral degrees.

During the 1983-84 academic year, our university initiated an innovative general education program that included a composition course in Spanish, our first language. IAUPR was the first university in Puerto Rico to require a composition course in our native language. Specifically, this course allowed our university to meet the following goal of this General Education Program: "To develop a person capable of communicating with propriety in Spanish or English and of using the other language at an acceptable level" (General Catalog, 2007-2009, p. 106). Composition courses in L1 had never been part of the college tradition in Puerto Rico, because it was assumed that students who were admitted to them already knew how to write well in any discipline. By doing this, our institution expressed concern about our students' written communication skills. From that moment on, the Vice Presidency of Academic Affairs of IAUPR also promoted writing across the curriculum. Later on, and after Christopher Thaiss was invited in 1988 to offer several workshops to faculty from across the disciplines, our institution approved a policy that stated:

> Writing will be part of our curriculum and should be used intensively so that it becomes a means of expression and a learning tool in all of the disciplines. Its use will facilitate the development of thinking skills while being used as a teaching and learning tool. This is based on the idea that knowledge and language are inseparable. In other words, what is known should be communicated in written form [Authors' translation] (Academic Excellence, 1988, p. 7).

It was in the Metropolitan Campus that this policy was accepted very enthusiastically by both of us as Directors of the Spanish and English Departments. Therefore, in 1990 and 1992, we organized, together with a group of professors from the Spanish and English Departments, the First and Second Conferences on the Teaching of Writing, which served as vehicles for faculty development. Both were key activities in acknowledging the importance of composition courses in our first language and the need of incorporating writing across the curriculum, not only in our university, but also in all institutions in Puerto Rico. During this period some of our guests included Peter Elbow, Paul Connolly, James Gray, Daniel Cassany, and Robert Tierney. We also received scholarships to take post-doctoral courses in the teaching of reading and writing, including seminars in the Institute for Writing and Thinking at Bard College in New York. All of these initiatives made us more aware that there was a need to supplement what the university had done up to that moment and to consider alternatives that would strengthen our General Education Program. It was at that time that we began to consider the development of a Writing Center for our campus.

THE DEVELOPMENT OF THE INTERDISCIPLINARY WRITING CENTER

In the summer of 1992, and with the sponsorship of the Vice Presidency of Academic Affairs, we began a research project that allowed us to develop a writing center model for our campus. Our research included visiting several centers in universities in the United States to observe their functioning, as well as to interview the directors. We visited the Writing Centers at Lehman College in CUNY, New York University, SUNY at Albany, the University of Southern California in Los Angeles, the University of California at Berkeley, the University of Texas at El Paso, and the University of Miami. In 1993 we also visited the Writing Center at Georgetown University in Washington, DC. The reading of A Guide to Writing Programs: Writing Centers, Peer Tutoring, and Writing across the Curriculum (Haring-Smith,1985) helped us choose these centers. Other factors we took into consideration when selecting these centers were their prestige, and that they were located in universities that had some similarities with ours; for example, the student population. Since many of them had Hispanic students, we were able to get information on how they taught writing in both L1 and L2.

The visits allowed us to gather information about where to locate our center and how to train the tutors and other personnel who would be working there. Because we interviewed directors and tutors and studied the organization of the centers, we also gathered much more information about the roles of Writing Centers. In addition, all of the directors shared with us hand-outs and other official documents that guided us in developing our own materials. All of the information collected and the work of Muriel Harris (1982) and Stephen North (1984) served as guides when we finally developed our model.

The mission of our Writing Center stated that we would help our students improve the quality of their written work by means of one-to-one tutorials during the writing process in both languages, English and Spanish. These tutorials would be given by trained undergraduate students. Other group orientations and workshops would be given to provide students with techniques to help them discover their own writing processes. In addition, our model of the writing center included a faculty-training component.

THE BEGINNING AND THE END

Our Writing Center was inaugurated in 1994 with the visit of Toby Fulwiler. The Center was assigned to the Dean of Studies office to make it clear that tutoring was available to students in all disciplines and not only to students taking Spanish and English courses. It had a director who was a full time professor of the Spanish Department and who had completed post-doctoral studies in the teaching of writing, plus two part-time coordinators, one for English and one for Spanish, who were in charge of the tutors. During the first three years all services were offered, and the number of students tutored increased year by year. The few graduate students who sought services received tutorials given by the coordinators, who had master's degrees in the teaching of Spanish and English. It is important to point out that the Center was a stronghold of both the writing process and writing across the curriculum. In other words, in the Center we were aware that the teaching of writing had to be transformed, so we organized professional development activities to help professors incorporate writing in their courses.

The Writing Center, the only one of its kind on the island, was open until 2000, when the administration indicated that for budgetary reasons it had to close. However, we have to indicate that very few faculty members and administrators understood its mission. Usually it was confused with the Spanish and English Language Laboratories that had been in operation since the 1970s on our campus. These were set up for basic level students to do remedial work to improve their writing skills. As a matter of fact, at the beginning of the 1990s, the teaching of writing as a process was hardly known in Puerto Rico, especially among the Spanish professors. Of course, this situation made it harder to incorporate writing across the curriculum.

Gradually, the budget for tutors decreased, provoking the reduction of one-to-one tutorials. At the same time, the direction of the Center fell into the hands of part-time Spanish or English faculty who only worked six hours a week and had no academic preparation in the field of writing. Basically, it was the responsibility of a "specialist" in the development of writing skills who was in charge of the Writing Center, because there were no tutors. This is further evidence that the idea of a writing center was not understood.

Sadly, all of these events led to the closing of the center, thus sending a formidable message to the professors who had included writing in their courses throughout the years. Harris (n.d.) helps us understand what happened:

> When there is a lack of understanding, outsiders tend to view the center as less important, capable of operating with limited funds and/or facilities, and able to cope with minimal assistance. In times of budget cuts, writing centers are more likely to be viewed as expendable because they are unlike

traditional credit-bearing courses. Thus, the tenuous nature of some facilities and their reduced levels of support can demoralize the staff and weaken the writing center's ability to do its work. Where there is a clearer understanding of what the writing center contributes, however, support is strong, and writing centers are likely to be given increased responsibilities (15).

The years that followed the closing of our center disrupted all we had done to incorporate writing across the curriculum. It is during this period that the composition course in Spanish was also eliminated as a graduation requirement university-wide. A world literature course was substituted for it. In addition, the university policy regarding writing across the curriculum was annulled at this time.

THE NEW BEGINNING

The efforts to transform the teaching of writing were left in the hands of a small group of professors who were committed to this end. In other words, we were left to work individually in our classrooms. We also continued publishing our work and attending conferences in Latin America and in the United States. Basically, we felt it was our responsibility to continue our own professional development, hoping that one day we would be able to resume our discussion of communication across the curriculum (CAC) throughout our campus.

In 2003, the UNESCO Chair for the Improvement of Reading and Writing in Latin America was established on our campus through our initiative. This event started a new dialogue about the importance of both processes as learning tools. To inaugurate the Chair a symposium was held in 2004, thus creating more interest in the writing process and academic writing. This activity coincided with a new administration that expressed great interest in reopening the Interdisciplinary Writing Center.

Finally, in March 2008, the Center was reopened based on the same model we had developed. One-to-one tutorials are given in Spanish and English—and this time in an extended schedule. Now the Center is open at night and on Saturday morning in order to service our graduate students, who only study during these periods on our campus.

Our experience has been rewarding once again. The number of tutorials has surpassed our expectations. Alliances have been made with the Teacher Preparation, Spanish, Music, and Psychology professors. At this moment our Internet webpage is under construction to serve our online students. We are also making plans to develop podcasts to strengthen our services.

Reopening the Center constitutes a new effort to incorporate writing as a learning tool in the curriculum, while we also take care of our students' needs during the writing process. The Center is also part of the restructuring of the services offered by the Faculty of Humanistic Studies and part of the new academic vision of our present administration. It is important to mention that the Language Laboratories have been eliminated, so our Writing Center occupies the place it should have in an educational institution that aspires to graduate its students with writing competencies.

WHERE WE ARE NOW

We are very satisfied with our achievements up to now. Nevertheless, we are aware that budgetary decisions sometimes do not allow us to offer the number of tutorials requested. There is still not a clear understanding that the tutoring sessions have to be given individually in both Spanish and English during the hours when the Center is opened. In addition, there is still no budget assigned for books and other educational materials.

We are also concerned that many faculty members still view the teaching of writing as being equivalent to teaching grammar. Therefore, these faculty believe that only Spanish and English professors should teach writing. All required Spanish courses have also been revised since 2000; they are all literature courses now. The syllabi indicate that writing and reading processes are included in all of them, but not all professors teach these. A strong grammar component has gradually been included in these courses in recent years, too.

Faculty development is still part of the Center, because the present administration has appointed us as members of a campus-wide Interdisciplinary Writing Committee. Therefore, we sense that the administration is trying to locate our CAC program in our Writing Center. The mission of this committee is to train professors who are interested in incorporating writing in their courses.

It is interesting to note that our participation in this committee has helped us reaffirm the results of a study that we recently completed with two other colleagues from other higher education institutions in Puerto Rico (Quintana, García Arroyo, Arribas, & Hernández, in press). In Puerto Rico, the teaching of reading and writing is still viewed from a very timid standpoint. All of the administrators of the institutions that we surveyed agreed that there is a great concern with CAC, and they also recognized that many of the students enrolled in their institutions need to improve these competencies. However, the participants in our study still view the writing process as being the same as learning grammar. In addition, the majority of the institutions that were surveyed still have Language Laboratories, including the other campuses of our institution. All emphasize remedial work, mostly grammar and punctuation exercises for which "correct" answers are sought to make sure, it is imagined, that students will obtain writing competence.

Some of the members of our campus Interdisciplinary Writing Committee also share this vision. They believe it is our responsibility, as Spanish and English professors, to make sure our students learn to write. In addition, they do not understand their role in helping students gain writing proficiency in their discipline. They all agree that students need to improve their writing skills, but they do not do anything about it. As a matter of fact, they have indicated that they do not include any writing activities in their courses because students do not know how to write. Therefore, our main challenge in this committee is to convince these members that writing is a learning tool in all disciplines. They also need to understand that the Writing Center can play a very active role in the development of the writing competencies of our student body.

Over the years we have finally understood that professors who write and publish their work are the ones who understand the importance of the role of writing in their disciplines. It is these professors who also understand the mission of the Writing Center; this is why they sponsor it.

Finally, it is important to point out that we have never doubted the value of the Writing Center. In the Center our students write and discover their strengths. There writing is promoted as an art and as a tool to obtain success in any field or profession. The Center gives them a wonderful opportunity to develop their intelligences, talents, and writing processes, most likely not developed in many traditional learning settings.

REFERENCES

InterAmerican University of Puerto Rico. (1988). *Circular letter A-108-88: Excelencia Académica [Academic Excellence]*. San Juan, PR: Author.

InterAmerican University of Puerto Rico. (2007-2009). *General catalogue*. San Juan, PR: Author.

Haring-Smith, T. (1985). *A guide to writing programs: Writing centers, peer tutoring, and writing across the curriculum*. Glenview, Ill: Scott, Foresman.

Harris, M. (1982). *Tutoring writing. A sourcebook for writing labs*. Glenview, Ill: Scott, Foresman.

Harris, M. (n.d.). *Statement: The concept of a writing center.* Retrieved from http://writingcenters.org/starting-a-writing-center/writing-center-concept/. (Originally published by the National Council of Teachers of English in 1988).

North, S. (1984). The idea of a writing center. *College English, 46*(5) 433–446.

Quintana, H., Garcia-Arroyo, M., Arribas, M., & Hernández, C. (in press). La alfabetización académica en las instituciones de educación superior en Puerto Rico en el siglo XXI [Academic reading and writing in higher education institutions in Puerto Rico in the twenty-first century]. In G. Parodi (Ed.), *Alfabetización académica y profesional en el siglo XXI: Leer y escribir desde las disciplinas [Academic and profesional reading and writing in the twenty-first century: Reading and writing in the disclplines].* Chile: Editorial Planeta.

CHAPTER 30.
ACADEMIC WRITING AT THE UNIVERSITY OF DUNDEE: A PERSPECTIVE FROM SCOTLAND

By Kathleen McMillan
University of Dundee (Scotland)

This profile essay explores the variety of Academic Writing provision in place at the University of Dundee, Scotland. The Academic Achievement Teaching Unit (AATU), under the Directorship of the Academic Secretary, supports the University of Dundee community by promoting on-campus development of academic literacies for all students. This provision includes credit-bearing academic literacy courses, support programmes, bespoke inputs, and discrete postgraduate writing courses. In addition, under the Royal Literary Fund's Fellowship Scheme for supporting writing development in Higher Education, the institution hosts part-time Royal Literary Fund (RLF) Writing Fellows. The profile charts how writing development work at the University of Dundee has come into being organically, in response to demand from academic colleagues and to student-led demand.

The student population in Scotland tends to reflect the demographic profile, by drawing the majority of its undergraduate students from the wider Scottish/UK community, and often from the local area in which the university is set. Postgraduate students present a more cosmopolitan profile, as institutions seek to exploit the international market to supplement income streams; this trend is reflected in taught and research degree programmes. Therefore, the academic needs of subsets within university communities are diverse and often without complementarity.

Students as a community are articulate in their demands for a high quality teaching and learning experience. However, they are not alone in possessing high expectations of their university education; teaching and research staff, too, have expectations as to performance of students and their ability to learn and to meet the standards of performance that judge them to be worthy of the target degree. In practice, this means a series of push-pull tensions, as university hierarchies seek to fulfil the requirements of central and regional governments in terms of recruitment and progression targets, while those involved in delivering courses strive to maintain levels of teaching and learning to standards that reflect the traditions of university education.

To add to these tensions, emergent factors have further influenced learning environments, as staff and students develop uses (and expectations about these uses) of technology in learning. Lecture notes are de rigeur posted on virtual learning sites, while podcast lectures and Twitter are beginning to reflect the outlook and expectation of the twenty-first century learner. Students make use of these different media to record ideas, contribute to discussions, and broker their learning by writing in ways that are not particularly well related to the traditional writing models of higher education. Yet, assessment modes still rely heavily on the written-word tradition as a means of demonstrating understanding and intellectual development.

THE INSTITUTIONAL CONTEXT

The University of Dundee, as one of the older Scottish universities, having separated from the University of St. Andrews in 1967, is no different from others in the sector in that it has to meet the demands of central (UK) and regional (Scottish) governments while responding to the requirements of its academic community. Recently, the university has restructured to four Colleges comprising 13 Schools, representing a range of disciplines including Life Sciences, Medicine, Dentistry, Social Sciences, Humanities, Engineering, and the Arts. The university has three campus sites.

The Academic Achievement Teaching Unit (AATU), under the Directorship of the Academic Secretary, supports the university community by promoting on-campus development of academic literacies for all students. The team consists of 4.75 full-time equivalent [FTE] staff: one senior lecturer with a remit for overseeing the provision of academic development (Head of Unit), two full-time lecturers (English language support for non-native speakers of English), and 1.75 Academic Skills Tutors, supplemented by hourly-paid freelance staff. Administration is covered by .5 FTE clerical staff with extended provision for large projects over the year. In addition, under the Royal Literary Fund's programme for supporting writing development in higher education, the institution hosts two part-time Royal Literary Fund (RLF) Writing Fellows (each for two days per week) and is grateful to the

RLF for its generosity in continuing to provide the services of the Writing Fellows.

SUPPORTING LEARNING: ORIGINS AND GRADUAL GROWTH OF AATU

AATU has developed organically, in response both to student-led demand and to demand from academic colleagues. The hard work of the AATU team has been successful in profiling the need for writing support and broader aspects of the acquisition of academic learning skills across the university. The AATU (under another name) originated in the late 1980s from modest requirements to meet the language needs of international students (English for Academic Purposes—EAP). Weekly tutorial classes were delivered within the University Language Unit, which specialised in the teaching of modern foreign languages (MFL). The EAP remit then morphed into a more inclusive one providing support in the development of academic literacies for all students. Subsequently, under one of several restructuring exercises, EAP tuition remained with MFL, while staff teaching academic literacies attained an independent identity within a centralised learning service. This model, in turn, was restructured, with the EAP component reunited with academic literacies activities, to the present configuration as AATU.

The chequered development of AATU demonstrates that, in earlier times, interest in the academic literacy needs of students tended to be confined to a minority of staff and to the international student community—rather than being an explicit policy of learning development across the student population. However, in 2007, the creation of a formal unit with the remit of providing academic literacies tuition to all students (international and home; undergraduate and postgraduate) based on the existing platform of writing development support, has contributed to the higher profile and more extensive activities that characterise AATU's current work.

Thus, institutionally, the work of AATU is regarded as a "good thing" in that it contributes to aiding student retention and to engaging with the Enhancement-led Institutional Review (ELIR) processes of quality assurance. However, this status has been achieved less as the outcome of a discrete policy than through the development of small, pilot projects launched proactively by AATU staff and championed by the Academic Secretary. As one success has been attained and the expertise, academic professionalism, and contribution of AATU staff recognised, further projects have become more readily supported and, thus, possible to implement.

Hence, University recognition of the importance of "academic literacy" as a pillar of the university learning experience has been constructed (Ivanic, 1998; Johns, 1997; Lea, 2004; Lillis, 2001; Street, 2001). The diverse demographic student profile provides a community whose learning histories may represent erratic assimilation of some basic concepts of learning, writing, and academic self-reliance. This is the challenge that AATU seeks to address through holistic approaches to supporting learning (McMillan, 2008). These encourage students to recognise that seeking assistance is a mature decision that will help them develop and succeed, rather than a de-motivating admission of failure. Students may "present" with one need, but reveal needs in other aspects of their learning; often, one of these is writing. While students may recognise for themselves or through staff feedback that there is a far bigger learning "picture," students may have yet to realise that

> Every time a student sits down to write for us, s/he has to invent the university . . . has to learn to speak our language, to speak as we do, to try on the particular ways of knowing, selecting, evaluating, reporting, concluding and arguing that define the discourse of our community. (Bartholomae, 1985, in Johns 1997, p. 20)

This is the challenge that AATU staff address through the pragmatic approach of identifying, and then meeting, learning needs in the broadest sense. Hence, the resultant AATU portfolio covers a range of diverse aspects of learning. This diversity takes account of the fact that students do not conveniently or predictably reach a simultaneous awareness of their learning needs, whatever these may be. Therefore, the essence of the AATU approach is to provide as many opportunities and routes into developing learning skills as possible. Writing plays a key role in this respect, since writing is the means by which students are most frequently assessed and, consequently, is the skill development to which they seem to give most credence.

PRACTICAL LEARNING: THE AATU PORTFOLIO

In its practical application, the AATU approach cleaves into four subsets as shown in Figure 1.

Each of the provisions identified in Figure 1 has contributed in some measure to the development of writing for those students who have, either individually or in their mainstream classes, participated in AATU teaching. The credit-

1. CREDIT-BEARING ACADEMIC LITERACY COURSES	2. SUPPORT PROGRAMMES
1.1 Personal Academic Student Skills 20-credit course for undergraduate students **1.2 Pre-sessional English Language Programme** Successful completion qualifies for admission **1.3 Access Programmes** Delivered online; successful completion of inputs to academic programmes qualifies for university admission	**2.1 Writing Programmes:** Writing by Appointment (WBA) Just Write (Royal Literary Fund sponsored) Write Right (Royal Literary Fund sponsored) **2.2 Numeracy Programme:** Count Me In **2.3 Examination Programmes:** Ready, Steady Exams Preparatory Resit Exam Programme (PREP) **2.4 English for international students** In-semester support programme of classes
3. BESPOKE INPUTS	**4. DISCRETE POSTGRADUATE WRITING COURSES**
3.1 Taught postgraduate Delivered within several courses including Design, Law, Education, Social Work **3.2 Undergraduate Programmes** Delivered across all Colleges with inputs in more than 12 Schools from levels 1- 4.	**4.1 Doctoral Programmes** Generic skills provision in academic writing for thesis level at 1st, 2nd and 3rd year levels of doctoral studies **4.2 Taught postgraduate** Civil Engineering for dissertation level Orthopaedic Surgery for dissertation level

Figure 1. Academic Achievement Teaching Unit Learning Models at the University of Dundee.

bearing Personal Academic Student Skills (P@SS) programme, introduced in 2003 (Figure 1: model 1), has been influential in raising the profile amongst those staff who acknowledge the value of developing academic literacies (http://www.dundee.ac.uk/aatu/pass.htm). The module is offered twice in an academic year and attracts students from Levels 1—3 from a range of disciplines. The 20 credits awarded for successful completion of the module contribute to the requirement to accumulate 120 credits at level 1 towards the final degree. The syllabus is delivered in three complementary threads: information-processing;

understanding "studentness," and academic writing (the latter incorporating significant inputs on language [grammar] and lexical development). Classroom teaching is supplemented by activities provided through the institutional virtual learning environment. The course attracts 80-100 students per year and has been commended by external examiners, one of whom commented that "this course is exemplary of the type of support we might wish were available to each student embarking on university study."

Pre-entry teaching takes place in English language courses for international students and, for home students, in a hybrid on-line/on-campus module on academic literacies entitled "Learning Plus." Both programmes (Figure 1: model 1) place considerable emphasis on learning to write well. Clearly, although these represent introductions to academic writing, the intention is that students will engage, where possible, with later 'writing in the disciplines' provision that exists within bespoke or discrete writing programmes.

Three support programmes (Figure 1: model 2), Just Write, Write Right, and Writing by Appointment, explicitly address the development of academic writing and have generated considerable activity since their inception. In 2004, the generosity of the Royal Literary Fund (RLF) provided the University with our first Writing Fellow, whose role was to help students develop their writing (www.rlf.org.uk). Since 2004, we have had five Writing Fellows, and the current arrangement is that we have two Writing Fellows at any one time working over the two-semester period of an academic year. Thus far, each Fellow remains in post for a two-year period. They offer two programmes (one each) —Just Write and Write Right—and appointments are made via an online booking system, so that the Fellows can optimize their time for working with students rather than on routine administrative tasks. They work with undergraduate and postgraduate students, with the focus on the development of style rather than explicit grammatical explanation of errors. The terms of the RLF agreement preclude working with specific groups who might be regarded as requiring specialist attention; notably, dyslexic students and students whose writing problems emanate from the fact that they are using English as an additional language. Such students are referred to our other in-house writing programme, Writing by Appointment.

In the RLF programmes and the in-house Writing by Appointment, students are seen on a one-to-one basis. This approach is well-received by students and deemed to be effective; its acknowledged success supports the view that in the modern, anonymous world of universities, the opportunity to work with a writing specialist on the student's own work is highly valued (www.dundee.ac.uk/aatu/writing.htm).[1]

Over the three writing programmes, an average of 300 students are seen each academic year, which in 2009-10 represented in excess of 780 appointments. The number of meetings will vary, since some students require support over a number of weeks. Students can book online or staff can refer students to AATU. Information about these programmes is delivered by corporate branded PLUS@Dundee[2] materials displayed prominently in sites available to staff and students (http://www.dundee.ac.uk/welcome2010/leaflet.htm).

The Challenge of Changing Staff Perceptions

However, for some academic staff, perceptions remain that these initiatives represent deficit models of teaching. These perceptions are incorrect. While some students do, indeed, register because they are weak in writing, others participate because they aspire to the highest grades possible and see the writing programmes as a route to fulfilling this aspiration. If deficit there is, then this lies in the shortfall in skills development in the school sector; higher education inherits that legacy (McMillan, 2006). Blame cannot be placed on students who have had limited school tuition in the fundamentals of writing; often these students write only what they can write, not necessarily what they know (McMillan, 2006).

Nevertheless, initially, some academics suggested that these writing programme interventions compromise the integrity of the work of students, claiming that such students gain an advantage over others who do not receive this help. These suggestions highlight the failure of some colleagues to recognize the approach as a construct of learning rather than provision of proof-reading, as they had assumed. Since the programmes are open to all students, then, it is counter-argued, no student is disadvantaged by the system, only by their choice not to seek an appointment. For some individual students who receive guidance on their writing and learning, this may well compensate in some measure for the skills shortfall that is increasingly evident among some sectors of the student population; even perceived "high achievers" need to recognize the importance of reflective thinking processes of planning and composing on writing (Sharples, 1999).

Yet raising staff awareness of academic support mechanisms that exist continues to be an uphill struggle for AATU practitioners. It is hoped that some recent institutional restructuring will address the student experience and the support mechanisms within that concept in a more comprehensive and coherent way that will help to push understanding of this aspect of learning higher on the continuous professional development agenda.

Bespoke Workshops and the "Writing in Disciplines" Approach

Further opportunities to disseminate writing support information are possible in bespoke workshops (Figure 1: model 3) where AATU staff collaborate with subject specialists in delivering a range of academic skills within the framework of the academic discipline and its timetable. There is a direct correlation between these team-teaching episodes providing large-group inputs and subsequent follow-on appointments for students wishing to address writing issues. Once students have had experience of AATU support, whether in 1:1 writing tutorials, bespoke class, or special courses such as P@SS and PREP, several seek further help at later points in their academic journey towards graduation.

Writing remains an issue for international students and, while AATU provides in-sessional English support classes (Figure 1: model 2) on different aspects of language acquisition, including writing, the numbers of students who seek places in this voluntary programme are not indicative of the numbers of international students who may be challenged by academic writing standards. This disparity has been attributed to the fact that, because both under- and postgraduate programmes are intensive, students do not have time to participate in generic language classes; conversely, some students do not acknowledge their difficulties with writing until much further on in the academic year, when it is too late to address these because of the time pressure of submission deadlines.

For these reasons, a 'Writing in the Disciplines' (WiD) approach to support the writing needs of undergraduate international students is being adopted, modeled on a long-standing initiative for taught postgraduate orthopaedic students and a newer pilot with taught postgraduate civil engineering students. These discrete writing modules involve international and home students (Figure 1: model 4). The inputs are integrated into the course timetable, and the aim is to do likewise for undergraduate programmes. The focus, in both instances, is to shift the overt emphasis from language acquisition in the traditional, generic English for Academic Purposes approach, by exploiting the students' strategic need to prepare and produce a dissertation that meets the required written standard. Therefore, as each stage of the dissertation is tackled, the explicit writing skills are developed incrementally to that end and, since the module is integrated into courses, the time spent in the subject-driven writing class is validated. The content can be tailored to meet the discipline requirements, with those students who are weaker being identified and given additional support through the one-to-one writing programmes.

POSTGRADUATE WRITING COURSES

Another dimension of the work of AATU is the provision of discrete postgraduate writing courses—in the form of 13 two-hour workshops on different aspects of thesis writing within the Generic Skills curriculum offered to all doctoral students regardless of nationality or language community in the four University Colleges as part of their professional development programme in years 1-3 of their studies. The workshops take students from the early stages of exploring their topic through the literature review (Organised Writing), the development of drafts as the research work begins to achieve outcomes (Scholarly Writing), and into the final phase with sessions on achieving coherence over the whole thesis (Thesis Overview). Again, working on the principle that students are more engaged if the material relates to them as individuals, the approach is to provide students with feedback on a short piece of un-edited writing (500-750 words). This provides diagnostic information that forms the basis of the workshop sessions.

Examination Preparation Support

> The AATU model of academic literacies development reflects the views of Johns (1997), who acknowledged that students need ". . . .strategies for understanding, discussing, organizing, and producing texts . . . the learning processes as well as products, form as well as content, readers' as well as writers' roles and purposes" (Johns, 1997:2-3).

This interplay is recognized particularly by students who participate in the Preparatory Resit Examination Programme (PREP) (Figure 1: model 2). This AATU support programme deals with students when they are at their most vulnerable. Although only two-weeks long, the PREP syllabus has to work through different academic literacies to ensure that students not only understand the critical thinking necessary for exam success, but also ensure that they can evidence this in their writing. For those students who successfully return to their studies after resits, this provides an introduction to AATU provision and, as a consequence, such students frequently seek further support with writing through AATU's one-to-one writing tutorials.

AATU also supports "unseen" students, namely, those who access the AATU "How to . . . " leaflets on essays, reports, and exams that are available on PLUS@ Dundee displays across the campuses (http://www.dundee.ac.uk/welcome2010/leaflet.htm). Additionally, our intranet sites, Advance@Dundee and Advance@ Dundee Postgraduate Portal, provide a resource on writing as an ever-present reference. Similarly, Write Attributes, a Virtual Learning Environment (VLE) module accessible to all students, provides guidance, with models, on citation and referencing. Designed to help students learn how to use the work of others in support of the discussion in their writing, it tackles plagiarism constructively.

MOVING FORWARD

The integrated approach of the AATU model is framed on an understanding that "there needs to be a facility within school and university curricula to introduce, develop, and enhance academic literacies for all those who may aspire to study in higher education at some point in the future" (McMillan, 2008). Writing is one such literacy. However, the problems that surround the development of writing lie not only with the constraints arising from students' lack of prior learning at school level, but also with the broadening genres within which students are expected to write (Ganobcsik-Williams, 2006), alongside the "hidden agenda" of limited resources that prevail in modern higher education. It is not enough that students have to write in traditional essay or report formats; their writing must be appropriate to the discipline—yet deal with the multitude of genres expected of them. Dealing with the different formats and expectations that lead from these genres presents, for many, confusion and inconsistency. For example, in some disciplines, students are asked to submit a standard essay, blog entries, and a piece of reflective writing within their first-year assessments. Feedback on any one of these diverse genres has little potential to be particularly useful to the others. Thus, students are often not given the opportunity (especially within the now common modular system of course delivery) to consolidate their writing skills in light of related feedback. Instead, within one module they are required to write in an entirely different way measured against criteria that can be vague, if not unclear. In addition, "mixed messages" within the guidelines, learning outcomes, and practices required by individual academics can confuse students further; for example, in use of voice, personalization, structuring of text, and general register. Hence, students are constantly challenged by criteria that, while perhaps seeming open and clear, are often, in practice, hidden and, to the novice writer, unfathomable.[3]

AATU initiatives have developed, therefore, not only to assist students, but also to encourage subject specialists to become more aware of their role in "unpacking" some of the mysteries of the writing required in their field, by helping students to understand the academic "voice," the related language, and the writing conventions. Thus, the roles of academic staff and academic skills practitioners are to act as interpreters of the academic mores that support the traditions of academic writing for undergraduate and postgraduate students and to model ways in which these need to adapt to meet the diverse range of genres and contexts of the modern university. At a time when so much is uncertain in higher education and the wider economy, it is imperative for employability that students develop these academic writing skills in all their diversity, and recognize that these skills need to be honed and shaped to transfer appropriately to professional contexts. How can this be done except by showing students that academia values and rewards excellence in writing?

NOTES

1. One unexpected outcome of the RLF scheme has been that the author of this essay has worked collaboratively since then on several commercial writing projects with our first Writing Fellow, Dr. Bill Kirton. Without the RLF initiative, this writing partnership opportunity would not have arisen.

2. PLUS@Dundee—Personal Learning for University Success at Dundee is a project that introduces students to the new learning environment of the University from the day of their arrival and progresses throughout the journey of their first academic year with support activities mostly delivered through AATU. A comprehensive set of information leaflets in addition to the "How to . . . ." leaflets positioned at information points across the institution gives students key information about University provision and signposts them to further information online or in support units.

3. The reality is that many students, especially at undergraduate level, are simply unaware of the not inconsiderable gaps in their writing skills, while staff make assumptions about the expected skill set that are at odds with the reality. This means that marking criteria and feedback often confuse more than assist.

REFERENCES

Ganobcsik-Williams, L. (2004). *A Report on the Teaching of Academic Writing in UK higher education.* London: Royal Literary Fund.
Ivanic, R. (1998). *Writing and identity: The discoursal construction of identity in academic writing.* Amsterdam: John Benjamin B.V.
Johns, A.M. (1997). *Text, role and context: Developing academic literacies.* Cambridge: Cambridge University Press.
Lea, M. (2004). Academic literacies: A pedagogy for course design. *Studies in Higher Education, 29*(6), 739-56.
Lillis, T. (2001). *Student writing: Access, regulation, desire.* London: Routledge.
McMillan, K. (2006). *The minority ethnic group experience in Scottish Higher Education.* Glasgow: University of Glasgow Doctoral Thesis.
McMillan, K. (2008). Changing identities: Intercultural dimensions in Scottish educational contexts. *Language and Intercultural Communication* I *8*(2), *119-135.*

Sharples, M. (1999) *How we write: Writing as creative design.* London: Routledge.
Street, B. (2001). *Literacy and development: Ethnographic perspectives.* London: Routledge.

CHAPTER 31.
CHANGING ACADEMIC LANDSCAPES: PRINCIPLES AND PRACTICES OF TEACHING WRITING AT THE UNIVERSITY OF CAPE TOWN

By Arlene Archer
University of Cape Town (South Africa)

This paper looks at the principles and practices of teaching writing in the Writing Centre at the University of Cape Town (UCT). It outlines some of the context of higher education in South Africa and how writing centres need to contribute to both access and redress of past inequities. In order to critically engage with writing, the UCT Writing Centre takes an "academic literacies" approach, which focuses on contextualized social practices, rather than decontextualized skills. This practice-based approach helps to explore the interdisciplinary nature of the work, as well as the changing representational landscape in higher education. The paper explores some of the impact the Writing Centre has had on student writing, and argues that the Centre contributes to higher education transformation through the mentoring of postgraduate students as future academics.

BACKGROUND AND CONTEXT

The Writing Centre at the University of Cape Town (UCT) is one of the oldest Writing Centres in South Africa and has been operating since 1994. Writing Centres are potentially a locus for change, political spaces with a transformatory agenda, which attempt to transform teaching and learning processes, whilst democratizing access to education. In most tertiary institutions in South Africa, the links with Academic Development have often given Writing Centres their unique character. From the 1980's, tertiary institutions developed units for Academic Development, or Academic Support as they were known then, in an effort to address the realities of educational transformation. The support model of these earlier programmes impacted Writing Centre identity. The walk-in centres functioned as an extension of the remedial, separate concept of Academic Development—they were seen as remediation centres to rectify language deficiencies in individual students. The quick fix model and deferment of responsibility for writing, the "sticky history of remediation that haunts writing centre work" (Grimm, 1999, p. 84), is something that the UCT Writing Centre has had to work against. In an effort to do this, the ethos of the centre is one of voluntary and confidential usage for all students, from all disciplines at all levels of study. The intensive training of the consultants ensures a degree of professionalism, as well as rigorous intellectual engagement with students' ideas.

Although the Writing Centre has been located in varying institutional places at different times in its history, it is currently based within a larger structure called the Language Development Group. This location has served to situate the work (Thesen & Van Pletzen, 2006). Although both the Language Development Group and the Writing Centre focus on developmental work (working in partnership with departments to develop language in the curriculum), the Writing Centre tends to have more of a "service" element. In particular, the one-on-one consultancy serves to accommodate individual students in unique ways.

The cognitive as well as the affective value of the one-on-one consultation is well-documented (Harris, 1995; Flynn, 1993). The complexities of different languages and discourses amongst students are well addressed by this model. The premise underlying the consultant-student relation is Lave and Wenger's argument that learning is located in the increased access of learners to participating roles in expert performances (1991, p.17). Thus, the most important role of consultants is to help students find their own voices as part of adopting a new academic identity. The philosophy of the student consultancy is that all students can improve their writing, whether they are highly experienced or complete novices. Sixty-four percent of our clientele are women, more than half speak English as a second language (although it is difficult to get the exact data on this), 30 percent are postgraduate students, and 45 percent hail from the Humanities faculty.

In 1999, the staffing model of the Writing Centre changed from three full-time staff members and two coordinators to one coordinator and 10 part-time postgraduate students. The reasons for this change were manifold. Firstly, it was felt that more than three years of one-on-one consulting led to consultant burn-out, whereas fresh consultants each year keep the energy of the project alive. Secondly, by employing 10 consultants, a range of disciplines could be accommodated in the Writing Centre. Thirdly, the Centre became a mentoring space for postgraduate students, creating a vibrant cross-disciplinary intellectual community, with many consultants using this as a training ground for moving into academic jobs within their disciplines. Lastly, the current model is extremely cost effective, and most of the funding for the part-time consultants is external. The source of this funding is a philanthropic organization that has consistently funded the Centre for more than a decade.

MISSION AND VALUES

Broadly, the Writing Centre aims to promote and facilitate access to higher education, within an ethos of social justice and national redress. Social, political and economic power is closely associated with knowledge of certain discourse forms and the Centre plays an important role in equity redress at UCT. Writing is one of the main means of assessment. Developing students' writing helps them to improve their academic performance and may mean that they stay in the tertiary system, and proceed to graduation. The Centre aims to assist by increasing students' understanding of writing as a process; enabling a "thinking-through-writing" approach; helping students to focus on the given task; heightening students' sense of audience in writing. We alert students to academic voice and plagiarism and help them understand how to select information from a variety of sources. Lastly, we improve students' sense of coherence, cohesion and logic in writing, and improve their ability to proof-read for some common grammatical errors. It is clear from the above that the Writing Centre is involved with emancipatory aspects of knowledge production, such as constructing arguments and thinking through ideas, as well as technical dimensions, such as the mechanics of writing. It is thus in a unique position to empower students within the Higher Education system.

There are three key challenges in the conceptualization of our Writing Centre's work. Firstly, the degree to which we need to provide students with access to dominant practices whilst at the same time enabling critique of these practices. Secondly, to make the tension between disciplinary conventions and the generic a productive one. Thirdly, to engage with the changing multimodal nature of student assignments.

CRITICAL ACCESS TO DOMINANT PRACTICES

The key question in terms of equity is how to provide access to dominant forms, while valuing and promoting the diversity of the representational resources of our students. There are social, educational, and political advantages of acculturation into university practices. If students are denied access, their marginalization is perpetuated in a society that values these practices. However, socialization into dominant practices contributes to maintaining their dominance and can uncritically perpetuate the status quo. By dominant practices, I mean dominant languages, varieties, discourses, modes of representation, genres and types of knowledge.

This places the work of the Writing Centre in a double-bind. On one hand, it would be in our learners' interests if we could help them to conform to the expectations of the institution. On the other hand, by doing so, we may be reproducing the ideologies and inequities of the institution and society at large, and uncritically perpetuating the status quo. Feeling the right to exert a presence in the text is related to personal autobiography, and therefore is often associated with the gender, class, and ethnicity of the writer. Students need to think of themselves as people who have the power and authority to be authors. They also need to be made aware of hidden cultural assumptions in socially powerful discourses and to be taught the "rules" of what is appropriate in a way that highlights their social constructedness (Delpit 1988; Kress, 1982; Lea & Street, 1998). One of the consultants reflected on how working at the Writing Centre made her critical of certain aspects of academic discourse and institutional practices.

> It forced me to know the "rules," it led to a critical look at why these rules are in place and whether they are still relevant or not. Understanding a system better automatically leads to questioning and exploring that system.

The Writing Centre consultants can talk to students about academic expectations in ways that acknowledge whose values are at stake. They can, for instance, critically highlight conventions around disciplines, genres, and academic discourse (such as the use of the third person, nominalizations, the passive). These conventions can be discussed in order to understand how and why they operate, and what "rules" would be the most appropriate for the students to apply in a particular context.

The approach described above is broadly known as an academic literacies approach (Lea & Street, 1998), which takes into account institutional relationships of discourse and power and the contested nature of writing practices. According to this view, a writer needs "to switch practices between one setting and another, to deploy a repertoire of linguistic practices appropriate to each setting, and to handle the social meanings and identities that each evokes" (Lea

& Street, 1998, p.159). This view also engages with diverse notions of reading and writing that are emerging from current social and technological changes.

WAYS OF INTEGRATING WRITING INTO THE DISCIPLINES

One of the central tensions of Writing Centres is the decontextualized nature of the operation, especially in a purely drop-in situation. Given that writing provides access to and a way of learning the structure of disciplinary thought that is typical of a discipline, such as ways of thinking, reasoning, interpreting and explaining, the separation from context could be problematic (Archer, 2008). We attempt to link writing and context through embedding workshops in courses, teaching in mainstream courses, developing feedback loops, and creating interdisciplinary spaces.

Although we run generic workshops on topics such as task analysis, reading, structuring an academic essay, academic argument, referencing and language use, we prefer to embed workshops within departments and courses. Large-scale lectures do not offer students many opportunities to practice academic discourse, whereas these kinds of workshops can create a space for students to make meaning of their disciplines. The consultants in the Centre also work together with mainstream lecturers in credit-bearing courses in order to stay in touch with the rhythms and challenges of tertiary teaching. This kind of collaboration is vital to prevent us from becoming disembodied from the rest of the university, and especially from the curriculum.

We work with one of the biggest first-year Humanities courses, Media and Society, for example. It addresses image literacy, writing skills and media writing. For the past seven years, the Writing Centre has organized a drafting exercise with between 400 and 500 first year students on the course. The peer-editing has been built into the tutorial structure of the course and feedback is also given by the tutors. Between 40 and 60 students from this course take advantage of the follow-up one-on-one consultations. This intervention has contributed to a drafting process for the first essay and a peer-review process to be adopted by the department, thus entrenching the approach within the course.

In general, the Writing Centre looks for opportunities to use its sites of practice as sites of institutional learning. The one-on-one consultancy is used to provide feedback to departments around the ways in which their students are grappling with particular tasks. To this end, we maintain a comprehensive database on student consultations, which includes demographic information as well as details on specific consultations. This database also enables us to track the developmental paths of individual students, sometimes across a number of years of their studies. Through these feedback loops, the one-on-one consultations can be justified in terms of data-gathering to inform institutional development.

In many ways, the interdisciplinary nature of the Writing Centre can be constructed as a strength rather than a weakness. By appointing consultants from a range of disciplines, we are able to access their disciplinary knowledge, and establish strong links to their departments. In the training programme we examine disciplinary discourses in depth, and the multidisciplinary nature of the group enables unique insight into writing practices. These feed into the numerous interdisciplinary workshops that we run at both undergraduate and postgraduate level

CHANGING REPRESENTATIONAL LANDSCAPES

The third challenge for our Writing Centre includes the extent to which we are equipped to deal adequately with new technologies and emerging multi-modal genres in Higher Education. Reading and writing practices are only part of what people have to learn in order to be literate, and thus we need to learn strategies to help students gain competency in multimodal composition. Many assignments use visuals as evidence, whilst other assignments are predominantly visual in nature, such as posters, storyboards, or assignments that include CD-roms or other media. Related to these changing assignments are new technologies that enable a range of possibilities for individuals creating documents, including variety in layout, image, colour, typeface, sound. The challenge for our Writing Centre is to train the consultants to deal with the changing nature of assignments. This includes learning about the appropriate use of visuals, and the integration of visuals in multimodal texts.

These multimodal challenges are in line with current thinking about Communication across the Curriculum (CAC) (McLeod, 2008; Reiss, Young & Selfe, 1998). CAC points to a widened notion of communication (including the visual design of written assignments) and the redefined nature of texts through new technologies. Although this thinking is more commonplace in the United States, it is new in South Africa, and our Writing Centre is one of the first to begin theorizing about the changing nature of texts and the implications for our work. We have received funding (in partnership with the Institute of Education, University of London) to re-evaluate Writing Centres in South Africa in the light of our changing representational landscapes, looking at how a range of forms of communication and media influence texts in specific disciplines and the implications of this for writing pedagogies and academic literacies. We are exploring the affordances of a range of modes in student assignments (particularly writing, image, colour and layout), the multimodal realization of academic voice, the complexity of visual-verbal linkages in texts and how these may differ across disciplines. We do not necessarily have the technological resources to show students how to use new tools, but aim to raise awareness of the ways in which multimodal texts are assembled.

IMPACT ON STUDENT WRITING: OUR ASSESSMENT

In the changing academic landscape, it has become imperative to evaluate the impact of Writing Centre work. However, there are numerous challenges involved in ascertaining our influence on student writing. Firstly, the one-on-one consultation is difficult to measure in any systematic way. Secondly, there are many factors affecting student writing other than visits to the Writing Centre, and it would be artificial to attempt to construct a control group. Students write in a range of courses, get feedback, do a range of reading, and it is difficult to ascertain the extent to which one or two visits to the Writing Centre have impacted their writing within this larger context. Thirdly, Writing Centre practice tends to be somewhat ad hoc, with some students coming for once-off consultations and others maintaining a relationship with the Centre throughout their degree.

In conducting an evaluation of our Writing Centre's work, I focused on a few in-depth case studies of student writing, which seemed more appropriate than looking at breadth of impact (see Archer, 2008). The evaluation was achieved through interviewing 40 first-year students on their perceptions of the Centre and its impact on their writing; looking at consultants' comments on the student writing; looking at grades obtained. Finally, it compared independent assessments of the students' improvement from first to final draft using three criteria: organisation, voice and register, and language use.

Both consultants and students identified organization as the most commonly addressed aspect of writing. The comparison of first and final drafts revealed that the majority of students show an improvement in the organisation of their essays. Many students do not have a good understanding of structure when they come into the university, but most of them grasp the basic concepts relatively easily and manage to improve on essay organisation. It appears that the Writing Centre helped most in the area of acquiring academic discourse within particular disciplines. Students seemed weakest in this regard in their first drafts (the average grade was 30.1%) and improved substantially through consultation with the Writing Centre (the average for the final essay was 50.9%). Students coming out of school tend to be unfamiliar with both academic discourse and the discourse of their discipline. They also battle with the use and correct citation of references. It is thus not surprising that consultations resulted in improved grades in the "voice and register" category.

However, improvements in voice and register can also be indicators of a process of "acculturation" at first year level. I have already made the point that discursive practices are ideological in the ways they serve to maintain existing social relations of power. Learning how each discipline presents students with appropriate knowledge, appropriate ways of organizing that knowledge, and appropriate ways of representing social relations between the writer and reader can either lead to acculturation into those knowledge practices or critical awareness thereof. One student maintained that the Writing Centre "changed the way I thought about putting information into essays." This summarises the Centre at its most useful, where it assists students to become adept at negotiating the epistemology of a particular subject, and inculcates understanding of how knowledge is linked to appropriate form. Many students indicated a shift towards a greater sense of autonomy and agency.

Grammar is often the main reason lecturers send students to the Writing Centre, yet few consultants and students mentioned this as a key component of their consultations. The external examiner found that in fact the smallest improvement took place in the "language use" category. Students who ask for help with grammar often have overriding problems with structure, voice, register and general understanding of the task. In these instances, working with grammar is of secondary priority until the student has a better grasp of larger academic literacy practices. Even when language problems are addressed, this by itself is unlikely to lead to a notable improvement of students' grammar, especially among second language speakers. While students who come to the Centre learn to express themselves in a more appropriate tone, improving grammar is a more long-term development as a result of increased practice in reading and writing.

It was evident from this study that the Writing Centre provides an invaluable service to undergraduate students, particularly in introducing them to academic literacy practices in a supportive environment. This was reflected in the students' marks, often making the difference between passing and failing assignments and even the whole course. Many students reported increased confidence in their own abilities to understand and write an assignment. This confidence is particularly important for students from disadvantaged educational backgrounds who feel overwhelmed by their own perceived lack of cultural capital (Bourdieu, 1991).

University of Cape Town (South Africa)

TRANSFORMATION OF HIGHER EDUCATION THROUGH MENTORING YOUNG ACADEMICS

In accordance with the developmental and equity focus of the UCT Writing Centre, we aim to develop future academics who are attuned to the academic literacy practices of their disciplines. There is a strong emphasis on equity, multilingualism and multidisciplinarity in the selection process of the consultants. The group is diverse in terms of gender, age, languages spoken and nationality (currently including people from South Africa, Zimbabwe, Kenya, Mauritius). The centre employs 10 postgraduate students from a range of disciplines (currently including linguistics, human genetics, educational technology, sociology, chemistry, democratic governance, adult education, environmental and geographical sciences, and social anthropology). They undergo intensive training throughout the year; training focuses on the theoretical underpinnings of Writing Centre work, including issues around access and redress, and the practical application of these. The topics include multilingualism, English as a second language, disciplinary discourses, multimodality, creative writing, referencing and academic voice.

Through the training we aim to develop a common language to theorize our practice and talk about teaching, learning and writing processes. Reflections from the consultants attest to how working in the Centre has led to the transformation of their academic identities as postgraduate students and educators, the refinement of their academic research and writing practices, as well as the development of their teaching (Lewanika & Archer, 2006):

> I have come to appreciate that knowing and knowledge
> exist amongst people . . . through the social interactions in
> the Writing Centre I have concluded and accepted that my
> understanding of literacy is ever-shifting and that the cliché
> "there are more questions than answers" will always ring true
> for me when attempting to understand the complex land-
> scape of literacy teaching and learning. . . .

This consultant's reflections reveal a transformation in his identity and practice as an educator. His interactions within the Writing Centre community changed his perception of teaching from an exercise in which he imparts knowledge, to one that acknowledges that he is an active participant in a mutual learning exercise.

In the last 10 years, we have produced 16 academic appointments at seven different tertiary institutions in a range of departments, including Academic

Development, Religious Studies, English, Film and Media, Law, Botany, Nursing, Civil Engineering, Environmental and Geographical Sciences, Sociology. These are academics well-trained in teaching writing and academic argument. Seven of these young academics were interviewed to ascertain the degree to which the Writing Centre had prepared them for and facilitated their entry into academia. All commented on the significance of the Centre to the development of their pre-existing ideas of academic discourse, particularly the barrier that this specialized discourse can pose to second-language English speakers. In addition to academic discourse, they felt they benefited from their Writing Centre experience insofar as it improved their own research, writing and teaching. It did this by allowing them to appreciate a wide number of different disciplines, to be explicitly aware of the rules that they took for granted in their own writing, and to shift the focus of their teaching from "teacher-centred" to "learner-centred." The specific experience of one-on-one teaching was beneficial in this regard. The Centre was regarded by all interviewed as a critically important space for mentoring new academics.

> The Writing Centre is a very important mentoring space. Academics generally aren't taught how to teach. The writing centre certainly made me more aware of how to deal with students and especially where they experience difficulties. It was also useful to see students from across the academic spectrum and different faculties. You realise that there are certain academic norms regardless of the department.

By training young academics, Writing Centres can facilitate equity appointments in higher education in South Africa, and also contribute to changing these teaching and learning environments.

CONCLUSIONS AND FUTURE PLANS

Writing Centres need to be grounded in critical discourses in order to understand and articulate individual cases and institutional practices. I have shown how we pursued this at UCT by developing a common theoretical basis through the training of consultants. This sense of common purpose needs to be inculcated nationally. Although Writing Centres in South African tertiary institutions have been operating for a good few years, it is only recently that Writing Centre practitioners have come together more as a community. There are now regional groupings that meet regularly, an active listserv and national seminars. UCT, together with Stellenbosch University, has taken the lead in putting together a national book outlining the approaches to and practices within Writing Centres in South Africa (Archer & Richards, 2011). The book serves to outline differing theoretical approaches to writing that underpin the various centres, as well as differing implementation of some of these theories in particular contexts. It reflects on good practice and also grapples with some of the tensions within Writing Centres, and between Writing Centres and institutions in terms of degrees of perceived legitimacy and authority. The hope is that putting together a book of this nature will help Writing Centres in South Africa to re-engage with our history of remediation and to redefine our practice theoretically.

In this profile, I have shown the ways in which our Writing Centre takes a multi-pronged approach to writing in the institution—providing one-on-one consultations, ad hoc and generic workshops at all levels, and more sustained departmental liaisons and curriculum development. There is no quick fix where writing is concerned; we need multiple sites in and out of the curriculum for raising awareness of writing. In addition, finding ways of designing interventions to accommodate and harness student diversity is critical. Effective teaching of writing involves a dialogue between the discourses of academia and those of students, offering those from disadvantaged backgrounds an empowering and critical experience, not just bridges to established norms. The Writing Centre plays a central role in this endeavour through its unique positioning in the institution, its interdisciplinary nature (which needs to be reconstructed as a strength rather than a weakness), and its ability to create coherent communities of researchers and writers. This chapter has argued that the UCT Writing Centre contributes to transformation in terms of research-led development, widening access, promoting excellence through equity, and ensuring the provision of key competencies in our graduates.

REFERENCES

Archer, A. (in press). Challenges and potentials of writing centres in South African tertiary institutions. *South African Journal of Higher Education, 24*(4), 495 - 510.

Archer, A., & Richards, R. (Eds.). (2011). *Changing spaces: Writing centres and access to higher education in South Africa.* Stellenbosch: SUN Press.

Archer, A. (2008). Investigating the impact of writing centre intervention on student writing at UCT. *South African Journal of Higher Education. 22*(2). 248–264.

Bourdieu, P. (1991). *Language and symbolic power.* Cambridge, Massachusetts: Harvard University Press.

Delpit, L. (1988). The silenced dialogue: Power and pedagogy in educating other people's children. *Harvard Educational Review, 58*(3), 280–298.

Flynn, T. (1993). Promoting higher-order thinking skills in writing conferences. In T. Flynn & M. King (Eds.), *Dynamics of the writing conference: Social and cognitive interaction* (pp. 3-16). Urbana, Illinois: NCTE.

Grimm, N. (1999). *Good intentions. Writing center work for postmodern times.* Portsmouth, NH: Heinemann-Boynton/Cook.

Harris, M. (1995). What's up and what's in: Trends and traditions in writing centers. In C. Murphy & J. Law (Eds.), *Landmark essays on writing centers* (pp. 27-36). Davis, California: Hermagoras Press.

Kress, G. (1982). *Learning to write.* London: Routledge.

Lave, J., & Wenger, E. (1991). *Situated learning: Legitimate peripheral participation.* Cambridge/New York/Victoria: Cambridge University Press.

Lea, M., & Street, B. (1998). Student writing and faculty feedback in higher education: An academic literacies approach. *Studies in Higher Education, 23*(2), 157–165.

Lewanika, T. and Archer, A. (2006). Communities of practice: Reflections on writing, research and academic practices in UCT Writing Centre. Presented at the Higher Education Learning and Teaching Association of Southern Africa (HELTASA) Conference, Tshwane University of Technology, 27 - 29 November.

McLeod, S. (2008, May). The future of WAC. Plenary address presented at the Ninth International Writing Across the Curriculum Conference, Austin, Texas. Accessed 14 November 2008. Retrieved from http://wac.colostate.edu/atd/articles/mcleod2008.cfm

Reiss, D., Young, A., & Selfe, D. (Eds.). (1998). *Electronic communication across the curriculum.* Urbana, Illinois: NCTE.

Thesen, L. and Van Pletzen, E. (Eds.). (2006). *Academic literacies and languages of change.* London: Continuum.

CHAPTER 32.
ACADEMIC COMMUNICATION STRATEGIES AT POSTGRADUATE LEVEL

By Isabel Solé, Ana Teberosky, and Montserrat Castelló
University of Barcelona, University of Barcelona, and Ramon Llull University (Catalonia–Spain)

This chapter describes an experience of teaching academic communication concepts and procedures as part of the compulsory syllabus of an interuniversity postgraduate (master's and doctorate) programme run by six universities in Catalonia (Spain). We shall first provide a necessarily concise description of the most relevant characteristics of the institutional and academic context in which our experience took place. We shall then set out the aims, contents, methodology and forms of assessment involved in teaching the subject Procedimientos y cánones de comunicación científica y académica (Procedures and canons of scientific and academic communication) for which we are responsible. In conclusion, we shall present an analysis of the achievements and limitations of the subject's current format within the more general context of postgraduate studies, which will allow us to identify the alternatives that in our judgement would increase its potential.

THE ACADEMIC AND INSTITUTIONAL CONTEXT

There is very little explicit teaching of reading, writing, or oral exposition strategies at Spanish universities. The few instances that do exist are mostly the result of initiatives taken by individual lecturers who do this sort of thing on a personal basis. The institutions in which we work also fit this model. There are many reasons underlying this and a detailed examination of them is beyond the scope of this chapter. In our opinion, a set of mistaken, albeit fairly widespread, beliefs among the educational community is responsible for the scant attention given to the specific teaching of academic communication strategies:

- The belief that the learning of oral and written language occurs only in the first few years of compulsory education, which leads oral and written language to be treated as an "object" of knowledge in these early stages. Thereafter these capacities acquire the status of learning "instruments" (and lose their former status).
- The consideration that oral and written language, as communication and (to a lesser extent) representation tools, remain invariable throughout a person's life, while what varies are the situations in which these tools are "applied."

The experience described in this chapter is based on radically different ideas, which are succinctly set out below (see section 2). This experience is part of an official postgraduate educational psychology programme formed by the Interuniversity Master's Degree in Educational Psychology (MIPE according to its Catalan and Spanish initials) and the Interuniversity Doctoral Degree in Educational Psychology (DIPE). This postgraduate course, which has been taught since the academic year 2004-2005, is a joint initiative by six universities in Catalonia (Spain) —the Autonomous University of Barcelona, the University of Barcelona, the University of Girona, the University of Lleida, Ramon Llull University, and Rovira i Virgili/Tarragona University—led by Barcelona University. It is aimed at students and professionals interested in acquiring a solid theoretical and practical grounding in the contributions of psychological knowledge to educational theory and practice, and also sets out to stimulate research and scientific production in the field of educational psychology.

There are fifty places available in the course every year and there exist specific admission criteria for selecting applicants, as the number of applicants always far exceeds the number of places. The students come from a mixture of geographical origins and educational backgrounds: there are students from Catalonia and other parts of Spain, but also from various European and Latin American countries (Portugal, the Netherlands, Sweden, Mexico, Brazil, Chile, Columbia, etc.); students of psychology, education or other related subjects; students who have just graduated and others who come back to university to complete their education following a period of employment. This means that the academic cultures co-existing in this postgraduate course are diverse, which makes it extremely rich and, at the same time, requires spaces where students, especially those doing a doctorate, can get to know and examine the academic requirements specific to the institutions where they are being educated.

Meeting this requirement and simultaneously responding to the students' wide variety of interests has implications for the organisation of the curriculum. This provides for two educational profiles, one of a professional nature, linked to psychoeducational intervention in a broad sense and leading to a master's degree upon satisfactory completion of 90 credits; the other of a more academic nature catering to research and linked to doctorate studies.

Students opting for a doctorate must take at least 60 postgraduate course credits—although most of them actually take the full 90 credits allowing them to obtain the master's degree—and carry out a research project in one of the 16 groups taking part in the DIPE (for more information, go to http://www.psyed.edu.es).

The postgraduate curriculum is organised as follows:
- compulsory common core credits: 20
- compulsory profile credits: 20, consisting of a practicum, of which there are two modalities: professional and research
- optional credits: 50, to be chosen from 42 subjects, each of which is worth five credits. Some subjects are professionally oriented, while others are research oriented, although at the present time most of them cater to both profiles.

All students, irrespective of the profile they choose—professional or research—must take the compulsory common core credits, which are divided into various subjects, some of a conceptual or methodological nature—Culture, Development and Learning in Educational Psychology; Methodology and Epistemology in Psychoeducational Research; Current Approaches and Trends in Educational Psychology— and others of a more applied nature: Professional Environments and Contexts in Educational Psychology; Procedures, Canons and Practices of Scientific and Professional Communication in Educational Psychology.

The fact that this last-mentioned subject (Procedures, Canons and Practices . . .) is compulsory shows that those responsible for the course think its contents are equally necessary whether students are intending to go into research (doctorate) or their interests lead them towards professional specialisation (master's degree). The experience acquired over several years' teaching on the master's and doctorate programmes had made it plain that postgraduate students often have difficulties in coping with the requirements of oral and written academic and scientific communication. Moreover, contrary to what might be expected, it is fairly common, even at the highest levels of formal education, for students to be ignorant of—or fail to use—the basic rules of citation, the documentary database search strategies specific to the discipline, or the necessary procedures for adequately organising documentary sources that are consulted in order to be able to extract information effectively whenever needed.

Of course, helping students to master these and other academic skills would require the teaching staff responsible for the various different subjects to coordinate in regard to the academic communication contents that need to be taught during the course and the order in which they should be introduced. This coordination is also necessary for those acting as tutors and supervisors of projects and doctoral theses. However, such coordination is difficult to achieve, and frequently there is not explicit agreement on what should be demanded of students in relation to these contents.

PROCEDURES AND CANONS: THEORETICAL BASIS AND TEACHING PLAN

Our proposal is based on the premise that reading and writing are inseparable from the social practices in which they occur and from the particular purposes that define these practices (Carlino, 2005; Kozulin, 2000). Reading and writing constitute a set of competencies that are socially constructed through participation in different textual communities—such as the academic community—sharing specific texts and practising particular ways of reading, interpreting, and producing them. Moreover, scientific writing is not just a vehicle for communicating elaborated knowledge, but an indispensable element for generating such knowledge. Using reading and writing in an epistemic sense compels those doing so not only to read and write certain texts; it leads to writing, reading, and thinking in a particular way. For all these reasons, students in postgraduate education are faced with new demands as readers and writers for which they require competencies that cannot be generalised from their previous experience and need to be learned; mastering such competences requires students to actually reconstruct the tools of representation and communication, not merely to apply them.

By means of this subject we intend to help students to become competent in the epistemic use of written comprehension and composition tools, and to familiarise them with the canons of formal oral and written communication. In particular, the aims set for the subject are:

1. Knowledge and analysis of the characteristics, canons, and requirements of academic texts in the psychology domain.
2. Knowledge of the basic tools for finding, selecting, and organising information that are useful in carrying out scientific research and in academic communication.
3. Knowledge and analysis of the characteristics of the processes involved in writing academic texts in the psychology domain.
4. Evaluation of the influence of conceptions about and attitudes towards writing for academic purposes, from both the process and product standpoints.

The contents are structured around four core concepts:
a) The characteristics of academic and scientific texts
   - The requirements of academic texts in psychology
   - Description of the general norms and canons
   - Examples of the variety of academic texts
   - Analysis of and reflection on examples, rules, and conceptions of academic writing in psychology
b) The processes of academic writing
   - The process of composing academic texts
   - Frequent paradoxes in the production of an academic text
   - Writers' identities and profiles
c) Reading academic and scientific texts
   - Exploratory reading and elaborative reading
   - Strategies for consulting and organising documentary sources
   - Reading to produce academic texts
d) Public presentation of academic and scientific work
   - The relations between the requirements of the text itself, regulation of the written composition process and the necessary strategies for communicating in academic contexts
   - Oral academic communication: analysis of norms and conventions

Teaching of the contents described above is done in four face-to-face classroom sessions—eight hours in all—plus the directed study and work time stipulated in the subject —a further 20 hours. Students must attend all four classroom sessions and carry out the assignments that are set. One assignment, which is of a general nature and is performed in groups of two or three at the end of the course, consists in analysing and inferring the structure of a scientific article given to them in disordered fragments. This activity is designed to help students identify important characteristics of academic texts. The other tasks set are more specific and are performed individually. They are linked to the development of the core concepts listed above and involve reflecting on contents and the composition process itself. The aim of both the general task and the more specific tasks is to help students to consolidate and use the most important knowledge from the different core sections. These tasks also have an evaluative dimension, as they are used to assess and grade the students' work.

The specific tasks are done before each session. There follows a description of the tasks set for the core contents in the 2009/10 programme:

BLOCK 1. THE CHARACTERISTICS OF ACADEMIC AND SCIENTIFIC TEXTS

Individual reading and production of texts to answer the following questions:

1. How many parts does each one contain?
2. How many linguistic operations? (definition, reformulation, explanation, summary, argumentation, comparison, contrast, description, enumeration, narrative, presentation of aims, presentation of procedures, presentation of instruments, etc.).
3. How many concepts? (conceptual vocabulary).
4. How many quotations?
5. Which connectors?

Working individually or in pairs, students are assigned two published scientific articles and asked to perform a textual analysis of them and describe their structure. For example, in the introduction section, they have to mark and label references to previous theoretical and/or empirical work, and also indicate whether a definition is given, and whether there are any descriptions, comparisons or contrasts. In the methodology and results section, they must underline the procedures, tasks and analyses carried out, the materials used and the instructions given, and whether any examples of tasks, productions, or behaviours are provided. They must also indicate the arguments and discussions in the Conclusions section. They are also required to categorise the citations in terms of integrated or non-integrated quotations, locate the connectors, and describe their semantic nature. Lastly, the students must indicate the key concepts and words in relation to the topic of the article. In order to perform this activity, they must read: El texto académico (*The academic text*, Chapter 1, by A. Teberosky in M. Castelló (2007). *Escribir y comunicarse en contextos académicos y científicos*. Barcelona: Graó, 17-46.

BLOCK 2. ACADEMIC WRITING PROCESSES

Individual reading and production of texts:
Assigned texts: Castelló, M. (2007). El proceso de composición de textos académicos [The process of composing academic texts]. In M. Castelló (Ed.), *Escribir y comunicarse en contextos académicos y científicos* (pp. 47-82). Barcelona: Graó.

Castelló, M. (2007). Los efectos de los afectos [The effects of affects]. In M. Castelló (Ed.), *Escribir y comunicarse en contextos académicos y científicos* (pp. 137-162). Barcelona: Graó.

The task involves various activities of different, though complementary, kinds, the aim of which is to promote reflection on the cognitive, affective, social and cultural nature of the process of written composition and relate this to the texts eventually produced. These activities are organised as follows:

a) After reading the set text, students write a brief summary of the research project they are carrying out—or will shortly be carrying out—in one of the modules on the master's degree (the practicum). These projects are usually done in the third semester and consist in a research project, in the case of the research itinerary, or an intervention project, in the case of the professionalising itinerary.

b) In order to have material for reflecting on the process, they must also keep a diary in which they make a note of the process they followed in writing the summary mentioned in the previous point. They are asked to record what happens to them (what they think, feel and do) from the time they start thinking about it until they consider the text finished. The instructions for this task instruct the students to do the following:

> Whenever you do any work on the summary, before finishing the work session, devote a few moments to making a note of everything you do (time spent, product achieved, steps taken, thoughts, feelings, expectations and your degree of satisfaction or dissatisfaction).

In addition, the students are asked to fill in a questionnaire about their profile as writers containing items related to four factors: conception of the composition process, emotions associated with writing, procrastination and self-image as a writer.

c) During the face-to-face teaching session, the students form pairs and analyse the similarities and differences between their diaries—the process followed and the associated feelings—and their final texts. After this they discuss the different factors dealt with by the items in the questionnaire and examine how they are linked to the different writer profiles, so that each student can assess their answers in the light of this information. Lastly, taking into account their reflections in pairs and the guided discussion with the whole group, they review their fellow students' texts and offer any suggestions for improvement they consider appropriate.

d) Following the classroom session, the students revise their own texts, bearing in mind the suggestions for amendments they have received, and write a final reflection on what they learned about their profile as writers.

All the documents—diaries, reflections, initial and final text—are handed in. The assessment is based on the level of reflection attained on both the process employed and the impact of that process on the texts, the amendments suggested in pair work, the changes introduced into the final texts, and the degree of justification for these changes.

BLOCK 3. READING ACADEMIC AND SCIENTIFIC TEXTS

Individual reading and production of texts:
Miras, M., Solé, I. (2007) La elaboración del conocimiento científico y académico [The production of scientific and academic knowledge]. In M. Castelló (Ed.), *Escribir y comunicarse en contextos académicos y científicos* (pp. 83-111). Barcelona: Graó.

Working in pairs or individually, students are asked to reflect on exploratory reading and elaborative reading, comparing the information in the reference article with their own experience, so they can identify difficulties or problems they have when doing this type of reading. On the basis of this reflection, they write a short piece (no more than two pages, but it can be shorter) succinctly defining each of the two types of reading and setting out their difficulties with them, if they have any. In this piece, students must also answer the following question:

> What would you ask of your (research or intervention) project director in regard to these two types of reading?

The text produced by the students is handed in to the lecturer at the end of the classroom session.

BLOCK 4. PUBLIC PRESENTATION OF ACADEMIC AND SCIENTIFIC WORK

Individual reading and production of texts:
Solé, I. (2007) La exposición pública del texto académico: del texto para ser leído al texto oral [Public presentation of academic texts: from the text for reading to the oral text]. In M. Castelló (Ed.), *Escribir y comunicarse en contextos académicos y científico* (pp. 113-135). Barcelona: Graó.

In the reading material, the students identify the components of the public presentation of academic work that cause them greatest doubts or difficulties, and these then become the subject of discussion in the classroom session.

CONCLUSION: BALANCE SHEET AND FUTURE PROSPECTS

The procedures and canons of scientific and academic communication was originally conceived as a workshop in which students and lecturers could further the competencies of the former by working together on the real problems posed by the production and dissemination—both oral and written—of academic and scientific knowledge in the context of a university postgraduate course. The aim was to cater also to the specialised communication requirements in the professional psychology sphere. In addition, the subject acted as a preparation for certain tasks—such as presenting and defending a research project or an intervention experiment before a tribunal of teaching staff—thereby adding a clearly evaluative dimension.

In our experience we have found that students show interest in
- learning and acquiring knowledge about the characteristics of academic and scientific texts
- learning the most important features to be taken into account in the processes leading to understanding them and producing them
- identifying and putting into practice appropriate strategies for finding, organising, and citing documentary sources.

However, meeting more ambitious goals would require changes in the present structure. Because of the short time available (eight hours in class and 20 outside), we have had to downscale our original plans in regard to both the scope of our objectives and the methodology employed.

As far as the objectives are concerned, we have gradually been focusing more and more on scientific and academic competencies, while professional competencies have been squeezed out. This does not mean that students who opt for the professional profile cannot derive any benefit from the subject; in their active life they will all have to read scientific articles, organise documentary sources, and speak in public. However, to be honest, we must acknowledge that our efforts are aimed at helping the students understand academic and scientific texts and be able to present and provide arguments in support of their research projects in prototypical academic situations.

As regards methodology, we have not been able to give the subject the workshop flavour to the extent we would have liked. The disparity between the scope of the contents and the time available, on the one hand, together with the large number of students to be catered to, on the other, caused us to impose a structure more akin to a seminar. In general, therefore, the core contents are dealt with by the lecturer presenting the most important aspects in the various classroom sessions, augmented by a discussion of the compulsory reading articles, which the students have to prepare prior to each session. The more procedure-oriented dimension –which enables students to practise oral presentations and the reading and writing strategies—is confined to the specific tasks mentioned in the previous section.

As might be expected, the restrictions we have described prevent the subject from achieving its full, intended purpose. For the subject to be more successful, the following conditions would be required:

1. more time allocated to the subject, making it possible to cover the more procedure-oriented dimension
2. a general reformulation of the subject so that its specific contents are integrated into the reading, writing, and oral communication tasks students have to prepare in other subjects.
3. an extension of the subject—as part of the reformulation described in point b—with a workshop to support the writing of doctoral theses and other academic texts (for example, abstracts and papers to be presented in public at conferences or scientific forums).

Each of these solutions has its problems, but there is no doubt that the second—especially if it also involves the third—is the most complex. An examination of this option and the decisions that are eventually taken must be part of a wider revision of the postgraduate course curriculum. At all events, we hope the experience we have built up will enable the subject to be expanded and improved. In this way, it would be possible to achieve the purpose for which it was originally devised and meet the demands of the students, almost all of whom appreciate the knowledge they acquire from taking the subject. They, as do we, regret that there is very little follow-up and support for them in the demanding reading and writing processes involved in producing academic knowledge.

REFERENCES

Carlino, P. (2005). *Escribir, leer y aprender en la universidad. Una introducción a la alfabetización académica [Writing, reading and learning in the university. An introduction to literacy instruction].* Buenos Aires: Fondo de Cultura Económica.

Castelló, M. (2007). El proceso de composición de textos académicos [The process of composing academic texts]. In M. Castelló (Ed.), *Escribir y comunicarse en contextos académicos y científicos [Writing and communication in academic and scientific texts]* (pp. 47-82). Barcelona: Graó.

Castelló, M. (2007). Los efectos de los afectos [The effects of affects]. In M. Castelló (Ed.), *Escribir y comunicarse en contextos académicos y científicos Writing and communication in academic and scientific texts]* (pp. 137-162). Barcelona: Graó.

Kozulin, A. (2000). *Instrumentos psicológicos. La educación desde una perspectiva sociocultural [Psychological tools. Education from a sociocultural perspective].* Barcelona: Paidós [Originally published in 1998 as *Psychological tools: A sociocultural approach to education.* Cambridge, MA: Harvard University Press].

Miras, M., & Solé, I. (2007). La elaboración del conocimiento científico y académico [The production of scientific and academic knowledge]. In M. Castelló (Ed.), *Escribir y comunicarse en contextos académicos y científicos [Writing and communication in academic and scientific texts]* (pp. 83-111). Barcelona: Graó.

Solé, I. (2007). La exposición pública del texto académico: Del texto para ser leído al texto oral [Public presentation of academic texts: From the text for reading to the oral text]. In M. Castelló (Ed.), *Escribir y comunicarse en contextos académicos y científicos [Writing and communication in academic and scientific texts]* (pp. 113-135). Barcelona: Graó.

CHAPTER 33.
MULTI-DISCIPLINARY, MULTI-LINGUAL ENGINEERING EDUCATION WRITING DEVELOPMENT: A WRITING PROGRAMME PERSPECTIVE

By Magnus Gustafsson and Tobias Boström
Chalmers University of Technology (Sweden)

The Centre for Language and Communication at Chalmers University of Technology is enabled by the university's curriculum structure to arrange productive collaborations that promote student development in language and learning throughout three- and five-year programmes, including successful completion of BSc theses. This profile describes two such in-depth collaborations, in mechanical and civil engineering. It goes on to describe the special challenges of providing the best interventions for the diverse students at the MSc level. That the Centre provides programmes in both Swedish and English is another important feature of its work.

INTRODUCTION

Chalmers University of Technology is a research university with a long history of engineering education. It is situated on the west coast of Sweden in Gothenburg, which is Sweden's second largest city with some 500,000 inhabitants. The institution was founded in 1829 and became a governmental university in 1937, only to become a private university owned by a foundation in 1994. The university's vision is "Chalmers—for a sustainable future" and its mission statement emphasizes its research profile, its educational appeal, and its professional context: "Chalmers shall be an outward-looking university of technology with a global appeal that conducts internationally recognised education and research linked to a professional innovation process" (Chalmers 2010a).

The annual report tells its readers that the research profile of the university is informed by its three initiatives—material and bio, systems and environment, industry and communication—as well as by its close collaboration with the research and development activities of the industries in the region (Chalmers, 2010b). Chalmers consequently runs four centers of excellence with industry, also works closely with the Swedish Ship-owners' Association, and works with a number of companies in the vehicle and safety centre as well as with the Volvo group on electronics, safety, and environmental issues. The sustainability profile of the university is also present in its work with the Alliance for Global Sustainability, as well as with the Swedish Hybrid Vehicle Centre.

It is not a large institution. The annual report (http://www.chalmers.se/en/about-chalmers/annual-report/Pages/default.aspx) statistics reveal that it numbers approximately 12,000 individual students with some 2,000 first year students. Approximately 25% of the students are women, with a slightly larger proportion of women at the PhD level (30%). The various engineering disciplines are taught through three- or five-year long programmes (there are two different categories of engineers in the Swedish work force). Across all the programmes and educations at the university (BSc Eng; BSc; MSc Eng; MSc; MSArch), there are almost 1,000 international students, most of whom are enrolled on one of the 44 international master's programmes. The university staffs some 1,500 teachers and researchers.

The university has a two-part structure, with the required courses within the departments on one hand and an educational organisation outside of the discipline on the other. The educational organisation outside the department places orders for courses with the relevant departments. For the undergraduate level this often means that a program buys courses from three or four departments, whereas for the master's level the programmes tend to be more specialised and involve fewer departments. So for instance, none of the engineering programmes deliver their own math courses in the first three years and instead buy or order these from the Department of Mathematical Sciences. Similarly, many programmes buy project management courses from the Department for the Management of Technology.

In this educational structure, our privileged situation at Chalmers allows us to set up writing in the disciplines, by which we deliver courses and modules for many programmes, allowing more than one encounter with language and communication as well as gradual and challenging progression through sequencing interventions, assignments, and courses. Our work relies partly on the professional applications of the engineering profession and on the current Swedish language law, which demands all agencies and institutions to promote Swedish as the official language, but also on the current European effort toward greater mobility and internationalization. This means that we must on one hand introduce communication for specific purposes in Swedish but subsequently turn to our international context and focus on English for specific purposes in an engineering/technical setting. Given the integration and progression, our language and communication activities are never isolated from the disciplines, and communication becomes a dimension of disciplinary knowledge.

WRITING AND LITERACY AT CHALMERS UNIVERSITY OF TECHNOLOGY

There is no equivalent to US general education in Swedish higher education. Therefore, students are admitted to a programme or to individual courses, and it is up to the individual programme manager to design learning outcomes and activities for the students. One of the consequences is that there is no predictable background in, for instance, writing instruction at a given point for a student in Swedish higher education, other than phrases in the higher education act. Similarly, literacy as a term has not had much impact, except information literacy. However, what has had greater impact is the emphasis in European higher education on generic and transferable skills. At Chalmers, and at many institutions with professional-oriented programmes, there is, also, a very strong sense of professional orientation that promotes meeting employability requirements.

Predictably, this kind of situation gives rise to a very instrumental and transactional view of writing and literacy. Most of the writing that gets done is focused on reporting learning for grading in connection to exams, project work, and theses. Assignments typically involve various types of reports and presentations, and there is often a strong connection to end-user applications of working in industry. In some programmes, there are projects in the third year or later with industrial representatives; many BSc and MSc theses are done at, with, or for industries, and all programmes have industrial representatives on their committees to help expand industrial networks.

The emphasis on transferability and employability in combination with a compartmentalised view of learning often leads to a situation where there is initially less writing and instead a greater focus on lectures and exams. As employment approaches, writing and discipline-specific communication are allowed more room in learning outcomes and learning activities. This situation is possibly understandable in view of the fact that it is primarily the programme managers, apart from faculty at the Centre for Language and Communication, who care for writing at the university. Beyond the higher education act and adaptation to European standards, there is no university commitment to writing or communication across the curriculum.

WRITING-TO-LEARN AND LEARNING-TO-WRITE IN SWEDISH AND ENGLISH

Adaptation to European education also means that writing tends to start with interventions in Swedish and, by the end of the three- year and five-year programmes, writing is also done in English. Initially, the assignments are restricted to smaller course projects; whereas, towards the third year and onwards, projects might involve BSc theses or MSc theses or other similarly demanding writing projects.

Our interventions vary in character. At times they are little more than a sequence of two or three courses in a three-year programme employing a rather superficial approach to writing that focuses on reporting and proficiency. Such designs give rise to a subsequent imbalance between learning-to-write activities and writing-to-learn activities. Increasingly, however, we are also fortunate to work with programmes where there are opportunities and conditions to integrate language and content more closely.

In such embedded contexts it is easier to promote a view of disciplinary language practice as informing the negotiation of and engagement with knowledge formation and hence learning. In these educational settings, our work with generic and transferable outcomes therefore becomes situated in a learning paradigm where the individual student needs to be able to access and contribute to a specific engineering discipline. Therefore, many of our courses and interventions are informed by basic CARS-applications (Swales, 1990; Swales & Feak 2004); by a peer learning framework (Boud, Cohen & Sampson, 2001); and by an effort to move beyond instrumental notions of literacy (Barrie, 2007; Lea & Street, 1998).

TWO ENGINEERING PROGRAMMES AT CHALMERS AND THEIR WRITING INTERVENTIONS

In this profile, we have chosen to focus the examples of our activities around the two main types of integration and progression that we have been able to promote. The five-year programmes with their integration into courses and the three-year programmes that are set up more around collaboration between separate courses. The three-year programmes are often very good; the student writing experience progresses well throughout the three years, even it is often communicated by us in our courses rather than primarily by the programme-specific faculty in their courses. However, since our efforts in three-year programmes have been profiled elsewhere (Ericsson & Gustafsson, 2008), we provide more description here of two of the five-year programmes.

Two interesting programmes to look at are mechanical engineering and civil engineering. These two programmes are relevant to our profile because they exemplify how we integrate activities inside "content courses" and work with faculty more, or in different ways, than we do in most three-year programmes. Both the programmes have also run educational development projects that have involved faculty from the Centre. The educational development project for mechanical engineering started in the 1990s with their commitment to the Conceive, Develop, Implement, and Operate (CDIO) initiative and involved reviewing the entire programme with all teaching faculty (Malmqvist et al, 2010). More than anything, the CDIO-effort has led to faculty being more involved with and aware of the communication dimension and the integrated learning we help design. In a similar manner, the educational development project for the civil engineering teaching faculty involved colleagues from the Centre who worked with programme faculty on course design of language and communication interventions

In both programmes, the actual interventions for the engineering students and the faculty are all connected to courses where students do projects. In their first year of mechanical engineering, we are involved in the planning and running of the course "Introduction to Mechanical Engineering," where groups of students work in Swedish to write up a design project. The course manager is a mechanical engineering professor and works with a team of faculty on the course including two colleagues from our Centre. After the initial planning stage, our work is primarily oriented towards students rather than faculty and involves setting up a peer review process and responding on second versions of reports. The first-year intervention for civil engineering focuses on an introductory course called "Building in Society," involving a large number of representatives from the department's various interests. The writing component is almost entirely oriented towards the written (and oral) presentation of the project they do in this survey type of course. The reports and presentations are presented to faculty from the department and from the Centre. Planning, supervision, and assessment are shared between us and civil engineering faculty throughout the intervention.

In the second year of the mechanical engineering programme, we are involved in a more demanding design project, and the course manager similarly works with a team of faculty and us. In this project, we do more work with faculty in providing joint feedback to students as well as sharing the assessment of oral project presentations. A specific effort has been to develop assessment criteria together with faculty; these criteria are used by faculty in summative assessment, as well as by students in formative assessment, where we scaffold a peer response workshop for the students.

In collaboration and discussion with the faculty, we decide the guidelines and requirements for the reports to be written by the students. For the civil engineering programme, the project is part of an advanced course in "Building Economy and Organization," and the project students do is a larger component of the writing-oriented course. Our work is very similar to the first-year intervention, including having jointly established criteria and assessment design. The decisive difference is that the stakes are higher in the second-year course; the requirements are more demanding, with an explicit emphasis on critical reading and argumentation.

Apart from the actual integration with content, the important faculty work in both these programmes is the co-assessment of reports or the design of criteria as well as reflection tasks for the various assignments. A possible disadvantage with these programmes is the similarity of tasks for the students across the two years. They do not face many different genres and text types, but they develop a firm sense of what counts as engineering communication in their respective disciplines.

Another problem with writing at Chalmers that these programmes exemplify is that while they are well designed for the first three years and there are integrated and often progressively more demanding interventions, there is hardly any corresponding work at the MSc-level. Needless to say, there are some very ambitious and professional course managers, but the Centre is rarely involved. Instead, our activities at the MSc-level are currently focused on providing six elective courses; these range from proficiency courses to advanced level technical communication courses.

THE BSC THESIS

For both these programmes, one factor that drives development is the recent new design of the BSc thesis in European higher education. As of 2007, all third year students have to write a 10-week credit (15 ECTS credits) individually-graded thesis. The key features involve projects advertised by supervisors and open to students from more than one programme, so we have cross-disciplinary project teams of up to six engineering students and shared writing and assessment guidelines across all disciplines. The Centre for Language and Communication has been integral to the design and development of this BSc thesis intervention and provides a seminar for supervisors across campus—writing guidelines, assessment criteria, and tutorials as well as lectures for students. All of this has been developed with the group of programme managers for the five-year engineering programmes. Our third intervention, then, for many of the engineering programmes is the scaffolding of the written documentation as well as the written and oral presentation of their BSc-thesis projects.

INCREASING FACULTY WORK AND OTHER SIGNS OF SUCCESSFUL PROGRAMME DEVELOPMENT

The requirement for a campus-wide, cross-disciplinary bachelor's thesis thus provides an opportunity to promote writing in all programmes and work towards more careful design of the writing interventions leading up to the BSc thesis. Thus, it is in the BSc thesis intervention that we see how the small but integrated courses we do in years one and two generate a good foundation. We also see how writing cultures differ between departments, and to some extent we have been able to adapt our activities accordingly.

So, for example, one of our successes is that three chemistry-related programmes contacted us to set up preparatory activities in the first year. Predictably, the Centre provides scaffolding for the first project report the students write in the first year by initiating a peer response process and a more deliberate writing process. The decisive difference with this intervention is that with these programmes we have designed a continuous annual fall seminar with PhD TAs who supervise the first writing efforts of the engineering students. The seminar focuses on how to integrate writing into the lab and how to promote learning as well as a shared instructional orientation among lab assistants during year one. While we do not yet see many of these PhDs as course managers or thesis supervisors, we do still see how a writing culture around the first-year chemistry students is beginning to form.

Another success we have been seeing is our being invited into other programmes to enhance the programme rather than just provide writing support. We see such examples in the Architecture and Technology programme (Swedish only) and in the most recent of Chalmers' three-year programmes—Economy and Production (Swedish only). In this programme, we do a short introductory intervention in the fall term of the first year and continue with a "course" in the second year that on the one hand integrates with a previous course and completes the documentation and presentation of an argumentative economic analysis industry case. More significantly, this second-year course also integrates seminar assignments and activities with a mathematical statistical analysis course. Here we get involved with assignments that focus less on learning-to-write and much more on enhancing learning with writing. The fact that programme and course managers are now also interested in such assignments makes our work more meaningful.

THE SHIFT TO TEACHING MSC PROGRAMMES IN ENGLISH

Much as the dean's decision to focus the BSc thesis assessment heavily on the written presentation affected the institution and us profoundly, a subsequent decision has been even more influential. In 2005, management decided that by fall 2007, all MSc-programmes would be delivered in English, to align more effectively with the European higher education arena and global education. Many education development projects have been initiated and some completed (Chalmers, 2010c). Our activities have been two-pronged. We were fortunate enough to be able to design and deliver "teaching in English" courses to faculty (Gustafsson & Räisänen, 2007). These courses are still in the staff development offer to faculty. For students, in view of our difficulties of establishing a sufficient number of integrated interventions at the MSc level, we decided to open **Chalmers Open Communication Studio (CHOCS)** (Chalmers, 2010d). CHOCS is a peer tutored writing-in-the-disciplines writing centre. It is a two-campus studio, staffing 8-10 student tutors from the engineering disciplines and catering primarily to students at the MSc-level.

In past years we have been focusing largely on students; however, we have also been able to increase our work with faculty and consider that one of our successes. Our meetings with BSc-thesis supervisors show us how their focus is initially often and justifiably on the documentation of the project and the accountability of the members in the projects. With a discussion of ways of enhancing learning through writing, they seem ready also to make more informed use of writing during the process leading up to the final presentation. Similarly, with the faculty we meet in our courses for "teaching in English," where we see an initial and necessary focus on proficiency, we see that gradually it also becomes rewarding to them to discuss issues like information structure, genre awareness, and actual critical reading. Such seminars tend to result in more enthusiastic supervisors, who see the strength of a communication-oriented approach and generate new integrated interventions or, at the very least, articulate better assignments that include using the writing centre—CHOCS—to scaffold the writing process and help promote writing-enhanced learning. As of 2010 we are also integral to a university-wide effort to promote high quality learning through constructive alignment (**Chalmers Learning Centre**, 2010), which offers additional venues for working with faculty to enhance learning with writing.

STUDENTS' VIEWS OF WRITING IN THE DISCIPLINES AT CHALMERS

For this section of the profile we summarize student comments to represent the student perspective. We show how students perceive the writing interventions they face and show to some extent how we have responded to the student feedback. This summary also allows us some room to articulate what happens at the MSc-level, where the writing interventions are less structured or not as explicitly designed by us at the Center for Language and Communication.

It comes as no surprise that many students in the civil and mechanical engineering programmes (described above) comment on the first-year writing experience as a useful one. Basically, this first-year writing intervention is seen, appropriately, as an introduction to the discipline focused on the writing of a report. Since writing reports is something engineers do very often, this first course, which includes many lectures about how to structure and formulate and formalize the written word, is greatly appreciated. While the two programmes described here do offer interventions also in year two, with a design for progression and greater complexity in the writing assignments, not all programmes do that yet or not all students experience the second year writing as different in terms of character or complexity. So, for some students, it is not until the writing of the BSc thesis near the end of year three that report writing is advanced to a significantly higher level. That is due to the mandatory meetings with the Center for Language and Communication, where feedback is provided in a professional manner.

Interestingly, when students have noted to us or to their programme managers the lack of year-two attention to writing, we can begin to address it in the various year-two interventions. The current second year interventions in various programmes exemplify different ways of bridging that gap. Such progression is crucial to developing writing ability even more before arriving at the BSc thesis intervention.

WRITING INSTRUCTION AT THE MSC LEVEL

Entering into the MSc level, where English is most often a second or sometimes a third language among student peers, most students find the first se-

385

mester quite frustrating. For instance, in addition to having to cope with compulsory writing assignments, which sometimes lack clear purposes or contain misaligned intentions, students who have been through the first three years and the writing interventions in them have to be "teachers" for those who have not had the privilege to study English in the context of basic sentence structuring and paragraphing. Such courses are available among the electives for the third-year students in the many engineering programmes before entering the MSc. Increasingly, we are beginning to hear students in their MSc-courses suggest that these currently elective communication courses should be made mandatory to all students at the MSc-level. Furthermore, the progression in the writing assignments at the MSc-level include genres other than reports; thus, mandatory writing interventions preparing students for genres like essays and articles make perfect sense as students are introduced to entirely new activity systems.

After the first semester is completed, there are some indications that convergence in both the oral and written proficiencies has occurred. However, it is all too often the case that the student "teachers" still end up as project managers and editors on written group assignments to maintain coherence and structure. Sadly, some students express a new sense of frustration, as they see how their personal development as writers is hampered due to the failure—at programme level—to increase the written proficiency level and requirements while adjusting to the heterogeneous student body. So, in an idealized MSc programme, we need, on the one hand, higher entry-level standards for communication and, on the other hand, a more structured scaffolding of the written progression for the various categories of students. The third need to address at a more consistent level, according to many students, is for the lecturers to be trained to design, give feedback to, and assess the increasingly more demanding and complex communication assignments at the MSc-level. If lecturers cannot keep up with the level required of students, awkwardness would surely arise that would not foster progression in the subject at hand nor in technical communication.

CONCLUDING REMARKS

From this brief profile it seems possible to say that designing a multi-disciplinary, multi-interventions, and engineering-education-specific writing programme for the first three years of undergraduate studies in Swedish higher education can be done successfully. The target of arriving at the third-year spring term prepared to take on the BSc thesis project in terms of its communication dimension is a feasible one that generates effective interventions in the first three years. These interventions prepare students well not only for the BSc thesis, but also for the writing at the MSc-level.

At the MSc-level, however, we have not been equally successful in our efforts to integrate the necessary writing interventions and find ourselves relying largely on electives and on the writing centre. Our intention, therefore, is to increase our work with faculty, for which we are in a good position. Our courses for "teaching in English" provide a natural meeting ground to discuss ways of enhancing learning at the MSc-level.

The main challenge right now appears to be addressing the heterogeneous student body at the MSc-level in terms of writing development and technical communication. We want the students who have been through the first three years at Chalmers to maintain their developmental momentum for writing competence. Our second challenge is to reach a larger number of the faculty at the MSc-level with our courses for "teaching in English" and, therefore, to increase our participation in educational development across Chalmers.

REFERENCES

Barrie, S. C. (2007). A conceptual framework for the teaching and learning of generic graduate attributes. *Studies in Higher Education.* 32(4), 439-458.

Biggs, J., & Tang, C. (2007). *Teaching for quality learning at university: What the student does. Third edition.* McGraw Hill, Maidenhead & New York. SRHE & Open University.

Boud, D., Cohen, R., Sampson, J. (2001). *Peer learning in higher education: Learning from & with each other.* London: Kogan Page.

Chalmers University of Technology. (2010a). *Mission statement.* Retrieved from http://www.chalmers.se/en/sections/about_chalmers/chalmers_strategies/mission

Chalmers University of Technology. (2010b). Annual Report. Retrieved from http://www.chalmers.se/en/sections/about_chalmers/annual_report6784

Chalmers University of Technology. (2010c). Chalmers open communication studio. Retrieved from http://wiki.portal.chalmers.se/CHOCS/

Chalmers University of Technology. (2010d). Chalmers impact. Retrieved from http://www.chem.chalmers.se/impact/

Chalmers Learning Centre. (2010). Kvalitetssatsning 2010—lärcentrerad undervisningsplanering [Constructive alignment—lärcentrerad teaching planning]. Chalmers University of Technology. Retrieved from http://www.chalmers.se/clc/SV/projekt-och-satsningar/larcentrerad4428

Ericsson, A., & Gustafsson, M. (2008). Tackling transfer and transferability: ESP/EAP design for learning beyond templates. In I. Fortanet-Gómez, & C. A. Räisänen (Eds.), *ESP in European Higher Education: Integrating language and content* (pp. 117–143). Retrieved from http://www.benjamins.com/cgi-bin/t_bookview.cgi?bookid=AALS%204

Gustafsson, M., & Räisänen, C. (2006). *More than medium of instruction: The Bologna process and teaching in English C-SELT Report.* Retrieved from http://document.chalmers.se/doc/802386713

Lea, M., & Street, B. (1998). Student writing in higher education: An academic literacies approach. *Studies in Higher Education, 11*(3), 182-199.

Malmqvist, J., Bankel, J., Enelund, M., Gustafsson, G., & Knutsson Wedel, M.(2010). Ten years of CDIO—experiences from a long-term education development process. Paper presented at the Sixth International CDIO Conference, Montreal, Canada. Retrieved from http://publications.lib.chalmers.se/records/fulltext/local_123264.pdf

Swales, J. M. (1990). *Genre analysis.* Cambridge: Cambridge UP.

Swales, J. M., & Feak, C. (2004) *Academic writing for graduate students: A course for nonnative speakers of English.* Ann Arbor: University of Michigan Press.

CHAPTER 34.
SHAPING THE MULTIMEDIA MINDSET: COLLABORATIVE WRITING IN JOURNALISM EDUCATION

By Daniel Perrin
Zurich University of Applied Sciences (Switzerland)

Blogs are being used for PR, online newsmagazines are booming, and young people are watching TV more and more often via Internet portals such as YouTube. Increasingly, publicity results from stories and news on the Internet. This development is unstoppable, just like when the market switched from black-and-white to color photography, from silent movies to sound films, and more recently from letters to e-mail. And, as always in journalism, anyone who understands how to exploit current technology for contemporary storytelling is in demand. The accelerating change calls for media—and journalists—fit enough to adapt to new circumstances. Professional practice and research show that multimedia mindsets foster applying three success factors: writing on all channels (see Section 1 of the article), working in teams (Section 2), and finding emergent solutions (Section 3). This has consequences for the design of writing courses in journalism education (Section 4) —including meaningful, relevant assessments, as an example will show (Section 5). The second part of this essay describes in detail a new joint programme in multimedia journalism designed by the Zurich University of Applied Sciences and the Zurich University of the Arts.

What is the difference between a blog and an item on a journalistic website? Not the information itself; everything right and wrong, important and unimportant to say or ask about almost any topic can be found in blogs and anywhere else on the Internet.

Why, then, use journalistic Brand X medium on the Internet, as opposed to non-journalistic Brand Y or Z? Because as a user, I assume that I will get more from Brand X than I would a mouse-click away. Only research and preparation, only such genuine journalistic performance, still separate a journalistic medium from YouTube and the rest of the net. Distribution costs nothing, trust means everything, and content is king like never before.

Newspapers and radio programs are becoming user interfaces for content management systems, for databases of journalistic stories, and for public storytelling (Singer, 2008). This development is unstoppable, just like when the market switched from black-and-white to color photography, from silent movies to sound films, and more recently from letters to e-mail. And, as always in journalism, anyone who understands how to exploit current technology for contemporary storytelling is in demand. Professional practice and research show (e.g., Brannon, 2008; Perrin, 2010, in press; Quinn, 2005; Singer, 2008; Tunstall, 2009;) that this is done with a multimedia mindset by applying three success factors: writing on all channels (see Section 1 of this article), working in teams (Section 2), and finding emergent solutions (Section 3). This has consequences for the design of writing courses in journalism education (Section 4) – including meaningful, relevant assessments, as an example will show (Section 5).

SUCCESS FACTOR ONE: WRITING ON ALL CHANNELS

Even convergent media need coherent texts, moving images, and suitable sounds. Editors-in-chief of leading publications in media-convergent journalism say that writing will be the key competence in the journalism of the future. By "writing" they mean the ability to present complex relationships not only with speech and written characters but also with sounds and images in an appealing, illustrative, and appropriately objective way.

First of all, this "writing" succeeds by using the familiar strengths of print, radio, and television journalism. As paradoxical as it may seem, these strengths are more urgently needed in convergent media than ever before. If journalists nowadays opt for a media item with sound but no images, they must know and make clear to their audience why audio information alone conveys the topic in the best way.

In the multimedia environment, journalistic items are organized similar to musical scores, but in all media: journalists present information, mediating between verified facts and the appearance of protagonists—usually the people concerned and the decision makers. In addition, there are other elements involved, such as experts, specialized knowledge, and transitions (Figure 1).

The text score of a quote story shows that an item often begins with a quote from someone representing the people concerned. Then the journalist might

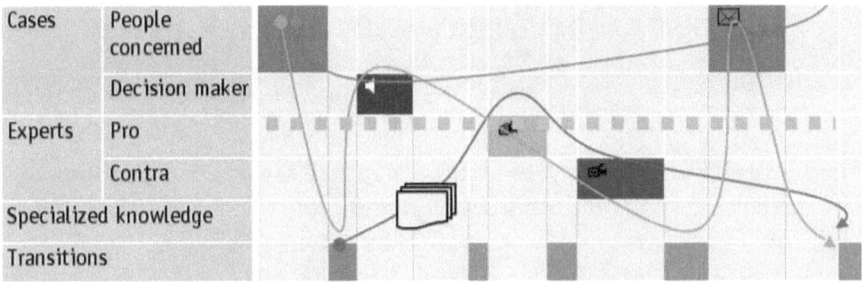

Figure 1: Score of a quote story with paradigmatic, syntagmatic, and navigational variants.

transition to the appearance of a decision maker, who the people concerned hold responsible for their misery. This is followed, for example, by specialized knowledge, introductory comments, an expert's opinions, a transition, a second expert, a transition, the people concerned again, additional specialized knowledge to round off the "score," and finally a summary statement.

A journalist might design the quote story not only for classically linear radio or television or for a newspaper, but also for her audience sitting in front of a multimedia computer. If so, she can prepare the main text as a written report, incorporate a quote from the decision maker as an audio file and the appearance of the experts as videos, and provide a link to a forum so that other people concerned can make comments.

In principle, a journalist operating in convergent media must continuously decide in favor of or against options within three new degrees of freedom:

- Paradigmatic variants offer "more of the same" on request, such as more background information or more comments from those involved (e.g. from blogs).
- Syntagmatic variants disclose what happens before and after what is linearly accessible; for example, the whole expert interview from which the journalist extracted only a single statement to incorporate into the media item.
- Navigational variants make it easier for users to skip or steer directly to certain parts of media items and thus to determine their own paths to gather the information they want.
- Every media item can be supplied with such a score. Journalists who master this universal tool of preparing media dramaturgy can design more clearly organized items, switch between media more easily, and exploit the strengths of all media more flexibly. Since complex production processes in journalism are increasingly based on division of labor, scores with many voices should be played ensemble, not solo.

SUCCESS FACTOR TWO: WORKING TOGETHER

Media convergent journalism is not for lone fighters. Almost no one can do everything perfectly, not in a single medium and most definitely not in multimedia settings. In the practice of leading media, successful convergence means a balanced and orchestrated interplay of professionals, each of whom brilliantly solves parts of the multimedia production task:

- shaping dramaturgical profiles that position one's own media product on the market, make it stand out, and distinguish it from the rest
- finding and delimiting topics, doing the necessary research, providing raw materials, and incorporating contributions from the audience
- preparing parts of the item to be read, listened to, or watched, as complementary voices of a multimedia score (see above)
- allocating assignments and bundling the results, so that the most suitable topics and dramaturgy run on all the right channels
- systematically updating and linking new media offers, indexing items for internal databases and for searches by users.

Multimedia assignment editors act as directors, conductors, and co-composers of such text scores. They allocate assignments to small teams and consolidate the results. Multimedia reporters work off-site, collecting morsels of information for all channels (e.g. still images, moving pictures, sounds, quotations).

In between, though, editors operate in familiar and new roles, using their knowledge of the topic, dramaturgical skill, their own material and that of others, and their media channels to create appealing, relevant, topical, and self-contained stories that will be retrievable on the net anywhere and anytime. They remain responsible for research, preparation, and maintenance way past the day the stories are published.

In this game, those who work well with others survive, because they are strong in their own fields and on the interfaces between their fields and those of their colleagues. This much is already clear. However, it is also clear—based on experience—that truly new things are still to come.

SUCCESS FACTOR THREE: FINDING EMERGENT SOLUTIONS

It took decades until serialized chronicles became independent news reports, until newspapers read aloud became listener-friendly radio, and until filmed radio became visually-interesting television. It might take further decades until a repertoire of dramaturgical patterns for journalistic items in convergent media can be developed and consolidated in daily editorial practice.

Such new patterns come into being *emergently:* the new whole is then more than the sum of its parts (O'Grady, in press). For journalistic writing this means that a successful item in digital space is more than just the additive mix of writing, sound, pictures, and interactiveness. It surpasses the accumulated advantages of its components with a fundamentally new quality. Such emergence, though, requires ideas, coincidences, courage to try things out, humility to learn, and, of course, time. Dramaturgy takes much longer to mature than technology does.

Anyone entering journalism today, wanting to stay in the field, or even educating and assessing new journalists should seize the opportunity of the present uncertainty and develop forms that exploit the added value of integrated media. An example of how to assess all three factors crucial for writing in convergent media will be presented using the case of a collaborative writing course, Text analysis and text production, in an MA program for arts journalists (who cover and critique music, literature, film, architecture, etc.).

COLLABORATIVE WRITING ON ALL CHANNELS: TRAINING THE MULTIMEDIA MINDSET

Text analysis and text production is one module of the Arts Journalism MA program that two Zurich universities (Zurich University of Applied Sciences and the Zurich University of the Arts) set up together for about 12 selected students per year (http://mae.zhdk.ch/).[1] The students come from Switzerland and other countries, but all speak German, as the courses are held in that language. The module described here prepares them to be journalists (online, print, radio, television) or PR-managers focusing on cultural issues.

It is in this module that attitudes, knowledge, and skills of journalistic writing are systematically reflected upon and taught. The Text analysis and text production module comprises fourteen full days spread over two semesters (Figure 2).

The first eleven days of the module are one-day workshops. Each workshop begins with a short theoretical block, followed by text analysis of case studies and collaborative text production as group assignments. The workshops end with a joint evaluation. During optional evening tutorials, students can receive feedback about their individual text products.

The workshops cover first the interplay of writing process, text product, and optimization (days 1 to 3); then micro- and macro-processes such as title and

	Perspective	Topic
1	Process, product, and optimization	writing process
2		systemic optimization
3		text product
4	Production process	micro: title design
5		macro: communication design
6	Text structure	e.g. reviews and comments
7		e.g. editorials and glosses
8	Text environment	e.g. word, picture, sound
9		e.g. information graphics
10	Text function	e.g. rhetoric
11		e.g. branding
12	Integration workshops	Convergent Media Production:
13		– conceptualization
14		– realization
		– implementation

Figure 2 Schedule of the Text analysis and text production module.

communication design (days 4 to 5); and exemplary aspects of text structure, function, and environment (days 6 to 11). The last three days of the module (12 to 14) are left for integration workshops with a single assessed assignment, which, at the same time, is the showcase for the module.

In the three integration workshops, each two weeks apart, the students produce a special section for the Swiss architecture magazine Hochparterre, with about ten items on the topic Emotion in architecture. The section is published on multiple platforms: the print version of Hochparterre and their multimedia website _http://www.hochparterre.ch as well as the didactically-motivated, experimental website http://www.redaktionzukunft.de ("redaktionzukunft" means *"newsroom of the future"*). The first integration workshop focuses on conceptualization, the second on realization, and the third on evaluation.

- In the first integration workshop, the students decide in workgroups and in plenary how to approach the assignment as a group and individually. The workgroups start with input they have prepared during the preceding weeks: group 1 with media management, group 2 with text design, group 3 with the journalistic profile of the special section. Moreover, all the students present their individual approaches to the topic *Emotion in*

architecture and outline what they would like to say as individual authors. Later on that day, the students align the ideas of the workgroups with the individual journalistic visions. They decide on and assign responsibilities and steps in the production process, on the profile of the product, and on the tasks each author has to accomplish.
- The second integration workshop focuses on the realization of the *Hochparterre* project. The students as individual authors or as members of the production team get advice on demand from the module leaders, who act as external advisors at this stage of the project—rather than as teachers, as in the previous workshops, or as assessors, which they will be in the last integration workshop. Before this final day of the module, the students submit the special section along with a writing diary in which they describe and reflect on their iterative learning process.
- The third and last integration workshop—which is the last day of the entire *Text analysis and text production* module—focuses on the evaluation of the *Hochparterre* project. Together, the module leaders and students evaluate what the entire project group, the three workgroups, and the individual authors have produced. This evaluation is presented in more detail below.

COLLABORATIVE EVALUATION: ASSESSING THE MULTIMEDIA MINDSET

How should the students' multimedia mindset, their ability to recognize the success factors in their collaborative production of the *Hochparterre* special section best be evaluated? In order to grapple with this complex issue of evaluation, we consider outcomes from three levels of text production: on the conceptualization level, the input from the three workgroups to the entire product group; on the realization level, the reflections on the iterative process of writing and learning that are recorded in the writing diaries; and on the product level, the individual texts and the entire special section.

An interdisciplinary group evaluates these outcomes: one is an expert in convergent media, one in conceptualization of communication, and one in writing processes. These three experts are the main leaders of the Text analysis and text production module. The other experts are the students themselves: they are experts in their own processes of learning. First, the module leaders agree on a grade for each of the evaluated outcomes and the students do the same. Then, the averages of the two groups' evaluations determine the final grades for each outcome.

The grades for the writing diaries and the individual texts apply to the individual students, whereas the grades for collaborative outcomes such as the group input or the entire special section apply for the respective groups. Thus, a grade of A for the text design input means an A for all the members of the text

Focus	Category of journalistic strategies and practices ...	... in convergent media
Process	Goal setting: What do I want to achieve by my item? What should it look like when finished? What sense does it make?	What do I want to achieve across media?
	Planning: How do I achieve my goals? Which is the best way to resolve the problem? How do I structure my item?	How do I split tasks across media?
	Formulating: How do I find my words? How can I stimulate my text flow?	How do I negotiate my workflow?
	Controlling: How can I improve my text? What do I consider a mistake and how can I eliminate it?	How can I improve the interplay across media?
	Defining the task: Who decides what I am going to do? How do I know what I am supposed to do?	Which is my task within the cross-media concerto?
	Implementing the product: How do I make sure that my work fits in what my collaborators do?	How do I implement my product in media clusters?
	Reading sources: When do I read sources? Which sources do I read? How do I read them? Why do I read them?	How do I gather linkable sources?
	Reading the text-so-far: When, why and how do I read my text-so-far?	How do I navigate through my product so far?
	Handling tools: How do I use as efficiently as possible the tools available? When do I use which tools?	How do I cope with recent, as yet unfamiliar tools?
	Handling task environment: How do I manage the different tasks I am supposed to carry out?	How do I update hot items?
	Handling the social environment: How do I interact with peers, superiors, interviewees? Who can help? Who expects what?	How do I collaborate in multimedia newsrooms?
	Optimize production costs by holding to space and time restrictions: How do I cope with the resources at hand?	How do I handle infinite hyper-space?

Figure 3 Set of text production criteria for the (self)evaluation, with highlighted subset for collaboration.

design workgroup, a B for an individual text or writing diary results in a B for that student, a C for the final special section results in a C for all of the students. The average of these three grades is the final grade for the module.

The reflections and discussions preceding the grading are based on a shared set of criteria. The set operationalizes the multimedia mindset and the success factors on a practical level of writing strategies and practices (see Figure 3, cf. Perrin, 2003; Perrin & Ehrensberger-Dow, 2008; Perrin, 2009 in press). For instance, the success factor of collaboration is operationalized as defining the task, implementing the product, and handling the social environment.

The following example illustrates the interplay of journalistic strategies and practices on the product level (e.g., *finding the sources*) and the process level (e.g., *goal setting, formulating and handling the social environment*). The student in question practiced and reflected on this interplay during his text production, and it was discussed in the evaluation in the last workshop as an example of an emerging practice to stage interviews in convergent media.

The student S.G. addressed an extraordinary topic and opted for an unusual format: an interview via e-mail. His topic is objectophilia, the intimate love a human feels for inanimate objects, in this case for the Twin Towers in New York. In his writing diary, the student reflected on the risks of his interview format:

Focus	Category of journalistic strategies and practices ...	... in convergent media
Product	Optimize factual recency and relevance by limiting the topic: Which topic, which aspects and details should I choose?	Which aspects do I cover with which media?
	Optimize discursive authenticity by finding the sources: How do I choose reliable sources and reproduce them?	How do I integrate the sources into my own items?
	Optimize author's uniqueness by taking own position: Which is my or our distinctive approach, perspective, hypothesis?	How do I achieve my USP across media?
	Optimize symbolic conventionality by staging the story: How do I design dramaturgy and style?	Which media transformation for which effect?
	Optimize accessibility by establishing relevance for the audience: What do I want to achieve for which audience?	How do I tune audience design across media?

Figure 3 (continued).

> Given that my focus was clearly on one case, specifically a single individual, I only considered two genres as possibilities: an interview or a profile. Since Sandro told me early on that he did not want to talk to me on the phone or meet with me, I decided on an e-mail interview—although I was aware of the inherent difficulties of this. (Translated from the original German diary entry.)

S.G. dedicated particular attention to the dramaturgy: "The first question has to set the tone, no unnecessary shifts, smooth transitions, space to rearrange things and delete bits . . . it's all about overcoming the deficiencies of an impersonal interview" (translated from the original German diary entry). In addition, S.G. edited and streamlined the answers of the interviewee linguistically (e.g., by eliminating redundancies). This procedure is common for transforming spoken interviews into writing, although wide segments of the audience and even authors are probably not aware of it.

In the discussion with the group, S.G. proposed a paradigmatic variant (see Figure 1) to make such staging procedures visible for the audience: readers would be able to access the literal transcription of the spoken interview behind the edited written text. The raw material would shimmer through the elegant final product—a variant of the interview genre inspired by the particularities and novelty of media convergence. A new solution for an old journalistic problem emerged from conflicting demands and the possibilities of convergent media.

To sum up, this way of assessing such programs shows that:
- students and experts differ only slightly in their grades
- students profit from the discussions during self-assessment when they reflect as a group on what they have produced individually and collaboratively and what they have reflected on in their writing diaries
- multimedia mindsets can be assessed through this multilevel and multi-perspective procedure systematically, explicitly, and convincingly for all parties involved.

Shaping the multimedia mindset with such assessments, workshops, and programs is what is required in the present professional environment. Convergent media challenge and enable us to come up with new solutions. Channels of distribution are becoming almost free of charge on the net: everything is everywhere. Branding in the media business results primarily from journalistic performance and audience design and from strong teams capable of writing for all channels with courage and openness for collaborative emergent solutions. Journalists who are fit in these areas will ensure the success of journalistic media.

The multimedia mindset makes the difference: in newsrooms—and in the corresponding educational programs.

NOTE

1. See the Kruse essay, this volume, for a description of the mission and structure of the Zurich University of Applied Sciences, as well as for a summary of the linguistic demography of Switzerland. Zurich University of the Arts (ZHdK) is a centre for teaching, research, and production excellence. While firmly anchored in Greater Zurich, its influence extends well beyond Switzerland to the wider international stage. ZHdK offers a broad range of degree programmes and further education courses in education, design, film, art & media, dance, theatre, and music. Closely interrelating teaching and research, ZHdK promotes transdisciplinary projects. Hosting over 600 events a year, ZHdK makes a significant contribution to cultural life in the city and region of Zurich. See the ZHdK website: http://www.zhdk.ch/?id=962.

REFERENCES

Brannon, J. (2008). Maximize the medium. Assessing obstacles to performing multimedia journalism in three US newsrooms. In C. Paterson & D. Domingo (Eds.), *Making online news. The ethnography of new media production* (pp. 99-111). New York: Peter Lang.

Mission Statement. (n.d.) *Mission statement of University of Zurich of Applied Sciences*. Retrieved from http://www.zhdk.ch/?id=962.

O'Grady, W. (in press). Emergentism. In P. Hogan (Ed.), *Cambridge Encyclopedia of Language Sciences*. Cambridge: Cambridge University Press.

Perrin, D. (2003). Schreiben als konfliktmanagement. Qualitätssicherung im printjournalismus [Conflict management in writing. Quality control in print journalism]. In H.-J. Bucher & K.-D. Altmeppen (Eds.), *Qualität im Journalismus. Grundlagen, Dimensionen, Praxismodelle* [*Quality in journalism: Basics, dimensions, practice*] (pp. 327-343). Wiesbaden: Westdeutscher Verlag.

Perrin, D. (2010 in press). "There are two different stories to tell here". TV journalists' collaborative text-picture production strategies. *Journal of Pragmatics*.

Perrin, D., & Ehrensberger-Dow, M. (2008). Media competence. In G. Rickheit & H. Strohner (Eds.), *The Mouton-de Gruyter Handbooks of Applied Linguistics: Communicative competence* Vol. 1 (pp. 277-312). New York: Mouton de Gruyter.

Quinn, S. (2005). *Convergent journalism: The fundamentals of multimedia reporting*. Frankfurt am Main et al.: Lang.
Singer, J. B. (2008). Ethnography of newsroom convergence. In C. Paterson & D. Domingo (Eds.), *Making online news. The ethnography of new media production* (pp. 157-170). New York: Peter Lang.
Tunstall, J. (2009). European news and multi-platform journalists in the lead. *Journalism, 10*(3), 387-389.

CHAPTER 35.
THE PLACE OF WRITING IN TRANSLATION: FROM LINGUISTIC CRAFTSMANSHIP TO MULTILINGUAL TEXT PRODUCTION

By Otto Kruse
Zurich University of Applied Sciences (Switzerland)

The School of Translation at the Zurich University of Applied Sciences is one of two Swiss institutions educating translators. The contribution describes the institute's literacy conception and the changes from linguistic parallelism to a model of multilingual literacy in which many forms of language interactions are reflected, not only translation. A first year writing program has been created that provides a variety of writing tasks focused on genre use in different domains (literary, academic, professional, and journalistic). The program places a strong emphasis on the connection of writing with linguistic knowledge acquired in the other parts of the study program. While the first part of the course may be characterized as genre training, the second one is devoted to creativity work leading to a group product in the form of a conjoint dossier. The program builds on a process approach, uses electronic portfolios, and places a strong weight on self-directed group activity. It is taught in three languages parallel.

THE INSTITUTION AND ITS GEOGRAPHIC, CULTURAL, AND ECONOMIC FEATURES

The Zurich University of Applied Sciences ZHAW was founded in 1998 as an amalgamation of the once separate schools of business, architecture, engineering, facility management, and translation. As a result of this merger the schools acquired university status, not only providing them with generous state funding but also extending their mandate to include research and continuing education alongside teaching. The legal framework for this development was provided by a federal law introducing the new type of a university of applied sciences in addition to the traditional universities. As a consequence, the formerly independent schools became departments of the new university, within which various institutes and competence centers were founded. The former School of Translation thus became the new Institute of Translation and Interpretation within the Department of Applied Linguistics. One of the newly founded competence centers within the Department was the Center for Professional Writing.

In the transition period from a vocational school to a university, faculty had to react to several challenges. They had to cope with the new standards of academic teaching and had to re-engineer the curriculum in accordance with the new laws of the Canton Zurich as well as within the framework of the Bologna Process that Switzerland had joined. Connected with this change was a reduction of the length of the study program from four to three years, which actually meant that the compulsory one-year period of study abroad had to be cancelled. Another change that had to be coped with was the transition from a collective leadership system to a hierarchical one, as required by Swiss law. Management became more flexible, albeit at the expense of transparency and collegiality in decision making.

Adaptation to the standards of university teaching demanded that the school-like teaching and learning procedures had to be changed to more independent, self-directed learning, which included seminar teaching, project-oriented learning, and thesis writing. These changes, however, were introduced in a tentative step-by-step process, as the guidelines for the reform process were anything but well defined. Research-oriented teaching and learning was one of the clear requirements imposed, but it was left up to the schools to find the discipline-specific ways of implementing this.

This new type of applied university proved to be very successful in Switzerland. Student numbers were and are still rising, and study programs were able to become highly selective. In 2007, new departments of Health, Applied Psychology, and Social Work were introduced. Today, the ZHAW hosts nearly 6,000 students and about 40 study programs at the bachelor and master level.

The cultural context of the School of Interpretation and Translation cannot be properly understood without considering the language situation of Switzerland. There are four national languages, French, German, Italian, and Romansh, each with a different weight. The dominant language, German, is spoken by about two-thirds of the Swiss population, French by about 20%, Italian by 6.6% and Romansh by only .5%.

All four languages are anchored in defined language regions and every canton has one or two official languages. Only a minority of cantons are factually bi- or multilingual (Wallis, Graubünden) and only some cities along the German/ French border are bilingual (Biel/Bienne, Freiburg/Fribourg). The public impact of the dominant languages German and French, however, is higher than that of the smaller languages, which seems to be the fate of all minority languages. This unbalanced situation has given language politics a high priority in Switzerland, which, throughout its history, has managed to prevent "language wars" by taking care to prevent the open dominance of one language over the others. This defensive attitude, however, led to multilingualism being considered something of a burden that blocks national unity. Only recently has the seeming disadvantage of multilingualism turned into an advantage for Switzerland as an economic and educational location (Dürrmüller, 1996).

Today, English is considered a fifth, unofficial national language, being used in the economy, tourism and higher education. In several cantons, English has now replaced one of the national languages as the first foreign language at school. Alongside English, many other languages are also present as a result of the high numbers of foreigners (20%) in Switzerland. The long tradition of well-managed multilingualism makes Switzerland an interesting model for the study of cultural differences in education. Multilingualism, however, does not mean that translation is obsolete. Quite the opposite is true. All public documents have to be translated into several other languages and the web sites of public institutions and business enterprises are usually maintained in three or four languages. This situation provides an excellent labour market for translators.

LITERACY AND WRITING IN THE TRANSLATION STUDY PROGRAM

The significance of literacy in a translation study program has received little attention, in spite of the obviously close connection between the two. Thinking in translation studies has a long tradition of stressing the independence of languages and the respective national or regional cultures. Translators are seen as mediators between these cultures; they need excellent knowledge and language skills in each. Both language skills and cultural studies are traditionally the main subjects of translation study programs. Even if translation is considered one of the oldest professions pursued by mankind, translation has only recently become a discipline in its own right (Snell-Hornby, 1988).

Before the School of Translation was remodeled, the objectives of the study program were mainly defined in terms of professional language and translation skills. Students had to acquire proficiency in two or three foreign languages (L2-L4) and received intensive training in translating from each of their foreign languages into their mother tongue and from their mother tongue into their first foreign language. "Literacy" in the study program was implicitly defined as linguistic knowledge and language proficiency.

Today, this has changed in several ways. First, all students are required to attain proficiency level (C2) in English, no matter which L2 and L3 they choose. Second, translation is now mainly seen in the framework of a communication model. Language skills are now seen as part of communication processes within/ between cultural systems or professional environments. To meet these communicative and professional demands, three specialisations have been recently defined:

- Multimodal communication: Management of the intercultural and interlingual transfer of information with different media
- Multilingual communication: Management of multilingual settings in business, education or culture
- Technical communication: Management and translation of technical content in multilingual fields.

Literacy is now seen as a matter of language use in social and institutional contexts instead of a matter of "pure" language skills. There is also a shift from a model of distinct, language-specific literacies to a model of multilingual literacy, in which the co-existence of different languages with their correspondent language practices is seen as the norm for individuals as well as for communities.

Although students still receive intensive language training separately in their own languages, courses with comparative approaches have also recently been included, such as one in comparative text analysis. Translation is usually performed from L2 and L3 to L1. Students do have to write, however, also in their L2 and L3 classes, at least for the purpose of language learning, and may, for the same reason, also translate from L1 to L2.

WHAT DO "LITERACY" AND ESPECIALLY "WRITING" MEAN TO STUDENTS AND TEACHERS?

That writing is part of translation or—even more—that translation is a writing profession, was always taken as a fact, but a fact not rooted in a writing or literacy theory. The only course connected to writing on the translation programme was "Text Redaktion," a course that taught text revision skills based on linguistic knowledge about grammar, text linguistics and style. "Text Redaktion" seemed to be the natural domain of translators' literacy, as they do not usually have to concern themselves with the first stages of the writing process: planning, the creation of ideas, text structuring, etc. In translation, the ideas, structure, audience, etc., are already in place and it therefore seemed unnecessary to teach them—in other words to make students actually work on their own texts. Consequently, the main kind of writing students had to perform was writing translations of published texts. The second was writing as a means of learning foreign language. The third form of writing consisted of the final thesis, an extended translation with annotations.

The kind of literacy standards typical for translation students was their high proficiency in two or three foreign languages and their highly developed reflective abilities in their mother tongue, principally in all normative aspects of language use. On the other hand, students had hardly ever written a text of their own beyond the school level. Finding ideas, structuring a text, expressing their own point of view, connecting to the texts of others, etc., were not required and never taught. In a writing workshop with translators, all of them alumni from the school of translation, I learned that they found even the most basic kinds of narrative or argumentative texts hard to write. They were skilled in producing perfect translations and delivering them in an accurate, error-free state to their clients. But they were not used to developing their own ideas or to writing as a means of communication. Literacy in the translation study programme meant educating language specialists (in several languages) without giving them their own voice or making them the authors.

Used to teaching academic writing in the sciences and social sciences of German universities (in which writing is traditionally a core element of teaching), I found that teaching writing to translation students posed a whole set of new challenges. When I taught my first writing course in this programme, I did not know how to legitimize writing and I did not know which genres to teach. The students expected to learn about correct writing, which meant polishing the surface until it shines. Language correctness was the dominant criteria for all kinds of student performance on this study programme. The focus on the writing process and on writing creativity which I initially offered did not seem to contribute substantially to this.

Moreover, I noticed that for students specializing in language skills a writing course that does not relate to their previously acquired knowledge of grammar, style, rhetoric, text analysis, etc., must indeed feel empty. For them, it is important to use writing not only as a means of producing some kind of message, but also as a way of integrating their different kinds of language skills. Creative writing exercises were especially hard for them to understand, as creative exercises often displace the writer from language norms in favor of enhanced expressiveness. I had to find a way of teaching writing that connected their quest for correctness with my ideals of process and creativity.

A third obstacle to introducing writing to the translation programme was the choice of the domain. Teaching writing at university level, as I had done before, meant teaching academic writing. Was this what translation students needed? Academic writing was important for theses and seminar papers, but as long as these were not an integral part of the curriculum, academic writing was not really needed. In addition, the writing competences of translators cannot easily be tied to a single domain. Translators need to be highly qualified as text specialists in different domains like business and law, technical writing, journalism, etc. It seemed impossible to prepare them in their core domain as this is done, for instance, on journalism study programmes, where students receive training in the dominant genres of news reports, comments, columns, features, or reportages. Focusing on the genres of a single domain would not apply to translators. They have to become generalists, able to understand and reproduce a great number of genres—that cannot be specified exhaustively. They need the skill to explore genres and genre systems in several domains and in several languages. This demands meta-linguistic abilities that do not follow the usual learning process of mastering genres, but need a deeper understanding of what genres are and how they may be examined.

WHERE AND WHAT DO STUDENTS WRITE IN OUR INSTITUTION – DISCIPLINES, GENRES, ASSIGNMENTS?

The transformation to a research-oriented institution with its respective teaching methods resulted in new developments, of which the following are worth mentioning:

- Research-oriented teaching: University teaching and learning demands a closer interconnection of teaching and research. This not only represented a change for the faculty, who were encouraged to carry out research projects themselves, but also for teaching, with translation no longer being considered simply a craft but a discipline comprising its own body of knowledge based on translation research. As a consequence, seminars were introduced to teach research skills.
- More self-directed learning: A second demand was the change from a school-like teaching arrangement to one with more student responsibility and self-directed learning. Less teaching in class and more independent work were required. In many classes, writing became the dominant mode of learning, for instance in translation projects, and of assessment,

where papers replaced multiple choice or gap-filling tests. Translation projects replaced translation exercises as the dominant form of learning.
- Bachelor thesis: The introduction of a bachelor thesis as a requirement for graduation started a long debate not only about the kind of writing expected but also about the kind of preparation necessary during the study programme. The thesis traditionally required was more a demonstration of craftsmanship than of the ability to understand ways in which the discipline creates knowledge. By contrast, the new bachelor thesis calls for a contribution to translation studies or to any of the other disciplines involved in the study programme. The introduction of the bachelor thesis made it necessary to offer seminars where students can learn what research means and how it is done.

WHO IN OUR INSTITUTION "CARES" ABOUT STUDENT GROWTH IN AND THROUGH WRITING? HOW IS THIS CONCERN—OR ITS LACK—SHOWN IN FUNDING, REQUIREMENTS, ATTITUDES AND ACTION?

The ZHAW Centre for Professional Writing was founded as a centre of excellence for research and continuing education. Coordinating writing within the study programme or providing tutoring for students has never been its mission. Plans for a student writing centre were discussed but were not realised, mainly for financial reasons. There is no lack of concern about writing, as writing is now a well-established field of teaching and learning, but the responsibility for student writing rested with the study programme directors and was not passed on to a writing centre.

The members of the Centre for Professional Writing were asked to add several new writing courses to the curriculum. Innovation came not only from the Centre itself but also from the other divisions, especially the English section, which soon used a variety of writing assignments in their courses. The different kinds of writing, however, were never co-ordinated.

Writing was introduced to the study program mainly by inviting the Centre for Professional Writing to offer writing courses. The first course was a two-semester offering on academic writing for the second-year-students, which was initiated in 2006. In groups of twenty, students were first introduced to the principles of academic writing and then, in the second semester, wrote a research-based paper in groups of four. In addition to the author, Gerd Bräuer and Michaela Baumann were involved in this course. After the second run it was decided to change this course to a research-oriented seminar in which writing instruction was reduced in favor of content. The first half of the course now follows the traditional way of seminar teaching, introducing students to a research field before making them, in the second half, choose their own topic and carry out a small research project. The second part consists basically of one-to-one tutoring of the students, directing their research and their writing processes. The course was no longer carried out by writing teachers but by faculty who, in turn, were able to develop their own skills in teaching research and writing.

A second innovation was the introduction of a new kick-off procedure for the bachelor thesis. Instead of leaving the students to choose a topic and a person to guide their writing process on an individual basis, a study week is organised in which faculty are invited to present their research fields and students asked to choose one of these as the subject of their own thesis. During this week, students have the opportunity to attend several workshops on methodology and to participate in colloquia and consultations with their future supervisors. At the end of the week, they submit a proposal for their thesis, which is then discussed with the supervisor. The third innovation was the construction of a new first-year introductory writing course to better support the transition from school to disciplinary writing. This course will be described in detail below.

WHEN AND HOW HAVE GROUPS OF TEACHERS MET TO DISCUSS AND PLAN WAYS TO HELP STUDENTS GROW AS WRITERS? WHAT HAS RESULTED?

The groups which discussed the writing issue consisted of those persons with the mandate to offer writing courses. To provide students with a learning-to-write experience specific to translation studies, a new course was designed for the first-year students. The course was to be offered for German-, French- and Italian-speaking students in their respective L1s. A group of five teachers developed the course in close coordination with the head of the study programme. In addition to myself, those involved were Michaela Baumann, Gerd Bräuer (both German), Vittorio Panicara (Italian), Christian Treffort (French) and Gary Massey (study programme director). The writing course that resulted from this collaboration is specially designed to meet the needs of a translation study programme (see Figure 1).

Three things were initially decided upon:
- The course was designed to give students enough time to take part in self-directed learning and to prevent school-like teaching. We therefore agreed to give lessons only every third week (in groups of 20) and have students work in small groups (of five participants each) in the two re-

maining weeks. After the first run, however, we changed this to a two-week rhythm, thus alternating classroom and small-group learning.
- Process-oriented teaching was used as the focus of the first semester, although this was interlinked with the teaching of genre norms and genre forms. This, we hoped, would help bridge the gap between writing and the linguistic or translation courses elsewhere in the curriculum.
- The course was to be genre-oriented in the first half and directed towards creative products in the second. The genre-oriented part was managed by means of an electronic portfolio. The creative product submitted after the second part was to be a "dossier," a collection of texts on a defined topic suited to the use of certain media (a brochure, newspaper, web site, etc.) and selected by the students themselves. Each student has to contribute at least two personally signed texts to this dossier.

In the first half of the course, the learning platform provides individual electronic portfolios, which here is defined as a forum to which students can upload their texts. They are encouraged to upload several versions of any text they write during the course. After one semester, students have usually posted between 15 and 25 texts to their portfolios, most of them in different versions and most of them commented on by their fellow students. Feedback is first provided in the small-group sessions and later, in electronic form, on the learning platform.

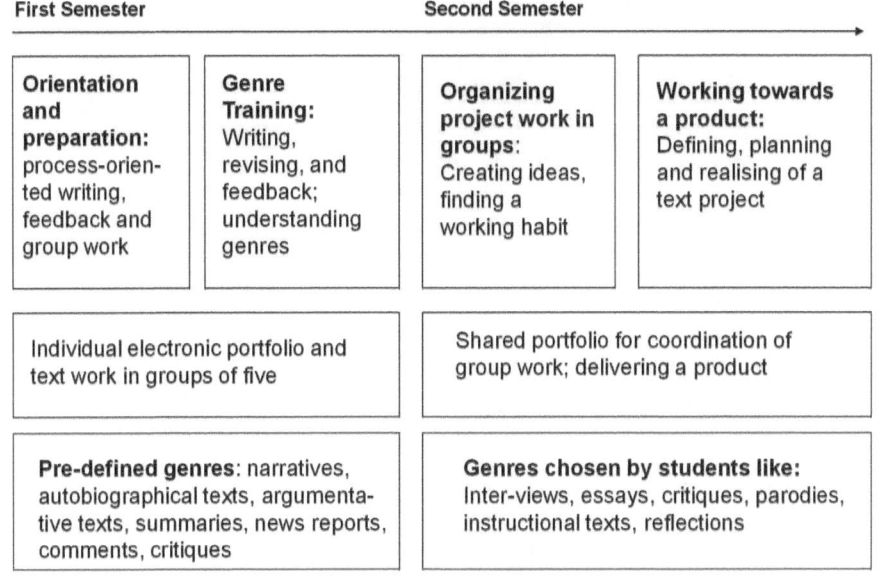

Figure 1. Course design for a translations tudy programme.

The first half of the course principally takes the form of genre training. A four-hour block is assigned to this every two weeks. Each block is usually devoted to introducing a domain (academic writing, creative writing, journalism, rhetoric) and certain genres (or genre families), together with some model texts, and to setting a defined writing assignment. All questions arising from the assignment and all theoretical issues can be discussed in the autonomous student groups. All written texts are instantly posted to the portfolios so that the lecturer can read them and respond to them before the next lesson. In this way, students are immediately informed about their products and given feedback on the level of comprehension they have achieved. Every training block begins with collective or individual feedback on the texts submitted. As seven 4-hour blocks are available, some of the trainings blocks are extended over six or even eight hours.

BLOCK 1

Introduction, process-oriented writing and feedback: This part gives students the chance to reflect on what writing at school is and what they have learned there, and to contrast this with their new tasks at university. It also contains an exercise in which they write a text in several steps, proceeding from the initial idea to structuring, drafting, receiving feedback and revising (a procedure taken from Ruhmann, 1997). This allows a discussion of relevant process aspects of writing to take place. In the last part of this four-hour block, students are instructed in the use of the learning platform and in the tasks they must perform in their small groups. The instructions for small-group work are very detailed at first, with students successively being given increasing autonomy (and responsibility) in organising their group sessions.

BLOCK 2

Narrative approaches: In the second block, students have to write an individual "literacy biography," exploring their family literacies, a procedure we have borrowed from Foster (2006, pp. 142 ff.). As an experience in creativity, they write a five-minute narrative text on a picture (from Allen, 1997) and then record a scene from their own experience of literacy or from a fictional story. This is supposed to introduce them to a few basic issues of creative writing: introducing characters, writing with all the senses, creating a setting, etc. The second teaching block is also used to introduce them to feedback and to increase their motivation to revise texts.

Block 3

Knowledge reproduction: Writing summaries and reflecting on knowledge constitutes the third block. Students are briefly introduced to the specifics of academic writing and the necessity of reproducing other texts. They perform an exercise in class called "text reproduction in slow motion," in which they reduce a text to its core elements and write their summaries on the basis of these (the procedure is described in Kruse & Ruhmann, 1999). This procedure allows all questions about quoting, understanding texts, reproducing texts, plagiarism and writing discursive texts to be discussed

Block 4

Argumentation: Writing arguments and critical essays is the focus here. Students are introduced to the traditions of rhetoric and the importance of argumentation. They are introduced to argumentation theory on the basis of a model provided by Booth et al. The text they write is a Plädoyer (a genre that has no exact correspondance in English; it might be translated best as "plea," an open text form that allows one to speak in favor of or against a statement).

Block 5

Journalism: Writing news reports and commentaries. The last block introduces journalism as a field of writing with highly regulated text norms. Participants learn to understand several journalistic genres like the news report, commentary, squib, and column, and have to produce a report and a commentary.

The second part of the course is mainly directed towards looking at text systems and at texts in context. The topics for their classes are as follows:

Block 1

Introduction to the course programme and to the task to be performed. The dossier they are to produce is explained and they are instructed that they can write on anything that is connected to writing or language and to our university. They may, for instance, write a dossier on writing in architecture, on foreign students studying at our university, or on the travel experiences of students going abroad. They receive some information on group creativity and use a brainstorming procedure to develop initial ideas.

Block 2

Each group prepares a presentation about the first ideas they have generated for their dossier. They are encouraged to visualise their ideas in order to optimise their understanding and subsequent discussion of them.

Block 3

Each group prepares a presentation about the most important genres in their dossier. They are instructed to look for descriptions or linguistic studies of the genre, to collect some good examples and to explain how the genre "works." Typical genres used for presentations are interviews, instructions, commentaries, overviews, introductions, summaries, reports, reportages, various narratives, satire and parody.

Block 4

Each group presents its first texts and receives feedback on them. The relationship between the texts and their context (dossier, media) is discussed. Issues of stance, voice and audience are discussed.

Block 5

Again, an integrated concept is presented (either in consultations with the supervisor or in plenary sessions with the other groups). Issues of structure, cohesion, media-specificity and text quality are discussed.

ON WHAT MODELS, THEORIES, AUTHORS AND PRINCIPLES HAVE COURSES OR METHODS BEEN BASED?

The principles the course is based on are manifold. The general directive was to create a space open to imparting new experiences in the use of written language. Unlike in other writing courses, we did not focus this course on a major domain like academic, creative, journalistic, technical, legal or business writing, but tried to use it to raise awareness of the differences among these domains. Translators may work in any of these fields but usually specialise in one. The most important principles the course is based on are the following:
- Independent, self-directed learning: The course should contain a high degree of autonomous learning and place as much responsibility for

learning success on the shoulders of the students as possible. This is a general prerequisite for academic learning but also the main ingredient of writing courses. In the German-speaking countries, the principles of this kind of learning in connection with writing are traditionally rooted in seminar teaching (Foster, 2006; Kruse 2006) and are outlined in many student handbooks for successful writing, such as Kruse (1994, 2007), Bünting, Bitterlich & Pospiech (1996), Frank, Haacke & Lahm (2007), Gruber, Huemer & Rheindorf (2009).

- Creativity development: As writing is always a process involving creativity, we had to make sure that the teaching of linguistic knowledge and of writing creativity was kept in balance. An important aspect of writing instruction is that students learn about keeping and breaking norms (see for instance Gardner, 1984, on creative writing). Writing creativity can develop only when text norms are not interpreted as laws. It also follows a developmental model of writing competence involving cognitive, aesthetic and social growth. Creativity is not an elementary or basic competence but an "emergent" feature that always involves a multitude of factors (Sternberg & Lubart, 1996, Kruse, 1997).
- Process-oriented text production: Understanding cognitive processes in writing and building up meta-cognitive awareness of writing are essential to produce effective writers. All kinds of training in writing have to be oriented towards integrating the sub-skills outlined in cognitive research and organising them in a sequential writing process that connects with learning, exploring and reflecting on a topic (Bräuer, 2003).
- Genre theory: We see genre as the interface between linguistics, context and writing. As genre is also a major field of instruction in linguistics, students are provided with knowledge on genres from several fields. In this area we rely on genre research and theory from Bazerman (1988), Swales (1990), Bazerman & Prior (2004) and Russell (1997).
- Collaboration and feedback: Several paedagogical theories of academic learning stress the importance of collaborative and learning communities as prime factors for successful learning (Bruffee, 1999, Miller, 2003). Understanding feedback is the most important prerequisite for collaboration in writing. Therefore, each writing course should contain some training in feedback and should connect writers through feedback. In addition, various form of collaboration such as group work, cooperative writing, writing projects, etc., should be offered. The most important goal of the first part of the writing course is simply to make students publish their texts early and overcome their fears of being exposed. This opens their minds for feedback.

WHAT HAVE BEEN OUR INSTITUTION'S SUCCESSES AND FAILURES IN TEACHING WRITING/STUDENT LITERACY?

Looking at the overall writing curriculum on the translation study programme, it is fair to say that writing has become a central concern. It has to be seen in the context of other innovations that needed to be introduced, such as independent learning and research-based teaching. A special issue in any translation programme is the presence of students with different mother tongues as well as of bilingual students who speak several languages at a native or near-native level. What has not yet been accomplished is a closer interrelation of writing and multilingualism. At the moment, writing is still performed separately in each language. Writing in L1 and L2 has still not been linked with translating and multilingual publishing. The creation of such a learning environment would be helpful not only to gain a better understanding of how language-related literacies may be interconnected but also to develop new forms of writing instruction.

REFERENCES

Bazerman, C. (1988). *Shaping written knowledge: The genre and activity of experimental article in science.* Madison, Wisconsin: University of Wisconsin Press.

Bazerman, C., & Prior, P. eds. (2004). *What writing does and how it does it: An introduction to analyzing texts and textual practices.* Mahwah, N.J.: Lawrence Erlbaum.

Bräuer, G. (2003). *Schreiben als reflexive Praxis: Tagebuch, Arbeitsjournal, Portfolio* (2. Aufl.). Freiburg im Breisgau, Baden-Württemberg, Germany: Fillibach Verlag.

Bruffee, K. (1999). *Collaborative learning. Higher education, interdependence, and the authority of knowledge* (2nd ed). Baltimore, London: John Hopkins University Press.

Bünting, K.-D., Bitterlich, A., & Pospiech, U. (1996). *Schreiben im Studium. ein Trainingsbuch [Scholastic writing. A practical guide].* Berlin Cornesen: Scriptor.

Dürrmüller, U. (1996). *Mehrsprachigkeit im Wandel. Von der Viersprachigen zur Vielsprachigen Schweiz.* Zürich: Pro Helvetia.

Frank, A., Haake, S., & Lahm, S. (2007). *Schlüsselkompetenzen: Schreiben in Studium und Beruf [Academic competency. Scholastic and professional writing].* Berlin: Metzler.

Gruber, H., Huemer, B., Rheindorf, M. (2009). *Wissenschaftliches Schreiben: Ein Praxisbuch für Studierende.* Vienna: Böhlau: UTB.

Miller, R. (2003). *Creating learning communities: Models, resources and new ways of thinking about teaching and learning.* Brandon, Vermont: The Foundation for Educational Renewal.

Ruhmann, G. (1997). Schreibproblemen auf der Spur: Betreuung und Beratung von Studierenden bei Schreibblockaden. In *Handbuch Hochschullehre. Informationen und Handreichungen aus der Praxis für die Hochschullehre* (pp. E 2.5, S. 1-26). Berlin: Raabe Fachverlag.

Russell, D. (1997). **Rethinking genre in school and society: an activity theory analysis,** *Written Communication, 14,* 504-554.

Snell-Hornby, M. (1988). *Translation studies: An integrated approach.* Tübingen, Baden-Württemberg, Germany: Stauffenburg.

Swales, J. (1990). *Genre analysis: English in academic and research settings.* Cambridge: Cambridge University Press.

CHAPTER 36.
A WRITING CENTER JOURNEY AT SABANCI UNIVERSITY, ISTANBUL

By Dilek Tokay
Sabanci University (Turkey)

This profile focuses on Sabanci University's [SU] Writing Center in Istanbul, which serves the university within another unit called the Center for Individual and Academic Development (CIAD). As the Writing Center's institutional, societal, and international roles and practices are reflective of its objectives in line with Sabanci University's vision and mission, a synopsis on the university and CIAD will serve as a prologue to closer focus on the Writing Center's work and an overall evaluation of what has been experienced as well as what still remains to be accomplished.

Sabanci University's founding raison d'être and operational philosophy is to be an innovative institution, responsive to the needs of its constituents and society through a participatory, team-based culture where interdisciplinary infrastructure is the backbone to create and disseminate knowledge. Established in 1996 by the Sabanci Foundation, the university began its first academic year in 1999 on a state-of-the-art campus. In its twelfth year now, SU has a total number of 3,470 students (2,836 undergraduate, 634 graduates) and 374 faculty members. The average number of students per faculty is 14, reflecting focus on small size and close interaction, which is electronically supported by 11,812 Internet connection points. As a member of the European Foundation for Quality Management, implementation of curriculum is in line with the Bologna Criteria for evaluation and enrichment of learning outcomes, pursuing education for all as well as lifelong learning (Sabanci University, 2011)

SU aspires to develop competent and confident individuals, capable of independent and critical reflection within the interdisciplinary framework of three Faculties: Faculty of Engineering and Natural Sciences (FENS), Faculty of Arts and Social Sciences (FASS), and the Faculty of Management (FMAN). For the incoming students to meet the expectations of the university, where instruction is in English, the School of Languages (SL) provides the Foundations Development Year Program. As Faculty Programs are built around a blend of disciplines that leverage scientific developments and equip students with a wide diversity of mental tools and skills, the Center for Individual and Academic Development (CIAD) is engaged in uplifting students' oral and written communication and research skills. The multi-functional role of CIAD's four units, including the Writing Center, is unique to SU among Turkish universities.

CENTER FOR INDIVIDUAL AND ACADEMIC DEVELOPMENT (CIAD)

The mission of CIAD is to support and facilitate SU students' adjustment to the uniquely participatory and interdisciplinary nature of SU. CIAD's subunits are (1) The Writing Center and Academic Support Program; (2) Disability Services Program; (3) Advisory System, comprising Academic Success Monitoring and Counseling, Foundations Development Year Counseling, Peer Tutoring, & Individual Counseling; and (4) the Course Evaluation System.

Activities of each sub-unit provide feedback to the other subunits. For example, through Peer Tutoring, students are directed to either the Writing Center for their skills development needs at all levels, or to the Academic Support Program, for remedial group activities concerning courses such as Physics or Calculus. For better self expression, time management, or study habits, Individual Counseling is the right address. Through the Course Evaluation System, the SU community has access to statistical reports on course evaluations, the types of instruction, and statistics on student satisfaction. Hence, CIAD, with a working team of 21 persons, promotes student-faculty-administration interaction for efficiency, productivity, and accessibility of methodological and pedagogical innovations.

SABANCI UNIVERSITY WRITING CENTER (SUWC)

The following synopsis of SUWC considers the Center's mission, programs, and future plans for viability and recognition.

Philosophy, History, and Strategies of the SUWC

All SU Faculty Programs necessitate critical thinking and academic writing. Forms include essays, project/internship/case reports, response or research papers, conference papers, and theses, as well as discussion-debate strategies, impromptu talks, presentations, and interviewing techniques.

To fulfill its goals of creating interest and establishing the concept of writing as a discipline, SUWC encourages and assists students to become expressive, persuasive, critical, and creative thinkers and writers both in English and Turkish. It facilitates students' development throughout their education at SU with programs focusing on Writing across the Curriculum or in the Discipline, plus thesis preparation, helping them seek for high achievement in careers or jobs in Turkey and abroad.

SUWC builds students' abilities to think, write, and speak in English through workshops, tutorials, study groups, and adjunct courses that promote student writing, by engaging them in contests, conference presentations, and publications. In these activities, sample student essays, proposals, reports, abstracts, response papers, presentations, CV or personal statements, and theses are used, accompanied by Essay Evaluation Checklists that serve as benchmarks.

In tutorials, SUWC does not proofread or edit student writers' work but helps them learn about writing by providing lead-in questions and ample samples in different genres, using different rhetorical styles, and initiating care for organization, structure, layout, and format, with documentation styles for integration of evidence as support, and citation techniques to avoid plagiarism.

The Writing Center has thrived within the frame of CIAD since its inception in 2000, serving the university community through five elements: (1) Foundations Development Year, (2) Undergraduate, (3) Graduate, (4) Career and Academic Advising, and (5) Creative Writing. By encouraging students to pursue competence in academic discourse and contribute to local and international networks through participating at conferences and organizing websites, SUWC fulfills its institutional responsibilities. Top administration's support from its groundwork until present, faculty's familiarity with the notion of Writing Centers, as well as the hard work of the Center's academic staff, have been crucial factors in SUWC's success.

LOCATION

Both CIAD and SUWC are conveniently located on the campus, and can workshop up to 60 participants; it has a Study Group Studio for 10. SUWC has access to all the SU studios for larger workshops. For the five academic staff of SUWC and the Help Desk, six offices are well-furnished and equipped with technology and internet.

Archives

SUWC has its program-based materials as workshop PowerPoint handouts, Study Group activity sheets, checklists, sample student outlines/essays, portfolios, reports, conference abstracts, presentations, CV and SOP samples, supplementary guidelines, reading lists, attendance lists, a database for statistics, semester-end reports, proposals, CDs of interviews with TAs and mock job interviews, and program leaflets. Materials are kept both electronically and in hard copy, including feedback letters and Evaluation Checklists as testimonials.

Composition

The five members of the SUWC academic staff have their degrees in English Literature, Law, Archeology, Mass Media, and Public Relations. Some have additional certificates and experience in English Language Teaching (ELT), teaching of English Literature, Expository Writing or Composition, and/or have been involved in curriculum design, materials production, and teacher training, with 8-40 years of experience per person. Throughout the years, SUWC has had a Coordinator, a Help Desk, and two to seven assistants for office work and peer-tutoring. The current assistants are SU Graduate Program students in Political Science, International Relations, and Cultural Studies, with BA degrees from universities such as Cornell, UC Berkeley, University of Chicago, University of Florida, Boston College, and Cambridge. Two assistants are junior and senior in SU, FENS, and FASS. Assistants' recruitment is a two-tier process: submission of CV and two essays, followed by two interviews to measure teaching and communication skills.

Activities/ Programs

The five program elements of SUWC are designed based on feedback collected from students, course assistants, and faculty at meetings, study groups, and tutorials. Each program holds six to 26 two-hour workshops with a range of eight to 257 students (course-based) per semester. The number of appointment-based tutorials has a range of 125-882 per semester. Study group sessions range between 16 and 77, with an attendance of 3-562 participants per semester. The number of students benefitting from any one of the SUWC services per semester is approximately 1,700 out of SU's 3,470 student population, mostly undergraduates.

Foundations Development Year Program (FDYP)

The goal of the FDYP is to support the English language development of FDY students to ensure a smooth transition between the academic English expectations of the FDY and undergraduate programs. Although this program promotes the growth of all interrelated English language skills, it focuses most strongly on advancing students' academic writing abilities.

Undergraduate Program (UP)

Similar to the relationships built by many established writing centers (see, e.g., Pemberton, 1995; Thaiss & Porter, 2010; and the Gustafsson/Boström , , McConlogue/Mitchell/Peake, and McMillan essays in this volume), the SU-WC's Undergraduate Program (UP) aims to strengthen students' writing skills through Writing in the Disciplines (WID) and Writing across the Curriculum (WAC), supporting their development as confident and effective communicators, researchers, and presenters, but primarily analytical and critical readers, thinkers, and writers with a voice. In workshops and tutorials, different strategies are practiced to help participants shape and refine their writing to achieve and maintain academic standards concerning content, organization, and format of their written work. Activities are designed in consideration of the interdisciplinary nature of the curriculum.

For example, English 101 and 102 are composed of workshops and tutorials concerning
- writing processes
- rhetorical styles
- documentation techniques
- research papers
- film analysis
- book reviews
- presentation skills
- effective interviews
- the Speakers' Corner

— all of these topics applicable in any discipline.

WAC Implementation

Within the interdisciplinary context of curricula at SU, students are required to write competently in all the courses. They are expected to write response/

research papers and essays, exam essays, case/project reports, and dissertations. SUWC's WID workshops started at the time of its foundation in 2000, with 11 workshops that found ground for WAC with the support of faculty.

WAC implementation is geared towards the needs of the following 15 courses, with their inception semesters in chronological order: HUM 201 Major Works of Western Literature (S 2002); SPS 101and102 Social and Political Sciences-Man and Society (F 2004); SPS 303 Law and Ethics (S 2002); POLS 302 Political Science (S 2002); HUM 203 Major Works of Ottoman Culture (S 2004), ANT 469 Writing Culture (S 2004); CULT 250 Oral History (S 2004); HUM 204 Major Works of Western Music (S 2005); HIS 227 History Goes to the Movies (F 2005); PROJ 102 Report Writing for FASS, FENS, and FMAN (F 2006); HUM 214 Major Works of the Opera (S 2009); HUM 224 Major Works of Twentieth Century Music (S 2010), IR 201International Relations Theory (F 2010), HUM 205 Major Works of the Cinema (S 2011). Each of these courses has one to four workshops.

Workshop attendance is made compulsory by the faculty teaching the course. If the times are inconvenient for the students, make-up workshops are arranged. Among all the courses for which WAC workshops are tailored, PROJ 102 (Report Writing for FASS) has the highest attendance.

Face-to-face tutorials are set by appointment. Each WAC tutorial is run by the responsible person of the program or a peer-tutor. The tutorial includes two hours of lead-in questions, attention pointers, and suggestions on the draft, with a revised version by the end of the session. Here, the aim has always been to make student writers "editors of their own work."

To encourage more courses to participate in WAC, we give best attendance awards and present facts and figures to the administration in our end-semester reports.

For the WAC project to turn into an institutionalized Program, concerned faculty have made the following recommendations:
- A University wide WAC Committee that would begin with an analysis of WAC programs in US universities
- A credit course for WAC TAs
- A credit course, Academic Writing, which could be made compulsory for undergraduates
- Funding for graduate assistants that would allow us to invite PhD candidates from US institutions with effective WAC training backgrounds

GRADUATE PROGRAM [GP]

The GP facilitates the acquisition of effective research principles, sound expression in scholarly discourse, and mastery of the specific conventions related to a graduate student's particular discipline. Such discourses include research/ course papers and assignments, theses and dissertations, journal articles for publication, and academic correspondence, as well as conference and classroom presentations. How the SUWC works with graduate students is in some ways unique to Sabanci, but its commitment to graduate education is similar to that in the Gustafsson/Boström, Solé/Teberosky/Castelló, and Thaiss/Goodman essays, among others, in this volume.

All graduate students send course papers, conference publications, and presentations, as well as grant and research proposals, to the SUWC for assistance. Writing tutorials for completion of the doctorate, proposals, and defense are also offered. Additionally, since 2005, GP offers the FMAN 621 Modules, Writing and Presentations for Doctoral Students. With GP support, doctoral students have published their research in academic journals. Since 2004, all second-year MBA students have received support in the form of individual tutorials and workshops in writing and the presentation of the cornerstone projects of the MBA: the Company Action Project (CAP) and the Value Added Presentations. All CAP Projects are read by GP faculty.

CAREER AND ACADEMIC ADVISING PROGRAM [CAAP]

The CAAP assists undergraduates and graduates in their career search as they prepare for employment or post-graduate education in Turkey or abroad. It provides support for graduate school and scholarship applications, internships, research, and grant proposals. Advising students in the decision-making and application process, the program contains a pedagogical component with workshops, study groups, and tutorials concerning preparation for standardized tests—GRE, GMAT, TOEFL, IELTS—plus writing the CV and personal statement, submitting sample papers, and practicing mock interviews. Based on 2004-2010 data, approximately 90% of the SU graduates accepted by postgraduate programs had used CAAP services.

CREATIVE WRITING PROGRAM (CWP)

The CWP's goal is to instill a love of writing with imagination and creativity, as well as clarity; CWP encourages students to develop their own voices and visions. The program aims to develop empathy and fosters an appreciation for human diversity, as students engage in the process of writing short stories, poems, personal essays, or novels. CWP has small interactive workshops and tutorials with undergraduate and graduate students, SU administrative staff, and the students of a foundations high school in the vicinity. The Program also designs two contests every academic year— one in short stories and the other in essay writing. The action plan for the program includes inviting prominent writers for panels, conferences, and Writing Contest Awards Ceremonies; such contests encourage writing in different literary genres such as poetry, mini-saga, novella, and poster design.

Professional Development - TA/ Peer-tutor Training

Professional Development activities occur in three categories. In Category I, TA Classroom Management Techniques workshops for all new FASS, FENS, and FMAN TAs, as well as SUWC assistants, are given at the SU Orientations in mid semester and the end of each semester. In Category II, workshops for TAs of the courses within the WAC program guide the TAs in composing written prompts and designing rubrics for assessment of students' written work. In Category III, we arrange group meetings for workshop and peer-tutoring assistants for each program. These sessions range between 4 and 9 per semester for specific strategies.

Evaluation and Assessment

The SUWC contacts faculty and students prior to the start of semesters for collection of feedback on past practices and expectations for the new programs. Contact with the students is maintained through e-mail or when the students drop in for feedback. The assessment of both the contents and the delivery of workshops and tutorials is a two-tier process: first, collection of student feedback on Workshop and Tutorial Evaluation Checklists, and second, checking the value added to student performance by consulting with the course instructors or TAs. Findings from this process show tremendous impact of workshops and tutorials on student achievement. Letters of satisfaction following each activity and letters asking for more sessions serve as testimonials shared in semester-end reports.

Local Outreach to Secondary Education and Other Organizations

The SUWC fulfills its societal responsibilities through its linkages with secondary education and universities in Istanbul and beyond through organizing seminars and workshops. Because writing has to start at an early age and Turkish secondary education curriculum disregards this fact, linkages with high schools are very important to equip the teachers with methods of teaching writing. Upon institutions' requests, activities are designed to discuss needs and curriculum design to find thematic overlaps with other courses, to tailor writing projects, and to assign meaningful class/group/home work. Strategies for the formation of a Writing Center are recommended. Current workshops and seminars have either continued weekly through the academic year, or have been presented as compact three-day or one-week programs. Educators, including administrators, have visited the SUWC to observe workshops or tutorials and review workshop materials. An SUWC effort has been instrumental in opening five high school and four university Writing Centers in Istanbul. More high school Writing Centers need to be established, and care must be spent not to let the newly-opened centers close by the change of institutions' administrators.

To reinforce these gains, in September 2011 we held our first Summer Institute for high school writing center enthusiasts. We allocated its three days to writing pedagogy enriched with creativity and critical thinking in Turkish courses. The institute will be followed by a series of subject-specific seminars to encourage WAC in Turkish secondary and higher education. The institute built on the gains of the recent SU Educational Reform Initiative Conference. 2011, which has been exemplary in establishing linkages with the teachers involved in Turkish secondary curricula.

The SUWC has also had some success in stretching teaching/learning spaces for other societal needs, as in CV and application letter writing, creative writing for municipalities and Non Governmental Organizations (NGOs), and presentation skills for the business sector.

International Outreach

From the very outset of the Center, international outreach has been a goal—widening its scope and recognition. The SUWC has been participating in international organizations and at conferences like INGED, EATAW, EWCA, IWCA, NCTE, and CCCC. Interaction of SUWC members with international colleagues has always been supported by SU's top administrators. SU encourages international outreach through funding because it values the international voice that its academic representatives gain for the university. As we mix with others, we add to the international common core of knowledge, and we then bring back what we have observed and admired as differences, to be shared by others at home and implemented as much as the circumstances allow.

The Center has also benefited from my own active involvement as a member of the European Association for the Teaching of Academic Writing (EATAW) and as Chair in 2005 of the European Writing Centers Association (EWCA).

The International Writing Centers Association (IWCA) honored me with the "one-time-only" Muriel Harris award in 2010 for my contributions to the organization.

Collegial ties established at conferences and strengthened through networking have brought SUWC prominent visitors from Turkey and abroad during the years 2004-2011. EWCA Chairs and Board members, the past CCCC and IWCA Chairs, Writing Center Directors from Europe and the US, and many international professors have enhanced professional sharing at the events designed by the SUWC in Istanbul, conveying their ideas for new action plans to others during their visits.

Networking through websites has additionally provided a professional medium for the discussion of effective teaching-learning strategies in writing centers. For example. since 2003, the SUWC website has had 290,334 unique visits and the EWCA website 199,151 (as of June 14, 2011). (See http://www.sabanciuniv.edu/writingcenter and http://www.ewca.sabanciuniv.edu.

EXPECTATIONS

The SUWC's growth in the past eleven years reflects the support by the university's administration. Keeping SUWC networked with an international audience is important, and so professional development of the staff through conference participation needs to be encouraged with funding. To establish further linkages with secondary and higher education, we need to recruit a technical staff to keep SUWC's homepage current and make it interactive, with links to other program websites and an online SUWC newsletter. In the tradition of electronic outreach by writing centers (e.g., Inman & Sewell, 2000; Thomas et al., 1998), we are also aiming to start an on-line service to set up tutorial appointments.

Such new initiatives as the online newsletter and the scheduled summer institute bring hope for the SUWC to carry on as even a better address in Turkey for promoting dialogue in the international writing community.

REFERENCES

Inman, J., & Sewell, D. (2000). *Taking flight with OWLS: Examining electronic writing center work.* Mahway, New Jersey: Lawrence Erlbaum.

Pemberton, M. (1995). Rethinking the WAC/writing center connection. *Writing Center Journal, 15*(2), 116-33.

Sabanci University (2011). *Sabanci University*. Retrieved from http://www.sabanciuniv.edu/eng/

Thaiss, C., & Porter, T. (2010). The state of WAC/WID in 2010: Methods and results of the US survey of the international WAC/WID Mapping Project. *College Composition and Communication, 6*(3), 534-70.

Thomas, S., DeVoss, D., & Hara, M. (1998). Toward a critical theory of technology and writing. *Writing Center Journal, 19*(1), 73-87.

CHAPTER 37.
WRITING PROGRAMS WORLDWIDE: PROFILE OF THE AMERICAN UNIVERSITY OF SHARJAH (AUS)

By Lynne Ronesi
American University of Sharjah (United Arab Emirates)

The American University of Sharjah (AUS) is a primarily undergraduate institution located in the emirate of Sharjah, in the United Arab Emirates, and accredited by the Commission on Higher Education of the Middle States Association of Colleges and Schools. AUS is an English-medium, co-educational, and culturally-diverse university that employs a traditional (US model) writing curriculum with a freshman writing sequence and a second-year English course dedicated to the communication needs of a field. Due mostly to a lack of exposure to writing in secondary school, many AUS students face steep learning curves as they try to meet the expectations of their writing courses and of the writing assignments in other discipline courses. Supplementing writing instruction are a well-established undergraduate-staffed Writing Center and a growing Writing Fellows program. As AUS undertakes initiatives to develop its role in the region, the need for greater attention to developing student writing is being highlighted.

Sheikh Dr. Sultan has articulated the principal values that should define the identity of AUS:
- Science and education must regain their rightful place in the advancement of our society and in shaping the lives of our children.
- The purpose of higher education is to reshape the minds of our youth in order for them to address personal and social challenges using the scientific method.
- AUS must be a center of research for solving the problems faced by society.
- AUS will have the autonomy and freedom needed to flourish as an independent university.

- AUS must be organically linked with the economic, cultural and industrial sectors of society in productive cooperation (Vision of the Founder, 2010)

AUS is a primarily undergraduate institution, with only 6% of enrolled students in graduate programs. In spring 2010, 4,742 undergraduates were enrolled: 43% in the College of Engineering; 30% in the School of Business and Management; 16% in the College of Arts and Sciences; and 11% in the College of Architecture and Design. During the spring 2010 semester, AUS faculty, staff, students, and alumni were asked to rank descriptive words in order to aptly describe AUS. Among the top-five ranked descriptors was "culturally diverse" (Chancellor's Snapshot, May 2010). Indeed, according to the AUS Institutional Research office, the top ten student nationalities of the 80 student nationalities represented during spring 2010 were Emirati (citizens of the UAE), Jordanian, Egyptian, Palestinian, Syrian, Pakistani, Indian, Iranian, Saudi Arabian, and Lebanese. Faculty members represented 49 nationalities (Fast Facts, Spring 2010).

This cultural diversity does not simply define AUS but can be noted throughout the United Arab Emirates. Sharjah, the emirate in which AUS is located, is one of the seven emirates comprising the United Arab Emirates (UAE), a largely coastal country situated on the Arabian Peninsula between Saudi Arabia and Oman. Once known as the Trucial States, the UAE gained independence from England and achieved nationhood in 1971. At that time, due to the small number of Emiratis, the government began to hire an international labor force to help create an infrastructure that would sustain the rapidly modernizing country. The workforce remains largely international, and English works as a lingua franca in the UAE. In fact, while students have the option of Arabic-medium and English-medium primary and secondary schools, all postsecondary institutions in the UAE are English-medium.

Sharjah, once known primarily for its ports and seafaring economy, receives revenues from oil and natural gas. More recently renowned for its emphasis on culture and learning, Sharjah was designated the Cultural Capital of the Arab World by UNESCO in 1998. The emirate contains a number of universities, museums, galleries, theatres, and restored heritage areas—a "context [that] facilitates the [AUS]'s intention to be an academic center at the intersection of ancient cultural traditions and contemporary intellectual currents" (About Sharjah, 2010).

LITERACY AND WRITING

As a university that is based on the American model, the concern for literacy focuses most specifically on English. However, as a university in the heart of the Arab world where the student body is 70% Arab, there are opportunities to study Arabic and learn about Arab heritage. An Arabic Heritage course, which can be taken in Arabic or in English, is a general education requirement for all AUS students. Also, the Department of Arabic and Translation Studies offers minors in Arabic language and literature and in English/Arabic translation, as well as a Master of Arts degree in English/Arabic translation. In general, despite the multicultural nature of our faculty and the fact that many speak Arabic as a first language, AUS faculty members publish in English. This certainly can be attributed to the effect of global English on academia; there are very few internationally recognized journals in languages other than English. At AUS, like most American universities, decisions about contract renewal and promotion revolve around publication in such journals.

While there are AUS students who engage in writing with a sense of pleasure and take advantage of the usual university venues for writing, such as the AUS literary magazine, student newspaper, and the annual Writing Center–sponsored writing contest, there are many students who are apprehensive of writing. There appears to be a variety of reasons for this trepidation; the most immediately recognizable is the lack of attention given to writing in their pre-collegiate schooling. Certainly, students from Arabic-medium schools often have weak writing skills due to their lack of exposure to English. Yet, many AUS students, even those educated in English-medium schools, begin their freshman year without basic skills in (1) structure (i.e., thesis statement, topic sentences, and transitions), (2) argumentation, and (3) source-based citation. Many do not completely understand the notion of plagiarism and have not assimilated the norms of intellectual ownership expected at an American-style university.

There appear to be a number of factors influencing this latter condition. It is understood that many regional secondary schools emphasize rote learning, which results in practices such as providing written essay models for students to memorize and re-write for evaluation purposes (Ronesi, 2009). Moreover, many students report receiving very few writing assignments in their pre-collegiate schooling and claim they were not taught the conventions associated with intellectual property. Another important factor is the collectivist nature of our students' societies. Collectivistic cultures, such as those in Arab countries, value collaboration and support through established networks over the more individualistic approach professed by North American society (McCabe, Feghali, & Abdallah, 2008). Subsequently, it is understandable that AUS students enjoy helping family and friends succeed and find it quite normal to ask for such help. As such, AUS students must learn to make a distinction between "helping behaviors" that truly help their peers (i.e., helping a friend brainstorm ideas for an essay or quizzing each other on the main ideas of a reading) and those behaviors that simply enable bad habits and lack of learning (i.e., writing an essay for a roommate who is under time pressure, or providing a friend homework answers). As new students grapple with assimilating all of the new concepts they encounter, they feel that writing at the university level is a monumental task.

Indeed, many AUS students face an extremely steep learning curve as they try to meet the expectations of their freshman writing courses and of the writing assignments in first-year discipline courses. Not surprisingly, with all the cognitive, social, and emotional demands on them, many students cannot reach academic standards for writing even after a couple of semesters. So, to many AUS students, writing engenders discomfort and a sense of inadequacy.

AUS follows a traditional US-model writing curriculum, with a freshman writing sequence (covering a continuum from basic writing to argumentation to research) and a required second-year English course dedicated to the general communication needs of a field (e.g., English for Engineers, Writing for Business). The freshman-year sequence includes four courses, and in all of them the development of critical thinking skills is emphasized: WRI 001 is a developmental course devoted to academic reading and writing, contextualized grammar instruction, goal setting, time management, and study skills; WRI 101 addresses reading and writing strategies through class discussion and formal and informal writing assignments; WRI 102 focuses on active reading, and intensifies critical thinking and analytical writing; and ENG 204 is devoted to the construction of an argumentative research paper (Undergraduate Course Descriptions, 2010). These courses comprise most of a 12-credit (four course) General Education requirement for English Language Competency and all emphasize the writing process with peer-review and multiple drafts.

A number of approaches have influenced the development of our writing courses. Professor Alaanoud Abusalim, Associate Director of Writing Studies and Curriculum Coordinator, notes that our curriculum and pedagogy draw mostly on the following: the cognitive school (Flower, 1994; Hairston, 1982, 1994) with a process approach and focus on meta-cognitive work; the expressive school (Elbow, 1998; Murray,1985) with an emphasis on free-writing, journals, and discussion boards in an attempt to help students locate their voice; and the social construction school (Berlin, 1996; Bizzell, 1992) which has shaped our understanding of the cognitive, socioeconomic, and cultural challenges our students face in becoming members of the academic discourse community (personal communication, June 25, 2010).

Over the years, the goals of the English Language Competency courses have been re-aligned periodically to suit the steadily increasing proficiency of more recent enrollees and to insure smooth flow between the courses. Placement exams prior to a student's first semester determine at which level the student begins. Most students are placed in WRI 101; for example, a typical student majoring in Economics might place into WRI 101 followed by WRI 102, ENG 204, and ENG 225 (Writing for Business). However, it is possible—though rare—for very strong students to be placed in WRI 102 in their first semester of their freshman year and to complete ENG 204 in their second semester. After that, what and how much a student writes is determined by the discipline a student chooses as a major and the pedagogical beliefs of the various professors the student encounters. Accordingly, students who major (or even minor) in International Studies report writing not only often but also critically and analytically. Yet, there are some majors in which students report relatively few writing assignments. However, it is not unusual that, within departments where students are not asked to write much, there may be a professor or two who bucks the trend and requires writing. Some professors believe strongly—often because of their own experiences—that writing is extremely important to the learning process, even as they admit that requiring writing in their classes is time-consuming and laborious. On the other hand, some professors express that other means of assessing student learning, such as multiple choice questions, are fairer to our students due to the potential for cheating or plagiarizing in writing assignments. There is also the argument that poor writing skills may hinder students from demonstrating their knowledge. Of course, this last argument highlights the need for providing AUS students more curricular opportunities to develop their writing if they are to graduate on an even par with cohorts in the US

WRITING ACROSS THE UNIVERSITY

While AUS has not instituted an official Writing across the Curriculum (WAC) program to support writing across the university, the College of Arts and Sciences (CAS) has generously supported the WAC endeavors of the Department of Writing Studies (DWS). In 2004, an undergraduate-staffed Writing Center was established; it has been growing steadily and now has a main location in the library and a satellite in the Language Building. The Writing Center is a dynamic hub which, in addition to providing session-based writing support on assignments, arranges workshops on various writing issues (e.g., rhetorical appeals, identifying logical fallacies, APA referencing), classroom visits by tutors to explain the Writing Center, and class presentations geared to specific aspects of writing as requested by professors. It has grown steadily and is well-utilized especially by students taking writing and English courses, but also increasingly by students in other courses. To expand Writing Center practice throughout the university and especially into classes that had not traditionally placed much emphasis on writing, DWS began running a Writing Fellows program in fall 2007. In conjunction, a training course for all undergraduate peer-tutors of writing was established with the goal of creating a coterie of students who could work in either capacity—Writing Fellow or Writing Center tutor—or as both simultaneously. This training course has become part of AUS curriculum and fulfills three credits of the 12-credit General Education requirement for English Language Competency mentioned earlier.

The Writing Center and the Writing Fellows Program are run by two different faculty members from the Department of Writing Studies. As the Writing Fellows Program director also recruits for and teaches the peer-tutoring class, the two professors work closely; in fact, the Writing Center and Writing Fellows program share tutors. During the course of an academic year, both professors are approached by colleagues from a variety of disciplines with questions about course-based writing (usually assignment development or assessment approaches) and for information on the types of support their particular tutors could lend. As AUS is not very large, word of mouth is a fairly effective means of promoting the programs, although both promote their services in fairly traditional ways: websites, e-mail reminders to faculty and students, posters, faculty newsletter articles, and occasionally AUS-based presentations. In February 2011, both professors were co-chairs for the second annual Middle East-North African Writing Center Association (MENAWCA) 2011 Conference held at AUS. This event not only provided more than 200 professors and students across the region a venue for discussion and learning, but also enlightened AUS about its own WAC endeavors.

It is fair to say there is interest and concern at many levels—from administration to faculty to students—about insuring that students have more curricular opportunities to develop their writing. From my vantage point, it is hard to determine what official route that interest and concern might take. AUS's relatively new and dynamic chancellor has begun to underscore the need for developing more of a research culture at the university, particularly locally-oriented research, and research that enhances the undergraduate experience. In addition, there has been a great deal of self-study at AUS with regard to promoting a culture of academic integrity. To the extent that I have been involved, discussions on both these topics serve to highlight the issue of writing at the university, and future developments in that area seem possible.

THE TEACHING OF WRITING: IMPACTS AND CHALLENGES

There is a strong feeling among those of us who teach writing at AUS that the nature of our courses contributes a great deal to the success of the AUS student. In learning to write, so much else is accomplished. In many cases, we writing professors provide our students' first exposure to employing critical thought to their learning and communication, as we ask them to evaluate their understandings and assumptions in light of a scholarly approach or of multiple perspectives. We introduce students to academic integrity and intellectual property issues and ask them to incorporate these notions into all their future accomplishments. In our capacities as writing professors, we individualize their learning, responding to their needs as writers, as students, as multicultural individuals learning to express their perspectives in a sensitive, principled, and scholarly way. Not only do we affect the learning of AUS students with limited or average proficiency in writing, but we also offer challenge and growth to many of our stronger writers, who, as peer tutors, grow as writers and individuals through their service to the AUS community.

Daily events corroborate the sense that the required AUS English Language courses and additional WAC endeavors play a pivotal part in our student's academic and personal growth. The following personal experiences come to mind: a chat with a Department of Writing Studies (DWS) colleague in which I learned that a strong writer and motivated student in my current Peer Tutor training class started out in the developmental course, WRI 001, only three semesters before; the student who, at the beginning of the semester, fearfully doubted his capability to write an argumentative research paper in ENG 204, and ultimately wrote one of the very best in the class; a student in the same class who admitted that his initial strong beliefs about his research topic were toppled in the light of the research evidence he uncovered; a Writing Fellow's report that she escorted a shy student she was working with to the Writing Center to help her make a first appointment there; and the proliferation of zany and creative Writing Center posters created by the tutors, which clearly convey the enthusiasm they have for their work. Events like these suggest that those AUS professors and students involved in the craft of writing have made untold impact on the lives of students, and that not only writing-based learning but also a culture of writing is unfolding at AUS.

Frustrations are fewer, but, of course, they exist: the senior who has managed to postpone his writing sequence until his final year, and whose writing is terribly undeveloped in view of his looming graduation date and the start of his career; the colleague from another department who presents me with an upper-level student's atrociously written paper and states that Writing and English faculty are responsible; the students who give short shrift to writing courses because they feel it is a useless imposition. These are all "downers" encountered on occasion.

THOUGHTS ON THE FUTURE OF WRITING AT AUS

Early in the fall 2009 semester, the different departments of the university took a retreat day for strategic planning. My department—the Department of Writing Studies—unanimously felt that we needed to play a greater role in promoting literacy at AUS beyond the introductory courses discussed above. We decided in our retreat that we wanted to increase our repertoire of classes, expand our peer-tutoring programs, and create a minor in Rhetoric and Composition, all goals to which we have made strides over the past months. That departmental retreat was a truly empowering one that seems to have played a pivotal role in galvanizing our motivation and spirit. My sense is that, while writing education becomes more apparent through the above-mentioned departmental goals, other internal and external forces will take shape that highlight the need for attending more closely to developing student writing at AUS.

My hope is that this attention will highlight that writing is "organically linked with the economic, cultural and industrial sectors of society in productive cooperation" (Vision of the Founder, 2010), as part of His Highness Sheikh Dr. Sultan Bin Mohammad Al Qassimi's vision of an education that culminates in the culture of productivity in the United Arab Emirates.

REFERENCES

The American University of Sharjah. (2010). *About Sharjah*. Retrieved from http://www.aus.edu/about/sharjah.php

The American University of Sharjah. (2010). *Chancellor's snapshot*. Retrieved from http://www.aus.edu/chancellor/snapshot_052010.php

The American University of Sharjah. (2010). *Fast facts*. Retrieved from http://www.aus.edu/about/sharjah.php

The American University of Sharjah. (2010). *Mission and goals*. Retrieved from http://www.aus.edu/about/mission.php

The American University of Sharjah. (2010). *Undergraduate Course Descriptions*. Retrieved from http://www.aus.edu/catalog/2009

The American University of Sharjah. (2010). *Vision of the founder*. Retrieved from http://www.aus.edu/about/vision.php

Berlin, J. (1996). *Rhetorics, poetics, and cultures: Refiguring college English studies*. Urbana, Illinois: NCTE.

Bizzell, P. (1992). *Academic discourse and critical consciousness*. Pittsburgh: University of Pittsburgh Press.

Elbow, P. (1998). *Writing without teachers* (2nd ed). New York: Oxford University Press.

Flower, L. (1994). *The construction of negotiated meaning: A social cognitive theory of writing*. Carbondale, IL: Southern Illinois Press.

Hairston, M. (1982, 1994). The winds of change: Thomas Kuhn and the revolution in the teaching of writing. In S. Perl (Ed.), *Landmark essays on writing process* (pp.113-126). Davis, CA: Hermagoras Press.

McCabe, D. L., Feghali, T., & Abdallah, H. (2008). Academic dishonesty in the Middle East: Individual and contextual factors. *Research in Higher Education, 49*, 451–467.

Murray, D. M. (1985). *A writer teaches writing: A complete revision* (2nd ed). Orlando, Florida: Houghton Mifflin Harcourt.

Ronesi, L. (2009). Multilingual tutors supporting multilingual peers: A peer-tutor training course in the Arabian Gulf. *Writing Center Journal, 29*(2), 75-94.

ACKNOWLEDGEMENTS

This author gratefully acknowledges Dr. Terri Storseth, Director of Writing Studies at the AUS, and Professor **Alaanoud A. Abusalim**, Associate Director of Writing Studies at AUS, for their comments and suggestions on this profile.

CHAPTER 38.

THE CITY UNIVERSITY OF NEW YORK: THE IMPLEMENTATION AND IMPACT OF WAC/WID IN A MULTI-CAMPUS U.S. URBAN UNIVERSITY

By Linda Hirsch and Dennis Paoli
Hostos Community College/CUNY and Hunter College/CUNY (US)

This profile will examine the ongoing WAC initiative at the City University of New York, the largest public urban higher education institution in the US and among the most diverse in students' language and cultural backgrounds. The essay provides an overview of WAC at CUNY's 23 campuses, including description of its unique Writing Fellows program, which employs PhD candidates from across disciplines. The authors give special focus to the implementation and impact of WAC principles and practices at two campuses: Hostos Community College, an urban, bilingual community college located in the south Bronx, one of New York City's poorest neighborhoods; and Hunter College, a senior college in mid-Manhattan with graduate programs and four professional graduate schools drawing students from throughout the City. As WAC Coordinators who were present at the inception of the now ten-year CUNY Initiative, we examine the insights gleaned from our experiences as well as the challenges and successes of this vast undertaking.

The City University of New York is the largest urban public university system in the United States, with a mission to provide access to quality higher education for the full range of the city's inhabitants, regardless of income, gender, or ethnic background. It serves more than 480,000 students at 23 colleges and institutions in New York City, including 11 senior colleges, six community colleges, the Macauley Honors College, the Graduate Center, and Graduate Schools of Journalism, Law, Professional Studies, and Public Health.

The university serves a diverse student body representing 205 countries, with African-American, white, and Hispanic undergraduates each comprising more than a quarter of the student body. According to CUNY statistics, 47% of undergraduates have a native language other than English, 41% work more than 20 hours a week, 63% attend school full time and 15% support children. Nearly 60% are female and 29% are 25 or older. Of first-time freshmen, 37% were born outside the US mainland and nearly 70% attended New York City public high schools.

It is against this background of an urban, multi-campus, diverse student body that CUNY sought to strengthen its students' writing proficiencies. Recognizing the vital role that writing plays both in a college education and in future academic and professional success, the CUNY Board of Trustees passed a resolution in 1999 establishing a CUNY-wide Writing Across the Curriculum (WAC) Initiative, which mandated that writing instruction be a University-wide responsibility and that writing proficiency become "a focus of the entire undergraduate curriculum" (http://policy.cuny.edu/text/toc/btm/1999/01-25). To bring its ambitious plan to fruition, the initiative was linked to a CUNY Writing Fellows Program, thereby placing CUNY doctoral students on each of the member campuses to assist in project execution.

This chapter will examine the breadth and depth of the CUNY-wide WAC Initiative by providing an overview of WAC at CUNY's campuses, followed by a special focus on the implementation and impact of WAC principles and practices at two campuses: Hostos Community College, an urban, bilingual community college located in the south Bronx, one of New York City's poorest neighborhoods; and Hunter College, a senior college in mid-Manhattan with graduate programs and four professional graduate schools drawing students from throughout the City. As WAC Coordinators who were present at the inception of the now ten-year CUNY Initiative, we examine the insights gleaned from our experiences as well as the challenges and successes of this vast undertaking.

WAC AT CUNY

In order to contextualize the WAC and Writing in the Disciplines (WID) programs at Hostos and Hunter, a brief description of CUNY's WAC Initiative, drawn from campus WAC web sites, reveals what may be common to all as well as particular interests and accomplishments of each.

While each CUNY campus has developed its own WAC initiative responsive to its particular institutional needs, the CUNY Writing Fellow is common to all. These advanced CUNY Ph.D. students represent a range of disciplines and are assigned to each of the undergraduate campuses and the CUNY Law School. Their duties are as varied as the campuses and may include collaborating with faculty on curriculum and assignments; tutoring students to develop writing abilities; supporting student preparation for entrance and exit writing-related exams; conducting faculty development workshops; developing and maintaining WAC websites; and undertaking research into aspects of WAC at CUNY. (For a description of the Writing Fellowship program and links to Fellow job descriptions, see http://www.cuny.edu/about/administration/offices/ue/wac.html.

This reliance on graduate PhD students rather than traditional undergraduate writing fellows, mentors, or associates is a unique aspect of the CUNY WAC Initiative that allows for greater flexibility in how Writing Fellows serve a program—while at the same time presenting new challenges and profound pedagogical shifts for both faculty and Fellows. The Writing Fellow/faculty collaborations have had a singular transformative effect on pedagogy and the future of the profession, by providing a professional development model for others engaged in similar academic intiatives (Hirsch & Fabrizio, 2010).

CUNY WAC programs' pedagogical underpinnings derive from a broad range of theorists and compositionists who view writing as a mode of communication and as a heuristic: a means of analyzing, understanding, and assimilating course material. They rely on a number of bibliographic sources, with many using John Bean's *Engaging Ideas* as a primary faculty development text. The Brooklyn College WAC Bibliography (http://bcwac.wordpress.com) is representative of the principles undergirding WAC at CUNY.

In essence, WAC programs at CUNY are a variation on a theme. Most campus WAC programs are coordinated with General Education or Coordinated Undergraduate Education (CUE) Initiatives. Almost all rely on Writing Fellow/faculty collaborations to assist faculty in integrating writing into their courses, develop and certify Writing Intensive (WI) courses, and provide opportunities for professional development. Programs are supervised by one or more WAC Coordinators from a number of disciplines (most frequently from the English department); the Coordinators attend monthly meetings with the University Dean for Undergraduate Education. Exchange of ideas, creation of University-wide Fellows' professional development activities, and collaboration on communal efforts such as assessment are functions of these meetings.

Program undertakings are also determined by local circumstances. For example, Baruch College, the university's "business school," situates WAC within its Bernard L. Schwartz Communication Institute and has focused on developing instructional media such as weblogs and wikis. Most senior colleges, including Lehman, Brooklyn, and John Jay, support the development of Writing in the Disciplines (WID) with the aim of customizing WAC practices to the needs of specific disciplines. At the CUNY Law School, Writing Fellows helped create and staff the Writing Center and work with post-baccalaureate professional students in presenting legal writing. LaGuardia Community College works extensively with electronic (e-) portfolios and quantitative writing assessment. Most programs engage in WAC research. Of particular interest to compositionists is the work done at Medgar Evers College. Drawing on James Britton's seminal The Development of Writing Abilities, Medgar Evers undertook a full-year research survey of writing at the college resulting in "WAC: A College Snapshot," in Urban Education, January, 2003. The CUNY site, http://www.cuny.edu/wac has links to all campus WAC sites as well as a report, Writing Across the Curriculum at CUNY: A Ten Year Review, which provides further programmatic details on WAC activities, WI requirements, and governance structures at each campus.

WAC AT HOSTOS COMMUNITY COLLEGE: STRENGTHENING UNDERGRADUATE WRITING PROFICIENCIES

Hostos Community College is an urban, bilingual college of 5,000 students established in 1968 to serve the needs of New York City's impoverished South Bronx community. Its mission is to provide educational opportunities for first and second-generation Hispanics, African Americans, and other New York City residents who have encountered significant barriers to education. Its student population is diverse and poor, with the largest numbers coming from the Dominican Republic, Puerto Rico, and Central and South America. Nearly 99% receive some form of financial aid. In addition to offering a rich liberal arts curriculum and career programs, Hostos, as the university's only bilingual college, permits English-language learners to enroll in Spanish-language college-level courses as they gain proficiency in English. Fifty-five percent of freshmen require developmental composition and 43% require developmental reading courses, thus posing particular challenges for a college implementing a WAC program.

While the college attracts many students to its two-year terminal-degree career programs, the majority plan on transferring to a four-year institution. Campus writing efforts focus on developing student ability to read and write proficiently in a variety of disciplines and genres including the changing forms of twenty-first century literacies such as blogs, wikis, and social networking sites. The College seeks to validate and draw on the diverse languages and dialects spoken by its students, including English-language learners (ELLs), students speaking Black Vernacular English (BVE), and Generation 1.5 language-learners. Recognizing that students must be adept in standard academic English if they are to succeed, the WAC program works with faculty to seek ways to reconcile students' language strengths and deficits. In accordance with its bilingual mission, the WAC Initiative also reaches out to faculty teaching courses in Spanish, so that these faculty are part of the campus-wide process of developing effective teaching practices, and so that students in these classes can further their Spanish-language writing skills and utilize principles of "writing-to-learn."

Writing at Hostos

The Hostos WAC Initiative reflects the university-wide philosophy that writing ability can only be developed through extensive writing practice across a broad range of academic experiences and that writing itself is a way of enhancing student comprehension of course material. WAC is situated throughout the college, encompassing developmental programs, ESL, liberal arts, the allied health professions, and dual degree Programs. Writing is encouraged at all levels of a student's academic experience: (1) generally throughout the curriculum, and (2) in specially designed "writing intensive" (WI) courses.

The development of WI courses that provide opportunities for both formal and informal writing has been a key component of WAC at Hostos. Students must complete two WI sections prior to graduation. (See http://www.hostos.cuny.edu/wac for a description of WI criteria and policies.) Having no such courses at the start of the University Initiative in 1999, the college currently offers 80 WI sections representing a wide range of disciplines and levels. Unlike senior colleges, which usually require that WI courses be upper-level, Hostos and some other community colleges permit students at the developmental English-level to enroll in selected WIs; these allow for early exposure to more complex writing tasks. Preferring to rely largely on full-time faculty, each department and academic program offers WI sections taught by the faculty who created them. WI sections are deemed highly valuable for their introduction to WID and for providing greater assurance that faculty are prepared to deal with WAC issues such as "covering the curriculum," "handling the paper load," and balancing the writing/multiple-choice testing requirements of accreditation agencies.

Yet from the outset the program's philosophy has been that students are best served when writing is not compartmentalized into WI sections and that opportunities for writing should be prevalent in all course offerings. The WAC Initiative encourages all faculty to collaborate with Writing Fellows to embed writing and reading into course work.

The amount and type of student writing varies by discipline. Along with electives, the English Department offers courses in developmental writing and freshman composition, and through collaboration with WAC is exploring ways of refining these courses to provide foundations for writing in other disciplines. Students are expected to write not only essays and research papers; through WI sections in certain disciplines they are exposed to such genres as lab reports in the sciences, lesson plans and observations in early childhood education, field reports and interviews in psychology and sociology, theater reviews in drama, and case studies in business and nursing. In addition, students may keep journals or logs and engage in other informal, non-graded writing activities.

As on most CUNY campuses, much of the success of developing WI sections, as well as incorporating WAC principles and practices, is the result of close collaborations between faculty and Writing Fellows. Hostos Writing Fellow responsibilities reflect the many seamless, and oftentimes unforeseen, ways in which Writing Fellows support the growth of student literacies and faculty receptiveness to changing pedagogies. Their influence extends beyond their work with individual faculty and reaches into areas including program assessment, workshops for students and faculty, and podcasts and library workshops on topics such as the research paper and avoiding plagiarism

A strength of any program is its ability to accommodate shifting priorities. The recognition of the pedagogical connections between reading and writing led to the Initiative's evolution from a Writing Across the Curriculum project to one that encompasses reading as well. As a result, in 2005 the program took on the in-house title of Writing and Reading Across the Curriculum (WRAC), resulting in even-greater curricular revisions.

Over the past ten years, the Hostos WAC project has sought to connect writing and reading with teaching and learning, and to develop a cadre of faculty from a variety of disciplines who are familiar and comfortable with principles of language-across-the-curriculum. Yet it came as no surprise that with the university's emphasis on high-stakes testing for exit from remediation, English Department faculty initially felt the greatest responsibility for improving student writing.

Faculty attitudes began to shift dramatically with the creation of the CUNY Proficiency Exam (CPE) in 2001. Its mandate as a community college graduation requirement (or movement from General Education to the major in the senior colleges) resulted in campus-wide recognition that the exam's emphasis on reading and writing across disciplines reflected sound pedagogical practice—

and that all departments were accountable for student success. Though the CPE was discontinued by the university's Board of Trustees in November 2010, the notion of broad faculty responsibility for student writing frames much of our work. The implications of the removal of this exam are yet to be determined.

At Hostos, funding for WAC activities derives from the college's allocation of the university's budget for Coordinated Undergraduate Education (CUE). Though funding for WAC is mandated in principle by CUE, each college may now determine the actual amounts given to WAC programs. In the face of city and state budget crises, the college's CUE allocation continues to diminish—including funding for WAC. Class size for WI sections, originally capped at 25, grows each semester with 27-28 students the current norm. The college provides funding for stipends for faculty engaged in WAC work (which have decreased from an average of $1,500-2,000 for a year's work to $500-1,000), for professional development and reassigned time for the two WAC Coordinators. The two-course WI requirement for graduation remains in effect, with waivers requiring approval by the WAC Coordinators. Administrative support is also reflected in support for campus-wide WAC activities such as Hostos involvement in National Council of Teachers of English (NCTE) National Day on Writing in 2009 and 2010, events which drew huge campus participation. (See http://www.hostos.cuny.edu/wac or YouTube for a video on our "Walls of Writing.")

AGENT FOR CHANGE

After a decade, the WAC Initiative has become increasingly integrated into the life of the college, fostering campus-wide dialogues on writing/reading and learning and becoming an agent for change as it encourages teachers to reflect upon their teaching practices and reshape pedagogies. The success and growth of the Initiative may be traced to its ever expanding role in strengthening undergraduate education by working closely with other college programs.

The English Department and the Department of Language and Cognition hold frequent course-level meetings to discuss student literacies and work closely with the Writing Center (WC). Writing Fellows often attend these meetings to provide an interdisciplinary perspective. Through WAC collaboration, plans are underway to provide greater integration of the WC with courses throughout the curriculum, and Fellows are providing workshops for WC tutors in elements of WID. Overall, the WAC Initiative encourages frequent dialogue among faculty to explore ways of fostering student growth as writers and readers by: (1) offering regularly scheduled professional development workshops throughout the academic year (on topics similar to those described at Hunter below) including ones for junior, adjunct, and evening faculty; (2) meeting with the WAC Advisory Committee composed of Department Chairs to determine WAC policies; (3) over-seeing the ad-hoc WI faculty Task-Force, which meets with colleagues who have designed WI syllabi to review and recommend them for WI designation; and (4) joining faculty in presenting WI syllabi to the college-wide Curriculum Committee for official WI designation. All of these avenues have resulted in conversations about writing that move beyond the English Department and beyond complaints about student writing to more fruitful discussions about effectively addressing these concerns.

VISION AND REVISION

In reviewing the past ten years of WAC at Hostos, there are moments of pride and also dismay. We have learned a great deal about what makes a successful WAC Initiative. Foremost is faculty support. Our model has been bottom-up and relies on working with interested faculty, an ever-widening circle over the decade. The WI requirement is viewed as an enrollment booster for WI classes; this results in greater faculty participation. We have created structures to institutionalize our work, including the WAC Advisory Committee and our insistence on going through college governance procedures on policies such as the conceptual frameworks of WIs and the graduation requirement. The congeniality of the WI Task-Force provides an environment conducive to open discussion of pedagogy and has led to much thoughtful conversation and assignment revision. Our experience indicates that many faculty are no more enthused than students about revising their work, and they benefit greatly from this non-judgmental opportunity to present their work to interested colleagues.

In addition to providing numerous avenues for faculty input and dialogue, the Hostos WAC Initiative also owes much of its success to its high visibility on campus through its integration with numerous campus agencies and initiatives including General Education, freshman composition, the library, workshops for mandated CUNY exams, professional development, the Writing Center, Freshman Academies, and College Now, a program for high school students taking college courses. In addition, publicizing our work through our website, videos, podcasts, manuals, and a newsletter, "From the Writing Desk," have contributed to the program's strength and viability.

The project also undertakes yearly formative and summative assessments by distributing and analyzing qualitative survey instruments to students and faculty and triangulating these with Writing Fellow assessments. These findings, shared with faculty and administrators, consistently reveal high satisfaction and perceived improvements in student writing as a result of enrollment in WI sections. The higher CPE pass rates for those taking WI sections have also provided quantitative support for the Initiative. All of these factors have resulted in college-wide authority and support for our work and have enabled us to avoid the "WAC-police" label too often assigned to WAC programs.

Growing Pains

Our great success with WI sections over the past ten years reminds us of the need to insure their vitality. Though faculty must attend professional development sessions and collaborate with a Writing Fellow for a section to receive WI designation, it is not easy to determine what happens over time as faculty teach the same WI year after year. Many CUNY campuses are grappling with how to maintain the integrity of these sections and insure that they still reflect WAC principles and practices such as opportunity for revision and informal "writing-to-learn" activities. Changes in pedagogy are hard-won, and student assessments indicate that in some WI sections there is not that much writing after all—with some faculty reverting to non-scaffolded, plagiarism prone, end-of-semester research papers as the primary writing activity. The WAC Coordinators are currently consulting with Chairs and Coordinators, the WAC Advisory Committee, and WI faculty to institute procedures to monitor the implementation of these sections over a period of time. Any recommendations will reflect broad faculty input and will go through college governance procedures. In this way we continue to insure that new requirements are faculty generated rather than imposed top-down and that the WAC Initiative maintains the faculty support crucial to its success.

With high pass rates on the university's CPE and ever-improving scores on the ACT reading and writing exams needed to exit remediation, the college would seem poised to have achieved many of its goals regarding student writing. There is a campus culture that acknowledges the value of writing and reading across the curriculum, as well as qualitative and quantitative measures demonstrating faculty and student satisfaction with WI sections. There are also increased opportunities for reading and writing in non-WI sections. Professional development sessions are well-attended, and campus participation in WAC events is broad and enthusiastic. Yet it would be impossible to conclude that our work is completed and that we are satisfied with student writing/reading proficiencies. Inexperienced readers and writers, our students still demonstrate a lack of ease and expertise in accessing difficult texts and demonstrating their comprehension and knowledge through writing. As our section on Hunter College indicates, student proficiency issues are by no means fully resolved upon admission to the four-year college. Upon transfer, many still struggle with senior college coursework and its greater expectations of writing and reading proficiencies. We have made great strides and have laid the foundation for a vast overhaul in how the teaching of writing is conceived and practiced at Hostos, but our work has only just begun.

WAC AT HUNTER COLLEGE

On every CUNY campus, in every WAC program, there are impressive examples of Fellows' success in managing this unique and challenging position and making a difference in the delivery of higher education's most prized outcomes: pedagogical and curriciular change, and student success. The exemplary successes of the WAC program at Hunter (http://rwc.hunter.cuny.edu/wac/index.html), one of CUNY's senior colleges, are due primarily to the Writing Fellows.

Hunter College, located in three campuses in Manhattan, is the largest college in the City University system, drawing over 21,000 students from all five of the city's boroughs and beyond. The college is one of seven CUNY institutions offering undergraduate and graduate degrees; it houses professional schools of Education, Health Professions, Nursing, and Social Work, as well as research centers specializing in genetics, gerontology, and Puerto Rican studies.

Founded in 1870 and for much of its history a women's college, Hunter shares the City University's mission: to provide academic opportunities for all of the City's students. And it therefore shares the challenges of the country's major institutions of public higher education: maintaining standards of learning across a large and varied curriculum for a large and diverse student population, and maintaining standards of instruction among a large (in Hunter's case nearly 1,700) and varied faculty, a substantial percentage of whom are part-time staff. Since the majority of courses in Hunter's curriculum require writing from a student body that comes from well over a hundred different linguistic backgrounds and exhibits a wide range of fluency in the English language and experience in writing academic prose; and since the instructors of those courses are from dozens of disciplines, often with limited experience assigning and assessing student writing, and less experience analyzing those assignments and assessments, the challenges to our Writing Across the Curriculum program are, as at Hostos, unsurprisingly large, diverse, and daunting.

"Significant Writing"

Hunter College has had a WAC program since 2000, and required writing intensive courses—called "Significant Writing" courses—since 2003. While most CUNY campuses certify writing intensive courses or faculty, Hunter does not, and therefore cannot require faculty development. The Significant Writing, or "W" course, requirements legislated by the College Senate are minimal: at least 50% of the grade must be based on written work; writing due dates must allow for "faculty feedback" on student writing; Freshman Composition must be at least a co-requisite; and the course must be offered on a regular basis. Given these requirements and the historical role of departments at the college in determining curriculum, individual departments— often individual instructors—determine the content of and pedagogy practiced in W-designated courses. There is no interdisciplinary WAC Committee, and the program has no basis from which to claim any college-wide authority. One consequence of this policy is that there is no set cap for enrollment in "W" courses, and while the optimal number of students in a writing-intensive course is debatable, such courses at Hunter can have up to 90 students per instructor. And while most of the over 900 sections of the roughly 200 Significant Writing courses offered in a standard semester are taught by experienced staff, many are taught by new and often inexperienced instructors. It is not uncommon that, given registration and hiring deadlines, instructors are placed in "W" courses without a clear idea of what that designation means, or indeed that they are teaching a writing- intensive course. To say nothing of courses throughout the curriculum that require student writing though they are not W-designated.

The Usual Suspects

Under these circumstances, the WAC program at Hunter has, over its first ten years, offered instructors of all courses, particularly targeting "W" courses, a menu of services and professional development opportunities, including workshop series and brown-bag lunches on academic writing-related issues such as assignment design, rubric development, and managing sentence-level problems in student writing; a one-day college conference and a college-wide roundtable on Writing in the Disciplines; consultation with departments and individual instructors on departmental and course-related writing issues; in-class workshops on specific writing assignments in conjunction with the college's Reading/Writing Center, as well as supplemental in-Center workshops on disciplinary and assignment-specific adaptations of the academic writing process; participation in interdisciplinary focus groups and departmental consultation on program and course assessment; and orientations for students on disciplinary writing and for faculty on standardized writing tests, specifically the now discontinued CPE, and on the foundations of academic writing as presented in Expository Writing, the college's Freshman Composition course.

The program offers faculty stipends for participating in professional development events, but the hourly rates are limited, leading to the welcome participation by part-time instructors and a core of Hunter faculty dedicated to progressive pedagogy, who have by now become "the usual suspects." The incorporation of funding for WAC in the university's Coordinated Undergraduate Education (CUE) Initiatives budget and therefore in the college's CUE budget has led to other responsibilities and opportunities for Hunter's program. Since the inception of CUE, the WAC program has supported and participated in college initiatives, including a Learning Communities pilot in the Freshman Block program, an e-portfolio pilot in Freshman Composition, a study and proposal for reorganization of the General Education Requirement (GER), and a diagnostic essay and Reading/Writing Center referral pilot in GER gateway "W" courses in History and Political Science.

THE WRITING FELLOWS

But by far the most transforming and enduring effects on course and curriculum design, classroom pedagogy, and student learning are those attributable to the work of the CUNY Writing Fellows. As discussed earlier, Fellows' roles differ from campus to campus, but generally, at Hunter and elsewhere, they provide consultation on WAC best practices to faculty and, in some, cases, tutorial services to students. Three narratives from the Writing Fellows Program at Hunter College give ample evidence of the capacity and potency of this model.

In 2001, a Writing Fellow PhD candidate in American Literature was assigned, upon request, to the Urban Public Health (UPH) Department in the Hunter College School of Health Sciences. The Fellow, working with the Department's Community Health Education (COMHE) program, well outside his field of academic expertise, would make a profound change in that program's curriculum. Besides offering tutorial services, he introduced COMHE faculty to low-stakes writing assignments, e.g., responses to readings, weekly letters, article summaries/analyses, and reading logs, leading to changes in their syllabi, the incorporation of peer critiquing and library workshops on informational literacy skills in their classes, and the scaffolding of higher-stakes assignments. Impressed with the changes effected in their individual courses, the UPH faculty asked the Fellow in his second year to help organize a study of their students' writing, leading to the development of shared writing goals, a rubric, the norming, led by the Writing Fellow, of senior UPH faculty using the assessment model, and the scoring of sample papers. After the experience, and in consultation with the Fellow, UPH professors re-conceptualized the undergraduate course of study in the COMHE Program, ultimately adding a course with a focus on research to the required curriculum, which then offered a more comprehensive, progressive approach to writing in the discipline. So the outcome of working with a Writing Fellow for the Urban Public Health Department was not just the introduction of WAC pedagogy and course adaptation, but programmatic change.

Humanities 110: Map of Knowledge is one of the college's "jumbo" courses, with enrollments often over 200 students. As taught for the last decade by a professor in the Philosophy Department, the course focuses on current issues in social policy and academia, takes a debate structure, and includes a number of critical writing assignments. Through the efforts of four different Writing Fellows, the development of the course and its writing component over three-quarters of that decade is an example of the ongoing refinement and improvement possible in a pedagogical model, even for a "jumbo" course. The first Fellow, from CUNY's graduate English Department, helped the professor clarify the grading criteria for the written debate reports and present them clearly in the assignments, and introduced a syllabus-busting "mock debate" format, in which class time was dedicated to student debate on a topic, to model break-out debates among the rest of the class. The Fellow also led an in-class workshop based on the reports submitted in the mock debate to demonstrate the features and quality of writing required. After her two-year appointment, a second Fellow, from Urban Education, was assigned to work with the course. In her service as a Fellow, she helped refine the criteria for writing assessment through norming sessions among the course's teaching assistants and the development of a rubric based on the refinements; added a critique element as well as a revision process to the debate report assignment, with workshop and tutoring support adapted to the new assignment design; and aligned documentation requirements for the class's research paper with the style (MLA) required in Freshman Composition (which is often taught in tandem with sections of Humanities 110 in the college's Freshman Block Program). A third Fellow, studying Environmental Psychology, continued this work while loading all the information and support materials onto the newly-developed course website. The current Fellow, another Urban Education student, is piloting a model for integrating the course's writing component with the features and goals of Freshman Composition, creating a team-led interdisciplinary series of workshops for students taking both courses. In the eight years a Writing Fellow has been assigned to

Map of Knowledge, this large-enrollment course has become more student-centered and participatory, its assignments more process-oriented and supportive, its assessment models clearer and more consistently applied, the course itself more interdisciplinary and integrated into the curriculum.

In 2007, Hunter's department of Instructional Computing and Information Technology (ICIT) reorganized and in the process ceased being able to provide workshops in MLA documentation to Freshman Composition classes, a service they had offered for years. ICIT asked the college's Reading/Writing Center and the WAC Program to collaborate on an on-line MLA tutorial that could substitute for the discontinued workshops. A Writing Fellow from Psychology was recruited to the project, and quickly became its manager, creating most of the content, contributing to the design, consulting on the contractors hired for the software training and the staff hired to build the tutorial, and organizing what would become a collaboration unique in the history of the college, between ICIT, the Library, the WAC Program, and the Reading/Writing Center, with beta-testing by instructors of Freshman Composition in the English Department. The result is a tutorial that is hosted on the Library web site (http://library.hunter.cuny.edu/tutorials/mla/mla_tutorial.html), is on all Freshman Composition course management sites, has been accepted into the prestigious ALA/ACRL Instruction Section's Peer-Reviewed Instructional Materials Online (PRIMO) project, and has become a model for future college on-line development projects. Not only was the Fellow successful in creating a viable alternative to the ICIT MLA workshops, she was instrumental in the development of a nationally recognized on-line learning platform, one that is now linked to dozens of academic websites across the country, and in creating an interdisciplinary, interdepartmental collaboration uncommon in our powerfully departmental institution.

Without the Writing Fellows Program, Hunter's WAC Program would appear desultory in its successes, which, while not inconsiderable, occur discontinuously here and there throughout, as opposed to consistently across, the curriculum.

CONCLUSION

While Hunter and Hostos are representative of WAC at CUNY and portray the tensions inherent in reframing conversations about writing, they are not necessarily the definitive CUNY senior or community college WAC experience. Each CUNY campus has its own model—with varying degrees of faculty participation, administrative support, and student success.

A 2007 poll of CUNY WAC Coordinators identified a number of common challenges. Primary were budget-related issues including faculty stipends, reassigned time for coordinators, the loosening of WI enrollment caps, the reliance on part-time staff with little WAC experience, and the difficulty in offering enough courses for students to meet WI requirements. Other concerns centered on institutionalizing WAC. Almost all campuses have a WI graduation requirement, and most certify WAC faculty or courses. Yet WAC experience is not a major factor in tenure or promotion decisions, in effect de-incentivizing participation.

There are also potential obstacles to the continuity of WAC programs brought on by CUNY policy changes that might dilute the highly successful Writing Fellows program. Beginning in 2011, a Writing Fellow's time on campus decreases from two years to one. Considering the time it takes to educate Fellows about WAC/WID and prepare them for their complicated, sensitive work with faculty, this reduction of time threatens the quality of all CUNY WAC programs.

The growth and continuity of WAC at CUNY over the last decade was made possible by the considerable talent in the field, available at CUNY, by virtue of the university's size and its history as a leader in the development of writing instruction and, of course, CUNY funding. With many of CUNY's acknowledged experts in Rhetoric and Composition and WAC retiring or leaving the position of WAC Coordinator, will the next generation of WAC directors be able to sustain growth and preserve what has been achieved?

Though these challenges cloud the future, some offer opportunities: the advent of CUE has given WAC programs greater visibility and influence in the development of General Education programs and professional development. There is ample evidence that changes made in the curricular incorporation of writing, reading, and WAC pedagogy will endure. The greatest promise lies in the fact that coordinators of WAC programs at Baruch, Hostos, Brooklyn College, and the City College of New York, among others, are former Writing Fellows, and that another generation of CUNY WAC practitioners, mentored by the experienced leaders in the field who helped build WAC at CUNY, will proceed to mentor the next generation and take WAC best practice to its next stage of evolution both in CUNY and beyond.

REFERENCES

Hirsch, L., & Fabrizio, A. (2010). The writing fellow/faculty collaboration in a community college: Paradigms of teaching and learning across the curriculum. In J. Summerfield & C. Smith (Eds.), *Making teaching and learning matter: Transformative spaces in higher education* (pp.145-170). New York: Springer Publishing.

Lester, N., Bertram, C., Erickson, G., Lee, E., Tchako, A., Wiggins, K.D., & Wilson, J. (2003). WAC: A College Snapshot. *Urban Education, 38,* 5-34, doi:10.1177/0042085902238684

CHAPTER 39.
WRITING AT UC DAVIS: WRITING IN DISCIPLINES AND PROFESSIONS FROM THE UNDERGRADUATE FIRST YEAR THROUGH GRADUATE SCHOOL

By Chris Thaiss and Gary Goodman
University of California, Davis (US)

Writing at this public research university—the largest among the ten campuses of the University of California—is taught in ways that reflect the university's "land-grant" mission. Our academic writing courses and writing-support activities serve tertiary and post-graduate students from more than 100 disciplines and from highly-diverse language and cultural backgrounds. While this profile describes ways that most academic departments contribute to our students' writing development, we pay particular attention to the several roles, some long-established and some new, of the University Writing Program (UWP), an independent department devoted to academic writing across disciplines and professions. We illustrate how UC Davis has re-interpreted the US model of "general education" to spread attention to student writing not only across disciplines but also vertically throughout the tertiary years and into services for PhD students from the humanities, social sciences, natural sciences, engineering, and agriculture. A PhD research emphasis in writing studies is also described, as is the Writing Minor for baccalaureate students.

The University of California goes back to the early years of the new state on the US Pacific coast. California became a state in 1850, just two years after the discovery of gold in the foothills of the Sierra Nevada had lured people from the eastern states and around the world to this rugged land. The closest port to the gold fields became in a few years a thriving city, San Francisco, with sudden pretensions to East Coast and European culture.

Just across San Francisco Bay, in the town of Berkeley, the University of California was launched in 1868, seen by civic leaders as an essential part of this cultural rise and by the US government as California's "land-grant" university. An essential part of the land-grant university's mission in the nineteenth century was to train new generations of agriculturists in the latest technologies and to redefine higher education as both "practical" and "classical," hence open to a broader swath of society than had had access to the older colleges on the East Coast in the US. Since California's richest agricultural lands lay across the coastal mountains from Berkeley, the state government was eventually convinced to establish a "University Farm" in the 500-mile-long Central Valley, the farming and ranching heart of the state (Scheuring, 2001, p. 20).

Thus came into being in 1906 the tiny branch of the University that would become the University of California (UC) at Davis, now in 2012 the largest of the ten campuses of the UC system. UC Davis, with more than 33,000 undergraduate, graduate, and professional students, offers more than 100 baccalaureate degrees, more than 80 PhD degrees, and degrees in law, medicine, veterinary medicine, and business management. The majority of students concentrate in the life and physical sciences, agriculture, and engineering, but robust baccalaureate and doctoral degree programs also flourish in the arts, humanities, and social sciences.

WHAT WRITING AND LITERACY MEAN AT UC DAVIS

Understanding the place of writing at UC Davis begins with acknowledging three factors:
1. the emphasis of the campus on a wide variety of tertiary degree and graduate programs, and how this variety has been interpreted in terms of "core literacies" to be achieved by all undergraduate students (as described later in this profile);
2. the American model of undergraduate studies, with "general education" a prime component; and
3. the cultural and linguistic diversity of the university, with more than 50% of all students coming from homes where English is not the first language—though the great majority of these students were born in California (Ferris & Thaiss, 2011). This diversity reflects not only the Spanish-speaking heritage of California, but also the waves of immigration over 150 years from the Pacific Rim nations, from the rest of the US, and from many other cultures across the continents.

University of California, Davis (US)

WHO CARES ABOUT STUDENT WRITING AT UC DAVIS?

US News and World Report, a public affairs magazine with international circulation, publishes annually "America's Best Colleges," a guide for prospective college students. Among its many categories for ranking US colleges and universities is "Writing in the Disciplines": according to the journal, "These colleges typically make the writing process a priority at all levels of instruction and across the curriculum. Students are encouraged to produce and refine various forms of writing for different audiences in different disciplines."

Since 2007, UC Davis has been listed as one of only 20 or so institutions considered distinguished in this category, as voted by a broad cross-section of higher education administrators. The institutions in this short list represent small privately-funded colleges, large private universities, and large public universities such as UC Davis. How each of these institutions enacts this commitment differs. (See McLeod et al., 2001; Thaiss & Porter, 2010; and the WAC Clearinghouse for examples of this variety.) In the case of UC Davis, the idea of "care" for student writing means a multi-stage curriculum and tutorial opportunities serving all students, from newly-admitted undergraduates to doctoral students writing dissertations.

Some of these courses and services are specifically for students whose first language is not English and are intended to help students achieve academic English proficiency. Other courses and services are specifically for graduate students, and these services focus on genres—journal articles, qualifying papers, dissertations—central to doctoral education. The largest portion of courses and services are open to all undergraduate students across all disciplines. Indeed, all undergraduate students are required to complete several courses devoted to text types and genres of academic writing. These various courses and services are outlined below.

In short, "care" for student writing is a cross-disciplinary commitment, with several offices and one academic department focused on this commitment, but with research and teaching faculty from many disciplines consciously developing student fluency, practice in writing processes, and genre literacy.

WHERE AND WHAT STUDENTS WRITE AT UC DAVIS—REQUIREMENTS, OPTIONS, DISCIPLINES, GENRES

This profile will describe requirements, programs, and services that have been tentatively begun, then grown and changed over thirty years. We look at these in terms of local and national contexts, changes in character and scope,

457

and ongoing challenges. Brevity allows only minimal analysis; we include links to sources that we hope will give a fuller picture. We will close by describing one of our most recent new programs, the Writing Minor.

ADMISSIONS TESTING FOR ACADEMIC WRITING IN ENGLISH

Applications for undergraduate admission to all branches of the UC are accepted from the top 12 1/2% of graduates of California secondary schools and from qualified students from outside the state and the US For over 100 years, most admitted students, despite their high academic standing in the secondary schools, have been required to take the Analytical Writing Placement Examination (AWPE), a timed essay examination used to determine placement in the appropriate first-year course dedicated to building awareness of and strategies to accomplish university-level writing. Each campus determines this configuration of courses differently, but all make distinctions based on AWPE scores. Leonard (2011) has written the most comprehensive history of the growth and changes in how this state requirement has been applied at UC Davis.

The range of placements is complex: the highest level of exam scorers (about 60%) may choose a course from several that introduce them to genre expectations either across disciplines or more focused on specific academic writing tasks, such as analysis of literary texts. The most popular of these courses is the introduction to academic writing across disciplines (UWP 1) offered by the University Writing Program, the autonomous department dedicated to teaching and scholarship in composition and rhetoric. The second level of AWPE scorers (about 30 %) is placed in a course that does not receive academic credit and is therefore considered remedial. This course is not taught by UC Davis faculty or graduate students, but is outsourced to another institution, Sacramento City Community College. These students must satisfactorily complete the non-credit course before being admitted to UWP 1 and similar courses. A third group of AWPE scorers (about 10%) are non-native speakers of English whose language skills are considered not yet adequate for the higher two levels. Each of these students is placed into one of three sequenced courses (all bearing academic credit) taught by ESL specialists in the Linguistics Department. Thus, a student placed into this developmental sequence may take as many as four ten-week courses before being eligible for the first-year academic writing course, such as UWP 1.

Because of budget restructuring in the current economic recession, this multi-step curriculum for the lowest group of AWPE scorers—now in place for more than 20 years—is being reconsidered. One possible proposal would bring the entire curriculum under the management of the University Writing

Program, so that placement and teaching could be coordinated and curriculum revision made easier.

THE REQUIRED FIRST-YEAR WRITING COURSE (E.G. UWP 1)

Typical of tertiary education in the US for more than a century (see, e.g., Brereton, 1996) is some form of mandatory first-year course (or courses) in academic writing, the primary goal of this course to prepare students for the assignments they are likely to receive in their major disciplines and in elective courses outside the major. Indeed, so common is such a course that the US Council of Writing Program Administrators (CWPA) has published a widely-used list of "student outcomes" for first-year writing, including objectives in five categories: Rhetorical Knowledge; Critical Thinking, Reading, and Writing; Writing Processes; Knowledge of Conventions; and Composing in Electronic Environments (http://www.wpacouncil.org/positions/outcomes.html). Because the common US model of undergraduate education dictates that prospective students apply to the university, not to a department or a faculty, such "general education" courses usually are populated by students representing a broad variety of degree programs, from the arts and humanities to the sciences and engineering.

Hence, assignments in these courses often give students freedom in choice of subject, but evaluate student writers on academic criteria that cross disciplinary boundaries. For example, one outcome from the CWPA list is to "understand a writing assignment as a series of tasks, including finding, evaluating, analyzing, and synthesizing appropriate primary and secondary sources." The typical US first-year writing course, including UWP 1 at UC Davis, expects students to learn these critical processes as they apply them to a range of topics that will differ by discipline and student interest.

REQUIRED WRITING IN THE UPPER DIVISION

However, where writing at UC Davis differs from typical US structure is in the portion of the general education writing requirement for the "upper division" (third-year students and above). The great majority of US universities place required general education writing courses in the first year only. At Davis and a growing number of other universities, this requirement is split between the first year and either the second or a later year (see Shamoon et al, 2000; Thaiss & Porter, 2010). When configured this way, the goals of the two levels differ. As we have theorized the difference here at UC Davis, the first-year course acclimates the student to university-level writing in general, while the upper-level course, taught in various versions, (1) focuses on discipline-specific genres and ways of thinking that students experience in their majors and (2) prepares students for rhetorical and genre expectations they are likely to encounter beyond graduation—in post-graduate education and professions. The high regard in which most students hold these courses, as expressed in course evaluations, reflects the importance to students of this dual aim.

In the upper division at UC Davis, students select from a broad and growing list of courses "in the disciplines and professions" (http://writing.ucdavis.edu/about-uwp/about/): to name a few, writing in science, writing in the health professions, writing for engineers, business writing, professional and technical writing, writing in history, writing in human development, writing in film studies, and writing in legal studies, as well as introductory and advanced courses in journalism.

All of these courses are taught in the University Writing Program, by faculty hired, reviewed, and promoted by the program. That the Writing Program has its own faculty, most of whom (30+) are tenured in the program or on tenure-like continuing appointments, is another difference from all but a few other US institutions. In most colleges and universities, general education writing courses are housed in the English department. Although how the independence (2005) of the Writing Program at Davis came about is to some extent unique (see http://writing.ucdavis.edu/about-uwp), what the emergence of the autonomous program shares with that of other similar US departments is the university's recognition that (1) "composition and rhetoric" is a research field distinct from most research concerns of US English departments and (2) the teaching of writing is relevant to all disciplines in the university (see O'Neill, Crow, & Burton, 2002), hence worthy of autonomy from any other single department.

The "Writing Experience" Requirement and WID Staff Development

"General education" at UC Davis, as at more than 400 other US institutions (Thaiss & Porter, 2010) also requires that undergraduate students complete a small number of courses, usually in their major degree programs, that demand a substantial amount of writing in appropriate academic genres—and that provide written feedback to student writers and the opportunity to revise for resubmission. Such courses, often labeled "writing intensive" or "writing emphasis" in the US, primarily focus on learning disciplinary content and methods, but writing is an important means of student thinking and expression in these courses (Townsend, 2001). At Davis, we use the term "writing experience" for such courses, and some 1,500 courses across more than 80 departments have been approved by cross-disciplinary committees to meet more stringent criteria beginning in 2011 (see http://ge.ucdavis.edu). Large lecture courses, advanced seminars, and senior "capstone" courses are all included as "writing experience" courses, as long as they meet the specified criteria for (1) number of graded words, (2) feedback on drafts and/or on scaffolded shorter assignments, and (3) the opportunity to revise. This breadth means that, in many departments, students are encountering process-based experience with disciplinary genres in lower-level, more advanced, and final-year courses in their fields.

The "writing experience" (WE) requirement, along with the required first-year and upper-division courses taught by the UWP, represents "literacy in words and images," one of the several "core literacies" that comprise the general education requirements for all UC Davis baccalaureate students (see http://ge.ucdavis.edu). The other core literacies include oral communication; visual literacy; scientific literacy; quantitative literacy; the "literacy" (critical understanding) of American history, culture, and governance; and the "literacy" of world cultures. Many of the courses that fulfill the WE requirement also fulfill one or more of the other core literacies (although each student may count a given course toward fulfilling only one of these core requirements; this rule means that students must take a number of courses across disciplines to meet the entire core).

Unlike teachers of the UWP first-year and upper-division courses, the faculty and graduate students who teach these "writing experience" (WE) courses in all those departments have not been formally trained in composition pedagogy. (In comparison, the graduate students who teach UWP 1 must complete two pedagogy seminars and be observed by program administrators in a later term.) What the many "writing experience" teachers have available to them are short-term workshops, consultation opportunities, and web-available materials, again offered by the UWP (http://writing.ucdavis.edu/programs-and-services/the-workshop-program) or by the university's Center for Excellence in Teaching and Learning (CETL: http://cetl.ucdavis.edu). While it would be ideal for all WE teachers to be certified for this pedagogy, the number of teachers far exceeds the resources of the UWP and CETL to reach them systematically, try as our UWP consulting faculty and the CETL staff do.

Writing Tutorials and Workshops at the Student Academic Success Center

All undergraduate students can also call on the tutoring services of the Student Academic Success Center (SASC) (http://lsc.ucdavis.edu/writing.html).

The full-time professional tutors and many trained undergraduate peer tutors review drafts of assigned writing from any UC Davis discipline for such features as focus, organization, coherence of argument, and English syntax and punctuation. Congruent with writing center tutorial philosophy in the US, the function of the tutor is to converse with the student about the draft so that the tutor can offer suggestions for improvement (Geller, Eodice, Condon, Carroll, & Boquet, 2006). In 2010-11, the UC Davis writing center gave almost 10,000 tutorial sessions to students from more than 100 degree programs.

The SASC also offers hour-long workshops for groups of students preparing for certain high-stakes essay examinations (e.g., for the L2 courses in Linguistics) and on other general topics of writing proficiency. Workshops for English L2 students are frequent.

Tutoring and Workshops for Graduate Students

Since the SASC focuses its tutorials and workshops on the 25,000 UC Davis undergraduates, similar services for graduate students across disciplines have become a further interest of the University Writing Program, in cooperation with the Office of Graduate Studies (OGS). Over the past eight years, gradually more of the time spent by the UWP on training opportunities for faculty to assign and "care for" the writing in their classes, as well as on services to the students themselves, has been given to the graduate level. To illustrate, the fall 2010 schedule of UWP/OGS workshops included (http://iccweb.ucdavis.edu/graduates/pds):

- Writing Scientific Papers
- Writing a Curriculum Vitae
- Revising and Organizing for Grad Students & Postdocs
- Overcoming Writer's Block
- Enhancing Your Use of Endnote
- Grammar and Sentence Crafting
- Writing a Research Statement in the Sciences & Engineering: Academic Job Search Series
- Articulating Your Research in the Humanities & Social Sciences: Academic Job Search Series
- Dissertation Writing Workshop and Retreat
- Grant Writing in the Sciences

Since 2007, the UWP has also staffed a Grad Writing Fellows tutoring service with PhD students trained in writing pedagogy. This service began with volunteers who had worked in writing centers at other universities; in 2009, the OGS began to provide funding for the tutors and in 2010 a permanent workspace. That tutorial services for graduate students across disciplines are far more recent at UC Davis than those for undergraduates reflects the (1) long-time acceptance by US tertiary education of responsibility for literacy development by undergraduates (e.g., Russell, 2002), (2) the scope and expense of undergraduate operations, and (3) only gradual realization by US graduate schools that lack of such assistance has kept retention and degree completion rates at disappointing levels.

TOWARD FULFILLING FURTHER AMBITIONS: THE PHD "DESIGNATED EMPHASIS" AND THE WRITING MINOR

Over the past three decades, close to one hundred US universities have developed PhD specialties in composition/rhetoric. Most of these programs are attached to English departments, given the historical placement of required English composition courses in these departments, as noted earlier. Some of the existing PhD specialties are free-standing programs that draw students from a number of disciplines. An annual issue of the journal *Rhetoric Review* provides descriptions of the various programs and their locations within institutions.

At UC Davis, the PhD "designated emphasis in Writing, Rhetoric, and Composition Studies" (WRaCS) was conceived in 2006, approved by the Graduate Council in 2008, and first offered to students that same year, with five to eight new students per year. Current students' research focuses in such areas as WAC/WID program design, writing placement theory and practice in higher education, adolescent literacy development, L2 writing methodology, and cultural rhetorics. Administered by the UWP, the designated emphasis has more than thirty affiliated faculty, from the faculties of Education, Linguistics, English, Cultural Studies, Techno-cultural and Film Studies, Performance Studies, and Spanish, as well as the UWP (http://wracs.ucdavis.edu).

Establishing an independent UWP also allowed the development of an undergraduate minor in writing, which began in 2009 (http://writing.ucdavis.edu/programs-and-services/uwp_writing_minor). Within the first year, more than 50 students graduated with the credential and 100 more declared their intentions to complete the minor. By the end of 2011, more than 150 students had completed the Minor. Like all minors at UC Davis, this minor allows students to concentrate study (20 units or five courses) outside their major; writing minors earn a credential that shows their concentrated work in writing. While the most common majors represented among our minoring students are Communication and English, many minors come from Political Science, International Relations, Psychology, Sociology, and various sciences.

The writing minor gives students advanced instruction and opportunities for practical experience. Students learn diverse genres in disciplines and professions; they learn to modify styles for varied audiences and formats. All courses for the minor are "upper division," although students also take the prerequisites for those courses. The curriculum includes four areas: writing in academic settings; writing in the professions; history, theory and design; and a writing-intensive internship outside the academy.

Many students choose internships in journalism: as reporters and editors of the student newspaper, *The California Aggie*, or for *UC Magazine*, local newspapers, radio and television stations, print magazines, and online publications. Internships in marketing and public relations are common, including work for University Communications and other campus organizations, for local visitors' bureaus, for local businesses and wineries.

Some enterprising students have gained writing experience in other professions through their internships: research and writing for law firms or district attorneys' offices, technical writing and editing, writing for political offices or campaigns, or grant-writing for the university, for specific scientific research projects, or for non-profit organizations.

While many students in the minor already have excellent writing skills, a significant number have chosen the minor because English is their second language or because they consider their writing poor.

> I never considered myself a writer. I did the minor because I knew writing was one of my weakest skills. Now I don't feel like that. I know how to write various forms, such as press releases. I never thought I had a strong grammar background, but this is an area in which I've also seen improvement. I believe this is because I was put in charge of editing the writing of others. I feel able to write on the job when I leave UC Davis. *Justin Chu, Nutrition major*

Because of the range of upper division courses in the disciplines and professions, students use the writing minor to prepare for careers in journalism, public relations, marketing, technical writing, editing, grant writing, and public policy analysis. Certification of the minor on students' transcripts establishes their credentials for writing-intensive jobs immediately after graduation, in non-profit organizations, businesses, and other fields.

> The minor is perfect toward preparing me for my dream

career as a book editor or publisher. To have the Writing Minor started during my second year seemed like a miracle, as it involves internships and certification of writing expertise, which I will definitely need as an advantage. *Elizabeth Orfin, English major*

The minor also enhances critical thinking skills and writing proficiency required for success in postgraduate programs and professional schools.

Writing is an essential skill in science. I think how you convey your research, your findings, and your observations greatly determines how professional you are. *Tacita Vu, Biological Science*

My writing has improved significantly. Critical and analytical writing not only helps you better convey your ideas to an outside population, but also trains your mind to be more analytical. *Enkhee Tuvshintogs, Biochemistry and Molecular Biology major*

CHALLENGES

As this profile shows, UC Davis's commitment to student writing and to research in this interdisciplinary field has grown over many years, with dramatic steps, such as creation of the independent UWP, to enhance its range and help ensure its future. Ambitions remain: e.g., for the Writing Minor to be built into a major degree program, for the PhD "designated emphasis" to become a free-standing degree, for funding to lower class sizes in required courses and workloads in "writing experience" courses. The main threat to this future, as in most places profiled in this book, is the ongoing financial crisis, which has forced a dramatic decline in public support and huge rises in student fees. In the midst of this crisis, the many cooperating faculty and staff across disciplines at Davis have maintained their imaginative devotion to student learning. Sustaining this ambition despite fewer resources will be our continuing challenge. However, as the student comments above illustrate, maintaining that commitment to growth in student writing and critical thinking will produce the next generation of thinkers and communicators to productively confront and, we hope, resolve crisis.

REFERENCES

Brereton, J. (1996). *The origins of composition studies in the American college, 1875-1925: A documentary history.* Pittsburgh: University of Pittsburgh Press.

Ferris, D., & Thaiss, C. (2011). Writing at UC Davis: Addressing the needs of second language writers. *Across the Disciplines* (special issue on WAC and 2nd Language Writers). Retrieved from http://wac.colostate.edu/atd/special.cfm

Geller, A., Eodice, M., Condon, F., Carroll, M., & Boquet, E. (2006). *Everyday writing center: A community of practice.* Logan, UT: Utah State University Press.

Leonard, D. (2011). Why we teach "ESL writing": A socio-historic discussion of an undergraduate ESL program. (Unpublished doctoral dissertation.) Davis, California: University of California, Davis.

McLeod, S., Miraglia, E., Soven, M., & Thaiss, C. (Eds.). (2001). *WAC for the new millennium: Strategies for continuing writing-across-the curriculum programs.* Urbana, Illinois: National Council of Teachers of English.

O'Neill, P., Crow, A., & Burton, L. (Eds.). (2002). *Fields of dreams: Independent writing programs and the future of composition studies.* Logan, UT: Utah State University Press.

Russell, D. (2002). *Writing in the academic disciplines: A curricular history.* Carbondale, IL: Southern Illinois University Press.

Scheuring, A. (2001). *Abundant harvest: The history of the University of California, Davis.* Oakland, CA: Regents of the University of California.

Shamoon, L., Howard, R., & Jamieson, S. (Eds.). (2000). *Coming of age: The advanced writing curriculum.* Portsmouth, NH: Boynton/Cook/Heinemann.

Thaiss, C., & Porter, T. (2010). The state of WAC/WID in 2010: Methods and results of the US survey of the International WAC/WID Mapping Project. *College Composition and Communication 61*(3), 534-70.

Townsend, M. (2001). Writing-intensive courses and WAC. In McLeod et al. (Eds.), *WAC for the new millennium: Strategies for continuing writing-across-the curriculum programs* (pp. 233-58). Urbana, Illinois: NCTE

WAC Clearinghouse. (n.d.). *WAC Clearinghouse.* Colorado State University. Retrieved from http://wac.colostate.edu

Writing in the Disciplines. (2011). America's best colleges 2012 issue. *US News and World Report.* Retrieved from http://colleges.usnews.rankingsandreviews.com/best-colleges/writing-programs

CHAPTER 40.
SECTION ESSAY: ACADEMIC LITERACY DEVELOPMENT

By Gerd Bräuer
University of Education, Freiburg (Germany)

This section essay provides an overview of the landscape of academic writing centers, writing programs, and writing initiatives in the German-speaking countries (Austria, Germany, Liechtenstein, Switzerland). The author sheds light onto some of the major motivations—on both individual and institutional levels—for the emergence of writing support in higher education and uncovers several tendencies in writing center work that seem to trigger institutional change with regard to writing. Peer learning, one of the major features of US-writing pedagogy, seems to have become a vital concept also in the German-speaking countries. Peer learning, especially as part of writing center work, is functioning as a strong catalyst for sustainable institutional and curricular development, leading not only to a change of individual writing practices but also to a redefining of the role of writing and maybe even to alternative writing cultures within institutions of higher learning.

The territory of the German-speaking countries I will be talking about in this section essay is about the same size as California.[1] It is the area that I traveled a lot over the past decade in order to participate in projects, conferences, and workshops. You can take a comfortable night train from the writing center at the University of Education in Zurich (Switzerland), in the south-western area of this geographic territory, to the writing center at the Europe University Viadrina in Frankfurt/Oder in Germany (not to be confused with the well-known airport hub Frankfurt/Main), located near the border to Poland, in the north-eastern corner of this international conglomerate of writing centers, writing programs, and other bold initiatives to support academic writing and writers in higher education.

I say bold here to indicate that this work has involved struggle against many obstacles at least since 1993, when the first European university writing center began its work in Bielefeld (Germany). Even in 2001, when I helped to set up the first writing center in European teacher education in Freiburg (Germany), I had to handle opinions among teaching faculty like the one that I received one day by email: "Dear colleague, it is wonderful to see what you do for our weakest students, but—please, please! —don't make this college look like a gathering place for fools. Many of our students CAN write and do it quite well and, therefore, don't need your support. All the others I'd rather see leave this university the sooner the better!"

Of course, all these students can write—some better than others—but everybody needs feedback and the challenge to revise. Luckily, opinions like the one just mentioned didn't hinder people in their efforts to progress to the present, where we find ourselves working in 39 writing centers across Austria (1), Germany (32), Liechtenstein (1) and Switzerland (5), collaborating closely in local networks, such as the one in Berlin-Brandenburg (Germany); in national forums, such as "Forum Schreiben" (http://www.forum-schreiben.eu) in Switzerland; and within international organizations, first and foremost the European Association of the Teachers of Academic Writing (EATAW, established in 1999) and the European Writing Centers Association (EWCA, since 2003). Several of the most active members of this German-speaking community have served on the boards of these large professional organizations.

These close collaborations resulted in international projects and initiatives such as "Scriptorium" (http://www.scriptorium-project.org), a professional development program for literacy student-teachers and in-service teachers; the foundation of a bilingual (German/English) scientific journal, *Zeitschrift Schreiben* (http://www.zeitschrift-schreiben.eu); a yearly conference for student peer-tutors (including its own journal on tutoring writing, JoSCH , journal.der.schreibberatung@googlemail.com); and the development of an extensive research data basis (http://www.ipts.rwth-aachen.de/) that connects professionals internationally outside the German-speaking area (see also Niederau and Jakobs in this book). The scientific publications that resulted from this collaboration have grown substantially since the 1980s, and most of them can be found in the database just mentioned. The most recent collaborative text that circled for months among several writing centers, stirring up fruitful internal and external discussion, focused on the declaration of quality standards for the training of peer tutors. The topic of this collaboration—peer tutoring—isn't a surprise when considering that the short history of this academic literacy movement in the German-speaking area was largely spurred by writing centers and peer learning concepts.

PEER LEARNING FOSTERED BY WRITING CENTERS AS A KEY CONCEPT FOR THE ACADEMIC LITERACY SUPPORT MOVEMENT

When I started a training program for peer writing tutors in 2002 at the Freiburg Writing Center (Germany), my main goal was to convince the participants about the process character of writing and, as a pedagogical consequence, the need to teach process writing in order to give students a chance to grow as writers—instead of drilling them in applying knowledge about text genres to successful written discourse (Bräuer, 2002). To better achieve my intention, I constructed the course around my own beliefs, materials, and methods, asking the students simply to follow the program by answering my questions and working on my tasks. I simply didn't know it any better at that time.

In the same year (2002), I participated in a workshop organized by the Bielefeld University Writing Lab with Paula Gillespie (Gillespie & Lerner, 2000) and Harvey Kail (Kail & Trimbur, 2000), two well-known experts on peer tutoring. Peer tutoring stands in the tradition of Kenneth Bruffee's approach to collaborative learning (1984), with peer learning—learning from and with each other (Boud et al., 2001) —in the center of attention. The peer learning concept and the research on peer-assisted mentoring and tutoring approaches (Falchikov & Blythman, 2000; O'Donnell & King, 1999; Topping & Ehly, 2001) heavily influenced US-based writing center development.

The lesson I learned at the Bielefeld Writing Lab workshop with Kail and Gillespie was fundamental with regard to the Socratic teaching method I originally applied to my training program for peer writing tutors that I just mentioned above: based on Bruffee's work and concepts developed out of it, such as community of practice (Lave & Wenger, 1991) and community of learners (Rogoff, 1994), I changed the focus of the training by applying peer learning strategies and thus opportunities for the students to discuss their own beliefs, experience, and knowledge in order to collaboratively develop methods and materials for the tutoring of writers and writing. The result was a radical conceptual change of the training program toward social constructivist learning, with peer interaction in person and on the web (in blogs, forums, and wikis) at the core—with me as facilitator and organizer on the sidelines. In other words: I gave up the role of one pretending to have all the answers on this very personal quest toward becoming a peer writing tutor. When I look at what many of the graduates of my training program do today as professionals in the field of academic literacy and beyond, I perceive a substantial and sustainable impact of the concept of peer learning on the development of writing centers, writing programs, and initiatives across the German-speaking area.

Not surprisingly, I see many of these colleagues engaged in redefining the role of writing in higher education in the German-speaking area being involved in writing centers as a place with a specific potential for fostering peer learning as a mode of academic literacy development across colleges and universities. At least in the German-speaking countries, writing centers, in my view, efficiently suggest and implement alternative ways of learning and instruction because they are extra-curricular. Other than a teaching faculty, they are in daily contact with students through one-on-one tutoring, workshops, seminars and self-learning materials.

If writing centers make their work transparent toward the teaching faculty, they can have a silent but nevertheless powerful and long-lasting impact on teaching practices (see also Bräuer & Girgensohn in this book). The writing lab at Bielefeld University (Bielefeld), with its powerful connections to the Center for Teaching and Learning, the Center for Student Advising and Counseling, the Career Center, and an initiative named "Toward a new culture of studying and teaching," is in my view the most impressive example in the German-speaking area of writing centers' innovation toward institutional change.

In the following sections of the essay, I will sketch current tendencies in the development of academic literacy that show peer learning, as part of writing center work, as a catalyst for sustainable institutional and curricular development that can lead not only to a change of individual writing practices, but also to a change in the role of writing—and maybe even to alternative writing cultures within institutions. Let me first briefly define what I mean by "change."

DEFINING A FRAMEWORK FOR UNDERSTANDING CHANGE

Curricular development and institutional development often go hand in hand (e.g., Altrichter et al., 2007), but they are certainly not automatic steps. While curricular development focuses primarily on change in individual classroom practice, institutional development concerns changing larger structures far beyond the individual classroom. Sometimes, the quantity and quality of change in individual teaching can spur change in the overall culture of learning and instruction and, therefore, trigger institutional change. In this bottom-up development, the changes made on an individual level will be "codified" by the institution's administration. The individual change becomes part of the official documents of the institution and, as such, sustainable: the development that has happened cannot be eliminated just because the agenda of the people in power in an institution may change in the future.

The other main scenario in the interplay between curricular and institutional development is top-down: it starts with an incentive on the administrative level, often triggered by outside experts who combine research and professional practice. Supported by a concept for change and a steering group, the institution's administration asks members of the teaching faculty to apply (or further develop) the suggested documents and measures of change.

How are these scenarios relevant to the integration of academic literacy measures in institutions of higher education? For the European context, I envision a unique potential for writing centers to pick up on grassroots initiatives or initiate change on the individual level of instruction, to further analyze the needs of individual faculty and learners, and to contextualize these with the appropriate research findings. This process facilitates a proposal to be made to the administration to consider long-term and sustainable change either on a larger curricular level (e.g., for a department or discipline) or for cross-institutional measures. Let me illustrate the two strategies for change with an example from the integration of university-wide portfolio systems at the University of Education in Freiburg (bottom-up) and at the Technical University of Darmstadt (top-down), both located in Germany.

Portfolio work in Freiburg as a grassroots initiative of the two institutes of education and languages has a history of almost 10 years. From the beginning, the Freiburg writing center supported this initiative with research on writing as reflective practice, faculty training, workshops for students, and peer tutoring. Based on the rich experience from this facilitation process, in 2008 the writing center presented a concept to the university administration for the implementation of a campus-wide e-portfolio system that would engage students in reflective practice throughout college training and beyond, and provide a conceptual backbone for instruction that switched, as part of the so-called Bologna process, to a modularized and competence-based approach. A first step in acknowledging this "bottom-up" portfolio concept is being made by adapting exam guidelines of individual degree programs that were recently set up in German Studies and German as a Foreign/Second Language.

At the TU Darmstadt, the procedure followed a somewhat reversed track, "top-down": Due to existing institutional structures, embodied by a so-called "dual mode strategy" (blended learning) (Ballweg et al., 2011, p. 190), an existing portfolio on e-learning competencies at the university and long-term portfolio practice in the teaching profession in the state of Hessen (Germany), the university administration assigned a steering committee to develop and assess a competency portfolio that would be kept throughout the entire college career, include the above-mentioned portfolio on e-learning, and prepare students for using the portfolio in the profession. In order to put this project into practice, faculty will be supported to design appropriate task arrangements and to use the e-portfolio web application "Mahara." The steering committee hopes not only to implement portfolio work into individual classrooms but also to initiate sustainable institutional change by defining and applying an alternative role of writing in teacher training, here especially in the format of "writing to learn" through reflective practice.

In both Freiburg and Darmstadt, tendencies in institutional development can be witnessed that Altrichter (2012) calls "intentional and systematic," "directed on long-term and structured development," by which "mediation between heterogeneous goals and expectations" is being practiced slowly but intensely, to build change in the overall culture of learning and instruction, where the concept of peer learning as part of writing center work can be a powerful change agent.

LITERACY MANAGEMENT AS A TOOL FOR INSTITUTIONAL CHANGE:

How can institutional change be carried out in a planned, efficient way? Curricular and institutional change are both pressing and central needs in today's academy in order to deal in a productive way with the growing challenges of "multiliteracies," which originate in a "multiplicity of communication channels and increasing cultural and linguistic diversity" (Cazden, Cope, Fairclough, & Gee, 1996, p. 60). The existence of multiliteracies indicates the need of managing the interplay of these different literacies among the three stakeholders of higher education: the individual learner, the educational institution (including teaching faculty and administration), and the profession(s). In order to be able to manage literacy—which Cazden et al. (1996) understand as the ability to read, write, and distribute information beyond language—we have to be aware of the existing flow of information within defined structures of an institution and beyond, especially among the stakeholders with regard to a certain phenomenon of change (e.g., the implementation of portfolios). In more specific terms: in order to be successful in the development of academic literacy in higher education, we need to know how to optimize the way people deal with information, form and formulate intentions, and comprehend, process, and fulfill the intentions of others.

The main task for literacy managers, who I see as change agents in the discourse among the stakeholders mentioned above, would therefore be two-fold: to construct and strengthen synergy, understood as the collaboration of people and their ideas, structures, methods, and materials; to deconstruct and therefore reduce dysergy, understood as the collision of people and their ideas, structures, methods, and materials. This negotiating role can be played out much better by extra-curricular entities such as the writing center than by structures that are part of the institutional hierarchy and the ongoing power struggle within this hierarchy.

Again, what is needed in today's academy more than ever is the negotiation of a multiplicity of discourses in which individual learners, institutions of education, and the professions are engaged with literacy managers. I personally envision writing center people as most well-prepared for this role: to juggle the potential, demands, and challenges of the different literacies such as computer literacy, digital literacy, multimodal literacy, visual literacy, and critical literacy, in order to solve problems with efficient handling of information through individuals within the larger framework of their institution.

Literacy managers perform a complex range of tasks: (1) analyze the current state of both handling information in general and text production, distribution, and reception, including visual, audio, spatial, and behavioral aspects of forms of representation of meaning, within their home institution and beyond; (2) assess the quality of the latter processes and try to determine a price tag for any loss of information and/or understanding of texts in order to quantify the urgency of change; (3) identify the current needs of the main stakeholders with regard to in-house communication and the flow of information beyond; (4) develop concepts and prototypes for optimizing the management of literacies within the organization, (5) test and assess procedures, methods, materials, and training programs in order to further develop and successfully implement them; and (6) initiate necessary structural change within the institution and facilitate steering groups in this matter.

The following list of current tendencies in an academic literacy environment in the process of dramatic change will show concrete areas of work for literacy managers either positioned in the writing center or collaborating with the writing center as a true powerhouse for institutional change: redefining the role of writing and writers in the academy, especially, as can also be seen below, through different forms of peer learning.

TENDENCIES IN INSTITUTIONALIZED SUPPORT FOR ACADEMIC WRITERS IN THE GERMAN-SPEAKING AREA

TENDENCY 1: FACE-TO-FACE FACILITATION OF WRITERS

Supporting academic writers through one-on-one interaction is probably the most striking achievement of this very young writing pedagogy movement in

German-speaking higher education. It is no surprise that the two possibilities of face-to-face writing support, peer tutoring and faculty mentoring (coaching), are sometimes still seen as conflicting alternatives. In the late 1990s, the number of institutions favoring faculty-based writing consultations was much higher than the number focusing on peer-based feedback. I see two reasons for this: (1) Aside from the Freiburg Writing Center (Bräuer, 2002), there was no other concept for training peer writing tutors in practice in the German-speaking area. (2) Interest in developing training programs was quite low because academic writing was still seen mostly as a set of rules provided and guarded by the academy.

Today, the number of institutions seeking ways to set up peer-based writing support is growing rapidly, and a discussion of standards for writing tutor training has begun among the most active writing centers. Some universities (e.g., Bielefeld and Bochum) already offer systematic training for teaching faculty in key aspects of process writing so that process-based and learner-based writing tasks will incorporate regular feedback of different kinds. With regard to support for faculty in writing pedagogy, the work by John Bean (1996, 2011) has become very influential in the German-speaking area.

Tendency 2: Online Tutoring

Asynchronous forms of tutoring writing have developed rapidly in recent years, with integration of e-learning platforms in higher education. While writing centers offer e-mail support for academic writers, though often limited to specific aspects of text production, the teaching faculty started to make use of peer-based asynchronous tutoring in discipline-specific forums on e-learning platforms.

Tendency 3: Extra-curricular Workshops

Many university writing centers have developed over the past few years extra-curricular workshops in which students participate voluntarily. The focus of these workshops is either on the introduction to academic writing or on specific aspects of the writing process in individual academic genres. Increasingly, university disciplines organize their own discipline-specific workshops and, sometimes, make them mandatory for students. This is especially the case with new genres (e.g., e-portfolio) or skills and tools (e.g., use of digital devices for academic literacy) in order to secure more comprehensive learning and instruction. As a consequence, at some universities, individual disciplines start their own writing centers, to provide a joint roof for and more structure to the different support initiatives. The most striking example of this initiative, in my view, is the writing center in the Institute of Sociology at the University of Göttingen (Germany).

TENDENCY 4: REQUIRED WRITING COURSES

At a growing number of universities, beginning students are required to take part in either (1) an introductory writing course or (2) a cluster of lectures and workshops, or (3) an autonomous writing group and/or collaborative writing project. A successful example of the first format is the course designed, scientifically assessed, and finally implemented by Helmut Gruber (Gruber, Huemer, & Rheindorf, et al., 2009) and his team at the University of Vienna (see also Gruber's chapter in this book). A unique version of the second format is the design of introductory clusters for academic writing at the Health Education Department and the Department of Applied Linguistics, both at Zurich University of Applied Sciences Winterthur (see also Otto Kruse in this book). A role model for the third format is Katrin Girgensohn's concept of autonomous writing groups at the European University Viadrina (see also my interview with Katrin Girgensohn in this book).

Mandatory "writing-intensive" courses for advanced students are still rare (see Hirsch and Paoli; Thaiss and Goodman in this book for US variations on this theme). There are two possible explanations: (a) within universities many faculty members and administrators view writing as a given skill which shall not require extra instruction during university studies; (b) among the teaching faculty there is a lack of knowledge about what writing pedagogy implies. Therefore, generic online courses, such as the one developed by Guillaume Schiltz (2006), called COLAC, have been implemented in advanced courses at the Universities of Basel and Zurich and in other places in Swiss higher education.

With regard to lack of writing pedagogy expertise among the teaching faculty, more and more local writing centers offer training in how to teach process writing and use writing task arrangements that offer alternative ways of text production based on the individual needs of different writer types (Schindler, 2011). Although most colleges and universities are not yet willing whole-heartedly to invest in structures of "writing-across-the-curriculum" (WAC) and/or "writing-in-the-disciplines" (WID), many colleagues are now eager to plan their seminars and lectures around task arrangements that define and make use of writing as a mode of learning and specific rhetoric tools for successful participation in discipline-specific discourse. (Bräuer & Schindler, 2011)

TENDENCY 5: WRITING GROUPS

Anne R. Gere (1987) defines writing groups as a communities of learners temporarily established, more or less voluntarily, and based on similar learning needs and goals of the participants. Interaction is organized through a set of agreements that are either preset by a facilitator (often representing an educational institution) or negotiated and agreed upon by the members of the writing group. Writing groups in a more structured format, guided by a workshop leader/facilitator, are an important element of the so-called Reform Pedagogy developed since the 1920s especially in alternative educational settings in the German-speaking area of Europe (e.g., Freinet pedagogy). Under the term "Schreibwerkstatt," the concept of guided group work in process writing saw a renaissance in the 1980s and is an integrated conceptual aspect of today's writing centers throughout the educational pyramid.

Based on this precedent, Katrin Girgensohn (2007) developed and thoroughly assessed a concept for autonomous writing groups in higher education, which forms one of the main pillars of the writing center at the Europe University Viadrina in Frankfurt/Oder (Germany, http://www.europa-uni.de/de/campus/hilfen/schreibzentrum/index.html). Girgensohn merits recognition for strengthening the self-dependent aspect of the original writing group approach of the Reform Pedagogy by maintaining the potential of peer learning and collaboration (Bruffee, 1984) and the pedagogical power of learner communities (Lave & Wenger, 1991). Meanwhile, Girgensohn's concept has been adopted by several German-speaking universities (see also my interview with Katrin Girgensohn in this book)

TENDENCY 6: SUPPORT OF OTHER STUDY SKILLS

Universities not only started to realize the importance of facilitating writing and writers but also the development of other key competences of academic work, e.g., reading, e-learning, digital text production, language learning, learning to learn, plus competences to safeguard success in entering the profession (e.g., writing of proposals and applications). Competences that directly influence the quality of academic writing have been central aims not only of writing centers but also of academic skills centers or language centers. The latter institution sometimes emerges from an existing writing center, as it may be the case in the near future at the University of Education in Berne (Switzerland), or out of original plans to pursue a writing center, as seen at the University of Freiburg (Germany). Which format the institution supporting writing and writers finally adopts often depends on long-term strategic decisions and goals, as can be witnessed at the Language Center of the Technical University of Darmstadt, where research and development of concepts of multilingualism clearly dominate the way academic writers are being supported within the "SchreibCenter" and the Online Writing Lab (http://www.owl.tu-darmstadt.de).

Tendency 7: Writing Projects with External Partners

This tendency is currently most often seen within teacher colleges and universities of education, where the goal of so-called "double literacy" is at stake: both mastering one's own academic writing process and knowing how to support writing development and text production of others. Projects that, on the one hand, meet an immediate need of the external partner, but also provide an opportunity for the university (students and faculty) to develop academic knowledge and professional skills, have been proven very useful. In addition to meeting a current need of the external partner (e.g., secondary school), they also provide incentive to ponder possibilities of sustainable development in at least two directions: to perpetuate a well-designed and assessed project and to gain new theoretical insights. A very powerful example for this tendency can be seen at http://www.ph-freiburg.de/schreibzentrum ("Laufende Projekte") under the rubric of "Zeitung in der Schule," where, together with a regional newspaper, projects in journalistic writing are being offered to local high schools. Results of this project also feed into another project (see "Internet-Zeitung"), a multilingual online newsletter for which students write about their experiences in dealing with different cultures and languages. Both projects provide excellent material for research on journalistic writing as a tool for discursive mobility (Monroe, 2002) and (pre-)academic writing. They also provide concrete incentive for bridging the gap between writing in high schools and at the university and for the training of peer writing tutors at the university writing center and at the writing centers of the participating high schools (Bräuer, 2003, 2006).

The largest initiative in the collaboration between colleges/universities and secondary schools so far in the German-speaking area is "Scriptorium" (Bräuer, 2009, Scriptorium, 2010). This network of about 50 online training courses for in-service teachers in literacy, partially provided in French, English, Italian, Finnish, Danish, Dutch, Spanish, and German, is a powerful way to find out the needs of international writing/reading support in and beyond the German-speaking area. International collaborators of this network—teaching faculty in primary, secondary, and/or higher education—share research findings and their rich experience in learning and instruction.

Tendency 8: Self-learning Material

Self-learning material presented to writers either in print or digital form often provides deep insight into the accomplishments of an institutional structure geared toward facilitating writing and writers. In a number of writing centers (e.g., see websites of writing centers in Bielefeld, Bochum, Frankfurt/Oder, Freiburg) self-learning material is being developed collaboratively by members of each writing center team. This procedure helps to shape not only the understanding of the individual writing tutors but also the mission of the institutional entity. When self-learning material becomes used and assessed purposefully, it provides valuable information for further developing tutoring strategies and the overall format of the writing center.

There is also an effort to move toward online writing labs (OWLs) in German-speaking higher education, which perform as a website with a carefully developed structure that leaves no single self-learning document without clearly defined didactical purpose and reference to other material. OWLs can be an efficient way of facilitating large numbers of students and/or students from different campuses, as seen at the University of Education of Northwestern Switzerland (http://www.schreiben.zentrumlesen.ch). This OWL works as a point of reference for both students and faculty; the didactical connection between the two sets of self-learning materials is carefully constructed. Ideally, using the student materials will be encouraged in class and as part of class-based tasks designed by the teaching faculty.

TENDENCY 9: WEB 2.0 TOOLS FOR TEXT PRODUCTION

A very special tendency can be seen in the use of WebQuests, an HTML structure which provides a compact framework for digital writing/learning arrangements. The writing center at the University of Education Freiburg (Bräuer & Schindler, 2011; SchreibQuest, 2010) and the University of Flensburg (Trepkau, 2010) (both located in Germany) provide insight into the pedagogical possibilities of focusing and contextualizing self-learning material online. Another web 2.0 tool, wikis, have developed growing impact in academic text production and, therefore, receives more and more attention within the teaching of academic writing, e.g., at the German universities in Greifswald (Endres 2010), and Dortmund (Beißwenger & Storrer 2010), as well as at the Swiss universities in Luzern and Rapperswil (Frischherz & Verhein 2010).

TENDENCY 10: WRITING CENTERS TAKING ON THE ROLE OF LITERACY MANAGERS

Assessing one's own conceptual development and daily practice with regard to literacy management has been a key issue of the writing center movement in higher education in the German-speaking area since the late 1990s. This can be seen in the following key publications on different issues of literacy management: Bräuer (1998), Björk, Bräuer, Rienecker, and Stray Jörgensen (2003), Abraham, Kupfer-Schreiner, and Maiwald, (2005), Kruse, Berger, and Ulmi (2006), Berning, Keßler, and Koch (2006), Doleschal and Gruber (2007), Frank, Haacke, and Lahm (2007), Jakobs, Lehnen, and Schindler (2010) and Bräuer and Schindler (2011). Due to this intense practice-based research, writing centers in specific, but also writing programs and other literacy initiatives, have a significant impact on certain aspects of institutional development. A few examples of this impact can be found in this book (see chapters by Otto Kruse, Helmut Gruber, Daniel Perrin, Ursula Doleschal) that either enhanced WAC and/or WID structures or the development of tutoring writing and writers. At the Technical University of Darmstadt, the work of writing center people, such as Sandra Ballweg, sparked a project for developing an e-portfolio concept to further enhance learning, instruction, and assessment procedures throughout the university (Ballweg, Scholz, Richter, & Bruder, 2011).

TENDENCY 11: WRITING RESEARCH

Also based on reflective practice carried out by writing centers as literacy managers, a broad range of research topics has emerged during the past decade. Some of the most recent research fields that are directly related to facilitating writing and writers include online/digital writing, the effectiveness of peer-tutoring of writing, procedural details of literacy management, aspects of L2-text production, influence of culture and domain on writing and writers, writer types and pedagogical consequences, and reflective practice (learning journal, e-portfolio). Nevertheless, direct collaboration between the writing center and writing researchers in combined research-development projects is still rare.

CONCLUSION

My concluding thoughts adhere to the central concern of literacy management under the circumstances and ways people both deal and interact with information and with others in the processing of information. I base this conclusion on the assumption that the academy aims for a better understanding of both theory and practice. The academy, embedded in research methodology, observes and describes reality, raises and answers questions to achieve new insights that are being used further in this continuing interplay of theory and practice. For the development of academic literacy in institutions of higher education in the German-speaking countries, I see the following two somewhat contradicting tendencies.

Stuck in a Traditional Role of Writing

The role of writing within the academy in the German-speaking area has been affected by the long-lived spirit of the Early Enlightenment of the eighteenth century, which views the writer as a medium through which inspiration speaks in a strong voice leading to an immediate result: a text with a clear message to its readers. This basic understanding of writing can still be witnessed in many different facets of the German-speaking academy—in some respects starker than ever, at least in places where the Bologna Reform has been misunderstood as "streamlining" what in the past was considered "individualized" learning through trial and error over too many semesters of college. This influence is true especially when the modularization of competency-based instruction now leads not only to a reduction in the number of individual writing tasks, but even to the elimination of entire task arrangements that, in the past, helped to shape academic literacy even if only through trial and error. Optional learning arrangements of the past, including short seminar papers and study group discussions, including summaries and commentaries eventually leading to an extensive end-of semester paper, are now often being replaced by large lecture classes with written exams as the only form of comprehensive writing—and even that expedience is eliminated when the test is conceptualized as multiple-choice.

In such a constellation, the institution will not see any incentive in the near future to change the role of writing into a learning tool that needs to be acquired through formal instruction and through different, individualized practices in the daily classroom. To see institutions act alternatively probably requires their sudden realization—a wakeup call—of the shrinking quality in learning and instructional outcomes based on the written exams and the final thesis. Unfortunately, since written exams often do not unveil contextualized understanding of the learner, and the final thesis in many universities of the German-speaking area does not count substantially in the final grade, I doubt that some institutions will, for now, even bother looking at the quality of academic literacy.

The Alternative: Less-structured Learning that Fulfills Individual Needs

The other tendency which can be witnessed since the Bologna reform started to unfold in German-speaking higher education is pointing in quite a different direction. With the support of mostly extra-curricular initiatives such as centers for writing, language, or academic skills, a growing number of students engage in a more informal, less-structured learning that feeds their real individual needs. As authentic, self-responsive learners, they decide whether they participate in an extra-curricular activity or not. This role has been experienced by many students recently as refreshing and stimulating, especially in contrast with the role they are supposed to play in a rigidly planned course of study in modularized BA and MA programs. This is a broad claim. However, one simple result from the Freiburg Writing Center underlines this value: the number of participants in writing workshops has doubled since the implementation of a modularized curriculum. Many of them, when being asked why they participate, express motives like those of the student quoted here:

> In this workshop I can pick up competences unavailable in seminars and lectures but that are actually needed in order to make full use of the instruction. I also like the idea that these workshops are being offered several times during the semester so that I can participate whenever I need them (and even come back if necessary).

Part of this second tendency is also the recognition from the teaching faculty that they actually need students with basic academic literacy skills from early on in their college careers in order to apply the modularized curriculum approach successfully. As a result, faculty either develop their own methods of writing instruction—often in some form of peer learning—in order to support their own teaching, or they make conscious use of the extra-curricular offerings provided by the institution, such as writing workshops and peer tutoring.

Another form of realization from the teaching faculty perspective is that the student's performance shown in an exam is a limited example of this person's learning effort and success. Here, portfolios have started to be used at least as a complementary form of evaluation, often including peer assessment.

There is a specific tendency coming from institutions of teacher training and the effort that can be witnessed there with regard to strengthening "double literacy" —the ability to write well and to facilitate others (peers and pupils in primary and secondary schools) to write well. This focus on double literacy has begun to show concrete results on the institutional level (e.g., portfolios as an officially recognized form of assessment) and in intensified collaboration with primary and secondary schools in the field of literacy development, often through peer learning and peer tutoring.

To conclude, it can be said that, even though a thorough realization and practical application of the procedural nature of writing has not yet taken place in higher education throughout the German-speaking region, the pressing needs stemming from the Bologna Reform make people—students and teaching faculty alike—act in a way that finally supports process writing and the long-term development of academic writers. It appears that, by means of extra-curricular activities, incentives are being placed that could lead, in the near future, not only to curricular change but also to a different culture of writing at the center of a different culture of learning and instruction. With a new generation of writers, informed and trained through writing programs and writing centers in secondary education, these tendencies will, hopefully, be strengthened and shaped further. As already witnessed in part during the massive student protest in 2010 throughout Austria, Germany and Switzerland, these students are going to demand places, structures, and resources in the academy to further develop writing competence as a necessary basis for success at the university and in their future professional careers. These students seem ready to take action, not least in the form of peer learning through writing that could again become a catalyst for institutional change in the future.

NOTE

1. I would like to thank all colleagues who provided feedback on my ideas and drafts. I am especially thankful to Birke Klima, Gerlinde Hollweg, and Marcy Scholz, who helped me a lot through highly efficient one-on-one tutoring.

REFERENCES

Abraham, U., Kupfer-Schreiner, C., & Maiwald, K. (2005). *Schreibförderung und Schreiberziehung. Eine Einführung für Schule und Hochschule.* Donauwörth, Bavaria, Germany: Auer Verlag.

Altrichter, H., Brüsemeister, T., & Wissinger, J. (Eds.). (2007). *Educational governance: Handlungskoordination und Steuerung im Bildungssystem.* Wiesbaden, Hesse, Germany: Verlag für Sozialwissenschaften.

Altrichter, H. (2012). In G. Bräuer et al. (Eds.), *Portfolio macht Schule* (pp. 33-40). Seelze-Velber, Lower Saxony, Germany: Friedrich Verlag.

Ballweg, S., Scholz, N., Richter, K. & Bruder, R. (2011). Schreibend lehren lernen. In G. Bräuer & K. Schindler (Eds.), *Schreibarrangements für Schule, Studium, Beruf* (pp. 188-204). Freiburg: Fillibachverlag.

Bean, J. (1996). *Engaging ideas. The Professor's guide to integrating writing, critical thinking, and active learning in the classroom.* San Francisco: Jossey-Bass.

Bean, J., & Weimer, M. (2011). *Engaging Ideas. The professor's guide to integrating writing, critical thinking, and active learning in the classroom,* 2nd ed. San Francisco: Jossey-Bass.

Beißwenger, M., & Storrer, A. (2010). Kollaborative Hypertextproduktion mit Wiki-Technologie. Beispiele und Erfahrungen im Bereich Schule und Hochschule. In E.-M. Jakobs, K. Lehnen, & K. Schindler (Eds.), *Schreiben und Medien. Schule, Hochschule, Beruf* (pp. 12-36). Frankfurt am Main: Peter Lang.

Berning, J., Keßler, N., & Koch, H. (2006). *Schreiben im Kontext von Schule, Universität, Beruf und Lebensalltag*. Berlin: LIT Verlag.

Boud, D., Cohen, R., & Sampson, J. (2001). *Peer learning in higher education: Learning from and with each other*. London: Kogan Press.

Bräuer, G. (2002). Drawing connections across education: The Freiburg writing center model. *Language and Learning Across the Disciplines, 5*(3), 25-34.

Bräuer, G. (2003). Centers for writing and reading—Bridging the gap between university and school education. In L. Björk, G. Bräuer, L. Rienecker, & P. Stray Jörgensen (Eds.), *Teaching academic writing in European higher education* (pp. 135-150). Amsterdam: Kluwer Academic Publishers.

Bräuer, G. (2006). The US writing center model for high schools goes to Germany: And what is coming back? *The Clearing House. A Journal of Educational Strategies, Issues, and Ideas (Special issue: The Writing Center and Beyond,* ed. Pamela B. Childers), 95-100.

Bräuer, G. (Ed.). (2009). *Scriptorium: Ways of interacting with writers and readers. A professional development program*. Freiburg i, Br.: Fillibachverlag.

Bräuer, G., & Schindler, K. (2011). *Schreibarrangements für Schule, Studium, Beruf*. Freiburg i. Br.: Fillibachverlag.

Bruffee, K. (1984). Collaborative learning and the conversation of mankind. *College English 46*, 635-52.

Cazden, C., Cope, B., Fairclough, N., & Gee, J. (1996). A Pedagogy of multiliteracies: Designing social futures. *Harvard Educational Review, 66*(1), 60-92.

Doleschal, U., & Gruber, H. (Eds.). (2007). *Wissenschaftliches schreiben abseits des Englischen mainstreams*. Vienna: Peter Lang.

Endres, B. (2010). Greifswald virtuell. Kollaboratives Schreiben im Wiki. In E.-M. Jakobs, et al. (Eds.), *Schreiben und Medien. Schule, Hochschule, Beruf (pp. 73-90)*. Frankfurt a.M.: Peter Lang.

Falchikow, N., & Blythman, M. (2000). *Learning together: Peer tutoring in higher education*. New York: Routledge.

Frank, A., Haacke, S., Lahm, S. (2007). *Schlüsselkompetenzen: Schreiben in Studium und Beruf*. Stuttgart-Weimar: Metzler.

Frischherz, B., & Verhein, A. (2010). Wiki-Web zur Projekt- und Poduktdokumentation. Ein didaktisches Konzept für die Schreibschulung im technischen Masterstudium. In E.-M. Jakobs, et al. (Eds.), *Schreiben und Medien. Schule, Hochschule, Beruf* (pp. 153-168). Frankfurt am Main: Peter Lang.

Gere, A. (1987). *Writing groups. History, theory and implications.* Carbondale and Edwardsville: Southern Illinois Press.

Gillespie, P., & Lerner, N. (2000). *The Allyn and Bacon guide to peer tutoring.* Boston: Allyn and Bacon.

Girgensohn, K. (2007). *Neue Wege zur Schlüsselqualifikation Schreiben. Autonome Schreibgruppen an der Hochschule.* Wiesbaden, Hessen, Germany: VS Research.

Gruber, H., Huemer, B., Rheindorf, M. (2009). *Wissenschaftliches Schreiben. Ein Praxisbuch für Studierende der Geistes- und Sozialwissenschaften.* Vienna: Böhlau, UTB.

Jakobs, E., Lehnen, K., Schindler, K. (2010). *Schreiben und Medien. Schule, Hochschule, Beruf.* Frankfurt am Main: Peter Lang.

Kail, H., & Trimbur, J. (2000): *Collaborative learning* (3rd. Ed.). Upper Saddle River, New York: Prentice Hall.

Kruse, O., Berger, K., & Ulmi, M. (2006). *Prozessorientierte Schreibdidaktik. Schreibtraining für Schule, Studium und Beruf.* Bern: Haupt Verlag.

Lave, J., & Wenger, E. (1991). *Situated learning: Legitimate peripheral participation.* Cambridge/New York/Victoria: Cambridge University Press.

Monroe, J. (Ed.). (2002). *Writing and revising the disciplines.* Ithaca, New York Cornell University Press.

O'Donnell, A., & King, A. (1999). *Cognitive perspectives on peer learning.* London: Erlbaum.

Rogoff, B. (1994). Developing understanding of the idea of communities of learners. *Mind, Culture, and Activity, 1,* 209-229.

Schiltz, G. (2006). *COLAC-Modell* . Retrieved from http://www.e-teaching.org/praxis/referenzbeispiele/colac

Schindler, K. (2011). Akademische Texte schreiben und beurteilen. In G. Bräuer & K. Schindler (Eds.), *Schreibarrangements für Schule, Studium, Beruf (pp. 240-255).* Freiburg i. Br.: Fillibachverlag.

SchreibQuest (2010). *SchreibQuest.* Retrieved from https://www.ph-freiburg.de/hochschule/weitere-einrichtungen/schreibzentrum/journalistische-werkstatt/zeitung-in-der-schule.html

Scriptorium (2010). *Scriptorium.* Retrieved from http://www.scriptorium-project.org

Topping, K., & Ehly, S. (Eds.). (2001). *Peer-assisted learning. A practical guide for teachers.* Cambridge, Massachusetts: Brookline Books.

Trepkau, C. (2010). WebQuests im Deutschunterricht. In E.-M. Jakobs, et al. (Eds.), *Schreiben und Medien. Schule, Hochschule, Beruf* (pp. 51-70). Frankfurt am Main.: Peter Lang.

CHAPTER 41.
SECTION ESSAY: WHO TAKES CARE OF WRITING IN LATIN AMERICAN AND SPANISH UNIVERSITIES?

By Paula Carlino
CONICET—University of Buenos Aires (Argentina)

This section essay briefly presents the Latin American and Spanish initiatives that are part of this volume. Before providing a general view of what is being done in regards to writing at Latin American and Spanish universities, I offer an account of my participation in the collective project that made this book possible. I first present my journey as a professor who strove to integrate reading and writing in an Educational Psychology course. I do this with the aim of offering an additional perspective on how certain university teachers in the region decide to help students read and write in their content courses, despite the lack of institutional support. In addition, my own story includes some suggestions on how to use this book, a topic I will return to in the conclusion.

HOW I GOT INVOLVED IN THIS BOOK: A LATIN AMERICAN TEACHER'S JOURNEY TO WAC

My participation in this book is rooted in my own enthusiasm and willingness to contribute to documenting, gathering, and communicating what is done with writing at the university level around the world. Through my personal history, I will explain how this enthusiasm was born.

In 1997 I started including in my Educational Psychology classes several reading and writing tasks to help students better understand the subject I was teaching. In order to do this, I had to learn from others. At that time, I did not know anyone who would do this in an explicit and systematic manner. Many professors in the social sciences did ask for a lot of reading and writing in their courses, but few of them oriented students to how to do it. When pedagogical assistance was provided, it tended to be sporadic and insufficient. I had never heard of the Writing Across the Curriculum (WAC) or Writing in the Disciplines (WID) movements. The universe of ideas proposed by WAC/WID authors was simply out of my reach, since during my undergraduate studies in Argentina or my graduate studies in Spain I never came across these readings.

However, my Psychology of Learning background had shown me that nobody learns just by receiving information in a passive way. Nobody learns by being a mere receiver of a given body of knowledge. Knowledge, in research and in learning, is not there to be taken. Instead, it needs to be created and recreated: the researcher creates knowledge and the students create their knowledge. None of them, researcher or student, receives knowledge that has been preformed. This is the epistemological essence of constructivism (Castorina, 2001; Ferreiro, 1999; Piaget & García, 1982).

According to this principle, it did not make sense to organize my classes around lectures only. I had to plan class activities and assignments that would get undergraduates to participate at both cognitive and social levels. I wanted to do so not as an extension of my teaching but as a core activity. I would help them work throughout the semester and not only during the week of the exam.

My graduate work on literacy was of great assistance to me in this task. The socio-cognitive activities that would lead students to learn the subject involved reading, writing, and exchanging ideas about the course concepts. Under certain conditions, reading and writing can prompt an intense cognitive activity (Bazerman et al., 2005; Langer & Applebee, 1987; Scardamalia & Bereiter, 1985; Wells, 1987) and I was attempting to recreate these conditions. But I would not just require those tasks without offering further guidance. I knew students needed to be oriented and receive feedback, since they were newcomers to the field and therefore would be somewhat lost without this support. I had often heard professors complain, "Students don't know how to write. They don't understand what they read—they don't read." Instead, I was convinced that many students did not do what teachers were expecting of them because they did not know how.

As a result, I decided to organize activities in a way that would allow students to participate. Thus, I guided students and provided feedback while they completed such activities as discussing readings, making connections among texts, and reviewing what they had written (Dysthe, 1996): all this, with the aim of helping them gradually understand the ideas of the course. By reading and writing about the subject, they could recreate the knowledge for themselves, something that a teacher could not directly transmit to them.

In brief, these literate activities were integrated into the course to help students understand and study its contents. Along the way, however, I discovered that these activities also contributed to another equally relevant purpose: helping students acquire new ways of thinking, making an argument, debating, explaining, and writing on topics related to the field. I realized that supporting their participation in literate tasks had led me to inadvertently teach a new content: how to interpret and produce the discourse of the discipline I was teaching.

QUESTIONS THAT A TEACHER ASKS HERSELF

During this journey, I began to ask myself: How best could I approach these goals? What writing and reading assignments should I ask from the students, and what kinds of help should I provide? How much time should I allocate for these activities and how much should I spend lecturing? How would these tasks relate to the exams? And above all, who could I learn from? There were other questions as well: How much time would I devote to design and implement these activities? Would I be able to do this in a work context in which I was totally alone and lacking institutional support? With whom could I share my experiences and discuss them?

I came up with two answers. On the one hand, I began an extensive Internet search in order to find out how professors from universities around the world were dealing with similar issues. I discovered the Australian Learning and Teaching Centres, the WAC programs in the United States, full text versions of conference papers, and countless websites where teaching practices were documented in detail. Entranced, I took on this task as a methodical exploration that lasted for two years. Whenever I found something relevant, I read it, and one website led to another. I selected, printed out, and organized materials, putting together a library of resources and a list of new links to continue exploring. As I went along, I decided what materials could help my teaching, and I modified them to try out in my classes. The response to my first set of questions was the following: I was going to learn to include work with reading and writing in my classes by testing variations of what other university professors had done, documented, and published on the Internet.

On the other hand, the response to the second set of questions was to turn my teaching into a research activity as well (Hutchings & Shulman, 1999). I first planned to make my Internet searches systematic and to categorize my discoveries about what was being done in distant lands. This later became part of the theoretical framework of a six-year action research project in which I documented and critically examined my own teaching practice. In addition, I wrote about all of this, presented at conferences, and submitted papers for publishing.

Written "conversations" with my readers and with authors who had inspired me were very encouraging, since I did not have any close peers from whom I could learn and by whom I could feel supported. I did find this support from colleagues from different countries. Therefore, reading and publishing not only fueled my research but also my teaching.

I decided to publish in Spanish, because it was difficult for me to write in English and because I hoped to spark dialogue in my own milieu. Looking back, this is how I would summarize my work for a period of six years (Carlino, 2005). This was my personal incentive for investing time and effort, though I expected to reap the benefits in terms of both my teaching and my potential contributions to the debates in the Writing Across the Curriculum field.

WHAT THIS STORY TELLS ABOUT OTHER TEACHERS IN IBEROAMERICA

I have shared my personal story because I believe it can help readers understand the context of teachers in many Spanish or Portuguese speaking countries. In these countries, professors face similar isolation in their academic contexts: limited institutional resources, scant activities for professional development, and a lack of knowledge of the epistemic power of writing and of WAC/WID programs in the English-speaking world.

I believe that the questions mentioned in the previous section are critical to encourage content course professors to care for how their students read and write. These are questions that all institutions should address in order to implement cross-curricular writing initiatives. The first set of questions—"How best could I approach these goals? . . . who can I learn from?" —refers to how a professor whose first and foremost subject is not reading or writing can learn ways to develop and actually integrate these activities in the classroom. The second set of questions—"How much time would I devote to design and implement these activities? . . . With whom could I share my experiences and discuss them?" —is about how to sustain such activities over time if a professor is alone and has no support or institutional recognition.

The following section describes profiles included in this book that show different initiatives that emerged from the personal conviction of their authors rather than from institutional policies—though some of them later gained university support. As a whole, the book explores both sets of questions and reveals that more than one path can be taken within different institutional contexts.

When I found out about Chris Thaiss' project, a project for researching, compiling, and disseminating the experiences of teaching writing and teaching with writing at universities across the world, I was thrilled. This book is part of the project, and I am sure it will be useful to many professors who not only want to integrate literacy work in their classes but also need to learn how to do so from others. In addition, I am convinced that the ideas brought here by each author will pave the way for institutions in our countries to understand that we will not get very far unless professors are accompanied in this challenge.

"DO NOTHING," "REMEDIAL," OR INTEGRATED MODELS IN IBEROAMERICAN UNIVERSITIES

In order to introduce the chapters on Latin America and the one on Spain, I will give an overview of what is happening in these places. According to the responses to the International WAC/WID Mapping Survey (see Thaiss essay in this volume) and the works presented at regional conferences, there is common concern about how university students read and write. This concern is what inspired the initiatives described in these chapters. Since the 1990s, different actions have been taken, some on the periphery and some more integrated. However, unlike what occurs in the US and Australia, Latin American and Spanish universities have fewer experiences and less institutional involvement for addressing questions concerning academic writing.

If we considered the classification of initiatives proposed by Skillen, Merten, Trivett, and Percy (1998)—the "do nothing" model, the "remedial" model, and the integrated model—we would include what generally occurs in the region in the second model. However, there are some isolated initiatives that represent the integrated model; in some countries the "do nothing" model is still predominant.

Regarding the "do nothing" model, Solé, Teberosky, and Castelló's essay (this volume) explains why Spanish universities and teachers often neglect writing instruction. They generally hold the belief that "learning oral and written language occurs only in the first few years of compulsory education; this belief leads oral and written language to be treated as an 'object' of knowledge in these early stages. Thereafter, these capacities acquire the status of learning 'instruments' (and lose their former status)." It is also assumed that "oral and written language, as communication and (to a lesser extent) representation tools, remain invariable throughout a person's life, while what varies are the situations in which these tools are 'applied'" (Solé, Teberosky & Castelló, this volume).

Similarly, in the "remedial" model, writing is seen as an autonomous code, ruled by universal conventions and with the normative level (spelling and grammar) appearing as its most visible attribute. Writing and reading, once dispossessed of their social nature, are often conceived of as general abilities that can be transferred to any context, as noted by Russell (1990). It is believed that these skills can be taught and learned in ad hoc curricular spaces, dissociated from the spheres in which reading and writing are required for specific purposes. In such spaces, the contents related to reading and writing are generally presented through exercises that break down and transfigure the real literate practices in order to teach them divorced from their situated uses.

For example, a recent survey done in Argentina (Carlino, Iglesia & Laxalt, 2010) found that 90% of 544 teachers across the higher education curriculum recognized that their students found it difficult to "read comprehensively and write clearly" in their courses. When asked what was done at the institutional level, 29% of the respondents stated that their institutions dealt with these problems and explained what was done. The most frequently mentioned initiatives were workshops and entry courses. Similarly, Fernandez Fastuca's (2010) study showed that ad hoc initial courses greatly predominated over other institutional initiatives. Carlino et al.'s (2010) survey also explored whether professors did something about their students' literacy problems, with 28% of the faculty declaring that they addressed reading and/or writing in content courses and describing what they did. Most commonly, professors' interventions took place at the "margins" of the literate assignments, with professors requesting tasks, giving guidelines, teaching writing techniques at the beginning, and assessing students' final products at the end. A smaller group of professors declared that they intervened during the writing process, devoting class time to literate tasks. Within this group, a reduced number of respondents explained that they promoted teacher-student interaction around disciplinary literacy.

In other words, very few of the professors in the sample discussed readings with their students, commented on their drafts, or mentioned teacher feedback as well as peer interaction as part of their classes. These results confirm what was found in a previous qualitative inquiry with university students and teachers (Carlino, 2010). The author found that although literate assignments were very common in Social Science courses in Argentine universities, professors rarely offered support for how to do them: guidelines were rare and feedback minimal.

In sum, those initiatives that address literacy in Argentine higher education institutions tend to take place outside the content areas and are dissociated from them. They are based on the idea that students can then transfer such learning to reading and writing in their disciplines. In addition, most professors in the disciplines require and assess students' reading and writing, but very few of them consider these practices as an object of their instruction. When they intervene, they often do so at the periphery of the assignments. Although these findings come from Argentina, they are consistent with what is usually presented regarding other Spanish-speaking countries in regional conferences and journals.

INITIATIVES IN IBEROAMERICA

In the following paragraphs I review the Latin American and Spanish initiatives, some of which are included in this book.

Writing Courses

Writing courses are the most frequent initiatives developed by tertiary institutions (Carlino, Iglesia & Laxalt, 2010; Fernandez Fastuca, 2010). These courses vary in length and are usually confined to the first year of the programs (Gonzalez, this volume) or required as entry courses at the undergraduate level (e.g., Narvaja, Di Stefano & Pereira, 2002). In addition, some universities offer writing courses at the graduate level (Carlino, 2008, and in press; Motta-Roth this volume; Solé, Teberosky & Castelló, this volume). Two theoretical viewpoints underpin writing courses: the remedial basic-skills approach and the genre-based developmental approach.

In the remedial basic-skills approach, writing is taught as an autonomous object of study, "a single universally applicable skill, largely unrelated to 'content,' [...] a separate and independent technique" (Russell, 1990, p. 55). As a result, students are expected to transfer this general writing skill to different disciplinary assignments.

In the genre-based developmental approach, on the other hand, writing is not taught as a generic skill but in context. Based on a situated learning perspective, writing courses are designed to help in the production of texts in a particular discipline, for a specific audience. Therefore, students have several opportunities to draft, receive feedback, and redraft their texts (e.g., Carlino, in press; Motta-Roth, this volume). It is along these lines that Solé et al. (this volume) highlight the importance of the length of postgraduate seminars to allow for nurturing the learning processes involved in academic communication.

Nevertheless, despite the fact that longer courses seem to be more encompassing, there is a potential problem associated with undergraduate or graduate programs offering writing courses: supporting student writing might fall only on the writing teacher's shoulders. Therefore, professors teaching content courses might not be held responsible for helping students to develop their writing—and those teaching writing courses most probably will experience a sense of insufficiency and isolation (González, this volume).

Writing Centers

The idea of a writing center with writing tutors is usually not known in Latin American or Spanish universities. Even the notion of receiving feedback, as a low-stakes reader's response to a student-author's text, is rare. Nevertheless, a handful of initiatives have appeared in recent years in countries such as Mexico (e.g., Galán Vélez & Ormsby, 2010) and Colombia (Molina, 2008). In addition, the history of the Puerto Rican writing center that García-Arroyo and Quintana offer in this volume exemplifies some of the difficulties that this type of initiative might face. Finally, most of the writing centers in Latin American and Spanish universities are based on the North American model and were preceded by local staff visiting several writing centers in the US.

Writing centers, as an expression of the WAC movement, should reach the writing done in the disciplines. However, in our region they are still seen by many professors as a remedial service to fix students' sentence-level problems. This is related to how writing is conceived. If writing is considered as a mere surface form dissociated from content, it is therefore confined to the writing center's domain, with few content-course professors taking care of it (García-Arroyo & Quintana, this volume).

Faculty Development

Other initiatives in Latin America aim at raising awareness among content-course professors and instructors regarding the feasibility of dealing with students' literacy in their own courses. To challenge commonsense assumptions, these initiatives discuss what literacy consists of, how reading and writing are learned, and why they may have an epistemic power, as well as whether they should be taught at the university level and across disciplines. At the same time, faculty development workshops show participants the most fruitful ways of assigning reading or writing and giving feedback to students. Thus, professors from various disciplines are helped to integrate literate assignments in their teaching with the aim of increasing students' learning in a specific field. These experiences are worth noting since they try to make all the disciplines responsible for supporting student academic literacy instead of confining it in a separate curricular space (writing course) or service (writing center tutoring).

However, since faculty development seminars are usually offered for only a few hours over a couple of months (e.g., Benvegnu, 2004; Marucco, 2004; Narvaez, this volume) and sometimes have an even shorter duration, professors are left on their own to put into practice what is theoretically discussed during the sessions.

For example, Narváez (this volume) questions whether the length and format of these seminars can affect teachers' instructional practices. The generally tight format in which most of the faculty development workshops are presented seems to be detrimental to this end. To overcome this limitation, Carlino & Martinez (2009) offered guidance as part of the process of changing cross-curricular instructional practices. Working with professors from various disciplines to help them integrate reading and writing in their classes, the authors approached the provision of faculty development as collective action-research for two years.

Excepting some very short workshops, these initiatives do not originate from university-wide policies, but from the determination of individual academic developers. As a consequence, they are sporadic, discontinuous, and reach few faculty members. In contrast, the next paragraph describes a unique institutional program in the region that promotes faculty development that accompanies teachers for longer periods of time.

Team Teaching

The essay by Moyano and Natale (this volume) depicts a writing program that offers assistance to course-content faculty over an 18-month period to integrate the teaching of writing into their courses. To achieve this integrative goal, the program fosters interdisciplinary partnerships between writing instructors and class professors. They collaboratively construct an inventory of genres and skills necessary for the course and design how to teach them. The writing instructor participates in the class on selected occasions to analyze with students the required genres. Three or four times a semester, for a minimum of three semesters, the class professor and the writing instructor work together until the professor is able to do the job alone.

This writing-across-the-curriculum program is a rare case in Latin America and Spain because it has gained clear institutional support to help students learn writing in context in all the subjects throughout the four years of study. It also contributes to faculty development through interdisciplinary collaboration.

It is worth noting that this example of team teaching resembles the Australian IDEALL project (Purser, Skillen, Deane, Donohue & Peake, 2008; Skillen et al., 1998;). Both initiatives take into account the principles of the "systemic approach: the shift in focus from working outside the curriculum to one that addresses the issues inside the curriculum [...] by collaborating with discipline staff; the importance of working at the faculty and department level to make these collaborations strategic; and the need to participate in and impact upon policy decisions" (Percy & Skillen, 2000).

WRITING INSTRUCTION INTERWOVEN IN DISCIPLINARY COURSES

Although faculty development actions are sporadic and limited, and team-based teaching is exceptional, there are some Iberoamerican professors who help develop student literacy in their content courses without any institutional support. Most of them have a Psychology, Education or Linguistics background. They draw on this knowledge to develop creative ways to enhance learning by offering guidance and feedback during the regular reading and writing tasks implemented in their classrooms (e.g., Carlino, 2005; Fernandez et al, 2004; Narváez, this volume; Padilla & Carlino, 2010; Vázquez & Jacob, 2007). They "interweave" literate activities through their courses and organize their classes to intervene during the processes of reading and writing. This concept contrasts with that of professors who only "sew" literate tasks on to their courses and intervene in a "peripheral" way, just requiring and assessing writing assignments. While in the "interwoven model" (Carlino, Iglesia & Laxalt, 2010) the professor helps students take part in the study practices she/he considers necessary to learn the subject, in the "sewed model" students are supposed to already have the necessary knowledge to do so on their own. The way professors in the disciplines include writing and reading in their classes—as integrated or intertwined activities or as added or sewed-on foreign elements—has clear consequences for the quality and equity of education. In the first case, the method nurtures the development of disciplinary literacy, while in the latter the method just demands it.

De Micheli and Iglesia (this volume) provide an unusual illustration of the interwoven writing model in a Biology course. They not only assign microthemes, in which students have to make connections among disciplinary concepts, but usually devote class time to collectively plan or review students' texts. They also give them quick written feedback, only assigning a grade in exams. In this way, students are given beforehand several opportunities to practice and receive feedback on the type of writing that later they will be required to do in the exams (for example, explaining practical situations through relating key concepts). Thus, they have the opportunity to study biology with the support of their teachers, who have also responded to their successive brief essays.

Experiences like this promote faculty-student and peer interaction around disciplinary literacy, constituting an example of dialogic teaching strategies (Dysthe, 1996). In the interwoven model, written assignments help students learn disciplinary content and go beyond just being a means of assessment. Students receive teacher support during the process of reading and writing, which allows them to understand the subject and, at the same time, develop their literacy. Furthermore, intertwining literate tasks in the courses leads to avoiding teacher-centered classes and encourages students to take a more active role in the course.

Finally, it is worth mentioning that since interwoven writing strategies are usually time-consuming, teachers who adopt this model often study their practices as part of their research commitment. Otherwise, it is very difficult for these faculty to sustain these teaching practices, especially with numerous students.

CONCLUSION

Latin American and Spanish universities have recently begun to address students' academic literacy needs. The essays by De Micheli and Iglesia, García-Arroyo and Quintana, González, Motta-Roth, Moyano and Natale, Narváez, and Solé et al. in this volume illustrate some of the most relevant initiatives collected in their countries. The essays show both the strong commitment by their authors and the irregular support by their institutions. It is in this regard that these profiles, as well as the whole book, can inspire teachers and institutions to develop their own ways of addressing literacy across the curriculum. The variety of examples and details offered by the authors in these pages will aid readers in foreseeing some challenges and opportunities. These vicarious experiences could encourage readers to experiment within their circumstances without beginning from zero.

Besides, the book can raise our awareness about what is being done or neglected in our own universities regarding students' writing. The range of perspectives presented over these chapters will hopefully allow us to see with fresh eyes what is done or not in our own institutional settings and acknowledge that what is occurring is just an option among others, and not something natural or necessary. This contrast will help us denaturalize familiar practices and open them to critique. Furthermore, the collection of profiles in this volume will be useful toward our questioning the ways of doing (or not doing) established in our institutions and perhaps inspire our advocating for institutional changes to better support the development of students' academic reading and writing.

ACKNOWLEDGEMENTS

I would like to thank Dr. Laura Colombo for generously helping me in editing the English version of this chapter.

REFERENCES

Bazerman, C., Little, J., Bethel, L., Chavkin, T., Fouquette, D., & Garufis, J. (2005). *Reference guide to writing across the curriculum*. West Lafayette, Indiana, and Fort Collins, Colorado: Parlor Press and the WAC Clearinghouse. Retrieved from http://wac.colostate.edu/books/bazerman_wac/

Benvegnu, M.A. (2004). Las prácticas de lectura en la universidad: Un taller para docentes. In P. Carlino (Ed.), *Leer y escribir en la universidad* (pp. 43-57). Colección Textos en Contexto nº 6. Buenos Aires: Lectura y Vida.

Carlino, P. (2008). Exploración de géneros, diario de tesis y revisión entre pares: Análisis de un ciclo de investigación-acción en talleres de tesis de posgrado. In E. Narvaja de Arnoux (Comp.), *Escritura y producción de conocimientos en carreras de posgrado*. Buenos Aires: Santiago Arcos. Retrieved from https://sites.google.com/site/jornadasgiceolem/posgrado

Carlino, P. (2010). Reading and writing in the Social Sciences in Argentine universities. In C. Bazerman et al. (Eds.), *Traditions of writing research* (pp. 283-96). Oxford: Routledge.

Carlino, P. (2012). Helping education doctoral students face writing and emotional challenges towards identity change. In M. Castelló & C. Donahue (Eds.), *University writing: Selves and texts in academic societies*. Sig-W Series Volume on Academic Writing. London: Emerald Group.

Carlino, P. Iglesia, P., & Laxalt, I. (2010, September). Leer y escribir en la formación de profesores secundarios de diversas disciplinas: Qué dicen los docentes que se hace. Memorias de las Jornadas Nacionales "Lectura, escritura y aprendizaje disciplinar." Facultad de Ciencias Humanas, Universidad Nacional de Río Cuarto, Córdoba, Argentina.

Castorina, J. A. (2001). Las versiones del constructivismo ante el conocimiento instituido y las prácticas sociales. *Contextos de Educación, 5*, 17-40.

Dysthe, O. (1996). The multivoiced classroom: Interactions of writing and classroom discourse. *Written Communication, 13*(3), 385-425.

Fernández, G., Izuzquiza, M. V., & Laxalt, I. (2004). El docente universitario frente al desafío de enseñar a leer. In P. Carlino (Ed.), *Leer y escribir en la universidad* (pp. 97-110). Colección Textos en Contexto nº 6. Buenos Aires: Lectura y Vida.

Fernández Fastuca, L. (2010). La enseñanza de la escritura académica en las universidades del área metropolitana de Buenos Aires. Unpublished master's thesis, Buenos Aires, Universidad de San Andrés.

Ferreiro, E. (1999). *Cultura escrita y educación*. México: Fondo de Cultura Económica.

Galán Vélez, R., & Ormsby, L. (2010). El centro de escritura como puente en la educación superior: El Centro de Aprendizaje, Redacción y Lenguas del ITAM. En Guadalupe Ruiz Cuellar, Guadalupe López Bonilla & Alma Carrasco Altamirano (Eds.), *Memorias del II Seminario Internacional de Lectura y Escritura en la Universidad*. Universidad Autónoma de Aguas Calientes.

Hutchings, P., & Shulman, L. (1999). The scholarship of teaching. New elaborations, new developments. *Change, 31*(5), 10-15. Retrieved from http://www.carnegiefoundation.org/elibrary

Langer, J., & Applebee, A. (1987). *How writing shapes thinking: A study of teaching and learning*. Urbana, Illinois: National Council of Teachers of English. WAC Clearinghouse Landmark Publications in Writing Studies. Retrieved from http://wac.colostate.edu/books/langer_applebee/

Marucco, M. (2004). Aprender a enseñar a escribir en la universidad. In P. Carlino (Ed.), *Leer y escribir en la universidad* (pp. 61-76). Colección Textos en Contexto nº 6. Buenos Aires: Lectura y Vida.

Molina, V. (2008). *Centro de Escritura Javeriano: Hacia un mejoramiento de las habilidades de estudiantes y profesores. II Encuentro Nacional y I Internacional de lectura y escritura en la educación superior*. Bogotá: Ascun, Redless.

Narvaja de Arnoux, E., Di Stefano, M., & Pereira, C. (2002). *La lectura y la escritura en la universidad*. Buenos Aires: Eudeba.

Padilla, C., & Carlino, P. (2010). Alfabetización académica e investigación acción: Enseñar a elaborar ponencias en la clase universitaria. In G. Parodi (Ed.), *Alfabetización académica y profesional. Perspectivas contemporáneas* (pp. 153-182). Santiago de Chile: Planeta. Retrieved from https://sites.google.com/site/jornadasgiceolem/universidad

Piaget, J., & García, R. (1982). *Psicogénesis e historia de la ciencia*. [*Psychogenesis and the history of science*.] México: Siglo XXI. Helga Feider (Trans.).(1989). New York: Columbia University Press.

Purser, E., Skillen, J., Deane, M., Donohue, J., & Peake, K. (2008). Developing academic literacy in context. *Zeitschrift Schreiben*. Retrieved from http://www.zeitschrift-schreiben.eu/Beitraege/purser_Academic_Literacy.pdf

Russell, D. (1990). Writing across the curriculum in historical perspective: Toward a social interpretation. *College English, 52*, 52-73.

Scardamalia, M. and Bereiter, C. (1985). Development of dialectical processes in composition. In D. Olson, N., Torrance and A. Hildyard (Eds.), *Literacy, language and learning* (pp. 307-329). Cambridge: Cambridge University Press.

Skillen, J., Merten, M., Trivett, N., & Percy, A. (1998). The IDEALL approach to learning development: A model for fostering improved literacy and learning outcomes for students. *Proceedings of the 1998 Australian Association for Active Research in Education Conference*. Retrieved from http://www.aare.edu.au/98pap/ski98343.htm

Vázquez, A., & Jakob, I. (2007). La escritura y el aprendizaje en el aula universitaria: Componentes cognitivos y didácticos. Innovación Educativa. *Instituto Politécnico Nacional de México, 7*(36), 21–35.

Wells, G. (1987). Apprenticeship in literacy. *Interchange, 18*(1/2), 109-123.

CHAPTER 42.

SECTION ESSAY: REFLECTING ON WHAT CAN BE GAINED FROM COMPARING MODELS OF ACADEMIC WRITING PROVISION

By Lisa Ganobcsik-Williams
Coventry University (England)

The purpose of this section essay is to consider a central question raised by the Writing Programs Worldwide *anthology and articulated in Chris Thaiss' "Introduction" to this volume. This question is, to what extent is it useful for those working in higher education to be aware of writing practices and models of academic writing provision in place at higher education institutions in other national contexts? To explore this question, I will then use examples of academic development work from profiles in this project from universities in the UK, Ireland, Australia, New Zealand, Belgium, and France.*

My own earliest reflections on how academic writing is learned and taught at the tertiary level in different countries occurred when I was an American exchange student at a British university in the 1980s.[1] Having been allocated reading lists and assigned essays to write, I was told by the academics teaching the courses I was taking, as well as by fellow students, that as far as writing was concerned I just needed "to get on with it." I found this experience, during which I grappled to understand what was expected of me as a writer and throughout which I struggled to write, to be in marked contrast to the pedagogy of the composition classes I had been required to take in my first year of study at a US university. In these classes, assignment structures, expectations, and argumentation were discussed and drafting processes scaffolded and monitored.

The experience of being a student writer in a foreign higher education system in which writing was not visibly taught proved to be a pivotal moment for me. Because of this experience, I came to recognise the need for students to become independent writers and to realise that students can be assisted in maturing as academic writers through explicit instruction and guided practice in writing. I carried this experience of learning to write academically, and of understanding that students can be assisted in learning to write academically, back with me to the US university at which I was studying; I became a peer writing tutor at the university's writing center while completing my undergraduate degree. As a student writing tutor, I began to understand more fully how fundamental writing support for university students is, and how empowering for students individualised attention to their writing can be (Borg & Deane, 2010). As an American writing tutor, I also realised that writing teaching, or "writing development work" as I later came to know it in the British context, can aid tutors and teachers themselves in improving as writers, communicators, and critical thinkers. (see, for example, Alpen, Breford & Tschirpke (2011); Devet, 2011; and Girgensohn, 2011).

Reflecting on my experience, however, led me to understand that the solution to supporting students as writers in various national higher education contexts was not simply to import models of writing instruction. As an American student in a UK university, I had not been looking for a composition class, but for guidance on expectations for writing in a higher education culture in which, at that time, students learned to write (or didn't) through acculturation.

When, in the 1990s, I began working in a UK university as a researcher and teacher of Academic Writing, I learned that this topic was not just something with which I was preoccupied, but that international interest in comparing models of writing instruction was growing. Professional organisations such as the European Association for the Teaching of Academic Writing (EATAW), the European Writing Centres Association (EWCA), and the Writing Development in Higher Education Network (WDHE) were being formed, and their biennial conferences, as well as the 2001 University of Warwick Writing Programme conference on "Teaching Writing in Higher Education," were attracting international delegates who were interested in sharing models and practices for teaching writing.[2] This interest was also beginning to surface at the Conference on College Composition and Communication (CCCCs), the major US-based conference for college and university writing teachers and scholars that has been held annually since 1949, as shown, for example, in the panel "Transnational Goals and Practices of Composition: An International Exchange" (Ede et al., 2002) and the half-day workshop "Changing Places: An International Exchange on the Teaching of College Writing" (Ede et al., 2003). Intellectual curiosity was also leading to collaborations on cross-cultural funded writing research and development projects such as the "Developing Academic Literacy in Context" (DALiC) project, "a comparative curriculum development exercise [. . .] involving a group of academic literacy specialists in the UK, the US and Australia" (Purser et al., 2008), which focused on the application, in different higher education contexts, of an embedded model of academic literacy teaching and learning that had emerged in Australian higher education (Skillen & Mahoney, 1997; Skillen et al., 1998 and 1999).

Articles published in English comparing both pedagogical and institutional approaches to developing students' writing in higher education in various countries were also beginning to appear. Examples of these, whose comparative nature is evident in their titles, include, "Learning from—Not Duplicating—US Composition Theory and Practice" (Mullin, 2006), "If not Rhetoric and Composition, then What? Teaching Teachers to Teach Writing" (Murray, 2006), "Peering Across the Pond: the Role of Students in Developing Other Students' Writing in the US and UK" (Devet et al., 2006), and "Writing Center Tutor Training: What is Transferable across Academic Cultures?" (Santa, 2009). Articles such as these explored and questioned specific instances of "importing" and "exporting" writing instruction models from one national higher education culture to another.[3]

In her article "'Internationalization' and Composition Studies: Reorienting the Discourse," Donahue (2009) further theorised the "import/export" concept of cultural exchange of writing pedagogies and provision. Citing Harbord (2008), Donahue acknowledged the attraction for "foreign experts" to share their expertise with colleagues in other countries, as well as the attraction for many colleagues of turning to foreign expertise to obtain advice on writing pedagogy, theory, and programme administration (Donahue, 2009, p. 222). She argued, however, that teachers and theorists of writing must move "'toward equal trade models of exchange" (Donahue, 2009, p. 231), and that, following Muchiri et al. (1995), we must "make claims in contextualized fashion, to remind [our]selves of what [we] take for granted," "become more self-conscious about the ways we use terminology, and resist an import-export model for an equitable exchange" model that puts us "in a learning position with respect to our colleagues around the globe" (Donahue, 2009, p. 232).[4]

As one of the co-editors of *Writing Programs Worldwide*, I have kept this set of principles in mind when offering feedback to authors on their profile essays and in learning from the many ways of teaching writing and approaches to organising the teaching of writing outlined in the profiles. My purpose in the remainder of this short essay is to investigate further the potential usefulness of exchanging cross-cultural writing development theory and practice by exploring themes and examples from the profile essays I commissioned. These profiles report on academic writing development work in universities in the UK, Ireland, Australia,

New Zealand, Belgium, and France. While some profiles focus on a particular sphere of activity, others discuss an array of writing development activities.

WRITING DEVELOPMENT IN RESPONSE TO HIGHER EDUCATION EXPANSION

One theme articulated in almost all of the profiles is that writing development is often called for—by students, by academics and professional staff in universities, by university managers, and by governments—in response to the massification of higher education and the increase in heterogeneity of the student body that such expansion brings.[5] Many profiles begin with a statement of how their institution's student body has grown and become much more diverse in terms of increased participation of indigenous people; foreign students; people from a variety of social classes, races, and ethnic groups; distance-learners; and students with varied experiences of educational preparation. Writing about AUT University, New Zealand, John Bitchener notes that AUT University "'has a multi-national and multi-cultural population: 42% pakehas (white New Zealanders), 10% Maori (indigenous New Zealanders), 11% Pasifika (Pacific Islanders), 27% Asians (East and South Asian countries) and 10% others," and that "[t]his range of backgrounds means that the university must cater for the diverse needs of its equally diverse student population" and "accept responsibility for ensuring that students have every chance of succeeding." Similarly, Marie-Christine Pollet notes that students at the Université Libre de Bruxelles, Belgium, are characterized by "a large diversity in their geographic, cultural and social origins" as well as in their educational backgrounds.

Karyn Gonano and Peter Nelson, writing from Queensland University of Technology, Australia, explain that their government's Bradley Review, Transforming Australia's Higher Education System, which was put into effect in 2009 "to widen participation in universities," has resulted "in an increasingly diverse range of students with an equally significant range of experiences." Gonano and Nelson discuss the impact of the internationalisation agenda in Australian higher education in terms of the development of English as a Foreign Language (EFL) writing support programmes at Queensland University of Technology. They identify, as does Mary Deane's and my profile of writing provision at Coventry University, England, the need for writing support not just for non-native speakers of English, but for all students.

That calls for writing development have been occasioned by growth in student numbers in higher education and by erosion of homogeneity in student populations is a claim that appears over and over again in Academic Writing and

Composition scholarship. Many scholars have written about this phenomenon as a catalyst for the development of Composition teaching and writing centers in US universities (see, for example, Boquet, 1999; Carino, 1995; Russell, 2002; and Yaher & Murdick,1991), while Skillen (2006) has argued that as a result of "the massification of the tertiary education system in the 1970s and 1980s" in Australia, the assumption that writing instruction was not necessary because "students at this level of education already had adequate writing skills acquired during secondary school" was questioned, and learning centres were set up in Australian universities (Skillen, 2006, p. 140). This claim has also been made in relation to the development, from the 1990s, of Academic Writing as a teaching and research field in UK higher education (Ganobcsik-Williams, 2006, p. xxi-5), and appears in many articles by European writing teachers and scholars in the Autumn 2011 inaugural issue of the *Journal of Academic Writing*, the journal of the European Association for the Teaching of Academic Writing.

WRITING CENTRES AND WRITING PROGRAMMES WITH MULTIPLE FUNCTIONS

A second theme apparent in the profiles is that of writing programmes and writing centres outside of the US taking on multiple functions. As Santa (2009) points out:"Most American writing centers stand in support of writing programs which include composition or writing intensive course instruction as mandatory features of an undergraduate curriculum. In most Continental writing centers, the writing centre *is the writing program"* (Santa. 2009, p.3).

That the writing centre is the hub for writing development work is also true of the first writing centre in Irish higher education. The Regional Writing Centre at the University of Limerick, Ireland, discussed in the profile by Íde O'Sullivan and Lawrence Cleary, names its priorities as supporting student writers, supporting postgraduate students in developing their writing and in training for tutoring writing, "faculty development on best practices for teaching with writing" and, in conjunction with the University's Centre for Teaching and Learning, academic staff development in scholarly writing. The Centre for Academic Writing (CAW) at Coventry University, England, as depicted in the profile by Deane and Ganobcsik-Williams, is also an example of a writing centre that functions as a department of writing studies. CAW's mission statement comprises a "whole institution" writing development commitment to supporting student writing, to carrying out staff development in the teaching of writing, and to facilitating staff and postgraduate writing for publication. The Academic Achievement Teaching Unit (AATU), at the University of Dundee, Scotland, detailed in Kathleen McMillan's profile, is classified as a teaching unit rather than a writing centre, but offers, through a partnership with Fellows from the UK's Royal Literary Fund Fellowship Scheme, one-to-one writing tuition for students, bespoke workshops in which AATU staff collaborate with academics to teach academic skills, and other types of writing and skills teaching.[6]

THE IMPORTANCE OF NATIONAL AND LOCAL INSTITUTIONAL CONTEXTS FOR WRITING DEVELOPMENT

Another theme common to all of the profiles is the importance of national and local institutional contexts for writing development. Many authors review their choices of pedagogical approaches and emphasise the need to fit writing pedagogies and writing development provision to particular contexts. Pollet, for example, notes that the Center for University Learning at the Université Libre de Bruxelles was established as a result of an internal institutional report and that its work has been affirmed by a national government mandate in "working to promote the success of students." Pollet explains how the Center's teaching practices have evolved through "normative" and "technicist" approaches into a "pragmatic" approach to providing linguistic and writing support for first-year, French-speaking students.

Another example of the emphasis on contextualising writing development is shown by Lisa Emerson, in her profile of academic writing teaching at Massey University, New Zealand. "Becoming an ethnographer: understanding the context," writes Emerson, who became involved in writing development work when a "colleague had returned from Sabbatical in the US fired up with a mission to start a writing centre to improve students' writing skills." Having subscribed to a US-based writing center listserv, Emerson notes that often:

> .... reading the email discussions felt more like eavesdropping on a conversation on an alien planet. The conversation may have been in English but the largely American cultural context in which it took place was beyond my comprehension: the terminology was opaque, and the assumption that a whole institutional infrastructure around writing was in place was unimaginable at that time in a New Zealand context.

Emerson notes, therefore, that she had to "invent" her role as a writing tutor and to become, in Elaine Maimon's words, an "ethnographer" of her home campus (McLeod & Soven, 1992, p. xi) in order to build "a New Zealand writing programme" informed by international scholarship but emerging "out of the context of a New Zealand university" and "carefully crafted to meet the needs of New Zealand students."

Emerson's experiences and observations correspond with those of Santa (2009), who found it inappropriate to use US Composition textbooks and writing tutor guides to teach and support Bulgarian, Romanian, Albanian, and Serbian university students and writing tutors in Bulgaria. As Santa (2009) argues, "[a]n increasingly international writing center practice demands elucidation of theory and practice which might best facilitate the work of new tutors and better conform to local academic practices and needs." (Santa, 2009, p. 1).

CROSS-FERTILISATION OF WRITING THEORIES AND PRACTICES

The concept of contextualised writing development relates closely to the final theme of the profiles that I would like to highlight, the importance of cross-fertilisation of writing theories and practices between higher education cultures. Within this group of profiles, the dominant and default provider of expertise about writing development is the US; this is, arguably, inevitable given that the US has well-developed programs, departments, and centers in which explicit tertiary writing teaching and tutoring takes place, underpinned by a long tradition of writing research and scholarship.[7] Many authors explain how they have been influenced by US theories and practices of teaching writing. In addition to my own and Emerson's experiences as discussed above, Theresa McConlogue, Sally Mitchell, and Kelly Peake note that the Thinking Writing programme team at Queen Mary, University of London drew "inspiration from Writing in the Disciplines at Cornell University;" Jonathan Worley credits the influence of a US writing center colleague in developing the writing centre and peer tutoring programme at St. Mary's University College, Belfast; and Lawrence Cleary and Íde O'Sullivan recount how, prior to setting up the writing centre at the University of Limerick, a visiting professor from the US met with their working group for "a week-long consultation" including "workshops on writing" and an exploration of how "university-wide support could be translated into a systematic, comprehensive approach to writing while addressing individual, disciplinary concerns."

For non-US-based writing teachers and researchers, one way in which to move beyond or alongside the US influence is to seek to learn more from one's own regionally- and nationally-based colleagues. In his section essay in this volume, Gerd Bräuer indicates the value of the collegial regional and local networks that have enabled close collaboration in developing writing centers in Austria, Germany, Liechtenstein, and Switzerland. As indicated by Pollet and by Françoise Boch and Cathy Frier's profile of the Université Stendhal, Grenoble III, France, a community of exchange between writing teacher-researchers also exists in Belgium and France.[8] In the UK, the WDHE network and groups such as the Interuniversity Academic Literacies Research Group (Aclits), as well as visits and discussions between writing development colleagues at various universities, have helped to create and maintain a community of writing teachers, scholars, and programme/centre managers.[9]

Another way to learn about writing development more broadly is to seek and compare expertise from a variety of cultural contexts. When setting up the Centre for Academic Writing at Coventry University, for example, I engaged a US writing center/ Writing Across the Curriculum (WAC) colleague and an Australian learning centre colleague as joint consultants,[10] and the writing centre benefited from my opportunity to learn about US writing programs, writing centers, and WAC administration as well as about Australian learning centres and models for organising the teaching of writing. On a larger scale, Pollet's profile essay suggests a cross-fertilisation of theory and theoretical traditions between Belgium and France (Littéracies Universitaires) and the UK (Academic Literacies),[11] while O'Sullivan and Cleary cite Academic Literacies and American Composition and Rhetoric perspectives as important influences on the teaching and research approaches taken at their Regional Writing Centre in Ireland.

Scholarship giving insight into writing pedagogies and ways of organising writing development in various cultures is increasing and becoming more widely available through publications such as the *Writing Programs Worldwide* anthology. By reviewing the group of profiles under consideration here, for instance, I have come to realise that there is an increasing focus on the writing of postgraduate students and academic staff. This focus includes doctoral thesis-writing as discussed by John Bitchener in his profile of AUT University, Auckland, New Zealand, as well as postgraduate and academics' development in writing for publication as discussed in the profiles about the writing centres at Coventry University and the University of Limerick.[12] As a result of Boch and Frier's profile of a writing research teaching intervention project, I have also gained insight into the concept of "scientific" writing research prevalent in European higher education.

To what extent, therefore, is it useful for those working in higher education to be aware of writing practices and models of academic writing provision in place at higher education institutions in other national contexts? In this essay, I have responded to this question through my reflection upon how the opportunity, as a student, to begin to compare writing instruction and ways of organising writing provision within universities in two different countries resulted in furthering my own development as a student writer and led me to recognise the benefits of supporting students with their writing in higher education. I have also reflected on the question of the value of cross-cultural awareness of writing pedagogies and institutional approaches to writing development by discussing four main themes and an array of examples taken from a selection of profile essays in this anthology. As these themes and examples show, there are now common inter- and trans-national issues being faced in academia that would suggest the benefit of comparing approaches, both within regions and nations and with other higher education cultures. Transnationalism is accelerating, and writing developers have much to learn from—and much to contribute to—other contexts for teaching writing.

NOTES

1. Donahue (2009) points out that a "broadly ignored area of [C]omposition work is that of US monolingual students' experiences when they go overseas to study or work and find themselves in universities and workplaces with different rhetorical, discursive, and sociolinguistic expectations, whether that work is being done in English or in another language. An 'English is English' mindset seems uniquely inappropriate for current international contexts" (p. 218). The personal reflections offered in this essay are a contribution to this area of Composition scholarship.

2. The WDHE was founded in 1994. The first, joint, EATAW/EWCA conference took place in 2001. For more information on these organisations and on the Warwick Writing Programme conference, see Ganobcsik-Williams (2006), pages xxiv-xxv.

3. Articles by Mullin (2006), as well as Heyda (2006) also cautioned that writing pedagogies and models of organising writing instruction within colleges and universities may not be appropriate for the contexts within which they are operating, let alone for implementation elsewhere. Heyda (2006), for example, argues that the "sentimental" tradition of required first-year composition classes in US universities is ineffective and that US institutions' focus on this model hinders the resourcing and development of other, he contends, more productive approaches to working with students on their writing.

4. While Donahue addresses her remarks in this article in *College Composition and Communication* to US Composition and Rhetoric teachers and scholars, I believe that these points apply to all writing developers.

5. For many higher education systems, "universalisation" rather than "massification" is the appropriate term. For a definition of the difference between "mass" and "universal" educational systems, see Peter Scott (1995, p. 2).

6. While other UK writing centres typically are engaged in a variety of activities, the Writing Centre at St. Mary's University College, Belfast, Northern Ireland, as discussed in Jonathan Worley's profile, focuses its expertise on peer tutoring in writing.

7. As Donahue (2009), citing Muchiri et al. (1995) points out, however, "[t]he absence of an 'industry' of first-year composition" in countries outside of the United States "is not the absence of the study and teaching of higher education writing," and some writing scholars have traced the histories of higher education writing instruction in various countries back hundreds of years (p. 222).

8. Donahue (2009) makes reference to this field of the study of university writing as 'la didactique de l'écrit' (p. 222).

9. Established in 1993, Aclits is convened by Mary Scott at the Institute of Education, University of London.

10. These colleagues were Professor Joan Mullin and Dr. Jan Skillen.

11. See the Call for Proposals for the "University Literacies" conference, held at the Université Charles de Gaulle, Lille III, 2-4 September 2010: http://evenements.univ-lille3.fr/litteracies-universitaires/en/?Call_for_proposals, which observes that "[r]esearch about university reading and writing practices, developed in French-speaking countries and in Europe in the field of 'didactics' in the past dozen years, are coming more and more into dialogue with this kind of research in the U.K. field of *Academic Literacies* . . . [and] the US field of *Composition Studies*."

12. For further discussion of thesis-writing pedagogies and approaches to supporting the scholarly writing of postgraduate students and academics, see, for example, Murray (2002, 2009) and Lillis and Curry (2006, 2010).

REFERENCES

Alpen, C., Breford, L., & Tschirpke, S. (2011, July). Peer tutoring: Through the eyes of the student tutor. Keynote Panel. The role of the student experience in shaping academic writing development in higher education: The sixth conference of the European Association for the Teaching of Academic Writing. Limerick, Ireland.

Boquet, E. (1999). "Our little secret": A history of writing centers, pre- to post-open admissions. *College Composition and Communication, 50*(3), 463-82.

Borg E., & Deane, M. (2011). Measuring the outcomes of individualised writing instruction: a multilayered approach to capturing changes in students' texts. *Teaching in Higher Education, 16,* 319-331.

Carino, P. (1995). Early writing centers: Toward a history. *The Writing Center Journal, 15*(2), 103-15.

Devet, B. (2011). What teachers of academic writing can learn from the writing center. *Journal of Academic Writing, 1(1),* 248-253.

Devet, B., Orr, S., Blythman, M., & Bishop, C. (2006). Peering across the pond: The role of students in developing other sudents' writing in the US and UK. In L. Ganobcsik-Williams (Ed.), *Teaching academic writing in UK higher education: Theories, practices, and models* (pp. 196-211). Universities into the 21st Century Series Houndmills: Palgrave Macmillan.

Donahue, C. (2009) "Internationalization" and composition studies: Reorienting the discourse. *College Composition and Communication, 61*(2), 212-243.

Ede, L., Ganobcsik-Williams, L., Gong, G., Ivanič, R., Lunsford, A., Paré, A., Russell, D., Skillen, J., & Van Kruiningen, J. (2003, March). Changing places: An international exchange on the teaching of college writing. 54th Annual conference on college composition and communication. New York.

Ede, L, Ganobcsik-Williams, L., Gong, G., Ivanič, R., Lunsford, A., Lea, M., Paré, A., and Skillen, J. (2002, April). Transnational goals and practices of composition: An international exchange. Panel Presentation. 53rd Annual Conference on College Composition and Communication, Chicago.

Ganobcsik-Williams, L. (2006). *Teaching academic writing in UK higher education: Theories, practices and models.* Universities into the 21st Century Series Houndmills: Palgrave Macmillan.

Girgensohn, K. (2011, July). Mutual growing: How student writing tutors' experience can shape writing centres. The role of the student experience in shaping academic writing development in higher education: The Sixth Conference of the European Association for the Teaching of Academic Writing. Limerick, Ireland.

Harbord, J. (2008, May) Speech. International writing across the curriculum conference. Austin, Texas.

Heyda, J. (2006). Sentimental education: First-year writing as compulsory ritual in US colleges and universities. In L. Ganobcsik-Williams (Ed.), *Teaching academic writing in UK higher education: Theories, practices and models* (pp. 154-166). Universities into the 21st Century Series Houndmills: Palgrave Macmillan.

Lillis, T., & Curry, M. (2006). Professional academic writing by multilingual scholars: Interactions with literacy brokers in the production of English-medium texts. *Written Communication, 2*(1), 3-35.

Lillis, T., & Curry, M. (2010) *Academic publishing in a global context: The politics and practices of publishing in English.* New York: Routledge.

McLeod, S. H., & Soven, M. (Eds.). (1992). *Writing across the curriculum: A guide to developing programs*. Thousand Oaks, California: Sage Publications.

Muchiri, M., Nshindi, M., Myers, G., and Ndoloi, D. (1995). Importing composition: Teaching and researching academic writing beyond North America. *College Composition and Communication 46*, 175-198.

Mullin, J. (2006). Learning from—not duplicating—US composition theory and practice. In L. Ganobcsik-Williams (Ed.), *Teaching academic writing in UK higher education: Theories, practices and models* (pp. 167-179). Universities into the 21st Century Series Houndmills: Palgrave Macmillan.

Murray, R. (2002). *How to write a thesis*. Maidenhead, UK: Open University Press.

Murray, R. (2006). If not rhetoric and composition, then what? Teaching teachers to teach writing. In L. Ganobcsik-Williams (Ed.), *Teaching academic writing in UK higher education: Theories, practices and models* (pp. 124-133). Universities into the 21st Century Series Houndmills: Palgrave Macmillan.

Murray, R. (2009). *Writing for academic journals*, 2nd ed. Maidenhead, UK: Open University Press/McGraw-Hill Education.

Purser, E., Skillen, J., Deane, M., Donahue, J., & Peake, K. (2008). Developing academic literacy in context. *Zeitschrift Schreiben*. Retrieved from http://www.zeitschrift-schreiben.eu

Russell, D. (2002). *Writing in the academic disciplines: A curricular history*, 2nd ed. Carbondale: Southern Illinois University Press.

Santa, T. (2009). Writing center tutor training: What is transferable across academic cultures? *Zeitschrift Schreiben*. Retrieved from http://www.zeitschrift-schreiben.eu

Scott, P. (1995) *The Meanings of mass higher education*. Buckingham: Open University Press.

Skillen, J. (2006). Teaching academic writing from the centre in Australian Universities. In L. Ganobcsik-Williams (Ed.), *Teaching academic writing in UK higher education: Theories, practices and models* (pp. 140-153). Universities into the 21st Century Series Houndmills: Palgrave Macmillan.

Skillen, J., & Mahoney, M. (1997). Literacy and learning development in higher education: An issue of institutional change. In P. Jeffrey (Ed.), *Higher education in new times, Proceedings of the 1997 AARE (Australian Association for Research in Education) Conference*. Retrieved from http://www.swin.edu.au/aare/conf97.htm

Skillen J., Merten M., Trivett N., & Percy, A. (1998). The IDEALL approach to learning development: A model for fostering improved literacy and learning outcomes for students. *Proceedings of the 1998 AARE (Australian Association for Research in Education) Conference.* Retrieved from http://www.swin.edu.au/aare/conf98.htm

Skillen J., Trivett, N., Merten, M. and Percy, A. (1999). Integrating the instruction of generic and discipline specific skills into the Curriculum: A case study. In *Cornerstones: Proceedings of the 1999 HERDSA (Higher Education Research and Development Society of Australasia) Conference.* Retrieved from http://www.herdsa.org.au/

Yahner, W., & Murdick, W. (1991). The Evolution of a writing center: 1972-1990. *The Writing Center Journal, 11*(2), 13-28.

ABOUT THE AUTHORS AND EDITORS

Arlene Archer co-ordinates the Writing Centre at the University of Cape Town, South Africa. She teaches in Applied Language Studies, Higher Education Studies, Film and Media. Her research includes drawing on popular culture and multimodal pedagogies to enable student access to Higher Education. She has published in such journals as *Language and Education, Teaching in Higher Education,* and *English in Education.*

Susaimanickam Armstrong, Associate Professor of English and Head-in-Charge, University of Madras, Chennai, Tamil Nadu, India, is a recipient of a Fulbright-Nehru Visiting Associate Professorship in Native American Studies at UC Davis, CA, US. He coordinates four language laboratories, soft skills, and elective courses at Tholkappiar Campus. He is a Governor-Chancellor nominee of the Planning Board of the Periyar University.

John Bitchener, Professor of Applied Linguistics at AUT University, Auckland, New Zealand, is the author of *Writing a Thesis or Dissertation in Applied Linguistics* and co-author (with Ferris) of *Written Corrective Feedback for Second Language Acquisition and Writing*. He has published many articles in SLA and academic genre discourse.

Françoise Boch is a lecturer in Language Sciences at the Université Stendhal in Grenoble (France) and a member of the Laboratoire LIDILEM (Linguistique et Didactiques des Langues Etrangères et Maternelles/linguistics and didactics of foreign and native languages). Since 2000, she has conducted studies on university writing (particularly scientific/academic writing) from the perspective of both linguistics and didactics.

Tobias Boström is an M.Sc. student in civil engineering at Chalmers University of Technology (Sweden) focused on design and construction project management. During the second and third years of this five-year programme, he participated in implementation of Supplemental Instruction at his department.

Gerd Bräuer was the chair of the European Writing Centers Association for 2006-2008. A professor of German Studies at Emory University in the US from 1995-2004, he currently directs the distance-learning program for teachers at the Writing Center at the University of Education in Freiburg, Germany. He is the initiator and coordinator of the Scriptorium project, dedicated to the development of a teacher training program in the fields of writing and reading pedagogy. His numerous publications on writing pedagogy and foreign language instruction include *Teaching Academic Writing in European Higher Education* (with Björk, Rienecker, and Stray Jörgensen) and *New Visions in Foreign Language Education* (with Karen Sanders).

Paula Carlino is a researcher with the National Council of Scientific and Technical Research, CONICET, at the University of Buenos Aires. She leads the GICEOLEM (Group for Students' Inclusion in Quality Education through Teachers Taking Care of Reading and Writing in the Disciplines), a group devoted to research and teacher development. Her interests include WAC/WID, academic literacies, action research, teacher education, and graduate students' experiences regarding their dissertations. She has lectured and consulted in several Latin-American universities. She has authored *Escribir, leer y aprender en la universidad. Una introducción a la alfabetización académica* [*Writing, Reading and Learning at the University. An Introduction to Academic Literacy*], which was distinguished as Best Book in Education 2005. Dr. Carlino has co-authored *Lectura y escritura, un asunto de todos* [*Writing and Reading. Everybody's Matter*], declared of Educational Interest by the National Senate of Argentina.

Montserrat Castelló is Professor at the Graduate School of Psychology and Educational and Sports Sciences, Ramon Llull University (Catalonia, Spain). From 2002-2008 she was Vicedean of Research and Doctoral Studies. Her publications focus on academic writing strategies and identity. Since 2008 she has been Editor in Chief of the journal *Cultura & Educación*.

Lawrence Cleary is a Writing Consultant at Ireland's first Regional Writing Centre at the University of Limerick. Cleary is involved in the design, delivery, and evaluation of writing-support interventions, including teaching academic writing at both undergraduate and postgraduate level, grounding writing centre initiatives in good practice and sound theory.

Mary Deane teaches at Oxford Brookes University, UK on the Postgraduate Certificate of Teaching in Higher Education (PCTHE) and the Associate Teachers (AT) course. In 2008 she won a Teaching Excellence Award at Coventry University, and her recent publications include *Academic Research, Writing, and Referencing* (2010), *Critical Thinking and Analysis* (2010), and the edited collection, *Writing in the Disciplines* (2011).

Ana T. De Micheli, PhD and Professor of Biology, has taught at the University of Buenos Aires since 1985. The commitment to her students as well as her colleagues has led her to enter upon participatory action research using different practical approaches such as reading comprehension and written production embedded in her teaching.

Ursula Doleschal is Professor of Slavic Linguistics at the Alpen-Adria Universität Klagenfurt (Austria) and director of the "SchreibCenter" since 2005. From 1990 until 2003 she worked at the Department of Slavic Languages at the

Wirtschaftsuniversität Wien (Austria), where her interest in academic writing and especially students' writing was triggered.

Associate Professor **Lisa Emerson** from Massey University, New Zealand, has been a key player in the development of academic writing in the tertiary curriculum in New Zealand since 1989. She is currently teaching the first Writing Center courses in New Zealand. Her research interests include science writing, plagiarism, and transition literacy.

Cathy Frier is a lecturer in Language Sciences at the Université Stendhal in Grenoble (France) and a member of the Laboratoire LIDILEM (Linguistique et Didactiques des Langues Etrangères et Maternelles). Her training is in both linguistics and the didactics of French. Her research concerns learning support in reading-writing at different educational levels.

Lisa Ganobcsik-Williams is Head of the Centre for Academic Writing, Coventry University, England. She has taught and tutored writing in both UK and US universities, and has published in journals including *Rhetorica*, *The Writing Center Journal*, and *Computers in Composition*. She has published an edited book, *Teaching Academic Writing in UK Higher Education: Theories, Practices and Models* (2006). From 2009-11, she served as Chair of the European Association for the Teaching of Academic Writing, and this, as well as her service on the executive boards of the European Writing Centers Association and the International Writing Centers Association, has enabled her to help raise international awareness of the work of European academic writing professional organisations.

Matilde García-Arroyo is an English professor at InterAmerican University of Puerto Rico, Metro Campus, where she teaches at the undergraduate and graduate levels. She combines her teaching responsibilities with the research she conducts in both the reading and writing processes in L1 and L2.

Katrin Girgensohn, founder and scientific director of the Writing Center at the European University Viadrina in Frankfurt (Oder), Germany, is chair of the European Writing Centers Association (EWCA). She published a workbook on creative writing, an anthology on writing center work with international PhD students, a novel, and several compilations of creative memoirs.

Co-editor of *Negotiating a Meta-Pedagogy: Learning from other Disciplines* (with Toni Glover), **Emily Golson** has published articles and book chapters in the *Journal of General Education*, *Advanced Composition*, *Computers and Composition*, *Kairos*, and *Comp Tales*, She has been Writing Center director at the American University in Cairo and chaired the first Department of Rhetoric and Composition in the Middle East.

Karyn Gonano is a Language and Learning Educator at Queensland University of Technology (Australia), delivering writing programmes across the university (e.g., to the Faculty of Built Environment and Engineering) and to the corporate sector. She won the Vice-Chancellor's Award for Excellence in recognition of exceptional sustained performance, and was nominated for an Australian Carrick Award for Programs that Enhance Learning.

Blanca González Pinzón has degrees in Philology and Languages, Classical Languages, and Social and Educational Development from the Universidad Nacional (Colombia). She researches reading and writing at all levels of education and currently directs the Reading and Writing Program at Universidad Sergio Arboleda.

Currently the Writing Minor and Internships Faculty Advisor in the University Writing Program at UC Davis (US), **Gary Goodman** teaches varied writing courses, including advanced writing in history, sociology, and women studies, and writing in the professions: journalism. For many years she coordinated the Writing Across the Curriculum Program.

Heather Graves is associate professor in English and Film Studies at the University of Alberta (Canada). In 2011, she served as the inaugural Scholar in Residence for Arts Research in Nanotechnology at the National Institute for Nanotechnology. Her research focuses on rhetoric and writing practices in the sciences.

Roger Graves is Director of Writing Across the Curriculum at the University of Alberta. Previously he served as Director of the Writing, Rhetoric, and Professional Communication program at the University of Western Ontario and as Director of the MA in New Media Studies at DePaul University in Chicago.

Helmut Gruber is Associate Professor at the Department of Linguistics at Vienna University. He received his PhD in Psychology and wrote his "habilitation" (second dissertation) in Applied Linguistics. His research interests include communication in politics and media, communication in the electronic media, academic writing in general, and students' academic writing.

Magnus Gustafsson is director of the Centre for Language and Communication at Chalmers University of Technology, Gothenburg, Sweden. Focusing on discipline-specific communication, he develops curricularly integrated communication interventions to enhance students' content learning while also facilitating good communication literacy with interventions ensuring progression and increasingly demanding learning outcomes.

Linda Hirsch, Professor of English at Hostos Community College/CUNY (US), coordinates the Hostos Writing/Reading Across the Curriculum Initiative. She researches language and cognitive needs of students across disciplines, including ELLs. Currently she is examining the transformative effects of WAC pedagogies on faculty and students. She also writes and hosts a televison program devoted to issues in education.

Lammert Holdijk, Associate Chair of the first and only department of Rhetoric and Composition in the Middle East, at the American University in Cairo, is involved in all aspects of departmental administration and faculty training. He teaches a core curriculum course called "Who Am I?: Self and consciousness across the disciplines." He gives guest lectures in other departments that reflect his outside interests: e.g., Jekyll and Hyde, Taoism, Sufism and love.

Patricia Iglesia is a biologist whose research area of interest is science education. She is a biology professor of first year courses at the University of Buenos Aires, where she has been working with writing tasks to promote learning of cellular biology since 2005. She is currently completing a master's degree in writing and literacy.

Eva-Maria Jakobs, full professor in Textlinguistics and Technical Communication at RWTH Aachen University, directs the Institute for Industrial Communication and Business Media and is a full member of the German National Academy of Science and Technology. She has published more than forty papers and books dealing with writing and text production in professional scientific writing, writing at the workplace, and writing in electronic environments. Jakobs is co-editor of the *Handbook of Writing and Text Production* to be published in 2013 by Mouton de Gruyter.

Carel Jansen, Professor in Business Communication, was until 2011 Vice-dean for Education at the Faculty of Arts of Radboud University Nijmegen, Netherlands. He is now head of the Department of Communication and Information Studies at the University of Groningen, and extraordinary professor with the Language Centre at Stellenbosch University, South Africa. He has published books and articles on professional communication and document design.

Associate Professor **Judith Kearns** chairs the Department of Rhetoric, Writing, and Communications at the University of Winnipeg (Canada). Her research interest in women's writing extends from the seventeenth-century memoirist Anne Halkett to contemporary Canadian journalist Christie Blatchford. Among the articles she and Brian Turner have co-authored are several on the history of their department.

Otto Kruse, Professor at the School of Applied Linguistics in the Zurich University of AppliedSciences, Switzerland, is head of the Centre for Professional Writing and teaches academic,technical, and creative writing. Current research interests are in the fields of comparative writing research and the analysis of national/disciplinary writing cultures.

Teresa McConlogue is a Thinking Writing advisor at Queen Mary, University of London, where she collaborates with academic colleagues to develop and research innovative courses. She is interested in how students are introduced to ways of thinking within a discipline and how they articulate their growing conceptions of disciplinary thinking through writing.

Kathleen McMillan, Director of Personal Learning for University Success at the University of Dundee, Scotland, has co-authored (with Jonathan Weyers) books on academic literacies; most recently, *Study Skills for International Students*. With Bill Kirton, the first Royal Literary Fund Writing Fellow at the University of Dundee, she has co-authored *Just Right*, a guide to tackling university writing assignments.

Sally Mitchell coordinates the Thinking Writing team at Queen Mary, University of London. She is currently conducting a study, with Sue Hudd at Quinnipiac University, Connecticut (US), of how higher education institutions think about and situate writing development initiatives, particularly in relation to their broader agendas for teaching and learning.

Désirée Motta-Roth, Associate Professor of English and Applied Linguistics at the Federal University at Santa Maria, Brazil, heads the Reading and Writing Laboratory. Researching for the Brazilian National Council for Scientific and Technological Development, she has written/co-edited books and articles on genre and discourse theory and multiliteracies.

Estela Inés Moyano's research areas are the discourse of disciplines and academic literacy at different educational levels. At the Universidad Nacional de General Sarmiento (Argentina), she has designed and led a literacy program across the university curriculum (PRODEAC). The pedagogic device for teaching literacy that she developed for this program has also been adapted to teach disciplines through reading and writing at different educational levels.

Elizabeth Narváez Cardona has led academic writing and scientific publication training courses for students and professors at Universidad Autónoma de Occidente. She is conducting the inter-institutional research project *Why do we read and write at the Colombian University? A contribution to the academic culture of the nation*, funded by the Colombian Department of Science, Technology and Innovation (COLCIENCIAS).

Lucía Natale is an applied linguist who specialises in language education, especially in early and academic literacy. Her research interests include writing teaching and discourse analysis. She is a Lecturer at the Universidad Nacional de General Sarmiento (Argentina), where she coordinates an institutional program for developing reading and writing across the curriculum.

Peter Nelson's background is in Education (TESOL) and Applied Linguistics, where he has worked both in Australia and internationally. For 15 years, he has coordinated the Language and Learning Unit in International Student Services at Queensland University of Technology, Brisbane. The unit collaborates closely with academic staff in faculties to develop timely, relevant and effective academic writing programs.

Íde O'Sullivan is Writing Consultant at Ireland's first Regional Writing Centre at the University of Limerick. She is involved in the design, delivery and evaluation of writing-support interventions, including teaching academic writing at both undergraduate and postgraduate levels, grounding writing centre initiatives in good practice and sound theory.

Dennis Paoli has been the Coordinator of the Hunter College Reading/Writing Center for 25 years and Co-coordinator of the college's Writing Across the Curriculum Program for 11 years. He is a former board member of the International Writing Centers Association and consultant for the City University of New York's Office of Assessment.

Kelly Peake, advisor in the Thinking Writing initiative at Queen Mary, University of London, maintains a particular interest in academic literacies, transitions into higher education, and the role of argument in developing disciplinary knowledge. She has worked in higher education in Japan, South Africa, and the UK, and holds an MSc in Applied Linguistics from the University of Edinburgh.

Daniel Perrin is Professor of Media Linguistics, Director of the Institute of Applied Media Studies IAM of the Zurich University of Applied Sciences, Secretary General of the International Association of Applied Linguistics (AILA), and Co-Editor of the *International Journal of Applied Linguistics*. Research and teaching areas include text linguistics, methodology of applied linguistics, and analysis of language in the media and in professional communication.

Hadara Perpignan, who passed away on December 25, 2010, after a difficult illness, was senior lecturer in the department of English as a Foreign Language at Bar-Ilan University (Israel), where she taught writing for academic purposes to doctoral candidates. She developed writing programs at Bar-Ilan University and the University of Haifa, as well as at the Catholic University of Rio de Janeiro, Brazil. Her research centered on teacher-written feedback to student writing, affective and social outcomes of writing instruction, and genre analysis of literary criticism.

Marie-Christine Pollet is a professor at the Faculty of Philosophy and Letters of the University of Brussels. She is the Director of the Centre de Méthodologie Universitaire et de Didactique du Français which aims at helping students develop their language competencies according to their disciplinary context.

Emily Purser is Lecturer (since 2002) in Learning Development at the University of Wollongong (Australia). She spent ten years in China and Germany teaching English, language theory & history, and Australian Studies. One focus of her current work is the learning needs of international students in Commerce and Informatics.

Hilda E. Quintana, Spanish Professor at the InterAmerican University of Puerto Rico, Metro Campus, teaches at the undergraduate and graduate levels. She is also the UNESCO Chair for the Development of Reading and Writing Abilities, a position that allows her to do research in both fields.

Lotte Rienecker, director of the Writing Centre at the University of Copenhagen, has since 1992 taught and published in (teaching) academic writing, university genres, writing processes, assessment criteria, writer's block, research questions, academic articles, etc. She works with university learning and teaching, supervisor's courses, feedback, PhD generic skills courses. Lotte Rienecker is currently chair of the Danish Universities Association for Learning and Teaching.

Lynne Ronesi, Assistant Professor at the American University of Sharjah (UAE), teaches writing, trains undergraduate writing tutors, and directs the Writing Fellows Program. She worked with undergraduate writing tutors at the University of Rhode Island, US, and at the Al Akhawayn University in Ifrane, Morocco.

Bella Rubin, Senior Lecturer at Tel Aviv University (retired), specializes in teaching academic writing to graduate students. Her research interests include responding to student writing, student/teacher perceptions of the outcomes of academic writing courses, bridging the gap between academic and workplace writing, and the development of academic writing as a discipline in Israel.

Aparna Sinha is pursuing her PhD in Education at the University of California, Davis (US), with designated emphases in Writing Studies and in Second Language Acquisition. She has a master's degree in English Literature with an emphasis in Composition and Rhetoric and a master's degree in TESOL certificate. She has been teaching composition for six years. Her dissertation research concerns student placement and assessment in first-year writing courses.

Isabel Solé, Professor at the University of Barcelona, teaches Educational Psychology and "the procedures and canons of scientific and academic communication." She studies the processes performed by students from secondary school to university to write after reading two or more texts. She has published books and scientific articles dealing with academic reading and writing.

Ingrid Stassen, lecturer in Business Communication at the Faculty of Arts of Radboud University Nijmegen, Netherlands, coordinated several projects funded by SURF (Utrecht, Netherlands) and EU-Minerva (Brussels, Belgium) on developing online writing centres and Quality Assessment of Digital Educational Materials. Her research focuses on (peer) feedback and text revision.

Peter Stray Jørgensen, writing consultant at the Academic Writing Centre of the University of Copenhagen (Denmark), has published on academic writing, university genres, writing processes, the teaching of academic writing and supervision, academic language, and oral presentation. He currently works with university learning and teaching, feedback, and assessment, as well as PhD and supervisor skills.

Ana Teberosky, Professor at the University of Barcelona, teaches subjects related to oral and written language acquisition. She also teaches "the procedures and canons of scientific and academic communication" in post-graduate studies. She has carried out research dealing with these subjects, published in books and scientific articles.

Chris Thaiss is Clark Kerr Presidential Chair and Professor in the University Writing Program at the University of California, Davis (US), where he is also a faculty member of the Graduate Group in Education and its concentration in Language, Literacy, and Culture. He teaches undergraduate courses in science writing and business/technical writing; graduate teaching includes composition theory/pedagogy/research and writing program administration. Author, co-author, or editor of twelve books, his most recent are *WAC for the New Millennium* (with S. McLeod, E. Miraglia, and M. Soven) and *Engaged Writers and Dynamic Disciplines: Research on the Academic Writing Life* (with T. Zawacki). His current research includes the International WAC/WID Mapping Project and a study of student writing in large-enrollment classes.

Dilek Tokay coordinates the Sabanci University (Turkey) Writing Center and its Undergraduate Program; at Sabanci since 1999, she worked at the Middle East Technical University (1970-1983) and Bosphorus University (1983-1999) as instructor, academic director, curriculum designer, materials producer, and teacher trainer. She was Chair of the European Writing Centers Association, 2005-2007.

Associate Professor in the Department of Rhetoric, Writing, and Communications at the University of Winnipeg (Canada), **Brian Turner** teaches rhetorical criticism, rhetorical theory, and environmental writing. He and Judith Kearns have co-authored several articles, the latest of them a rhetorical study of *Globe and Mail* columnist Christie Blatchford for the *Canadian Journal of Communication*.

Jonathan Worley is Senior Lecturer in Written Communications and Writing Centre Director for Saint Mary's University College, Belfast. He has degrees in English literature from the University of New Hampshire and Rutgers University and has been teaching both literature and academic writing in Northern Ireland since 1992.

Wu Dan received her PhD from Clemson University in 2010 and returned to China. She is now Dean of Humboldt College at Xi'an International Studies University and teaches in the School of English Studies. Her research interests include the internationalization of WAC, second language writing, and higher education political culture.

Trudy Zuckermann, retired head of the English department of Achva Academic College of Education, and retired senior lecturer in English at the Hebrew University of Jerusalem, received her doctoral degree from Temple University in 1986. She has worked in many different educational settings in the United States and Israel. Her research interests include curriculum and program development, academic writing, and teacher education.

INDEX

A

academic literacies (theory) 18, 79, 81, 84, 96, 110, 195, 204, 263, 267, 343, 349, 353, 506, 508
agriculture. *See "writing in (fields of study)"*
applied linguistics 31, 73, 79, 105, 107, 110, 211, 263, 288, 307, 316, 402, 475
Archer, Arlene 357, 359, 361, 363, 364, 513
architecture. *See "writing in (fields of study)"*
arts. *See 'writing in (fields of study)"*
assessment,
  student 44, 48, 56, 82, 101, 158, 169, 178, 187, 194, 208, 309, 381, 389, 424, 452, 481
  program 43, 119, 126, 157, 161, 164, 230, 297-299, 359, 424, 441, 446

B

Bazerman, Charles ii, 21, 22, 26, 31, 33, 109, 112, 113, 115, 161, 166, 221, 413, 414, 486, 496
Bean, John 194, 199, 441, 474, 482
Ben-Yehuda, Eliezer 271, 273, 274, 275, 276, 277, 292
Bereiter, Carl 84, 90, 172, 179, 486, 497
biology. *See "writing in (fields of study)"*
Bielefeld (Germany) University Writing Centre 90, 236, 468, 469, 470, 474, 478
Bitchener, John 309, 310, 311, 502, 506, 513

Boch, Françoise 220, 221, 506, 513
Bologna Process 7, 17, 29, 88, 89, 94, 388, 402, 417, 471, 480
Bourdieu, Pierre 84, 85, 90, 360, 364
Bradley Review 46, 53, 67, 502
Bräuer, Gerd 8, 74, 76, 180, 225, 226, 228, 229, 230, 231, 237, 238, 296, 407, 408, 413, 414, 469, 470, 474, 475, 477, 478, 479, 482, 483, 484, 505, 513
Bruffee, Kenneth 236, 238, 413, 469, 476, 483
business. *See "writing in (fields of study)"*

C

Carlino, Paula 8, 12, 26, 27, 32, 35, 41, 150 155, 158, 161, 166, 368, 374, 488, 490, 491, 493, 494, 496, 497, 514
Castelló, Montserrat 102, 150, 155, 370, 372, 374, 375, 423, 489, 491, 496, 514
chemistry. *See "writing in (fields of study)"*
Cleary, Lawrence 264, 266, 270, 503, 505, 506, 514
communication across the curriculum (CAC) 126, 337, 358, 364, 380
community of practice (theory) 47, 466, 469
Conference on College Composition and Communication (CCCC) 8, 12, 425, 426, 500
creative writing 14, 44, 71, 182, 185, 213, 217-220, 225, 236, 245, 254,

523

284, 330, 361, 405, 410, 413, 419, 423, 425
cultural studies. *See "writing in (fields of study)"*

D

Deane, Mary 67, 192, 193, 194, 195, 199, 200, 201, 211, 493, 497, 500, 502, 503, 508, 510, 514
De Micheli, Ana 494, 495, 514
digital literacy *See "writing with technology"*
dissertation 108, 113, 171, 177-179, 255, 258, 301-311, 345, 423, 457, 462. *See also "thesis"*
Doleschal, Ursula 69, 73, 74, 76, 77, 81, 479, 483, 514
Donahue, Christiane 12, 13, 98, 102, 103, 496, 501, 507, 508, 509

E

economics. *See "writing in (fields of study)"*
Emerson, Lisa 317, 322, 504, 505, 515
electronic tools *See "writing with technology"*
engineering *See "writing in (fields of study)"*
English for academic purposes (EAP) 274, 285, 288, 343, 388
ePortfolio *See "portfolio"*
European Association for the Teaching of Academic Writing (EATAW) 6, 13, 20, 233, 266, 271, 289, 425, 468, 500, 503, 507
European Writing Centers Association (EWCA) 13, 425, 426, 468, 500, 507

F

faculty development 125, 187, 334, 338, 449, 492, 493, 494. *See also "professional development"*
Foster, David 80, 89, 90, 410, 413
Foster, Steve 194, 195, 199, 200
Freire, Paulo 105, 108, 115
Frier, Catherine 217, 221, 506, 515

G

Ganobcsik-Williams, Lisa 8, 190, 191, 199, 200, 201, 211, 270, 350, 351, 503, 507, 509, 510, 515
García-Arroyo, Matilde 340, 492, 495, 515
genre (instructional approach or theory) 122, 135, 150, 153, 169, 179, 193-196, 216, 226, 254, 286, 291, 298, 303-305, 350, 356, 382-386, 401, 405-406, 413, 442, 457-460, 469, 474, 491, 493
Gere, Anne 233, 234, 238, 475, 484
Gillespie, Paula 236, 469, 484
Girgensohn, Katrin 225, 231, 232, 233, 234, 237, 238, 470, 475, 476, 484, 500, 509, 515
Gonano, Karyn 50, 53, 502, 515
Gonzalez Pinzón, Blanca 158, 159, 161, 166, 491, 495, 516
Goodman, Gary 423, 475, 516
Graves, Heather 138, 516
Graves, Roger 118, 124, 126, 127, 131, 138, 516
Gruber, Helmut 72, 73, 76, 77, 83, 84, 87, 90, 413, 415, 475, 479, 483, 484, 516
Gustafsson, Magnus 381, 384, 388, 421, 423, 516

H

Halliday, M. A. K. 24, 26, 32, 81, 90, 112, 115, 145, 146
Harris, Muriel 295, 300, 335, 336, 339, 340, 354, 364, 426
high school writing centers or programs 165, 230, 237, 239-248, 423-425, 446, 477, 483. *See also "secondary school" and "lycée"*
Hirsch, Linda 441, 453, 475
history *See "writing in (fields of study)"*
humanities *See "writing in (fields of study)"*
Hyland, Ken 26, 32, 73, 77

I

Iglesia, Patricia 490, 491, 494, 495, 496, 517
International Network of WAC Programs 8, 22
international students 43-53, 56-59, 63, 140, 190, 204, 254, 262, 284, 288, 315, 343, 345, 346, 348, 378
International WAC/WID Mapping Project 5, 10-18, 427
International Writing Centers Association 6, 426
Israel Forum for Academic Writing 271

J

Jakobs, Eva-Maria 243, 248, 249, 250, 468, 479, 483, 484, 517
journalism. *See "writing in (fields of study)"*

K

Kail, Harvey 236, 469, 484

Kearns, Judith 118, 127, 132, 133, 135, 137, 138, 517, 521
knowledge-transforming strategy 84, 90, 172
Kruse, Otto 71, 77, 89, 231, 243, 248, 249, 250, 290, 399, 411, 413, 475, 479, 484, 517

L

Lahire, Bernard 96, 103
Lave, Jean 354, 364, 469, 476, 484
law. *See "writing in (fields of study)"*
Lea, Mary 81, 90, 109, 110, 115, 262, 263, 270, 344, 351, 356, 364, 380, 388, 509
Lillis, Theresa 198, 200, 204, 211, 344, 351, 508, 509
linguistics 15, 18, 28, 31, 57, 72, 75, 79, 81, 85, 296, 143, 144, 147, 148, 213, 215, 285, 404, 413, 458, 463, 494 *See also "applied linguistics," "systemic functional linguistics," and "text linguistics"*
littéracies universitaires 95, 98, 102, 506, 508
lycée 213, 216 *See also "high school" and "secondary school"*

M

major in writing or rhetoric. *See "writing or rhetoric major"*
Martin, J. R. 24, 26, 32, 33, 81, 82, 90
mathematics (maths). *See "writing in (fields of study)"*
McConlogue,, Teresa 421, 505, 517
McLeod, Susan 22, 26, 33, 166, 314, 322, 358, 364, 457, 466, 505, 510, 521

McMillan, Kathleen 344, 347, 350, 351, 421, 504, 518
minor in writing or rhetoric. *See "writing or rhetoric minor"*
Mitchell, Sally 205, 210, 211, 421, 505, 518
Monroe, Jonathan 194, 195, 200, 477, 484
Motta-Roth, Désirée 107, 113, 114, 115, 491, 495, 518
Moyano, Estela 25, 26, 28, 29, 31, 32, 33, 34, 493, 495, 518
multilingual(ism) 361, 401, 403, 404, 414, 437, 476, 477, 509
multimedia 389-400
multimodal (instructional approach) 227, 355, 358, 359, 361, 404, 473,
Murray, Donald 325, 326, 327, 328, 330, 331, 432, 437
Murray, Rowena 196, 200, 266, 270, 501, 508, 510

N

Narváez Cardona, Elizabeth 148, 150, 152, 155, 156, 492, 493, 494, 495, 518
Natale, Lucia 28, 29, 33, 493, 495, 518
Nelson, Peter 44, 49, 50, 51, 53, 502, 518
North, Stephen 206, 211, 230, 238, 263, 270, 335, 340
nursing. *See "writing in (fields of study)"*

O

online writing *See "writing with technology"*
online writing lab (OWL) 171, 197, 321, 474, 476, 478
oral presentation(s) 18, 48, 171, 283, 373, 381, 383
O'Sullivan, Íde 264, 266, 270, 503, 505, 506, 519
Oz, Amos 275, 277, 292

P

Palmquist, Mike 20
Paoli, Dennis 475, 519
Peake, Kelly 200, 209, 211, 421, 493, 497, 505, 510, 519
peer learning (instructional approach) 19, 23, 27, 47, 49, 51, 65, 73, 74, 80, 124, 126, 129, 134, 135-136, 186, 195, 197, 210, 228, 232, 236, 237, 254, 256, 263, 265, 267, 283, 287, 314, 318, 319-321, 328-330, 335, 357, 380- 385, 418, 420, 424, 432, 434, 435, 450, 452, 462, 467, 469-472, 474, 477, 479, 481, 490, 494, 500, 505, 508
Perpignan, Hadara 285, 291, 519
Perrin, Daniel 231, 243, 248, 249, 250, 390, 397, 399, 479, 519
Petelin, Ros 45, 53
physics. *See "writing in (fields of study)"*
Plato 7, 21
PLEA (Program of Academic Reading and Writing) (Columbia) 157-167
PRODEAC (Program to Develop Academic Literacy Across the Curriculum) (Argentina) 23-34
political science. *See "writing in (fields of study)"*
Pollet, Marie-Christine 95, 101, 102, 103, 502, 504, 506, 519
portfolio (instructional approach) 120, 184, 185, 187, 228, 230, 286, 401,

409, 410, 414, 420, 442, 450, 471, 472, 474, 479, 481
process writing (theory or instructional approach) 18, 28, 65, 75, 82, 90, 109, 120, 122, 125, 131, 134, 149, 150-152, 159-162, 164, 165, 169, 171, 185, 192, 204, 218, 233, 234, 245, 280, 282, 293, 297, 299, 326, 327, 335, 336, 339, 347, 355, 361, 369, 370, 374, 384, 391, 394, 396, 401, 405, 413, 421, 432, 449, 451, 457, 459, 461, 469, 474, 477, 490, 494, 499
professional writing 73, 132, 137, 150, 171, 192, 261, 286, 402, 407
professional development (faculty or staff) 16, 19, 45, 52, 69, 73, 74, 124, 125, 126, 133, 204, 230, 241, 244, 263, 266, 269, 287, 290, 296, 334, 408, 424, 425, 441, 444, 445, 461, 467, 471, 492, 493, 505
psychology. *See "writing in (fields of study)"*
Purser, Emily 64, 66, 67, 194, 200, 493, 497, 501, 510, 519

Q

Quintana, Hilda 333, 338, 340, 492, 495, 520
Quintilian 7, 21, 135

R

REDLEES (Reading and Writing in Higher Education Network) (Columbia) 157, 165, 166
rhetoric 73, 82, 85, 90, 118, 122, 129, 130-137, 145, 170, 173, 175, 181-188, 192, 263, 304, 314, 394, 405, 410, 411, 419, 421, 434, 436, 453, 458, 459, 460, 463, 475, 501, 506, 507
Reinecker, Lotte 170, 172, 173, 175, 179, 180, 479, 483, 514, 520
Ronesi, Lynne 431, 437, 520
Royal Literary Fund (U.K.) 192, 200, 341, 342, 345, 346, 504
Rubin, Bella 285, 520
Russell, David ii, 7, 22, 90, 113, 115, 133, 138, 158, 161, 167, 413, 415, 463, 466, 490, 49, 497, 503, 509, 510

S

Scardamalia, Marlene 84, 90, 172, 179, 486, 497
Schmandt-Besserat, Denise 7, 22
Science *See "writing in (fields of study)"*
Scriptorium 230, 231, 237, 468, 477
secondary school(s) 31, 74, 125, 158, 165, 214, 228, 229, 328, 429, 430,, 458, 477, 481. *See also "high school" and "lycée"*
SFL *See "systemic functional linguistics"*
situated learning (theory) 364, 484, 491
social networking 9, 66.443
social science *See "writing in (fields of study)"*
sociology *See "writing in (fields of study)"*
Solé, Isabel 372, 375, 423, 489, 491, 495, 520
staff development 189, 191, 193-195, 198, 210, 384, 460., 503. *See also "professional development"*
Stassen, Ingrid 295, 300, 520
Stray Jørgensen, Peter 170, 172, 173, 179, 180, 479, 483, 514, 520

Street, Brian 81, 90, 115, 263, 270, 344, 352, 356, 357, 364, 380, 388
Swales, John 26, 27, 33, 304, 311, 380, 388, 413, 415
systemic functional linguistics (SFL) 23, 26, 30, 81, 82, 86, 90. *See also* "linguistics"

T

teacher training 153, 231, 287, 328, 420, 472, 481. *See also* "professional development"
Teberosky, Ana 370, 423, 489, 491, 521
technical communication (field of study) 141, 184, 240, 241, 254, 268, 382, 386
technical writing ii, 185, 240, 257, 258, 285, 288, 406, 460, 464
technology. *See* "writing in technology" or "writing with technology"
terroir 6, 8, 11
text types 76, 84, 169, 206, 279, 286, 382, 457. *See also* "genre"
text linguistics 79, 404. *See also* "linguistics"
Thaiss, Christopher 8, 12, 21, 22, 175, 180, 334, 421, 423, 427, 456, 457, 459, 460, 466, 475, 488, 489, 499, 521
thesis (degree requirement) 51, 71, 73, 111, 125, 140, 169, 169-180, 226-232, 255, 266, 268, 282, 283, 301-311, 345, 348, 349, 382-384, 386, 402, 405, 407, 419, 480, 506, 508. *See also* "dissertation"
translation (field of study) 89, 106, 216, 258, 259, 401-415, 431
Turner, Brian 118, 127, 132, 133, 135, 137, 138, 517, 521

W

WAC Clearinghouse 18, 20, 457
WAC/WID 20, 439, 454, 463, 486, 488, 489 *See also* 'International WAC/WID Mapping Project," "Writing Across the Curriculum" and "Writing in (fields of study) disciplines"
Wenger, Etienne 354, 364, 469, 476, 484
WID *See* "Writing in (fields of study) disciplines"
workshop(s). *See* "writing workshops (instructional approach)" and "professional development" (workshops for teachers)
Worley, Jonathan 505, 508, 521
writing across the curriculum (WAC) ii, 8, 12, 18, 26, 33, 45, 53, 77, 117, 119, 124, 125, 126, 132-136, 138, 144, 157-166, 169, 183, 230, 264, 268, 270, 272, 279, 290, 296, 313, 314, 317, 334, 337, 419, 421, 424, 433, 435, 439-454, 479, 485, 487, 492, 493, 506, 509. *See also* "WAC/WID"
writing center (also, centre) 15, 19, 52, 69-78, 79, 88, 117, 123, 126, 131, 135, 139-146, 165, 169-180, 181, 189-201, 225, 226, 229, 236, 261-270, 274, 279, 287, 290, 293-300, 313-323, 325-331, 333-340, 353-364, 384, 407, 417-427, 429, 433, 442, 445, 450, 462, 467-484, 492, 500, 503, 505, 508
writing course(s) 14, 31, 73, 79, 85, 87, 109, 111, 118, 119-122, 131, 133, 140, 142, 171, 182, 184, 231, 251, 255, 274, 278, 280, 282, 284, 287,

291, 314, 316, 317, 319, 326, 341, 345, 348, 389-400, 401-415, 429, 432, 449, 455, 458-460, 475, 491
writing, creative. *See "creative writing"*
writing fellow(s) 19, 269, 341, 342, 346, 429, 434, 439-447, 450-453, 462
writing group(s) 225, 231-237, 475
writing in (fields of study):
  agriculture (rural sciences) 106, 317, 456
  architecture 383, 393, 394, 411
  arts 62, 119, 134, 295, 389, 393
  biology 35-42, 125, 205-209, 285, 288, 322, 465, 494
  business 14, 52, 71, 81, 84, 143, 153, 182, 184, 185, 190, 216, 246, 262, 286, 288, 313, 316, 398, 403, 406, 412, 425, 432, 433, 441, 444, 460, 464
  chemistry 106, 121, 285, 361, 383, 465
  cultural studies 232, 256, 403, 420, 463
  disciplines (WID) (program) 194, 195, 230, 266, 279, 289, 317, 347, 348, 421, 422, 440, 442, 443, 455, 460, 475, 486 See also "WAC/WID"
  economics 44, 72, 81, 254, 286, 288, 433
  engineering 14, 25, 46, 50, 107, 151, 167, 184, 239, 242, 262, 268, 285, 288, 291, 345, 348, 362, 377-388, 455, 462
  history 84, 85, 88, 100, 101, 131, 211, 254, 284, 289, 328, 422, 450, 460, 461, 464
  humanities 14, 119, 134, 169, 174, 177, 183, 184, 216, 242, 258, 267, 274, 284, 289, 318, 354, 357, 451, 462

journalism 44, 131, 135, 136, 137, 216, 239-250, 254, 259, 389-400, 406, 410, 411, 460, 464
law 144, 164, 194, 195, 201, 286, 287, 297, 345, 362, 406, 422, 441, 442, 464
mathematics 121, 125, 134, 200, 384
nursing 199, 284, 289, 362, 444, 448
physics 107, 114, 121, 134, 418
political science 126, 140, 422, 450, 463
psychology 230, 254, 338, 366-375, 444, 451, 463, 485, 486, 494
science 64-66, 122, 125, 311, 317-318, 460
social sciences 14, 36, 84, 87, 131, 134, 176, 184, 256, 262, 267, 279, 282, 284, 287, 297, 318, 405, 455, 462, 485, 490, 496
sociology 72, 361, 444, 464, 474
technology 55, 71, 197, 263, 286, 288, 361, 452, 502
writing-intensive (course or requirement) 133, 293, 299, 441, 443, 449, 460, 464, 466, 475, 503
writing or rhetoric major 19, 131, 136, 465
writing or rhetoric minor 19, 181, 185, 436, 455, 463-465
writing module 16, 19, 65, 85-87, 152, 193, 203, 205-209, 257, 265-269, 345-348, 371, 378, 393-397, 423
writing online *See "writing with technology"*
writing process. *See "process writing"*
writing, professional. *See "professional writing"*
Writing Research Across Borders (conference) 6, 13, 21, 145

writing studies (discipline or program) 117-120, 122-126, 133, 432-437, 455, 463

writing, technical. *See "technical writing"*

writing to learn (instructional approach) 35, 40, 133, 134, 139, 144, 205, 264, 266, 317, 380, 443, 472

writing with technology 8, 20, 47, 55, 63, 86, 87, 155, 160, 165, 171, 175, 185, 193, 197, 198, 208, 227, 230, 245, 262, 266, 277, 290, 293, 338, 342, 361, 364, 389-400, 401, 409, 417, 426, 442, 452, 459, 464, 473, 474, 476, 477, 478, 479

writing workshop(s) (instructional approach) 16, 19, 36, 45, 52, 70, 74, 95, 120-126, 141, 151, 160, 165, 170, 175, 182, 193, 196, 204, 218, 236, 240, 244, 265, 280, 287, 288, 296, 302, 303-310, 326, 335, 347, 349, 357, 363, 374, 382, 393, 394, 405, 419, 444, 446, 451, 461, 462, 470, 474, 481, 490, 493, 500, 504

Wu, Dan 144, 146, 521

Y

Yang, Dafu 144, 145, 146

Z

Zawacki, Terry Myers 12, 175, 268
Zuckermann, Trudy 279, 292, 522

www.ingramcontent.com/pod-product-compliance
Lightning Source LLC
Chambersburg PA
CBHW030102010526
44116CB00005B/66